WOODROW WILSON CENTER SERIES

A culture of rights

Other books in the series

A culture of rights

The Bill of Rights in philosophy, politics, and law—1791 and 1991

Edited by
MICHAEL J. LACEY and KNUD HAAKONSSEN

WOODROW WILSON INTERNATIONAL CENTER
FOR SCHOLARS

AND

CAMBRIDGE
UNIVERSITY PRESS

Published by the Press Syndicate of the University of Cambridge
The Pitt Building, Trumpington Street, Cambridge CB2 1RP
40 West 20th Street, New York, NY 10011-4211, USA
10 Stamford Road, Oakleigh, Victoria 3166, Australia

First published 1991
First paperback edition 1992

Printed in Canada

Library of Congress Cataloging-in-Publication Data

A Culture of rights: the Bill of Rights in philosophy, politics, and
law, 1791 and 1991 / edited by Michael J. Lacey and Knud Haakonssen.
p.   cm. – (Woodrow Wilson Center series)
Includes index.
ISBN 0-521-41637-X
1. Civil rights – United States – History.   I. Lacey, Michael
James.   II. Haakonssen, Knud, 1947–   .   III. Woodrow Wilson
International Center for Scholars.   IV. Series.
KF4749.C85   1991
342.73′085–dc20
[347.30285]   91-25265
                                          CIP

A catalog record for this book is available from the British Library.

ISBN 0-521-41637-X hardback
ISBN 0-521-44653-8 paperback

WOODROW WILSON INTERNATIONAL CENTER FOR SCHOLARS

BOARD OF TRUSTEES

The Center is the "living memorial" of the United States of America to the nation's twenty-eighth president, Woodrow Wilson. The U.S. Congress established the Woodrow Wilson Center in 1968 as an international institute for advanced study, "symbolizing and strengthening the fruitful relationship between the world of learning and the world of public affairs." The Center opened in 1970 under its own presidentially appointed board of trustees.

In all its activities the Woodrow Wilson Center is a nonprofit, nonpartisan organization, supported financially by annual appropriations from the U.S. Congress and contributions from foundations, corporations, and individuals. Conclusions or opinions expressed in Center publications are those of the authors and do not neccessarily reflect the views of the Center staff, fellows, trustees, advisory groups, or any individuals or organizations that provide financial support to the Center.

Woodrow Wilson International Center for Scholars
1000 Jefferson Drive, S.W.
Washington, D.C. 20560
(202) 357-2429

Contents

Acknowledgments

This volume is the result of a series of scholarly workshops organized by the Woodrow Wilson Center's Division of United States Studies to commemorate the bicentennial of the Bill of Rights. Thanks are due, first, to the authors whose work appears in the pages that follow, not merely for their scholarly contributions but also for the patience and good humor they showed along the road to publication. The editors also wish to thank the other members of the workshops, whose advice and criticisms were so helpful in discussing the essays as they underwent development: Charles Blitzer, James MacGregor Burns, A. E. Dick Howard, Stephen Conrad, Maeva Marcus, Gordon Wood, John Pocock, Walter Berns, and Mark Tushnet. We also acknowledge our gratitude to the Exxon Education Foundation for its generous support.

Introduction

History, historicism, and the culture of rights

MICHAEL J. LACEY and KNUD HAAKONSSEN

Nothing is more deeply rooted in the American political tradition than the vocabulary of rights. In part because of its role in the founding and grounding of that tradition in the eighteenth century, the language of rights has been worked especially hard in political debate ever since. Slaves cited violations of their natural rights in hopeless petitions to Congress. Abolitionists and their states' rights adversaries both spoke in rights terms. Later on, when leaders of the union movement invoked labor's right to organize as the key to securing social justice for the new industrial working class, their opponents in the corporations invoked the individual's right to work free of union obligations.

As these examples indicate, the stakes in arguments over the proper use of rights claims have been high,[1] and the importance of the objectives sought through the rhetoric of rights has not diminished over time. The major social movements of recent decades have been steeped in that rhetoric as evidenced in the continuing conflicts triggered by the civil rights movement as its reach extends deeper into the life of the workplace, by the long and narrowly unsuccessful drive of the women's movement for an Equal Rights Amendment, by environmentalists' assertion of rights on behalf of threatened species of plants and animals, and by the claims

---

[1] For an important and wide-ranging set of essays on the significance of the Constitution for American development and on the impact of changing conceptions of rights related to the problems of minorities, women, labor, and other groups in American culture, see the special bicentennial issue of the *Journal of American History* on the Constitution and American life, vol. 74, no. 3 (December 1987).

of people who advocated women's right to choice regarding abortion and the counterclaims of those who advocate a fetal right to life.

Although Western in its origins, the language of rights is now a virtually global phenomenon. Woodrow Wilson at Versailles spoke of the right to self-determination. The ideals of decolonization and nation building after World War II were typically formulated in rights terms. And after each of the world wars many nations made concerted attempts to strengthen and elaborate the legal framework of the international community, attempts in which charters of rights played an important role, as in the post–World War II development of an integrated European community. In the recent upheavals in the Communist world the revolt against oppression and incompetence and the assertion of aspirations of suppressed nationalities and ethnoreligious groups have been voiced routinely as rights claims. Apart from the ideal of democratic self-government—itself often understood as a basic right—there is no more universal feature of politics in the late twentieth century than rights.

Although talk about rights is common, its meanings are commonly ambiguous and unconstrained, used by individuals and groups deeply divided in their basic perspectives on events. No one observing the contemporary American scene would suggest that the pervasiveness of the language of rights points to the existence of a coherent underlying philosophy of morals and politics shared by those who use the terms, even by those who use them most carefully. Quite the contrary. To ask for the difference between rights and wants is to open up difficult problems of reasoning, problems that are poorly served by the appeal to common sense. The dominant intellectual institutions in contemporary culture are academic, and few truths are held to be self-evident in the postmodern university. Exactly this point is made in an influential article on the paradox of the persistence of rights talk in a cultural environment that is profoundly skeptical of its metaphysical rationale.[2] The article begins with the observation that what long served as the basic premise for rights discourse—the existence of an objective moral order accessible to reason and amenable to formulation in terms of rights and duties—has become a highly controversial assertion in the contemporary American university setting. There, as some of the chapters that follow show, traditions of inquiry indifferent or hostile to rights concepts have long held sway.

---

[2] See Thomas Haskell, "The Curious Persistence of Rights Talk in the 'Age of Interpretation,'" in ibid., 984–1012.

Despite skepticism about the philosophical grounding of rights, however, we continue to talk of these rather mysterious, intangible entities as if we were thoroughly familiar with them, never more so than in the day-to-day affairs of politics and public policy. One of the many reasons for this characteristic way of performing in the drama of our politics is the special symbiotic connection that was established between ideas of rights and American institutions at the nation's founding. The United States Constitution and its first ten amendments, the Bill of Rights, not only are potent symbols of nationhood based on American understandings of the political ideals of the Enlightenment but also are working charters for the operation of increasingly powerful institutions—charters that are referred to constantly for guidance in sorting out social and political conflicts. In other words, the American institutional setup—given the prominence it accords the Supreme Court and the practice of judicial review—strongly encourages the persistence of ideas of rights, both popular and professional, and virtually requires that foundational questions regarding rights be asked from time to time by anyone seriously concerned about the relationship between social theory and practice.

We mention the ambiguities and contradictions of popular understandings not to disparage commonsense usage or to suggest that the more theoretically self-conscious academic uses of the language of rights have resolved those ambiguities and contradictions but, rather, to draw attention to the inherent complexity of rights thinking and consciousness as subjects for study. The title of this volume was selected to convey a sense of orientation among the complexities of the subject. "Culture of rights" can be interpreted in two ways: The phrase can refer to a way of life informed by a set of beliefs and values in which the language of rights plays a prominent role; as already indicated there are many such cultures of rights. Alternatively, culture is also the activity of cultivating—in this case, of developing a rights-related, philosophical jurisprudence adequate to meet the practical problems of providing for both continuity and change in the evolving legal order.

Taken either way, the culture of rights poses difficult questions for historical understanding. One of the principal aims of this book is to indicate and illustrate why this is so. The chapters that follow examine the ambiguities of the American culture of rights at two points in time, the late eighteenth century and the late twentieth. The authors have tried to point out the inherent complexity of the subject, the relations between rights discourse and other powerful cultural idioms, and the continuing pluralism of perspectives about the grounding and utility of rights. Reporting such pluralism faithfully is possible only by calling on scholars from different academic disciplines—law, philosophy, history, and political theory.

The Wilson Center's project that produced this book was undertaken as a scholarly contribution to the bicentennial of the Bill of Rights (15 December 1991). The project probed the current state of scholarship on several of the contexts in which the Bill of Rights has been read, including a few particularly important ones. Care has been taken to ensure that the notes to each chapter give guidance to the scholarly literature on the broad subjects covered. Even so, the book does not aim at unraveling the many meanings of the first ten amendments as they might have been understood in 1791 or may be understood today. And the book is emphatically not a potted collective history of the Bill of Rights. It is concerned only with two broadly conceived moments in the cultural history of that document. There are three reasons for this choice of focus: One has to do with the historiography of the Bill of Rights; one, with its history; and one, with its historicity.

The historiography of the Bill of Rights is large but in various respects uneven. Some important analyses of discrete provisions of the document have been published—on the freedom of religion and the press, for example—and some provisions remain neglected as subjects of study.[3] And yet, taken in the round, historical scholarship on the Bill of Rights is not as rich as one might expect, given its present importance in the American scheme of things. The historical trajectory of the document—its changing placement within the dynamics of American constitutionalism as a whole—is well known. This knowledge is such as to give pause to the historian who would trace the vicissitudes of the document's provisions as if to do so were a simple matter, calling for no more than close observation of a rather straightforward march of official interpreters and their findings through the decades, one at a time. No such march occurred, and this brings us to the second reason we have limited ourselves to two moments in the history of the document.

Through most of American history the Bill of Rights played little if any role in the broader scheme of national development. The preparation and adoption of the Bill of Rights were vital and perhaps decisive acts

---

[3] For a review of historical research on the birth of the Bill of Rights, see James H. Hutson, "The Birth of the Bill of Rights: The State of Current Scholarship," in *Prologue: Quarterly of the National Archives* 20, no. 3 (Fall 1988): 143–61.

of political maneuver that made possible the ratification of the Constitution itself, but thereafter the Bill of Rights fell into a kind of oblivion, as many well-informed contemporaries, Federalists and Anti-Federalists alike, thought it would. It did so because, by design, its provisions did not reach to the sovereign legal doings of the several states, and under the federalism of the Constitution, the states were entrusted with the vital powers affecting civil liberties and much else. We often forget just how sweeping the powers of the states were in pre–Civil War America, and how minimal the powers of the national government. Jefferson, to take but one example, took the federal division of labor to mean that the states were concerned with domestic policy, the federal government with foreign affairs. "The federal is, in truth, our foreign government, which department alone is taken from the sovereignty of the separate States," he wrote to a correspondent in 1824. "I recollect but one instance of control vested in the federal, over the State authorities, in a matter purely domestic, which is that of metallic tenders."[4]

An extreme view of the autonomy of the states, particularly as connected to the problem of slavery, was, of course, the issue that finally brought about the Civil War, and it was the post–Civil War amendments to the Constitution, particularly the Fourteenth, that settled, or at least put on a new footing, the underlying problem of the reach of federal jurisdiction. It did so via clarification of the meaning of citizenship. Whereas the exact locus of citizenship was not addressed in the original Constitution and had proved problematic in the compound republic, the Fourteenth Amendment made it clear that American citizenship was dual citizenship, applying to both national and state governments, and that the national government was primary with respect to any problems of securing the rights of citizenship.

Centralization of authority proceeded, though slowly. Today it seems to many observers that federalism, once the potent principle, has become rather like a vestigial organ among the living tissues of the Constitution, while the Bill of Rights, once something of a useless appendix, has become a symbol of the Constitution itself. It was the twentieth-century "nationalization of the Bill of Rights" by the Supreme Court via its "incorporation doctrine," a series of complicated and increasingly far-reaching interpretations of the requirements of the Fourteenth Amendment, that

[4] Quoted in Michael Kammen, *A Machine That Would Go of Itself: The Constitution in American Culture* (New York: Vintage, 1987), 59.

brought about this basic shift in perspective. A recent account of the changing character of constitutionalism in American culture describes the pattern of change as a movement from a constitutionalism of powers to a constitutionalism of rights.[5]

In short, while certainly not denying that the Bill of Rights showed signs of life between the end of the eighteenth century and our own time—and while acknowledging especially the importance of the Fourteenth Amendment—we are convinced that our two chosen moments are indeed the momentous ones. What is more, they are in a sense inherently connected, and this brings us to the third argument behind our chosen scheme of things.

Major movements in American public life almost inevitably refer to origins and foundations. In the American Republic the understanding and justification of function can hardly be divorced from the understanding of foundation, and foundation cannot be separated from validating origin. The fact that the origin *was* the foundation at a particular, discernible time will always lend great attraction to attempts at seeing new foundations and directions as validated by some relation of fidelity to the origins.

One of the most remarkable features of the United States is that, alone of the major democratic states, it has an assignable beginning in history. It emerged not from the mist of ancient custom but from self-conscious design, a design solemnly recorded and expressed in the founding documents themselves. All countries feel the need for a usable past in the sense of agreed, sustaining traditions, but America's search for a usable past has an additional element of specificity and design. It must be usable with reference to these known origins, to the foundational myth in which the Founders bestowed on subsequent generations their vision of liberty and the common good. Any quest for understanding of the Bill of Rights and its role in the transformation of American constitutionalism is therefore inevitably a historical quest. Whatever view Americans may adopt on the great questions of the day concerning the relationship between the original intention and the current meaning of the Constitution and the Bill of Rights, they will be united in seeing the special authority of these great instruments of government as in some sense deriving from the fact that they were foundational.

---

[5] See Morton Keller, "Powers and Rights: Two Centuries of American Constitutionalism," *Journal of American History* 74, no. 3 (December 1987): 675–94.

The tension between foundational myths and the changing perceptions of historical truth has given American historiography much of its peculiar energy. The founding event and its dramatis personae are now venerated, now vilified in the continuing search for a past that speaks to the exigencies of the present. Accusations of mistaking myth for history have often had a peculiarly paradoxical ring to them, because they have in fact been criticisms for not getting the "meaning" of the foundation "right." The fact is that the past is past, and in the deepest sense it can never be rendered perfectly clear "as it actually happened." We see the evidence of the past from particular points of view, and we can detach the mythical, or parts thereof, from the historical in those points of view only when new perspectives, suggested by the strains of our contemporary experience, have been adopted and tried out.

If the Bill of Rights and the Constitution to a significant degree are contextualized by their own history as perceived at any given time, and if such history is inevitably in a dialectic tension with the demands for a workable foundational myth, then the choice of focus for a scholarly inquiry into the culture of rights is easy. The eighteenth-century moment is unavoidably fundamental and must be selected, and our own moment is simply unavoidable. So far as the long period in between is concerned, it would certainly have been interesting to revisit and refine our knowledge of all the turning points that, since the Civil War, have contributed to the nationalization of the Bill of Rights and added to its increasing potency as a shaping factor in American life. But exploring this large and so far only imperfectly charted terrain would require work different in scale and kind from that undertaken here.

The reader will also note that this book focuses on the constant reshaping of the relationship between rights enshrined in a legal instrumentality such as the Bill of Rights and rights as extralegal entities. This concern with the philosophical foundation of rights runs through the discussion at various levels and turns up repeatedly as a question of great practical and theoretical importance. The relationship between legal rights written into a text and "higher" rights may appear to some readers to be one of the perennial questions in political philosophy and thus above historicization. And yet one of the favorite ways of seeking out the timeless character of this relationship has been to point to its formulation in earlier periods, especially at the founding period. This tendency to seek historical warrant for truths supposed to be *above* the flux of history—something more fixed and universal, permanent, and reliable as a guide to action than the particularities and contingencies of history can of themselves disclose—is, of course, neither new nor exclusively American, but it has become a pervasive feature of American rights culture.

What went into inventing the Bill of Rights? As indicated by the text that follows, particularly Chapters 2 and 3, by James Hutson and Jack Rakove, the Founders seem to have combined in a process of bricolage the selective use of old traditions, elements of makeshift, and gambles on the future. The Bill of Rights was not added to the Constitution as a display of doctrinal agreement on matters of first principle. Its provisions are too curious a mixture of the obviously fundamental and the oddly specific and time-bound to suggest otherwise.

Then, too, there was an adventitious and tactical quality in stories of what went into the construction of the Bill of Rights—a quality forced by the bitter struggle of the Federalists and Anti-Federalists, as each impugned the motives and vision of the other. It was a document, as James Hutson puts it, "that could not stand in the esteem of either its sponsors or opponents." The push of expediency that went into the composition of the Bill of Rights, however, and the elements of bungle and murk that hovered over its passage and adoption should not be taken as signs that the Founders were not genuinely solicitous of rights. On the contrary, it is abundantly clear that concepts of rights played a central, constitutive role in shaping their outlook on morals and government.

Perhaps it is best, therefore, to start not with politics but with philosophy. Whereas the political historian is necessarily concerned with bringing to the forefront of consciousness the tactics, expediencies, and practical difficulties involved in the invention of the Bill of Rights, the philosophical historian is concerned with capturing how rights concepts held together and with understanding the conceptual structure of the prevailing tradition of thought. In doing a different *kind* of history, such a thinker provides a different kind of access to the broad tradition of rights thinking in which the Founders lived. The philosophical historian asks, What kinds of rights theories would have been intelligible to the Founders? The answers, provided in this instance in Chapter 1, by Knud Haakonssen, suggest the need for revising to some degree our understanding of the ideological context of the founding.

Much current scholarship on the ideology of the Revolutionary and early national period typically distinguishes the strains of liberalism, republicanism, Scottish realism, and evangelical Christianity as the principal elements in the picture. Relations among these outlooks are generally unclear, although an atmosphere of battle for the soul of American politics hovers over much of the writing. Precisely because each has a bearing on present-day evaluations of what was "really" going on in the founding period, and thus plays a part in the continuing search for a usable past, each has its scholarly champions. Too often, however, the outlooks are assumed to have been so incompatible and opposed to one another in rather simple ways that one wonders how the contemporaries could have conversed. Liberalism, for example, and liberalism alone, was seen as connected to the natural-law tradition. For too long liberalism was taken as the legacy of John Locke's natural-rights ideas and was generally viewed as inadequate for serving the public good, because of its individualistic emphasis and its concern for rights of property. In contrast, republicanism, though equally concerned with autonomy and property, was seen as a workable alternative inheritance that favored the requirements of the common good over the claims of individualism.

It is increasingly doubtful whether this characterization of liberalism is fair to John Locke, who was unquestionably influential in American life; more to the point, it is clear from Haakonssen's opening chapter that reducing the natural-law tradition to the confines of Locke's second *Treatise of Government* would be deeply unfair to that tradition. It was a far richer, more complex and influential body of thought than has often been appreciated. Haakonssen provides a brief historical dictionary of rights concepts and their interrelations for the seventeenth and eighteenth centuries that suggests how central to the thought and practice of the period was the framework of natural law, rights, and duties he outlines. This variegated body of thought, profoundly influenced by the theological currents of its time, was both the outcome of a search for a supraconfessional basis for politics and morals and a response to the recurrent challenges to the notion that there were universally valid grounds for politics and morals. The framework encompassed prescriptive and descriptive elements, and it served as a kind of proto–social science for scholars throughout early modern Europe.

Although generally ambitious of transcending confessional divisions, natural-law theory was firmly anchored in natural religion. It was part of the overall arrangement of nature by "nature's God" to which reason and science gave humanity access. The source of natural law was God, who imposed it on rational beings as an obligation to pursue the common good. And the subject of natural law was the proper discharge of each person's duty or office or station in life as a contribution to the common good. Natural rights were derived from natural law as correlatives to such natural duties, and thus they were by no means the hallmark of the "atomic" individual of liberal lore.

Natural law was altogether less individualistic and less antiauthoritarian than it was subsequently taken to be and thus more compatible with other contemporary currents of thought. More particularly, it was quite capable of encompassing various forms of traditionalism, including British constitutionalism. It was important precisely because of its ecumenical ambitions and its character as a formal body of thought. Although liberalism, republicanism, and evangelicalism were not taught as academic subjects, natural jurisprudence *was*. As far as the *cultivation* of this mainstream view of the proper context of rights thinking was concerned, the institutions that mattered were those that educated the young gentry of the period: the Scottish universities, latitudinarian Cambridge and the dissenting academies in England, and the colonial colleges in America.

Gradually, of course, this secularized religion itself was further secularized, and in a complex and subtle fashion cleared the way for the later emergence of subjective-rights theories proper—those holding that rights are the primary moral features of humanity. This point of view, as Haakonssen indicates, was anticipated in different ways, but it could not become part of mainstream thought so long as it was seen as a source of moral anarchy and, in effect, as a denial of the divine origins of morals. Eighteenth-century anxieties on this point are comparable to doubts within the community of twentieth-century liberalism—treated in Chapter 5 of this volume by William Galston—over its distinction between politics and morals as separable domains. In both cases it is thinking about the foundations of rights claims that is at issue.

The Founders, Haakonssen suggests, rather unwittingly contributed to the mechanics of this process of secularization. The new civil order they established spurred its development, helping to usher in a more recognizably modern culture of rights and eventually modernity itself. In their attempts to formulate a position from the materials available in the received tradition, to make the past usable in the predicament in which they found themselves, the Founders—most famously, Jefferson—gave a new individualistic "spin" to the old idea of the inalienability of rights. The formerly communitarian aspect (i.e., people had been understood to have an inalienable right and duty to be sociable and to provide for the common good) gradually receded from view. The providentialism of the received tradition—its assumption that clashes between rights ideally could be harmonized with the proper use of "right reason" along the lines of Christian utilitarianism—gave way to the notion that perhaps such clashes were unresolvable. Finally, a new idea of autonomy, understood in purely naturalistic terms, began to make some headway.

Whereas Chapter 1 is concerned with the conceptual structure of the natural-law tradition as broadly conceived over two centuries (and thus primarily with the basic ideas of the great European "forefathers" of the American understanding of natural jurisprudence), Chapters 2 and 3 shift attention to the complexities, ironies, and ambiguities that went directly into the invention of the Constitution and the Bill of Rights under turbulent conditions of conflict. James Hutson points out that, like our contemporary period, the eighteenth century in America was a time in which "the public's penchant for asserting its rights outran its ability to analyze them and to reach a consensus about their scope and meaning." His survey confirms (1) that Americans assumed that rights were derivative, not made or invented but discovered as already present in human nature, and (2) that they did not fully understand the theological and philosophical subtleties of the problem.

Whether or not natural law was adequately grasped as a way of thinking, it became the basic source of legitimacy in America's thinking about rights. As the crisis of the Revolution approached, the Americans were intellectually unprepared for the challenge of establishing a new system of governance that was about to confront them. Clearly such governance would deal with rights, but just how and on what grounds? There was no "intercolonial position paper" to which to refer to sort out the problem. Nonetheless, Hutson argues, under the press of events between the Stamp Act crisis and the early years of independence a common popular understanding on rights and governance developed. He details the reasons Americans deepened their dependence on natural-law concepts (rather than staying within the confines of English constitutionalism) as the dispute escalated into open revolution and the colonists found themselves to be living, in effect, in the "state of nature" mentioned in their books.

In the moment between independence and the formation of the first state governments, "state of nature" contractarianism became a live issue and a spur to thinking about the problems involved in the very concept of enumerating natural rights, inventing new purposes for bills of rights as reserved natural rights, sorting out differences between alienable and inalienable rights, and much else. Hutson reviews the experience of Americans with the bills of rights in the early state constitutions, distinguishes these from the conflicting political purposes associated with the proposed federal government's bill of rights, and discusses the conflict between Federalists and Anti-Federalists in light of recent scholarship—all as background to a present-day appreciation of just what a "strange document" the Bill of Rights is.

The whole idea of enumerating rights of the individual in written bills was once an innovation of considerable import, but there are serious difficulties in establishing just where the innovation fitted within the overall experience of the Founders. It was different from the English Declaration of Rights of 1689, which asserted some rights of Parliament against the Crown, and from the colonial charters of governance. It emerged somewhat haphazardly out of the experience of war and establishment of the new states. The Founders themselves were often divided as to the aims and efficacy of the process and the weight that ought to be assigned to this new instrument that subordinated government to rather abstract principles. Plainly, the idea of enumerated rights and their proper interpretation has special salience for today's American debates over constitutional philosophy, with the advocates of a jurisprudence of original meaning at one extreme and the advocates of more free-wheeling styles of interpretation at the other. As Jack Rakove makes clear in Chapter 3, this controversy over the principles of judicial interpretation clarifies the tensions between history as an academic discipline, with a sense of proportionality and emphasis on how things fit together in the past, and history as an instrument for use in contemporary problem solving.

Although the jurisprudence of original intent, as it has come to be called, makes certain claims to being old-fashioned and representing tradition, in some respects it is a recent phenomenon that grew up as a part of the reaction in recent decades against aspects of the rationale from which an innovating Supreme Court derived basic rights (particularly the right to privacy) and justified its role in protecting them. As Rakove points out, originalism has an inherent bias that tends to equate valid rights with enumerated rights, and hence with the Bill of Rights. Another bias in originalism equates the true meaning of a particular clause with its original meaning, the latter having been permanently fixed at the point of adoption.

The Founders did not make these assumptions. In fact, their thinking about the enumeration of rights was much more tentative and ambiguous than one might have expected. "Where we look for answers," Rakove points out, "the framers and ratifiers of the late 1780s were still struggling with questions whose novelty and complexity had already carried them away from the received wisdom of their time." He focuses not on which rights the Founders believed they had (he insists that there was a strong underlying consensus on this subject) but on the more fundamental problem of isolating for study their thinking about how to secure and protect rights.

This problem inspired the creativity of the generation, and Rakove notes that whereas we naturally think of the protection of rights in terms of the history of judicial review, the Founders thought of the problem in terms of the history of representation, focusing their hopes on republican ideas of legislative sovereignty. He examines the process of social learning that was under way between the 1760s and the 1790s and details how this process was reflected in changing constitutional thought and practice. The pressures of war and recovery had generated a torrent of intrusive legislation on the part of the fledgling states, and the quarrelsome experience of legislative sovereignty in these early years had led some contemporaries to question the adequacy of representation as an all-purpose idea for ensuring that rights were exercised and protected. As a result, they began to think of alternatives or supplements to it.

One of these contemporaries, of course, was James Madison. As he was the father of the Constitution and the rather reluctant godfather who presided over the formulation and enactment of the Bill of Rights, his analyses of the problem were especially influential. Madison's ideas of constitutional design and his theory of faction are familiar; less familiar are his thoughts about rights and their protection. Rakove makes it clear that Madison thought deeply about rights, and that his thinking took shape in the midst of this first crisis of American republicanism as a critique of representation, which had been its central premise. Rakove traces the complex evolution of Madison's views that brought him finally and unenthusiastically to the Bill of Rights, an institutional device he had once dismissed contemptuously as a mere "parchment barrier" unlikely to impede the will of majorities mobilized in legislatures.

Chapter 4, by Charles Griswold, treats the other great intellectual presence among the Founders—Thomas Jefferson, the leading natural-rights theorist of the day. A philosopher, not a historian, Griswold has written a chapter that differs in kind and aim from the others in this collection. He is concerned with Jefferson's philosophy of life and his understanding of the self and moral obligation. He is especially concerned with the lack of coherence in the Jeffersonian vision with reference to what many contemporaries, Jefferson among them, knew to be the great moral challenge to the pervasive rights talk of the era, namely, slavery. How did Jefferson—the author of the Declaration of Independence, the foundational statement of American natural-law doctrine; the friend and correspondent of Madison, who encouraged him to push the Bill of Rights project through to its completion—think about implementing his rights-based theory of justice in the midst of the messy, contradictory real world of politics and prudential calculation? What kind of moral reasoning is bound up with the Jeffersonian style of natural-rights philosophy, and if that reasoning were to be taken seriously and systematically, what would it look like?

Griswold's treatment of Jefferson's casuistry with reference to slavery is intended not to expose simple hypocrisy (the man was neither simple nor hypocritical) but to pinpoint the incoherence in Jefferson's philosophy itself—its attempted synthesis of Epicurean ideas, a radically stripped-down and "naturalized" Christianity, and a "moral sense" theory of natural law, natural rights, and obligation—a compound that worked in the direction of the emerging subjective-rights theories to which Haakonssen refers in his chapter. This compound led to continuing rationalization of slavery as a wrong that could be lived with rightly, in the interest of higher values. While Jefferson is, strictly speaking, no more representative of the culture of his day than Madison or Franklin or John Witherspoon, like them he is nonetheless exemplary of certain deep currents within that culture. His empiricism, his materialism, his belief that moral principles are rooted in natural passions or sentiments, his understanding of happiness (as tranquillity) to be the chief aim in life, his appeals to utility, his assumptions about progress as something operating on automatic pilot—all these characteristics he shares with many people in our own time. The difficulty he had in holding his beliefs together in a synthesis that dealt adequately with the problems of practice has been handed on to those who followed him. "We are left," Griswold notes, "with the task of articulating a notion of the self, its virtues, and its happiness capable of avoiding Jefferson's quandaries."

The last three chapters in the volume deal in various ways with the present-day culture of rights, and each confirms in its different fashion

Griswold's point about the continuing need for an adequately grounded philosophy of rights and justice. Just as the colonial colleges were vital institutions in the cultivation and propagation of eighteenth-century understandings of the ideology of rights, so the twentieth-century university is the major locus of both the criticism of received understandings and the construction of new ones.

So vast and various is the academic literature in philosophy and political theory produced in the course of the polymorphous "rights revival" of the last generation that it is difficult to achieve a sense of orientation vis-à-vis the phenomenon as a whole. Chapter 5, by William Galston, provides a map to enable readers to perceive the rights terrain and grasp how its many features stand in relation to one another. Deep skepticism about the grounding of rights claims has long been a feature of the university environment, and Galston surveys the many objections to rights—epistemological, ontological, moral, and political—that have been developed as a result.

Criticism alone will not do, however, at least not if it abandons the vocabulary of rights altogether. As noted earlier, the American institutional setup, with its roots in the founding, exerts a powerful pull back to rights questions, a pull that is felt sooner or later by everyone concerned with the relationships between theory and practice in its American context. Galston makes the important observation that inherited confusion about the scope of rights, the apparently intended *incompleteness* of those enumerated in the Bill of Rights, is one of the "key points at which American constitutionalism is compelled to confront moral and political philosophy." American theorists and reformers in some sense *must* have a philosophy of rights if they are to make any headway. With this point in mind, Galston surveys current theories of rights with respect to their philosophical foundation, their understanding of the scope and content of rights, and their treatment of the bearers of rights—a question that has been rendered ever more complex in light of controversies over the rights of minorities, women, children, people with disabilities, and the like.

As a political theorist, Galston is concerned not simply with how the current debate over the meaning of rights is organized, but with what it offers and fails to offer in the present crisis of American liberalism. His treatment makes clear the sense in which the multidimensionality of thinking about rights in the founding period has been lost in important respects, with the result that an atmosphere of one-sidedness and incompleteness now hovers over the conversation. Liberal practical philosophy has always excelled at the defense of individual rights, but it has often evaded the need to distinguish liberty from license. Unless the problem of the "rightness of rights" is confronted more fully and deeply than it has been, he suggests, the future of the culture of rights is not bright.

William Fisher, in Chapter 6, treats another department of university life, the law school, so vital in the continuing search for a philosophical jurisprudence. Like Galston, he offers a map of an immense and poorly charted terrain—the field of American legal theory as it has been developed since the 1920s. Like Galston, he offers *more* than a map, in this case a new set of insights into the connections between academic legal theory and the evolution of the Supreme Court's interpretations of the Bill of Rights.

Ironically, critiques of rights are more deeply rooted in the law schools' traditions of inquiry than in other sectors of the university, and here, too, deep skepticism about the philosophical grounding of rights and a seething pluralism of perhaps incommensurable viewpoints appear to hold sway. With few exceptions, the work of Ronald Dworkin being one of them, one is unlikely to encounter theories formulated ab initio and explicitly in rights terms. In the complex situation set forth by Fisher, a kind of indirection prevails toward rights and their placement in legal theory. The beginnings of critical reasoning have to do with questions put to the legal process that were felt to be more searching and fundamental than the abstract inherited vocabulary of rights. The most extensive, influential, and highly developed body of work in this legacy is that of the "Legal Realists" of the 1920s and 1930s. Fisher examines in detail their critique and program, and the implications of realism for the understanding of rights. He demonstrates the ways in which the Critical Legal Studies movement of recent decades has inherited and extended the criticisms of the Legal Realists and, like them, has been unable to develop a serviceable constructive jurisprudence. And he explains the ways in which the five most clearly delineated schools of postwar legal theory relate to one another and to rights debates more generally.

Does the cultivation and criticism of rights thinking that go on in the law schools make any difference for the culture as a whole? Do they have anything to do with the changing interpretations of the Bill of Rights? Fisher argues that indeed they do, that the proposals made by law teachers concerning the proper construction of these provisions eventually find their way into the Supreme Court's reasoning, via young law clerks and citations to debates in the law reviews. He marshals evidence for the argument by searching out connections between each of the five schools described and recent opinions of the Court regarding freedom of speech, "takings" of property, and the controversial rights of privacy and personhood. Given the diversity and fragmentation of the academic scene, together with the incommensurability of many of the viewpoints welcomed there, Fisher notes that the Court's tendency to borrow selectively from the culture of the law schools has aggravated the intellectually unsatisfying character of current doctrine and highlighted the need for more ambitious and comprehensive theory.

The final chapter of the book is a venture into comparative cultural history and politics by Alan Ryan. At its best, comparative analysis helps to bring out the strangeness in the familiar and to loosen the hold of assumptions taken for granted—a fitting approach to thinking about rights. Ryan contrasts British and American attitudes to bills of rights, judicial review, and the interplay of judicial and party politics. The American Revolution began because the rights of Britons did not fit into the realities of life in the colonial portions of the empire, and the Americans sought other grounds for building up their own culture of rights. Given Britain's lack of a written constitution and a bill of rights, Ryan asks, are the rights of today's Britons any less extensive and secure than those of their American contemporaries? Yes and no, he suggests, depending on the issue in question. Discussion of the abortion question, the regulation of police, and the balancing of free speech with considerations of public order and national security bring the points home.

How do we account for the variations? The interactions of institutions and intellectual traditions are important. In the long run, it is the persistence of anticontractualist views of authority that seems most impressive in Britain—the continuing antipathy to the idea that preexisting rights, however derived, set limits to government authority. Whereas America's philosophical radicals spoke in terms of natural rights ("nonsense on stilts," in Bentham's judgment) and protections against government, Britain's emphasized a strain of legal positivism appropriate to an institutional setup with parliamentary supremacy at its core.

As Ryan points out, although Britain does not have a culture of rights in the same sense as America does, it has, nonetheless, recently been acquiring such a culture, with the gradual adoption of something roughly equivalent to the Bill of Rights in the offing. In a style reminiscent of the doubts and hesitations experienced by Madison and others who wondered about the strength and likely influence of mere parchment barriers designed to protect enumerated rights, Ryan speculates on the likely consequences of this expected turn in British constitutionalism. And so we have come full circle.

1

From natural law to the rights of man:
a European perspective on American debates

KNUD HAAKONSSEN

ENGLISH AND AMERICAN JURISPRUDENCE

As the first ten amendments were making their way through the provisions of the new Constitution they were to amend, American jurisprudence was being systematically formulated by the recently appointed professor to the new chair of law at the College of Philadelphia. With much rhetorical force and eclectic learning, James Wilson presented a public course of lectures, one important aim of which was to give an American answer to the jurisprudence of Sir William Blackstone. In doing so, he effectively provided one of the earliest sustained analyses of the contrast between the American cultivation of rights as the basis for social ethics and politicolegal institutions and the British reliance on a combination of common law and policy. Wilson would, in fact, have recognized all the leading themes in the latest such analysis, by Alan Ryan in the last chapter of this volume.

Nowhere is the theoretical scope of Wilson's polemics brought out more dramatically than in his discussion "of the natural rights of individuals."[1] Here Blackstone is joined by Edmund Burke's recent *Reflections on the Revolution in France* as the epitome of British thinking. Wilson understands the two British thinkers to be maintaining that all or—allowing for Blackstone's lack of clarity in the matter—at least all significant natural rights are given up in civil society in return for such fundamental legal rights as those contained in Magna Charta, that is,

[1] James Wilson, "Lectures on Law," in *Works,* ed. J. Dewitt Andrews, 2 vols. (Chicago, 1896), 2:296–336.

19

"civil privileges, provided by society, in lieu of the natural liberties given up by individuals."[2] Thus in his eyes the British held rights to be a kind of communal property to be granted to individuals and individuals to be "nothing but what the society frames."[3] It is as a contrast to this view that he formulates the well-known "American" ideas of human beings as the carriers—in society and out of it—of certain inalienable natural rights, and of civil society and its government as the means "to secure and to enlarge the exercise of the natural rights of its members."[4]

The striking thing about American jurisprudence, then as now, and the thing that has been seen as the main difference from British jurisprudence, is this emphasis on basic rights. For long periods this jurisprudence has been taken as the key to understanding both political thought and action in America in the last third of the eighteenth century. When major challenges to such interpretations have been launched, normally to establish the independent efficacy of politics and the political vis-à-vis jurisprudence and the law, a central problem has been to explain the prima facie prominence of rights talk. In these grand debates comparatively little attention has been paid to the concept of rights itself. The purpose of this chapter is to sketch some of the argumentative structure surrounding this concept in the eighteenth century. This will show that the status of rights was different from that commonly assumed, and that at least some of the divisions in the major scholarly disputes run along rather anachronistic lines.

The central point is that in the mainstream of natural jurisprudence in the eighteenth century natural rights derived from natural law and natural duty. Natural rights were understood as part of a morally well-ordered universe structured and lent certainty by the law of nature. Natural-rights theory was much less individualistic and antiauthoritarian than it has later been taken to be. Furthermore, the natural-law theory, of which it was part, was developed by a wide variety of British thinkers so as to accommodate a great deal of traditionalism, including that inherent in English constitutionalism and common-law thought. This cluster of doctrines constituted a formidable hindrance to the development of a subjective rights theory proper, that is, a theory according to which rights are the primary and basic moral feature of humanity. However, a number of steps toward such a theory were taken, and it is in the resulting

---

[2] Ibid., 302.
[3] Ibid., 303.
[4] Ibid., 307.

complex situation that we have to locate some important attempts by Americans to conceptualize their position. One such step was the strong emphasis upon the inalienability of certain rights—an idea that was already part of traditional natural-law theory and became crucial in a revolutionary situation. Another was the suggestion that the moral world might not be well ordered even in principle or, in other words, that clashes between rights might not simply be due to human folly or blindness but might be ultimate and unresolvable. A third move in the direction of a subjective-rights theory was the emergence of the idea of autonomy understood as the ability to impose obligation upon oneself, not as an effect of the moral law but as the foundation for all morals.

The moral philosophical paradigm based upon natural law was so dominant that these steps were taken uncertainly and with difficulty—the last two with such difficulty, in fact, that it remains uncertain when they were clearly made. In order to understand why this should be so, one must have an appreciation of the complexity of the natural-law tradition as it was developed into the conventional moral philosophy in which educated Britons and Americans alike were reared. Natural law became a prevalent academic form of moral philosophy in the eighteenth century, as it was taught in the two major Scottish universities and in many English dissenting academies and American colleges, as well as in latitudinarian Cambridge. Natural law was, in fact, schoolbook stuff, for it was generally taught to boys aged fourteen to eighteen as part of the arts curriculum that prepared them for all further education. It was thus crucial in forming a moral outlook and provided a framework into which other moral ideas had to fit or in which they must be tested. This applies not least to any innovations on a central point like the idea of rights.

PROTESTANT NATURAL LAW

The great natural-law theories of the seventeenth century are part of the attempts to formulate coherent moral-political theories within Protestantism. At the same time there are many continuities between scholastic and Protestant natural law, and it should be remembered that the major syntheses of the former appeared only in the sixteenth century in the great schools of Spain, culminating in the work of Francisco Suárez, as late as 1612.[5] It may therefore appear difficult to explain how natural

[5] For the following section, see K. Haakonssen, "Divine/Natural Law Theories in Ethics,"

law could be part of the breakup within Christianity, and in particular how for two centuries it could be an important part of the basic moral training of the educated classes in a cultural sphere whose religious reformation had such antinomian origins. Recent scholarship has put us in a better position to understand this.

Scholastic natural-law theory was problematic for a number of reasons. Perhaps most fundamental, it was an obvious target for the sort of moral skepticism that had been revived in the Renaissance and continued to have great influence in the formulations given it by thinkers like Montaigne and Charron. Scholastic natural law seemed to presuppose a degree of knowledge about God, the world, and human nature, which it was only too easy for skeptical criticism to undermine. Not least, it operated with an idea of God and of the relationship between God and man that could hardly be considered "natural" unless it could be shown to be pervasive outside the Christian world. One of the main points of modern skepticism was that this could not be done. Religious and moral notions were so relative to time and place that no theoretically coherent account could be given of them. A continuing ambition of modern natural law was, therefore, to overcome such skepticism.

Protestant natural law's answer to skepticism started from the fundamental Protestant objection to scholastic natural law, that the latter seemed to presuppose a moral continuity between God and man. For Protestant thinkers the starting point was the complete discontinuity between God and man, a discontinuity that made it impossible to give a rational account of human morality by reference to God and His eternal law. Only faith could bridge the gulf between man and his Creator. This led to a continuing ambiguity in Protestantism toward natural law as a rational account of morals. On the one hand, such an undertaking seemed impossible and pointless, since nothing but faith could sustain morality. On the other hand, precisely the circumstance that no ultimate account seemed attainable put pressure on thinkers to attempt whatever was possible in purely human and temporal terms. Thus if no amount of calculating human rationality could establish the link between man's behavior and God's reward or punishment, then man had either to live by faith alone or to find a purely human and temporal foundation for reward and, especially, punishment.

in M. Ayers and D. Garber, eds., *Cambridge History of Seventeenth-Century Philosophy* (Cambridge: Cambridge University Press, forthcoming), chap. 7, section 4.

We may see this ambiguity from a different angle. On the one hand, Protestant moral theology, and Luther's in particular, is an ethics of duty par excellence. There is here no room for degrees of perfection and improvement through good works, as in Catholic thinkers. Nothing that man can be or make of himself will justify him before God. If anything justifies—and according to some, nothing can—only faith does, and that only by God's grace. Our duty toward God is thus infinite, and we may view our temporal life as a network of unfulfillable duties, which natural-law theory may put into systematic form and give such worldly justifications as our limited understanding will permit. It is in this general perspective that we must view the overwhelming emphasis on duty in modern natural law. Notions of virtue were to be interpreted in terms of duty; rights derived from duty; prima facie supererogatory acts were to be seen simply as special duties. These are the basic ideas in what may be called the mainstream of modern natural-law theory and thus to a large extent in eighteenth-century moral philosophy.

There was, however, an entirely different line of thought. If our duty is really infinite and unfulfillable, then it is hard to see it as a possible guide to action; it provides no criterion for what behavior to choose. We can therefore live only by faith, and according to some even this was only for the elect few. This strongly antinomian line was adopted by a great many sects in the Reformation as well as later, and must undoubtedly be regarded as a target of no less importance than moral skepticism to Protestant natural-law theory. In fact, antinomian tendencies continued to create strains within the polite Calvinism of the high Enlightenment, which had otherwise adopted conventional natural-law theory for the teaching of moral philosophy. In America these strains came to the fore in the thought of John Witherspoon, and, as we shall see later, this was not without relevance to the theory of rights.

Our understanding of this connection is vastly complicated by another factor. The challenge of Renaissance skepticism was met not only by theories of natural law of the sort just mentioned but also by theories of natural rights.[6] Hugo Grotius and Thomas Hobbes in particular put

---

[6] For the pre-Grotian history of rights, see especially the work of B. Tierney, "Villey, Ockham and the Origin of Individual Rights," in J. Witte and F. Alexander, eds., *The Weightier Matters of the Law ... A Tribute to Harold Berman* (Decatur, Ga.; Scholars Press, 1987), 1–31; idem, "Conciliarism, Corporatism, and Individualism: The Doctrine of Individual Rights in Gerson," *Cristianesimo nella storia* 9 (1988): 81–111: and "Origins of Natural Rights Language: Texts and Contexts, 1150–1250," *History of Political Thought* 10 (1989): 615–46. Cf. R. Tuck, *Natural Rights Theories* (Cambridge: Cam-

forward the idea that it can be ascertained, *pace* the sceptics, that men have certain minimal rights, on the basis of which a common moral world is worked out. This was, however, a dangerously radical idea that was deprived of much of its force by a subversive rewriting of history, in the case of Grotius, and by incomprehending rejection, in the case of Hobbes. Partly for prudential reasons, Pufendorf, writing in the 1670s and 1680s, created the idea that he was continuing a natural-law theory begun by Grotius in the *De jure belli ac pacis* in 1625, and this led to the myth of a coherent natural-law tradition within Protestantism, stretching from Grotius to the late eighteenth century. We can only understand the full significance of this myth, which still persists, if we appreciate the fundamental division which it was meant to obscure.[7]

EARLY RIGHTS THEORY: GROTIUS AND HOBBES

The answer to skepticism given by Grotius and Hobbes may be briefly restated as follows: Since men as a matter of empirical fact exhibit a variety of forms of moral behavior and maintain moral, including social and political, institutions, the moral philosopher may legitimately inquire whether there is some moral fact, some moral feature of humanity, that is necessarily presupposed in all such behavior and institutions. Such a minimally necessary morality would seem to escape skeptical denials. If we accordingly abstract from existing moral forms, we will find a condition where men, concerned with their self-preservation, have to assert their respective claims, or rights, concerning themselves, each other, and the goods of the world. In order to do so rationally, they have to enter into agreements with each other about the creation of a civil society with an absolute sovereign power that will ensure harmony between conflicting claims. There is thus at least a minimal core of morality consisting of rights to self-preservation and the rational pursuit thereof. This is sufficient for social life, and it is universal because it follows necessarily from human nature itself.

For both these thinkers, rights are features of human nature; they are something men have. If they did not have them, that is, did not pursue

bridge University Press, 1979), chap. 1, and Tierney's criticism, "Tuck on Rights: Some Medieval Problems," *History of Political Thought* 4 (1983): 429–41.
[7] Concerning the rewriting of the history of moral philosophy, see especially R. Tuck, "The Modern Theory of Natural Law," in A. R. D. Pagden, ed., *The Languages of Political Theory in Early Modern Europe* (Cambridge: Cambridge University Press, 1987), 99–119.

these claims rationally, human life would be impossible. Grotius elaborates this by suggesting that a right is not only a claim in the interest of self-preservation, but the mental power (right reason) to make such a claim rationally, which means the power to judge one's own claim vis-à-vis the claims of others. The motivation to exercise this latter ability is provided by a natural inclination toward sociability, which is as empirically ascertainable as the drive toward self-preservation. In its subjective aspect, a right is thus in effect a moral power that, when exercised, does not conflict with the similar exercise of the moral powers of others. In its objective aspect a right is the well-judged exercise of the moral power, and this falls into three general groups, powers over oneself, powers over things, and (contractually created) powers over others.[8]

These rights, of course, do not exhaust our morality. In addition to recognizing rights of others that do not infringe on the similar rights of ourselves, we have a certain ability to recognize claims that do or might so infringe. These are quasi or imperfect rights which, unlike perfect rights, are not absolutely necessary to the very existence of social life and which consequently are less certain and universal. Our moral faculty recognizes that it is inherently good to honor both perfect and imperfect rights. Consequently such behavior may be considered as prescribed by the Author of our nature, that is, as a law of nature. For Grotius the concept of natural law is thus derivative from rights, and he stresses that the behavior prescribed by God is obligatory in itself—that is, without God—and that this circumstance distinguishes it from the prescription of divine positive law.[9] But although Grotius is relatively clear in his account of morals in terms of rights and self-imposed contractual obligations, his willingness to accommodate the notion of a divinely issued natural law, albeit in an argumentatively subordinate position, was sufficient to get him enrolled as the founder of "the" modern school of natural law.

While Hobbes agreed with Grotius that individuals in a state of nature can recognize the equal right of others to self-preservation, they have, in the view of the former, no objective or intersubjective means of judging

---

[8] The account of Grotius's theory of rights is mainly based on *The Rights of War and Peace* [1625], ed. J. Barbeyrac, 3 vols. (London: W. Innys et al., 1738), Book I, chaps. 1 and 2, section i. Cf. Tuck, *Natural Rights Theories*, chap. 3; idem, "Grotius, Carneades, and Hobbes," *Grotiana*, N.S. 4 (1983): 43–62; Haakonssen, "Hugo Grotius and the History of Political Thought," *Political Theory* 13 (1985): 239–65.

[9] Grotius, *Law of War and Peace*, Prol. XI-XII, XLIX, and LI.

when others are simply defending their own right and when they are aggressors; they can only judge from an overriding concern for their own safety. Hobbes has to seek a political solution to this impasse in his moral theory, namely the creation of an absolute sovereign. By contrast, Grotius thought that individuals can agree on a range of minimal rights issues in the state of nature, so that the eventual establishment of civil institutions simply secures these.[10] For Grotius there are two reasons why men in the state of nature can agree not only *that* others have the right to self-preservation and the rights that follow therefrom, but also to a significant extent, on *what* those rights are in particular circumstances. First, transgressions against such rights are inherently wrong—so inherently wrong that not even God could make them acceptable. Grotius is, in anachronistic terms, a moral realist. Second, men have the moral power to recognize such objective values. They have the ability to see what is good for others, as well as for themselves, and this ability is commonly recognized. Hobbes, on the other hand, gives a completely subjectivist account of what is good and bad and of moral judgment. Of course he introduces into this scheme a notion of natural law, which is "right reason" bidding individuals to close off some of their endless options or rights by seeking peace with others. However, in itself this injunction does not help so long as we have no objective standard for recognizing when others are or are not following the same injunction. Only when the natural law becomes institutionalized, that is, when it has become the sovereign's law, do we have such a standard.

To contemporaries and most successors Hobbes seemed to have arrived at a skepticism (what today is called relativism) even worse than the Renaissance variety that Grotius had seen as his target. Natural law seemed to have been largely emptied of meaning, and it had become exceedingly difficult for most to see how human nature, on Hobbes's account of it, would even allow the formation of social relations. In fact, Hobbes's radicalization of the subjective-rights theory made it so feared that for more than a century only a few thinkers could even understand it properly. A typical example is Richard Cumberland who, in the English-

---

[10] See Tuck, *Hobbes* (Oxford: Oxford University Press, 1989), 63–4. The account of Hobbes is based mainly on *The Elements of Law Natural and Politic*, ed. F. Tönnies (Cambridge: Cambridge University Press, 1928), 1:14–17, 19, and 2:1, 10; *De cive* [1641], ed. H. Warrender (Oxford: Oxford University Press, 1983), 1:1–3, and 2:5–6, 14; *Leviathan* [1651], ed. C. B. Macpherson (Harmondsworth: Penguin Books, 1968), 1:13–14, and 2:17–18, 26.

speaking world, was for long seen as the third man, along with Grotius and Pufendorf, in the seventeenth-century founding of "the" modern school of natural law.[11] Cumberland simply found it hard to take seriously Hobbes's suggestion that from the hand of nature everyone in a sense has a right to anything he wants. One thing is our natural power to act: "But when we are enquiring into the Rights of Acting, the Question is, which among the Actions which are in our Power, are lawful? Any Answer to this Question, without respect had to some Law, at least that of Nature, is absurd."[12] If rights were not "guarded by the Laws of Nature," then they would clash and the result would be Hobbes's war of all against all. Along with many others, however, Cumberland thought that the latter idea was empirically refutable and, furthermore, that an unresolvable conflict of rights was simply impossible, since it would show that God was inconsistent. God would, in that case, have created a world in which two or more people would have contradictory "right reasons." Such contradictions arise only from human error, since each man's "right reason" is, in fact, delegated from God's reason, or is part of God's reason.[13]

NATURAL-LAW THEORY: PUFENDORF

The development of subjective-rights theories like those of Grotius and Hobbes was quelled not only by disbelief but, as the quotations from Cumberland show, by a theory in which rights are derived from natural law. This line of argument had many variations, Cumberland's being one of them. However, it was the forceful formulation by Samuel Pufendorf, Cumberland's contemporary, that made natural-law theory one of the most important moral-philosophical idioms of the Enlightenment.[14]

---

[11] See Haakonssen, "Sociability and Obligation in Richard Cumberland's Natural Jurisprudence," in H.-E. Bödeker and I. Hont, eds., *Unsocial Sociability, Natural Law and the Eighteenth-Century Discourse on Society* (London: Routledge, forthcoming), and L. Kirk, *Richard Cumberland and Natural Law* (Cambridge: James Clarke, 1987).

[12] Richard Cumberland, *A Treatise of the Law of Nature* [1672], trans. J. Maxwell (London: R. Phillips, 1727), I:xxxv; cf. I:xxviii.

[13] Ibid., II: vi-viii.

[14] Concerning Pufendorf's influence, see, e.g., R. Derathé, *Jean-Jacques Rousseau et la science politique de son temps* (Paris: Librairie philosophique Vrin, 1988); Haakonssen, "Natural Law and the Scottish Enlightenment," in D.H. Jory and C. Stewart-Robertson, eds., *Man and Nature*, Proceedings of the Canadian Society for Eighteenth-Century Studies, 4 (1985): 47–80; I. Hont, "The Language of Sociability and Commerce: Samuel Pufendorf and the Theoretical Foundations of the Four Stages Theory," in Pagden, ed., *Languages of Political Theory*, 253–76; B. Lindberg, *Naturrätten i Uppsala 1655–1720*

Often Pufendorf's system of jurisprudence was used eclectically and its philosophical underpinnings replaced by, or fused with, other philosophical theories, including some ideas from Cumberland, as we shall see; but the system itself and the notion of the primacy of law, natural law, were planted firmly at the center of Enlightenment moral thought, thanks to the enormous popularity of Pufendorf's treatises in all of Protestant Christianity (and beyond).

Pufendorf's answer to the skeptical challenge was, in effect, to point out that the moral world, like the physical, exhibits a certain orderliness and then to enquire what must be presupposed if we are to account for this order.[15] The answer is that just as there are laws in accordance with which physical phenomena take place, so there are laws of moral phenomena. While the former are causal laws, however, the latter must be prescriptive, since their subjects are agents of free will. If free agents were not subject to prescriptions, their actions would simply be random physical events. Furthermore, the idea of a prescription or law implies a legislator, namely, God. The basic law of nature follows from human nature and its circumstance, that is, from the fact that man is naturally impelled to seek his self-preservation and the fact that he cannot achieve this in isolation. The basic law is to be sociable.

All this may allegedly be understood rationally without the aid of revelation and is thus a supraconfessional and, indeed, universal basis for all morals. The same applies to at least the immediate derivations from this basis. The first law of nature is a commandment to be sociable with humanity wherever it is encountered, that is, both in ourselves and in others, which means that we have duties partly to ourselves, partly to

(Uppsala: Acta Universitatis Upsaliensis, 1976); K. Luig, "Zur Verbreitung des Naturrechts in Europa," *Tijdschrift voor Rechtsgeschiedenis/Revue d'histoire du droit* 40 (1972): 539–57; M. Medick, *Naturzustand und Naturgeschichte der bürgerlichen Gesellschaft. Die Ursprünge der bürgerlichen Sozialtheorie als Geschichtsphilosophie und Sozialwissenschaft bei Samuel Pufendorf, John Locke und Adam Smith* (Göttingen: Vandenhoeck and Ruprecht, 1973).

[15] The discussion that follows is based mainly on Samuel von Pufendorf, *The Law of Nature and Nations* [1672], ed. J. Barbeyrac, trans. B. Kennet, 5th ed. (London: J. and J. Bonwicke et al., 1749), Books I–III, and on *The Whole Duty of Man according to the Law of Nature* [1673], ed. J. Barbeyrac, trans. A. Tooke, 5th ed. (London, 1735), Book I. The principal monographs on Pufendorf are H. Denzer, *Moralphilosophie und Naturrecht bei Samuel Pufendorf* (Munich: C. H. Beck, 1972); L. Krieger, *The Politics of Discretion, Pufendorf and the Acceptance of Natural Law* (Chicago and London: University of Chicago Press, 1965); and P. Laurent, *Pufendorf et la loi naturelle* (Paris: Librairie philosophique J. Vrin, 1982). An excellent brief presentation of the basics in English is J. B. Schneewind, "Pufendorf's Place in the History of Ethics," *Synthèse* 72 (1987): 123–55.

others.[16] Duties to ourselves mean duties to cultivate our person in both its physical and its moral aspects, because such cultivation is the point of God's creation of us and, by extension, because it is necessary for our association with others. It should here be explained that in this form of natural-law theory, there is a distinction between the "obligator" who puts us under the obligation to do our duty, and the beneficiary of this duty. God is the obligator to the duties of natural law, whereas the beneficiary is either oneself (duties to self) or others (duties to others). The benefit that the beneficiary has is his *right*. From this point of view a right is that which there is a duty to yield, whether to oneself or to others. Rights are, however, also derived from duties and law in a different way. That which we have a duty to do, we must have a right to do, and in this sense a right is a moral power to act, granted by the law of nature in order to fulfill the duties imposed by this law. Rights thus have both a passive and an active side, both of which are directly derived from duties conceived as impositions of natural law.

Pufendorf divides the general field of rights into four categories of deontic powers: power over one's own actions (*libertas*); power over another person's actions (*imperium*); power over one's own things (property or *dominium*); power over another person's property (*servitus*).[17] The three last are adventitious, that is, they are instituted by individuals through contractual and quasi-contractual arrangements, and they therefore presuppose the first power. *Libertas* encompasses the absence of subjection in one's command of one's own physical and moral personality—one's life, actions, body, honor, and reputation. This right, or cluster of rights, does not depend on the agreement of others; it exists in a person by nature or innately, inasmuch as everyone is by nature subject to the law of nature.

The connection between duty and right is made even closer through another feature of Pufendorf's work. The Latin word *officium*, which is normally translated as *duty*, often means something wider than duty in

---

[16] After the first publication of his major treatise *De jure naturæ et gentium* in 1672, Pufendorf added duties to God, and this tripartite division of the duties became entrenched for the next century and more. Pufendorf himself undoubtedly had difficulties with the idea of separate duties to God. For one thing they were a sort of umbrella for the other duties: to know and, consequently, to obey God meant first of all to do the duties to oneself and to others. Furthermore, Pufendorf remained as firm as his Lutheran upbringing would lead one to expect in his belief that there could be no moral society with God; duties to God must therefore mean something entirely different from duties to humanity.

[17] Cf. K. Olivecrona, "Die zwei Schichten im naturrechtlichen Denken," *Archiv für Rechts- und Sozialphilosophie* 63 (1977): 79–103.

the modern sense, namely, the offices, roles, or stations that we occupy in life. These offices encompass not only duties but also the accompanying or entailed rights. The basic offices of life fall into three categories, that of being *tout court* a human being under natural law, that of being a member of a family (as spouse, parent, child, sibling, master, servant), and that of being a member of a political society (as citizen, sovereign, all manner of magistrates, soldier, and so on). These offices provide the framework for Pufendorf's detailed analyses of the specific natural jurisprudential relations of persons, of "oeconomical" relations in the traditional sense of the household economy, and of civic relations. Self-consciously inspired by stoicism, this theory fitted directly into the Christian stoicism of the Enlightenment and lived on in the popular practical ethics of the eighteenth century as Pufendorf's most pervasive legacy, though often on philosophical foundations different from his own. In order properly to appreciate this central feature of Enlightenment moral thought, it is necessary to keep in mind the relations between natural law, duties, and rights outlined earlier.[18]

THE FORMATION OF AN EIGHTEENTH-CENTURY PARADIGM

The impact of Pufendorf's natural-law theory is a matter of great complexity, not least as far as the English-speaking world is concerned. As generally in this chapter, we have to concentrate more on conceptual structure than historical processes. Schematically we may say that in the critical debate about Pufendorf there were two problems of particular importance to the theory of rights. The common answer to one of these strongly reinforced the derivative character of rights just sketched. The diverse answers to the other could have worked in the opposite direction but generally did not, thus creating an interesting explanatory task for the historian. The first problem concerned the knowledge of natural law, the second the obligation to it.

First, a voluntarist theory like Pufendorf's presupposed some knowledge of God's sanctions for the law. However, as he himself acknowledged, because knowledge of an afterlife was gained only through

---

[18] Cf. Haakonssen, "Natural Law and Moral Realism: The Scottish Synthesis," in M. A. Stewart, ed., *Studies in the Philosophy of the Scottish Enlightenment* (Oxford: Oxford University Press, 1990), 61–85; and idem, Introduction, in Thomas Reid, *Practical Ethics. Being Lectures and Papers on Natural Religion, Self-Government, Natural Jurisprudence, and the Law of Nations,* ed. with Introduction and Commentary by K. Haakonssen (Princeton, N.J.: Princeton University Press, 1990), 52ff.

revelation, the much-wanted separation of natural law from revealed— as opposed to natural—religion was not achieved. The obvious solution to this problem seemed, for an empirically minded age, to be to trace God's sanctions in the present life. This had, in fact, already been attempted in a simple-minded fashion by Cumberland. For him there was an empirically ascertainable approximate correlation between virtue and happiness and vice and unhappiness. At least the correlation was so close that it could only be by design, and this design could by analogy be extended beyond the present life. The moral world is in principle, or ideally, a well-ordered one—often referred to as the common good of all rational beings—in which there is harmony between the moral judgments of all individuals. Or, put negatively, it is a world in which there are no unresolvable moral conflicts, no irreducible moral dilemmas. Only misguided judgment prevents this world from being ours, but the empirically ascertainable providential order of the world means that we may be sure that every right moral judgment somehow contributes toward the realization of this world.

This idea was elaborated in ever more detailed and sophisticated ways and was disseminated by thinkers like Francis Hutcheson throughout the Anglo-American world, as we shall see examples of below. It was evidently one of the major stumbling blocks for the development of anything like a subjective rights theory of the sort we have encountered in Grotius and Hobbes. The hallmark of the latter is that there is no guarantee even in principle that men's individual moral judgments can harmonize. It is precisely for this reason that people must create their own human guarantees through contractual devices that close off some of their limitless possibilities. If we know in advance that harmony in principle is possible, then the moral pursuit is an entirely different one from that of contractual trade-offs ad infinitum (or at least for as long as human life endures); rather, it is a matter of fulfilling one's duty to seek this harmonious common good. Furthermore, if a rights theory could be sustained, it would seem to make morals in principle independent of religion, even natural religion, while a theory of law and duty would fit a variety of religious beliefs. Against this background the horror and incomprehension, which often characterized the reaction to Hobbes during the seventeenth and eighteenth centuries, and of which we earlier saw a typical example in Cumberland, becomes more intelligible.

The other problem in the reaction to Pufendorf, to which we referred earlier, concerns the obligation to natural law. This is one of a cluster of connected problems that can only be indicated here. As a problem in voluntarist theories like Pufendorf's the point was seen as follows. If individuals are to be under a moral obligation to God's law and not simply subject to His superior power, then they must have an understanding of the justifiability of God's law and its sanctions. Such understanding, however, seems to imply a moral ability in human beings prior to all natural law and, indeed, independent of God considered as moral authority.

Speculation about man's innate moral power was, of course, one of the most prominent features of British moral thought both in connection with and independently of natural-law theory. From the late seventeenth and throughout the eighteenth century, British thinkers were divided over the nature of the moral power—whether it was a feature of reason or whether it was to be understood by analogy with perception and, if the latter, how such a "moral sense" was related to reason. However, the important point here is the common assumption that individuals do have such a distinctive moral power. Whatever its precise nature, such a power would seem to be an obvious foundation for rights: it would be by means of the moral power that people would stake their claims, or rights, and relate their own rights to those of others through contracts and the like. Furthermore, as we saw earlier, Grotius's early rights theory contained a notion of moral power or ability, thus providing a precedent for this line of argument.

Despite all this, neither moral sense theories nor their "rationalistic" counterparts developed into subjective-rights theories of the Grotian and Hobbesian variety. It is true that thinkers often linked their concept of rights to the function of the moral power, but both had to be understood in terms of the law of nature. Typical and highly influential was Hutcheson's argument: "From the constitution of our *moral faculty* ... we have our notions of *right* and *wrong,* as characters of affections and actions." However, "This is the *rectum,* as distinct from the *jus* ... : the *jus* ensues upon the *rectum.*" Hutcheson then goes on to show how subjective rights, *jura,* "ensue upon" that which is right, *rectum,* when the latter contributes to the common good. Since the common good is the primary prescription of the law of nature, we can see that "*rights* as moral qualities, or *faculties* [that is, *jura*] [are] granted by the law of nature."[19] In other words, the

[19] Francis Hutcheson, *A System of Moral Philosophy,* 2 vols. (London: A. Millar and T. Longman, 1755), 1: 252–6; cf. *A Short Introduction to Moral Philosophy* (Glasgow: R. Foulis, 1747), 118–20 (and 109–10). Cf. Haakonssen, "Natural Law and Moral Real-

moral sense gives us spontaneous ideas of right actions, but which of these actions are in fact rights that we (or others) have depends upon their contribution to the common good, which is the duty prescribed by the law of nature.[20]

The derivative status of natural rights vis-à-vis natural law and its duties may be further illustrated and confirmed in a wide variety of eighteenth-century thinkers, including many of importance in America. Morton White has done so with particular sharpness in the case of Locke and the important Jean-Jacques Burlamaqui.[21] Here we might add further variety by pointing to a thinker from the Anglican fold, Thomas Rutherforth, who is thoroughly ordinary and typical (and, like Grotius, Pufendorf, Locke, Hutcheson, and Burlamaqui, taken for granted by James Wilson as a household name amongst his educated audience).

As Regius Professor of Divinity at Cambridge from 1756 to 1771 Rutherforth was at the heart of Cambridge latitudinarianism,[22] whose philosophical basis is spelled out in his main works in the form of a by now traditional theory of natural law, "or the Knowledge of Right and Wrong" (as Isaac Watts defined it):[23]

The actions of men are, in their own nature, either good, or bad, or indifferent. ... The law of nature ... enjoyns all those actions, which are morally good, and forbids all those which are morally bad. By this means the former become duties, and the latter crimes.... But when any actions, which are indifferent in themselves, are commanded or forbidden by any express revelation of Gods will; those actions likewise ... become duties, and ... crimes: however, as the actions in themselves, or in their own nature, affect the common good of mankind neither one way or other, as they have nothing in them either morally good or morally bad; this sort of duties are called positive duties.[24]

ism." The best general monographs are W. Leidhold, *Ethik und Politik bei Francis Hutcheson* (Freiburg, Munich: Karl Alber, 1985), and W. R. Scott, *Francis Hutcheson: His Life. Teaching and Position in the History of Philosophy* (Cambridge: Cambridge University Press, 1900).

[20] It is worth noting that Hutcheson himself did not comprehend Grotius as a subjective-rights theorist but saw him as a precursor of his own. *A System of Moral Philosophy*, 1:255.

[21] Morton White, *The Philosophy of the American Revolution* (New York: Oxford University Press, [1978] 1981). Cf. "Inalienable Rights" below.

[22] See John Gascoigne, *Cambridge in the Age of the Enlightenment: Science, Religion, and Politics from the Restoration to the French Revolution* (Cambridge: Cambridge University Press, 1989), especially chap. 5: idem, "Anglican Latitudinarianism and Political Radicalism in the Late Eighteenth Century," *History* 71 (1986): 22–38.

[23] I. Watts, *The Improvement of the Mind, or, a Supplement to the Art of Logick* (London, 1741), 341.

[24] Thomas Rutherforth, *Institutes of Natural Law*, [1754] 2d. ed. (Cambridge: J. Archdeacon, 1774), 17–18.

The forms of behavior which are pointed out by natural law as good are those that bring happiness, on the whole, to ourselves and to our neighbor, and that please God.[25] In other words, Rutherforth presents the usual combination of moral realism and Christian utilitarianism, as it has come to be known,[26] and on this basis he goes on to clarify the relationship among law, right, and obligation:

> Our actions or our possessions are just, where they are consistent with law; and consequently the right which any person has to do any action, or to possess any thing, is nothing more than his power of doing this action, or possessing this thing consistently with law. Right and moral power are expressions of like import. A mans natural power extends to every thing, which his strength enables him to perform, whether the law allows it or not. But his moral power extends to such things only, as his strength enables him to perform consistently with law. For in a moral sense, or in reference to such rules as a man is strictly obliged to observe in his behaviour, he is not supposed to have any more power than what the law allows him to exercise.[27]

In these circumstances it is not surprising to find that "obligation and right are correlative terms: where any person has a right, some one or more persons are under an obligation, which corresponds to that right" and vice versa.[28] Rutherforth draws the traditional distinctions between

---

[25] Ibid., 9–13. For Rutherforth's influence on Paley, see D. L. Le Mahieu, *The Mind of William Paley* (Lincoln: University of Nebraska Press, 1976), 124.

[26] Cf. Blackstone, to add but one other genre in which we find this combination (we might as well have taken, say, Philip Doddridge's textbook for the dissenting academies): God "has laid down only such laws as were founded in those relations of justice, that existed in the nature of things antecedent to any positive precept. These are the eternal, immutable laws of good and evil, to which the creator himself in all his dispensations conforms.... He has so intimately connected, so inseparably interwoven the laws of eternal justice with the happiness of each individual, that the latter cannot be obtained but by observing the former; and, if the former be punctually obeyed, it cannot but induce the latter. [Accordingly] he has not perplexed the law of nature with a multitude of abstracted rules and precepts, referring merely to the fitness or unfitness of things, as some have vainly surmised; but has graciously reduced the rule of obedience to this one paternal precept, "that man should pursue his own happiness." This is the foundation of what we call ethics, or natural law." Blackstone. *Commentaries on the Laws of England*, 4 vols. (Oxford: Clarendon Press, 1765–69), 1: 40–41. How could Bentham not give credit for this! For Doddridge, see *A Course of Lectures on the Principal Subjects in Pneumatology, Ethics, and Divinity* [1763], 2 vols., 4th ed. (London: G. G. and J. Robinson et al., 1799), 1: 188ff. Cf. also J. E. Crimmins, "John Brown and the Theological Tradition of Utilitarian Ethics," *History of Political Thought* 4 (1983): 523–50.

[27] Rutherforth, *Institutes of Natural Law*, 27. Cf. Jefferson: "Of liberty then I would say that, in the whole plenitude of its extent, it is unobstructed action according to our will, but rightful liberty is unobstructed action according to our will within limits drawn around us by the equal rights of others." Letter to Isaac H. Tiffany, 4 April 1819, in *The Political Writings of Thomas Jefferson*, ed. E. Dumbauld (Indianapolis, New York: Bobbs-Merrill, 1955), 55.

[28] Rutherforth, *Institutes of Natural Law*, 29–30.

perfect and imperfect rights and duties, natural and adventitious rights, and alienable and inalienable rights, both sides of the distinction in each case being entirely dependent upon natural law. The consequence of the logical primacy of law is that right and duty become not only correlative in this sense but, in the case of the basic rights, interchangeable with duties in the manner we have already explained.[29] We should therefore not be surprised to find, in a chapter devoted to a discussion "Of the Right which a Man has in his own Person," a subheading, "Duty towards ourselves," under which Rutherforth sets out rights and duties in a way that reveals the nature of his theory very clearly:

It seems to be self-evidently true, that no man can have a right to manage his own person, or to dispose of it in such a manner, as will render him incapable of doing his duty. For his duty is a restraint, which arises from the law of nature: he cannot therefore have any right to free himself from that, unless he has a right to free himself from all restraints, which the law of nature has laid him under. The consequence of this is, that a mans right to his life or his limbs is a limited right; they are his to use, but not his to dispose of. As they were given him to use, whoever deprives him of them does him an injury. But then, as they are not his to abuse or dispose of, it follows, that he breaks through the law of nature, whenever he renders himself incapable of complying in any instance with that law, which the author and giver of his life and limbs, has required him to observe. ... A duty, which we can release ourselves from at pleasure, is unintelligible; it is in effect no duty. the law of nature could not in any respect be binding upon a man, if we suppose him to have such a right in his own person, that he may at any time, by his own voluntary act, lawfully release himself from the whole obligation of it, or in any respect render himself incapable of performing it.[30]

We can hardly find a clearer expression of the common dogma that a self-imposed obligation cannot be the foundation of morals,[31] from which it was inferred that rights must in some sense be derivative from some higher moral standard.

RIGHTS AND CONTRACTARIANISM

The prevalence of this line of argument in the eighteenth century leads to some reconsideration of the basics of much moral-political thought in

---

[29] Cf. Jean-Jacques Burlamaqui, *The Principles of Natural and Politic Law*, [1747–48], 2 vols., trans. T. Nugent [1748], 2d. ed. (London: J. Nourse, 1763), 1: 74: "There are rights which of themselves have a natural connexion with our duties, and are given to man as means to perform them."
[30] Rutherforth, *Institutes of Natural Law*, 146–7.
[31] Cf. "Self-Government and Obligation" below.

the period. Rights are not simply powers granted, but powers granted for a purpose; they have a right use, namely, that of contributing to an overall moral order. Consequently they are never granted as open-ended powers, but always in conjunction with matching duties—duties to use them properly and duties on others then to respect them. As John Witherspoon put it in his lectures at Princeton: "Right in general may be reduced, as to its source, to the supreme law of moral duty; for whatever men are in duty obliged to do, that they have a claim to, and other men are considered as under an obligation to permit them."[32]

It is the package deal of rights and duties in a person that is so often referred to as that person's office, role, station, or even character, but since, as we have mentioned, the Latin *officium* was also often translated as "duty," we find a great deal of linguistic confusion. While the sense of "the rights and duties of one's office" is immediately intelligible, "the obligations of one's office," not to speak of "the moral obligations of duty,"[33] are somewhat desperate attempts to keep separate the particular actions which one's office, in the sense of station, require—and not only desperate but unfortunate, for "obligation" had a separate function to indicate the moral necessity one is under in fulfilling a duty.

Once we think about the impositions of natural law as offices, the individualistic contractarianism that traditionally is ascribed to natural-law theory looks rather different. The relations constituting the family or the more extensive society cannot simply be understood as negotiated deals abridging the potentially open-ended claims of individuals. Rather they are specifications of the relationship among the offices imposed upon individuals by natural law. This idea is exactly what made it so easy to interpret all contracts as tacit, implied or quasi-contracts, and this interpretation again made it easier to evade criticism of the unhistorical character of contractarianism and promoted the assimilation of the prescriptive use of history into natural-law contractarianism.

Once again we have to contend with fluid and uncertain language. Tacit contract is not always clearly distinguished from implied contract, and in modern scholarship the latter has all but disappeared, except

---

[32] John Witherspoon, *An Annotated Edition of "Lectures on Moral Philosophy,"* ed. J. Scott (Newark, London, Toronto: University of Delaware Press and Associated University Presses, 1982), 110.

[33] As, for example, in Hume, *A Treatise of Human Nature* [1739–40] (Oxford: Clarendon Press, 1978), 568. Similarly, Witherspoon wanted to derive "the nature or obligation of duty" from human nature; see *Lectures on Moral Philosophy*, 79.

among legal historians who remember its civil-law ancestor, quasi-contract.[34] However, using various Roman-law materials, natural lawyers and moral philosophers through the seventeenth and eighteenth centuries slowly and by apparently uncertain steps, which I have indicated elsewhere,[35] achieved an interesting distinction. The central point is that a tacit contract is simply an unspoken contract, that is, it is an event involving the will of the contracting parties which gives rise to an obligation.

By contrast an implied contract is not an event; it is rather a purely implied and fictional thing which is inferred from a relation between two or more parties, of such a nature that it is *as if* it were based on a contract, though, in fact, it is not. An implied contract therefore does not presuppose an act of will in the same way that both explicit and tacit contracts do. An implied contractual obligation may simply be a situation one happens to find oneself in. The nature of such obligations can therefore not be inferred from what the contracting parties did intend to will; it must rather be inferred from the nature of the situation in which they find themselves, that is, from the role or office they have in that situation. If you find yourself alone faced with a disaster on your absent neighbor's property, you have an obligation of care as if you had promised him to look after the place. You find yourself to be a child of parents you did not choose, but you have the obligations of a child as if you had, because a child is what you are. You are a citizen/subject and have the obligations of this office, because that is what you are. Questions of voluntariness arise, of course, but the point of this approach is that voluntariness is not a matter of either/or, but of more or less. Within a range of voluntariness that cannot be specified a priori for all cases, once a person signals that he or she is playing a certain role, the performance is judged in terms of the obligations that generally pertain to that role.

This is where history comes in. Our notions of the many offices which make up human life are inevitably based on experience, and so it is by using the ways institutionalized in the past that a king can signal his office and be understood, just as it is with the barber hanging out his

---

[34] See the splendid article by Peter Birks and Grant McLeod, "The Implied Contract Theory of Quasi-Contract: Civilian Opinion Current in the Century before Blackstone," *Oxford Journal of Legal Studies* 6 (1986):46–85.

[35] See Haakonssen, Introduction, 66–8 and 70–1: and Commentary, 356–8 and 405–7, in Reid, *Practical Ethics;* and, again, Birks and McLeod, "The Implied Contract Theory of Quasi-Contract."

sign, or the spouse who continues to behave in the ways expected of this role. It is not the passing of time which creates obligation; the obligation arises from the office discharged as if we had contracted to do it; but we can only discharge the office because the past tells us what it is. I submit that this is the general tenor of a great deal of so-called contractarianism in the eighteenth century. Once the natural-law legacy from Pufendorf and others concerning the offices imposed by natural law is read in this way, it can assimilate most forms of traditionalism in morals and politics, including traditional English constitutionalism, as we shall see below.

It is of course a moral philosophy which was tailor-made for a conservative Enlightenment.[36] With its emphasis upon the recognizable offices of life and society, it seemed to make traditional social arrangements both understandable and justifiable. At the same time the suggestion of a possible balance between duties and rights lent credibility to the ideal of moral improvement through enlightenment and thus to the justifiability of social betterment. The philosophical foundations were mainly laid in the moral philosophy classes of the Scottish universities and especially in the work of Francis Hutcheson and Thomas Reid,[37] but the general train of ideas became the stable core in the popular moral philosophy that penetrated to an ever-growing reading public.

A good example is David Fordyce's *Elements of Moral Philosophy*. Fordyce taught moral philosophy at Marischal College in Aberdeen and was one of many direct links between the Scots enlighteners and the

---

[36] See J. G. A. Pocock, "Post-Puritan England and the Problem of the Enlightenment," in P. Zagorin, ed., *Culture and Politics from Puritanism to the Enlightenment* (Berkeley: University of California, 1980), 91–111; idem, "Clergy and Commerce: The Conservative Enlightenment in England," in Ajello et al., eds., *L'Età dei Lumi: studi storici sul settecento europeo in onore di Franco Venturi,* 2 vols. (Naples: Jovene Editore, 1985), 2:523–68; idem, "Conservative Enlightenment and Democratic Revolutions: The American and French Cases in British Perspective," *Government and Opposition* 24 (1989): 81–105. Cf. also Pocock, "Josiah Tucker on Burke, Locke, and Price: A Study in the Varieties of Eighteenth-Century Conservatism," in his *Virtue, Commerce, and History. Essays on Political Thought and History, Chiefly in the Eighteenth Century* (Cambridge: Cambridge University Press, 1985), 157–91.

[37] See J. Moore, "The Two Systems of Francis Hutcheson: On the Origins of the Scottish Enlightenment," in Stewart, *Studies in the Philosophy of the Scottish Enlightenment,* 37–59; Haakonssen, "Natural Law and Moral Realism," in ibid., 61–85; R. B. Sher, "Professors of Virtue: The Social History of the Edinburgh Moral Philosophy Chair in the Eighteenth Century," in ibid., 87–126. For Reid, see Haakonssen, Introduction, in Reid, *Practical Ethics.* For the general context, see Sher, *Church and University in the Scottish Enlightenment: The Moderate Literati of Edinburgh* (Edinburgh: Edinburgh University Press, 1985).

English dissenters. His work on moral philosophy was first written for *The Preceptor*, a comprehensive popular course in all the arts and sciences aimed at "trying the Genius, and advancing the Instruction of Youth," and engineered by the author and publishing entrepreneur Robert Dodsley.[38] Subsequently another Scots dealer in ideas with an eye for a wider market, William Smellie, used Fordyce's work—in the meantime also published as a successful book[39]—for the extensive article on "Moral Philosophy" in his new *Encyclopaedia Britannica*.[40] And the unitarian minister and educator John Prior Estlin gave Fordyce's conventional version of a very conventional moral philosophy further coverage by basing his "familiar lectures" on it.[41]

Even wider circulation resulted from the adoption of such ideas into one of the most popular genres of the time, the "conduct-books" for women, many of which analyzed women's domestic and social relations in terms of the proper discharge of offices, directly derived from the standard section on "oeconomical jurisprudence" in any system of natural jurisprudence.[42] This part of natural jurisprudence was also the source of professional ethics, of which medical ethics considered as systems of mutually related offices—or implied contracts—between doctor and patient was only the most spectacular.[43]

[38] *The Preceptor: Containing a General Course of Education. Wherein the First Principles of Polite Learning Are Laid Down in a Way Most Suitable for Trying the Genius, and Advancing the Instruction of Youth*, 2 vols. (London: R. Dodsley, 1748). Concerning Fordyce, see W. H. G. Armytage, "David Fordyce: A Neglected Thinker," *Aberdeen University Review* 36 (1956): 289–91; J. C. Stewart-Robertson, "The Well-Principled Savage, or The Child of the Scottish Enlightenment," *Journal of the History of Ideas* 42 (1981): 503–25; P. Jones, "The Polite Academy and the Presbyterians, 1720–1770," in J. Dwyer, R. A. Mason, and A. Murdoch, eds., *New Perspectives on the Politics and Culture of Early Modern Scotland* (Edinburgh: John Donald, 1982), 156–78.

[39] David Fordyce, *Elements of Moral Philosophy* (London, 1754). For the use of this work at Harvard, see D.W. Robson, *Educating Republicans. The College in the Era of the American Revolution, 1750–1800* (Westport, Conn.: Greenwood, 1985), 16–17, 82, and 168.

[40] *Encyclopaedia Britannica*, 3 vols. (Edinburgh: A. Bell and C. Macfarquhar, 1771), 3:270–309. See R. L. Emerson, "Science and Moral Philosophy in the Scottish Enlightenment," in Stewart, *Studies in the Philosophy of the Scottish Enlightenment*, 11–36, at 25–28; A. Murdoch and R. B. Sher, "Literary and Learned Culture," in T. M. Devine and R. Mitchison, eds., *People and Society in Scotland* (*A Social History of Modern Scotland*, 3 vols., 1760–1830) (Edinburgh, 1988), 1:127–42, at 137.

[41] John Prior Estlin, *Familiar Lectures on Moral Philosophy*, 2 vols. (London, 1818).

[42] A useful survey of the sheer extent of this genre is in W. St. Clair, *The Godwins and the Shelleys: The Biography of a Family* (London: Faber and Faber, 1988), 504–10.

[43] My information on these matters comes from work in progress by Lisbeth M. Haakonssen.

In an entirely different genre, even the most influential system of international law, that of Vattel, largely follows this pattern.[44] Finally we may refer to an ambitious attempt by the latitudinarian divine Thomas Gisborne to map the whole of "the Duties of Men in the Higher and Middle Classes of Society in Great Britain, resulting from their respective stations, professions, and employments," beginning with the duties of the sovereign and ending with those of "persons engaged in trade and business" and of "private gentlemen."[45]

The authors of such works had generally been taught moral philosophy in a Scottish university or a dissenting academy. The most philosophically sound presentation was that of Thomas Reid in Glasgow, which I have dealt with at length elsewhere.[46] As for the dissenting academies, we know that many of the most important of these regularly taught natural law in the way just outlined.[47] The moral philosophy section of the most popular of textbooks in the academies, Philip Doddridge's *Course of Lectures on the Principal Subjects in Pneumatology, Ethics, and Divinity,* followed the established pattern of duties to God, to others, and to ourselves, based on a straightforward Christian utilitarianism, and this was typical of the academy curricula in moral philosophy.[48]

---

[44] Emerich de Vattel, *The Law of Nations, or Principles of the Law of Nature applied to the Conduct and Affairs of Nations and Sovereigns,* [1758], 2 vols. (London, 1759–60). See the Introduction for a survey. Vattel organizes much of his material into the state's duties to itself and to others, with duties to God incorporated into the former (Book I, chap. 12). The traditional difficulty of understanding the relationship between the conventional and the natural in the law of nations has to be looked at again in the light of the notions of office and implied contract.

[45] Thomas Gisborne, *An Inquiry into the Duties of Men in the Higher and Middle Classes of Society in Great Britain, Resulting from their Respective Stations, Professions, and Employments,* 2 vols. (London, 1794: 6th ed., 1811). The full list of duties includes those of the sovereign, Englishmen as subjects and fellow citizens, peers, members of the House of Commons, executive officers of government, naval and military officers, the legal profession, justices of the peace and municipal magistrates, the clerical profession, physicians, persons engaged in trade and business, and private gentlemen. The philosophical foundations are given in exactly the manner to be expected in Gisborne's *The Principles of Moral Philosophy Investigated, and Applied to the Constitution of Civil Society* (London, 1789; 4th ed. by 1798). And one is not surprised that he added, for good measure, the 400 pages of *An Enquiry into the Duties of the Female Sex* (London: T. Cadell, Jr., and W. Davies, 1797), which reached 11 editions in 19 years.

[46] Haakonssen, Introduction, in Reid, *Practical Ethics.*

[47] For a brief survey, see Anthony Lincoln, *Some Political and Social Ideas of English Dissent 1763–1800* [1938] (New York: Octagon, 1971), chap. 3. Cf. H. McLachlan, *English Education under the Test Acts, Being the History of the Non-Conformist Academies 1662–1820* (Manchester: Manchester University Press, 1931); and J. Seed, "Gentlemen Dissenters: The Social and Political Meanings of Rational Dissent in the 1770s and 1780s," *Historical Journal* 28 (1985): 299–325.

[48] Philip Doddridge, *A Course of Lectures on the Principal Subjects in Pneumatology,*

Many more examples could be given of the pervasiveness of this conventional moral philosophy and its adaptation of the natural-law framework. In the present context its political-constitutional use is, however, of the greatest importance, especially as we find it in the great Whig oracle Blackstone himself. After ridiculing the mere idea that civil society has its beginnings in historical contracts and briefly sketching instead a Scottish-type "stages" theory of society, he writes:

But though society had not it's formal beginning from any convention of individuals, actuated by their wants and fears; yet it is the *sense* of their weakness and imperfection that *keeps* mankind together; that demonstrates the necessity of this union; and that therefore is the solid and natural foundation, as well as the cement, of society. And this is what we mean by the original contract of society; which, though perhaps in no instance it has ever been formally expressed at the first institution of a state, yet in nature and reason must always be understood and implied, in the very act of associating together: namely, that the whole should protect all it's parts, and that every part should pay obedience to the will of the whole; or, in other words, that the community should guard the rights of each individual member, and that (in return for this protection) each individual should submit to the laws of the community; without which submission of all it was impossible that protection could be certainly extended to any.[49]

To us this notion of implied contractual obligations, inferred from a more or less tradition-bound notion of the office that implies the obligation, may well appear as the death of "real" contractarianism. But then we have probably been brought up on too much Hobbes for our own good as eighteenth-century scholars. My point is just that a Hobbesian theory of subjective rights as the basis for contractual relations is foreign to what is conventionally known as the great age of contractarianism. This is further underlined by Blackstone's discussion of rights in the first chapter of his great work. After explaining natural rights in the conventional natural-law terms with which we are now familiar, he sketches the major steps by which these rights have been declared through English history. For Americans at least such declarations could only mean that the natural rights had been surrendered and then returned as a grant

---

Ethics, and Divinity 1:169–312. Doddridge, typically, also meant his course to be a guide to the literature for the students' self-education. His copious reading lists to this part of the course most frequently cite Pufendorf's *De jure* and *De officio,* with Grotius's *De jure* a close second, followed by Fénélon, Locke's *Second Treatise,* Hutcheson, Hoadly, Barbeyrac, Grove, and others.

[49] Blackstone, *Commentaries,* I:47–48. Cf. D. Lieberman, *The Province of Legislation Determined: Legal Theory in Eighteenth-Century Britain* (Cambridge: Cambridge University Press, 1989), chaps. 1–2.

from civil government. This point was the central target of James Wilson's critique, as we saw at the beginning of this chapter.

NATURAL-LAW THEORY AND MORAL PHILOSOPHY IN AMERICA

The derivative nature of rights and the watering down of contractarianism were intimately connected and, when used to assimilate the English constitution into the traditional natural-law framework, it constituted one, if not the, major stumbling block for the American attempt to formulate a theory of natural rights as the foundation for American civil society and its constitution. The Americans broke the connection between traditionalism and the derivative character of rights, and they got rid of the former—or at least reduced it significantly. But apparently nobody achieved a radical theory of subjective rights of the sort whose beginnings we encountered in Grotius and Hobbes. Philosophically rights remained derivative.[50]

This is, of course, not surprising, for Americans drew upon the same natural-law tradition as their British contemporaries, and they shared its development into the broader, conventional moral philosophy outlined earlier. In saying this, I am not trying to enter into the rather common monocausal, or at least single-track, patterns of explaining American intellectual life, American independence, or American constitutionalism. I have no method of intellectual calibration that allows me to measure the relative significance of the roles played in these wider contexts of natural law, common law, evangelicalism, liberalism, or republicanism, of whatever stripe. My explanandum is a good deal narrower than the intellectual origins of American ideology of independence. On the assumption that natural-law theory and the moral philosophy built on it had a presence of some significance in America in the later eighteenth century, my main concern here is to explain the conceptual structure of such theories and so contribute to a characterization of the culture of rights in which events like the adoption of the first ten amendments took place.[51] But I am happy to add that such a concern is a necessary pre-

---

[50] In Britain there was at least one notable exception to this generalization, namely, Adam Smith. However, Smith's theory had several unusual features, and it was never developed in published form. See Haakonssen, *The Science of a Legislator: The Natural Jurisprudence of David Hume and Adam Smith* (Cambridge: Cambridge University Press, 1981), especially 99–103.

[51] Even with this modest agenda I may be in conflict with J. P. Reid's interesting attempt to reduce everything to common-law ideas; see his *Constitutional History of the American Revolution: The Authority of Rights* (Madison: University of Wisconsin Press, 1987),

liminary to considerations of how natural-law theory related to other moral and political theories.

Whatever the exact role of natural law and the associated moral philosophy in the great events in North America in the last third of the eighteenth century, the assumption mentioned seems well founded and is widely documented in the literature.[52] Perhaps the most important point to remember is that this material was, in effect, school-learning. Several important American colleges, following the Scottish and dissenting pattern already discussed, taught a natural law–based moral philosophy as part of the arts curriculum.[53] Apart from general political talk of rights, the theory of rights outlined here was thus the first, and certainly the first systematic, exposition of the topic to which significant parts of the American intelligentsia were exposed while still boys in their teens.[54]

e.g., p. 95: "There was little substantive difference between natural rights and positive rights. To dissect a natural right was to find a British right and it was natural because the British possessed it. . . . Natural rights were the reflection, not the essence; they were the confirmation, not the source, of positive rights." Even if this view were correct—and it is hard to square with the central texts—the historian must still ask whether the loose natural-rights talk makes sense on the premises of those using it, why people indulged in it at such great length from an early age, and *how* many people of the time could see the theories of natural law and British constitutionalism to be compatible.

[52] The literature bearing on this wide topic is extensive. Much of it is marred by a lack of distinctions between various strands of European natural-law thought and by neglect of the connection between some of these and eighteenth-century moral thought. Philosophically the outstanding discussion is White, *Philosophy of the American Revolution*, but see also N. Fiering, *Jonathan Edwards's Moral Thought and Its British Context* (Chapel Hill: University of North Carolina Press, 1981); B. Kuklick, *Churchmen and Philosophers: From Jonathan Edwards to John Dewey* (New Haven, Conn.: Yale University Press, 1985), chaps. 1–6; E. Flower and M. G. Murphey, *A History of Philosophy in America,* 2 vols. (New York: Putnam, 1977), vol. 1. Of the more broadly historical studies I have used in particular B. Bailyn, *The Ideological Origins of the American Revolution* (Cambridge, Mass.: Harvard University Press, 1967); H. F. May, *The Enlightenment in America* (New York: Oxford University Press, 1976); and G. Wood, *The Creation of the American Republic, 1776–1787* (Chapel Hill: University of North Carolina Press, 1969). Cf. also D. Walker Howe, "European Sources of Political Ideas in Jeffersonian America," *Reviews in American History* 10 (1982): 28–44; and F. McDonald, *Novus Ordo Seclorum: The Intellectual Origins of the Constitution* (Lawrence: University of Kansas Press, 1985).

[53] See in general H. Miller, *The Revolutionary College: American Presbyterian Higher Education, 1707–1837* (New York, 1976); and D.W. Robson, *Educating Republicans* (Westport, Conn.: Greenwood Press, 1985), especially 82–7, 123–6, 148–52, 162–71, 191–4 and 206–9. Cf. also D. C. Humphrey, *From King's College to Columbia, 1746–1800* (New York: Columbia University Press, 1976); M. A. Noll, *Princeton and the Republic 1768–1822* (Princeton, N.J.: Princeton University Press, 1989); D. Sloan, *The Scottish Enlightenment and the American College Ideal* (New York: Teachers College Press, 1971).

[54] It is not surprising that the Revolution principles often were seen as less than revolutionary. As Jefferson repeatedly emphasized late in his life, his work on the Declaration of Independence was meant "not to find out new principles, or new arguments, never

It is uncertain and controversial how much direct influence was exerted by the seventeenth-century natural lawyers, especially Pufendorf and Locke.[55] However, whether Americans read the original texts or learned their ideas from textbooks like those of Hutcheson, Rutherforth, Fordyce, or Burlamaqui—to mention only the few already referred to—the common theoretical framework for teaching and learning was certainly natural-law theory. It was generally based on Christian utilitarian principles of one sort or another, and, if not, such principles were still expounded at length as the central object of the lecturer's criticism—and followed by the usual system of duties.[56] An early example of the former is Francis

before thought of, not merely to say things which had never been said before; but to place before mankind the common sense of the subject, in terms so plain and firm as to command their assent, and to justify ourselves in the independent stand we are compelled to take." Letter to Henry Lee, 8 May 1825, in *The Writings of Thomas Jefferson,* ed. A. E. Bergh, 20 vols. (Washington, D.C.: Thomas Jefferson Memorial Association of the United States, 1907), 16:118. Cf. also letter to James Madison, 30 August 1823, ibid., 15:462.

[55] Concerning Pufendorf, see H. Welzel, "Ein Kapital aus der Geschichte der amerikanischen Erklärung der Menschenrechte," in R. Schnur, ed., *Zur Geschichte der Erklärung der Menschenrechte* (Darmstadt: Wissenschaftliche Buchgesellschaft, 1964), 238–59; Clinton Rossiter, *Seedtime of the Republic* (New York: Harcourt, Brace, 1953), especially 212ff.; A. Haddow, *Political Science in American Colleges and Universities 1636–1900* (New York and London: Appleton-Century-Crofts, 1939); D. Klippel, *Politische Freiheit und Freiheitsrechte im deutschen Naturrecht des 18. Jahrhunderts* (Paderborn: Ferdinand Schöningh, 1976), chap. 3. Concerning Locke, see, for example, J. Dunn, "The Politics of Locke in England and America in the Eighteenth Century," in J. W. Yolton, ed., *John Locke: Problems and Perspectives* (Cambridge: Cambridge University Press, 1969), 45–80; D. Grimm, "Europäisches Naturrecht und Amerikanische Revolution: Die Verwandlung politischer Philosophie in politische Techne," *Ius Commune* III (1970): 120–51; T. L. Pangle, *The Spirit of Modern Republicanism: The Moral Vision of the American Founders and the Philosophy of Locke* (Chicago: University of Chicago Press, 1988); Pocock, *Virtue, Commerce, and History.*

[56] The American connections with the Scottish Enlightenment have been cultivated with particular intensity. There are several surveys of the literature, but see especially D. Walker Howe, "Why the Scottish Enlightenment Was Useful to the Framers of the American Constitution," *Comparative Studies in Society and History* 31 (1989): 572–87, and R. B. Sher, "Introduction: Scottish-American Studies, Past and Present," in Sher and J. R. Smitten, eds., *Scotland and America in the Age of the Enlightenment* (Princeton, N.J.: Princeton University Press, 1990), 1–27. Of particular interest for the following are Garry Wills, *Inventing America: Jefferson's Declaration of Independence* (New York: Vintage Books, [1978] 1979), and the criticism by R. Hamowy, "Jefferson and the Scottish Enlightenment," *William and Mary Quarterly* 36 (1979): 503–23; P. J. Diamond, "Witherspoon, William Smith and the Scottish Philosophy in Revolutionary America," in Sher and Smitten, *Scotland and America,* 115–32; D. F. Norton, "Francis Hutcheson in America," *Studies on Voltaire and the Eighteenth Century,* 154 (1976): 1547–68; C. Robbins, " 'When It Is That Colonies May Turn Independent': An Analysis of the Environment and Politics of Francis Hutcheson (1694–1746)," *William and Mary Quarterly* 11 (1954): 214–51; and S. C. Stimson, " 'A Jury of the Country': Common Sense Philosophy and the Jurisprudence of James Wilson," in Sher and Smitten, *Scotland and America,* 193–208.

Alison's lectures at the College of Philadelphia from the 1750s onward; a contemporary example of the latter is Thomas Clap's teaching at Yale, soon to be followed by Witherspoon's at Princeton, which we shall encounter later.[57] By the end of the century such adaptations of natural-law theory had acquired the same quality of academic orthodoxy as they had somewhat earlier in Britain. The ethical and political sections of Samuel Stanhope Smith's undergraduate lectures at Princeton bear a very close resemblance to those of several of his older Scottish colleagues, especially Thomas Reid,[58] and James Wilson's systematization of American jurisprudence in 1790–1 represents, in its theoretical aspects, an excellent summing-up, complete with a virtual guide to the literature, of the tradition with which we have been concerned here.[59]

Having grown up with natural-law theory and the associated moral philosophy, it is hardly strange that Americans found use for such ideas in their own writings and, eventually, in the documents of independence and constitution building. It is of course in these fields, and especially the latter, that the great historiographical controversies are raging concerning the relative importance of different traditions. The unwary reader

[57] See Sloan, *Scottish Enlightenment and American College Ideal*, 88–94; Norton, "Hutcheson in America," and Thomas Clap, *An Essay on the Nature and Foundation of Moral Virtue: Being a Short Introduction to the Study of Ethics: for the Use of the Students of Yale-College* (New Haven: B. Mecom, 1765). A further interesting perspective on this matter, which cannot be pursued here, is that these three intellectual leaders were of different theological orientations, Alison an Old Side Presbyterian, Clap a strongly antirevivalist Congregationalist, and Witherspoon a Scottish evangelical who in America was expected to align himself with New Side Presbyterianism and yet managed to include elements of Butlerian and Hutchesonian moral philosophy.

[58] Samuel Stanhope Smith, *The Lectures, Corrected and Improved, Which Have Been Delivered for a Series of Years, in the College of New Jersey: On the Subjects of Moral and Political Philosophy*, 2 vols. (Trenton: D. Fenton, 1812). Like Reid, Smith massively increased the treatment of the philosophy of mind. Reid's lectures were not published at the time; see Reid, *Practical Ethics*. The most important discussion of Smith is Noll, *Princeton and the Republic*.

[59] There was more than this, of course, to Wilson's teaching. Cf. the important studies by S. A. Conrad, "Polite Foundation: Citizenship and Common Sense in James Wilson's Republican-Theory," *Supreme Court Review, 1984* (1985): 359–88; and "Metaphor and Imagination in James Wilson's Theory of Federal Union," *Law and Social Inquiry* 13 (1988): 1–70; and by Stimson, " 'A Jury of the Country' "; and *The American Revolution in the Law: Anglo-American Jurisprudence before John Marshall* (London: Macmillan, 1990), 127–36. Wilson draws on a wide variety of sources. By far his most frequent reference is Blackstone, followed by the ever present Bacon. Then come John Millar for legal history, Pufendorf for legal theory, Reid for epistemology and moral psychology, and Cicero for everything. Behind these come Burlamaqui, Paley, Grotius, Vattel, Beccaria, Burke, Gibbon, Heineccius, Locke, Hooker, Wooddeson, Montesquieu, Pope, Rutherforth, Shaftesbury, Hume, Rousseau, Hutcheson, Kames, Barbeyrac, Bolingbroke, Hobbes, plus a number of legal sources.

is tossed around between "liberal," "republican," and "evangelical" interpretations of American action and mind.[60] Of these, the liberal line of argument traditionally promoted the importance of natural rights. However, after a decade or more out of the scholarly limelight, liberalism has returned, broadened and bettered, according to many. It has supposedly benefited from the growing understanding of the Scottish Enlightenment and its influence in America and can accordingly now see that the liberal individual of revolutionary and independent America exercised his rights with a moral sense. Since moral-sense theory, furthermore, can be seen as a theory of virtue, and since "republicanism" is centrally concerned with virtue, some rapprochement between the two great "isms" has appeared possible.[61]

This syncretic move has its problems. It still assumes that it makes sense to talk of liberalism in this context, and that whatever else this might have been about, it was also concerned with natural rights. But liberalism is a nineteenth-century construct that is best kept out of these discussions, and the Scottish philosophy that influenced Americans was only concerned with rights within the natural-law and duty framework outlined earlier. Americans did not change this framework, and it was this inherited natural *law* that could provide a certain assimilation of republicanism. Throughout the eighteenth century the languages of duty and of virtue were practically interchangeable—for moral-sense theorists as well as ethical rationalists—and it never seemed to trouble those of a neoclassical republican tendency, like Hutcheson, to switch from the jurisprudential concept of duty to the republican concept of virtue.[62] Virtuous behavior was duty, and the performance of duty was virtue. Rights had their place in this scheme, but it was a logically subordinate one, as we have seen. It is thus primarily the anachronistic use of a vaguely rights-based liberalism which has made it appear to scholars that there was a deep division between it and republicanism. This is not to deny that the traditions of natural law and republicanism have different clas-

---

[60] Excellent overviews are provided by J. T. Kloppenberg, "The Virtues of Liberalism: Christianity, Republicanism and Ethics in Early American Political Discourse," *Journal of American History* 74 (1987): 9–33; and P. S. Onuf, "Reflections on the Founding: Constitutional Historiography in Bicentennial Perspective," *William and Mary Quarterly* 46 (1989): 341–75.

[61] See Kloppenberg, "The Virtues of Liberalism," especially pp. 28ff. For the wider debate on the relationship between republicanism and liberalism, see also Onuf, "Reflections on the Founding," 346–50.

[62] See Haakonssen, "Natural Law and Moral Realism," and, for a contrasting view, J. Moore, "The Two Systems of Francis Hutcheson."

sical and early modern ancestries, or that there remained republicans with no use for natural law. The point is that by the eighteenth century the popular moral philosophy based on natural law, which was taught in the colleges, was not only no hindrance to republican politics; its notion of the duty to virtue provided more of a philosophical foundation for the latter than it had had before.[63]

This harmony was not to last. Just as the emerging emphasis on rights disrupted the assimilation of English common-law traditionalism into a natural-law framework, so it eventually led to a new phenomenon, liberalism, at loggerheads with much of the republican legacy. This was the outcome of the search for a rights theory, not the cause of it. In order to conceptualize the search itself, we must remain within the theoretical framework already outlined. In other words, we must explain how rights could become argumentatively effective although they were justified in terms of law and duty. However, in order to underline how complex and difficult a matter it was to break with this tradition and approach a subjective-rights theory proper, we shall also indicate two imperfect steps in that direction. The final sections of this chapter will therefore be devoted to three lines of argument. The first concerns the inalienability of rights, the second questions the Christian-utilitarian idea of rights as derivative from a common good prescribed by natural law, and the third deals with the ideas of individual autonomy and the ability of individuals to impose obligations upon themselves.

INALIENABLE RIGHTS

The problem concerning the inalienability of rights was central to Americans' understanding and justification of their dispute with Britain, as James Wilson explained.[64] If certain basic rights were to be the moral touchstone by means of which the conduct of all instituted authority was to be checked, such rights must exist on a basis that made them transcend all institutions of authority. They must somehow be inherent to the human species and thus continue to be justifiably held by persons in society as well as out of it. Furthermore, the institutions of civil society

---

[63] Cf. Haakonssen, "Natural Jurisprudence in the Scottish Enlightenment: Summary of an Interpretation," in D. N. MacCormick and Z. Bankowski, eds., *Enlightenment, Rights, and Revolution: Essays in Legal and Social Philosophy* (Aberdeen: Aberdeen University Press, 1989), 36–49.

[64] Cf. White, *Philosophy of the American Revolution*, chap. 5; and idem, *Philosophy, "The Federalist," and the Constitution* (New York: Oxford University Press, 1987), 32–34.

must be seen primarily as safeguards for such rights. This argument was at the heart of the theoretical rationale of the American rebellion against British authority and the institution of a new civil society. The question then was, How could one justify the proposition that certain rights are basic in this sense, and which rights are these?

The answer is, in a way, simple to the point of triviality within the natural-law tradition we have been tracing.[65] It was, in fact, only the great need of the Founders, particularly Jefferson, to formulate in theoretical terms the crucial locus of British transgression that brought the point to the fore. Even then it was hardly explained. It was a matter of course in theory, which now needed to be asserted in practice. Yesterday's matter of course is commonly today's puzzle, and so it has often been in this case. If natural rights are derivative from the duties imposed by natural law in the sense that rights are powers granted by the law in order to fulfill its duties and thus its purpose, then the rights are necessary to human life under the natural law, that is, to all moral life. There can therefore be no moral justification for alienating such rights. A right is a duty and a duty a right.

It should here be pointed out that there was considerable terminological confusion concerning the phrase *natural rights*. In the broadest sense, natural rights were those that people had in the state of nature as distinct from the positive rights instituted by civil society. In this sense, natural rights encompassed rights to property and contractual rights— rights that were excluded by the other common and more restrictive sense of the term. For natural rights were also distinguished from adventitious or acquired rights, which are the result of human activity or arrangements—typically the acquisition of property or the establishment of contracts—while natural rights pertain to persons without any such initiatives being taken. Some of the rights which are natural in this sense can, however, be alienated while others cannot, and it is this group we occasionally have referred to noncommittally as "basic."[66]

---

[65] In the following discussion I agree with Morton White, ibid., concerning the most basic point, that the inalienability of rights derives from the dependence of rights upon duties. I work the thesis out somewhat differently from White, and I do not go into the details of these differences, as they would require considerable discussion.

[66] Cf. Witherspoon's explanation: "The distinction between rights as alienable and unalienable is very different from that of natural and acquired. Many of the rights which are strictly natural and universal may be alienated in a state of society for the good of the whole as well as of private persons; as for example, the right of self defense; this is in a great measure given up in a state of civil government into the hands of the public" (*Lectures on Moral Philosophy*, 111). Witherspoon is bound to have confused his students

Clearly only a limited number of natural, nonadventitious rights can be inalienable. In fact, of *specific* rights, only the rights to life and liberty could be considered inalienable within the natural-law theory presupposed here. We have a duty, and consequently a right, to maintain God's creation as we find it in ourselves. Similarly we have a duty, and hence a right, to maintain ourselves as moral agents under natural law and consequently cannot justifiably give up all of our liberty: a vestige must always remain in the form of the right of judgment. This was the reason why there could not be natural slavery; a being without a minimum of moral judgment about himself or herself is simply not a person or moral agent. This minimum must be preserved even in life-long servitude—the legitimacy of which was commonly allowed. In addition it was not uncommon to think that if a person was already morally "dead," having made himself a non-person through incurable moral depravity, then slavery was in order; it was, in effect, moral death in place of physical.

In addition to the two basic rights of life and liberty we also have a duty, and therefore a right, to seek out the means to maintain these two rights for ourselves. As far as our physical being is concerned, we must appropriate things around us. This right is commonly referred to as a right to property though, strictly speaking, as an *inalienable* right it can never be more than a right to *seek* property (plus, according to some, a right to subsistence). As for our moral being, we must seek the means to independence of judgment, namely freedom of opinion and speech.

There is, however, a clear difference between the two basic duties/ rights to life and liberty and the derivative duties/rights to the means of maintaining life and liberty. The derivative duties/rights form a kind of framework rights because they may be implemented through a variety of institutional arrangements. Consequently Jefferson for the purposes of the Declaration of Independence had to choose the broad and somewhat vague phrase, the right to "the pursuit of happiness" (which could also encompass the pursuit of both physical and moral means). This broadening and the implied exclusion of a specific inalienable right to private property was controversial, but entirely consonant with the natural-law doctrine sketched earlier. Although the right to the pursuit of happiness, considered as a framework-right, is indeed necessary and

when he added, "and the right of doing justice to ourselves or to others in matters of property is wholly given up." Property is precisely an acquired right, but it is "natural" in the wider sense of obtaining in the state of nature. Cf. Thomas Reid, *Practical Ethics*, 188–203; and Haakonssen, Introduction, in ibid., 58ff.

inalienable, the specific forms it takes in any given place will be a matter of human action, and the specific rights to which they lead (for example, communal versus several property) are, therefore, both alienable and adventitious.[67] Similarly all other rights, while ultimately deriving their justification from the basic, inalienable rights and, hence, from the law of nature, are adventitious devices to implement the law.

This solution to the problem of rights is the most coherent interpretation that can be given of the central, mainly Jeffersonian, formulations of the American standpoint. It provided a basis for the common rejection of English traditionalism and conventionalism, of the sort we have met with in Blackstone, as far as the ultimate natural rights are concerned. It thereby also gave meaning to contractarianism of a kind somewhat closer to the modern notion than the implied contractarianism outlined earlier. The contract supporting civil government was between individuals who retained an identifiable core of rights, for the sake of whose protection other rights were alienated to create government. At the same time, by limiting the natural rights proper to the well-known three, it underlined the alienable and adventitious character of the rest and so allowed wide scope for the assimilation of the historically contingent.[68]

In a sense this solution simply follows the logic of traditional natural-law theory: Certain basic rights are inalienable because they are duties under natural law, and all other duties/rights derive their ultimate justification more or less directly from these. None of the American theoreticians put forward a clear idea of rights as underived, primary features of the human person, and one inevitably gets the impression that some of the apparent moral certainty stemmed from the fact that Americans stayed well within the comfortable moral world of traditional natural-law theory with its assurance of an in-principle harmony of individual rights and duties.

If this account is correct, the question remains why Americans (and

---

[67] As Jefferson explains, well knowing the traditional rhetoric concerning property, "It is a moot question whether the origin of any kind of property is derived from nature at all.... By an universal law, indeed, whatever, whether fixed or movable, belongs to all men equally and in common, is the property for the moment of him who occupies it, but when he relinquishes the occupation, the property goes with it. Stable ownership is the gift of social law, and is given late in the progress of society." Letter to Isaac McPherson, 13 August 1813, in *Writings of Jefferson*, 13:333. Cf. White, *Philosophy of the American Revolution*, 213–28.

[68] Cf. Jefferson's dictum that "[our government] is a composition of the freest principles of the English constitution, with others derived from natural right and natural reason." "Notes on Virginia," in *Writings of Jefferson*, 2:1–261, at 120 (Query VIII).

a growing number of Britons) increasingly claimed life, liberty, and the pursuit of happiness (or some more or less clearly conceived equivalent) as *rights* when they might as well have asserted them as duties. One obvious answer is that it was rhetorically and polemically more forceful to point out that your just claims were being denied than that your duties were being taken out of your hands. Another, theoretically much more interesting, answer can be found by attending to an apparently unconnected question, which also arises from the present interpretation, namely, What became of the duties to others?

As we have seen, it was a common point in natural-law theory that we have a basic duty to preserve God's moral creation wherever we encounter it, in ourselves and in others, which means that we have to be sociable and promote the common good. However, the basic inalienable rights in American theory are all derivative from our duties to ourselves only. Here the equality of basic rights comes in. Since life, liberty, and the pursuit of happiness are equally duties for all, they are equally rights for all, and accordingly there is a duty on everyone not to disturb this equality, that is, to leave all others to enjoy their basic rights. The primary duty to others is simply to leave them alone.[69]

Behind this doctrine lies the assumption that God's moral creation is best nurtured when each person looks after his own part of it, namely himself. This assumption is in fact twofold. The first is that, if each person did not look after his or her own basic duties/rights, then he would simply not have a complete moral personality; and the more people are in that condition, the further away is the optimal common good. This fundamental natural-law—and in the end Protestant—idea of the necessity of personal judgment in morals always favored the rights-side of the Janus-faced notion of duty/right. It also provided an opening for further development, as we shall see later. The other assumption is that in practical terms it is most realistic and efficient that each person cultivates his or her own life, liberty, and pursuit of happiness. It is most realistic because it is taken for granted that self-love is one, if not the most, fundamental

---

[69] Cf. Jefferson: "No man has a natural right to commit aggression on the equal rights of another; and this is all from which the laws ought to restrain him; every man is under the natural duty of contributing to the necessities of the society; and this is all the laws should enforce on him; and, no man having a natural right to be the judge between himself and another, it is his natural duty to submit to the umpirage of an impartial third. When the laws have declared and enforced all this, they have fulfilled their functions; and the idea is quite unfounded, that on entering into society we give up any natural right." Letter to Francis W. Gilmer, 7 June 1816, in *Writings of Jefferson*, 15:24.

feature of human nature. Consequently it is also most efficient because people on the whole are more motivated to pursue their own good than that of others. When eventually combined with an economic theory of the market, this aspect of rights theory became recognizably political in the narrower sense. Possessive individualism did come about, though a couple of centuries too late to fit the scholarly bill.[70]

A standard controversy, of course, concerned the moral situation when these assumptions did not hold and especially when individuals were not the best judges of their own good, whether because of ignorance or because their judgment was irrelevant, as in illness or famine.[71] The logic of traditional natural-law theory was that such persons still had basic rights under natural law. The duty/right to life entailed at least a right to subsistence, and the duty/right to liberty entailed at least that one could not sell one's person but only one's services. To that extent, if no further, I am my brother's keeper. As we know, this logic was not always appreciated in practice.

However, it was obviously assumed that on the whole the strict or perfect duties to others, that is, duties essential to the very existence of society, were discharged by simply respecting the basic rights of others. In this light it is not strange that life, liberty, and the pursuit of happiness should be emphasized as rights rather than as duties, though duties they also were.

EVANGELICALISM AND CHRISTIAN UTILITARIANISM

A cornerstone in the natural-law theory discussed here is the proposition that the law of nature prescribes duties and grants matching rights that, when properly taken care of, contribute to the general common good or greatest happiness in God's creation. As part of the general providentialism of the age, this idea was found as much in America as in Britain. As long as rights were thought of within this scheme, there was no real

---

[70] I am, of course, referring to C. B. Macpherson's interpretation of seventeenth-century political thought, *The Political Theory of Possessive Individualism: Hobbes to Locke* (Oxford: Oxford University Press, 1962). In a more general explanation of American political thought, the ideas set out in the text should be related to Revolutionary thinkers' understanding, and possible readjustment, of the balance between self-interest and the public good in republican theory, as discussed in R. C. Sinopoli, "Liberalism, Republicanism and the Constitution," *Polity* 19 (1987): 331–52; and L. Banning, "Some Second Thoughts on Virtue and the Course of Revolutionary Thinking," in T. Ball and J. G. A. Pocock, eds., *Conceptual Change and the Constitution* (Lawrence: University of Kansas Press, 1988), 194–212, especially 199–201.

[71] We disregard conditions like childhood, insanity, and various forms of dependence, because they raise questions of a different sort, namely, when a person is a person.

chance of developing a subjective-rights theory proper. In such a theory there would be no guarantee that the maze of individual rights, or claims, even in principle could exist harmoniously as part of the common good. On the contrary, in such a theory no such assumption could be made the justifying ground for rights, and in its absence individuals, starting from no other moral assumptions than their own and others' several claims, would seek temporal, historically contingent guarantees through contractual arrangements of moral (social and political) institutions.

Insofar as the eighteenth century had any clear idea of such a rights theory, it associated it with irreligion and Hobbesian chaos and the concomitant authoritarianism. The reaction of Cumberland, described earlier, would still have been typical a century later.[72] Alternatively eighteenth-century moralists would have associated such ideas of the moral primacy of the individual spirit and its claims with religious "enthusiasm" and generally antinomian evangelicalism.

There is a long-standing tradition in American scholarship for seeking the springs of individualism, independence, and self-government in one or another form of evangelical religion.[73] The question here is, however, a different and much more modest one, whether there were any conceptual points of contact between evangelicalism and natural law. While evangelicalism is often represented as a doctrine of the Christian virtues, it was by the same token also a doctrine of Christian duty. The emphasis on duty was a quite fundamental point in common with natural law, and this in practice provided evangelicals who became teachers with an opening for preserving elements of both lines of thought. At the same time they could use evangelical religion to undermine natural law, and it is, in fact, from this quarter that we encounter a clear blow at the

---

[72] See notes 12 and 13 above.
[73] The pioneering study is P. Miller, *Errand into the Wilderness* (Cambridge, Mass.: Harvard University Press, 1956). As an outsider I have found P. U. Bonomi's *Under the Cope of Heaven: Religion, Society, and Politics in Colonial America* (New York: Oxford University Press, 1986), particularly useful, not least for its explanation of the fusion of Old Light rationalism and New Light emotionalism with Whig resistance ideology. Cf. also A. Heimert, *Religion and the American Mind: From the Great Awakening to the Revolution* (Cambridge, Mass.: Harvard University Press, 1966); N. O. Hatch, *The Sacred Cause of Liberty: Republican Thought and the Millennium in Revolutionary New England* (New Haven: Yale University Press, 1977); W. G. McLoughlin, *Revivals, Awakenings, and Reform: An Essay on Religion and Social Change in America, 1607–1977* (Chicago: University of Chicago Press, 1978), chaps. 2–3; R. H. Bloch, *Visionary Republic: Millennial Themes in American Thought, 1756–1800* (Cambridge: Cambridge University Press, 1985); and H. S. Stout, *The New England Soul: Preaching and Religious Culture in Colonial New England* (New York: Oxford University Press, 1986).

conventional Christian-utilitarian basis of natural law. It was delivered
at one of the main centers for the education of the new American mind,
in John Witherspoon's lectures on moral philosophy to the Princeton
undergraduates.

Witherspoon's lectures are notoriously eclectic, and he was not a good
enough moral thinker to make a coherent whole of what he picked up
from his many sources.[74] He was, however, quite clear-headed enough
to see where the real dividing line lay between his own evangelical notions
of man's duty and those of mainstream natural-law moralists, of whom
his former compatriot and opponent, Francis Hutcheson, was the ar-
chetype. In the main, Witherspoon's course follows the natural law—
derived organization that was standard in Scottish moral philosophy
courses and in the many textbooks and treatises, of which we encountered
several examples earlier. He obviously thought that it was important to
instruct his students in the usual system of duties and rights and that he
could simply adjust the theoretical foundations. While it cannot be said
that he worked out the implications of his scattered objections to conventional theory, these objections are of obvious importance as disturbing
elements in the theoretical situation surrounding American ideas of
rights.[75]

Witherspoon begins his lectures traditionally enough by identifying
the subject of moral philosophy as being "the laws of Duty" that reason
derives from human nature independently of, though in consonance with,
revelation. However, he goes on to stress that moral philosophy has its
limitations because of the complexity of human nature, which we only
know in its fallen and corrupt state, and

this depravity...must be one great cause of difficulty and confusion in giving
an account of human nature as the work of God. This I take to be indeed the

[74] Concerning Witherspoon generally, see Noll, *Princeton and the Republic,* chaps. 3–4;
Diamond, "Witherspoon, William Smith"; R. K. Donovan, "The Popular Party of the
Church of Scotland and the American Revolution," in Sher and Smitten, eds., *Scotland
and America,* 81–99; N. C. Landsman, "Witherspoon and the Problem of Provincial
Identity in Scottish Evangelical Culture," in ibid., 29–45; T. P. Miller, "Witherspoon,
Blair, and the Rhetoric of Civic Humanism," in ibid., 100–114; L. E. Schmidt, "Sacra-
mental Occasions and the Scottish Context of Presbyterian Revivalism in America," in
ibid., 65–80; Sher, "Witherspoon's Dominion of Providence and the Scottish
Tradition," in ibid., 46–64; and J. Scott, Introduction, in Witherspoon, *Lectures on
Moral Philosophy,* 1–61.
[75] My emphasis here is on Witherspoon's contrasts with natural-law theory and Hutchesonian moral philosophy. If instead he is contrasted with evangelical and New Side
attitudes and with Jonathan Edwards, he of course comes out a good deal closer to the
former theories. See Noll's excellent discussion in *Princeton and the Republic,* 36–52.

case with the greatest part of our moral and theological knowledge. Those who deny this depravity, will be apt to plead for every thing, or for many things as dictates of nature, which are in reality propensities of nature in its present state, but at the same time the fruit and evidence of its departure from its original purity. It is by the remaining power of natural conscience that we must endeavour to detect and oppose these errors.[76]

Witherspoon goes on to sketch a theory of conscience that owes much to Bishop Butler. In the process he rejects moral-sense theories, especially that of Hutcheson. His principal objection is that such theories tend to assume that that which appears (feels) good to the human mind in its present state *is* good in an absolute sense. He allows that human beings are provided with a moral sense which offers some moral guidance, but it is in need of correction by reason. Although this correction is fallible too, reason and sense combine to jolt into action whatever they have left of a conscience, or sense of duty, after Adam brought death into the world.

Accompanying this thought is the point we are after here. Because of people's sinfulness, the moral world is complex and confused and our moral powers are weak and easily deceived. In such a world it is impossible for individuals to discern a common good which could guide their moral sense and judgment, although they may try when nothing else points to a decision. As Witherspoon says, in a passage where he typically tries to have it a little both ways:

True virtue certainly promotes the general good, and this may be made use of as an argument in doubtful cases, to determine whether a particular principle is right or wrong, but to make the good of the whole our immediate principle of action, is putting ourselves in God's place, and actually superseding the necessity and use of the particular principles of duty which he hath impressed upon the conscience.[77]

Witherspoon does not deny that we should and can enlighten our conscience, or that we should hold fast to the belief that conscience is God's voice speaking through us. But we should not think that we can make God's purpose, the greatest common good, into *our* purpose in our actions. We simply have to do our duty as we see it by the limited light of our conscience. This is God's law. What it adds up to is God's business, not ours. Witherspoon made the point pithily in his fast-day sermon at

---

[76] Witherspoon, *Lectures on Moral Philosophy*, 66.
[77] Ibid., 87.

Princeton on 17 May 1776: "There is the greater need to take notice of this that men are not generally sufficiently aware of the distinction between the law of God and his purpose."[78] This statement is his indictment of those polite moral philosophers like Hutcheson who thought they could build a system of natural law and its duties on the idea of the common good that God has in store for humankind. They entirely forgot that humankind is fallen and corrupt and that individuals have to grope their way without such rationally established moral certainty.

Witherspoon got no further than this with his rethinking of the basis for natural law. His ideas are not particularly remarkable in themselves, but they deserve notice because of the explicit attempt to introduce them into the conventional system of natural law, and because this attempt was made as part of the teaching of moral philosophy at such a prominent institution. The point is that at the time no other line of thought had much chance of breaking the Christian-utilitarian foundation for natural law and of persuading people to consider seriously the possibility that the moral world of humankind may be, if not chaotic, at least without guarantee of order, even in principle. It is beyond the scope of this chapter to investigate how far evangelicalism was successful in this regard, let alone what it did to create a climate later for the development of a proper subjective-rights theory.

SELF-GOVERNMENT AND OBLIGATION

The last argument that tended to chip away at the conventional natural-law theory in favor of a subjective-rights theory will be presented not through an American voice but through one much heard in America in the late eighteenth century. I refer to the Swiss thinker Jean-Jacques Burlamaqui.

A central feature of eighteenth-century moral thought is, as we have seen, the apparently paradoxical proliferation of theories stressing the moral autonomy of the individual while retaining the natural-law foundation for morals. However, neither the supposed moral sense, nor reason, nor conscience provided as much autonomy as might at first appear; for most thinkers the moral power derived its strength from guidance by natural law. This went hand in hand with another feature of traditional

---

[78] Witherspoon, "The Dominion of Providence over the Passions of Men," in *The Selected Writings of John Witherspoon,* ed. T. Miller (Carbondale and Edwardsville: Southern Illinois University Press, 1990), 126–47, at 127.

natural-law theory, the idea that obligation presupposes a superior authority. The common assumption was that a necessary condition for the obligation of natural law was that it issued from God's authority, and that all other obligations, that is, those undertaken by individuals, derived their force from the binding character of natural law. Only very few early modern thinkers, Grotius among them, clearly articulated the idea that there could be obligation without reference to divine authority. It is true that many, probably most, rejected outright voluntarism of the Pufendorfian kind, but they did so by the redeployment of a scholastic distinction, between the content and the form of natural law. The content of the law was the specification of what was good and virtuous and could be grasped by people's native moral power (however conceived). But in order for this specification to be obligatory upon them as a guide to action, it had to have the form of law, and obligatory law required a lawgiver of supreme authority, namely, God.[79] The idea that human beings could have sufficient autonomy to impose obligations upon themselves without any ultimate reference to a higher law and authority was extremely difficult to accept, for it was assumed that if they had such autonomy, morals would be possible without reference to any deity—as Grotius had also pointed out. Since an account of morals in terms of subjective rights required the ability to enter into contractual obligations without reference to a higher law, this common line of thought was one of the main hindrances to the development of a subjective-rights theory.

One can point to a number of attempts in the later eighteenth century to formulate the idea of sui generis obligation, but, as with the other elements in a subjective-rights theory discussed here, it is not possible to point to one particular breakthrough that goes the whole way, at least in the Anglo-American world. The closest might be said to be Richard Price's theory of obligation and self-determination,[80] but he too has a

[79] See Haakonssen, "Divine/Natural Law Theories of Ethics." Cf. James Wilson, who, discussing Pufendorf and political obligation, says, "Consent is the sole principle, on which any claim, in consequence of human authority, can be made upon one man by another. I say, in consequence of human authority: for, in consequence of the divine authority, numerous are the claims that we are reciprocally entitled to make, numerous are the duties, that we are reciprocally obliged to perform. But none of these can enter into the present question. We speak of authority merely human. Exclusively of the duties required by the law of nature, I can conceive of no claim, that one man can make upon another, but in consequence of his own consent." "Lectures on Law," *Works*, 1: 190; cf. his tortuous but remarkable discussion of self-imposed obligation in ibid., 102–3.

[80] Richard Price, *A Review of the Principal Questions in Morals* [1758], ed. D. D. Raphael (Oxford: Clarendon Press, 1974), chaps. 5 and 6; *Observations on the Nature of Civil Liberty, the Principals of Government, and the Justice and Policy of the War with America*

moral safety net, though of a Platonist cut.[81] This apart, the attempt by
Burlamaqui is, however, of significance, partly because it is clearly stated,
partly because it occurs within the framework of a natural-law theory,
and finally because Burlamaqui was so significant for the American
intellect.[82]

Burlamaqui's great two-volume work presents a full system of "natural
and politic law," which in its external form largely follows the systematics
which had become traditional since Pufendorf. Behind the conventional
facade is an often sharply argumentative mind, as can be seen in the case
of particular interest here, the notion of obligation upon which all morality rests. His starting point is an account of what we might call practical
reason. Human action, as opposed to mere bodily locomotion, is goal
directed, it has some sort of aim or purpose, however vague, and a rule
of action is simply pointing out the connection between action and aim.

This being premised, I affirm that every man who proposes to himself a particular
end, and knows the means or rule which alone can conduct him to it, and put
him in possession of what he desires, such a man finds himself under a necessity
of following this rule, and of conforming his actions to it. Otherwise he would
contradict himself; he would and he would not; he would desire the end, and
neglect the only means which by his own confession are able to conduct him to
it.

(London: T. Cadell, 1776), 2–6; *Additional Observations on the Nature and Value of
Civil Liberty, and the War with America* (London: T. Cadell, 1777), 1–15.

[81] See, e.g., *Additional Observations,* 11.

[82] See Burlamaqui, *The Principles of Natural and Politic Law.* Burlamaqui was professor
at the University in Geneva and contributed significantly to its reputation as, in Jefferson's
words half a century later, one of "the two eyes of Europe," the other eye being Edinburgh.
After the French Revolution had spilled over into Geneva, Jefferson actively promoted
the idea of importing the whole of the Geneva faculty, at George Washington's expense,
and locating it "so far from the federal city as moral considerations would recommend
and yet near enough to it to be viewed as an appendix of that, and that the splendor of
the two objects would reflect usefully on each other." Letter to George Washington, 23
February 1795, *Writings of Jefferson,* 19: 113; see also the letters to Wilson Nicholas,
22 November 1794, and M. D'Ivernois, 6 February 1795, 9:291ff. and 297ff. I should
perhaps point out that within 50 years Burlamaqui's great work appeared in 38 editions
(the next 50 adding another 19) in eight countries and was translated from the original
French into seven other languages. There were seven American editions from 1792
onward. There is one solid modern monograph on Burlamaqui: Bernard Gagnebin,
Burlamaqui et le droit naturel (Geneva: Editions de la Frégate, 1944), and a useful chapter
in A. Dufour, *Le mariage dans l'école Romande du droit naturel au XVIIIe siècle* (Geneva:
Librairie de l'Université, Georg, 1976), 65–82. See also R. F. Harvey, *Jean Jacques
Burlamaqui: A Liberal Tradition in American Constitutionalism* (Chapel Hill: University
of North Carolina Press, 1937), which gives the bibliographic information (see 188–92).
The best discussion of Burlamaqui's influence on American thought is in White, *Philos-
ophy of the American Revolution,* passim. See also U. M. von Eckardt, *The Pursuit of
Happiness in the Democratic Creed* (New York: F. A. Praeger, 1959), chap. 8.

The acknowledgment of a rule of action under such circumstances is thus a "reasonable necessity" or an obligation, "because obligation, in its original idea, is nothing more than a restriction of liberty, produced by reason, inasmuch as the counsels which reason gives us, are motives that determine us to a particular manner of acting, preferable to any other."[83] This is the natural condition of humankind. It is inevitable that reason in this sense regulates our behavior, and "consequently reason alone is sufficient to establish a system of morality, obligation, and duties; because when once we suppose it is reasonable to do or to abstain from certain things, this is really owning our obligation."[84]

Burlamaqui goes on to confront all the traditional objections to the notion of self-imposed obligation: that the very idea of obligation implies an agent who obliges and who is distinct from the obligee; that one cannot have a contract with oneself; that one cannot impose a necessity on oneself, because a removable necessity is not a necessity; that obligation implies a law and law a superior. Acknowledging that these are indeed the received opinions,[85] Burlamaqui rightly points out that they beg the question and goes on to explain:

> It is true that man may, if he has a mind, withdraw himself from the obligations which reason imposes on him; but if he does, it is at his peril, and he is forced himself to acknowledge, that such a conduct is quite unreasonable. But to conclude from thence that reason cannot oblige us, is going too far; because this consequence would equally invalidate the obligation imposed by a superior.[86]

The consequence is that a voluntarist account of natural law is impossible, for even our obligation to God as moral legislator is a self-imposed obligation (and the same, of course, applies to human legislators). The Covenant had been turned into a philosophical theory, and Hobbes would have been amused.[87]

[83] Burlamaqui, *Principles of Natural and Politic Law*, 1: 207–8.
[84] Ibid., 210.
[85] Cf. the quotation from Rutherforth above at note 30 and the one from Wooddeson below in note 90.
[86] Burlamaqui, *Principles of Natural and Politic Law*, 1: 213; cf. 65–6.
[87] For a typical late example of the sort of public mind that would be receptive to a philosophical theory of self-government, we may take the notable abolitionist Granville Sharp. For him all law and authority, including God's, are based on covenant. Consequently he must reject Pufendorf's authoritarian voluntarism—of which the idea of Parliament's absolute sovereignty is a consequence—and warn his readers of "the Errors of this celebrated Civilian, because the studying of his Works ... is at this time considered as a material part of Education in our Universities; so that *the rising Generation* of the very best Families in this Kingdom are liable to imbibe (as it were with the Milk of Instruction) these poisenous Doctrines." *A Declaration of the People's Natural Right to*

Most of the elements in Burlamaqui's argument may have been anticipated in various earlier rationalist theories of ethics, such as those of Leibniz, the Cambridge Platonists, Samuel Clarke and his followers, and, indeed earlier still, by Suárez. But the Swiss thinker is unusually clearheaded in insisting that his line of argument means that all morals rest on rationally self-imposed obligation. As we saw above, he also appreciates that in that case there is no further guarantee of the moral life than human rationality. This point is, however, considerably obscured by a good deal of the usual sunny providentialism concerning the essential harmony between individual rational judgments, including the correlativity between rights and duties.[88]

This combination of a strong theory of human moral self-government with a tradition-bound theory of how such self-government works out is characteristic of the deep philosophical ambiguity of the so-called rights-of-man theories of the later eighteenth century. Those, like Burlamaqui and cognate spirits among rational dissenters, who were finding their way to the idea of moral autonomy and the possibility of self-imposed obligation, found it hard to accept the implication that self-government makes moral harmony an open-ended task and not a justifying ideal. Those, like Witherspoon, who were able to toy with the idea of a more or less chaotic moral world in which all semblance of order was man-made and transitory, found the strength to do so in the eschatology of evangelical religion. However, from whichever side they came, their idea of the moral self easily adopted the old political rhetoric of self-government and gave the latter an individualistic sense it had not had. For a short season people of many persuasions—although differing about key terms like *right, self-government,* and *nature*—could agree with Jefferson that "every man, and every body of men on earth, possesses the right of self-government. They receive it with their being from the hand of nature. Individuals exercise it by their single will; collections of men by that of their majority."[89]

---

a Share in the Legislature (London, 1774), xx–xxi. Elsewhere he attacks the common combination of Christian utilitarianism and (residual) voluntarism, using as his starting point the passage in Blackstone's *Commentaries* quoted above in note 26: Sharp, *A Tract on the Law of Nature, and Principles of Action in Man* (London: B. White, E. and C. Dilly, 1777), 57ff.

[88] Burlamaqui, *Principles of Natural and Politic Law,* 1: 71. In Burlamaqui, as in many earlier and later thinkers, there is always some ambiguity as to whether the correlativity thesis is purely definitional or whether it is a statement about the (ideal) moral world.

[89] Jefferson, "Opinion Upon the Question Whether the President Should Veto the Bill,

The man who saw most clearly what this could lead to—and disliked what he saw—was Edmund Burke, who thought it had to do with a new idea of the rights of man. He was both right and wrong. Many people certainly talked of such rights, and a few even talked of the rights of women. This chapter has been concerned with the history of the ideas of rights, not with the discourse about them, but if my argument is correct, few people understood exactly what they were talking about. There were, if not good, at least intelligible reasons for this situation, as I have tried to show. In the end the talk may have led to a more coherent theory, but that end probably lies well beyond the eighteenth century. On the whole the conceptual structure of natural law-duty-right, with its comfortable orderliness, persisted on both sides of the Atlantic, as shown in the lectures of Blackstone's successors, of Witherspoon's successor, and of James Wilson.[90] As Wilson said, "The laws of nature are the measure and the rule; they ascertain the limits and the extent of natural liberty."[91] Within this framework, however, American thinkers managed to rid themselves of the traditionalism the British had grafted onto it and thus to create a culture in which rights talk could flourish, whatever it meant.

Declaring That the Seat of Government Shall Be Transferred to the Potomac, in the Year 1790." 15 July 1790, in *Writings of Jefferson*, 3: 60.

[90] Opening his lectures as Vinerian Professor of Law at Oxford in 1777 with a lecture on "The Laws of Man's Nature," Richard Wooddeson warned his students: "Those, who think man's sociability ... might suffice to preserve some order and justice in the world [note: Grotius, *De iure belli ac pacis*, Prol., VI, VIII, XI], and those, who speak of obligation arising from the mere approval of reason [note: Burlamaqui, *Natural Law*, Part 2, chap. 7, i.e., the chapter quoted above at notes 84 and 86], both sorts of speculatists, excluding natural theology from the argument, seem to deal in unprofitable refinements, not considering things as they are, but upon a subject so serious inventing and dwelling on arbitrary suppositions. Besides, if rules so founded could obtain, they could not properly be termed laws, which cannot be abstracted from the authority of a lawgiver. It may be added, that in unlettered minds the conceptions of moral right and wrong immediately raise impressions of the pleasure or displeasure of the Deity; which cannot be wholly ascribed to habitual association; for it does not rest there." *Elements of Jurisprudence Treated of in the Preliminary Part of a Course of Lectures on the Laws of England* (London, 1783), 6–7. Cf. Robert Chambers, *A Course of Lectures on the English Law Delivered at the University of Oxford 1767–1773*, ed. T. M. Curley, 2 vols. (Oxford: Oxford University Press, 1986), 1: 83ff. (Lecture 1); Stanhope Smith, *Lectures on Moral and Political Philosophy*, especially 2:94ff. (Lecture 18); and Wilson, "Lectures on Law," *Works*, 1: 95ff., especially 104ff. (Lecture III). See also Noll's splendid discussion of Stanhope Smith's synthesis, a "Republican Christian Enlightenment," *Princeton and the Republic*, especially chap. 10.

[91] Wilson, *Works*, 1: 276.

2

●━○━●━○━●━○━●━○━●━○━●━○━●━○━●━○━●━○━●━○━●━○━●━○━●━○━●━○━●━○━●━○━●

The Bill of Rights and the American
Revolutionary experience

JAMES H. HUTSON

THE PERVASIVENESS OF RIGHTS TALK
BEFORE AND AFTER THE REVOLUTION

A recent book on the framing of the United States Constitution claims that "from the beginning...the language of America has been the language of rights."[1] Although this statement may not be applicable to seventeenth-century America, in which one authority finds rights "very rarely" discussed,[2] few scholars would deny that it accurately describes the situation in the eighteenth century—especially the period after the passage of the Stamp Act in 1765.

The eagerness of eighteenth-century Americans to claim rights exasperated those trying to govern them. As early as 1704, James Logan, an agent of William Penn, ridiculed Pennsylvanians' obsession with the "Rattle of Rights and Privileges";[3] three years later, this same functionary assailed the "infatuated people of this province" for their "ridiculous contending for rights unknown to others of the Queen's subjects."[4] That the colonists had inflated ideas of their rights was, in fact, a stock complaint of royal officials as long as the king's writ ran in America.

---

[1] Philip B. Kurland and Ralph Lerner, eds., *The Founders' Constitution* (Chicago: University of Chicago Press, 1987), 1: 424.
[2] Benjamin F. Wright, Jr., *American Interpretations of Natural Law* (New York: Russell and Russell, 1962), 7.
[3] Quoted in Gary Nash, "The Rattle of Rights and Privileges: Pennsylvania Politics, 1701–1709," in Stanley N. Katz, ed., *Colonial America Essays in Politics and Social Development* (Boston: Little, Brown, 1971), 265.
[4] Ibid., 266.

Reverence for rights was not grounded, however, in widespread intellectual mastery of the subject; there were frequent assertions and admissions that Americans did not fully understand the object of their devotion. But the Americans perceived that they could not afford to wait for perfect enlightenment before claiming rights in opposition to the pretensions of an intrusive British government. Thus, the eighteenth century was a period (not, perhaps, unlike our own) in which the public's penchant for asserting its rights outran its ability to analyze them and to reach a consensus about their scope and meaning. As the century progressed, especially after independence set off searching debates in the states about the formation of new governments, Americans reached a common understanding about some aspects of the rights question that informed the drafting of the Bill of Rights in 1789. To understand what the drafters of that document meant requires, therefore, an explanation of the context from which the Bill of Rights emerged, an investigation that must begin in the reign of George III and pick its way through a complicated clutter of ideas emanating from moral philosophy, jurisprudence, political theory, and theology.

On whose authority can it be said that Americans did not comprehend the rights they claimed? On Thomas Hutchinson's, for one. "I am sensible," Hutchinson lectured the Massachusetts legislature on 6 March 1773, "that nice Distinctions of Civil Rights and Legal Constitutions are far above the reach of the Bulk of Mankind to comprehend."[5] Because Hutchinson soon retired to London as a Loyalist, his statement might be dismissed as so much Tory superciliousness, but modern scholars have agreed with him. Assessing the events in 1773 upon which Hutchinson was commenting, they have concluded that "the people at large . . . were too little informed in political theory to have possessed any clear ideas [about rights], and so they voted in ignorance for opinions presented to them by a handful of local leaders."[6] Just how much difficulty the people at large had in dealing with the rights question is revealed by a plaintive letter to a Baptist minister from a backcountry delegate to the Massachusetts Constitutional Convention of 1780. "I am sensible," wrote Noah Allen to the Reverend Isaac Backus, that "the work is grate and my gifts Small and I am inexperienced in work of this sort Dear brother I pray you to favor me with your mind on the subject Expesualy what are the

---

[5] *Boston Gazette,* 15 March 1773.
[6] Richard D. Brown, *Revolutionary Politics in Massachusetts* (Cambridge, Mass.: Harvard University Press, 1970), 94.

Rights of the people and how that Bill of Rights ought to be drawn."[7] That Allen's perplexity was widespread is attested by pleas from various Massachusetts towns to the draftsmen of the 1780 constitution to describe rights in language "so explicitly as the lowest capacity may fully understand," to use words "levelled as much as may be to the Capacities of the Subjects in common."[8]

Problems in comprehension were no less severe in Virginia, prompting one pundit to suggest during the debates on the ratification of the Federal Constitution in 1788 that the term *bill of rights* be dropped because "the bulk of the people do not understand abstruse, or lengthy political disquisitions," and that *fundamental truths* should be substituted for *bill of rights* and these "truths" expressed "in a few words, yet plain and pithy."[9] The same complaints were voiced in Pennsylvania, where a Whig pamphleteer, writing in 1775 over the signature Antoninus, deplored the inability of persons of "inferior condition" to form adequate conceptions of their rights, and castigated the leisured members of Pennsylvania society for their similar ignorance of the subject. These privileged people, Antoninus suggested, should "peruse Lord Somer's Judgement of Nations, a two shilling pamphlet, Locke on Government about the same bulk; they would need no more excitement to study their birthrights."[10]

Study, then, was the key to understanding rights—study of major thinkers in British political and intellectual history. But research might not be enough, as William Bollan discovered in 1762. A "learned man of indefatigable research" who was serving as Massachusetts agent in London at the time, Bollan proposed to write a book "establishing... the native equal and permanent rights of the colonists against all Opponents," but found that "the facts and arguments necessary on this occasion... are so numerous and various, and many of them so difficult in their nature, that the completion of a work of this kind will unquestionably require great leisure, labor, and application," qualities which Bollan could not muster.[11]

[7] Noah Allen to Isaac Backus, (1780?), quoted in Oscar and Mary Handlin, eds., *The Popular Sources of Political Authority: Documents on the Massachusetts Constitution of 1780* (Cambridge, Mass.: Harvard University Press, 1966), 412–13n.

[8] Ibid., 803, 903.

[9] "Sentiments of the Many," *Virginia Independent Chronicle*, 18 June 1788, in Herbert Storing, ed., *The Complete Anti-Federalist* (Chicago: University of Chicago Press, 1981), 5: 275.

[10] *Pennsylvania Journal*, 11 October 1775.

[11] Charles G. Washburn, ed., *Jasper Mauduit, Agent in London for the Province of the*

The "numerous and various" opinions on rights vexed American thinkers for the rest of the century. "I consider that there are very few who understand the whole of these rights," James Wilson complained in 1787. "All the political writers, from Grotius and Puffendorf down to Vattel, have treated on this subject, but in no one of these works, nor in the aggregate of them all, can you find a complete enumeration of rights appertaining to the people as men and citizens."[12] Even leading European commentators admitted that their own writings were not very helpful. Francis Hutcheson, for example, a leading figure of the Scottish Enlightenment who is said to have influenced strongly Madison and Jefferson, conceded in his *System of Moral Philosophy* (which Bollan probably consulted) that "our notion of right [is] a complex conception" and that it was "hard to determine the several claims of men and the nice degrees of them, about which there must be a great diversity of sentiment."[13]

Formidable though the subject of rights was, John Adams contended in 1765 that many Americans were having trouble coming to grips with it, not because they were unable to understand it but because they were unwilling to try to do so. "We have been afraid to think," claimed Adams. "We have felt a reluctance to examine into the grounds of our privileges and the extent to which we have an indisputable right to demand them."[14] Scholars have agreed with Adams, arguing that in the years before 1763 Americans were "noticeably hesitant about spelling out the rights and liberties they claimed."[15] Why was this so? Adams cited "certain prudent reasons" for his countrymen's diffidence.[16] Some Americans, he believed, were opportunists, seekers after political loaves and fishes, who did not want to antagonize potential patrons in the British colonial administration by raising the rights issue. Others, Adams implied, recoiled from a searching investigation of rights when they saw where it might lead. Pronouncements like that issued by the Massachusetts legislature in the quiet year 1762, that the foundation of American rights was "to be under

Massachusetts Bay 1762–1765, in Massachusetts Historical Society, *Collections* 74 (1918), 28–29.

[12] James Wilson, speech, Pennsylvania ratifying convention, 4 December 1787, in Merrill Jensen, ed., *Documentary History of the Ratification of the Constitution* (Madison: State Historical Society of Wisconsin, 1976), 2: 470.

[13] Frances Hutcheson, *A System of Moral Philosophy* (2 vols., London, 1755), 1: 258.

[14] John Adams, *Dissertation on the Canon and Feudal Law* (21 October 1765), in Robert Taylor et al., eds., *Papers of John Adams* (Cambridge: Harvard University Press, 1977), 1: 123.

[15] Lawrence H. Leder, *Liberty and Authority* (Chicago: Quadrangle Books, 1968).

[16] Taylor et al., eds., *Papers of John Adams*, 1: 123.

no other legislative power but that established by Consent in the Commonwealth"[17]—seemed to point in the direction of independence, a course that was anathema to almost everyone in the colonies before hostilities broke out with Britain in 1775. Better close the door than admit such mischievous light.

Consequently, when Britain precipitated the imperial crisis in 1764–65 by taxing the colonies, Americans were caught intellectually unprepared: they knew they had rights, but they had no coherent, authoritative statement, nothing resembling an intercolonial position paper, on the origin, sum, and scope of those rights. To forge a common understanding on rights, to reach a continental consensus, became one of the principal challenges confronting American thinkers from the Stamp Act to the drafting of the Bill of Rights a quarter century later.

RIGHTS, NATURE, AND ITS LAWS

The Stamp Act, announced in Parliament in 1764 and passed in 1765, taxed legal instruments, business documents, and newspapers in the colonies and subjected violators of the act to trial in the vice-admiralty courts, where judges, applying Roman law, sat without juries. This statute started the rights controversy on the most elementary level because everyone in America believed that Magna Charta and other foundation documents of the British constitution forbade the taking of an Englishman's property without his consent. Because the colonists were Englishmen and because they were not represented in Parliament, the Stamp Act violated their constitutional rights. So plain was this proposition that people in Britain, including the officials who drafted the Stamp Act, agreed with it, although they countered with the specious argument that American rights had not been violated after all because the colonists were "virtually" represented in Parliament. Trial by jury, which was not available in vice-admiralty courts, was not so simple and was characteristic of the problems raised in the colonies by the rights arguments. Once again, Americans held that Magna Charta guaranteed Englishmen the right to trial by jury. But how inclusive was this right? Did trial by jury secure a trial in the neighborhood (vicinage) of the accused, an issue raised by the Dockyards Act of 1772, which apparently permitted the transportation of Americans to England for trial? And did trial by jury presuppose

---

[17] Washburn, ed., *Jasper Mauduit*, 40.

a right to challenge jurors, an issue raised in the ratifying conventions in 1787–8? Some Americans asserted that unless the right to challenge was spelled out, it did not exist. Others argued that this right was inherent in the concept of jury trial, a "necessary appendage" of the institution,[18] and existed without specification. It was not easy to tell who was right and who was wrong.

As the dispute with America intensified, George III's ministers attempted to tighten their controls in the colonies. Refractory Massachusetts required special attention. The Bay Colony's legislature paid the salaries of the judges of its superior court. To deprive the locals of this lever of financial control over the administration of justice, the ministry proposed in 1772 to pay the judges itself. Massachusetts Whigs believed that royal payment of judges serving during royal pleasure might subvert the rule of law by creating an irresponsible and tyrannical judiciary. The ministerial proposal was, in their view, politically and morally wrong, but did it violate their rights? The British constitution was no help here, for it certainly permitted the king to pay his servants. Massachusetts Whigs, therefore, used another voice in the repertoire of rights to remonstrate against the payment of the judges. Speaking through the Boston Committee of Correspondence, they issued on 20 November 1772 a statement, which they circulated through Massachusetts and the other colonies, listing the "Natural Rights of the Colonists as Men"[19] and protesting that the payment of the judges violated those rights.

In issuing statements in the language of natural rights, Americans, according to John Phillip Reid, "went off the constitutional deep end."[20] What Reid apparently means is that because natural rights (and the law of nature from which they were derived) were unwritten and hence undefined, they could be used to dignify any desire, to package any prejudice—as, for example, when the citizens of Andover, Massachusetts, announced in 1780 that it was "one of the natural and civil rights of a free People" to limit public office to Protestants,[21] or when a writer in

---

[18] Edmund Randolph, speech, Virginia ratifying convention, 24 June 1788, in Jonathan Elliot, ed., *The Debates in the Several State Conventions on the Adoption of the Federal Constitution* (Philadelphia, 1896), 3: 602.

[19] "The Rights of the Colonists, A List of Violations of Rights and a Letter of Correspondence," in Harry A. Cushing, ed., *The Writings of Samuel Adams, 1770–1773* (New York, 1906), 2: 350–355.

[20] John Phillip Reid, *The Constitutional History of the American Revolution: The Authority of Rights* (Madison: University of Wisconsin Press, 1986), 88.

[21] Andover town meeting, 1 May 1780, in Handlin and Handlin, eds., *Popular Sources of Political Authority*, 904.

the *Boston Gazette* claimed in the same year that Congregational ministers had "a natural and unalienable right" to be paid salaries by the state legislature.[22] A term so protean could not help introducing confusion and contradiction into the rights discourse, for although it might seem to the Boston Committee of Correspondence in 1772 that judges violated the people's "essential natural right" by receiving salaries from the king,[23] a few years later popular leaders in Virginia insisted that "all men have a natural inherent right of receiving emoluments from any one."[24] Or, to cite another example, one Maryland political leader in the 1780s argued that the people had a natural right to issue instructions to their elected representatives, while another leader vigorously denied that any such natural right existed.[25]

Thomas Hutchinson, whose efforts to rebut the Boston Committee of Correspondence manifesto led to a protracted controversy with the Massachusetts legislature in 1773, gave his British correspondents the impression that by employing the natural-rights argument Massachusetts Whigs had unscrupulously attempted to change the terms of debate by introducing a foreign element into the dispute. Hutchinson certainly knew better, however, for in 1762 as a member of the Massachusetts Council, he helped compose a state paper that vigorously asserted natural rights,[26] although he later admitted that "no precise ideas seems to have been affixed" to the term.[27] However defined (or undefined), natural rights were common currency in American political discourse on the eve of the Stamp Act crisis. James Otis's claim in his widely read *Rights of the British Colonies Asserted and Proved* (Boston, 1764) that Americans possessed "natural, inherent, and inseparable rights as men and citizens"[28] was understood by all his readers as a truism.

Reid accuses historians of overemphasizing the "nonsense" of natural

---

[22] "Iraeneus," *Boston Gazette*, 27 November 1780.

[23] Cushing, ed., *Writings of Samuel Adams*, 354–5.

[24] Edmund Randolph, speech, Virginia ratifying convention, 15 June 1788, Elliot, ed., *Debates in the Several State Conventions*, 465.

[25] See the exchanges between William Paca and Alexander Hanson in the *Maryland Gazette* (Baltimore), 13, 20 February, 18 May, 22 June, 3, 31 August 1787, and in the *Maryland Gazette* (Annapolis), 28 June, 2, 16 August 1787.

[26] Instructions to Jasper Mauduit, 14 June 1762, in Washburn, ed., *Jasper Mauduit*, 39–40.

[27] Edmund S. and Helen M. Morgan, eds., *The Stamp Act Crisis* (Chapel Hill: University of North Carolina Press, 1953), 123.

[28] Bernard Bailyn, ed., *Pamphlets of the American Revolution 1750–1776* (Cambridge: Harvard University Press, 1965), 1: 444.

rights during the Revolutionary controversy.[29] In his opinion, the primary authority for rights between 1763 and 1776 was the British constitution; it followed, therefore, that "the revolutionary controversy was concerned with positive constitutional rights, not abstract natural rights."[30] Not so, argues Harry Jaffa: "Natural law always took precedence in the order of importance. The primacy of rights and right, understood in the light of the law of nature, was the argument of the American Revolution from the beginning."[31] Thomas Grey had reached a similar conclusion ten years earlier: natural law "renewed and fortified . . . by the political and legal theories of the Enlightenment . . . largely animated American Whig thought during the pre-1776 independence struggle."[32]

The dispute among contemporary scholars over the primacy of rights sources repeats a debate in the First Continental Congress between natural-law advocates John Adams and Richard Henry Lee and proponents of the British constitution Joseph Galloway, James Duane, and John Rutledge.[33] The First Continental Congress split the difference between the two groups of disputants by agreeing to found American claims on both the "immutable law of nature" and the "principles of the English Constitution."[34] The British paid little attention to the First Continental Congress's distinctions, however, and as they moved toward a military solution of the colonial problem, Americans moved toward a reliance on natural law as the chief source of their rights. Typical of this trend was Alexander Hamilton's assertion in 1775 that "the sacred rights of mankind are not to be rummaged for, among old parchments, or musty records. They are written, as with a sunbeam, in the whole volume of nature, by the hand of divinity itself."[35]

---

[29] John Phillip Reid, "The Ordeal by Law of Thomas Hutchinson," in Hendrik Hartog, ed., *Law in the American Revolution and the Revolution in the Law* (New York: New York University Press, 1981), 33.

[30] Reid, *Constitutional History of the American Revolution*, 90.

[31] Harry Jaffa, "What were the 'Original Intentions' of the Framers of the Constitution of the United States?" *University of Puget Sound Law Review* 10 (Spring 1987): 384.

[32] Thomas C. Grey, "Origins of the Unwritten Constitution: Fundamental Law in American Revolutionary Thought," *Stanford Law Review* 30 (May 1978): 850, 892.

[33] See, for example, John Adams's Notes of Debates, 8 September 1774, in Paul Smith et al., eds., *Letters of Delegates to Congress, 1774–1789* (Washington, D.C.: Government Printing Office, 1976), 1: 46–48.

[34] Bill of Rights (and) List of Grievances, [27 October?] 1774, in James H. Hutson, *A Decent Respect to the Opinions of Mankind* (Washington, D.C.: Government Printing Office, 1975), 53. The First Congress also included "the several charters or compacts" as a source of rights.

[35] Alexander Hamilton, "The Farmer Refuted," [23 Feburary] 1775, in Harold C. Syrett

Independence cemented the preference for natural law. "How in the world," Jaffa asks, could Americans be expected "to appeal to their rights under the laws of England at the precise moment that they were telling the world they were no longer Englishmen?"[36] The situation was, in fact, more complicated than this statement suggests, for Americans claimed throughout the Revolutionary controversy that their quarrel was not with the British constitution but with the unprincipled politicians who were defiling it. In fact, the mother country's constitution was extolled at the Constitutional Convention in 1787 and for decades thereafter. These tributes, however, were almost always paid to the institutional contrivances of the British constitution that were designed to control the excesses of democracy. Admiration for the stabilizing properties of the document, mostly confined to political conservatives, did not translate into a willingness of the citizens of the new republic, stirred by a nascent nationalism, to concede that they were beholden to the British for their rights. Rather they considered, with James Wilson, that "by the Revolution [they] have regained all their natural rights,"[37] that by repudiating British authority they had "nobly resumed those rights which *God* and *nature* bestowed on man."[38] "As soon as the independence of America was declared in 1776," explained Thomas Hartley, "from that instant all our natural rights were restored to us."[39] The citizens of the new American nation, warned a Massachusetts pamphleteer, had "too strong a sense of the rights of nature, of the sufferings experienced for their re-establishment," to tolerate any trifling with them.[40] Americans believed, in short, that one of the results of independence was the recovery of their natural rights.

THE STATE OF NATURE AND ITS LAWS

If "the natural rights philosophy seized the minds...of the rebellious patriots of 1776," as Leonard Levy has recently argued,[41] a contributing factor was the use Americans made of the theory of the state of nature

et al., eds., *The Papers of Alexander Hamilton* (New York: Columbia University Press, 1961), 1: 122.

[36] Jaffa, "What were the 'Original Intentions,'" 383.

[37] Wilson, speech, Pennsylvania ratifying convention, 28 November 1787, in Jensen, ed., *Documentary History of the Ratification of the Constitution*, 2: 391.

[38] *Pennsylvania Evening Post*, 24 July 1777.

[39] Hartley, speech, Pennsylvania ratifying convention, 30 November 1787, in Jensen, ed., *Documentary History of the Ratification of the Constitution*, 2: 430.

[40] "Helvidius Priscus," in ibid., 15: 332–3.

[41] Leonard Levy, *Original Intent and the Framers' Constitution* (New York: Macmillan, 1988), 279.

to explain the events of 1776. The Thomas Hobbes employed the state of nature as a major presumption in his *Leviathan,* but most Americans absorbed the more benign version of the concept used by John Locke in his *Two Treatises of Government.*[42] For the purposes of this chapter, the following features of the Lockean state of nature should be noted: it preceded society; no organization of any sort existed in it—only individuals or extended families; these individuals had rights that were bound only by the law of nature; individuals chose to abandon the state of nature because, with no impartial arbiter to resolve controversies, the weak were at the mercy of the strong; in leaving the state of nature, these same individuals concluded compacts with one another (Locke postulated separate compacts of society and government) in which they surrendered some of their natural rights to a government that became responsible for protecting the remaining unalienated rights.

The state of nature began appearing in American writing less than thirty years after the publication in 1690 of Locke's *Two Treatises.* John Wise used it in 1717 in his *A Vindication of the Government of the New England Churches,*[43] and other colonial pulpits were conduits for the concept. By the middle of the eighteenth century, writes Edmund S. Morgan, "Locke's political doctrines were assimilated by American clergymen and dispensed in their sermons along with older ideas."[44] In 1764 it was reported that New Englanders believed themselves entitled "to form a new government as full to all intents and purposes as if they had been in a state of nature and were making their first entrance into civil society."[45] The state of nature was so commonplace by 1769 that one South Carolina politician patronizingly informed an adversary that it "has been so often transcribed by one from another that time is misspent to prove it; and those, who ever did think, or are capable of reflecting upon it, stand in no need of having it thus retailed in this enlightened age."[46] Tories like Thomas Hutchinson, Joseph Galloway, and Samuel Seabury were as adept at invoking the concept as Whigs.[47]

---

[42] The best edition of Locke's *Two Treatises* and the one consulted in writing this paper is Peter Laslett, ed., *Two Treatises of Government* (Cambridge: Cambridge University Press, 1967).

[43] Wise, *A Vindication . . .* (Boston, 1717), 33, 43.

[44] Edmund S. Morgan, "The American Revolution Considered as an Intellectual Movement," in Esmond Wright, ed., *Causes and Consequences of the American Revolution* (Chicago: Quadrangle Books, 1966), 176.

[45] Bernard Schwartz, ed., *The Bill of Rights: A Documentary History* (New York: Chelsea House Publishers, 1971), 1: 179.

[46] Robert Weir, ed., *The Letters of Freeman, Etc.* (Columbia, S.C.: University of South Carolina Press, 1977), 87.

[47] On Hutchinson, see the instructions to Jasper Mauduit in Washburn, ed., *Jasper Mauduit.*

Not every American believed that a state of nature literally existed at some point in the past. James Otis, for example, labeled the doctrine "a piece of metaphysical jargon and systematic nonsense." Yet Otis conceded that the state of nature was an indispensable fiction: even if imaginary, it "hinders not but that the natural and original rights of each individual may be illustrated and explained in this way better than in any other."[48] Madison's teacher, John Witherspoon, also taught the uses of a state of nature as a necessary fiction: "It is impossible to consider society as a voluntary union of particular persons, without supposing those persons in a state somewhat different, before this union took place—there are rights therefore belonging to a state of nature, different from those of a social state."[49]

Many Americans regarded the British Parliament's passage of the Intolerable Acts in 1774 to be an act of aggression that converted the fictional state of nature into fact. This was the view of Patrick Henry, who, at the First Continental Congress in September 1774, declared: "Government is dissolved. Fleets and Armies and the present State of Things show that Government is dissolved. . . . We are in a State of Nature."[50] The state of nature was a popular topic among Henry's Virginia constituents, for on 1 September 1774 a writer in Virginia's leading newspaper warned that "if the king violated his sacred faith" with the American colonies, "he dismembers them from the empire and reduces them to a state of nature."[51] From the eye of the storm, Massachusetts Whig leader James Warren wrote John Adams on 16 October 1774, "It can be no longer a question whether any People ever subsisted in a State of Nature. We have been and still remain in that Situation."[52] And on 21 January 1775 John Adams wrote a British correspondent that in the province "four hundred thousand people are in a state of nature."[53]

Some people in Massachusetts believed that a state of nature could be self-induced. The town of Pittsfield, for example, on 15 August rec-

On Seabury and Galloway, see Samuel Seabury, *A View of the Controversy in a Letter to the Author of a Full Vindication* (New York, 1774), 8; Joseph Galloway, *A Candid Examination of the Mutual Claims of Great Britain and the Colonies* (New York, 1775), 34.

[48] Otis, *The Rights of the British Colonies Asserted and Proved* (1764), in Bailyn, ed., *Pamphlets of the American Revolution*, 1: 422, 439.

[49] Jack Scott, ed., *An Annotated Edition of Lectures on Moral Philosophy by John Witherspoon* (Newark, Del.: University of Delaware Press, 1982), 122.

[50] Henry, speech, 6 September 1774, in Smith, *supra* note 33, 27–8.

[51] "Vox Vociferantis," *Virginia Gazette*, 1 September 1774.

[52] Quoted in Taylor et al., eds., *Papers of John Adams*, 2:191.

[53] Ibid., 2: 215.

ommended that its citizens assist in closing the royal courts: "The Courts of Justice [should] immediately cease," Pittsfield resolved. "The People of this Province fall into a state of nature."[54]

The experience of being in what they conceived to be a state of nature made a strong impact on the citizens of Massachusetts, because at the state constitutional convention in 1780 a delegate bragged about "the peaceable behavior of the people of the State, when our charter was vacated by an act of the King and Parliament and we were reduced in great measure to a state of nature."[55] Swelling with pride over the successful drafting and adoption of the state constitution, Thomas Dawes the next year recounted how "we often read of the original contract, and of mankind, in the early ages, passing from a state of nature to immediate civilization." The citizens of Massachusetts, Dawes continued, "have reduced to practice the wonderful theory. The people have convened in a state of nature, and, like our ideas of the patriarchs, had actually drawn and signed a glorious covenant."[56] Seven years later, at the convention to ratify the federal Constitution, the Bay State delegates were reminded that when "we dissolved the political bands which connected us with Great Britain, we were in a state of nature."[57]

From one end of the colonies to another, Americans after 1774 considered that the actions of George III had reduced them to a state of nature. In New York it was said that "upon the declaration of independence... our situation resembled a people in a state of nature."[58] In Pennsylvania in May 1776 James Wilson contended that if the movement toward independence was successful, "The People will be instantly in a State of Nature."[59] And in Maryland it was asserted that "when the people of these states dissolved their Connection with the Crown of Great Britain by the Declaration of Independence, they found themselves as to Government in a State of Nature."[60] A writer in Berkshire County, Massachusetts, suggested in homespun language what Americans believed

---

[54] John L. Brooke, "To the Quiet of the People: Revolutionary Settlements and Civil Unrest in Western Massachusetts, 1774–1789," *William and Mary Quarterly*, 3d Ser., 46 (July 1989): 438.

[55] A member of the Convention to Nathaniel Willis, 3 January 1780, in *Boston Independent Chronicle*, 10 February 1780.

[56] Quoted in Gordon S. Wood, *The Creation of the American Republic 1776–1787* (Chapel Hill: University of North Carolina Press, 1969), 289.

[57] Samuel Nason, speech, 1 February 1788, Elliot, ed., *The Debates in the Several State Conventions*, 2: 134.

[58] "Sydney," *New York Journal*, 13–14 June 1788.

[59] Quoted in Smith, et al., eds., *Letters to the Delegates of Congress*, 3: 670.

[60] *Maryland Journal and Baltimore Advertiser*, 19 October 1787.

had happened to them in 1776: "The Declaration of Independence Operated to all Intents and Purposes to throw all the Declared Independent States into a State of Nature.... Hear then Goes Charter Covenants, Compacts Laws and Constitution. All is Redust to a perfect State of Nature."[61]

In a state of nature Americans had, as Locke postulated, the law of nature and it alone. It was axiomatic to citizens of the new republic that "these Independent States... have fallen into a state of Nature.... We Revert to the Eternal Law of Nature to which we are always and Invariably subject."[62] The law of nature was, of course, the source of those natural rights that Americans believed independence had restored to them. The origin of the new nation's rights was simple, James Madison said in 1785; they were the "gift of nature."[63] Since Americans believed that the law of nature embodied the will of God, was "dictated by God himself," as Blackstone described it,[64] many identified God—the more secular-minded substituted the "Creator" of the Declaration of Independence—as the source of American rights. The following phrases recurred like a refrain before and after 1776: "we hold them [rights] immediately from God"; they are the "free absolute gift of God"; they are "inherited from heaven."[65] Rights, then, for the founding generation were grounded in religion, if not the religion of the New Testament, as some insisted, at least in Judeo-Christian morality.

BILLS OF RIGHTS AND RIGHTS SURRENDERED

The constitutions the new states began adopting in 1776 signaled their emergence from the state of nature (whether real or theoretical) to which British oppression had reduced them. Bills of rights were added to most, though not all, of the new constitutions, and they contained all the contradictory and incoherent thinking about rights that existed before

---

[61] Quoted in Theodore M. Hammett, "Revolutionary Ideology in Massachusetts: Thomas Allen's 'Vindication' of the Berkshire Constitutionalists, 1778," *William and Mary Quarterly,* 3d Ser., 33 (July 1976): 521.

[62] Ibid., 525.

[63] Madison, "Memorial and Remonstrance against Religion Assessments," 20 June 1785, in Robert Rutland and William Rachel, eds., *Papers of James Madison* (Chicago: University of Chicago Press, 1973), 8:304.

[64] William Blackstone, *Commentaries on the Laws of England,* ed. Stanley N. Katz (Chicago: University of Chicago Press, 1979), 1: 41.

[65] *Four Letters on Interesting Subjects* (Philadelphia, 1776), 3: 15; "A Country Gentleman," *Continental Journal* (Boston, 1776), 17 October 1776; "Whitlock," *Pennsylvania Evening Post,* 24 May 1777.

1776. Scholars have been struck by the "sporadic and confused" nature of the new bills of rights. Gordon Wood observes that the new documents contained a "jarring but exciting combination of ringing declarations of universal principles with a motley collection of common law procedures."[66] If they contained too much for Wood's taste, they included too little to suit Leonard Levy. Reproving the drafters of the documents for proceeding "in an incredibly haphazard fashion that verged on ineptness,"[67] Levy deplored the omissions in the state bills of rights:

Two states passed over a free press guarantee; four neglected to ban excessive fines, excessive bail, compulsory self-incrimination, and general search warrants. Five ignored protections for the rights of assembly, petition, counsel, and trial by jury in civil cases. Seven omitted a prohibition of ex post facto laws. Nine failed to . . . condemn bills of attainder. Ten said nothing about freedom of speech, while eleven were silent on double jeopardy.[68]

People at the time were not satisfied with the first bills of rights either. The citizens of Albemarle County, Virginia, for example, in the fall of 1776 sent instructions to their delegates in the state assembly complaining that although the recently adopted Virginia Declaration of Rights "will be an honorable Memorial to the memory of its Compilers . . . we find, that the true sense of it is not understood; for which reason a good many still remain ignorant of their rights."[69] What were the people of Albemarle unable to comprehend? Perhaps they could not tell how secure their rights were, for by using the verb *ought* with respect to certain rights—trial by jury "ought to be held sacred," excessive bail "ought not to be required"—the drafters of the Declaration seemed to make the enjoyment of rights optional. There were also doubts in the Old Dominion about the relationship of the bill of rights to the state constitution, which raised the question of whether the bill of rights was in any sense a fundamental law. "Virginia," said Gov. Edmund Randolph, "has a bill of rights, but it is no part of the Constitution. By not saying whether it is paramount to the Constitution or not, it has left us in confusion."[70] The relationship

---

[66] Wood, *Creation of the American Republic*, 271.
[67] Leonard Levy, *Freedom of Speech and Press in Early American History: Legacy of Suppression* (1960; Cambridge, Mass.: Harvard University Press, 1963), 281.
[68] Leonard Levy, *Essays on the Making of the Constitution* (2nd ed., New York: Oxford University Press, 1987), 269.
[69] Albemarle County Instructions [September–October 1776], in Julian P. Boyd., ed., *The Papers of Thomas Jefferson* (Princeton, N.J.: Princeton University Press, 1952), 6: 286.
[70] Randolph, speech, Virginia ratifying convention, 9 June 1788, Elliot, ed., *The Debates in the Several State Conventions*, 3: 191.

of the bill of rights to state constitutions troubled officials in other jurisdictions as well. In Maryland, Judge Alexander Contee Hanson asserted that it had been strongly argued that the constitution "was indeed binding; but the declaration of rights was only declaratory."[71] Massachusetts "declared her bill of rights as no part of her Constitution."[72] Pennsylvanians, in contrast, considered their bill of rights their preeminent document. In Philadelphia in October 1776 a group of writers using the signatures Casca, Lucius, and Camullus,[73] argued in the local newspapers that their state's bill of rights was superior to their state constitution, a "trunk" as compared to the constitutional "branches" of the tree. According to Camullus, "The fundamentals are contained in a Bill of Rights. A constitution is only the executive part of a bill of rights." New Yorkers had yet another view of the matter, contending that their state needed no bill of rights, because "the constitution to be formed would operate as a bill of rights."[74]

Another confusing aspect of the first state bills of rights was what appeared to be their strong British flavor. Sections from the English Bill of Rights of 1689, the Habeas Corpus Act of 1679, and even Magna Charta seemed to have been imported wholesale into the first bills, raising the question of whether the British constitution was not, after all, the source of rights in independent America. The eminent Continental jurist Georg Jellinck dismissed such a conclusion as "superficial," because there was a fundamental difference in spirit between the English and American bills of rights. The American instruments recognized the individual's "inalienable and indefeasible rights. The English laws know nothing of this. They do not wish to recognize an eternal, natural right, but one inherited from their fathers."[75]

Americans of the Revolutionary generation tended to interpret the British constitution as being, no less than their own fundamental charters, grounded in nature. Most Revolutionary Americans did not subscribe to our modern view that rights can be created; rather, they believed that in

[71] "Aristides to the Citizens of Maryland," *Maryland Journal and Baltimore Advertiser*, 4 March 1788.

[72] Randolph, speech, 9 June 1788, in Elliot, ed., *The Debates in the Several State Conventions*, 3:191.

[73] Lucius and Camullus, *Dunlap's Pennsylvania Packet*, 15, 29 October 1776; Casca, *Pennsylvania Evening Post*, 31 October 1776.

[74] "Sydney," in Storing, ed., *The Complete Anti-Federalist*, 6: 109.

[75] Georg Jellinck, *The Declaration of the Rights of Men and of Citizens* (Westport, Conn.: Hyperion Press, 1979), 45, 48.

formulating rights, individuals merely declared the presence of what Madison called "pre-existent rights" (hence the preference of many states for the phrase "declaration" of rights in describing their earliest bills of rights).[76] Because rights were not considered to be created or invented, the British were thought to have appropriated to their use natural, preexistent rights; therefore, in the American view, the British constitution was itself a natural-rights document. As the Massachusetts Assembly asserted in 1765, Americans "have a just value for those inestimable rights which are derived to all men from nature, and are happily interwoven in the British Constitution."[77]

This notion persisted and was specifically applied by American writers to the English Bill of Rights. A "Maryland Farmer," for example, argued in 1788 that the famous English document was "an enumeration of those conditions on which the individuals of the empire agreed to confirm the social compact," a list of "these their natural rights—not vested in Society, but reserved to each member thereof."[78] The idea took root in the United States that all rights and liberties, those variously called after 1776 civil, positive, and political, as well as those that appeared to be derived from British documents, were more or less natural rights. Alexander Hamilton made this point when he declared that "civil liberty is only natural liberty, modified and secured by the sanctions of civil society,"[79] and James Wilson reaffirmed the point at the Pennsylvania ratifying convention in 1787 by stating that "civil liberty is natural liberty itself."[80]

The idea that all rights and liberties were natural or naturally derived had by 1787 become the analytical tool Americans used to make sense of the bills of rights they had reflectively written in 1776. Bills of rights, it was widely held by 1787, were in theory repositories of reserved natural rights. How this notion evolved from the confused and conflicting ideas about rights abroad in 1776 is worth noting. The starting point was the

---

[76] James Madison, speech, House of Representatives, 8 June 1789, in Robert Rutland, ed., *Papers of James Madison* (Charlottesville, Va.: University Press of Virginia, 1979), 12: 204.

[77] Answer of the Massachusetts House, 23 October 1765, in Cushing, ed., *Writings of Samuel Adams*, 1:18–19.

[78] Quoted in Storing, ed., *The Complete Anti-Federalist*, 5:11.

[79] Quoted in Robert Rutland, *The Birth of the Bill of Rights 1776–1791* (Boston: Northeastern University Press, 1983), 42–3.

[80] Wilson, speech, 24 November 1787, in Jensen, ed., *Documentary History of the Ratification of the Constitution*, 2: 358–9. That civil liberty was "no other than natural liberty" was a conventional notion at the time of the American Revolution. See, for example, Blackstone, *Commentaries*, ed. Katz, 1: 121.

pervasive concept of the state of nature. As already noted, Locke postulated that individuals who left the state of nature surrendered some of their rights to society but retained others.

Americans subscribed to this idea. George Mason, author of the Virginia Declaration of Rights, America's first bill of rights, believed that individuals who formed societies "entered into compacts to give up some of their natural rights, that by union and mutual assistance they might secure the rest."[81] Civis, writing in the *Virginia Gazette,* 18 May 1776, asserted that "the use of speech is a natural right, which must have been reserved when men gave up their natural rights for the benefit of society." When "an Observer" wrote in a Boston paper two years later that "every natural right, not expressly given up, remains,"[82] he was merely repeating what had been claimed for years in the Bay State. The Boston Committee of Correspondence, for example, had declared in 1772 that "every Natural Right not expressly given up or from the nature of a Social Compact necessarily ceded remains,"[83] a sentiment affirmed the next year by the "Old Friend" who claimed that the "People have a Right to all their natural Rights which they have not given away."[84] The whole notion of keeping some and giving away other natural rights had become a cliché long before Madison wrote in 1785 of men "entering into Society on equal conditions; as relinquishing no more, and therefore retaining no less, one than another, of their natural rights."[85]

What were the natural rights retained by individuals who had entered society? In theory there were two kinds: alienable and inalienable. Alienable natural rights were those that individuals could have ceded to society if they wished; inalienable natural rights were so fundamental to human welfare that they were not considered to be in the power of individuals to surrender. George Mason included three inalienable rights in the Virginia Declaration of Rights: life, liberty, and "the means of acquiring and possessing property."[86] Mason appears to have borrowed this trio from Blackstone's three "absolute" rights: personal security (life

---

[81] Robert Rutland, ed., *The Papers of George Mason* (Chapel Hill: University of North Carolina Press, 1970), 1: 229.

[82] *Boston Independent Chronicle,* 22 January 1778.

[83] Cushing, ed., *Writings of Samuel Adams,* 2: 352.

[84] *Boston Gazette,* 8 February 1773.

[85] Rutland and Rachel, eds., *Papers of James Madison,* 8: 300.

[86] William F. Swindler, ed., *Sources and Documents of United States Constitutions* (Dobbs Ferry: Oceana Publications, 1979), 10: 49.

and limb), personal liberty, and personal property. The same threesome, described variously as "natural, inherent and inalienable rights" (Pennsylvania) and "natural, essential, and unalienable rights" (Massachusetts),[87] appeared in five of the seven remaining state bills of rights, suggesting that from the beginning Americans recognized that, at a minimum, declaration of rights must contain these inalienable natural rights.

Quite soon it became apparent to some Americans that around natural rights they could construct a theory about what the state bills of rights were. Writing as Ludlow in the *Pennsylvania Journal,* 21 May 1777, Benjamin Rush complained that his state's "Bill of Rights has confounded the *natural* and *civil* rights in such a manner as to produce endless confusion in society." Presuming to speak as an expert on the subject, the future author of the *Rights of Man,* Thomas Paine, replied over his familiar signature Common Sense that "a Bill of Rights . . . should retain such natural rights as are either consistent with or absolutely necessary toward our happiness in a state of society."[88] The *Essex Result,* published the next year in Massachusetts, agreed with Paine. "Sometimes," said the authors, we mention "the surrendering of a power to control our natural rights, which perhaps is speaking with more precision than when we use the expression parting with natural rights." Whether power or right was surrendered (Americans considered the two synonymous), the individual had "remaining after entering into political society, all his unalienable natural rights" and "over this class of unalienable rights the supreme power hath no control, and they ought to be clearly defined and ascertained in a Bill of Rights."[89]

As this line of thinking became prevalent in America, we find citizens instructing their representatives, as the people of Bellingham, Massachusetts, did in 1779, to see that a "Bill of Rights be formed where in the Natural Rites of Individuals be clearly ascertained."[90]

Observers were impressed with their fellow citizens' assiduous efforts to refine their thinking about bills of rights. A Maine newspaperman, for example, claimed in 1788 that "during the last fifteen or twenty years it has been the business of the ablest politicians . . . to discover, and draw

---

[87] Ibid., 8:278; 5: 93.
[88] *Pennsylvania Journal,* 4 June 1777.
[89] *Essex Results,* in Handlin and Handlin, eds., *The Popular Sources of Political Authority,* 330–32.
[90] Ibid., 413.

a line between, those rights which must be surrendered, 'and those which may be reserved.' "[91] As a result of those efforts by 1787 something approaching a national consensus had emerged that whatever else a bill of rights might include, its distinguishing characteristic was that it contained reserved natural rights.

FEDERALISTS AND ANTI-FEDERALISTS

The consensus was evident in the debates over the ratification of the federal Constitution in 1787–8. "A bill of rights may be summed up in a few words," Patrick Henry declared in the Virginia ratifying convention. "What do they tell us? That our rights are reserved."[92] Pennsylvania Anti-Federalist leader Robert Whitehill agreed, describing a bill of rights as "an explicit reservation of those rights with which the people ought not, and mean not to part."[93] A bill of rights, added Whitehill's colleague, John Smilie, is "necessary as an instrument of original compact and to mention the rights reserved."[94] According to the influential Anti-Federalist pamphleteer the "Old Whig," bills of rights contained "those liberties which it is of the greatest importance for Freemen to retain to themselves, when they surrender up a part of their natural rights for the good of society."[95] And "Brutus," perhaps the ablest of all Anti-Federalist writers, defined bills of rights as "expressly reserving to the people such of their essential natural rights, as are not necessary to be parted with."[96] Borrowing a phrase from Blackstone, Richard Henry Lee summarized the Anti-Federalist position by declaring that bills of rights were "express declarations of that Residuum of natural rights, which is not intended to be given up to society."[97] Federalists shared this opinion. A "Citizen

---

[91] Thomas B. Wait to George Thatcher, 15 August 1788, quoted in John P. Kaminski, "Restoring the Declaration of Independence, Natural Rights and the Ninth Amendment," in Jon Kukla, ed., *The Bill of Rights: A Lively Heritage* (Richmond: Virginia State Library and Archives, 1987), 144.

[92] Patrick Henry, speech, Virginia ratifying convention, 14 June 1788, in Elliot, ed., *The Debates in Several State Conventions*, 3: 448.

[93] Robert Whitehill, speech, Pennsylvania ratifying convention, 28 November 1787, in Jensen, ed., *Documentary History of the Ratification of the Constitution*, 2: 393.

[94] John Smilie, speech, Pennsylvania ratifying convention, 30 November 1787, in ibid., 2: 441.

[95] Storing, ed., *The Complete Anti-Federalist*, 3: 34.

[96] Ibid., 2: 373.

[97] Richard Henry Lee to Samuel Adams, 5 October 1787, in Jensen, ed., *Documentary History of the Ratification of the Constitution*, 13: 323. For Blackstone's usage, see *Commentaries*, ed. Katz, 1: 125.

of Pennsylvania" expressed it as well as any when he asserted that upon declaring independence in 1776 Americans

found themselves, as to Government, in a State of Nature; yet they were very sensible of the Blessings of civil Society. On a Recommendation of Congress... the Inhabitants of each Colony respectively, formed a Compact for themselves, which Compacts are our state Constitutions. These were original Agreements among Individuals, before actually in a state of Nature. In these Constitutions a Bill of Rights (that is a Declaration of the unalienated Rights of each Individual) was proper and indispensably necessary.[98]

What happened to those rights that *were* surrendered to society? By 1787 a consensus had also emerged about their status. Locke's theory posited that these rights were surrendered to the "Legislative or Supreme Power of a Common-Wealth."[99] In the years after 1776 Americans defined their legislatures in terms of the "Blackstonian doctrine of legislative omnicompetence," which was "in the ascendant" throughout the Revolutionary period.[100] In all parts of the country Americans stressed the plenitude of power enjoyed by the legislative branch.

"The Legislature," asserted Noah Webster in 1787, "has all the power, of all the people," the reason being, Alexander Contee Hanson explained, that "when people entered into a compact of government" they "thereby parted with the whole legislative power."[101] In the Confederation Congress in September 1787 Nathaniel Gorham said that "in state governments ... the legislature had unlimited power."[102] Some months later in the Virginia ratifying convention, George Nicholas declared that in his state "all powers were given to the government without exception."[103] This was also the opinion of the major Anti-Federalist writer, the "Federal Farmer," who informed his readers that in the states the people "often give general powers, indeed all power, to the government."[104] "When general legislative powers are given," James Wilson told the Pennsylvania

---

[98] Quoted in *Maryland Journal and Baltimore Advertiser*, 19 October 1787.

[99] Laslett, ed., *Two Treatises of Government*, section 131, 371.

[100] E. S. Corwin, "The Progress of Constitutional Theory between the Declaration of Independence and the Meeting of the Philadelphia Convention," *American Historical Review* 30 (April 1925): 517.

[101] Wood, *Creation of the American Republic*, 381, 291.

[102] Nathaniel Gorham, speech, 27 September 1787, in Jensen, ed., *Documentary History of the Ratification of the Constitution*, 1: 335.

[103] Speech, Virginia ratifying convention, 14 June 1788, in Elliot, ed., *The Debates in Several State Conventions*, 3: 450.

[104] Quoted in Storing, ed., *The Complete Anti-Federalist*, 2: 323.

ratifying convention, "the people part with their authority, and . . . retain nothing."[105]

Nothing, Wilson should have added, except the natural rights they reserved in their bills of rights. "Indefinite powers," stated the Federalist spokesman Charles Pinckney in the South Carolina ratifying convention, were "given to the government, except on points that were by express compact reserved to the people."[106] Anti-Federalists agreed with Pinckney: "It is certainly true," wrote the "Old Whig," "that in establishing the powers of government, the rulers are invested with every right and authority which is not in explicit terms reserved."[107] Rights, claimed the "Impartial Examiner," should be "expressly reserved, for it is a maxim, I dare say universally acknowledged, that when men establish a system of government, in granting powers therein they are always understood to surrender what they do not so expressly reserve."[108] "A state government is designed for ALL CASES WHATSOEVER," added "Plain Truth," "consequently what is not reserved is tacitly given."[109] The Federalists and Anti-Federalists agreed, then, on the theory of the bills of rights adopted by the American states, a theory that was a marriage of Blackstone and Locke. Both groups held that the American bills of rights reserved certain natural rights and that those rights not expressly reserved were considered to be transferred to an omnicompetent, Blackstonian legislature vested with "general powers."

If Federalists and Anti-Federalists agreed about the nature of American bills of rights, how can historians claim that the issue divided them during the ratification campaign? Anti-Federalists, it is true, assailed the new constitution because of the absence of a bill of rights, and Federalists aggressively refuted their charges. But what was at issue in the dispute was not contrasting understandings of the nature of bills of rights but a disagreement over who the parties to the new constitution were. The Anti-Federalists claimed that in writing the Constitution the Federalists had flouted their instructions, which called for a mere revision of the Articles of Confederation, and had taken the unprecedented step of dis-

---

[105] Speech, 4 December 1787, in Jensen, ed., *Documentary History of the Ratification of the Constitution*, 2: 470.
[106] Speech, 16 January 1788, in Elliot, ed., *The Debates in Several State Conventions*, 4: 259–60.
[107] Storing, ed., *The Complete Anti-Federalist*, 3: 33.
[108] Ibid., 5: 176.
[109] "Plain Truth," 10 November 1787, in Jensen, ed., *Documentary History of the Ratification of the Constitution*, 2: 218.

solving the social compact and throwing the country into a state of nature in which individuals were obliged to come together and reconstitute the social and political order. The creation of the Constitution was, in Anti-Federalist eyes, nothing more than a replay on a continental scale of the creation of the state governments, the only difference being "in the number of the parties concerned."[110]

The framers of the Constitution, Luther Martin asserted, assumed that "all the people of this continent were in a state of nature, and we were forming one government for them as individuals . . . nearly the same as was done in most of the States when they formed governments over the people who compose them."[111] "We the People," agreed William Findley in the Pennsylvania ratifying convention, "supposes us in a state of nature" and the Constitution as "a compact between individuals entering into society."[112] If the federal Constitution was, in theory, the state constitutions writ large—if it was a compact of individuals leaving a state of nature—the other lessons of the state constitutions followed, of course. If the individuals forming the constitution reserved no rights by adopting a bill of rights, all rights and powers were ceded to the new federal government. Explained Massachusetts Anti-Federalist "Agrippa" in language that by 1788 had become hackneyed: "Any system therefore which appoints a legislature without any reservation of the rights of individuals surrenders all power . . . to the government."[113] Without a bill of rights it was indisputable, Anti-Federalists argued from the common American understanding of the state bills of rights, that the new federal government would acquire absolute power—would become an "iron-handed despotism." To forestall such a development, a bill of rights was, Anti-Federalists insisted, absolutely indispensable.

If Anti-Federalist premises were granted—if the new constitution was considered, like the state governments, a compact of individuals leaving a state of nature and granting government general powers—then Federalists were prepared to concede that a bill of rights should have been added at Philadelphia. Said James Iredell, "If we had formed a general legislature, with undefined powers, a bill of rights would not only have

---

[110] John DeWitt, in Storing, ed., *The Complete Anti-Federalist*, 4: 21.
[111] Luther Martin, "Genuine Information," in Max Farrand, ed., *The Records of the Federal Convention of 1787* (New Haven: Yale University Press, 1966), 3: 193.
[112] Speech, 1 December 1787, in Jensen, ed., *Documentary History of the Ratification of the Constitution,* 2: 446.
[113] Storing, ed., *The Complete Anti-Federalist*, 4: 96.

been proper, but necessary; and it would have then operated as an exception to the legislative authority in such particulars. It has this effect with respect to some of the American constitutions, where the powers of legislation are general."[114] But Federalists scorned the Anti-Federalist premises. "The absurd idea of the federal constitution being a government of individuals," complained a Maryland Federalist, "seems too nugatory to merit a serious reflection."[115]

But if individuals did not create the Constitution, who did? The people did, the Federalists answered. But the people as creators must not be viewed as acting as "unassociated individuals" (Luther Martin's term)[116] but as in a corporate capacity, in what James Wilson called an "assemblage of societies."[117] James Madison authoritatively elaborated this idea in *Federalist 39*, observing that assent was given to the Constitution "by the people, not as individuals composing one entire nation, but as composing the distinct and independent states to which they respectively belong. It is to be the assent and ratification of the several States, derived from the supreme authority in each state—the authority of the people themselves."[118] Or, as Madison explained in the Virginia ratifying convention, the Constitution was created by the people, acting not as individuals "composing one great body, but the people as composing thirteen sovereignties."[119] Therefore the Constitution, as the product of a collective people, could not, in theory, be a vehicle of individual rights, a fact obvious to common scribblers in the newspapers. "In the proposed Compact among the same thirteen individual sovereignties no Bill of Rights of Individuals has been or could be introduced," asserted a Federalist writer in a Baltimore newspaper. But this commentator recognized that a state government was a different matter, for "in Articles of Agreement among a Number of People forming a Civil Society, a Bill of Rights of Individuals comes in of course, and it is indispensably necessary."[120]

---

[114] Speech, North Carolina ratifying convention, 28 July 1788, Elliot, ed., *The Debates in Several State Conventions*, 4: 149.

[115] "A Plebian," *Maryland Journal* (Baltimore), 14 March 1788.

[116] Observations, 3 June 1788, in James H. Hutson, ed., *Supplement to Max Farrand's The Records of the Federal Convention of 1787* (New Haven: Yale University Press, 1987), 4: 292.

[117] Speech, Pennsylvania ratifying convention, 24 November 1787, in Jensen, ed., *Documentary History of the Ratification of the Constitution*, 2: 352.

[118] Quoted in Jacob Cooke, ed., *The Federalist* (Middletown, Conn.: Wesleyan University Press, 1961), 251.

[119] Speech, 16 June 1788, Elliot, ed., *The Debates in Several State Conventions*, 3: 94.

[120] "A Citizen of Pennsylvania to the People of America," *Maryland Journal and Baltimore Advertiser*, 19 October 1787.

The Baltimore writer stated the Federalist position exactly. Bills of rights were "indispensably necessary" in the states, created as they were by individuals leaving a state of nature; they were inappropriate in a federal constitution created by a collective people acting through the agency of state governments. The Federalists' support for state bills of rights gave the lie to Anti-Federalist accusations that they were enemies to rights in general. The Federalists were, as scholars have recognized, "civil libertarians"[121] who could genuinely claim, as John Marshall did at the Virginia ratifying convention, "the title of being firm friends of liberty and the rights of mankind."[122] Their assertions that "the natural, and unalienable rights of mankind form the most eligible ground on which we now stand"[123] were not hollow. Federalists believed, however, that the definition and protection of these rights was the duty of the states, whose bills of rights, they universally contended, had not been superseded by the federal Constitution, as the Anti-Federalists monotonously charged. That the definition of rights and the content of bills of rights might vary from state to state, and that some states might even forgo bills of rights, the Federalists accepted with equanimity as the inevitable result of the system they were creating. Justice Brennan's recent observation that "our federalism permits diversity"[124] in rights from state to state was their credo.

Believing that rights were a state responsibility, the framers said little about them in Philadelphia. According to one authority, the framers' "immediate business gave them little occasion" to discuss rights.[125] What was their "immediate business"? Power, they would have responded. "Every member who attended the Convention," said Charles Cotesworth Pinckney at the South Carolina ratifying convention, "was from the beginning sensible of the necessity of giving greater powers to the federal government."[126] To some Federalists the Constitution was nothing more than a "great power of attorney."[127] In 1789 Madison

---

[121] Levy, *Essays*, 260.

[122] Quoted in Wood, *Creation of the American Republic*, 524.

[123] (Tench Coxe), "A Democratic Federalist," 26 November 1787, in Jensen, ed., *Documentary History of the Ratification of the Constitution*, 2: 298.

[124] William J. Brennan, "The Bill of Rights and the States: The Revival of State Constitutions as Guardians of Individual Rights," *New York University Law Review* 61 (1986): 551.

[125] Benjamin F. Wright, Jr., *American Interpretations of Natural Law* (New York: Russell and Russell, 1962), 126.

[126] Speech, 17 January 1788, in Elliot, ed., *The Debates in Several State Conventions*, 4: 282.

[127] James Iredell, speech, North Carolina ratifying convention, July 23, 1788, in ibid., 4: 148.

described it as a "Bill of Powers [that] needs no bill of R[ig]hts."[128] It was in the language of power that Federalists responded to Anti-Federalist strictures about the absence of a bill of rights in the Constitution.

The Federalist argument was adumbrated during the final days of the Philadelphia convention by Roger Sherman, who parried a demand that a written guarantee for the freedom of the press be included in the Constitution with the reply that "it is unnecessary. The power of Congress does not extend to the Press."[129] This line of reasoning was employed by James Wilson in the major Federalist apologia he delivered at the Pennsylvania Statehouse on 6 October 1787. According to Wilson, Americans "invested their [state] representatives with every right and authority which they did not in explicit terms reserve." But "in delegating federal powers," he continued, "congressional authority is to be collected... from the positive grant expressed in the instrument of union. Hence, it is evident, that in the former case everything which is not reserved is given, but in the latter the reverse of the proposition prevails, and everything which is not given, is reserved."[130]

Federalists savored this last phrase. "There cannot be a more positive and unequivocal declaration of the principle of the adoption," said Madison in the Virginia ratifying convention, than that "everything not granted is reserved."[131] This aphorism became the Federalists' principal polemical weapon to "prove" that a bill of rights was unnecessary. If in creating the Constitution the people granted only limited and enumerated powers (keeping the rest to themselves), why adopt a bill of rights to protect those large areas of American life to which the granted powers did not extend? "Why," asked Hamilton in *Federalist* 84, "declare that things shall not be done which there is no power to do?"[132] "Where there is no power to attack, it is idle," Wilson added, "to prepare the means of defense."[133] Believing that a bill of rights was unnecessary, Federalists also concluded that it would be dangerous, reasoning that the principle

[128] Notes for speech in Congress (8 June 1789), in Rutland et al., eds., *Papers of James Madison*, 12: 194.

[129] Speech, 14 September 1787, in Farrand, ed., *The Records of the Federal Convention*, 2: 618.

[130] Jensen, ed., *Documentary History of the Ratification of the Constitution*, 2: 167–8.

[131] Speech, Virginia ratifying convention, 24 June 1788, in Elliot, ed., *The Debates in Several State Conventions*, 3: 120.

[132] Cooke, ed., *The Federalist*, 579.

[133] Speech, Pennsylvania ratifying convention, 4 December 1787, in Jensen, ed., *Documentary History of the Ratification of the Constitution*, 2: 471.

of the state bills of rights—everything not reserved was granted—posed the danger that, if valuable rights were omitted from any enumeration or listing in a bill of rights, they could be considered to have been surrendered to the government. The case against a bill of rights seemed so clear to the Federalists that they did not conceal their contempt for the counterarguments in its favor. Bills of rights, Federalists jeered, were "absurd and dangerous," "idle and superfluous," "preposterous and dangerous," not to mention being full of "inutility and folly."[134]

THE BILL OF RIGHTS

Ridicule could not assuage the public's anxiety about the absence of a bill of rights, and the Federalists were obliged, beginning in the Massachusetts ratifying convention in February 1788, to promise their opponents that they would consider adding rights amendments to the Constitution after it was ratified. Minorities in various state conventions suggested more than two hundred amendments (many duplicating one another), which were collected in a pamphlet published in Richmond and used by James Madison as he guided the Bill of Rights through the First Congress, which convened in New York in April 1789. Acclaimed as the Father of the Bill of Rights, Madison was a reluctant parent. In the Virginia ratifying convention he joined in denouncing proposals for a bill of rights as "unnecessary and dangerous," although he muted these criticisms in a letter to Jefferson.[135] He also suffered politically at the hands of supporters of bills of rights in Virginia. Patrick Henry prevented the Virginia legislature from electing him to the U.S. Senate and forced him to run for a House seat in a district gerrymandered in favor of the Anti-Federalists. To win election Madison was forced to betray his understanding by promising the local voters that he would support a bill of rights in Congress. This he dutifully did, by introducing rights amendments in the House of Representatives on 8 June 1789.[136]

---

[134] James Iredell, speech, North Carolina ratifying convention, 28 July 1788, in Elliot, ed., *The Debates in Several State Conventions*, 4: 149; Benjamin Rush, speech, Pennsylvania ratifying convention, 30 November 1787, in Jensen, ed., *Documentary History of the Ratification of the Constitution*, 2: 434; Wilson, speech, Pennsylvania ratifying convention, 28 November 1787, in ibid., 2: 388; Henry Lee, speech, Virginia ratifying convention, 9 June 1788, in Elliot, ed., *The Debates in Several State Conventions*, 3: 186.

[135] Speech, 24 June 1788, in ibid., 3: 626. For Madison's letter to Jefferson, 17 October 1788, see Boyd, ed., *Papers of Thomas Jefferson*, 14: 18.

[136] For the amendments of 8 June and Madison's speech introducing them, see Rutland, ed., *Papers of James Madison*, 12: 197–210.

In introducing these amendments Madison rejected out of hand the model of the state bills of rights, which were placed as discrete entities at the head of state constitutions. Like a modern Procrustes, he compressed the rights amendments into the frame of the Constitution to make them as indistinguishable as possible, structurally and theoretically, from that document. Madison, for example, on 8 June 1789, tucked what became the Bill of Rights' first eight amendments "into article 1st, section 9, between clauses 3 and 4." Article I, section 9, is, of course, the part of the Constitution that limits the powers of Congress, forbidding it to prohibit the slave trade for twenty years, to pass bills of attainder, to tax exports from the states, and so on. During the ratification debates some participants considered these "express restrictions" on the powers of Congress to be a truncated bill of rights—what Patrick Henry called a "congressional bill of rights."[137] What better place, then, Madison appears to have reasoned, to insert rights amendments than in Article I, section 9, where their presence would permit the system to "remain uniform and entire; it will certainly be more simple when amendments are interwoven into those parts to which they naturally belong, than it will if they consist of separate and distinct parts."[138]

Weaving rights amendments into Article I, section 9, gave the Bill of Rights the curious shape it assumed as it finally emerged from Congress. To make the amendments inserted into Article I consistent with the language already there, Madison was obliged to express rights not positively and unconditionally, as they were phrased in the state bills of rights, but to use language that seemed to link them to restraints on power and to make them in some sense dependent on the forbearance of government. Thus Madison used the following locutions: "nor shall the full and equal rights of conscience be in any manner, or on any pretext infringed"; "the people shall not be deprived or abridged of their right to speak, to write, or to publish their sentiments." Madison asserted that rights existed but implied that they were not absolute and that they could be jeopardized unless Congress was prohibited from infringing them (as it already was, by the language of Article I, section 9, prohibited from interfering with the slave trade or from taxing exports).

As Madison's rights amendments made their way through Congress

[137] Speech, Virginia ratifying convention, 15 June 1788, in Elliot, ed., *The Debates in Several State Conventions*, 3: 461.
[138] Madison, speech, House of Representatives, 13 August 1789, in Rutland, ed., *Papers of James Madison*, 12: 333.

in the summer of 1789, they were extracted from Article I, section 9, and placed at the end of the Constitution. In the case of religion, the press, and speech, Congress also deleted Madison's assertions that these were rights but retained his language, tailored to Article I, section 9, that Congress had no power to infringe them. This is the reason that freedom of religion, press, and speech are not claimed as rights in the First Amendment—that they stand on no other foundation than that Congress, in the manner of Article I, section 9, is forbidden to interfere with them. That they are rights must be inferred from Congress's obligation to refrain from exercising power; they are rights, in short, only in the sense of being correlatives of congressional duty.

Madison's amendments of 8 June contained the precursor of what became the Bill of Rights' Ninth Amendment. At the end of the amendments inserted in Article I, section 9—amendments that, as revised, became the first eight amendments of the Constitution—Madison added the following sentence: "The exceptions here or elsewhere in the constitution, made in favor of particular rights, shall not be construed as to diminish the just importance of other rights retained by the people; or as to enlarge the powers delegated by the constitution; but either as actual limitations of such powers, or as inserted merely for greater caution." As refined by the First Congress, these words became the Ninth Amendment: "The enumeration in the Constitution of certain rights shall not be construed to deny or disparage others retained by the people."

Both the embryonic language of 8 June and the Ninth Amendment repudiated the philosophy of the state bills of rights—that what is not reserved is granted—for both documents stated that, in addition to rights reserved (i.e., enumerated), other undefined rights were retained by the people. Some modern scholars contend that the undefined rights declared in the Ninth Amendment to be retained by the people must be natural rights or some other species of unwritten rights,[139] but this argument collapses in the face of Madison's resolve, noted in his interweaving rights

---

[139] Leonard Levy, for example, has argued that the Ninth Amendment "is the repository for natural rights." Levy, *Original Intent and the Framers' Constitution* (New York: Macmillan, 1988), 278. Another scholar has claimed that the Founders "wrote the Ninth Amendment to affirm the natural rights doctrines of the Declaration of Independence." See Kaminski, "Restoring the Declaration of Independence," in Kukla, ed., *The Bill of Rights*, 150. For a recent assertion that the Ninth Amendment can be considered as a source of unwritten rights in general, see Lawrence G. Sager, "You Can Raise the First, Hide Behind the Fourth, and Plead the Fifth: But What on Earth Can You Do with the Ninth Amendment?" *Chicago–Kent Law Review* 64 (1988): 239–64.

amendments into Article I, section 9, to preserve the integrity of the Constitution by crafting amendments to be consistent with it.

As we have seen, a fundamental conviction of Madison and the Federalists was that the Constitution was created not by individuals leaving a state of nature but by the people acting collectively through their state governments, and that therefore the natural rights of individuals had no place in the Constitution. At the Philadelphia convention during the deliberations of the Committee of Detail, Edmund Randolph stated the Federalist position precisely: "We are not working on the natural rights of men not yet gathered into society, but upon those rights modified by society."[140] Leonard Levy has recently shown how convention delegates scrupulously observed this distinction by proposing only measures to protect rights incident to civil society, such as freedom of the press and the inviolability of the writ of habeas corpus. "No natural rights were constitutionally protected,"[141] Levy asserted, nor were any proposed to be protected in the meetings at Philadelphia.

In 1789 American society was further removed from the state of nature than it had been in 1787, because the adoption of the Constitution had overlaid the existing state governments with a powerful new national government. Therefore to conceive of a bill of rights or of any other law passed by the federal Congress in 1789 as addressing the concerns, or protecting the rights, of individuals emerging from a state of nature was ludicrous. Individual natural rights were the concern of the states, as Madison acknowledged in notes prepared for his speech introducing his amendments of 8 June. State bills, he observed, summarizing the received wisdom, protected "Natural rights retained—as Speech, Con[science]."[142] Because amendments containing natural rights would be incompatible with the federal Constitution, Madison omitted them from his amendments. That he did so deliberately can be seen from the use he made of the Virginia ratifying convention's proposed amendments.

Madison had these amendments at his elbow when preparing his amendments, for he incorporated parts of them word for word. What he did not incorporate from the Virginia document was its assertion of "certain natural rights" shared by all men, the familiar trio of life, liberty, and property, borrowed from the Virginia Declaration of Rights of 1776 and included in many of the other state bills of rights.

---

[140] Farrand, ed., *The Records of the Federal Convention*, 2: 137.
[141] Levy, *Essays*, 265–6.
[142] Rutland, ed., *Papers of James Madison*, 12: 194.

The Virginia convention's amendments assert: "There are certain natural rights ... which are the enjoyment of life, and liberty, with the means of acquiring, possessing, and protecting property, and pursuing and obtaining happiness and safety."[143] As revised by Madison for inclusion in his amendments of 8 June, the passage read: "Government ... consists in the enjoyment of life and liberty, with the right of acquiring and using property, and generally of pursuing and obtaining happiness and safety." Madison, in a word, stripped rights of their natural status when drafting the Bill of Rights.

As Madison's amendments progressed through Congress in the summer of 1789, one attempt was made to restore natural rights. On 21 July the House appointed a select committee to consider Madison's proposals. A committee member, Roger Sherman, presented a bill of rights patterned after the state bills. Sherman's bill of rights used the conventional formula that "the people have certain natural rights which are retained when they enter into society" and listed several, including the "right of conscience," speech, and assembly. Sherman's draft was rejected[144] and, so far as we know, no other attempt was made in Congress to insert natural rights into the Bill of Rights.

RIGHTS AND POWERS

If the other rights "retained by the people" mentioned in the Ninth Amendment are not natural rights or collateral unwritten rights, what are they? One clue is the linkage between rights and power in the embryonic Ninth Amendment language of Madison's proposals of 8 June. Another is the Virginia ratifying convention's amendment from which Madison copied some of his Ninth Amendment language of 8 June: it used the word *power,* where we should have expected the term *right.* The rights retained in the Ninth Amendment seem, therefore, to have been intimately related, in Madison's mind, to power, although we have been assured by scholars as diverse in their interests as Bernard Bailyn and John Hart Ely that power and right are utterly incompatible. The two concepts, Bailyn insisted, occupied "innately antagonistic spheres ... the one [power] must be resisted, the other [right] defended, and the two

[143] Amendments, 27 June 1788, Elliot, ed., *The Debates in Several State Conventions,* 3: 657.
[144] For the Sherman draft, see *New York Times,* 29 July 1787.

must never be confused."[145] In fact, Revolutionary Americans fused the two concepts, and they did so not because they were confused—as they often were, when they engaged in rights discourse—but because they had on their side the authority of the foremost students of rights in the Western intellectual tradition.

The concept of an individual right is thought to have been first formulated by the fourteenth-century nominalists, one of whose leading spirits was William of Ockham. Ockham's admirers claim that he wrote the first "systematic account of subjective rights," his *Opus Nonaginata Dierum,* in which he described the "notion of a jus [right] in something by using the word potesta [power]."[146] Other scholars believe that Jean Gerson created modern rights theory in 1402 in a volume in which he defined right as a "dispositional facultas or power, appropriate to someone and in accordance with right reason."[147] From Gerson the line defining right as power runs through Thomas Hobbes (right is "the liberty each man hath, to use his own power, as he will himself, for the preservation of his own nature")[148] to those seventeenth- and eighteenth-century natural-law commentators and popularizers who so strongly influenced the Revolutionary generation: Pufendorf, Vattel, Burlamaqui. Pufendorf explained that because "the several kinds of Power have, for the most part, a particular Name . . . we have thought it convenient to give it the name Right."[149] Burlamaqui, whose impact on Jefferson, James Wilson, and others was substantial, wrote simply: "We must define Right a power."[150] Blackstone, whose *Commentaries* contained passages lifted without attribution from Burlamaqui, asserted that the rights of man consist "properly in a power of acting as one thinks fit, without any restraint or control, unless by the law of nature."[151]

Confining rights/power within the bounds of the law of nature (dictated, Blackstone believed, by God) gave rights a moral dimension, which every writer back to William of Ockham had proclaimed and to which

---

[145] Bernard Bailyn, *The Ideological Origins of the American Revolution* (Cambridge, Mass.: Harvard University Press, 1967), 57–8; John Hart Ely, *Democracy and Distrust* (Cambridge, Mass.: Harvard University Press, 1980), 36.

[146] Richard Tuck, *Natural Rights Theories: Their Origin and Development* (Cambridge: Cambridge University Press, 1979), 22–3.

[147] Ibid., 25.

[148] Ibid., 130.

[149] Samuel Pufendorf, *The Law of Nature and Nations,* 5th ed. (London, 1749), 11–12.

[150] Jean-Jacques Burlamaqui, *The Principles of Natural and Politic Law,* 5th ed. (Cambridge, 1807), 1: 48.

[151] Blackstone, *Commentaries,* ed. Katz, 1: 121.

Americans of the Revolutionary generation were committed. Vattel spoke their mind when he said that right was "nothing more than the power of doing what is morally possible."[152] So, too, did Burlamaqui, who wrote that although he had no quarrel with those who "understand by power pretty near the same thing, as we understand by right," it was imperative not to "confound simple power with right," for right required "agree-ableness to a rule, which modifies the physical power, and directs its operations in a manner proper to conduct a man to a certain end. It is for this reason we say that right is a moral quality."[153]

Subscribing to this point of view, Americans believed that a right was the power to do right. Throughout the Revolutionary period they equated right and power in their political discourse. Observe Richard Henry Lee's interpretation of the British Parliament's notorious Declaratory Act of 1766, which asserted Parliament's power to bind the colonies "in all cases whatsoever," a charter of power if there ever was one. Yet Lee called the act a "Bill of Rights declaring the power of Parliament."[154] Two decades later the equation of right with power was pervasive. Consider the following examples: *Federalist* 2: "people must cede to it [government] some of their natural rights, in order to vest it with the required powers";[155] Nathaniel Gorham (a Massachusetts delegate to the Philadelphia convention), 27 February 1787: "A bill of rights in state governments was intended to retain certain powers";[156] John De Witt, the Massachusetts Anti-Federalist pamphleteer, 1788: "The people, although fully sensible that they reserved every title of power they did not expressly grant away, yet afraid that the words made use of, to express those rights so granted . . . ";[157] Thomas Hartley, Pennsylvania ratifying convention, 30 November 1787: "If no power was delegated to the government, no right was resigned by the people";[158] James Wilson, Pennsylvania ratifying convention, 11 December 1787: "Where power is not delegated to

---

[152] Emmerich de Vattel, *The Law of Nations, or, Principles of the Law of Nature* (London, 1811), xj.

[153] Burlamaqui, *Principles of Natural and Politic Law*, 1: 48–49.

[154] (R. H. Lee), *The Farmer's and Monitor's Letters to the Inhabitants of the British Colonies* (Willamsburg, Va., 1768 [?]), preface.

[155] Cooke, ed., *The Federalist*, 8.

[156] Jenson, ed., *Documentary History of the Ratification of the Constitution*, 1: 335. On 28 November 1787, James Wilson asserted in the Pennsylvania ratifying convention that "a bill of rights annexed to a constitution is an enumeration of the powers reserved." Ibid., 2: 388.

[157] Storing, ed., *The Complete Anti-Federalist*, 4: 22.

[158] Jensen, ed., *Documentary History of the Ratification of the Constitution*, 2: 430.

our rulers, the rights still remain in the people";[159] Patrick Henry, Virginia
ratifying convention, 25 June 1788: "I contend there are many essential
and vital rights which are omitted. One is the power of direct taxation";[160]
Edmund Randolph, Virginia ratifying convention, 24 June 1788: "All
powers come from the people, and whatever is not granted by them
remains with them; that among other things remaining with them are
liberty of the press, right of conscience, and some other essential
rights";[161] William Maclaine, North Carolina ratifying convention, 28
July 1788: "The powers of Congress are limited and enumerated. We
say we have given them these powers, but we do not say we have given
them more. We retain all these rights which we have not given away to
the general government."[162] The identity of right and power was asserted
dogmatically by the Anti-Federalist pamphleteer the "Impartial Examiner," who claimed that a "natural right is [a] power or claim established
by the law of nature,"[163] and by Davie in the North Carolina ratifying
convention who declared that "every man of common sense knows that
political right is political power."[164] Madison told George Washington
on 5 December 1789 that any distinction between "powers granted and
rights retained" was "altogether fanciful."[165]

The founding generation's equation of rights and power clarifies the
meaning of the Ninth Amendment. It was, as we have said, a disclaimer
of the philosophy of the state bills of rights that everything not reserved
was granted to the government. Had there been no Ninth Amendment,
Madison and his colleagues feared that it could be assumed that the
people retained only the rights contained in the first eight amendments;
every other right/power would, according to the example of the state
bills, be ceded to the government, which would become a leviathan in
possession of virtually unlimited power. The assertion in the Ninth
Amendment that other rights/powers were retained by the people ex-
ploded the possibility that a federal government of unlimited or "general"
powers was being created on the state government model. As soon as
people outside Congress saw the Ninth Amendment, they perceived that

[159] Ibid., 2: 570.
[160] Elliot, ed., *The Debates in Several State Conventions,* 3: 650.
[161] Ibid., 3: 598.
[162] Ibid., 4: 145.
[163] Storing, ed., *The Complete Anti-Federalist,* 5: 177.
[164] Elliot, ed., *The Debates in Several State Conventions,* 4: 238.
[165] Madison to Washington, 5 December 1789, in Rutland, ed., *Papers of James Madison*
    12: 459.

this was its purpose; it was, said Edmund Randolph in the Virginia General Assembly, a "reservation against constructive power."[166] No one considered the amendment a repository of natural or unwritten rights, as indeed it was not.

What was the extent of those rights/powers declared by the Ninth Amendment to be retained by the people? The answer was supplied by the Tenth Amendment. The curious aspect of the Tenth Amendment was that it was a kind of anti–bill of rights. It repeated the stock Federalist charge used during the ratification campaign to deny that a bill of rights was needed: powers not granted to the government were reserved to the people. This being so, it was absurd to list rights to be protected against an abuse of power that did not exist. During the ratification contest partisans on both sides recognized that language similar to the Tenth Amendment would obviate the necessity of a bill of rights. The Articles of Confederation, said Spencer of North Carolina, stated "that all was not given up to the United States was retained by the respective states. If such a clause had been inserted in the Constitution, it would have superseded the necessity of a bill of rights."[167] Yet the Tenth Amendment was needed as a gloss on the Ninth. Scholars have recognized that the two amendments are "complementary"[168] but have not appreciated that the Tenth Amendment was designed to explain the Ninth. To the question posed by the Ninth Amendment—What other rights and powers are retained by the people?—the Tenth Amendment answers: all powers not delegated to the United States.

A HOUSE DIVIDED

The Bill of Rights is a strange document indeed. The first eight amendments are a list of rights in a form resembling that advocated by Anti-Federalists. The Ninth Amendment is a disclaimer, denying that the federal Bill of Rights is similar to any of the other American bills of rights adopted since independence. The Tenth Amendment is an anti–bill of rights, a repetition of the argument used by the Federalists to repudiate a bill of rights during the ratification controversy. No wonder that Roger Sherman, in a House debate on 13 August 1789, criticized the document

---

[166] Ibid.
[167] Elliot, ed., *The Debates in Several State Conventions*, 4: 152.
[168] Rauol Berger, "The Ninth Amendment," *Cornell Law Review* 66 (November 1980), 2–3.

as a potpourri of "heterogeneous articles," an incongruous concoction like the great idol in the book of Daniel.[169] Sherman might have found an equally apt analogy in the New Testament, for the Bill of Rights was a house divided against itself, a document that could not stand in the esteem of either its sponsors or its opponents.

The adoption of the Bill of Rights was a defeat for those Anti-Federalist politicians who had aroused popular anxiety over the Constitution's alleged failure to protect civil liberties in the hope of mobilizing an opposition that could be maneuvered into revising the document to enhance state power. Once it became apparent that Congress would pass a bill of rights that protected individual rather than states' rights, Anti-Federalist leaders began "depreciating the importance of the very protections of individual liberty that they once demanded as a guarantee against tyranny."[170] Speaking for many of his colleagues, Anti-Federalist Senator William Grayson of Virginia dismissed the amendments sent to the states as "good for nothing and, I believe, as many others do, that they will do more harm than benefit."[171]

Nor did the Federalists consider the passage of the Bill of Rights a famous victory. There was constant exasperation with, and sniping at, Madison for pushing the Bill of Rights through the First Congress. Fellow Federalists accused him of headline hunting and denounced his proposals as "watergruel amendments," "milk and water amendments," and placebos prescribed for "imaginary ailments."[172] They persisted in considering a bill of rights absurd and dangerous, and they justified passing it as a means of placating the misguided Anti-Federalist rank and file, an exercise they cynically described as tossing a tub to a whale.[173] Wearied of rowing against the tide of friend and foe, Madison confided to a correspondent on 19 August 1789 that the Bill of Rights business was a "nauseous project."[174]

Federalists in Congress were not inclined to take much credit for a measure they passed with so little enthusiasm, and their Anti-Federalist

---

[169] Joseph Gales, comp., *Annals of the Congress of the United States* (Washington, D.C., 1834), 1: 708.

[170] Leonard Levy, *The Emergence of a Free Press* (New York: Oxford University Press, 1985), 228.

[171] Ibid., 229.

[172] Kenneth R. Bowling, "'A Tub to the Whale': The Founding Fathers and Adoption of the Federal Bill of Rights," *Journal of the Early Republic* 8 (Fall 1988): 237, 244.

[173] Ibid., 223–4, 236, 238.

[174] Madison to Richard Peters, 19 August 1789, in Rutland, ed., *Papers of James Madison*, 12: 346–7.

adversaries wrote the Bill of Rights campaign off as a bad investment of their time. Taking their cue from Congress, the state parties received and ratified the Bill of Rights so unceremoniously that, except in Virginia, they left scarcely any evidence of what they had done. The Bill of Rights forthwith fell into a kind of national oblivion, as Michael Kammen reminded us in 1987, not to be "discovered" until the beginning of World War II.[175] A census taken in 1941 of the thirteen copies of the Bill of Rights sent to the states in October 1789 revealed that the document had been literally forgotten; only four copies could be found, although a diligent search, propelled by patriotic ardor, uncovered copies in Rhode Island, New Jersey, and South Carolina, the last named "crumpled, and torn" and caked with "much dust."[176] Of course, since World War II, as the result of actions of the Supreme Court too familiar to be described, the Bill of Rights has enjoyed a remarkable resurgence in our national consciousness.

What of natural law, considered by Americans in the years after 1776 to be the bedrock of rights in the new nation? A recent scholar has found natural law prospering in American jurisprudence from 1789 to 1820, despite the persistence of the confusion, noted by Justice Iredell in *Calder v. Bull* (1798) about its precise contours.[177] G. Edward White has described it as a principle of considerable, though declining, jurisprudential importance up to the Civil War.[178] Today natural law and natural rights are said to be rejected by spokesmen of every ideological stripe.[179] The result is that natural law, considered indispensable to the Founders' generation, is now dismissed as unnecessary, while the Bill of Rights, considered unnecessary in 1787, is now held to be indispensable. Such reversals are not uncommon in the history of ideas, nor are they unknown in the history of law. What they indicate is that the most strongly held convictions often change and that the current reverence for the Bill of Rights cannot be taken for granted in the future.

---

[175] Michael Kammen, *A Machine that Would Go Of Itself: The Constitution in American Culture* (New York: Knopf, 1987), 337.

[176] Elizur Smith to Solon Buck, 5 July 1945, Manuscript Division, Library of Congress.

[177] Suzanna Sherry, "The Founders' Unwritten Constitution," *University of Chicago Law Review* 54 (1987): 1175.

[178] G. Edward White, *The Marshall Court and Cultural Change 1815–35* (New York: Macmillan, 1988), chap. 10.

[179] Harry Jaffa, "Judicial Conscience and Natural Rights: A Reply to Professor Ledewitz," *University of Puget Sound Law Review* 11 (Winter 1988): 221.

3

Parchment barriers and the politics of rights

JACK N. RAKOVE

HISTORICAL QUESTIONS

As an episode in political history, the adoption of the Bill of Rights between 1789 and 1791 does not present particularly difficult or puzzling questions. In the standard interpretation, the Bill of Rights was a product of the expedient, even cynical, political maneuvers of both Federalists and Anti-Federalists; once proposed by the First Federal Congress in 1789 after the heroic efforts of James Madison, the Bill of Rights generated little public interest during its ratification and quickly passed into legal and political irrelevance.[1] By far the more challenging questions raised by the history of the Bill of Rights concern not its origins in the distant world of the eighteenth century but the reasons for its recovery

In addition to being grateful to the members of the Woodrow Wilson Center workshop, I wish to thank Thomas Grey, Ralph Lerner, Robert Post, and John Phillip Reid for useful comments, suggestions, and even criticisms—not all of which, I fear, I have successfully answered. Section 5 of this chapter derives from my essay "The Madisonian Theory of Rights," *William and Mary Law Review* 31 (1989–90): 241–66, and I thank the editors of that periodical for their permission to draw so extensively from it here.
[1] James H. Hutson, "The Birth of the Bill of Rights: The State of Current Scholarship," *Prologue* 20 (1988): 143–59, provides a good historiographical survey, while suggesting that too great an emphasis has been placed on the explicitly political aspects of the adoption of the Bill of Rights. Robert A. Rutland, *The Birth of the Bill of Rights, 1776–1791* (Chapel Hill: University of North Carolina Press, 1955), is the standard narrative history; see also Leonard W. Levy, "The Bill of Rights," in Levy, *Constitutional Opinions: Aspects of the Bill of Rights* (New York: Oxford Unversity Press, 1986), 105–34. Two recent collections of essays survey the progress of ratification of the Constitution in the states, touching on the significance of the call for a bill of rights as warranted: Michael A. Gillespie and Michael Lienesch, eds., *Ratifying the Constitution* (Lawrence: University Press of Kansas, 1989); Patrick T. Conley and John P. Kaminski, eds., *The Constitution and the States: The Role of the Original Thirteen in the Framing and Adoption of the Federal Constitution* (Madison, Wis.: Madison House, 1988).

and prominence in our own time. Indeed, were it not for the central place held by disputes about the Bill of Rights in present-day law and politics, the conventional account of its adoption would still seem satisfactory and sufficient. Conversely, the intensity of our current debates has turned the seemingly prosaic circumstances surrounding the adoption of the Bill of Rights into a source of nervous unease. Surely, we sense, there must have been more to the story than this.

One response to the perceived inadequacies of a merely political account of the adoption of the Bill of Rights takes the form of particularistic inquiries into the "original meaning" of the individual clauses that have become the subject of current controversy. This approach presumes that each right codified in the text possessed an independent history that can be studied in isolation from the others, and asks how the formulations of 1789 reflected the development of legal thinking in specific areas.[2] Such an approach is especially useful where the provisions adopted were innovative by eighteenth-century standards, as was, for example, the establishment clause, or the broad terms in which Madison consciously cast the Fourth Amendment's protection against "unreasonable searches and seizures," or the Fifth Amendment's prohibition against self-incrimination.[3]

Although significant gaps remain in our understanding of how concepts of particular rights evolved during the Revolutionary era, this monographic approach has served the fields of legal and constitutional history well. Yet insofar as these studies have been inspired by the contemporary debate over rights, they may also distort or mistake the questions that most need asking about Revolutionary Americans' ideas of rights. For although all questions about original meaning are inherently historical, they are not the kinds of questions that historians ordinarily ask. Few if any historians would find it worthwhile to ask exactly what the estab-

---

[2] The most influential works in this vein are those of Leonard W. Levy, especially *Origins of the Fifth Amendment: The Right against Self-Incrimination* (New York: Oxford University Press, 1968), and *Emergence of a Free Press* (New York: Oxford University Press, 1985), a significantly revised version of his controversial *Legacy of Suppression: Freedom of Speech and Press in Early American History* (Cambridge, Mass.: Harvard University Press, 1960). A useful collection of essays on the original meaning of particular rights is Jon Kukla, ed., *The Bill of Rights: A Lively Heritage* (Richmond: Virginia State Library and Archives, 1987). One avenue of research that might prove promising would involve asking whether or to what extent the federal Bill of Rights provided the model for state constitutions adopted after 1789.

[3] Leonard W. Levy, *Original Intent and the Framers' Constitution* (New York: Macmillan, 1989), 242–50 ff.

lishment clause or the right to bear arms or the prohibition against "unreasonable searches and seizures" meant in 1789 or 1791, were it not for the fact that such issues as school prayer, gun control, or drug testing are hotly disputed today.[4]

A strictly historical inquiry into the original meaning of a particular right does not presuppose that the same meaning, if and when it can be recovered, should be binding today; it simply asks why a particular clause was adopted while marking a baseline from which its subsequent evolution can be traced and assessed. But in recent years the demand for a return to a "jurisprudence of original intention" has raised the stakes of historical research by insisting that the true meaning of a particular clause was somehow fixed at the moment of adoption, and that the task of interpretation is to apply that meaning to contemporary issues. Equally important, many proponents of "originalism" also hold that the only rights deserving constitutional recognition and protection are those explicitly mentioned in the text of the Constitution.[5]

Both these claims imply that the central problem of rights in the Revolutionary era was to identify, enumerate, and define with textual precision the rights that Americans felt were crucial to the protection of their liberty. The inherent bias of originalism thus equates American ideas of rights with the Bill of Rights. From the vantage point of contemporary jurisprudence, this bias may seem sensible; but from the vantage point of history, the equation of the problem of rights with the issue of enumeration is questionable. With its pressing need to find determinate meanings at a fixed historical moment, the strict theory of originalism cannot

---

[4] I do not mean to suggest that these present concerns have produced what is often called "law office history," but that our general interest in these questions can be explained as a function of contemporary issues rather than as a manifestation of the inherent importance—relative to other events of the time—of the subject itself.

[5] As theories of constitutional interpretation, both these claims lie beyond the realm of definitive historical resolution. But insofar as all appeals to original intent are appeals to the evidence of the past, historical interpretation can both sustain and subvert the assumptions on which originalism rests. Historical evidence may conceivably demonstrate that some clauses *were* understood in a reasonably consensual way circa 1789 and after; or it may prove that the Constitution and its clauses were subject to conflicting interpretations ab initio, and thereby illustrate the impossibility of freezing that one pristine moment of understanding that a theory of originalism seemingly requires. For a representative sampling of various issues and positions in this debate, see the essays collected in Jack N. Rakove, ed., *Interpreting the Constitution: The Debate over Original Intent* (Boston: Northeastern University Press, 1990). For perhaps the strongest statement asserting the primacy of originalism and the limiting power of the enumeration of rights, see Robert H. Bork, *The Tempting of America: The Political Seduction of the Law* (New York: Free Press, 1990).

capture everything that was dynamic and creative—and thus uncertain and problematic—in Revolutionary constitutionalism; nor can it easily accommodate the diversity of views that, after all, best explains why the debates of this era were so lively.[6] Where we look for answers, the framers and ratifiers of the late 1780s were still struggling with questions whose novelty and complexity had already carried them away from the received wisdom of their time.

One of these questions was indeed identical with the issue so much disputed today: whether the enumeration of specific rights within the Constitution was understood to relegate all other rights left unmentioned to an inferior status. Yet if this question was very much part of the debate about the need for a bill of rights in 1788 and 1789,[7] it was neither the sole nor even the most important problem that the Americans confronted during their revolutionary experiment in designing republican governments. The colonists entered the imperial crisis of 1765–76 confident that they knew what their rights were; in the decade after independence, they modified these original ideas only modestly. What did evolve, far more dramatically and creatively, were their ideas of where the dangers to rights lay and how rights were to be protected.

As was the case with every other aspect of constitutional theory— representation, sovereignty, federalism, the definition of a constitution itself—American ideas about rights and their protection evolved continuously if unevenly throughout the Revolutionary era, from the Stamp Act controversy of the mid-1760s to the organization of political parties in the 1790s.[8] At the outset of this period, Americans, as good Whigs, believed that arbitrary acts of magistracy—that is, of the Crown and its officials in the colonies—posed the greatest danger to rights. The claim

---

[6] As Gordon S. Wood has aptly observed, "When confronted with these constrasting meanings of the Constitution, historians . . . are not supposed to decide which was more 'correct' or more 'true.' Our task is rather to explain the reasons for these constrasting meanings and why each side should have given to the Constitution the meaning it did." Wood, "Ideology and the Origins of Liberal America," *William and Mary Quarterly*, 3d ser., 44 (1987): 632.

[7] On this point, see especially the 28 July 1788 speech of James Iredell in the first North Carolina ratifying convention, which presciently imagines how later interpreters might plausibly but wrongly conclude that the only rights that had mattered to the original adopters of the Constitution were those they explicitly included in the proposed bill of rights; reprinted (in part) in Philip B. Kurland and Ralph Lerner, eds., *The Founders' Constitution* (Chicago: University of Chicago Press, 1987), 1: 475–6.

[8] Nowhere is this sense of development more powerfully captured than in the two concluding chapters of Bernard Bailyn, *The Ideological Origins of the American Revolution* (Cambridge, Mass.: Harvard University Press, 1967).

that Parliament could legislate for America "in all cases whatsoever" exposed a new threat to colonial rights, but it did not shake the deeper conviction that the greatest security for the collective rights of the people still lay in the process of representation. Americans repeatedly argued that they could be adequately represented only in their own elected assemblies, never in a distant Parliament, where their rights would always be subject to violation by majorities representing the distinct interests of the mother country. It took a decade of experience under the new state constitutions written at the moment of independence to expose the dual dangers that so alarmed James Madison in 1787: that the abuse of legislative power was more ominous than arbitrary acts of the executive, and that the problem of rights was a matter less of protecting the ruled from the rulers than of defending minorities and individuals against the impassioned or self-interested desires of popular majorities acting through government. When set against this broader shift in the way that Americans thought about rights, the issue of which rights deserved explicit constitutional mention appears distinctly secondary.

How this transformation in the broader understanding of the problem of rights led Madison, his colleagues in the Federal Convention, and like-minded Federalists to dismiss formal statements of rights as mere parchment barriers is the central theme of this chapter. After first describing how the colonists thought about the protection of rights before independence, it asks how the experience of the Revolution led to a reconsideration of these traditional ideas. The concluding section then considers how Madison fashioned a new synthesis of the problem of rights after 1785 and why his initially disparaging view of the utility of bills of rights was modified by the constitutional debates of the late 1780s.

DEFINITIONS OF RIGHTS IN COLONIAL AMERICA

In *Federalist* 37, his brief but acute meditation on the epistemology of the science of politics, James Madison sought to explain why attempts to delineate the "three great provinces" of government or "the several objects and limits of different codes of law and different tribunals of justice" repeatedly "puzzle" even "the greatest adepts in political science" and "the most enlightened legislators and jurists." Madison traced "the obscurity which reigns in these subjects" to three distinct causes: "indistinctness of the object, imperfection of the organ of conception, [and] inadequateness of the vehicle of ideas." The science of politics was necessarily untidy, Madison understood, because the objects it studied were inherently complex, because human faculties of observation and analysis were fallible, and because language itself was a source of "unavoidable inaccuracy."[9]

Writing at a point in the ratification campaign when Federalists still opposed a bill of rights, Madison naturally avoided citing the case of rights as another example of the difficulties of classifying political phenomena. He could easily have included it, however, had he wished to; and indeed, on the specific issue of language, one of his reservations about enumerating constitutional rights was the danger of reducing a broad claim of right to any specific textual formula. More than that, Madison and other Federalists found the task of classifying rights genuinely daunting. The rights to which eighteenth-century Americans laid claim, whether as British subjects or as citizens of an independent republic, were diverse and complex. Nor did rights pertain to individuals alone. Communities, corporate bodies, and institutions of government all had rights, which were exercised on behalf of both the collective groups so constituted and their individual members.[10] A farmer in, say, Medway, Massachusetts, who voted for his town's representative in the General Court was simultaneously exercising an individual right of suffrage and participating in a communal right of representation; arguably he also had a stake in both the legislator's right to speak freely when he attended the General Court in Boston and the assembly's sole right to levy whatever taxes would burden its constituents.

Recent scholarly commentators on the origins of American constitutionalism have emphasized the complexity and diversity of the rights Americans claimed. Take, for example, the synthetic chapter canvassing "The Rights of Englishmen" in Forrest McDonald's *Novus Ordo Seclorum*.[11] Although hardly exhaustive, this brisk survey manages to describe both rights of property and civil liberties in a short compass. To speak of the former, McDonald observes, one must describe the corporate right

---

[9] Benjamin F. Wright, ed., *The Federalist* (Cambridge, Mass.: Harvard University Press, 1961), 268–70.

[10] Indeed, a powerful case can be made that, in the Anglo-American tradition, rights were regarded first and foremost not as qualities belonging to individuals but rather as the collective property of the people. I am grateful to John Reid for clarifying this point to me in private correspondence.

[11] Subtitled *The Intellectual Origins of the Constitution* (Lawrence: University Press of Kansas, 1985), 9–55.

of the public to govern the use of property through regulation of markets, sumptuary laws, the granting of monopoly privileges, and various forms of takings: forfeiture, eminent domain, and, most important, taxation, which, in turn, implicated the fundamental right of representation. Private rights of property included such prosaic matters as "grazing, wood gathering, hunting, passage, and the use of water."[12] Far more exalted were the civil rights that defined the relationship between citizens and subjects, on the one hand, and the state, on the other: the right of habeas corpus and other procedural safeguards against the coercive power of government. Of these, "The genuinely crucial right was that of trial by jury."[13] In Britain and America, rights of conscience had gained broad and principled recognition by the eighteenth century, even if dissent was often merely tolerated instead of accepted as an absolute right, and even if the exemptions that dissenters enjoyed varied from place to place with the strength of local establishments. Within the realm of political life, freedom of speech was still regarded as a privilege of legislators more than of citizens, while freedom of the press meant only a prohibition on prior restraint from publication, not a broad defense against prosecution for the various forms of libel.

Any discussion that reveals how "the rights of Englishmen" subsumed concepts as diverse as *estover* (the right to gather wood) and the limited yet vital definitions of freedom of the press has already illuminated the inherent complexities of the subject. But for all its elegance, McDonald's survey does not explain how these diverse notions affected the development of American ideas of *constitutional* rights. To understand rights in this sense, one has to ask how colonial ideas reflected both the intense debate precipitated by the Stamp Act of 1765 and, more broadly, the constitutional history of England and the British Empire.

Perhaps the most important and certainly the most detailed examination of the pre-Revolutionary debate over rights is found in the writings of John Phillip Reid. In a series of monographs, Reid has catalogued the multiple claims of rights the colonists invoked; traced these claims to their primarily English sources; and vindicated American positions as faithful expressions of traditional doctrines that had become problematic not because the colonists were grasping for pretexts to justify resistance, but rather because British constitutional theory was itself changing in

[12] Ibid., 37ff.
[13] Ibid., 36–40.

radical ways. In these writings, which are archaeological in depth and intensely taxonomical in approach, Reid confirms just how deeply the language of rights and liberties suffused American thinking—so much so that modern readers may find it hard to comprehend both the intense precision and flabby abstraction with which these terms were repeatedly invoked.[14]

At the most general level, Reid argues, the imperial debate brought two rival conceptions of the British constitution into irreconcilable conflict. Adhering to traditional English notions, Americans saw themselves defending a body of customary rights that history, common law, and precedent had secured beyond the reach of governmental interference. But this insistence upon their inherent rights as Englishmen[15] collided with the emerging doctrine of parliamentary supremacy and "the constitution of arbitrary power that the British constitution was about to become."[16] Once that doctrine was arrayed in all its splendor, the traditional notions that the Americans espoused verged perilously close to anachronism. Where law itself had been regarded as a set of customary restraints on the exercise of arbitrary power, it was now being transformed into the mere command of the sovereign.[17]

Although Reid avoids asking how the revolutionaries confronted problems of rights once they began drafting their own constitutions of government,[18] his conclusions remain significant for that problem on several grounds.

Reid demonstrates, first, that rights were regarded as being constitutional in nature, and indeed, that the British constitution itself was a

---

[14] "Liberty fascinated eighteenth-century English-speaking people as much as an abstraction as a practical constitutional principle. . . . The extent to which eighteenth-century legal, constitutional, and political commentators discussed liberty in the abstract is simply amazing." John Phillip Reid, *The Concept of Liberty in the Age of the American Revolution* (Chicago: University of Chicago Press, 1988), 11.

[15] Reid's emphasis on "the Englishness of [the] Rights" the colonists claimed is consciously designed to challenge the view, still dearly held in some circles, that natural rights provided the dominant conceptions of the rights that Americans cherished. See Reid's essay. "The Irrelevance of the Declaration," in Hendrik Hartog, ed., *Law in the American Revolution and the American Revolution in the Law* (New York: New York University Press, 1981), 46–89.

[16] John Phillip Reid, *Constitutional History of the American Revolution*, vol. I, *The Authority of Rights* (Madison: University of Wisconsin Press, 1986), 237.

[17] Reid, *Concept of Liberty*, 60–3.

[18] Thus Reid deems the Declaration of Rights of the First Continental Congress of 1774 far more important than the state bills of rights of 1776, "as these were concerned with future principles of governance, not with the prerevolutionary controversy." *Authority of Rights*, 18.

constitution of rights: "the basic theory, stated often enough in the eighteenth century," was "that the constitution and rights were one."[19] The
security of rights and the right to security were the very end of the
constitution and the measure of its legitimacy.[20] But precisely because
the eighteenth-century constitution was in process of transformation,
Reid insists on the importance of distinguishing law that was either
"fundamental" or "constitutional" from acts that were still legal even
while violating the former norms. "To say that a statute or a governmental action was unconstitutional was to say that it was contrary to
the constitution, it was not to say that it was illegal." Yet in both Britain
and America, the conviction survived that there remained a category of
fundamental law that was "immutable law beyond the reach of any
institution of government."[21] Thus the paradox: rights deemed constitutional could be either rendered vulnerable by statute or exalted as
fundamental, depending on how parliamentary supremacy was balanced
against the vestigial but potent norms of the customary constitution.

Reid's work bears on emerging American doctrine in a second significant way. For all its abstraction and "circuity," for all the nuances and
paradoxes of definition that Reid lovingly details, the language of rights
was clearly pervasive in Anglo-American political culture, and this fact
alone explains why bills of rights formed an organic part of the new state
constitutions that the Americans drafted in the mid-1770s. Simply put,
the omission of statements of rights in the new charters would have been
far more surprising than their presence. If rights were constitutional by
nature, a constitution that was intended to secure them would naturally
include some statement of rights—even though the rights there proclaimed can be described, as Gordon Wood has aptly noted, as "a jarring
but exciting combination of universal principles with a motley collection
of common law procedures."[22]

Finally, Reid's effort to identify the multiple sources of the rights
Americans claimed establishes the point of departure from which the
significance of emerging American conceptions can best be seen. For the
pre-Revolutionary debate, Reid argues, the crucial problem is not to

[19] Ibid., 5.
[20] Ibid., 34–8; Reid, *Concept of Liberty,* 68–73.
[21] Reid, *Authority of Rights,* 75–8.
[22] Gordon S. Wood, *The Creation of the American Republic, 1776–1787* (Chapel Hill:
University of North Carolina Press, 1969), 271. Reid would respond to this slightly
dismissive characterization by arguing that rights were always regarded as being essentially procedural.

identify the rights Americans claimed. "The rights were British rights and well known," Reid observes. "Why Americans were entitled to them was more controversial and more complicated."[23] The heart of his analysis of "the authority of rights" requires examining the ten sources on which the colonies relied, sometimes admittedly for rhetorical effect, but more profoundly as expressions of the multiple *constitutional* foundations for their claims. The very diversity and complexity of these sources help to clarify the theoretical dilemma that the Americans encountered *after* independence. How would the promulgation of written constitutions at precise (and literally memorable) moments of historical time affect the status and extent of rights whose authority had previously rested on more elusive and diffuse foundations? The American innovation promised to simplify and clarify the authority of rights, and to close and perhaps even erase the distance between rights that were fundamental and rights that were merely constitutional. Yet the explicit designation of particular rights as constitutional created at least a latent possibility that other rights that were equally venerable but ignored in the new frames of government would be relegated to a lesser status. Could a right that was not explicitly constitutional remain fundamental?

Confined as his analysis is to the Revolutionary debate with Britain, Reid does not ask how Americans perceived the problem of rights *after* 1776. Nor does he venture an answer to the question that seems so crucial to the contemporary debate over rights: whether the authors of the federal Bill of Rights understood that the adoption of particular rights would or would not relegate other equally fundamental rights left un-enumerated to an inferior (or less than constitutional) status. But other legal scholars, most notably Thomas Grey and Suzanna Sherry, have carried the story forward from 1776 to 1789 (and beyond). In their account, Americans continued to recognize that their resort to the novel device of a written constitution did not annul the authority of other sources of fundamental or inherent rights—notably the principles of both the common-law tradition and natural law. Ideas of rights broader than any positive enumeration of rights survived in the form of an "unwritten constitution" to which American jurists still accorded substantial weight.[24]

---

[23] Reid, *Authority of Rights*, 65–6.
[24] See especially Thomas C. Grey, "Origins of the Unwritten Constitution: Fundamental Law in American Revolutionary Thought," *Stanford Law Review* 30 (1978): 843–93; idem, "The Original Understanding and the Unwritten Constitution," in Neil L. York,

THE CONSTITUTIONAL PROTECTION OF RIGHTS

Much more, of course, could be written—and indeed has been written—about the particular rights that Americans claimed, the sources of those rights, and the way in which conceptions of specific rights were affected by the course of the Revolution. One could ask how the Second Amendment's affirmation of a right to bear arms reflected radical Whig assumptions about the virtue of a citizen militia, or why the Third Amendment's prohibition on the quartering of soldiers in civilian homes was derived from the problem of housing loutish British soldiers in colonial cities.[25] But the rest of this chapter is more concerned with asking how Americans thought rights in general were to be protected than with cataloguing or mapping the various rights they claimed.

At the start of the Revolutionary controversy, American ideas about the protection of rights were derived largely from their perceptions of the complementary constitutional histories of both the mother country and its colonies. Nothing better illustrates how much our approach to the protection of rights has departed from the original understandings of the eighteenth-century Americans than the substantially different emphases that our very ideas of constitutional history express. Where we define that history first and foremost as the development of judicial doctrine, the revolutionaries understood the constitutional history of rights as a history of representation. Before hope or confidence in the judicial protection of rights could become the defining trait of American constitutionalism, Americans first had to question their orthodox belief that representation was the great and potentially sufficient source of security for all rights.[26]

Representation: the first defense. Of all the rights the colonists claimed before 1776, the crucial and most controverted was the right to be sub-

---

ed., *Toward a More Perfect Union: Six Essays on the Constitution* (Provo, Utah: Brigham Young University Press, 1988), 145–73; and Suzanna Sherry, "The Founders' Unwritten Constitution," *University of Chicago Law Review* 54 (1987): 1127–77.

[25] For discussion of these issues, see Robert E. Shalhope, "The Ideological Origins of the Second Amendment," *Journal of American History* 69 (1982–83), 599–614; Lawrence Delbert Cress, "A Well-Regulated Militia: The Origins and Meaning of the Second Amendment," in Kukla, ed., *A Lively Heritage*, 55–65; and B. Carmon Hardy, "A Free People's Intolerable Grievance: The Quartering of Troops and the Third Amendment," ibid., 67–82.

[26] Here again my interpretation of what might be called the starting position of American thinking about the protection of rights owes a great deal to the work of John Phillip Reid, especially his treatment of *The Concept of Representation in the Age of the American Revolution* (Chicago: University of Chicago Press, 1989).

jected only to laws enacted by their own duly elected assemblies. By defending the privileges of these assemblies, Americans asserted both their rights as a people and the transcendent importance they attached to the belief that the protection of popular rights required representative government. As a matter both of constitutional theory and of history, this hallowed axiom of Whig thought had been decisively confirmed in the great struggles between the Stuart kings and their parliamentary foes, and beyond that, in the centuries-long effort of Parliament—and especially the Commons—to recover ancient rights lost after the descent into Norman dominion. The individual rights discovered in common law mattered too, of course; and a number of commentators, including William Blackstone, fretted that excessive lawmaking by Parliament was undermining the consistency and security of common law itself.[27] But in a deeper sense, the collective survival of English rights and liberty depended on the *political* capacity of Parliament to check arbitrary royal encroachment. Just as the rules of common law governed the king's judges as they dispensed royal justice, so the vindication of parliamentary supremacy in the Glorious Revolution of 1688–89 guaranteed the collective rights of the people.

The most important precedent the colonists could look to for an explicit affirmation of constitutional rights was thus the Declaration of Rights of 1689. The declaration asserted both parliamentary and popular rights, but its crucial feature was that *all* the rights it proclaimed were to be protected against abuse by the Crown. There, in the arbitrary acts of the king and his subordinates, lay the preponderant threats to the rights and liberties of his subjects and their representatives. By making the prior acceptance of this statement of rights a condition for the accession of William and Mary to the Crown, the Convention Parliament understood full well that the monarchy would henceforth be bound to honor the *constitutional* rights recognized in the declaration. The declaration, in that sense, was more than a bill of grievances directed against the Stuarts; it also satisfied the traditional terms of a compact between the ruled and their magisterial (royal) rulers.[28]

Colonists who regarded themselves as equal heirs with their English countrymen to the Glorious Revolution had every incentive to appropriate its constitutional settlement in their own struggles with royal of-

---

[27] David Lieberman, *The Province of Legislation Determined: Legal Theory in Eighteenth-century Britain* (Cambridge, Eng.: Cambridge University Press, 1989), 1–67.

[28] Lois G. Schwoerer, *The Declaration of Rights, 1689* (Baltimore: Johns Hopkins University Press, 1981), 101.

ficials in America. Because political strife in the colonies so often took the form of institutional conflicts between assemblies and governors, the seventeenth-century constitutional disputes framed the dominant paradigm within which political arguments were conducted. The model of extensive parliamentary privilege set the standards to which all colonial assemblies aspired. If the rights of Englishmen depended on the rights of Parliament, American rights similarly required that colonial assemblies enjoy equal privileges vis-à-vis Crown and proprietary governors.[29] So, too, the colonists applied the idea that all government was founded on a compact between rulers and ruled to describe the conditions under which their ancestors, migrating under the auspices of the Crown, had secured, retained, or "purchased" the English rights they carried with them.[30]

The imperial debate. Americans forged their attachment to these principles when claims of royal prerogative represented the chief threat to their rights. Yet no great shift was needed when the new threat from Parliament eclipsed the older one from the Crown: the danger still lay to rights of autonomy that were equated with legislative privilege. What was new after 1765 was the specter of a Parliament that, as a lawmaking body itself, could not merely obstruct the exercise of colonial legislative powers, as the governors had long done, but actually usurp them. Even then, however, the colonists opposed Parliament under the same principles that Parliament had once asserted against the Crown. The security

---

[29] The literature on the general topic of the rise of the colonial assemblies and their quarrels with the representatives of the Crown is massive. Two books by Jack P. Greene, the synthetic *Peripheries and Center: Constitutional Development in the Extended Polities of the British Empire and the United States, 1607–1788* (Athens: University of Georgia Press, 1986), and his earlier monograph, *The Quest for Power: The Lower Houses of Assembly in the Southern Royal Colonies, 1689–1776* (Chapel Hill: University of North Carolina Press, 1963), provide the best introduction. It could, of course, be argued that the "ancient" rights claimed by Parliament and confirmed to it by the Glorious Revolution were either less venerable or less legally secure than their advocates asserted; see Schwoerer, *Declaration of Rights*, 58–101, which surveys the sources of particular claims. In theory this circumstance would have made it more difficult for the colonists to claim that equivalent or identical rights had been vested in their assemblies ab initio; in practice, both American and English Whigs had good reason not to press their historical scholarship too far but simply to state their claims as given. As Bernard Bailyn has argued, the constitutional sources of political strife in eighteenth-century America can be traced to the retention by Crown authorities in America of prerogative powers that the Glorious Revolution and its aftermath had rendered archaic in Britain; Bailyn, *The Origins of American Politics* (New York: Alfred A. Knopf, 1968), chap. 2.

[30] Reid, *Authority of Rights*, 114–68.

of their collective rights required effective representation in a legislative body of their own choosing.

This prior history affected the development of American ideas about the protection of rights in several crucial but not entirely consistent ways. Although the Whig tradition imbued Americans with a powerful residual suspicion of executive power, for a time the logic of the imperial controversy led them to turn to the Crown to secure their rights. So, too, while the colonists naturally opposed Parliament by affirming the customary rights of their own assemblies, their *political* explanations of the sources of Parliament's assault on American liberties raised troubling questions about the risk of legislative misrule. Finally, the Americans' long-standing reliance on the authority of their original charters and other documents asserting their rights and privileges began to lead them toward a new understanding of constitutionalism itself.

Perhaps the most curious aspect of the imperial quarrel was the enhanced image of the Crown that the colonists were led to espouse. While accommodation with Britain remained their avowed goal—as it did well into 1775—the colonists struggled to find a constitutional basis on which to abide within the empire, still subject to its governance, yet with their legislative rights secured. In this quest they earned little help "across the water": spokesmen for the British position eliminated any basis for compromise by refusing to "draw a line" between what Parliament could and could not do.[31] American hopes for reconciliation thus came to depend, constitutionally and politically, on the Crown. It was up to George III to avert calamity by intervening as a patriot king on the side of the colonists, redressing their grievances, vetoing parliamentary acts violating their rights, and halting the conflict before the police action in Massachusetts escalated into civil war. More important, to repair the *constitutional* flaws exposed by a decade of inquiry into the structure of the empire, the Crown must assume an enhanced role in its government, acting, in Jefferson's phrase, as "the balance of a great, if well-poised empire."[32]

---

[31] By 1775 the best the Americans were prepared to offer was to abide by the navigation acts regulating imperial commerce, with the understanding that American adherence was the product of voluntary consent rather than simple obedience. See the discussion in Jack N. Rakove, *The Beginnings of National Politics: An Interpretive History of the Continental Congress* (New York: Alfred A. Knopf, 1979), 35–8, 57–9, 72–3.

[32] Thomas Jefferson, *A Summary View of the Rights of British America* (Williamsburg, 1774), reprinted in Julian Boyd, ed., *The Papers of Thomas Jefferson* (Princeton, N.J.:

This wildly improbable solution was defective on two counts. Urging the Crown to act against Parliament meant asking George III to defy the Glorious Revolution itself. For a king schooled in the duties of limited monarchy, this notion was politically unacceptable and constitutionally inconceivable.[33] Second, little in their history suggested that Americans would happily embrace this vision of royal authority once it served its immediate purpose: anyone familiar with colonial politics could safely predict that old conflicts between the assemblies and governors would soon revive. However much Americans venerated a patriot king, his minions would face the same contentious opposition they had encountered before. The sole form of kingship Americans would accept was one that vigorously protected their customary rights against all external dangers, royal or parliamentary.[34]

On balance, then, this belated willingness to resort to the king as a potential security for rights was too expedient and problematic to relax long-standing fears of royal power. It was far more a response to the exigencies of the imperial debate than a considered reassessment of the positive role that executive power could play in protecting rights. In 1776 such a notion was still heretical, amply condemned by the colonists' Whiggish reading of their own history and Britain's. Americans were far more obsessed with the demonstrated abuse of executive power than the potential betrayal of legislative trust. As Madison noted a decade later, "Want of *fidelity* in the administration of power" was the principal "grievance" the colonists had felt under the empire.[35] Americans drew the appropriate lessons both in the institutional design of the new state constitutions and in their accompanying statements of rights. There was no analogue to the patriot king in the original scheme of American republicanism, no notion that an executive above party would preserve the balance on which liberty depended.[36] The state constitution writers

Princeton University Press, 1950–), 134–5; Rakove, *Beginnings of National Politics*, 35–6.

[33] John Phillip Reid, "Another Origin of Judicial Review: The Constitutional Crisis of 1776 and the Need for a Dernier Judge," *New York University Law Review* 64 (1989): 987–8; Greene, *Peripheries and Center*, 143.

[34] Ibid., 124–8; for a case study tracing how notions of "the rights of the people" were defined largely as a reaction against the perceived corruption of royal officials, see Richard L. Bushman, *King and People in Provincial Massachusetts* (Chapel Hill: University of North Carolina Press, 1985), 88–132.

[35] Madison to Caleb Wallace, 23 August 1785, in William Hutchinson, William M. E. Rachal, Robert Rutland, et al., eds., *The Papers of James Madison* (Chicago: University of Chicago Press, and Charlottesville: University of Virginia Press, 1962–), 8: 350–1; hereafter cited as *Papers of Madison*.

[36] By this I do not mean to suggest that the ideal of the patriot king, associated first and

of 1776 revealed their continuing suspicion of executive power by strip-ping the governors of anything smacking of prerogative and reducing their authority to the literal execution of legislative will. This same ob-session with the executive was reflected in the slightly anachronistic qual-ity of the early bills of rights. Insofar as they were modeled on the traditional English formula, they were designed to protect popular rights against executive abuse. Yet how dangerous would a republican executive be, when in nearly every respect its power was subordinated to legislative control?

The American aversion to executive power had one additional source. Well before the Stamp Act, Americans had come to believe that avaricious ministers of state wielding improper influence had seriously compromised the independence of Parliament.[37] Steeped in the opposition literature that placed ministerial corruption first among the political evils afflicting Britain, they were prepared to expect the worst of Parliament almost from the outset of the controversy.

This cynical perception encouraged some colonists to reconsider more critically the relationship between representation and rights. The ability of any representative body to protect popular rights required more than legislative independence. It also depended on the conditions of represen-tation—that is, on all the constitutional and legal provisions that deter-mined how legislative bodies debated and acted and how faithfully they served the public good. The defects of representation in the House of Commons—the vices of rotten and pocket boroughs and other inequities of apportionment; the servile dependence of placemen, pensioners, and creatures of aristocratic patronage; the lack of accountability created by the Septennial Act and a narrow franchise—had long been familiar to Americans. Indeed, of the many issues in dispute between Britain and America before 1776, representation was probably the one area in which, in both theory and practice, the two societies had most manifestly diverged.[38]

Yet from this perception of the defects of the British practice of rep-

foremost with the writings of Bolingbroke, did not survive the revolutionary interregnum, only that it is difficult to discover its imprint in the institutional arrangements of the new republics. As a constitutional value, the ideal had to be resurrected in the 1780s. See, in general, Ralph Ketcham, *Presidents above Party: The First American Presidency, 1789–1829* (Chapel Hill: University of North Carolina Press, 1984).

[37] This is, of course, the central explanation of the Revolution offered in Bailyn, *Ideological Origins*, 1–159.

[38] Reid, *Concept of Representation*, especially 119–46; Bailyn, *Ideological Origins*, 161–75.

resentation, American constitution writers could still draw two divergent conclusions about the protection of rights. The belief that the conditions of American politics *were* different from those prevailing "at home" reinforced the orthodox conclusion that representation afforded the most effective protection for popular rights. Yet rather than dismiss the vices of the British system as a problem for the mother country alone, some Americans took them seriously enough to ask whether their legislatures, too, could be made to pursue the same inimical ends.

Revolutionary constitutionalism: the first phase. The remedies that the Americans adopted in 1776 promised to spare the new republic the vices of the parliamentary system by narrowing the distance between constituents and legislators. To a remarkable extent, the early state constitutions combined republican confidence with republican mistrust.[39] By emphasizing the relative homogeneity of American interests and the ability of legislators to re-present the society, republicanism supposed that legislators and constituents would share common concerns and values—including a common stake in their mutual rights. The metaphors of representation that Americans repeatedly invoked reinforced this expectation. Imagining legislatures as "mirrors" or "miniatures" of society, the Americans expected legislators to protect both popular rights and the public good. Yet the very devices that would keep the mirror unclouded, the miniature true to scale—annual elections, rotation in office, the right of instruction, equitable apportionment, and a broad franchise—also betrayed doubts about the feasibility of the enterprise. A half-century's criticism of Parliament had prepared Americans to wonder whether their own assemblies also could go astray. "If once the legislative power breaks in upon [the constitution]," warned the author of the acute *Four Letters on Interesting Subjects,* "the effect will be the same as if a kingly power did it."[40] So, too, the Virginia Declaration of Rights could insist

---

[39] This formulation parallels, I believe, Gordon Wood's efforts to trace the American attachment to republicanism and its promise of "moral reformation" to the contradictory images that the colonists held of themselves simultaneously, as a people who seemed uniquely virtuous (or capable of acting virtuously), yet who were also actively pursuing the self-interest that republicanism abhorred. This tension or contradiction was also manifested, Wood argues, in the conflicting ideas of representation discussed here, that is, in the conflict between the residual attachment to the ideal of virtual representation, as a norm of legislative conduct, and the pressures, apparent from the start, to make the legislatures susceptible to popular will. Wood, *Creation of the American Republic,* 91–124, 178–96.

[40] *Four Letters on Interesting Subjects* (Philadelphia, 1776), 24.

that in order that the members of both the executive and the legislature "may be restrained from oppression, by feeling and participating [in] the burdens of the people, they should, at fixed periods, be reduced to a private station, return into that body from which they were taken."[41]

If the equivalence between executive and legislature in this article is striking, so also is its expectation that the proper remedy to the dangers it foresees lies in the political practice of rotation (which in Virginia was constitutionally required only for the senate, not the lower house). Neither the Virginia Declaration of Rights nor the Virginia constitution proper suggested that a formal limitation of legislative power might better prevent the legislative abuse of rights. If a legislature violated its trust, the proper republican remedy lay in the citizenry, voicing its concerns through the medium of annual elections. Indeed, orthodox republicanism regarded this one device as a sufficient protection for all popular rights. "While all kinds of governmental power reverts annually to the people, there can be little danger of their liberty," observed "Demophilus," one of the more radical republicans of 1776. "Because no maxim was ever more true than that, WHERE ANNUAL ELECTION ENDS, SLAVERY BEGINS." In this sense, rights of suffrage and representation were arguably superior to any others: if these were explicitly guaranteed, others could be safely omitted. "If the government be free, the right of representation must be the basis of it," one New Hampshire writer observed; "the preservation of which sacred right, ought to be the grand object and end of all government."[42]

Even in 1776, some Americans understood how closely the details of suffrage and apportionment were tied to questions of rights. Spokesmen for rural interests, like the author of *The People the Best Governors,* argued that it should be left to legislative discretion to determine whether populous towns deserved additional representation. But other writers, recalling both the rotten boroughs of England and Crown efforts to block the creation of new districts in America, thought otherwise. The crucial point was elegantly stated in the last of the *Four Letters on Interesting Subjects:*

A constitution should lay down some permanent ratio, by which the representation should afterwards encrease or decrease with the number of inhabitants;

---

[41] Kurland and Lerner, eds., *Founders' Constitution,* 1: 6.
[42] Demophilus, *The Genuine Principles of the Ancient Saxon, or English Constitution* (Philadelphia, 1776), 24; *New Hampshire Gazette,* 4 January 1783, quoted in Wood, *Creation of the American Republic,* 164.

for the right of representation, which is a natural one, ought not to be dependent upon the will and pleasure of future legislatures. And for the same reason perfect liberty of conscience, security of person against unjust imprisonments, similar to what is called the Habeas Corpus act; the mode of trial in all law and criminal cases; in short, all the great rights which man never mean, nor ever ought, to lose, should be *guaranteed*, not *granted*, by the Constitution, for at the forming a Constitution we ought to have in mind, that whatever is secured by law only, may be altered by another law.[43]

Here emerging American doctrine is stated with remarkable clarity. Rights of representation need special security against legislative abuse because they are essential; but on closer examination, other rights also merit the same protection against prospective acts of the legislature.

The same animus informed the celebrated resolutions with which the Concord, Massachusetts, town meeting first explained why a constitution could not be drafted by "the Supreme Legislative," but required instead the meeting of a special convention. In its resolves of 21 October 1776, the town meeting offered three reasons for its position:

First, because we conceive that a Constitution in its proper Idea intends a System of principles Established to Secure the Subject in the Possession and enjoyment of their Rights and Priviliges, against any Encroachment of the Governing Part— 2d Because the same Body that forms a Constitution have of Consequence a power to alter it. 3d—Because a Constitution alterable by the Supreme Legislative is no Security at all to the Subject against any Encroachment of the Governing part on any, or on all of their Rights and priviliges.[44]

With extraordinary elegance, the Concord meeting thus recognized that rights could be endangered by legislative act, but more than that, it also grasped the more sophisticated point that the act of declaring constitutional rights legislatively could in fact weaken rather than enhance their juridical status, leaving them vulnerable to revision by a future legislature.

Yet in the context of 1776 these positions were relatively advanced. The central, indeed controlling, element of this first phase of Revolutionary constitutionalism was its "restructuring of power" in a manner that simply presumed that legislatures could faithfully represent the just interests and rights of their constituents. The idea of directing statements of rights explicitly against legislative power was more than most writers

---

[43] *Four Letters on Interesting Subjects*, 21–2.
[44] Oscar Handlin and Mary Handlin, eds., *The Popular Sources of Political Authority: Documents on the Massachusetts Constitution of 1780* (Cambridge, Mass.: Harvard University Press, 1966), 153.

of early state constitutions imagined. Having rallied opposition to Britain around the right of each colony to exercise comprehensive and exclusive legislative power, they felt little need to make the limitation of that power a vital principle of the new constitutionalism. It was enough to purify its exercise by curbing corrupt executive influence, retaining the safeguard of bicameralism, and by supposing that a vigilant citizenry would defend its rights should a legislature actually run amok. The idea of protecting rights by enumerating specific powers of legislation, or by fencing off areas beyond its reach, was a concept that Americans were only beginning to grasp.

Still, the very act of writing state constitutions involved a delegation of power, and that in turn made it possible to ask whether even legislative power could be limited. Here, too, the prior history of colonial politics influenced how Americans first conceived the problem of rights. For the idea of measuring acts of government against the standard of written constitutions was not woven from whole cloth in 1776. A century of disputes between assemblies and governors had made recourse to the authority of the original colonial charters a staple weapon in the American arsenal. These charters and other declarations of colonial rights were repeatedly invoked, both to justify the claimed powers of the colonial assemblies and to codify the individual civil rights that Americans insisted they had retained in migration. These texts did not "create" the rights Americans claimed, but rather described rights they had always possessed and never forfeited. But the more the colonists resorted to the evidence of charter as proof of their rights, the easier it became to consider written constitutions as prescriptive as well as descriptive texts.[45]

From the idea of a written constitution as fundamental law would eventually develop the doctrine of judicial review, which in turn formed so crucial and eventually controlling an element of the American theory of rights. But from the vantage point of 1776, the role that the judiciary should play in the protection of rights was as yet poorly defined and highly problematic.

The initial uncertainty about the place of the judiciary in a republican constitution had multiple sources.[46] Again, the retrospective qual-

---

[45] Bailyn, *Ideological Origins*, 193–8.
[46] The entire question of the origins of American ideas of an independent judiciary deserves more careful consideration. For obvious and good reasons, scholars have long been fascinated, indeed obsessed, with the origins of the doctrine of judicial review, which

ity of American thinking—its natural tendency to recall past abuses rather than anticipate future dangers—left Americans uncertain whether they had more to hope for or fear from an independent judiciary exercising discretionary judgment. Under the colonial regime, members of the higher courts were Crown appointments, so that American demands that judges hold office during good behavior or not receive royal salaries typically meant only that judges should be independent of the Crown. Whether judicial dependence on elective legislatures would prove equally dangerous was another matter. An advanced thinker (and professionally self-conscious attorney) like John Adams could boldly assert that "the judicial power ought to be distinct from both the legislative and executive, and independent upon both, that so it may be a check upon both,"[47] but other writers were more cautious.

Two sets of reasons militated against elevating judicial power to full constitutional equality with the other branches. The first stemmed from the residual difficulty of distinguishing judicial from executive power. The authority of "the celebrated Montesquieu" notwithstanding, judicial power was still regarded as merely another aspect of executive power. To render judges as officeholders independent of executive (or legislative) control was not the same thing as saying that the act of judging was a qualitatively distinct function. "However we may refine and define," observed the author of the Four Letters on In-

can certainly be seen as the most innovative and potentially momentous element in the constitutional theory of judicial power. Yet given the prior ambivalence in American attitudes toward the judiciary, perhaps it would be useful to ask whether acceptance of the idea of judicial review was not itself contingent on, or a manifestation of, a broader shift in the appreciation of the nature and uses of judicial power. On this point, J. M. Sosin, *The Aristocracy of the Long Robe: The Origins of Judicial Review in America* (Westport, Conn.: Greenwood Press, 1989), provides a useful survey, though one still concerned, as the subtitle indicates, with the hoary question of judicial review. The endlessly fascinating subject of the origins and evolution of judicial review has also been treated in no fewer than four recent books by political scientists: Christoper Wolfe, *The Rise of Modern Judicial Review: From Constitutional Interpretation to Judge-Made Law* (New York: Basic Books, 1986); Robert Lowry Clinton, *Marbury v. Madison and Judicial Review* (Lawrence: University Press of Kansas, 1989); Sylvia Snowiss, *Judicial Review and the Law of the Constitution* (New Haven: Yale University Press, 1990); and Shannon C. Stimson, *The American Revolution in the Law: Anglo-American Jurisprudence before John Marshall* (Princeton, N.J.: Princeton University Press, 1990). Of course, in the early Republic the role of the judiciary in a republican society was at least as hotly disputed as it remains today, as is clearly demonstrated in Richard E. Ellis, *The Jeffersonian Crisis: Courts and Politics in the Young Republic* (New York: Oxford University Press, 1971).
[47] [Adams], *Thoughts on Government* (Philadelphia, 1776), reprinted in Kurland and Lerner, eds., *Founders' Constitution*, 1: 109.

teresting Subjects, "there is no more than two powers in any government, viz., the power to make laws, and the power to execute them; for the judicial power is only a branch of the executive, the Chief of every country being the first magistrate."[48] Second, and equally important, many Americans rejected the idea that courts should be free from legislative correction or review. The author of the quasi-populist *The People the Best Governors* expressed a widely held view when he argued that judicial discretion in interpreting the law, which was made necessary because the "circumstances [of cases between man and man] are so infinite in number, that it is impossible for them all to be specified by the letter of the law," ineluctably led judges into "assum[ing] what is in fact the prerogative of the legislature, for those, that made the laws ought to give them a meaning, when they are doubtful."[49] Jefferson made essentially the same point when discussing the need to make punishment "strict and inflexible, but proportioned to the crime." "Let mercy be the character of the lawgiver"—that is, the legislature—"but let the judge be a mere machine. The mercies of the law will be dispensed equally and impartially to every description of men; those of the judge, or of the executive power, will be the eccentric impulses of whimsical, capricious designing man."[50] To the modern reader, it is an open question whether Jefferson's image of the judge as machine is more striking than his equation of judicial discretion with the arbitrary will of unrestrained executive power.

When it came to fixing the place of judicial power in a republican constitution, then, American ideas were susceptible to being pulled in divergent directions. At the outset, the familiar association of judicial and executive power, reinforced by fears and historical memories of the abuse to which both could be put, probably weighed more heavily than the formulaic statement of the benefit of judicial independence that first appeared in the Virginia Declaration of Rights. Before Americans could better appreciate the role that an independent judiciary could play in protecting rights, they first had to ponder the defects of the legislative supremacy that was the central feature of all the early

---

[48] *Four Letters on Interesting Subjects,* 21.
[49] *The People the Best Governors: Or a Plan of Government Founded on the Just Principles of Natural Freedom* ([Hartford], 1776), 12–13.
[50] Jefferson to Edmund Pendleton, 26 August 1776, in Boyd, ed., *Papers of Jefferson,* 1: 505.

state constitutions—which was exactly what the course of the Revolution made possible by forcing the legislatures to make unprecedented demands on the entire society.

LEGISLATIVE SUPREMACY IN PRACTICE

Taken by itself, the idea of legislative supremacy to which eighteenth-century British and American Whigs were devoted did not mean that the principal task of government—or even of the legislature—was to legislate. It meant, rather, that the legislature should be able to prevent the other branch(es) of government from taking arbitrary actions injurious to the rights and liberties of citizens and subjects. This checking function was as central a legislative duty as positive lawmaking.[51] And although in both countries the volume of lawmaking increased throughout the eighteenth century, reigning ideas about the nature and purposes of legislation remained traditional. Members of the House of Commons or the provincial assemblies were not elected to enact legislative programs, nor was the ability to frame bills or secure their adoption taken as the measure of their political talent. The ordinary business of any legislative session was largely spent dealing with petitions requesting authority to undertake some enterprise promising particular benefits within the small compass of local communities. Other requests commonly involved appeals by individuals of decisions taken by local courts. Legislatures responded to these requests by granting new trials or resolving matters on their own authority, thereby revealing (with all due respect to Montesquieu) that the theoretical line separating judicial and legislative power was as blurred and permeable as the line separating judicial and executive power. When statutes affecting the entire community were enacted, they were likely to be either acts of appropriation or taxation, or corrections of some common-law procedure.[52]

---

[51] Reid, *Concept of Representation*, 28–30.

[52] William Nelson's accounting of "the legislative product" of the 1761 session of the Massachusetts General Court reveals how widely these notions of lawmaking differed from the modern concept of positive legislation. "The great bulk of the General Court's acts in that year were essentially administrative, involving questions of raising and appropriating money, organizing and granting jurisdiction to local units of government, and responding to specific local needs. The Court also acted on a number of occasions in a quasi-judicial capacity when it granted new trials to litigants in pending actions. In that year it passed only three acts that were arguably legislative in the sense that they changed law or made new law—an act making robbery a capital offense, an act prohibiting the arrest of royal soldiers or sailors for debt, and an act for incorporating the Society for the Propagation of Christian Knowledge." William E. Nelson, *Americani-*

Yet this Anglo-American conception of the limited scope of lawmaking may mask important differences between the two countries in the actual exercise of legislative power. Bernard Bailyn's analytical comparison of the instability of colonial politics with the relative harmony of Georgian Britain illustrates the central point. Parliament played a far more modest role in governance, Bailyn suggests, than did its sister institutions across the Atlantic. "Parliament did, of course, pass some laws relating to social and economic development," Bailyn notes, but in the authoritative judgment of Sir Richard Pares, "most of this legislation was private, local, and facultative, setting up local agencies, such as turnpikes, paving, enclosure, or improvement commissioners where such things appeared to be desired by the preponderant local interests." The American assemblies, however, "were led willy-nilly, by the force of circumstance, to exercise creative powers, and in effect to construe as public law what in England was 'private, local and facultative.'" The very need to organize a new society inclined the colonists to accept a broader role for legislative regulation than most Britons yet accorded to Parliament.[53]

Other historians have suggested that this contrast between Parliament and the colonial assemblies is overdrawn. The greater comfort that Americans felt with the exercise of positive legislative power before 1776 resulted less from their advanced thinking on this subject than from their distrust of the other (imperial) elements of their constitutions.[54] British and American attitudes toward legislation, in other words, differed more in degree than kind. Yet regardless of how progressive or traditional colonial concepts of legislation can be said to have been, it seems evident that crucial departures in American thinking about the scope of legislative

---

zation of the Common Law: The Impact of Legal Change on Massachusetts Society, 1760–1830 (Cambridge, Mass.: Harvard University Press, 1975), 14.

[53] Bailyn, Origins of American Politics, 101–4.

[54] In addition to the portrait of legislation drawn in Nelson, *Americanization of the Common Law*, see Thomas L. Purvis, *Proprietors, Patronage, and Paper Money: Legislative Politics in New Jersey, 1703–1776* (New Brunswick: Rutgers University Press, 1986), 176–99; Allan Tully, *William Penn's Legacy: Politics and Social Structure in Provincial Pennsylvania, 1726–1755* (Baltimore: Johns Hopkins University Press, 1977), 98–102; and Robert Zemsky, *Merchants, Farmers and River Gods: An Essay on Eighteenth-Century Politics* (Boston: Gambit, 1971), 10–27. The validity of the comparison between British and American attitudes toward legislation requires a systematic assessment of legislative output in the two societies. For a view suggesting that historians have underestimated the legislative role of the eighteenth-century Parliament, see Lieberman, *Province of Legislation Determined*, 13–28. For all its old-fashioned quality, the subject as a whole merits further study. As Purvis aptly notes, "Little is presently known regarding either the disposition of petitions or the general range of statutes enacted by provincial governments in eighteenth-century America."

power took place after 1776. For just as the early state constitutions removed any effective limitations on legislative dominion, so the course of the Revolution demanded the vigorous exercise of lawmaking authority in the modern, positive sense.

The massive burdens that wartime mobilization placed on both society and government were without precedent in the entire colonial past. Once the sobering recognition that victory would not come easily or cheaply replaced the sunshine patriotism of 1774–76, the assemblies were repeatedly impelled to use their legislative initiative to frame the laws required to mobilize the resources and manpower for a protracted struggle. The real stuff of wartime lawmaking did not involve drafting enlightened statutory codes to compact the legislative debris of the colonial era into suitably concise and republican form, as in Jefferson's famous project for Virginia; nor did the amateur lawmakers who came and went every session spend much time thinking about ways of improving the republican manners of their constituents. Instead, matters at once more prosaic yet urgent preoccupied their attention: currency emissions and the measures required to halt their depreciation; laws setting the terms of military service, meeting congressional requisitions for men and supplies, regulating prices and markets in an unhappy effort to balance the rival needs of military commissaries, farmers, and urban artisans; and whatever other expedients the war required. Within each state, this legislation was intrusive and burdensome to an extent previously unimaginable.

Among all the areas on which the assemblies were forced to act, the most sensitive and important concerned taxation, public debts, paper currency, and the control of markets—in other words, the broad arena of public finance and economic regulation. The controlling circumstances against which the legislatures struggled were the open-ended demands of the war and the inherent inflationary pressures generated by national and state reliance on currency finance.[55] The irony of the Revolutionary

---

[55] For all that has been written on state politics during the Revolutionary War, more attention could well be paid to the problem of mobilization and regulation at the state level—that is, to the *use* of power—as opposed to the more familiar themes of struggles for "democracy" or the opening up of the political system to new groups. The best study for these purposes is Richard Buel, Jr., *Dear Liberty: Connecticut's Mobilization for the Revolutionary War* (Middletown, Conn.: Wesleyan University Press, 1980). See also Ronald Hoffman, *A Spirit of Dissension: Economics, Politics, and the Revolution in Maryland* (Baltimore: Johns Hopkins University Press, 1973); and Edward C. Papenfuse, "The Legislative Response to a Costly War: Fiscal Policy and Factional Politics in Maryland, 1777–1789," in Ronald Hoffman and Peter J. Albert, eds., *Sovereign States in an Age of Uncertainty* (Charlottesville: University of Virginia Press, 1981), 134–56.

predicament was precisely that to secure the great right to be free from parliamentary taxation and legislation, the Americans had to accept (at least over the short run) a host of economic restraints and financial measures far more onerous than anything that Britain would ever have imposed. At one time or another, almost every segment of American society found cause to feel aggrieved either by the policies the states were forced to pursue, or by their inability to control the most palpable economic consequences of the war: rising prices, a depreciating paper currency, shortages of goods, and the like. Sensitive to the complaints of their constituents, the assemblies were reluctant to levy taxes commensurate with the costs of war, but this caution did not lessen the disturbing impact the war had on masses of ordinary families. After all, the inflation that inevitably resulted from the reliance on currency finance was itself, as Benjamin Franklin observed, "a kind of imperceptible Tax."[56] Nor did the coming of peace in 1783 magically relieve the state legislatures of all their burdens, because they still faced the problem of retiring the staggering public debt incurred during eight years of war.

A grasp of the substance and the scope of all the legislating required by the war and its aftermath is vital to understanding how the problem of rights could be reformulated by the 1780s. The crucial consideration is that the legislatures had to govern actively, and to make law in areas where nearly every decision was bound to afflict one segment of the community or another. It was in this sense that the war and the recovery efforts of the mid-1780s translated legislative supremacy from an abstract constitutional principle into an empirical description of a functioning republican government. At the same time, it subverted the belief, so dear to the republicanism of 1776, that a properly constituted legislature could at once mirror society *and* pursue the general good to which all classes and individual communities could uniformly adhere. No legislature could possibly distribute the burdens of the war equally among its people or avoid convincing some segments of society that their interests were being treated unjustly. Nor could the assemblies long escape the criticisms, resentments, and simply ornery complaints that measures impinging so deeply on the conduct of private affairs inevitably evoked. And because so much of the legislation of the war period directly affected property—whether through inflation, taxation, price controls and other restrictions on commerce, or

---

[56] Quoted in Ralph V. Harlow, "Aspects of Revolutionary Finance, 1775–1783," *American Historical Review* 35 (1929): 62–3.

the collection of critical supplies—people aggrieved by particular decisions could readily agree that the damage done to their immediate interests
was also an assault on their rights.[57] When Americans increasingly questioned how well their legislators were truly representing their interests—a
process that Gordon Wood has aptly described as the "disintegration of
the concept of representation"—they were probably driven less by the
logic of popular sovereignty or the working out of other constitutional
ideas than by complaints about the inability of the legislatures to manage
all the economic evils the war had produced.[58]

This concern for economic rights, though crucial to the politics of
constitutional reform after 1783, was itself only one aspect of a broader
transformation in American thinking. For the failures of republican lawmaking during the decade after independence encouraged a new appreciation of the nature and scope of legislative power itself and a more
critical understanding of the danger that legislative acts—rather than the
arbitrary decisions of executive and judicial officials—posed to rights. At
the same time, the political divisions that were either generated or reinforced by the Revolution undermined the image of a homogeneous people
with a mutual interest in protecting the collective rights of the people
against arbitrary acts of government. The lessons on which new ideas
about rights could be based were no longer drawn solely from the prior
history of English and Anglo-American politics; now they included as
well the potent examples of recent experience.

JAMES MADISON AND THE BILL OF RIGHTS

The significance of Madison. To formulate the problem of rights in this
way is already to give its solution a strongly Madisonian twist.[59] For

---

[57] The most remarkable example of this perception of the relation between economic legislation and rights of property can probably be found in the extended correspondence
between Charles Carroll of Annapolis, reputedly one of the largest landowners in the
entire nation, and his politically active son, Charles Carroll of Carrollton, over the
injustice of Maryland financial legislation. See the account in Ronald Hoffman, *A Spirit
of Dissension.*

[58] Wood, *Creation of the American Republic,* 363–76. Here as elsewhere, Wood's illuminating account of the directions in which American thought was moving after 1776
pays insufficient attention to the specific issues of public policy to which both public
officials and their constituents were responding. See Jack N. Rakove, "Gordon S. Wood,
the 'Republican Synthesis,' and the Path Not Taken," *William and Mary Quarterly,* 3d
ser., 44 (1987): 617–22.

[59] This section draws on a number of essays I have written about various aspects of Madison's constitutional thought. Especially important for the purposes here is "The Mad-

although Madison was hardly alone in condemning the character of state lawmaking, both his analysis of the principal threats to rights in a republic and his condescending attitude toward bills of rights rested on an acute appreciation of the nature of legislative power and on a still more powerful explanation of the social sources of legislative misrule. Three major convictions controlled Madison's general theory of rights. First, purposeful legislation, rather than capricious exercise of the coercive authority of the state, posed the greatest danger to rights. Second, the central problem of rights was not to protect the people against their rulers but to protect one segment of the people against another—or more directly, to protect individuals and minorities against popular majorities who could claim to embody the people themselves. Third, consistent with the arithmetical logic of his theory of faction, rights would be most in jeopardy where government was most immediately responsive to the wishes of its constituents—that is, within the democratic polities of the states rather than the extended republic that would, Madison hoped, insulate the national government from populist pressure. None of these positions had been part of the original American understanding of rights circa 1776.[60] Taken together, they indicate how far American thinking—or at least its leading edge—had since advanced.

It could, of course, be objected that placing too great an emphasis on Madison is wrong, because after all he was only one participant among many. Moreover, if his ideas were so advanced, he can hardly be described as a representative thinker.[61] Nevertheless, two powerful reasons justify giving his ideas and actions close attention. First, were it not for Madison, a bill of rights might never have been added to the Constitution. Among the members of the First Federal Congress in 1789, Madison almost alone believed that prompt action on amendments was politically nec-

---

isonian Theory of Rights," *William and Mary Law Review* 31 (1989–90): 241–66. See also "Mr. Meese, Meet Mr. Madison," *Atlantic* 258 (December 1986): 77–86; "The Great Compromise: Ideas, Interests, and the Politics of Constitution Making," *William and Mary Quarterly*, 3d. ser., 44 (1987): 424–57; and "The Madisonian Moment," *University of Chicago Law Review* 55 (1988): 473–505. I have also benefited from reading Paul Finkelman, "James Madison and the Bill of Rights," *Supreme Court Review* (1990): 301–47.

[60] It can be argued, though, that the Loyalists, by dint of theory and experience alike, would have then been prepared to subscribe to the second and third propositions.

[61] This is a potentially significant objection from the vantage point of a strict theory of originalism, which, following Madison's own position in the early 1790s, holds that the authoritative original understandings of the Constitution must be found in the shared opinions of its ratifiers or, more generally, the broad body of public opinion they represented.

essary. Nearly all his colleagues favored deferring the entire subject until the new government was safely operating—by which point, the perceived need for a bill of rights might well have evaporated. But Madison insisted that Congress had to act sooner not later, and the amendments Congress eventually submitted to the states in September 1789 followed closely the proposals he had introduced in June. Madison was not merely one participant among many or even primus inter pares; he was the crucial actor whose aims deserve scrutiny for that reason alone.

The enormous influence that Madison's writings hold over modern interpretations of the Constitution offers a second reason for examining his approach to the issue of rights in some detail. To the historian, the problem with this emphasis is not that it is undeserved but rather that so much of the Madison midrash surrounds a mere handful of texts. But the nuances of his thought cannot be reduced to the binary logic of *Federalist* 10. Madison never regarded himself as "an ingenious theorist" whose best work was "planned in his closet or in his imagination."[62] For all his bookishness, he was very much a public man whose ideas reflected his continuous engagement in politics. Like any intellectual, he valued consistency, but his thought was dynamic and can only be explained contextually.

A coherent historical explanation of Madison's developing position must solve two central puzzles. The first involves explaining how his intense commitment to the protection of rights and his analysis of the "vices of the political system of the United States" led him by 1787 to dismiss bills of rights as so many "parchment barriers" with little if any practical value. The second requires asking how Madison thereafter reluctantly agreed that additional statements of rights should be appended to the Constitution, and further, what role he hoped a bill of rights could henceforth play in American politics.

The young liberal. Madison's interest in issues of rights can be traced to an early age. The young man who completed his studies at Princeton in 1772 returned to Virginia deeply committed to the cause of religious

---

[62] These phrases appear in *Federalist* 37, in Wright, ed., *The Federalist,* 271. Cf. the penultimate paragraph in David Hume's essay, "Whether the British Government Inclines More to Absolute Monarchy or to a Republic," where Hume, expressing his preference for monarchy, observes: "Let us consider, what kind of republic we have reason to expect. The question is not concerning any fine imaginary republic, of which a man may form a plan in his closet." David Hume, *Essays Moral, Political, and Literary,* Eugene F. Miller, ed. (Indianapolis: Liberty Press, 1987), 52.

liberty—a commitment that in fact predated his interest in either politics or constitutional theory. His first notable action in public life was to secure an amendment to the Virginia Declaration of Rights of 1776, altering the article that originally promised "the fullest toleration in the exercise of religion" to the broader affirmation that "all men are equally entitled to the free exercise of religion, according to the dictates of conscience." But Madison's crucial contribution to religious liberty came in the mid-1780s, when he led the successful opposition to a bill providing public funds for all teachers of Christianity, and then capitalized on this victory to secure passage of the celebrated Virginia Statute for Religious Freedom, originally drafted by Thomas Jefferson in 1779.[63]

Madison expressed his ideas about religious liberty most fully in his *Memorial and Remonstrance against Religious Assessments* of 1785, which he published anonymously to rally public opposition against the pending general assessment bill. From the vantage point of a general theory of rights, the *Memorial* provides a curious mixture of conventional and original ideas. Its most explicitly political passages clearly echoed the language of the dispute with Parliament by casting the question of religious liberty in the familiar terms of a struggle between overreaching rulers and a citizenry that needs to be roused to protect its rights. Lawmakers who would enact such a law were "Tyrants," Madison wrote, and "the People who submit to it are governed by laws made neither by themselves nor by an authority derived from them, and are slaves." Virginians should "take alarm at the first experiment on our liberties," and thereby emulate the patriots of a decade earlier, who "did not wait until usurped power had strengthened itself by exercise, and entangled the question in precedents." So, too, Madison suggested that a failure to check the assembly in this one instance might lead to other, unforeseen dangers: an assembly that violated this one right could "sweep away all our fundamental rights" as well.[64]

Yet if the rhetoric of the *Memorial* was conventional, in other respects

---

[63] On Madison's early views, see his letters to his college friend William Bradford of 1 December 1773; 23 January 1774; and 1 April 1774, *Papers of Madison*, 1: 101, 106, 112. The Virginia Declaration of Rights can be found in ibid., 172–5. The progress of disestablishment in Virginia has been extensively studied; see especially Thomas C. Buckley, *Church and State in Revolutionary Virginia, 1776–1787* (Charlottesville: University of Virginia Press, 1977); and the essays collected in Merrill D. Peterson and Robert C. Vaughan, eds., *The Virginia Statute for Religious Freedom: Its Evolution and Consequences in American History* (New York: Cambridge University Press, 1988).
[64] *Papers of Madison*, 8: 299–304.

the campaign against the general assessment led Madison toward more radical conclusions. The idea of describing legislators as "rulers" was itself highly problematic; it was precisely because they were representatives, rather than rulers in the traditional sense, that Madison and his allies could appeal to public opinion to reverse their initial judgment in favor of assessment.

The troubling question the general assessment bill raised was to explain how rights were to be protected if the institution customarily regarded as the bulwark of popular liberty took the part of "tyrant." That question could be answered in two ways, one conventional, the other innovative. The conventional answer was to mobilize the people to defend their rights—the strategy that in fact sent the assessment bill to defeat. Madison's *Memorial* was circulated as a petition, and, in conjunction with other similar petitions that collectively gained more than ten thousand signatures, this graphic expression of popular sentiment proved decisive. The more radical answer and superior solution, however, pointed toward the action that Madison thereafter took by pressing the assembly to take up the bill for religious freedom. At the core of Madison's (and, of course, Jefferson's) support for disestablishment and free exercise lay the radical conviction that the entire sphere of religious practice could be safely deregulated, placed beyond the cognizance of the state, and thus defused as both a source of political strife and a danger to individual rights. By treating religion as a matter of opinion only, Madison and Jefferson identified the one area of governance where it became possible to imagine how the realm of private rights could be enlarged by a flat constitutional denial of legislative jurisdiction. The Statute for Religious Freedom thus promised to convert the general premise that all government rested on a delegation of authority from the people into a specific refusal to permit government to act over an entire area of belief and behavior.

Madison's interest in the formal limitation of legislative power in behalf of rights also found expression in his August 1785 letter discussing a constitution for Kentucky. "If it were possible," Madison wrote,

it would be well to define the extent of the Legislative power but the nature of it seems in many respects to be indefinite. It is very practicable however to enumerate the essential exceptions. The Constitution may expresly restrain them from medling with religion—from abolishing Juries from taking away the Habeas corpus—from forcing a citizen to give evidence against himself, from controuling the press, from enacting retrospective laws at least in criminal cases, from abridging the right of suffrage, from seizing private property for public use without paying its full Valu[e] from licensing the importation of Slaves, from infringing the Confederation &c &c.

Save for the references to religion and slavery, this listing of rights is not exceptional; what distinguishes it instead is the recognition—not present in the state bills of rights—that it is against the legislature that explicit prohibitions must be made. Equally notable is Madison's ensuing recognition that in constructing a constitution, "The Judiciary Department merits every care. Its efficacy is Demonstrated in G. Brittain where it maintains private Right against the corruptions of the two other departments & gives a reputation to the whole Government which it is not in itself entitled to."[65]

The vices of the political system. The crucial departures in Madison's thinking about rights, however, occurred *after* 1785, and they carried him away from the lessons he seemingly had learned by that point—as well as away from the republican orthodoxy of 1776. Rather than inferring from the rejection of the assessment bill that appeals to public opinion could protect popular rights against legislative abuse, Madison now concluded that the greater danger to liberty came from the people themselves, acting through their elected representatives. He similarly came to doubt whether any formal limitation of legislative authority— through either the enumeration of particular legislative powers or the constitutional exemption of specific rights—could restrain a legislature bent on mischief from enacting unjust laws. And as Madison considered these dual problems of legislative *and* popular misrule, he further concluded that the greatest danger to liberty would necessarily arise within the states, where the wrong kinds of majorities—again, both popular and legislative—could more readily form to pursue their vicious ends.

The disparaging opinion that Madison now formed about bills of rights was a consequence of the profound analysis of republican politics

---

[65] Madison to Caleb Wallace, 23 August 1785, in ibid., 351–52. Madison here echoes the comments of William Livingston, the venerable New Jersey Whig, writing as "Scipio" in the *New Jersey Gazette* of 14 June 1784, in defense of fixed salaries for state judges: "The purity of their courts of justice," Livingston wrote of England, "is now perhaps the only remaining band that (amidst the wreck of publick and private virtue) holds together the pillars of that tottering nation." Carl E. Prince et al., eds., *The Papers of William Livingston* (New Brunswick, N.J.: Rutgers University Press, 1988), 5: 137. Compare Alan Ryan's discussion of judicial independence in contemporary British constitutional practice in Chapter 7 of this volume.

on which these more fundamental insights rested. If he grew more skeptical about the value of bills of rights, it was not because he found it difficult to enumerate individual rights worth protecting, but because he increasingly doubted that any formal declaration, however carefully stated or comprehensive, could counteract the real forces threatening their security in a republican polity.

In reaching these conclusions, Madison drew on his own experience in the Virginia assembly and on his observation of the course of legislation, particularly economic legislation, in other states. Indeed, a mounting dismay with state legislation, legislatures, and legislators was the engine driving all his creative responses to the crisis of republicanism—his ideas of federalism, separation of powers, and representation as well as rights. Surveying "the vices of the political system" in the early months of 1787, Madison concluded that the "multiplicity," "mutability," and most important, "injustice" of the laws that the states had enacted since 1776 had called "into question the fundamental principle of republican government, that the majority who rule in such Governments are the safest Guardians both of public good and of private rights."[66] His concern about the security of private rights was rooted in his palpable fear that fundamental rights of property were being jeopardized by the rise of populist forces in the states. Paper-money laws, debtor-stay laws, and the specter of Shays's Rebellion in Massachusetts all alarmed him. So did the grim prospect he sketched at the Federal Convention when he warned that even in the United States a factious majority might eventually form from "those who will labour under all the hardships of life, & secretly sigh for a more equal distribution of its blessings."[67] The constitution writers of 1776 had erred in assuming that by protecting "the rights of persons" they would also protect "those of property." Now he understood "that in all populous countries the smaller part [of society] only can be interested in preserving the rights of property."[68] Although other classes of rights remained of concern to Madison, his analysis of the sources of the dangers to rights of property was (arguably) paradigmatic for the development of the program of constitutional reform that he carried to Philadelphia in the spring of 1787.

---

[66] From his memorandum on the "Vices of the Political System of the U. States [April 1787]," in *Papers of Madison*, 9: 353–4.

[67] Speech of 26 June 1787, in ibid., 10: 77.

[68] Observations on Jefferson's Draft of a Constitution for Kentucky [October 1788], in ibid., 11: 287–8.

When rights of property were at stake, Madison feared, neither the specific enumeration nor the explicit denial of positive legislative powers would provide adequate safeguards. In this sense, his solution to the problem of religious liberty—to deny government any authority to legislate for religion—could never wholly apply to public finance and economic regulation.[69] His clearest statement on this point appears in *Federalist* 10. Madison closed his famous passage describing the sources of faction and the way that different forms of property divided society into different "interests" by noting, "The regulation of these various and interfering interests forms the principal task of modern legislation, and involves the spirit of party and faction in the necessary and ordinary operations of government." But he then denied that acts of economic regulation were solely legislative in character. "What are so many of the most important acts of legislation," Madison asked, "but so many judicial determinations, not indeed concerning the rights of single persons, but concerning the rights of large bodies of citizens; and what are the different classes of legislators, but advocates and parties to the causes they determine?" The examples of economic regulation that Madison cited reveal that he regarded *all* decisions of economic policy as implicating questions of private rights: laws relating to creditors and debtors, to the protection of domestic manufactures and the restriction of foreign goods, to the apportionment of taxes—all involved questions of justice, and thus of rights.[70] Economic rights were fundamentally different from rights of conscience, then, in at least one critical sense: Although government could safely abstain from religious matters, it could never avoid having to regulate the "various and interfering interests" of a modern society; and any legislative decision would necessarily affect not merely the interests but also the rights of one class of property holders or another.

This strikingly modern perception of what legislatures could *do* re-

---

[69] Madison still *hoped* that the diversity of economic interests in the national Republic would have the same beneficial effects as "a multiplicity of sects," but his gloomier comments about the future security of property rights suggests that he may have been more confident that Protestant sectarianism would continue to work in wonderfully divisive ways than he was about the social and political consequences of economic development. Nathan O. Hatch, *The Democratization of American Christianity* (New Haven: Yale University Press, 1989), provides a provocative account of the fusion between Jeffersonian-Madisonian principles, on the one hand, and the sectarian creativity of the Second Great Awakening, on the other. On Madison's economic ideas, see Drew McCoy, *The Elusive Republic: Political Economy in Jeffersonian America* (Chapel Hill: University of North Carolina Press, 1979).

[70] Wright, ed., *The Federalist*, 131–2.

flected not only discontent with the sheer busyness of American lawmaking, but a fundamental recognition of "the impossibility of dividing
powers of legislation, in such a manner, as to be free from differing
constructions, by different interests, or even from ambiguity in the judgment of the impartial." In the realm of economic legislation, the interests
to be regulated were so complex, and the ends and means of legislation
so intertwined, that no simple formula seemed likely to defeat the "infinitude of legislative expedients" that artful lawmakers could always
deploy.[71] Nor did Madison expect the executive and judiciary to be able
to counteract the injustice of the legislature. Its very rulemaking power,
he observed in *Federalist* 48, enabled the legislature to "mask under
complicated and indirect measures, the encroachments which it makes
on the co-ordinate departments. It is not unfrequently a question of real
nicety in legislative bodies, whether the operation of a particular measure,
will or will not extend beyond the legislative sphere."[72]

By its very nature, then, legislative power was too supple and plastic—
too "indefinite"—ever to be neatly confined. But Madison's analysis
thrust deeper still. It was not enough to identify the danger that excessive
legislation posed; Madison also felt compelled to explain its *political*
sources. Because republican politics was necessarily the politics of representation, this concern, in turn, led Madison to ask why the essential
safeguard of representation—the first and most formidable line of defense
for the protection of rights—had been found wanting.

Madison traced much of the blame for the sorry condition of public
affairs to the character of state lawmakers, too many of whom sought
office only for "ambition" and "personal interest" rather than from
sincere consideration of "public good." Those who were not demagogues
or self-seekers were too often inexperienced backbenchers with little understanding of public issues and less inclination to withstand the improper
influence either of designing leaders or of their own electors.[73] As many
commentators have observed, Madison's quite Burkean ideal of national
representation was designed to "extract from the mass of the Society the
purest and noblest characters which it contains," and to allow them to

---

[71] Madison to Jefferson, 24 October 1787, *Papers of Madison*, 10: 211–12.
[72] Wright, ed., *The Federalist*, 344; and see the parallel discussion of the problem of
delineating powers in *Federalist* 37 in ibid., 269.
[73] *Papers of Madison*, 9: 354.

serve under conditions that would effectively insulate their deliberations from the populist pressures of their constituents.[74]

Yet as "vicious" as state lawmaking and legislators seemed, Madison now thought that the ultimate danger lay not in unchecked rulers but in society itself. "A still more fatal if not more frequent cause" of unjust legislation, he wrote in April 1787, "lies among the people themselves." His theory of faction was designed to explain why this was the case. As is well known, Madison located the sources of factious behavior in the passions and interests of the citizenry, and he argued that smaller communities—whether the city-states of antiquity or of the early modern era, or the substantially larger American states—were more vulnerable to injustice than an extended national republic would be, simply because in a smaller society it would be easier for such factious majorities to form. The peculiar danger in a republic was that "whenever . . . an apparent interest or common passion unites a majority," few if any checks existed "to restrain them from unjust violations of the rights and interests of the minority, or of individuals."[75]

Although Madison could easily illustrate this proposition from his voluminous reading in the history of ancient and modern republics, its relevance to American politics in 1787 manifestly reflected his bleak assessment of the legislation that the states were enacting to deal with the economic and financial problems of the postwar years. What these problems enabled him to perceive was how certain issues of public policy could lead to the coalescence of popular factions in society, which would then actively compete to manipulate the legislature to secure the desired ends. It is doubtful whether such a perception would have been readily attainable had recent experience not made it appear realistic. True, some precedents for it could be found in Anglo-American history before the Revolution—in mercantilist legislation or in an exceptional episode such as the Massachusetts Land Bank controversy of 1740 or the repeal of the parliamentary Jew Bill of 1753. But arguably it was the Revolution

---

[74] For closer analysis of Madison's ideas of representation, see Rakove, "The Great Compromise," 429–36, and idem, "The Structure of Politics at the Accession of George Washington," in Richard R. Beeman et al., eds., *Beyond Confederation: Origins of the Constitution and American National Identity* (Chapel Hill: University of North Carolina Press, 1987), 261–94.

[75] *Papers of Madison,* 9: 355–7; these quotations from the memorandum on the "Vices of the Political System of the U. States" were, of course, the first statement of the ideas better known from their reformulation in *Federalist* 10.

itself that provided the most compelling lessons. The urgency and pervasive impact of the problems the Revolution created, and the legislatures' inability to overcome them, all alerted Madison to both the scope of legislative power and its susceptibility to popular influence.

This dual obsession with the nature of legislative power and the populist sources of unjust legislation was also reflected in Madison's approach to the problem of federalism. For Madison, the problem of protecting rights was first and foremost a problem of finding ways to curb injustice *within* the individual states. However powerful a national government the Federal Convention might propose, Madison understood that most laws affecting property—as well as all other ordinary activities of society—would still emanate from the states. Second, the arithmetical logic of his theory of faction predicted that majorities willing to commit injustice would still readily form within the states. From these perceptions came the two proposals that Madison thought would protect rights far more effectively than any formal bill of rights could ever promise to do: an unlimited national legislative veto on all state laws and the establishment of a joint executive-judicial council of revision, armed with a limited veto over national laws and a participatory role in the national review of state laws.

Radical remedies. At the start of the Federal Convention, Madison regarded the veto on state laws as the one indispensable measure for the preservation of private rights against "vicious" state legislation. Armed with such a power, the national government could act as a "disinterested & dispassionate umpire in disputes between different passions & interests in the State"—that is, within the *individual* states—and thus curb "the aggressions of interested majorities on the rights of minorities and of individuals."[76] From the vantage point of 1776, it would be difficult to imagine a more offensive proposal, especially when Madison explicitly linked his veto with the similar prerogative power the Crown had wielded over colonial legislation (and against which his friend Thomas Jefferson had complained so bitterly in the Declaration of Independence). The proposed council of revision seemed equally obnoxious to the orthodox doctrine of separated powers. As much as Madison believed in this principle, he also understood that mere textual declarations of the need to keep the three branches of government distinct would always prove in-

[76] Madison to Washington, 16 April 1787, in ibid., 9: 383–4.

adequate. His dismissal of formal constitutional statements of this principle echoed his impatience with bills of rights: both erected "parchment
barriers"[77] that could always be easily pierced if other methods of securing balanced government were not provided. Rather than trust the
two weaker branches to correct an unjust law after it was enacted, Madison instead preferred to involve them directly in legislation through the
proposed executive-judicial council of revision. If many legislative decisions were truly judicial in nature, he reasoned, why not bring the judiciary into the lawmaking process itself, in the hope that sound judicial
counsel could prevent the adoption of unjust laws in the first place?

If these proposals illustrate Madison's impatience with trite axioms
of constitutional thought, they also reveal how far his impassioned analysis of the vices of republicanism had carried him beyond the boundaries
of what was politically feasible in 1787. At the convention, both the veto
over state laws and the council of revision encountered decisive criticism.
Their rejection left Madison fearful that the Constitution "will neither
effectually answer its national object nor prevent the local mischiefs which
every where excite disgusts agst. the state governments."[78]

In one of the most remarkable of all his political papers—his letter to
Jefferson of 24 October 1787—Madison went out of his way to defend
the absolute veto on state laws, and he did so with a conviction that
helps to explain why he could dismiss the practical value of a bill of
rights so easily. It was true, he observed, that the Constitution did afford
some basis for the protection of economic rights, by prohibiting the states
from issuing paper currency and enacting laws impairing the obligation
of contracts. Yet even if these restrictions proved "effectual as far as they
go, they are short of the mark," Madison observed. "Injustice may be
effected by such an infinitude of legislative expedients, that where the
disposition exists it can only be controuled by some provision which
reaches all cases whatsoever. The partial provision made, supposes the
disposition which will evade it." Because a provision reaching "all cases
whatsoever" would not have to identify the specific rights deserving
protection, Madison's reservation about enumerating rights was the cor-
ollary of his concern that an "infinitude of legislative expedients" could

[77] It is significant that Madison used this term both in *Federalist* 48 to describe the inad-
equacy of the statements in the state constitutions prescribing the separation of powers
and in his 17 October 1788 letter to Jefferson (discussed extensively later) registering
his persisting doubts about the utility of bills of rights.
[78] Madison to Jefferson, 6 September 1787, *Papers of Madison,* 10: 163.

always be deployed to circumvent a formal ban proscribing the exercise of particular powers. In effect, Madison feared that an enumeration of rights would prove restrictive and effective in a way that the enumeration of legislative powers could not. Nor would it do to trust the federal judiciary to remedy wrongs: "It is more convenient to prevent the passage of a law [through a national veto], than to declare it void after it is passed," he observed, and this was "particularly the case, where the law aggrieves individuals, who may be unable to support an appeal agst. [against] a State to the supreme Judiciary."[79]

From this defense of his pet scheme for a veto Madison went on to present Jefferson with his first statement of his theory of faction.[80] Only once in this letter, the central theme of which is the protection of rights, did Madison refer to the issue of a bill of rights, when he noted that George Mason, his colleague in the Virginia delegation, "considers the want of a Bill of Rights as a fatal objection" to either his own signing of the Constitution or its ratification. Madison clearly regarded this objection as specious. No *federal* bill of rights could reach the real and subsisting dangers to American liberty unless it somehow restrained the legislative power of the states and the vicious impulses of the local majorities whom they too faithfully represented. No partial list of prohibitions on the state legislatures could be efficacious—especially in the crucial realm of rights of property—given the plasticity of legislative power and its intrusive impact on the economy.

Subsisting doubts and grudging acceptance. Nearly a full year passed before Madison provided Jefferson with a more powerful set of reasons for questioning the utility of a federal bill of rights—even as he moved to commit himself to the task of securing appropriate amendments to the Constitution. When Madison sat down on 17 October 1788 to respond to the arguments that Jefferson had made in support of a bill of rights, a full year of public debate on the subject had barely altered his original opinion.[81] He had "always been in favor of a bill of rights," he wrote (at least a shade disingenuously), "provided it be so framed as not

---

[79] Ibid., 10: 211–12; on the veto, see especially Charles F. Hobson, "The Negative on State Laws: James Madison, the Constitution, and the Crisis of Republican Government," *William and Mary Quarterly*, 3d ser., 36 (1979): 215–35.

[80] Only four weeks later that theory would be published in the tenth number of *The Federalist*.

[81] Quotations from this letter in this and the following paragraphs can be found in *Papers of Madison*, 11: 297–300.

to imply powers not meant to be included in the enumeration." This qualification, of course, invoked the central claim that Federalists had opposed to the call for a bill of rights. Madison then explained why he had still "not viewed it in an important light." To some extent he accepted James Wilson's argument that a bill of rights was less necessary for the federal government because it was vested with limited powers and because the independent existence of the states would "afford a security" against an abuse of federal power. Moreover, there was "great reason to fear that a positive declaration of some of the most essential rights could not be obtained in the requisite latitude," especially if "rights of conscience" were considered.

But Madison saved for last the one argument that expressed his most profound doubts. "Experience proves the inefficacy of a bill of rights on those occasions when its controul is most needed," he observed. "Repeated violations of these parchment barriers have been committed in every State." The crucial point followed:

Wherever the real power in a Government lies, there is the danger of oppression. In our Governments the real power lies in the majority of the Community, and the invasion of private rights is *cheifly* to be apprehended, not from acts of Government contrary to the sense of its constituents, but from acts in which the Government is the mere instrument of the major number of the constituents. This is a truth of great importance, but not yet sufficiently attended to: and is probably more strongly impressed on my mind by facts, and reflections suggested by them, than on yours which has contemplated abuses of power issuing from a very different quarter.

By this last comparison, Madison set his own recent observations about American politics against the inferences Jefferson had drawn from his four years of service as American minister in France—inferences that allowed Jefferson to cast the problem of rights in the traditional terms of protecting the ruled from the rulers. In a monarchy, Madison continued, a bill of rights could serve "as a standard for trying the validity of public acts, and a signal for rousing the superior force of the community" against "abuses of power" by "the sovereign." But in a republic, "the political and physical power" were both lodged "in a majority of the people, and consequently the tyrannical will of the sovereign is not [to] be controlled by the dread of an appeal to any other force within the community."

If Madison's deepest concern was still for the security of property— because, in the familiar words of *Federalist* 10, "the most common and durable source of faction has been the various and unequal distribution of property"[82]—he nevertheless applied this general analysis of the prevailing force of public opinion to other categories of rights. He remained convinced, he told Jefferson, that some form of religious establishment could yet be adopted in Virginia, if the assembly "found a majority of the people in favor of the measure" and "if a majority of the people were now of one sect," notwithstanding the "explicit provision" protecting rights of conscience in the state constitution and "the additional obstacle which the law has since created" through the Statute for Religious Freedom. He questioned whether it would be useful to cast the provisions for rights that Jefferson wanted to incorporate in the federal Constitution in "absolute" terms. "The restrictions however strongly marked on paper will never be regarded when opposed to the decided sense of the public," Madison warned, "and after repeated violations in extraordinary cases, they will lose even their ordinary efficacy." "No written prohibitions on earth" would deter a people alarmed by civil turmoil from supporting a suspension of habeas corpus, nor would an article prohibiting standing armies as a danger to popular liberty do much good if Britain or Spain massed forces "in our neighbourhood."

What value, then, would a bill of rights have in a republic? Madison asked rhetorically. He saw two uses for it "which though less essential than in other Governments, sufficiently recommend the precaution." The first can be described as educative: "The political truths declared in that solemn manner acquire by degrees the character of fundamental maxims of free Government, and as they become incorporated with the national sentiment, counteract the impulses of interest and passion." By his own standards, this formulation seems remarkably optimistic: everywhere else in his concurrent political writings he concluded that ordinary citizens would rarely find appeals to principle more persuasive than the impulses of interest and passion.[83]

Madison was equally doubtful about the second rationale he conceded for a bill of rights: that occasions could arise when "the danger of oppression" would lie more in "usurped acts of the Government" than "the interested majorities of the people," or even when "a succession of artful and ambitious rulers, may by gradual & well-timed advances, finally erect an independent Government on the subversion of liberty." But

---

[82] Wright, ed., *The Federalist*, 131.
[83] The obvious texts to be consulted on this point include *Federalist* 10, 49, and 50.

Madison treated even this prospect more as a speculative possibility than a serious threat. In the American republics, the greater danger by far was that government would experience a progressive "relaxation" of its power to restrain the populace "until the abuses of liberty beget a sudden transition to an undue degree of power."

With these strictures in mind, Madison was prepared to endorse the call for a bill of rights, if suitably framed, and to assume personal responsibility for the adoption of appropriate amendments. Yet this grudging acceptance of political necessity reflected no sudden realization that a national bill of rights would have great practical value. The original failure of the Federal Convention to accept the programmatic reforms he valued most—the national veto and the council of revision—could not be remedied by the adoption of a federal bill of rights that would not reach the cases (or, in a sense, the arena) where most rights would remain at greatest risk. Legislation affecting rights of property, rights of conscience, and the other legal procedures (civil and criminal) to which Americans would be subject remained the province of the state legislatures, and Madison simply could not see how the acceptance of cautionary limitations on the exercise of national power would do much good.

Given the continuing force of these reservations, Madison's public declaration favoring amendments can easily be interpreted as a campaign conversion inspired by his difficult contest against James Monroe for election to the First Congress. That is what many of his colleagues suspected. Senator Robert Morris of Pennsylvania, for example, scoffed that Madison had "got frightened in Virginia and 'wrote a Book'"—that is, issued public letters revising his known views about amendments.[84] Yet as important as political considerations, both local and national, were in persuading Madison to take the lead in promoting the adoption of amendments, the depth of his libertarian convictions was never in doubt. When the time came to enumerate rights meriting explicit constitutional recognition, he had no problem drafting an expansive list of civil rights in language that by contemporary standards can only be described as advanced. His subsisting objections to bills of rights were more pragmatic and functional than principled. Madison simply regarded the adoption of a federal bill of rights as an irrelevant antidote to the real dangers to

---

[84] Morris to James Wilson, 23 August 1789, Willing, Morris, and Swanwick Papers, Pennsylvania Historical and Museum Commission, Harrisburg.

rights that republican politics would generate. Unless it applied to the states, it would not reach the political arena where the greatest threats lay. Nor could he imagine how rights of property could ever be codified with the same relative ease and precision with which the procedural guarantees of more conventional civil rights could be stated.

Just as Madison's deepest reservations survived intact, so he found it impossible to dissemble when the time came (both in Virginia and Congress) to present his reasons first for accepting and then for sponsoring the requisite amendments. For all the pain that his personal stewardship of the eventual bill of rights caused him, Madison did not shrink from offering a final and largely unmodified defense of his essential views. Rather than endorse the Anti-Federalist claim that a Constitution lacking a bill of rights would prove dangerous, he carefully explained why standard Federalist arguments against amendments were at once plausible yet less than persuasive. He stressed that the most important reason for proposing amendments was to reconcile to the Constitution all those "respectable" citizens whose "jealousy . . . for their liberty . . . though mistaken in its object, is laudable in its motive." Similarly, Madison used his speech introducing amendments to reiterate central elements of his own teachings about republican government. He reminded his colleagues, and the public who would read his speech in the newspapers, that any declaration of rights needed to be aimed against the legislative branch, not against the relatively weak executive. But in fact, Madison continued, "the greatest danger" to liberty was "not found in either the executive or legislative departments of government, but in the body of the people, operating by the majority against the minority."[85]

Far from seeking to assuage public opinion or Anti-Federalist arguments at any cost, Madison thus restated the convictions that still informed his analysis of the essential problem of rights. So, too, he sought once again to place further restrictions on the abuse of state power by proposing an additional amendment declaring, "No state shall violate the equal rights of conscience, or the freedom of the press, or the trial by jury in criminal cases." Though far more limited than his proposed national veto on state laws, this measure marked one last effort to salvage something from his earlier critique of the preeminent dangers to rights within the states. In subsequent debate, Madison boldly described this

---

[85] Speech in the House of Representatives, 8 June 1789, in *Papers of Madison*, 12: 196–209, quotations at 198, 204.

clause "as the most valuable amendment on the whole list." Would the people not be equally grateful, he asked, if "these essential rights" were secured against the state as well as the national governments? This logic prevailed in the House but not the Senate, which acted to protect the rights of its legislative constituents in the state assemblies against national encroachment.[86]

In his speech of 8 June, Madison did make one notable point he had not endorsed previously. If a declaration of rights was "incorporated into the constitution," he observed, "independent tribunals of justice will consider themselves in a peculiar manner the guardians of those rights; they will be an impenetrable bulwark against every assumption of power in the legislative or executive; they will be naturally led to resist every encroachment upon rights expressly stipulated for in the constitution by the declaration of rights."[87] The inspiration for this statement came from Jefferson.[88] But however attractive this prospect seemed in the abstract, Madison did not expect the adoption of amendments to free judges to act vigorously in defense of rights, at least over the short run. The true benefits of a bill of rights were to be found in the realm of public opinion, whose mysterious workings Madison—following David Hume—found so compelling. Beyond the immediate boost in allegiance to the new government that the prompt approval of amendments would produce, Madison hoped and expected a bill of rights to reinforce the stability of government over a much longer period. "In proportion as Government is influenced by opinion, must it be so by whatever influences opinion," Madison privately noted in December 1791. "This decides the question concerning a bill of rights, which acquires efficacy as time sanctifies and incorporates it with the public sentiment."[89] As greater popular respect for the justice and importance of protecting individual and minority rights did develop over time, perhaps the judiciary would eventually act as

---

[86] Ibid., 202, 208, 344.

[87] Ibid., 206–7.

[88] "In the arguments in favor of a declaration of rights [included in Madison's letter of 17 October 1788]," Jefferson had written on 15 March 1789, "you omit one which has great weight with me, the legal check which it puts into the hands of the judiciary." Ibid., 13.

[89] This observation appears in the notes Madison kept for his *National Gazette* essays of 1791–2; ibid., 14: 162–3. In the printed essay on "Public Opinion," the corresponding passage reads: "In proportion as government is influenced by opinion, it must be so, by whatever influences opinion. This decides the question concerning a *Constitutional Declaration of Rights*, which requires [*sic; acquires* was probably the intended word] an influence on government, by becoming a part of the public opinion." Ibid., 170.

Madison very much hoped, yet initially doubted, it would. But the greater benefit would occur if acceptance of the principles encoded in rights acted as a restraint on political behavior, tempering improper popular desires *before* they took the form of unjust legislation.

If this interpretation is correct in suggesting that Madison placed his greatest hopes for the Bill of Rights in its educative value,[90] it may also explain why he insisted that Congress take up the subject of amendments during its inaugural session. The logic of this demand was consistent with the concern for public opinion that figured so prominently in his constitutional thinking in the late 1780s. By linking the adoption of amendments so closely with the ratification of the Constitution and by treating both as extraordinary exercises of rational deliberation and choice, Madison hoped to attach to this conception of rights "that veneration which time bestows on every thing, and without which perhaps the wisest and freest governments would not possess the requisite stability."[91]

THE RELEVANCE OF HISTORY

Two centuries later, no one doubts that the Constitution has attained this "requisite stability," but it would be more problematic to suggest that the Bill of Rights enjoys a similar degree of "veneration." The controversies that ceaselessly swirl around claims of constitutional rights— whether asserted or denied, protected or endangered—now provide the most volatile and contentious issues of American politics. Given the evolving complexity of current theories of rights, and the capacity of our constitutional system to give every interest a voice somewhere in its multiple repositories of power (local, state, or federal; judicial, legislative, or administrative), there is every reason to think that controversies over rights will ever remain divisive. Yet if a consensus about rights will always prove unavoidably elusive, in certain respects the modern evolution of the Bill of Rights has followed a Madisonian trajectory. Indeed, a strong case can be made that the most Madisonian element of the Constitution

---

[90] Nor is it clear that this conviction was his alone. Herbert Storing has also suggested, on the basis of his deep reading of Anti-Federalist writings, that "the fundamental case for a bill of rights is that it can be a prime agency of that political and moral education of the people on which free republican government depends." Herbert J. Storing, ed., *The Complete Anti-Federalist*, vol. I, *What the Anti-Federalists Were For* (Chicago: University of Chicago Press, 1981), 69–70.

[91] Wright, ed., *The Federalist*, 349 (from the 49th essay).

is found in the Fourteenth Amendment, and that the extension of the Bill of Rights to the states, under its aegis via the "incorporation" doctrine, is entirely consistent with the general role that Madison originally intended the national government to play in protecting individual and minority rights.[92] So, too, the idea that the fundamental rights enumerated in the first eight amendments were exemplary and illustrative rather than exhaustive and restrictive expresses a deeper principle that Madison sought to codify explicitly in the formula of the Ninth Amendment—so long ignored but now so intriguing a source of constitutional scrutiny.[93]

Historians are always happy to describe the relevance of the ideas and events they study to contemporary issues, the more so when they witness complex historical evidence being abused or at least grossly oversimplified for political ends. But they are happier still when issues arising in the present occasion a fresh look at that evidence and a better understanding of the events and developments that evidence represents. To trace the rapid evolution that took place after 1776 in American thinking about the protection of rights is to appreciate again how fertile and innovative this period of republican experimentation was. To recast the problem of rights in the new terms that Madison helped to fashion required both a theoretical originality and a pragmatic, questioning approach to pressing political issues. As it is today, so it was in the beginning. By its very nature, the language of rights seeks the eloquent forms of moral principle and philosophical abstraction; but those who speak that language must also master a more vernacular dialect whose rules reflect the play of interest, opinion, passion—and politics.

[92] From a Madisonian perspective, there are two ways to view the relationship between the current debate over constitutional rights and the original intentions of this most influential framer of the Constitution and its amendments. Whether Madison would relish the idea that judges could "create" new rights, rather than merely recognize and protect preexisting but unenumerated rights, is certainly a good—indeed challenging—question. But the idea so central to recent conservative claims—that the federal judiciary should defer to local democratic preferences even where questions of rights may be implicated—strikes me as being the antithesis of the central Madisonian principle, namely, that the real dangers to rights would arise primarily within the states and that the best solution to this condition would require the creation of a national government capable of intervening to protect individuals and minorities against the abuse of factious majorities within the states and local communities.

[93] See the essays collected in Randy E. Barnett, ed., *The Rights Retained by the People: The History and Meaning of the Ninth Amendment* (Fairfax, Va.: George Mason University Press, 1989).

4

Rights and wrongs: Jefferson, slavery,
and philosophical quandaries

Rights and wrongs: Jefferson, slavery,
and philosophical quandaries

CHARLES L. GRISWOLD, JR.

Such is the government for which philosophy has been searching, and humanity
been sighing, from the most remote ages. Such are the republican governments
which it is the glory of America to have invented, and her unrivalled happiness
to possess.   James Madison[1]

Americans! your republican politics, not less than your republican religion, are
flagrantly inconsistent.   Frederick Douglass[2]

The civil status of a contradiction, or its status in civil life: there is the philosophical problem.   Ludwig Wittgenstein[3]

The vocabulary of rights constitutes a continuous thread through the
maze of contemporary American political culture. So pervasive is that

The research for this chapter was supported by a grant from the Faculty Research Program
in the Social Sciences, Humanities, and Education at Howard University and a fellowship
from the National Endowment of the Humanities. The final draft was completed during
my term as a Fellow at the Woodrow Wilson Center. I am grateful to all these sources for
their support. Earlier drafts benefitted greatly from comments offered by the members of
the working group composed of the other contributors to this volume (as well as J. G. A.
Pocock). Bill Galston's detailed suggestions were especially welcome. Knud Haakonssen's
editorial and philosophical points led to many improvements as well. My thanks also to
Howard DeLong, a lengthy correspondence with whom has been extremely useful, and to
Lance Banning, Howard McGary, and David Roochnik for helpful comments. I bear sole
responsibility for any errors remaining in this chapter.
[1] Essay in the *National Gazette*, 20 February 1792, in *The Papers of James Madison,* ed.
   Robert A. Rutland et al. (Charlottesville: University of Virginia Press, 1983), 14: 234.
[2] "Fourth of July Oration" (1852) in *What Country Have I?: Political Writings by Black
   Americans,* ed. H. J. Storing (New York: St. Martin's Press, 1970), 35.
[3] *Philosophical Investigations,* I. 125, 3d ed., trans. G. E. M. Anscombe (New York:
   Macmillan, 1968).

vocabulary that mutually exclusive sides of the same issue are normally argued by appeals to rights. The abortion debate is a prominent example. Positions on every issue, no matter how seemingly trivial, follow a similar pattern. Jefferson's open-ended list of rights in the Declaration of Independence seems now to stretch on indefinitely,[4] indeed beyond the human species to animals and even nonliving entities. Correspondingly, we have not wanted for laments about the perceived vacuousness of contemporary rights discourse, or for judgments that rights discourse is inherently corrupt.[5] Natural rights, we are told, are both cause and effect of a disintegrating society lacking any shared sense of community values. The bill of particulars continues further: Rights talk supplies no rational way of mediating disputes, and as a consequence, power politics (exercised through the megabureaucracies, the media, and "popular movements" led by altruistic, dedicated activists) replaces deliberation; rights talk fuels an endless culture of litigation, and of hopelessly arcane (not to mention expensive) legal interpretation; in practice it amounts to little more than a rationalization of the oppression of the poor and powerless by the rich and powerful; it is founded on epistemological and theological assumptions that were prevalent in the early Enlightenment but are now discredited.

Whether to abandon a key phrase in the vocabulary of American republicanism—an unlikely prospect, to be sure—or to attempt a restriction of its scope will depend in part on how we understand the past from which that vocabulary springs.[6] Some who see our present discourse as

---

[4] I refer to the beginning of the Declaration's second paragraph: "We hold these truths to be self-evident: that all men are created equal; that they are endowed by their creator with inherent & inalienable rights; that *among these* are life, liberty, & the pursuit of happiness" (emphasis added). From Jefferson's *Autobiography,* in *Thomas Jefferson: Writings,* ed. Merrill D. Peterson (New York: Library of America, 1984), 19. Unless otherwise noted, all page references to Jefferson's writings in this chapter are to Peterson's edition.

[5] The best known recent indictment along the latter lines is offered by Alasdair MacIntyre, *After Virtue* (Notre Dame: University of Notre Dame Press, 1984), chaps. 5–6. As the following sentences in my text suggest, criticisms have also been made from a number of other perspectives stretching from the Marxist to the postmodernist. See, for example, M. Horkheimer and T. W. Adorno's *Dialectic of Enlightenment,* trans. J. Cumming (New York: Herder and Herder, 1972), 85 passim. Also relevant here is Mark Tushnet's "An Essay on Rights," *Texas Law Review* 62 (1984): 1363–1403.

[6] One could, of course, set out a view of justice that claims to articulate systematically the intuitions of the public culture of a democratic society, without engaging in further historical excavation. Compare John Rawls's "Justice as Fairness: Political, not Metaphysical," *Philosophy and Public Affairs* 14 (1985): 225: "Justice as fairness is a political conception in part because it starts from within a certain political tradition" (Rawls's discussion makes it plain that the American tradition is at issue). But the selection of the supposedly representative intuitions risks being one sided, as William Galston points out

corrupt tend to think of the disease as coeval with the American founding and even further as rooted in the poverty or impracticality of rights discourse altogether. This type of argument is advanced not only by MacIntyre but also by the "classical" critics of that vocabulary, namely, Hume, Burke, Bentham, Hegel, and Marx. No amount of adjusting or restricting and no amount of reversion to "original" rights schemas could, the argument goes, relieve us of the burdens imposed by the vocabulary. Thus the poverty of rights talk may be graphically illustrated (and this point becomes crucial for my purposes here) by the fact that the architects of classical American liberalism—Jefferson, Madison, Washington, to mention only a few—owned slaves. From Marx's standpoint in particular, the failure thus signaled is not one of implementation of rights talk; slavery is simply an especially graphic illustration of the inner collusion between the "ideology" of "natural rights" and oppression.[7]

The fact that America's treatment of blacks is as much a part of our heritage as the principles of the Declaration of Independence—a heritage whose inner tension continues to be felt in myriad ways—may be interpreted in a more benign way. As Jefferson, Douglass (by 1852), and many others have argued, the American history of oppression represents the privation, not the negation, of the culture of rights defined by the Declaration and embedded in the Constitution. The poverty (if indeed it is such) of contemporary American political discourse might be taken as an indictment not of rights talk as such but rather of our decayed understanding of what such talk was meant to accomplish. Our current appeals to rights to justify contrary positions on every issue imaginable may be taken as the consequence of mistaken notions as to how rights are best implemented legally and institutionally. The theory of rights has nevertheless done valuable work in the past and can do so again. From this standpoint, definitional questions as well as questions of implementation must be addressed in saving the theory.

The issue of efficacious implementation is as old as the debates about the Bill of Rights. Obviously, the Bill of Rights has been central to the

---

in "Pluralism and Social Unity," *Ethics* 99 (1989): 725 passim: "But is the absolute priority of freedom over truth [entailed by Rawls's theory] really the polestar of liberal-democratic public culture?" Rawls distorts "our shared understandings," which include holding (contra Rawls) the principles of the Declaration of Independence to be universal truths.

[7] See Marx's discussion of the constitution of Pennsylvania in "Bruno Bauer, *Die Judenfrage*," in *Karl Marx: Early Writings*, trans. T. B. Bottomore (New York: McGraw-Hill, 1964), 23–6 and context.

dominance of the language of rights in American culture, especially in this century.[8] "Publius's" qualms as articulated in *Federalist* 84 anticipate later objections, and possibly prophesy correctly the developments just lamented. Two of Publius's points are relevant here: The first is compressed into the statement that in the body of the Constitution (including the preamble) we have "a better recognition of popular rights than volumes of those aphorisms which make the principal figure in several of our State bills of rights and which would sound much better in a treatise of ethics than in a constitution of government."[9] In other words, enumeration of rights is too theoretical a project for a working political document. The conceptual and semantic complexities render any such enumeration more properly the subject of philosophical than political discourse. In a political context, enumeration leads to arcane interpretation and, we may infer, invites multiplication of "rights" until they fill "volumes." The dangers are particularly pressing given the intrinsic ambiguity of language against which Publius warns in *Federalist* 37, and all the more so when combined with our natural propensity to disagree in political matters.[10] As Publius goes on to say in *Federalist* 84, definition of a right is in the abstract virtually impossible: "Who can give it [liberty of the press] any definition which would not leave the utmost latitude for evasion?" (p. 514). Inherently fine distinctions better suited for a treatise on ethics provide occasion for political conflict and even, Publius warns in no. 84, for perversely standing intentions on their head: enumerating rights may be taken to imply that the federal government has authority in areas where it has none (pp. 513–14).[11] Language that is tidy in theory becomes exceedingly messy in practice.

The foregoing objections to inclusion of a Bill of Rights in the Constitution may be said to concern the *implementation* of a conception of justice. The existence of these rights is not debated (and presumably was

---

[8] For some discussion of this point, see Michael Kammen's *A Machine That Would Go of Itself: The Constitution in American Culture* (New York: Vintage Books, 1987), 336–56.

[9] *The Federalist Papers,* ed. Clinton Rossiter (New York: New American Library, 1961), 513. Subsequent references are to this edition.

[10] So imprecise is language that "when the Almighty himself condescends to address mankind in their own language, his meaning, luminous as it must be, is rendered dim and doubtful by the cloudy medium through which it is communicated" (p. 229). On disagreement, see *Federalist 10,* p. 79.

[11] For further discussion of the *Federalist*'s criticisms of inclusion of a Bill of Rights, see Gordon S. Wood, *The Creation of the American Republic 1776–1787* (Chapel Hill: University of North Carolina Press, 1969), 536–43.

agreed on by Federalists and Anti-Federalists); what is at issue is the proper way of putting theory into practice.[12] If, in Lincolnian spirit, we conceive of the Constitution as a "machine,"[13] geared toward implementing (as the preamble suggests) "justice" understood in accord with a theory of natural rights—say, a theory of the sort articulated in the Declaration of Independence—the problem Publius is flagging may be thought of as a second-order theoretical issue, namely, the issue as to how a (first order) theory of justice is to be put into practice (the latter understood concretely enough to include a complex historical setting). The question is one of the appropriate "inventions of prudence" (*Federalist* 51).

The problem of implementing a theory of rights in a concrete, suitably messy historical situation—say, a situation that includes a well-entrenched system of slavery, a struggling economy, the threat of civil war or at least of widespread faction, and possibly a renewed war with a powerful enemy—may seem to be not a philosophical but a technical or strategic matter. Such is not the case, however. I have referred to Publius's remark in no. 37 concerning the intrinsic equivocality and imprecision of words. He also speaks there of the immense complexity of the "works of nature,"[14] the intrinsic obscurity of the "institutions of man," and the limitations of the human understanding. Publius is explicit that these facts about the world and human beings have political implications: "We must perceive the necessity of moderating still further our expectations and hopes from the efforts of human sagacity" (p. 228). Publius's warnings against inclusion of a Bill of Rights in the Constitution are immediately followed, in the final number of the *Federalist,* with an emphatic recommendation of the virtues of moderation and prudence in light of human imperfection (p. 523); the improbability that an equally auspicious historical juncture will recur; and a general reflection, taken directly from Hume, on the sheer difficulty and length of the process of trial and error by which societies *gradually* learn to govern themselves.

---

[12] References to natural rights and natural law in the *Federalist* are to be found in nos. 2 (p. 37), 28 (p. 180), 40 (p. 253), 43 (pp. 279–80), 51 (pp. 324–35).

[13] Borrowing from the title of Kammen's *A Machine That Would Go of Itself.* The relationship between the Declaration and the Constitution is controversial, of course. For argument in support of the proposition being advanced, see Morton White, *Philosophy, the Federalist, and the Constitution* (New York: Oxford University Press, 1987), 30–1, 211 passim.

[14] Among which is the human mind: "The faculties of the mind itself have never yet been distinguished and defined with satisfactory precision by all the efforts of the most acute and metaphysical philosophers" (p. 227).

Thus Publius's fears about a separate Bill of Rights and, more generally, his repeated recommendation of prudence and moderation—*the* political virtues in the *Federalist*—are heavily committed philosophically.

The "second order" issue concerning the efficacious implementation of rights theory is obviously linked to the ways in which that theory is defined. It is possible for tensions to exist between the philosophical assumptions of a rights theory and the assumptions governing the implementation of that theory. Indeed, it is has been held that this is a problem in the American founding itself.[15]

In this chapter I propose to focus on one key figure in the American Enlightenment[16] who had a great deal to do with the formulation and propagation of rights theory, who thought and wrote about the problem of implementing that theory, and who did so with reference to *the* problem in the efforts in the post-Revolutionary period to implement the theory, namely, slavery. To be sure, Jefferson was not present at the Constitutional Convention, but he strongly supported the addition of a Bill of Rights.[17] More broadly, if we read the Constitution (including the Bill of Rights) as the "machine" intended to implement principles of justice as broadly defined by the Declaration of Independence, we have further warrant for focusing on Jefferson. Two of the three accomplishments for which Jefferson wished to be remembered—authorship of the Declaration and of the Virginia Statute for Religious Freedom—are "rights" documents that have surely done much more than affect our

---

[15] For example, the culminating quotation from Hume in *Federalist* 85 confers a strong Scottish tone on a cluster of themes concerning the virtues, human nature, political institutions, history, knowledge, and nature that surround any theory as to how moral theory ought to be practiced. The tension arises in part from the fact that Hume's arguments for prudence and moderation in politics are connected to an epistemology that denies the existence of natural rights and natural law (understood as Locke understood them), and indeed of the entire social contract tradition. White concludes his discussion of the *Federalist* with precisely this puzzle.

[16] The American Enlightenment is a complicated affair, of course. Henry F. May, for example, distinguishes four distinct phases, or at least types, of Enlightenment in the early republic. See *The Enlightenment in America* (New York: Oxford University Press, 1976). These distinctions can be overlooked here.

[17] See his letter to Madison of 20 December 1787 (pp. 915–16), the central points of which are repeated in letters to James Alexander Donald, 7 February 1788 (p. 919), to Washington of 4 December 1788 (p. 930), to Francis Hopkinson of 13 March 1789 (p. 941), and again to Madison on 15 March 1789 (pp. 943–44). Jefferson's criticisms of the Constitution's lack of a Bill of Rights became public knowledge and a topic of debate, to which Jefferson responded in a letter to George Washington of 9 September 1792 (pp. 996–7). It is not clear whether Jefferson thought of the rights named in the Bill as "natural" rights; at the very least the right to freedom of religion would seem to fall in that category for him.

recollection of Thomas Jefferson.[18] Through them, as well as through his regular invocations of "rights," Jefferson has profoundly influenced the creation of our culture of rights. Moreover, Jefferson wrote philosophically about the sources of rights theory as well as the "second order" problem of implementing that theory. He provides us with a partly completed synthesis of ancient and modern thought intended as a basis for a sound affirmation of both the theory and the practice of rights. Jefferson thus offers an excellent subject for reflection on these issues and a reasonably generous window to the sources of American political culture.[19]

As mentioned, Jefferson owned slaves, even as he wrote frequently about slavery in ways that explicitly connect with the "how to implement rights in a complex historical situation" issue. The latent inconsistency between theory and practice here would not be so bothersome in the case of lesser men who owned slaves. Jefferson, however, knew that slaveowning was wrong in principle—on that point he did not waver— and at odds with the ethical principles to which he had dedicated his life.[20] Jefferson's famous passion for justice, outstanding intelligence, well-documented strictness of morals and character, and tremendous learning all heighten the inconsistency between his words and deeds— an inconsistency to which he himself fully admitted and which has struck many others then and now. The historical issues have, of course, been extensively studied in the literature—indeed, an entire book has been devoted to the topic, not to mention numerous articles and chapters of other books.[21]

---

[18] See Jefferson's own proposed epitaph, in *Writings*, 706.

[19] I use the term *window* advisedly. A window provides a perspective to the spectacle on the other side. At the same time, some windows make for better viewing than others.

[20] The issues of moral principle and implementation of principle are evident in Jefferson's famous letter to John Holmes of 22 April 1820: "I can say, with conscious truth, that there is not a man on earth who would sacrifice more than I would to relieve us from this heavy reproach, in any *practicable* way. The cession of that kind of property, for so it is misnamed, is a bagatelle which would not cost me a second thought, if, in that way, a general emancipation and *expatriation* could be effected; and gradually, and with due sacrifices, I think it might be. But as it is, we have the wolf by the ears, and we can neither hold him, nor safely let him go. Justice is in one scale, and self-preservation in the other" (p. 1434).

[21] The book referred to here is John C. Miller, *The Wolf by the Ears: Thomas Jefferson and Slavery* (New York: Macmillan, 1977). In addition to the works cited below, other important studies on the topic include David B. Davis, *Was Thomas Jefferson an Authentic Enemy of Slavery?* (Oxford: Oxford University Press, 1970), and his "Slavery and 'Progress,'" in *Anti-slavery, Religion, and Reform: Essays in Memory of Roger Anstey*, ed. Christine Bolt and Seymour Drescher (Hamden, Conn.: Archon Books, 1980), 351–66; William W. Freehling, "The Founding Fathers and Slavery," *American Historical Review* 77 (1972): 81–93; Bernard Bailyn, *The Ideological Origins of the American*

My purpose in this chapter is not to reexamine the historical evidence but to examine Jefferson's philosophical synthesis that, as already suggested, underlies his view about the nature of rights and their implementation in an imperfect world. It does not suffice to say that Jefferson's ownership of slaves and his stance toward the institution (and these two issues are to be distinguished, as I shall argue) are a reflection of hypocrisy *and nothing more*. For that judgment may well assume a theory as to how a doctrine of natural rights is to be acted on—what it means to stand on principle, in effect—that Jefferson did not share. In fact, Jefferson self-consciously espoused a "prudential" theory of moral deliberation that committed him to take seriously the conceptual messiness of concrete cases, the importance of the consequences of actions, and other factors. He rejected the "immediatist" view of the resolution of the slavery question to the effect that the moral thing to do under the circumstances is to act on principle without regard for consequences. Judged by that immediatist standard, Jefferson was a hypocrite, and his protestations to the contrary, philosophical or not, are rationalizations. Analogous interpretive choices arise with respect to other Enlightenment figures, including John Locke.[22] My view is that Jefferson's position deserves to be taken seriously in its own right, however, before the hypocrisy conclusion is drawn.[23]

Revolution (Cambridge, Mass.: Harvard University Press, 1971), 232 ff.; John P. Diggins, "Slavery, Race, and Equality: Jefferson and the Pathos of the Enlightenment," *American Quarterly* 28 (1976): 206–28; C. B. Galbreath, "Thomas Jefferson's Views on Slavery," *Ohio Archeological and Historical Quarterly* 34 (1925): 184–202. For some of the earlier remarks about the divergence between the theory of the American founding and American practice, see Samuel Hopkins, "The Slave Trade and Slavery," in *Family Articles on Slavery* (Boston: Congregational Board of Publication, 1854), 613–24; Thomas Paine, "African Slavery in America," in *Writings of Thomas Paine*, ed. Moncure Conway (New York: Putnam's, 1894), 1:4–9.

[22] In various ways, Locke participated in the slave trade. See Wayne Glausser, "Three Approaches to Locke and the Slave Trade," *Journal of the History of Ideas* 51 (1990): 199–216. Glausser discusses three explanatory schemes: (1) that Locke's behavior is a personal moral lapse and nothing more; (2) that Locke's writings provide some justification for the slave trade, but only by a tortured logic at odds with the central thrust of his theories; and (3) that his writings provide, as part of their very fabric, a justification of slavery. Most readers of Jefferson choose the equivalent of (1), possibly with the additional observation—the equivalent of (2)—that there are racist passages here and there in Jefferson's writings.

[23] The long juridical interpretation of the Bill of Rights and the framers' intent also concerns itself with the second-order issue. But given the disagreements within that tradition, particularly with respect to slavery, we are compelled in order to adjudicate among them to regress to the level of philosophical theory. See Robert McColley, *Slavery and Jeffersonian Virginia* (Urbana: University of Illinois Press, 1973), 137, who notes that Justice Taney thought that the Founders could not have intended the Declaration to apply to

As an illustration of this last proposition, it may be pointed out that the alternatives Jefferson understood himself to face on this question are still with us in other forms. The debate between gradualists and immediatists reproduces itself, for example, in current arguments about the relative virtues and vices of an American policy of "constructive engagement" versus "disengagement" toward South Africa.[24] The immorality of apartheid is not the issue; the issue concerns the right thing to do by way of extirpating the institution.

My purpose is not to exculpate Jefferson but to understand his views, allowing him as rich an argument as he demands, and in a way that elicits philosophically the genuine tensions and complexities at play. I conclude that even when interpreted as generously as possible, Jefferson's rationale not just for his personal ownership of slaves but also for the institution of slavery is unpersuasive. And I argue that this failure is directly traceable to the underlying incoherence of his philosophical position, a position that is an attempted synthesis of Epicureanism and a "moral sense" theory of natural rights extracted in part from a "demystified" Christianity.[25] Jefferson's synthesis of Epicurean tranquillity,

---

blacks, for if they had, they (the Founders) would have been hypocrites. Taney's decision would follow if a certain theory about moral action is accepted; but that was not the theory proposed by Jefferson, as we shall see. David B. Davis notes in *The Problem of Slavery in the Age of the Revolution, 1770–1823* (Ithaca: Cornell University Press, 1975), 166, that in the 1830s to 1850s abolitionists cited Jefferson's words in their favor, while their opponents cited Jefferson's deeds, ascribing the Declaration of Independence to Jefferson's youthful enthusiasm.

[24] Moral philosophers have paid a good deal of attention recently to the anti-Kantian view that in reality moral reasoning is an extremely messy affair, little assisted by universal rules and heavily infected with a spectrum of contingencies and variously valued goods all of which must somehow be appropriately weighted and sorted. If there are no clear a priori rules for acting morally in an imperfect world, reflection on historical situations as well as literary representations (especially those in drama) become important to understanding what it would mean to judge well. History and literature do not simply provide illustrations for an abstract treatise in ethics; they provide an important experiential basis for understanding the nature of moral judgment. Jefferson's struggles with slavery, then, seem to provide an excellent opportunity for understanding not only issues in American political culture and history or issues in rights theory, but issues in moral deliberation. This is particularly so because, since Kant, prudence has rarely been taken by philosophers as a virtue, though ordinary language still preserves a moral connotation of the term. For a sample of the discussion, see the papers in "Ethical Theory: Character and Virtue," *Midwest Studies in Philosophy* 13 (1988).

[25] My intention is neither to write a short history of ideas that influenced Jefferson nor to ignore the fact that he did not write a systematic treatise on ethics rigorously addressing the issues in question. Hermeneutically, I shall assume that Jefferson's ideas on the issues to be examined should be reconstructed as though they might form a coherent whole (an assumption that can be falsified), as parts, so to speak, of a single text that Jefferson

prudence, and moral sense collapses under the pressure of the slavery issue.[26]

The failure of his philosophical resources to meet the overwhelming challenge of the day suggests, ultimately, that his notion of what it means to be a "self" is unpersuasive. As my task in this paper is archeological, I cannot also explore the extent to which Jefferson's philosophical failure has affected us today. I limit myself to noting that although other figures in the American founding would undoubtedly have found Jefferson's position bizarre or repugnant (or both), its constituent elements—the role of science, the materialism, the origin of moral principles in natural

could have acknowledged as his "meaning" had he worked through his views more systematically. The ideas in a single text may, of course, evolve without a sacrifice of unity—particularly if the later ideas represent the full articulation of what their earlier formulations aimed for. I shall also attempt to take Jefferson at his word, as when he claims to be an Epicurean. Several of the themes central to my discussion—moral sense, the existence of natural rights and the wrongness of slavery, and errors of conventional Christianity—seem constant from the early to the late Jefferson (in the case of religion, see the relevant entries in Jefferson's "Literary Commonplace Book"). For discussion of the general hermeneutical issue, see the introduction to my *Self-knowledge in Plato's Phaedrus* (New Haven, Conn.: Yale University Press, 1986). At the same time, I grant from the outset that evidence contrary to my interpretation can be found in Jefferson's writings; unfortunately, this is an obstacle that every interpretation of Jefferson must face. My aim is to reconstruct a Jefferson so as to tell a coherent story that accounts for the gist of Jefferson's most important pronouncements on the issues I examine and that takes seriously his self-understanding (none of which excludes the possibility that his self-understanding is defective). I take the position that historical and rational reconstruction are inseparable in fruitful interpretation. On that point see Richard Rorty's "The Historiography of Philosophy: Four Genres," in *Philosophy in History*, ed. R. Rorty, J. B. Schneewind, and Quentin Skinner (Cambridge: Cambridge University Press, 1990), 52–3, n. 1.

[26] My argument may thus be taken as an interpretation of David B. Davis's view that "Negro slavery in the eighteenth and nineteenth centuries posed a genuine moral problem that reflected deep tensions in Western culture and involved the very meaning of America." *The Problem of Slavery in Western Culture* (Ithaca: Cornell University Press, 1966), 28. The paradoxes I explore should be distinguished from Edmund S. Morgan's point that it was "slavery that enabled Virginia to nourish representative government in a plantation society, slavery that transformed the Virginia of Governor Berkeley to the Virginia of Jefferson, slavery that made the Virginians dare to speak a political language that magnified the rights of freemen, and slavery, therefore, that brought Virginians into the same commonwealth political tradition with New Englanders." Morgan, "Slavery and Freedom: The American Paradox," *Journal of American History* 59 (1972): 29. Similarly, I do not mean to explore the paradox evident in Adam Smith's argument (echoed later by Tocqueville) that "the condition of a slave is better under an arbitrary than under a free government" (*An Inquiry into the Nature and Causes of the Wealth of Nations*, 2 vols., ed. Roy H. Campbell and Andrew S. Skinner [Indianapolis: Liberty Press, 1981], 2: 587), or his argument that slavery is much more difficult to extirpate in a free society than one governed tyrannically (*Lectures on Jurisprudence*, ed. Ronald L. Meek, David D. Raphael, and Peter G. Stein [Indianapolis: Liberty Press, 1982], 186–7).

passions or sentiments, the appeals to utility, the equation of happiness with tranquillity, the privileging of the "private" over the "public"—are widespread in both the Enlightenment and in contemporary modernity.

My discussion begins with Epicurean philosophy and Jefferson's points of intersection with it. Next comes a discussion of Jefferson's "supplement" to Epicurus, that is, his "other regarding" moral sense theory and his synthesis of Epicurus and moral sense theory. The last part of the first section serves as a transition to the issue of moral action in an imperfect world and examines the differing "virtues of self" available to Jefferson and his immediatist opponents on the slavery issue. In the second section, I examine the implementation of Jefferson's Epicurean moral sense theory with respect to the problem of slavery—the "second order issue" (the issue as to how best to implement moral principle). I also examine some boundary conditions on the invocation of prudence—some taken from Jefferson's "Opinion on the French Treaties" and others stipulated by Jefferson himself (one concerns the importance of preserving the Union; the other deals with the expatriation of the slaves). Then I consider Jefferson's ownership of slaves and his words and deeds with respect to the institution of slavery. In the third section I discuss the difference between prudence and rationalization with specific reference to Jefferson's handling of the slavery issue; I argue that Jefferson's rationalization of his actions reveals the incoherence of his overall philosophical synthesis. I conclude by briefly tracing the fault line of Jefferson's attempted synthesis through his views on public service (including his own service) and public education.

PRINCIPLES

"As you say of yourself, I too am an Epicurian."[27]

Epicurus and Jefferson. After declaring himself an Epicurean in this letter to William Short, Jefferson proceeds to show why Short's understanding

---

[27] Jefferson, letter of 31 October 1819, to William Short (p. 1430). Jefferson's Epicureanism is stressed by Charles A. Miller, *Jefferson and Nature: An Interpretation* (Baltimore: Johns Hopkins University Press, 1988), 23ff. For further discussion, see (in addition to the sources cited below) Gilbert Chinard's "Jefferson among the Philosophers," *Ethics* 53 (1943): 255–68; and Henry C. Montgomery, "Epicurus at Monticello," *Illinois Studies in Language and Literature* 58 (1969): 80–7. On the general issue of the transmission of Epicurus's views, see Howard Jones, *The Epicurean Tradition* (New York: Routledge,

of Epicurus is fundamentally wrong in its equation of indolence with happiness. Jefferson provides an accurate if extremely skeletal summary (some twenty years old, according to Jefferson's own testimony in this letter) of some central teachings of Epicurus. I flesh out the skeleton somewhat as I discuss the main points.

In Jefferson's summary we are told, first, that happiness, understood as freedom from mental anxiety, is the aim of life. The summum bonum is tranquillity, which is understood as the absence of mental anxiety (*ataraxia*) and freedom from physical pain (*aponia*). This tranquillity Epicurus takes to be pleasurable.[28] This is the linchpin of the system. That happiness is the summum bonum is a fact determined by nature; we are constructed as creatures whose chief aim is happiness so understood.[29] The desire for happiness is prerational, part of our affective makeup. But nature does not give us a clear understanding of what happiness consists of; reflection and experience are required to see that the goods proposed by the imagination and the senses—wealth, power, physical pleasure—do not yield happiness and must be restricted. Happiness requires a comprehensive ordering of the soul so that all remaining desires are satisfied. Thus the nature of happiness is not subjective, it is something about which mistakes are systematically made, something that requires self-knowledge to achieve. Epicurus is in this sense a rationalist: our affective beliefs are dependent on our cognitive beliefs about self and

Chapman, Hall, 1989). On Lucretius, see Wolfgang B. Fleischmann, "The Debt of the Enlightenment to Lucretius," *Studies on Voltaire and the Eighteenth Century* 25 (1963): 631–43. My (and Jefferson's) main source for Epicurus's writings is Diogenes Laertius. The main points of Epicurus's teaching that I am summarizing would have been available to Jefferson. The *Sententiae Vaticanae* are not in Diogenes and were not available to Jefferson, but they play only a minor role in my summary of Epicurus. Sowerby lists three editions of Diogenes Laertius (one in Greek and Latin, another in Latin, a third in French) as being in Jefferson's library. Millicent E. Sowerby, *Catalogue of the Library of Thomas Jefferson*, 5 vols. (Washington, D.C.: Library of Congress, 1952–9), 1:15–16.

[28] *Letter to Menoeceus* 128–9, p. 87. All quotations from Epicurus are taken from *Epicurus: the Extant Remains*, trans. and ed. Cyril Bailey (Oxford: Clarendon Press, 1926).

[29] Of course this controversial view would require a great deal of explanation, far more than I can offer here. My purposes are much more limited. I note that Epicurus assumes that we want happiness for ourselves understood as extended through time (for our future as well as present self), an assumption that, Thomas Nagel has argued in a different context, underlies the possibility of prudence. Nagel, *The Possibility of Altruism* (Oxford: Clarendon Press, 1970), chap. 6. Responses to Nagel include Janet Broughton's "The Possibility of Prudence," *Philosophical Studies* 43 (1983): 253–66; and Richard Kraut, "The Rationality of Prudence," *Philosophical Review* 81 (1972): 351–9. As this debate is not essential to the purpose here, I have sidestepped it.

the world.[30] Epicurean eudaemonism requires reason—"prudence"—for its fulfillment.

For Epicurus a chief fruit of happiness is self-sufficiency or freedom.[31] To be happy is to cease to desire those things that make one dependent on other people (and also lead one to make other people dependent on oneself). Indeed, the tranquil person does not even fear death, for reasons I shall briefly discuss in a moment. To be happy is to be invulnerable to fortune; ideally, the sage could remain tranquil under any external conditions. Diogenes Laertius ascribes to Epicurus the view that "even on the rack the wise man is happy."[32]

In addition to his profession of Epicureanism and his summary of Epicurus, Jefferson seems regularly to equate happiness with tranquillity.[33] Hence his eudaemonism is not fruitfully interpreted along Aristo-

---

[30] Phillip Mitsis notes that "Epicurus views the virtues as cognitive states." In *Epicurus' Ethical Theory* (Ithaca: Cornell University Press, 1988), 64, n. 15.

[31] See the *Letter to Menoeceus* 132–5, pp. 91–3; *Sen. Vat.* LXXVII, p. 117; and the *Kuriai Doxai*, p. 99, n. XVI: "In but few things chance hinders a wise man, but the greatest and most important matters reason has ordained and throughout the whole period of life does and will ordain." Freedom understood as independence from the pursuit of false pleasures and from dependence on others for the provision of those pleasures in turn assumes the possibility of a free act of choice on the part of the agent. How that freedom of will is to be reconciled with Epicurus's physics is a controverted subject; Jefferson would have faced a similar difficulty had he worked through the issue.

[32] *Lives*, X.118, p. 165.

[33] On Jefferson's equation of happiness with tranquillity, see (in addition to his self-characterization as an Epicurean) his letter to Madison of 9 June 1793 (p. 1010); letter to John Randolph, 25 August 1775 (p. 749); the letter to P. S. Du Pont de Nemours, 18 January 1802, p. 1101 ("freedom and tranquillity" are the goal of the political experiments in France); the letter to Spencer Roane of 6 September 1819; the letter to Benjamin Rush, 21 April 1803 (p. 1124: the precepts of the ancient philosophers "related chiefly to ourselves, and the government of these passions which, unrestrained, would disturb our tranquillity of mind. In this branch of Philosophy they were really great"); letter to Edward Dowse, 19 April 1803 (*Jefferson's Extracts from the Gospels*, ed. Dickinson W. Adams and Ruth W. Lester [Princeton: Princeton University Press, 1983], p. 330); to William Duane, 12 August 1810 (pp. 1227–8); letter to William Short, 28 November 1814 (p. 1358); letter to Benjamin Waterhouse, July 19, 1822 (*Extracts*, p. 407). Consider, too, Jefferson's "Dialogue Between Head and Heart" in the letter to Maria Cosway (12 October 1786), in which the Head says that "the art of life is the art of avoiding pain: and he is the best pilot who steers clearest of the rocks and shoals with which he is beset. Pleasure is always before us; but misfortune is at our side: while running after that, this arrests us. The most effectual means of being secure against pain is to retire within ourselves, and to suffice for our own happiness." "Everything in this world is a matter of calculation.... Put into one scale the pleasures which any object may offer; but put fairly into the other pains which are to follow, and see which preponderates" (p. 872). The Heart objects that morals stem from the heart, not the head, and that "to you she [nature] allotted the field of science; to me that of morals... in denying you the feelings of sympathy, of benevolence, of gratitude, of justice, of love, of friendship, she has excluded you from their controul. To these she has adapted the mechanism of the heart. Morals were too essential to the happiness of man to be risked

telian lines,[34] and the evidence weighs against a Stoic interpretation.[35] Once it is recognized (as Jefferson saw) that Epicurus's morals are actually quite strict, the temptation to see the doctrine as leading to a thoroughly un-Jeffersonian laxness of personal morals is removed.

on the uncertain combinations of the head. She [nature] laid their foundation therefore in sentiment, not in science. That she gave to all, as necessary to all: this to a few only, as sufficing with a few" (p. 874). Charles Miller argues (with insufficient evidence) that the Heart represents the Epicurean viewpoint (*Jefferson and Nature*, p. 99).

[34] Compare Adrienne Koch, *The Philosophy of Thomas Jefferson* (New York: Columbia University Press, 1943): "The happiness of others, which he [Jefferson] singled out as the essence of a virtuously motivated action, was a part of the secular, practical, and modern morality which Jefferson admired. He valued it as a realistic reinforcement of the loftier Christian morality, the latter remaining indisputably the most perfect pattern of conduct, while the former represented the desirable average compromise which a wise legislator would be glad to have realized by the citizens of a state. That is why Aristotle's 'eudaemonism' is a closer approximation to Jefferson's use of the happiness concept than the more contemporary 'hedonism' was" (p. 42). In the note to this passage Koch remarks, "Sometimes Jefferson interpreted happiness in the Epicurean sense," but adds that "Jefferson always approached Epicureanism via Gassendi, in its Christianized and Stoicized version, so that nothing really conflicting with the eudaemonistic has a place in Jefferson's system." On Stoicism, see the following note. I see no evidence that Jefferson *always* approaches Epicureanism in that manner, though he was indeed fond of Gassendi; and in any case I shall argue that he self-consciously synthesized Epicureanism and Christianity in such a way as to alter the latter's orthodoxies radically. It seems to me that the Aristotelian element is only superficially present in Jefferson's synthesis.

Of course, Jefferson once mentioned Aristotle in the course of his famous letter to Henry Lee (8 May 1825): the Declaration places "before mankind the common sense of the subject" and is "an expression of the American mind"; "all its authority rests then on the harmonizing sentiments of the day, whether expressed in conversation, in letters, printed essays, or in the elementary books of public right, as Aristotle, Cicero, Locke, Sidney, etc." (p. 1501). It is also possible that Jefferson was thinking of Aristotle's argument in the *Politics* about the necessity of farmers, and all the virtues they embody, to a free republic. In "The Intellectual Origins of Jeffersonian Democracy" (Ph.D. diss., Yale University, 1943), Douglass Adair argues that "Jefferson and Madison were concerned with him [the "honest farmer"]...not because they themselves were planters from Piedmont, Virginia, but because they were eighteenth-century inheritors of an agrarian tradition that runs directly back to the fourth century before Christ when Plato and Aristotle, Xenophon and Thucydides, attempted with varying degrees of scientific precision to delineate man as a political animal" (p. 30). But consider Jefferson's other reference to Aristotle, in the letter to I. H. Tiffany of 26 August 1816: "But so different was the style of society then and with those people from what it is now and with us that I think little edification can be obtained from their writings on the subject of government. They had just ideas of the value of personal liberty, but none at all of the structure of government best calculated to preserve it.... The introduction of this new principle of representative democracy has rendered useless almost everything written before on the structure of government, and in a great measure relieves our regret if the political writings of Aristotle or of any other ancient have been lost or are unfaithfully rendered or explained to us. My most earnest wish is to see the republican element of popular control pushed to the maximum of its practicable exercise. I shall then believe that our government may be pure and perpetual." The letter is cited in *The Political Thought of American Statesmen*, ed. Morton J. Frisch and Richard G. Stevens (Itasca, Ill.: Peacock, 1973), 35–6.

[35] Whether Stoicism should play a role in a reconstruction of Jefferson's position is a complicated question. I limit myself to pointing out that while in the letter to Short (31

Happiness thus requires "virtue," and the test of virtue is its utility—
that is, its ability to bring about mental tranquillity. Jefferson lists four
Epicurean virtues: prudence (*phronesis*), temperance, fortitude, and justice. In his "Letter to Menoeceus" Epicurus states:

> Of all this [the pursuit of freedom from anxiety, i.e., happiness] the beginning
> and the chief good is prudence. For this reason prudence is more precious than
> philosophy itself. All the other virtues spring from it. It teaches that it is not
> possible to live pleasantly without at the same time living prudently, nobly, and
> justly, nor to live prudently, nobly, and justly without living pleasantly; for the
> virtues have grown up in close union with the pleasant life, and the pleasant life
> cannot be separated from the virtues. (p. 57)

Prudence is not, as with Kant, merely a skill in achieving any end the
agent desires.[36] This Kantian sense inevitably reduces to the computation
of what will lead to one's own happiness, that is, to self-interest narrowly
conceived.[37] Rather, for Epicurus prudence evaluates desires and possible

----

October 1819) Jefferson expresses a desire to translate Epictetus, he does not say, "I am
a Stoic." Jefferson says here of Seneca that he is "a fine moralist, disfiguring his work
at times with some Stoicisms" (p. 1431), and in a letter of 9 January 1816, to Charles
Thomson, Jefferson says that he would like to "subjoin [to his "Philosophy of Jesus"]
a translation of Gosindi's Syntagma of the doctrines of Epicurus, which, notwithstanding
the calumnies of the Stoics and caricatures of Cicero, is the most rational system remaining
of the philosophy of the ancients, as frugal of vicious indulgence, and fruitful of virtue
as the hyperbolical extravagances of his rival sects" (p. 1373). In the letter to John Adams
of 8 April 1816, Jefferson remarks: "And the perfection of the moral character is, not
in a Stoical apathy, so hypocritically vaunted, and so untruly too, because impossible,
but in a just equilibrium of all the passions" (p. 1382). These remarks do not convey a
high praise of the Stoics, though Jefferson clearly had enough interest in them to keep
reading their texts (in his 1 April 1818 letter to Wells and Lilly, Jefferson indicates that
he has been studying Cicero [p. 1413]). However, because the *summum bonum* of the
Stoics—self-sufficiency and tranquillity of mind—resembles that of the Epicureans, and
because the Stoic and Epicurean list of the virtues also are similar, Jefferson's interest in
Stoicism is not surprising.

[36] Kant says that "skill in the choice of means to his own greatest well-being may be called
prudence, in the narrowest sense." *Fundamental Principles of the Metaphysic of Morals,*
trans. T. K. Abbott (Indianapolis: Bobbs-Merrill, 1949), 33. The sentence that follows
reads: "And thus the imperative which refers to the choice of means to one's own
happiness, that is, the precept of prudence, is still always *hypothetical;* the action is not
commanded absolutely, but only as means to another purpose."

[37] See *Fundamental Principles*: "The word *prudence* is taken in two senses: in the one it
may bear the name of knowledge of the world, in the other that of private prudence.
The former is man's ability to influence others so as to use them for his own purposes.
The latter is the sagacity to combine all these purposes for his own lasting benefit. This
latter is properly that to which the value even of the former is reduced" (p. 33, n. 4).
Philosophers since Kant have for the most part reduced prudence to the level of skill, a
connotation that seems prevalent in the popular use of the term, although our everyday
speech has not entirely succumbed, as is suggested by William E. Davie, "Being Prudent
and Acting Prudently," *American Philosophical Quarterly* 10 (1973): 57–60.

courses of action in light of the agent's summum bonum. Presumably the prudent person leads a unified life in which the virtues are harmonized with each other. The basic values or goals are naturally given us by our desires or emotions (among which Jefferson includes moral sense) and clarified by reflection (of the sort exhibited in Epicurus's writings), whereas the means are provided by prudence. As Jefferson insists, "Nature has constituted *utility* to man the standard and best of virtue."[38] Self-interest and virtue coincide.

"Natural justice," in turn, is "a compact resulting from expediency by which men seek to prevent one man from injuring others and to protect him from being injured by them."[39] From this Epicurus infers—presumably against Plato, who is also one of Jefferson's favorite targets—that neither justice nor injustice exists in the abstract, and that neither is good or evil in and of itself. Their goodness and badness result solely from their utility relative to the summum bonum of individual happiness (this is not a utilitarian scheme, of course, as the agent is concerned solely with his own happiness). Epicurus's teaching about justice is thus entirely unmetaphysical. Epicurus claims that an adherent of this teaching will be perfectly just (though the meaning of the term *just* may vary in different societies), for he recognizes that injustice simply is not worth the price in terms of mental tranquillity. It is rational to be just. But what is justice? Again, Epicurus has no "Platonic" answer to this question, nothing to say about it in the abstract. Epicurus's teaching about justice is in one sense strictly conventionalist; the just is whatever a given community takes to be just. Whether an agent will obligate himself to follow the given rules of justice depends on his understanding of whether doing so furthers his tranquillity (the costs of deviating from the given rules will also be a factor).[40] Contracts and promises do not in themselves generate any obligation on the part of the Epicurean.[41]

Given the distinction between true and false happiness and the connection between cognitive and affective states, the Epicurean can claim

---

[38] The quotation is from Jefferson's letter to Thomas Law, 13 June 1814 (p. 1338). For a similar point see his letter to William Short, 4 August 1820 (p. 1437).

[39] *Kuriai Doxai*, XXXI, p. 103.

[40] Consequently, the Epicurean cannot be wholly indifferent to threats of physical punishment. While he does not fear death and claims invulnerability to the acts of others, in general he finds it less disturbing to avoid transgressing the given rules of justice and risking punishment. He seeks to avoid physical pain and to satisfy the "natural and necessary" desires, including the desire for life. (Whether this is really reconcilable with the invulnerability premise may be doubted.)

[41] As noted by Mitsis, *Epicurus' Ethical Theory*, 80.

that he will have no motive to do injustice, understood as the taking of the property (defined broadly) or lives of others. Presumably, a society of Epicureans would be entirely free from internal strife and would not require rules of justice. So justice is useful to the Epicurean as a member of a society of non-Epicureans.[42] It is important to stress for the purposes here that (putting aside any self-imposed obligations resulting from friendships) the Epicurean has no theory as to the intrinsic "moral worth" of others, and this is the point at which Jefferson saw the need of a "supplement." From the Epicurean standpoint, there is nothing wrong in principle with slavery or with owning slaves. In fact, Diogenes Laertius reports that Epicurus owned slaves.[43] It might or it might not be just for an Epicurean to own slaves. It is hard to imagine that an Epicurean would find grounds to wage a battle against the institution of slavery.

More generally, Epicurus would seem to have little interest in statecraft and still less motivation to engage in it, because it would appear to interfere with the pursuit of true happiness. Or at least he would see reason to engage in statecraft only so far as is required by prudence. The goal the individual pursues is fundamentally private, because it amounts to the cultivation of the individual's own soul. Whatever commitments to the promotion of the happiness of others this teaching entails would be based on deliberation about how the friendships or deeds in question lead to one's own tranquillity. What occupation of life best exhibits self-sufficiency? Epicurus does not say; his own life consisted of quiet reflection, writing, and teaching. It seems easiest to imagine a life of this sort unfolding in a context shielded from the bustle of the city.[44] The Epicurean emphasis on the private life weighs heavily against the valuation of honor, not to mention the other goods mentioned earlier. One imagines that an Epicurean might find the life of a gentleman farmer fitting to the pursuit of happiness.

The parallels with Jefferson are striking, although Jefferson's deeds are not in harmony with this teaching. From an Epicurean standpoint the private stands above the public, and indeed in an important sense,

---

[42] See ibid., 89–90, for useful citations and discussion of this point.

[43] Diogenes also notes that Epicurus treated them well and that he manumitted several on his death. *Lives* X.10 (p. 147), X.21 (p. 155), X.118 (p. 165). At X.3 (p. 143) Diogenes reports that Epicurus allowed a slave to be his student.

[44] Jefferson's praise of the farmers is praise, in part, for self-sufficiency as the ground of virtue. The picture of the farmer thus takes "freedom" from the realm of the psychological and shows how it might be exhibited in the world. See Jefferson's letter to John Jay of 23 August 1785 (p. 818).

the public is a hindrance to the private pursuit of happiness.[45] As Jefferson would seem to have agreed, the polis is not the arena that virtuous persons require in order that the excellence of their souls may flourish and the agent's happiness may be found.[46] Politics is drudgery—a view in many ways congenial to Jefferson.[47] Correspondingly, Epicurus was accused of shirking his civic duty.[48] For the unreconstructed Epicurean, the art of statesmanship might at best consist in devising a set of rules that will allow individuals to be as free as possible from the power of others, and so to be free in the deeper sense implicit in happiness. It would therefore be appropriate for the Epicurean to encourage a system in which the liberating pursuit of knowledge—especially science—was protected, and

[45] Jefferson expressed over and over his desire to leave public life and to return to the more satisfying sphere of the private. Compare Lucretius's discussions in book V of *On the Nature of the Universe* about the futility of the search for political power and fame, and praise for the modest tranquillity of the non-ambitious. In these pages he also suggests that the rule of kings is inherently unstable and that the pervasiveness of violence led men to form a social contract or constitution "based on fixed rights and recognized laws."

[46] Consider Jefferson's remark in a letter to David Rittenhouse of 19 July 1778 (p. 763) that "nobody can conceive that nature ever intended to throw away a Newton upon the occupations of a crown." Similarly, see the letter to James Monroe of 20 May 1782: "If we are made in some degree for others, yet in a greater are we made for ourselves. It were contrary to feeling and indeed ridiculous to suppose that a man had less right in himself than one of his neighbors or indeed all of them put together. This would be slavery and not that liberty which the bill of rights has made inviolable and for the preservation of which our government has been charged." To think otherwise is "to annihilate the blessing of existence; to contradict the giver of life who gave it for happiness and not for wretchedness; and certainly to such it were better that they had never been born" (p. 779). Note the emphasis on happiness and the Epicurean sense of privacy associated with the term (the context of the letter, in fact, concerns the extent to which public service, with all the "private misery" and destruction of "mental quiet" it entails, is a duty for the individual). See, too, John P. Diggins, *The Lost Soul of American Politics: Virtue, Self-Interest, and the Foundations of Liberalism* (New York: Basic Books, 1984), 42: "Jefferson stripped the traditional idea of virtue of its essential political content. The arena in which virtue manifests itself is not the public sphere but the private circle of effort and reward . . . the 'moral sense' merely informs man what is in his own interest, not what is in the interest of the 'general good' as defined by classical philosophers of the Old World."

[47] If so, then Jefferson's participation in public life becomes difficult to explain. I return to the problem at the end of this chapter. The demotion of public service for Jefferson and others among the framers is also noted by Diggins, *The Lost Soul of American Politics*, 62–3. James Nichols remarks on the depreciation of political life in Lucretius as well. *Epicurean Political Philosophy* (Ithaca: Cornell University Press, 1972), 145.

[48] See Epictetus's *Discourses* III.vii.19–23. Diogenes Laertius tells us that the Epicurean wise man will not "make elegant speeches. . . . Nor will he take part in public life. . . . Nor will he act the tyrant." *Lives* X.118–19, pp. 165–7. David Konstan notes that "the Epicurean injunction against the political life did not mean that the school was actively hostile to established political authority." *Some Aspects of Epicurean Psychology* (Leiden, Netherlands: Brill, 1973), 52.

so a system in which religious zeal was prevented from arming itself with political power. The corresponding art of statesmanship would require a thorough knowledge of human history and of the various attempts to construct workable regimes. Similarly, history is a subject Jefferson recommends with great enthusiasm.[49]

Jefferson's moral-sense "supplement" to Epicurus (discussed later) prohibited him from taking a straightforward Epicurean stance toward his ownership of slaves or the institution of slavery. There is, then, only partial overlap between Epicurus and Jefferson on the issue of slavery. But he did retain Epicurus's insistence on the centrality of prudence as a virtue, including as a virtue of statecraft. That Jefferson's politics was thoroughly infused with notions of prudence is evident most famously from his use of the term in the Declaration of Independence: "Prudence indeed will dictate that governments long established should not be changed for light and transient causes" (the point is echoed in the letter to Samuel Kercheval of 12 July 1816). But it is also evident from the reasons he gave for his position on the slavery issue. Jefferson approached that issue, among others, with the mind of a practicing statesman informed by a thorough knowledge of Western history, and so by a sense of what is and is not possible to accomplish at any given moment. He assumes that at different historical periods different forms of government are suitable. Writing to Pierre-Samuel Du Pont de Nemours (24 April 1816) Jefferson says,

But when we come to the moral principles on which the government is to be administered, we come to what is proper for all conditions of society. . . . I believe with you that morality, compassion, generosity, are innate elements of the human constitution; that there exists a right independent of force; that a right to property is founded in our natural wants . . . ; that no one has a right to obstruct another . . . ; that justice is the fundamental law of society. . . . These, my friend, are the essentials in which you and I agree; however, in our zeal for their maintenance, we may be perplexed and divaricate, as to the structure of society most likely to secure them. (pp. 1386–7)

Jefferson goes on in this letter to discuss the constitution of Spain, which contains a novel provision; he affirms it on the basis that it is what is needed in Spain at the time. And with reference to de Nemours's

---

[49] Jefferson recommends, as part of his general plan for public education, that at the first level of schooling (that to which the bulk of students will be exposed) students be taught not religion, but history (Query XIV of the *Notes*, pp. 273–4). Jefferson indicates that a knowledge of history is crucial to the people's ability to rule themselves.

proposed constitution for the "Equinoctial republics," Jefferson says: "Like Solon to the Athenians, you have given to your Columbians, not the best possible government, but the best they can bear" (p. 1388). Jefferson thinks that constitution unsuitable for the United States, however (p. 1385). For similar prudential reasons, Jefferson was not averse to letting the king of France retain a limited role in the new republic, and argued that the changes in France should be brought about in a carefully controlled way.[50] He writes to William Short (3 January 1793) that he deplores the killing of the innocent that has occurred in the course of the French Revolution, but adds: "The liberty of the whole earth was depending on the issue of the contest, and was ever such a prize won with so little innocent blood? My own affections have been deeply wounded by some of the martyrs to this cause, but rather than it should have failed, I would have seen half the earth desolated" (p. 1004). In another letter to de Nemours (18 January 1802, p. 1101), Jefferson states: "What is practicable must often controul what is pure theory; and the habits of the governed determine in a great degree what is practicable. Hence the same original principles, modified in practice according to the different habits of different nations, present governments of very different aspects."

Central to the purposes here are Jefferson's remarks in the letter to John Holmes of 22 April 1820. Jefferson says that he wishes Americans to be relieved of the reproach of owning slaves "in any *practicable* way" (p. 1434). When the opportunity for purchasing the Louisiana territories arose, Jefferson acted, even though he did not believe that the action met the standards of the Constitution strictly interpreted, and he wanted a retroactive amendment to the Constitution legitimating the action (see his letter to John C. Breckinridge of 12 August 1803 [pp. 1136–41]). In his letter to Samuel Kercheval of 12 July 1816 Jefferson says, "I am certainly not an advocate for frequent and untried changes in laws and constitutions. I think moderate imperfections had better be borne with; because, when once known, we accommodate ourselves to them, and find practical means of correcting their ill effects. But I know also, that laws and institutions must go hand in hand with the progress of the human mind" (p. 1401). It is true that Jefferson, like others among the Founders, saw the United States as an "experiment," but one with a good probability of succeeding, given the various empirical factors (including

[50] See the letter to Lafayette of 14 February 1815 (pp. 1360–6).

the character of the citizens) involved.[51] Speaking with reference to various measures concerning domestic manufactures, Jefferson says that "the maxim to be applied will depend on the circumstances which shall then exist; for in so complicated a science as political economy, no one axiom can be laid down as wise and expedient for all times and circumstances, and for their contraries" (letter to Benjamin Austin, 9 January 1816). Examples supporting the contention that Jefferson was committed to a non-Kantian, "prudence" view as to how one puts a moral principle into practice, could be multiplied.[52]

Jefferson's Epicurean might thus reason as follows: In an imperfect world over which one person has very limited control, prudence will often require a course of action that is far from ideal but justifiable in that it is the best practicable under the circumstances. The gap between an ideal world (in which tranquillity, natural rights, and prudence are perfectly reconciled) and our real world means not only that all choice-worthy goods cannot be realized simultaneously and that some goods must receive less than their due at least in the short run, but also that improving the situation is a matter not entirely within the individual's control. As a consequence, prudence may well require tolerating great evils such as slavery in the name of justice. The remedy for great evils may require (supposedly) lesser evils such as—to use one of Jefferson's examples—the forcible expatriation of black people from the land of their birth (America), the separation of mothers from their children, and

---

[51] See Jefferson's letter to Madison of 28 February 1796 (p. 1034).

[52] For further references to prudence by Jefferson, see the letter to John Lynch, 21 January 1811, with reference to creating a settlement for blacks on the coast of Africa, in which Jefferson notes that the fact that few blacks would voluntarily consent to the move, or would be capable of self-government, "should not, however, discourage the experiment, nor the early trial of it; and the proposition should be made with all the prudent cautions and attentions requisite to reconcile it to the interests, the safety and the prejudices of all parties" (p. 1241). In the letter to Walker Jones of 2 January 1814, Jefferson says of George Washington: "Perhaps the strongest feature in his character was prudence, never acting until every circumstance, every consideration, was maturely weighed; refraining if he saw a doubt, but, when once decided, going through with his purpose, whatever obstacles opposed. His integrity was most pure, his justice the most inflexible I have ever known, no motives of interest or consanguinity, of friendship or hatred, being able to bias his decision. He was, indeed, in every sense of the words, a wise, a good, and a great man" (pp. 1318–19). In the letter to Lafayette of 14 February 1815 concerning the French Revolution, Jefferson notes that he urged at the time that a compact with the king be made and that several other measures for step by step improvement be taken, for "this was as much as I then thought them [the people] able to bear." But those "unpractised in the knowledge of man" ignored the hazards and did not weigh "the imprudence of giving up the certainty of such a degree of liberty, under a limited monarchy, for the uncertainty of a little more under the form of a republic" (p. 1361).

the like. Prudential action would not have to measure itself solely by the agent's happiness and the duties owed others, but it would have to distinguish between levels of good states of affairs relative to these criteria. Given the vastly complex context of empirical life, the path to the highest good is bound to contain a complex sequence of causes and effects, of means and ends. Thus one might recognize that slavery is evil but that the preservation of the political order sanctioning slavery is just, *if* it is probable that preserving the present order will make the abolition of slavery more likely.[53] That is precisely how Jefferson argued, especially concerning the controversy over whether Missouri should be admitted to the Union as a state sanctioning slavery. Indeed, Jefferson's Epicurean may hold that because the goodness of actions consists in their utility relative to the end of tranquillity and consistent with the strictures of moral sense, strictly speaking it is immoral (not to mention irrational) to act imprudently, with an eye solely to abstract principles of right and wrong.[54]

There also exists broad (though not complete) agreement between Jefferson and Epicurus on the destructive role of organized religion and the positive, liberating role of science. Epicurus clearly thinks that adherence to conventional religion is not a necessary condition of morality. Atheists, too, can be moral, a point made by Jefferson.[55] Moreover,

---

[53] See the statement in the "Opinion on the French Treatise" (1793) that "Questions of natural right are triable by their conformity with the moral sense and reason of man" (p. 428). Although Christian virtue may teach us to treat our fellow humans with benevolence, reason must judge which actions are, in the imperfect world in which we live, most useful in instituting benevolence. As noted earlier, Jefferson would argue that in *not* freeing most of his slaves, he was in effect acting as benevolently as the situation permitted.

[54] As already noted, in the letter to Holmes of 22 April 1820, Jefferson emphasized that the solution to the slavery problem must be *practicable,* and concluded by contrasting the meager benefits of acting according to a moralistic passion inspired by pure theory with those of acting prudently: "I regret that I am now to die in the belief, that the useless sacrifice of themselves by the generation of 1776, to acquire self-government and happiness to their country, is to be thrown away by the unwise and unworthy passions of their sons, and that my only consolation is to be, that I live not to weep over it. If they would but dispassionately weigh the blessings they will throw away, against an abstract principle more likely to be effected by union than by scission, they would pause before they would perpetrate this act of suicide on themselves, and of treason against the hopes of the world" (pp. 1434–5).

[55] For Jefferson's defense of the view that atheists can be moral, see his letter to Thomas Law, 13 June 1814 (p. 1336). Compare the famous passage of *Notes on the State of Virginia,* Query XVII (p. 285): "The legitimate powers of government extend to such acts only as are injurious to others. But it does me no injury for my neighbour to say there are twenty gods, or no god. It neither picks my pocket nor breaks my leg. . . . Reason and free enquiry are the only effectual agents against error. Give a loose to them, they

Epicurus argues that religion as conventionally conceived destroys happiness. The doctrine of immortality, heaven, and hell is not only unprovable scientifically but dangerous psychologically. Recognition, and acceptance, of our finitude frees us from the fear of death (which is really the fear of what may come after death), and is thus the precondition of true morality. Epicurus's love of natural science is sanctioned by the necessity to rid the mind of religion, which in his terms is the equivalent of superstition.[56] Science enlightens and liberates. Like Jefferson, then, Epicurus must take a dim view of the mystifications of religions, as well as of "metaphysical" philosophers (the chief philosophical mystifier being, for Jefferson, Plato). Certainly Jefferson believes that he has found such a religion in the "pure" Christianity stripped of all the "heresies" with which religious sects have infected it.[57]

For Epicurus, science frees the mind of superstition and so makes for tranquillity. One infers that science also destroys rationales by which non-Epicureans control other non-Epicureans. I take it that Jefferson sees science as operating in a similar ground-clearing manner. Shortly before he died, Jefferson wrote to Roger C. Weightman, "All eyes are opened, or opening, to the rights of man. The general spread of the light of science has already laid open to every view the palpable truth, that the mass of mankind has not been born with saddles on their backs, nor a favored few booted and spurred, ready to ride them legitimately, by the grace of

will support the true religion, by bringing every false one to their tribunal, to the test of their investigation." As Eugene R. Sheridan notes in his Introduction to the *Extracts* (pp. 10–11), Jefferson's myriad enemies found this statement thoroughly offensive and used it, especially in the 1800 election, in their efforts to portray Jefferson as an atheist whose election would lead to the destruction (possibly by God) of the Republic. I shall later return to the coherence of Jefferson's stance on the civic religion issue.

[56] *Letter to Pythocles* 116, p. 81; and ibid. 85, p. 57: "We must not suppose that any other object is to be gained from the knowledge of the phenomena or the sky, whether they are dealt with in connexion with other doctrines or independently, than peace of mind and a sure confidence, just as in all other branches of study."

[57] See, for example, his letter of 29 March 1801, to Elbridge Gerry: "The mild and simple principles of the Christian philosophy would produce too much calm, too much regularity of good, to extract from it's disciples a support for a numerous priesthood, were they not to sophisticate it, ramify it, split it into hairs, and twist it's texts till they cover the divine morality of it's author with mysteries, and require a priesthood to explain them. The Quakers seem to have discovered this. They have no priests, therefore no schisms. They judge of the text by the dictates of common sense and common morality" (p. 1090). In a letter to Mrs. Samuel H. Smith, 6 August 1816 (p. 1404), Jefferson wrote, "For it is in our lives, and not from our words, that our religion must be read. By the same test the world must judge me. But this does not satisfy the priesthood. They must have a positive, a declared assent to all their interested absurdities. My opinion is that there would never have been an infidel, if there had never been a priest." Neither Epicurus nor Jefferson was committed to outright atheism, however.

God" (p. 1517). The light of science shows us that nature has furnished each of us with an understanding of our end—happiness—and at least embryonically with the means (the capacity for prudence and virtue). There is no hierarchy sanctioned by supernatural forces according to which some are by nature allotted a lower place in the great chain of being. The liberating role of science consists, we are to infer, in the dissolution of mystifications created by self-interested persons for their own advancement and accepted by non-Epicureans as a result of their lack of scientific knowledge and lack of reflection on the nature of true happiness. Nature and reflection are a sufficient guide to happiness and peace. Once we have removed the wrong sorts of motivations from our own selves, as well as destroyed the rationale for oppressive action, egoism diminishes and benevolence arises.

For Epicurus, science establishes that phenomena previously attributed to immaterial entities such as "gods" or "soul" have perfectly "natural" explanations. Epicurus is a materialist. There is no immaterial soul; the composition and character of the human self are purely material and are to be understood in accordance with the laws of nature.[58] Epicurus does not claim that scientific knowledge is apodictic; he is an empiricist and promises probability only, all knowledge being crucially dependent on the senses. His scientific research suggests the hypothesis that the world is composed entirely of atoms and the void. Human nature is just a particular arrangement of atoms in space. The study of human nature will be part natural science and part anthropology. Clearly the latter will require a knowledge of natural history and of the history of cultures, languages, and the like.[59]

Jefferson shared Epicurus's materialism. In his letter to John Adams of 15 August 1820, Jefferson says that the only existence he admits to is that of matter and the void, and that his only basis for knowledge of the world is sensation. Thought is to be explained in material terms. "When once we quit the basis of sensation, all is in the wind. To talk of *immaterial* existence is to talk of *nothings*. To say that the human soul, angels, god, are immaterial, is to say they are *nothings,* or that there is no god, no angels, no soul. I cannot reason otherwise: but I believe I am supported in my creed of materialism by Locke, Tracy, and Stewart" (pp. 1443–4).[60] Jefferson also asserted "I am a Materialist" in his letter to

[58] *Letter to Herodotus* 63, p. 39.
[59] Consider, for example, the *Letter to Herodotus*, 30, on the origins of language.
[60] Koch has provided a good discussion of Tracy in *The Philosophy of Thomas Jefferson,*

William Short of 13 April 1820.[61] Jefferson claims that the "heresy of immaterialism" is not the true teaching of Christianity at all, and adds that he will "rid himself of the Pyrrhonisms with which an indulgence in speculations hyperphysical and antiphysical so uselessly occupy and disquiet the mind" (p. 1444). The alliance with the "ideologues" is a natural one for an Epicurean.[62] These extraordinary passages suggest that Jefferson saw little tension between his characterizations of himself as both an Epicurean and a Christian.[63] Thus, when he says that Epicurus

chap. 8. Jefferson was extremely enthusiastic about Tracy's thoroughly anti-metaphysical notion of "ideology." Tracy refers to himself as a continuator of the work of Bacon, Condillac, and Locke (Koch, p. 66). The central thrust of his epistemology is positivistic, and explicitly rejects teleology (Koch, p. 67). Tracy classifies ideology as a branch of zoology, and tries to transform the philosophical study of ideas into the scientific observation of the natural history of the mind (Koch, p. 68). The political implications of Tracy's approach directly threatened claims to "self-evident or transcendental knowledge" held by vested interests in church and state (Koch, p. 73). On the issue of materialism, see further Jefferson's letter to John Adams of 8 January 1825 (p. 605 of *The Adams-Jefferson Letters*, ed. Lester J. Cappon [Chapel Hill: University of North Carolina Press, 1988]), where Jefferson discusses with enthusiasm Flourens's work on the nervous system of animals, and particularly the experiments on the connection between the ability to think and the brain. (Flourens removed part of the brain; the animal was partially incapacitated, though still functioning in other respects.) With reference to these experiments, Jefferson wrote, "I wish to see what the spiritualists will say to this. Whether, in this state, the soul remains in the body deprived of it's essence of thought or whether it leaves it as in death, and where it goes?" Jefferson very much liked the "ideologues," and wrote to Canabis (a member of that group) that he enjoyed Canabis's book on "the relations between the physical and moral faculties of man," adding: "That thought may be a faculty of our material organization, has been believed in the gross" (12 July 1803; and Peterson, p. 1135).

[61] *Extracts*, 391.

[62] For further discussion, see Miller, *Jefferson and Nature*, 27–9. For relevant texts and some discussion, see Gilbert Chinard, *Jefferson et les Idéologues* (New York: Arno Press, 1979).

[63] There appear to be two stumbling blocks to this dual membership, namely, the immortality of the soul and the notion of a separate God. First, Jefferson attributes to Jesus the teaching that the soul is immortal in a sense that permits rewards and punishments, that is, retains personal identity (letter to Benjamin Waterhouse, 26 June 1822 [p. 1458]). An Epicurean could admit to impersonal immortality—upon death, one's atoms (there being no immaterial soul), which are indestructible, are simply reabsorbed into the nature and continue on as constituents of other things. One wonders whether Jefferson might have put down the teaching of *personal* immortality as one of the few imperfections in Jesus's teachings, imperfections whose existence Jefferson explains with reference to an extremely delicate political situation in which Jesus found himself (letter to William Short, 4 August 1820 [p. 1437]). In his letter to Short of 13 April 1820, Jefferson indicates that he does not agree with Jesus in every respect: "I am a Materialist; he takes the side of spiritualism; he preaches the efficacy of repentance towards forgiveness of sin, I require a counterpoise of good works to redeem it etc. etc." (*Extracts*, 391–2). Jefferson goes on to suggest that the parts of Jesus's doctrines he rejects, that is, the "false" parts, are due to the excesses of Jesus's biographers. In any event, Jefferson could certainly admit to personal "immortality" in the sense of unending fame. Second, at one point Jefferson affirms (without, as he says, appeal to revelation), a loose form of the argument from

needs "supplementing" with the basic Christian regard for the happiness of others, he presumably means that the true Christian teaching does not supersede or conflict with Epicurus.

"I am a Christian, in the only sense he [Jesus] wished any one to be."

"I am of a sect by myself, as far as I know."[64]

The supplement. Jefferson thought that Epicurus's teaching was incomplete with respect to its understanding of our moral obligations toward others.[65] As we have seen in our discussion of Epicurus's notion of justice, Epicurus's moral views are developed from the standpoint of the agent's regard for his own happiness. Jefferson thought it necessary to supplement Epicurus with an other-regarding moral principle that may be summed up under the rubric of "moral sense." This means that Jefferson will have three fundamental principles in his system: tranquillity, prudence, and moral sense (closely connected to natural rights for him). Of course, more is packed into Jefferson's appropriation of the "supplement"

---

design (letter to John Adams, 11 April 1823): in observing the workings of nature it is impossible "for the human mind not to believe that there is, in all this, design, cause and effect, up to an ultimate cause, a fabricator of all things from matter and motion, their preserver and regulator while permitted to exist in their present forms, and their regenerator into new and other forms." He continues: "Of the nature of this being we know nothing" (p. 1467). An Epicurean could admit that our psyche is shaped in such a way that as we observe the world unscientifically we often cannot help *feeling* or inferring the existence of that Cosmic Designer (so long as we admit to knowing nothing about the Designer), for the feeling or inference is merely a comment on the structure of our minds. It would seem that an Epicurean could not admit to a separate (let alone immaterial) God, unless in the sense of a separate natural force somehow responsible for the ordering of the universe and its continued existence (a doctrine of "energy," for example). Such a separate natural force might well be referred to as "nature's God" (a phrase understood as synonymous with "nature"), or, somewhat loosely, as "the Creator."

[64] Jefferson to Benjamin Rush, 21 April 1803 (p. 1122); and Jefferson to Ezra S. Ely, 25 June 1819, in *Extracts*, 387.

[65] In the letter to Rush (21 April 1803), Jefferson makes a similar point about the limitations of the ancient philosophers (Pythagoras, Socrates, Epicurus, Cicero, Epictetus, Seneca, and Antonius are named) as he does in the 1819 letter to Short: "Their precepts related chiefly to ourselves, and the government of those passions which would disturb our tranquillity of mind. In this branch of philosophy they were really great. In developing our duties to others, they were short and defective. They embraced, indeed, the circles of kindred and friends, and inculcated patriotism, or the love of our country in the aggregate, as a primary obligation: toward our neighbors and countrymen they taught justice, but scarcely viewed them as within the circle of benevolence. Still less have they inculcated peace, charity and love to our fellow men, or embraced with benevolence the whole family of mankind" (p. 1124).

than a moral-sense version of Epicurean friendship. The supplement also provides him with the doctrine of natural rights.

Clearly, orthodox Christianity and Epicureanism do not mesh well. Jefferson overcomes the difficulty by stripping Christianity of everything in it that implies revelation or a violation of observable natural law (violations such as miracles, the virgin birth, and the divinity of Christ), implies that religion contains truth inaccessible to a sensible and reasonable person, or implies that the divine is a "mystery" (including, for Jefferson, the doctrine of the Trinity).[66] Jefferson was convinced that most of the teachings conventionally associated with Christianity were distortions invented by the clerics partly out of desire to increase their own standing (they being the only ones who understand the Word) and partly out of flights of imagination.[67] What remains is, according to Jefferson, the moral essence of Christianity, namely, the praiseworthy virtues of benevolence, sympathy, humility, and charity and the condemnation of worldly ambition, honor, and pursuit of wealth.[68] The "true Christian" teaching, in effect, amounts to Jefferson's moral-sense doc-

[66] See Jefferson's letter to Peter Carr, 10 August 1787 (p. 902), for the view that every assertion of religion must be examined by reason and must accord with the laws of nature. The recommended reading list Jefferson attached to the letter includes under "Morality" the Socratic dialogues and books by Cicero, Kames, Helvetius, Locke, and Lucretius. Under the "Religion" category are books by Locke, Middleton, Bolingbroke, Hume, Voltaire, and Beattie. This is scarcely a list intended to lead the reader to any of the established doctrines of Christianity. For Jefferson's "syllabus" of the true teachings of Jesus see his letter to Rush of 21 April 1803 (pp. 1122 ff.). Similarly, see Jefferson's letter to Short of 4 August 1820, on "the course of nature" as the criterion of truth. That Jefferson felt comfortable with the Gospels only after they had been significantly edited should come as no surprise in light of his attempted synthesis.

[67] See Jefferson's letter to Joseph Priestley, 9 April 1803 (p. 1121); Jefferson's letter of 12 October 1813, to John Adams (pp. 1300 ff.), which links Platonism to false Christianity. In his letter to Mrs. Samuel Smith, 6 August 1816 (p. 1404), Jefferson writes: "I have ever thought religion a concern purely between our God and our consciences, for which we were accountable to him, and not to the priests"; in his letter to Adams of 11 April 1823, he writes: "The truth is that the greatest enemies to the doctrines of Jesus are those calling themselves the expositors of them.... But we may hope that the dawn of reason and freedom of thought in these United States will do away with all this artificial scaffolding, and restore to us the primitive and genuine doctrines of this the most venerated reformer of human errors" (p. 1469). See also the letters referred to in the preceding note. In the letter to Ely of 25 June 1819, Jefferson asserts again that efforts to define the nature of God—metaphysics, in short—are the causes of schisms between believers (in *Extracts*, 387).

[68] Jefferson liked the Unitarians. See his letter to Benjamin Waterhouse of 26 June 1822: "I rejoice that in this blessed country of free inquiry and belief... the genuine doctrine of one only God is reviving, and I trust that there is not a *young man* now living in the United States who will not die an Unitarian" (p. 1459); "the doctrines of Jesus are simple, and tend all to the happiness of man" (p. 1458; I note that Jefferson calls this letter a "sermon"). See also Jefferson's letter to Thomas Cooper, 2 November 1822 (p. 1464).

trine, and that doctrine could be made compatible with a range of views from atheism to agnosticism to Deism. Jefferson presents the moral sense doctrine as antithetical to the thesis that the basis of morality is self-love or egoism, a thesis that he thinks is empirically false in any event. As a matter of fact human beings do act, though not always, out of genuine regard for others.[69] But how does the moral-sense doctrine supplement Epicurus's view of the self? How does "nature" understood along Epicurean lines offer a basis for normative propositions about "natural rights" (a phrase Epicurus would undoubtedly have found very strange)? To answer these questions, Jefferson's "supplement" must be examined.

These questions bring us to a central puzzle in Jefferson's moral theory, namely, the connection between nature and morality. How can a theory of natural rights, which presumably has normative content, be generated from a materialistic theory that simply describes what *is* rather than what *ought* to be the case? How can an empiricist have a theory of "nature" that is arrived at noninductively and is at the same time an empirical generalization?[70] If the phrase *laws of nature* is used without equivocation in both a scientific and an ethical context, how can laws of nature serve as a moral standard for action? Can a theory of rights be generated from observation of "human nature" conceived of non-teleologically, without reference to metaphysics, revealed religion, or "soul"? To understand Jefferson's notion of prudence, we have to understand his natural rights theory, and so the sense in which he assumes that natural rights do and do not obligate moral choice in the real world. And to do this we must look at Jefferson's comments about the relationship among natural rights, natural law, and moral sense.

As already mentioned, Jefferson does not think it possible to provide a metaphysical interpretation of "nature" or "rights"; his Epicureanism and demythologized Christianity rule out a theological interpretation (in his mind closely connected to the metaphysical, especially Platonic); and he nowhere ventures the sort of teleological strategy proposed by Aris-

---

[69] See the letter to Thomas Law of 13 June 1814 (pp. 1336–7).
[70] I wish to avoid beginning with Charles Miller's statement that "in religion and ethics, in aesthetics, politics, and economics, in all the regions of value, Jefferson was ignorant of any problems associated with deriving a statement of value from a statement about being. Rather, and without thinking about it, he adhered to a variety of ethical naturalism, according to which nature gives direct and certain guidance on matters of human choice" (*Jefferson and Nature*, 91). My procedure is to assume that Jefferson understood the direction in which he wished to go (that of a naturalized ethics) and the direction he wished to avoid (that is, a theological ethics)—and then to see how far he succeeds.

totle. Let me try to clarify the sources of Jefferson's notion of nature, and with it his notions of natural law and natural rights, with an examination of several important texts. I begin with the sense of nature implied by the natural-law formula.

Jefferson sees in nature a basis for both science and morality, and the phrase *law of nature* is used in both contexts, never with any indication that substantially different senses of *law* or *nature* might be at work. Speaking with reference to the Bible, Jefferson holds that claims about occurrences that violate the laws of nature (or the "course of nature") should be dismissed. The laws of nature do not permit us knowledge of the spirit-world.[71] The laws of nature can characterize geographical configurations—which themselves may play an important part in political developments—as well as the connection between the habits humans or animals form and the characters they end up with.[72] We observe that human beings can live in societies that are closer to nature's laws or further removed from them, that is, in less and more civilized nations.[73] The laws of nature are to be distinguished from the conventional laws, the latter being, from the moral standpoint, subservient to the former.[74]

Jefferson frequently mentions the right to voluntary expatriation or emigration. This "right which nature has given to all men" seems to stem

---

[71] See the letters to Peter Carr, 10 August 1787 (p. 902); to William Short, 4 August 1820 (p. 1435); and to Isaac Story, 5 December 1801 (*Extracts*, 325).

[72] See Jefferson's letter to Short, 13 April 1820 (*Extracts*, 393), and to John Langdon, 5 March 1810 (p. 1221). On the issue of geography, consider Jefferson's remark in the letter to John C. Breckinridge, 12 August 1803, to the effect that the United States will exercise "the natural right we have always insisted on with Spain, to wit, that of a nation holding the upper part of streams, having a right of innocent passage thro' them to the ocean" (p. 1137). Presumably that natural right is ultimately to be derived from the right of self-preservation possessed by the individuals constituting the society (the society having been formed for the purpose of securing their mutual self-preservation). In the "Draft of the Kentucky Resolutions," we read that "every State has a natural right in cases not within the compact... to nullify of their own authority all assumptions of power by others within their limits" (p. 453); and in Jefferson's "Response to the Citizens of Albemarle" (12 February 1790), we are told that "the will of the majority, the Natural law of every society, is the only sure guardian of the rights of man" (p. 491).

[73] Letter to William Ludlow, 6 September 1824 (p. 1496): "These [savages] he would observe in the earliest stage of association living under no law but that of nature, subscribing and covering themselves with the flesh and skins of wild beasts."

[74] Letter to John B. Colvin, 20 September 1810 (p. 1231): "A strict observance of the written laws is doubtless *one* of the high duties of a good citizen, but it is not *the highest*. The laws of necessity, of self-preservation, of saving our country, when in danger, are of higher observation. To lose our country by a scrupulous adherence to written law, would be to lose the law itself, with life, liberty, property and all those who are enjoying them with us; thus absurdly sacrificing the end to the means." On the relationship between the law of self-preservation and conventional law, see also the beginning of the "Opinion on the French Treaties."

in the way just noted from the individual's rights to self-preservation, liberty, and pursuit of happiness, as well as from the fact that one's place of birth is not chosen by the individual and so entails no obligation on one to remain there.[75] This reasoning suggests that there is a hierarchy of individual rights. Indeed, the natural rights of individuals seem to be the basis of the conventional rights of societies. The rights of societies to control their own lands and institutions, to have representative government, and so forth seem to derive from the rights of individuals to "life, liberty, and the pursuit of happiness."[76]

Thus nature or, as Jefferson occasionally says, nature's law is the source of rights (by means of the moral sense). One of the most interesting examples of his (attempted) derivation of rights concerns his thesis, repeated several times throughout his life, that "the earth belongs to the living." That notion is closely tied to Jefferson's intense dislike of national debt, banking interests, and commerce, as well as to his praise of the self-sufficient life of the farmer. His view that each generation is entitled to write its own constitutions and laws follows from the thesis in question. In a letter to John W. Eppes of 24 June 1813 Jefferson writes: "But what limits, it will be asked, does this prescribe to their powers? What is to hinder them from creating a perpetual debt? The laws of nature, I answer. The earth belongs to the living, not to the dead. The will and power of man expire with his life, by nature's law" (p. 1280). Further on in the same letter, Jefferson adds, in reply to the question of whether one generation is bound by the debts or laws of the preceding generation: "Every one will say no; that the soil is the gift of God to the living, as much as it had been to the deceased generation; and that the laws of nature impose

[75] See the *Summary View*, 105–6. A similar sentiment is repeated in the "Bill Declaring Who Shall Be Deemed Citizens of this Commonwealth": "And in order to preserve to the citizens of this commonwealth, that natural right, which all men have of relinquishing the country, in which birth, or other accident may have thrown them, and, seeking subsistance and happiness wheresoever they may be able, or may hope to find them," no citizen shall be prevented from emigrating (p. 374).

[76] In the *Summary View* Jefferson says: "From the nature of things, every society must at all times possess within itself the sovereign powers of legislation. The feelings of human nature revolt against the supposition of a state so situated as that it may not in any emergency provide against dangers which perhaps threaten immediate ruin" (p. 118). And "From the nature and purpose of civil institutions, all the lands within the limits which any particular society has circumscribed around itself are assumed by that society, and subject to their allotment only" (p. 119). At the start of the "Opinion on the French Treaties" we read that "between society and society the same moral duties exist as did between the individuals composing them while in an unassociated state...Compacts then between nation and nation are obligatory on them by the same moral law which obliges individuals to observe their compacts" (p. 423).

no obligation on them to pay this debt. And although, like some other natural rights, this has not yet entered into any declaration of rights, it is no less a law, and ought to be acted on by honest governments" (p. 1282).

Writing on the same subject to James Madison some twenty-four years earlier (6 September 1789), Jefferson claims that it is "self evident" that the earth belongs in usufruct to the living. He allows, of course, that governments may, for this or that reason of utility, establish laws regulating the transfer of property; but these laws do not have the force of "natural right" because they are not based on self-evident natural law (p. 959).[77] Between society and society, and generation and generation, "there is no municipal obligation, no umpire but the law of nature" (p. 962). Natural rights, then, can belong only to the living.[78] In another

[77] So far as I am aware, this passage contains the only use of the term *self-evident* in Jefferson's writings, other than in the Declaration of Independence. For Madison's sober and pragmatic reply of 4 February 1790 to Jefferson's letter, see *The Mind of the Founder: Sources of the Political Thought of James Madison,* ed. Marvin Meyers (Hanover, N.H.: University Press of New England, 1981), 176–9. For example, Madison remarks: "If the earth be the gift of *nature* to the living, their title can extend to the earth in its *natural* state only. The *improvements* made by the dead form a debt against the living, who take the benefit of them. This debt cannot be otherwise discharged than by a proportionate obedience to the will of the Authors of the improvements." The distinction between natural and conventional law is nicely illustrated in Jefferson's discussion of patents on ideas; see his letter to Isaac McPherson of 13 August 1813. Jefferson points out that although it is a "moot question whether the origin of any kind of property is derived from nature at all," it is agreed that "no individual has, of natural right, a separate property in an acre of land, for instance." So far as natural right goes, however, property in a particular piece of land exists only while it is occupied. Conventional law may, for reasons of utility, confer stable ownership. Nature has made ideas nearly as public as land. While an idea is kept secret in a man's head, he may be said to have exclusive right to it. Once it is divulged, it belongs to all. For nature has "benevolently" constructed things in such a way that ideas can be easily shared without diminishing them, like the air in which we breathe and move. "Inventions then cannot, in nature, be a subject of property. Society may give an exclusive right to the profits arising from them, as an encouragement to men to pursue ideas which may produce utility" (pp. 1291–2). Jefferson's arguments for the "More General Diffusion of Knowledge"—that is, for publicly supported education—are of necessity utilitarian. Public education, which is most useful in helping people to exercise their natural rights freely, is also a way of destroying the "pseudo-aristocracy" and substituting the natural aristocracy of "the veritable aristoi" (see Jefferson's letter to John Adams of 28 October 1813). Jefferson denies that talents, which are unevenly distributed by nature among mankind, provide their possessors with a natural right to rule others.

[78] In his letter to P. S. Du Pont de Nemours of 24 April 1816, Jefferson says that "a right to property is founded in our natural wants, in the means with which we are endowed to satisfy these wants, and the right to what we acquire by those means without violating the similar rights of other sensible beings" (p. 1387). It is worth mentioning that Jefferson was much worried about the excessive accumulation of property and saw no natural right to infinite accumulation of property. The regulation of the accumulation of specific property was for him a utilitarian issue. Hence he denies that the abolition of entail—a

letter on the subject, to Samuel Kercheval of 12 July 1816, Jefferson answers: "The dead have no rights. They are nothing; and nothing cannot own something. Where there is no substance, there can be no accident" (p. 1402). And again, in a letter to John Cartwright of 5 June 1824, we learn that conventional laws cannot be unchangeable because "the Creator has made the earth for the living, not the dead. Rights and powers can only belong to persons, not to things, not to mere matter, unendowed with will. The dead are not even things" (p. 1493). The key terms here are *will* and *powers*. Death is as natural as life, and the condition of the deceased is as natural as that of the living. Why, then, grant natural rights only to those living, those who have "will" and "powers"?

The sentence following that just quoted from Jefferson's letter to Cartwright reads: "The particles of matter which composed their bodies, make part now of the bodies of other animals, vegetables, or minerals, of a thousand forms. To what then are attached the rights and powers they held while in the form of men?" Jefferson is excluding, in full accordance with his Epicureanism and demystified Christianity, one possible answer to his rhetorical question, namely, an immortal soul. Soul could be considered to be the "substance" of human nature that lives on after the dissolution of the body. In any event, for Jefferson, life is the presupposition of liberty, that is, the exercise of the will, and liberty would seem to be the presupposition of the pursuit of happiness. Even within the list of natural rights in the Declaration of Independence, then, there seems to be a logical order grounded in an understanding of the sense in which nature is the foundation for rights.[79]

Presumably, in the absence of living possession of will, inner liberty, conscience, ideas, and powers, natural rights are lost because the living can no longer see the dead as subjects of choice, sociality, and so forth; the dead cannot be "sympathized" with in the relevant sense.[80]

---

development that he did so much to effect—deprived anyone of their natural rights (*Autobiography*, 32).

[79] In the *Summary View* Jefferson says: "That these are our grievances which we have thus laid before his majesty, with that freedom of language and sentiment which becomes a free people claiming their rights, as derived from the laws of nature, and not as the gift of their chief magistrate" (pp. 120–1). Several sentences further Jefferson refers to "the rights of human nature" (a phrase used on p. 116 as well, with reference to the injustice of slavery); thus the "laws of nature" here must mean "the laws of human nature."

[80] There may be a connection between Jefferson's argument (as I have just reconstructed it) and the fact that Jefferson leaves open the list of natural rights. The attribution of rights would seem to depend, for him, on our ability to sympathize and on the capability of the entity sympathized with to be the subject-of-a-life. And this scheme might lead to the discovery of new rights. Our determination of the entity's ethical status might

Jefferson's argument sustaining the inference from nature to morality is painfully sketchy here, and his position has correspondingly puzzled many commentators. Thus far the inference seems quite unpersuasive, but Jefferson has another card to play. The connection between nature and rights seems effected through two observations about the constitution of human nature. Nature has "created" us so that we possess a "moral sense," a faculty or characteristic that Jefferson sometimes refers to as "conscience" or simply as moral "feelings." "Common sense" seems to function for Jefferson as a nearly analogous term. The moral sense provides all human beings, or nearly all, with the perception of the difference between right and wrong.[81] For Jefferson, it is the possession of the moral sense that makes an animal human. That a particular person proceeds as though lacking any moral sense does not, Jefferson thinks, disprove the rule.[82] He takes it as an empirical truth that moral sense is the species

itself depend heavily on our ability to sympathize, so that, for example, a particularly vivid imagination might enable people to sympathize with and see as ethical subjects certain higher primates, who would then be thought of as having rights. Further, the specific rights to be attributed to accepted rights-bearers might itself be a function of the ability to sympathize; well-attuned sympathy might lead one, say, to attribute to a person in dire need of health care a right to that health care.

[81] In a letter to Peter Carr of 10 August 1787, Jefferson remarks: "The moral sense, or conscience, is as much a part of man as his leg or arm. It is given to all human beings in a stronger or weaker degree, as force of members is given them in a greater or less degree" (p. 901). Toward the start of the "Opinion on the French Treaties" we read that "For the reality of these principles [concerning the relationship between positive and natural law] I appeal to the true foundations of evidence, the head and heart of every rational and honest man. It is there Nature has written her moral laws, and where every man may read them for himself" (p. 423). And further on in the same treatise: "Questions of natural right are triable by their conformity with the moral sense and reason of man. Those who write treatises of natural law, can only declare what their own moral sense and reason dictate in the several cases they state. Such of them as happen to have feelings and a reason coincident with those of the wise and honest part of mankind, are respected and quoted as witnesses of what is morally right or wrong in particular cases. Grotius, Puffendorf, Wolf, and Vattel are of this number. But where they differ, and they often differ, we must appeal to our own feelings and reason to decide between them" (p. 428). In Query XI of the *Notes* Jefferson says, with reference to the Indians who live without government and written law: "Their only controuls are their manners, and that moral sense of right and wrong, which, like the sense of tasting and feeling, in every man makes a part of his nature" (p. 220). In Query XIII of the *Notes* (p. 251) we read that "it is the natural law of every assembly of men, whose numbers are not fixed by any other law" to determine what will count as a quorum. Occasionally Jefferson refers to "natural reason" (e.g., Query VIII of the *Notes* [p. 211]); the phrase seems equivalent to "moral sense."

[82] I refer to his letter to Thomas Law of 13 June 1814. Jefferson agrees that the creator did not plant the "moral instinct" in *every* man, for "there is no rule without exceptions." Although some people are born without sight, hearing, or hands, they nevertheless "enter into the general definition of man. The want or imperfection of the moral sense in some men ... is no proof that it is a general characteristic of the species" (pp. 1337–8). Jefferson

difference in our case. As far as I can tell, this doctrine of moral sense and natural law remains constant throughout all of Jefferson's writings from the earliest to the latest.[83] Our possession of moral sense is a result of the operation of laws of nature—the laws according to which we are constituted; according to which humans have evolved; or, in another formulation, the laws according to which we are "created."[84] Given my earlier observations about Jefferson's view of religion and of his materialism, it seems that he uses "nature," "nature's God," and "the creator" interchangeably.[85] Jefferson can and does characterize human nature in

did seem to think that there has been an improvement of humankind through history, culminating in the American experiment; but this seems not to be an improvement in the moral sense as such. In the letter to P. S. Du Pont de Nemours, 24 April 1816, Jefferson remarks: "Although I do not, with some enthusiasts, believe that the human condition will ever advance to such a state of perfection as that there shall no longer be pain or vice in the world, yet I believe it susceptible of much improvement, and most of all, in matters of government and religion; and that the diffusion of knowledge among the people is to be the instrument by which it is to be effected" (pp. 1387–8). Also, in the "Report of the Commissioners for the University of Virginia," 4 August 1818, we read: "Education generates habits of application, of order, and the love of virtue; and controls, by the force of habit, any innate obliquities in our moral organization. We should be far, too, from the discouraging persuasion that man is fixed, by the law of his nature, at a given point; that his improvement is a chimera, and the hope delusive of rendering ourselves wiser, happier or better than our forefathers were" (p. 461).

[83] As is also suggested by May, *The Enlightenment in America*, 296.

[84] In his letter to Benjamin Austin of 9 January 1816, Jefferson refers to the actions of England and France as "setting at defiance all those moral laws established by the Author of nature between nation and nation, as between man and man" (p. 1371). And at the start of the "Opinion on the French Treaties" we read: "The first of these only [the Moral law of our nature], concerns this question, that is to say the Moral law to which Man has been subjected by his creator, and of which his feelings, or Conscience as it is sometimes called, are the evidence with which his creator has furnished him" (p. 423). Thus the "laws of nature and of nature's God" phrase in the first paragraph (in Jefferson's reproduction of the document in his *Autobiography*) of the Declaration of Independence should be read (on substantive as well as grammatical grounds) as "the laws of nature and [the laws] of nature's God." The "nature's God" phrase used here is possessive or subjective genitive and seems to mean "the God belonging to nature." (This first paragraph contains the only use of the word *God* in the Declaration.) In the second paragraph of the Declaration we read once of all men being "created" equal, and once of a "creator" who endows men with their inalienable rights. The creator in question is nature. The Declaration closes with a loose reference to "divine providence." Of course, it is possible that Jefferson and his colleagues thought that the readers of the Declaration would interpret "creator" in a more conventional sense, and even that Jefferson wished readers to do so, without himself subscribing to that conventional sense. But the "nature's God" phrase seems striking enough to arrest the moderately attentive reader (although it was used, by Alexander Pope, for example, before Jefferson). From a more conventional Christian standpoint one would presumably speak of "God's nature" or "the nature created by God" rather than "nature's God."

[85] The point is controversial, of course. Morton White argues that Jefferson's "moral sense" doctrine of natural law and natural right is suggested in good part by Burlamaqui's more conventional theses that "these duties [toward God, oneself, and other humans] are inferable by reflection on the *nature* and *states of man,* which indicate the intentions of

religious vocabulary, but on the reading I am proposing he is not compelled to.[86]

Further, Jefferson assumes that we are social or other-directed animals
who by nature care about others and their evaluations. In some passages
this characteristic of human nature seems to be assimilated to the moral
sense.[87] I take it that this caring will require sympathy (or better, em-

God with respect to man. . . . Moreover, having proposed these as ends for man, God
wills that man *should* labor for his own preservation and perfection in order to obtain
all the happiness of which he is capable according to his nature and estate." *The Philosophy of the American Revolution* (New York: Oxford University Press, 1981), 162.
White notes that Burlamaqui took God to be powerful, good, and wise; such an assumption seems hard to make in Jefferson's case, particularly if God is taken to be an
individualized and active agent (an assumption that is difficult to reconcile with Jefferson's
materialism). As White restates the Burlamaquian/Jeffersonian position: "We examine
the essence God has given man and the states in to which he has put man, infer his
intentions with respect to man, and then infer what God was led to decree, using along
the way the premise that God, by his nature, can do nothing but good and nothing in
vain" (p. 180). I am suggesting, by contrast, that Jefferson moves directly from moral
sense to natural law and natural right, in a way closer to Pufendorf's strategy of arguing
for natural law from human sociability (a strategy criticized by Burlamaqui; see White,
p. 183), and probably still closer to Hutcheson. (For further discussion of Burlamaqui,
see Chapter 1 in this volume.)

[86] Jefferson closes the *Summary View* by remarking: "The God who gave us life gave us
liberty at the same time; the hand of force may destroy, but cannot disjoin them." The
rights to freedom of thought and religion stem from the same basic source—nature (given
my reading of what Jefferson means by "God"). In the "Bill for Establishing Religious
Freedom" the argument for freedom of religion depends in part on the premise that
"Almighty God hath created the mind free" (p. 346). The freedom of the mind is a
characteristic of human nature and is valued by moral sense; therefore people have a
right to freedom of thought and belief. To interfere with that freedom is, as the Bill
makes clear, to interfere with other natural rights as well (e.g., Jefferson refers to "those
priviledges and advantages to which, in common with his fellow citizens, he [the indi-
vidual] has a natural right" [p. 347]. In Query XVII of the *Notes* Jefferson states: "The
error seems not sufficiently eradicated, that the operations of the mind, as well as the
acts of the body, are subject to the coercion of the laws. But our rulers can have authority
over such natural rights only as we have submitted to them. The rights of conscience
were never submitted, we could not submit. We are answerable for them to our God"
(p. 285). Jefferson did not make the correct workings of the moral sense depend on the
existence of an immortal soul or a separate Creator and did not include such teachings
in his educational schemes. His philosophy of history does seem connected, rather loosely
to be sure, with the notion of an ordering principle, which along Epicurean lines could
be interpreted in accordance with a belief (perhaps not scientifically warranted so much
as psychologically ineluctable) that progress is generally taking place and seems guided.
This sense of history is important to his doctrine of moral action, discussed later.

[87] See the letter to Thomas Law, 13 June 1814 (p. 1337): "Nature hath implanted in our
breasts a love of others, a sense of duty to them, a moral instinct, in short, which prompts
us irresistibly to feel and to succor their distresses. . . . The Creator would indeed have
been a bungling artist, had he intended man for a social animal, without planting in him
social dispositions." Those few persons deficient in moral sense must be educated to see
its truth, or presented with a system of punishments and rewards that will appeal to
their self-interest narrowly understood until they acquire the habit of acting in accordance
with moral sense.

pathy), and so an exercise of the imagination. I conjecture that if Jefferson were to spell out the steps leading to his normative conclusion about the existence of natural rights that we are obligated to respect, it would be through a Hutchesonian strategy—one in keeping with his obvious predilection for a naturalized ethics, his Epicurean suspicion of any theological arguments for ethical norms, his materialism and interest in seeing psychology founded on biology, his view that basic ethical principles are taught to the heart rather than the head (i.e., by moral sense), and his notion that we are naturally social.[88] The line of reasoning would seem to go as follows: It is through our ability to empathize with others—to see them as being human like us; as possessing moral sense; as being capable of choice, ethical understanding, and responsibility—that we draw the inference that others are to be treated in a certain way. This is not so much an attempt to infer a normative thesis directly from an observation about certain traits as an observation that a properly constituted, impartial, and enlightened community would accord recognition to certain traits. We Jeffersonians—enlightened by science, freed from the fictive hierarchies proposed by the superstitious or by metaphysical Platonizers—find it self-evident that persons (defined as possessing, at a minimum, moral sense) have rights, given the way nature has constituted us. Obligation is derived from moral sensibility enlightened in the appropriate way.[89]

[88] The influence of Hutcheson on Jefferson may well be indirect; so far as I know, Jefferson never quoted from Hutcheson. Jefferson possessed Hutcheson's *Short Introduction to Moral Philosophy in Three Books,* his *Synopsis Metaphysicae,* and the *Inquiry into Our Original Ideas of Beauty and Virtue* (Sowerby, *Catalogue of the Library of Thomas Jefferson,* 2: 1, 12, 13). Some discussion of the relationship between Jefferson and Hutcheson may be found in Garry Wills's *Inventing America: Jefferson's Declaration of Independence* (New York: Doubleday, 1978). I note that Hutcheson offered a strong critique of Aristotle's justification of "natural slavery" and of the institution of slavery. See Wylie Sypher's "Hutcheson and the 'Classical' Theory of Slavery," *Journal of Negro History* 24 (1939): 263–80. On that point see also Davis, *The Problem of Slavery in Western Culture,* 375–8. Aristotle's argument was widely cited in support not just of the enslavement of blacks but of Indians as well. See Lewis Hanke, *Aristotle and the American Indians: A Study in Race Prejudice in the Modern World* (London: Hollis & Carter, 1959).

[89] I note two striking omissions in Jefferson's account so understood. First, a notion of the common good does not seem to play an important role in the argument (in contrast with Hutcheson, but in keeping with Jefferson's Epicureanism). The pursuit of happiness figures prominently in his writings, but seems not to do the work that we would expect from a notion of the common good. Second, Jefferson does not avail himself of his Epicureanism by making pleasure and pain the basis for rights. That strategy, for which there is Hutchesonian precedent, would be proto-utilitarian in character and would mesh nicely with the emphasis on prudence. It would also provide Jefferson with a reason for keeping open the list of rights and of the species of rights bearers. Hutcheson was an

An argument along these lines does not provide the sort of justification a Kantian would require.[90] The argument gives an important place to the imagination in ethical reflection (as similar arguments in Hume and Smith do). The empirical determination that another person possesses moral sense would seem to require an imaginative grasp (what Smith calls "sympathy") of the other's world by which the other's capacity for moral feeling, sense of responsibility, and the like are understood. Jefferson does not explore the consequences of this point, but the path is certainly open to an important role, in Jefferson's supplement to Epicurus, for an aesthetics based in the imagination.[91]

In any event, because Jefferson takes it to be empirically true that blacks possess moral sense, he infers that they possess natural rights, regardless of any other respects in which blacks are (supposedly) inferior.[92] Before we see how Jefferson thought the principle of moral equality was best applied in practice, let us examine further his attempted synthesis of Epicurus and moral-sense Christianity.

Jefferson's synthesis. An effort to integrate the "moral sense" view with the Epicurean might proceed in the way Jefferson indirectly suggests in

"animal rights" exponent, for example. For some discussion of Hutcheson (and some of his predecessors) on animal rights, see *Thomas Reid: Practical Ethics*, ed. Knud Haakonssen (Princeton, N.J.: Princeton University Press, 1990), 378, n.3.

[90] For a discussion of the problem of equality and of the problem of drawing normative conclusions from factual statements about human beings, see Bernard Williams, "The Idea of Equality," in *Problems of the Self: Philosophical Papers 1956–1972* (Cambridge: Cambridge University Press, 1973): 230–49.

[91] See Jefferson's letter to Robert Skipwith, 3 August 1771 (pp. 741–2), in which Jefferson commends literature as a vehicle for exciting the "sympathic emotion of virtue" in the reader.

[92] In Query XIV of the *Notes on the State of Virginia*, Jefferson says that blacks may be inferior to whites in both body and mind but indicates there (and more unambiguously in other writings) that they possess the essential trait of "moral sense" (p. 269). For example, in his letter to Henri Gregoire of 25 February 1809, Jefferson says: "Be assured that no person living wishes more sincerely than I do, to see a complete refutation of the doubts I have myself entertained and expressed on the grade of understanding alloted to them by nature, and to find that in this respect they are on a par with ourselves." After noting that his observations were expressed only with hesitation given their limited empirical basis, he adds: "whatever be their degree of talent it is no measure of their rights. Because Sir Isaac Newton was superior to others in understanding, he was not therefore lord of the person or property of others" (p. 1202). But with respect to the physical beauty of blacks, Jefferson says without ambiguity that whites are superior, a judgment that seems associated with his fear of miscegenation and his correlative insistence on expatriation. On the questions of physical beauty and of the mixing of the races, see Query XIV of the *Notes* (pp. 264–5); the letter to Monroe of 24 November 1801 (p. 1097); and the letter to Edward Coles of 25 August 1814 (p. 1345).

the letter to Thomas Law of 13 June 1814, namely, through refinement of the "broader sense" of egoism that Jefferson there attributes to Helvétius (p. 1337). Correspondingly, prudence will not amount simply to the agent's pursuit of happiness at the expense of any consideration of others. The performance of moral acts with regard to others gives us pleasure in a psychological, not a pecuniary or bodily, sense. Jefferson says that "this is indeed true," and goes on to assert that we derive pleasure from others because of the natural moral sense implanted in us. Human beings by nature possess moral sense and so sociability, and their happiness depends on acting morally. That is, one could attempt to reconcile Epicurus and "true Christianity" by defining happiness or tranquillity so that it includes the pleasure of performing selfless action, given that our "sociability" is part of our natural makeup.[93] Epicurus's stress on friendship is expanded and diluted so as to encompass the "family of man," a broadened care for others that is somehow a component of the agent's summum bonum. The sentiments of benevolence and the like are, Jefferson wants to insist, in our self-interest—they are part of our pursuit of happiness. To repeat, duty and self-interest coincide when rightly understood.[94] Jefferson's synthesis as I have construed it continues to

---

[93] Presumably this would require abandonment of Epicurus's association of happiness with invulnerability, because the happiness of others cannot be entirely within our control. Furthermore, it would seem difficult for Epicurus to defend a more than instrumental view of friendship (as some of my language above suggests). That is, it is difficult to see how Epicurus could make room for the type of friendship Aristotle describes as being a joint pursuit of a shared good; even though Epicurus does tell us that "all friendship is desirable in itself, though it starts from the need of help" (*Sent. Vat.* XXIII, p. 109). (For discussion of Epicurus's difficulties in accounting for friendship, see once again Mitsis's *Epicurus' Ethical Theory,* chap. 3 and pp. 117–28.) The tension between happiness and friendship is already evident in Epicurus. Jefferson's supplement to Epicurus adds further strain to the position. In the end the strain overwhelms Jefferson's attempted synthesis.

[94] See Jefferson's letter to Caesar A. Rodney, 10 February 1810, in which he says, with reference to America's struggle with Britain: "All those calculations which, at any other period, would have been deemed honorable, of the existence of a moral sense in man, individually or associated, of the connection which the laws of nature have established between his duties and his interests, of a regard for honest fame and the esteem of our fellow men, have been a matter of reproach on us, as evidences of imbecility. As if it could be a folly for an honest man to suppose that others could be honest also, when it is their interest to be so" (p. 1217). The three dependent clauses beginning with "of" should be understood as parts of an extended parallel construction. See also the letter to Jean Baptiste Say of 1 February 1804: "Morality listens to this [the view that in America laborers should be concentrated in the agricultural sector], and so invariably do the laws of nature create our duties and interests, that when they seem to be at variance, we ought to suspect some fallacy in our reasonings" (p. 1144). In the letter to George Logan of 12 November 1816 (*Extracts,* 381) Jefferson refers to "the truth of the maxim that virtue and interest are inseparable."

privilege the Epicurean side in at least this sense, namely, that the happiness of the individual remains the summum bonum.

As already intimated, Jefferson's version of moral sense and natural rights does not require sacrificing his materialism, antidualism, suspicion of metaphysics, critique of orthodox religion, or affirmation of science. The supplement preserves Jefferson's effort, so characteristic of the Enlightenment, to redeem nature; for nature is so structured as to provide us with all we need to function as social and happy beings. Deviations from moral sense are taken not as an indication of the presence in the human soul of an intrinsic or natural tendency to evil, but as an indication of ignorance. The supplement does expand the role that imagination and sentiment will play. It both retains and expands the complexity of the role of prudence with respect to deliberation about how an individual or community may best act on the imperatives of moral sense, not just within the framework of natural rights (understood as side constraints) but also in the implementation of these rights. Prudence would remain central to an individual's understanding of the status that moral sense and the imperatives it illuminates have in the well-ordered life.

Another element present in Jefferson's synthesis, namely, his views about historical progress, should be made more explicit before we continue. Jefferson seems to have thought that the capacity for the right exercise of moral sense had progressed; the increasingly humane treatment of prisoners of war was an example.[95] Jefferson never quite abandoned his optimism that Americans eventually had to see the light with respect to slavery. The Founders had made known the principles of justice; the next generation would, if properly led, implement them with respect to slavery. Jefferson also suggested that great evils do not go unpunished forever. He seemed to arrive at this point in part via inductive

---

[95] See Koch, *The Philosophy of Thomas Jefferson*, 18. In the letter to Samuel Kercheval of 12 July 1816, Jefferson discusses the "progress of the human mind" and the necessity that laws change to suit it (p. 1401). See also the letter to John Brazier, 24 August 1819: "To the moralist they [the Greek and Latin languages] are valuable, because they furnish ethical writings highly and justly esteemed: although in my opinion, the moderns are far advanced beyond them in this line of science" (p. 1424); and the letter to P. S. Du Pont de Nemours of 24 April 1816 (pp. 1387–8). Consider also Jefferson's letter to John Adams of 8 April 1816: "I think with you that it is a good world on the whole, that it has been framed on a principle of benevolence, and more pleasure than pain dealt out to us. There are indeed . . . gloomy and hypocondriac minds, inhabitants of diseased bodies, disgusted with the present, and despairing of the future; always counting that the worst will happen, because it may happen. To these I say How much pain have cost us the evils which have never happened? My temperament is sanguine. I steer my bark with Hope in the head, leaving Fear astern" (pp. 1381–2).

generalization from the past and in part through hope: "Had Bonaparte reflected that such is the moral construction of the world, that no national crime passes unpunished in the long run, he would not now be in the cage of St. Helena."[96] Jefferson articulates a similar point in the famous passage in Query XVIII of the *Notes on the State of Virginia*.[97] But he does not present us with anything like a philosophy of history. Presumably, the moral-sense doctrine, combined with belief in the progress of science and the disutility of wrongdoing, are elements of his vaguely articulated view.

Nevertheless, his view about the course of history is important to a doctrine of prudential action in the political sphere. Because political prudence as Jefferson understands it is deliberation about contingent events, he needs a view about contingency that tells him not simply whether patterns of events exist through time, but whether improvement in the patterns can be expected as a result of intelligent choice. The reasonableness of Jeffersonian prudence here depends on two assumptions: (1) that causes are connected to effects in some knowable way and (2) that the vast network of interconnected events is so structured that it is rational to expect that prudent action may lead to desirable results. If one held that the world is in the process of decaying very rapidly, spinning off into chaos, it would make little sense to argue that moral

[96] Letter to François De Marbois, 14 June 1817 (p. 1410). See also the conclusion of the "Answers and Observations for Démeunier's Article on the United States in the *Encyclopédie Methodique*, 1786." Jefferson there remarks, in reference to the extirpation of slavery: "But we must await with patience the workings of an overruling providence, and hope that that is preparing the deliverance of these, our suffering brethren" (p. 592).

[97] "And can the liberties of a nation be thought secure when we have removed their only firm basis, a conviction in the minds of the people that these liberties are of the gift of God? That they are not to be violated but with his wrath? Indeed I tremble for my country when I reflect that God is just: that his justice cannot sleep for ever: that considering numbers, nature and natural means only, a revolution of the wheel of fortune, an exchange of situation, is among possible events: that it may become probable by supernatural interference! The Almighty has no attribute which can take side with us in such a contest—But it is impossible to be temperate and to pursue this subject through the various considerations of policy, of morals, of history natural and civil. We must be contented to hope they will force their way into every one's mind. I think a change already perceptible, since the origin of the present revolution. The spirit of the master is abating, that of the slave rising from the dust, his condition mollifying, the way I hope preparing, under the auspices of heaven, for a total emancipation, and that this is disposed, in the order of events, to be with the consent of the masters, rather than by their extirpation" (p. 289). What are we to make of Jefferson's reference to "supernatural interference," given his materialism and his implicit denial of a separate and purposive God? I prefer the line of interpretation set out earlier, though ultimately, as I suggest later, Jefferson is not consistent on the question of whether citizens' belief in such a God matters (whatever the truth of the question is).

principles and practice can be brought together through prudential action. If we ask ourselves whether action X was a rational choice even though, as we now know in retrospect, it failed to bring about the desired end, we could answer affirmatively by saying that it was the best choice given the circumstances and information available at the time. But that affirmative answer loses a great deal of force unless we also assume that it is rational to expect that things can get better. Prudence would then become a merely defensive, literally conservative, strategy—a means for fending off for as long as possible the inevitable decay.

Jefferson's assumptions about history seem closely tied to his prudence-centered view of moral and political action, especially with respect to the slavery issue. Assuming that things would get better helped make it possible for him to postpone taking any radical steps to free his slaves immediately, to campaign vigorously for universal emancipation, and so forth. Of course, Jefferson did not assume that things would get better without the conscious efforts of Americans; he was also clear that in the absence of such conscious efforts, things would get worse. He was convinced, for example, that the slaves would get their freedom one way or the other, and not in the distant future either. The historic improvement in the situation takes place in the realm of the human—the science of morals has progressed, the moral sense is more finely honed, human rights are much better understood than at any previous time, and so forth. These examples provide the main evidence that moral progress (at least as reflected in the political arena) is possible. Progress itself is defined by reference to the Epicurean doctrines, supplemented by the teachings of moral sense and sociability.[98]

By way of transition to the question of the coherence of this synthesis in light of the slavery issue, let me turn to Jefferson's differences with early abolitionists. This will help me flesh out Jefferson's view of the virtues of self.

Moral action and virtues of self: how to do the right thing. The preceding section indicates that Jefferson's notion of Christianity does not require that what is right in theory be acted on without regard to the complexities

---

[98] Correspondingly, history would be an important subject for the Epicurean to study. Lucretius does present us with a historical narrative of the development of civilization, though presumably not with the intent of providing evidence of "progress" to be used in support of prudent statesmanship. On the complex relation between Lucretius and Epicurus, see Diskin Clay's *Lucretius and Epicurus* (Ithaca: Cornell University Press, 1983).

of the empirical situation. Of course, it is also true that much of Christian teaching as traditionally understood did not require the abandonment of prudential morality, and so of slavery.[99] However, a number of the abolitionist movements active during Jefferson's life were sustained by an interpretation of Christianity that did not leave much room for a prudential view of moral action, particularly the Quakers and the various evangelical or revivalist sects that grew out of the Great Awakening. In the course of his summary of John Wesley's *Thoughts upon Slavery*, David B. Davis notes that Wesley thought that "no argument of utility could justify debasing a rational creature to the level of a brute." And several lines further: "But Wesley's most compelling thoughts had nothing to do with reason or nature. His ultimate message was that the sins of this world would soon be judged."[100] Davis goes on to show that the revivalist movement as a whole (including the Methodists) had as one of its chief targets "the trend toward natural religion." "They were revolting not only against moral decay and the laxness of a worldly and self-contented clergy, but also against the entire drift of British thought from Locke and Tillotson to Shaftesbury, Bolingbroke, and Hutcheson." And "If the philosophy of benevolence was associated with an expanded view of man's capacity for virtue, the very core of evangelicalism was a renewed conviction of original sin."[101] Sin came to be interpreted as self-

---

[99] For an outstanding treatment of the connection between Christianity and the slavery issue, see Davis, *The Problem of Slavery in Western Culture*. It should be noted that some of the proponents of the "positive good" theory of slavery came close to arguing that in principle Christianity sanctions the enslavement of blacks, for, they argued, although God created all men equal, He also made it clear that the descendants of Ham were to be slaves; further, the Bible does not provide a clear-cut condemnation of all slavery for all time. As John Miller notes (*Wolf by the Ears*, 53), "Jefferson's scientific views were entirely compatible with a separate creation of the various races of man." This could not have been so if he had accepted the theory of monogenesis affirmed in the Bible, that is, if he had accepted the Bible as truth. His "purified" Christianity thus left the equality of human beings resting on a quasi-empirical basis.

[100] Davis, *Slavery in Western Culture*, 383.

[101] Davis, *Slavery in Western Culture*, 383–4. Davis adds that the revivalists "interpreted man's predicament within the old framework of sin and grace, and consequently spoke a language which was meaningful to those who had never heard of Locke or David Hume." For a discussion of similar themes in connection with the Transcendentalists, see Stanley M. Elkins, *Slavery: A Problem in American Institutional and Intellectual Life*, 3d. ed. (Chicago: University of Chicago Press, 1976), 157–93. As Davis puts it in "The Emergence of Immediatism in British and American Antislavery Thought," in *From Homicide to Slavery: Studies in American Culture* (New York: Oxford University Press, 1986): "The policy of gradualism was related to certain eighteenth-century assumptions about historical progress, the nature of man, and the principles of social change; but we have also noted a subjective, moral aspect to antislavery thought that was often revealed as an immediate consciousness of guilt and a fear of divine punish-

centeredness and greed, both being at the heart of slaveowning; salvation required profound inner changes and (at a minimum) immediate cessation of the sinful activity.[102] The human being was seen as the scene of inner turmoil and moral struggle between good and evil—a scene an Epicurean would surely have taken as a sign of deep conceptual confusion. To make a complex story short, acting in accordance with the true principle of salvation meant maintaining a personal opposition to slavery, an opposition exhibited without prevarication in practice.[103] From that standpoint there can be no prudential justification for possession of slaves, let alone for involvement with the slave trade. Jefferson certainly took a dim view of the revivalists, and his comments about the Quakers are mixed.[104]

ment" (p. 246). And "immediatism was something more than a shift in strategy. It represented a shift in total outlook from a detached, rationalistic perspective on human history and progress to a personal commitment to make no compromise with sin. It marked a liberation for the reformer from the ideology of gradualism, from a toleration of evil within the social order, and from a deference to institutions that blocked the way to personal salvation" (p. 255).

[102] The term *immediate* was used in this connection by abolitionists including Anthony Benezet. See Davis, "The Emergence of Immediatism," 240. As Davis notes in these pages, *immediate* might mean different things, from declaration of absolute personal opposition to slavery to the conviction that "slavery should be abolished absolutely and without compromise, though not necessarily without honest preparation" (p. 239). The latter construal begins to introduce a notion of prudence. I am more interested for present purposes in the former construal, but acknowledge hidden complexities. For one could argue that immediate action is sometimes prudent, and that it would belong to prudence to determine whether an immediatist, or gradualist, approach is warranted. The point here is that the choice would not be made, for Jefferson, by reference to the sorts of virtues of self, or theological beliefs, that hold for his antagonists in this debate.

[103] Davis, *Slavery in Western Culture*, 386, n.48: "One may note that the nineteenth-century abolitionist, A. A. Phelps, said that carrying out the decision for immediate emancipation was like acquiring sanctification after conversion." See Davis's discussion in these pages for the various qualifications of the view that evangelical religion in practice encouraged the antislavery movement in a way that required immediate emancipation of the slaves. For the connection between the antislavery movement and the Quakers, see Davis, *Slavery in the Age of the Revolution*, chap. 5, for example: "It would be difficult to exaggerate the central role Quakers played in initiating and sustaining the first antislavery movements" (p. 215). In the twenty years or so preceding the American Revolution, the Quakers took steps to free themselves from any involvement with slavery, as part of their policy of self-purification. Of course they also took numerous steps to extirpate the slave trade and the institution of slavery itself, though they did not always call for the immediate emancipation of all slaves. In the same book Davis also notes that "Quaker lobbyists were apparently responsible for the temporary and unpopular Virginia law of 1782 allowing private manumissions." By 1788 Virginia laws had barred any members of emancipation societies from being jurors in freedom suits and "had virtually prevented humanitarians from advising or aiding blacks in any legal action for freedom" (p. 197).

[104] Jefferson criticizes the Quakers in the following vein: "You observe very truly, that both the late and present administration conducted the government on principles *professed* by the Friends. Our efforts to preserve peace, our measures as to the Indians, as to slavery, as to religious freedom, were all in accordance with their *professions*" (letter

The point I wish to make here is that, in adopting a completely demystified version of Christianity, Jefferson rejected a theory of the virtues of self that might have required him to free his own slaves forthwith (and quite possibly to educate and otherwise prepare them for their freedom), and to speak out much more vigorously and frequently against the institution.[105] Because he did not accept the doctrines of revelation, sin, salvation, guilt, and the Last Judgment—none of which would make any sense from his Epicurean starting point—Jefferson did not feel compelled to abandon his doctrine of prudential action. Jefferson was in a position to own slaves all his adult life and still think of himself as having lived as purely moral a life as is practicable.

Jefferson's deep antipathy toward what he calls "fanaticism" is an objection to, among other things, the notion that the moral thing to do in an imperfect world is to act according to pure moral principle without regard to the this-worldly consequences of one's actions.[106] The "good

to Samuel Kercheval, 19 January 1810 [p. 1214]). For Jefferson's criticisms of revivalist religion, see his letter to Thomas Cooper of 2 November 1822 (pp. 1463 ff.). Of course, the historical issues are complicated here, for revivalist movements may have contributed directly to the notion of "individual freedom" so important to the founding. William G. McLoughlin remarks in his "The Role of Religion in the Revolution" that "the Great Awakening, sometimes seen as a religious reaction to Arminianism and sometimes as the upthrust of the Enlightenment in the colonies, was really the beginning of America's identity as a nation—the starting point of the Revolution" (in *Essays on the American Revolution,* eds. Stephen G. Kurtz and James H. Hutson [Chapel Hill: University of North Carolina Press, 1973], 198). McLoughlin goes on to argue that as a result of the Awakening "every individual was assumed to be in direct relationship to God and responsible only to him, and therefore their collective will was God's will. Or so, in its extreme and logical form, this theory evolved by the time of Thomas Paine's *Common Sense* and came into practice by the age of Jackson" (p. 200).

[105] At least given Jefferson's various assumptions about the side constraints I discuss later. Jefferson could, again, find it prudent to act immediately on a given issue; the point is that if he were to do so with respect to slavery, it would be for very different reasons than those animating the immediatist camp.

[106] Jefferson intensely disliked Calvinism, whose "demoralizing dogmas" include, according to Jefferson, the thesis that "faith is every thing, and the more incomprehensible the proposition, the more merit in its faith," as well as the view that "reason in religion is of unlawful use" (letter to Benjamin Waterhouse, 26 June 1822 [pp. 1458–9]). In his letter to Thomas B. Parker of 15 May 1819, Jefferson remarks on the "reveries, not to say insanities of Calvin and Hopkins; yet the latter, I believe, is the proper term. Mr. Locke defines a madman to be one who has a kink in his head on some particular subject, which neither reason nor fact can untangle.... This was the real condition of Calvin and Hopkins, on whom reasoning was wasted.... Were I to be the founder of a new sect, I would call them Apriarians, and, after the example of the bees advise them to extract the honey of every sect. My fundamental principle would be the reverse of Calvin's that we are to be saved by our good works which are within our power, and not by our faith which is not within our power" (*Extracts,* 385–6). For Jefferson, Calvinism stands for intolerance—the very opposite of reasonableness—that is, for the pure and self-righteous adherence to principle as opposed to the recognition of the

will" is not always good without qualification. Jefferson credits Jesus with understanding, in opposition to the Jews, "the social utilities which constitute the essence of virtue," and so with allowing a place for reason—prudence—in morality. Jefferson's criticisms of Judaism amount at least in part to a criticism of what we would think of as the Kantian view concerning the irrelevance of consequences to moral evaluation in morality. Jefferson's criticisms of Plato can be viewed as including a similar element. Jefferson had read the *Republic* and disliked it very much—and, at least on the surface, the radical political recommendations of the *Republic* dispense with every prudential maxim of politics.[107] Jefferson thought that the "science of morals" was one area in which the moderns had progressed significantly beyond the ancients. Because, as discussed earlier, Jefferson also tells us that the basics of morality are provided by Epicurus and Jesus, the progress in question must have taken place in our understanding of the means for implementing morals. Jefferson no doubt has in mind the political machinery set out in the Constitution, as well as the principles described by the Declaration of Independence. His belief that a carefully thought out "science" of morals is necessary, as well as carefully crafted institutions to embody these morals, commits him to the sorts of views about (1) the fallibility of knowledge of empirical states of affairs and of the "nature" of things, about (2) the accumulation of insights through the historical process of trial and error, and about

imperfection of both self and world as well as the difficulties of implementing morality in such a world: "Such is the malignity of religious antipathies that, altho' the laws will no longer permit them, with Calvin, to burn those who are not exactly of their Creed, they raise the Hue and cry of Heresy against them, place them under the ban of public opinion, and shut them out from all the kind affections of society." Letter to George Thacher, 26 January 1824 (*Extracts*, 415). In his letter to John Adams of 22 August 1813, Jefferson says: "But I have read his [J. Priestley's] Corruptions of Christianity, and Early opinions of Jesus, over and over again; and I rest on them, and on Middleton's writings, especially his letter from Rome, and to Waterland, as the basis of my own faith" (*Extracts*, 348). In *Thomas Jefferson and his Library* (Hamden, Conn.: Archon Books, 1977), Charles B. Sanford remarks that "it turns out that Jefferson had more sermons in the religious section of his library than any other type of work.... The authors whose sermons Jefferson collected were mostly Anglican clergymen but there were also Presbyterian, Congregational, Catholic, Unitarian, Dutch Protestant, Episcopalian, and Quaker clergy." Among these were sermons on the issue of slavery (pp. 136–7).

[107] On Judaism, see Jefferson's letter to William Short, 4 August 1820 (pp. 1435–8); letter to Benjamin Rush, 21 April 1803 (p. 1124). Jefferson links Calvin to Plato in his letter to John Davis, 18 January 1824 (*Extracts*, 413). In numerous letters Jefferson links Platonism, Judaism, and the corruptions of the true teachings of Jesus. For Jefferson's comments on the *Republic*, see his letter to John Adams, 5 July 1814 (pp. 1341–2).

(3) the importance of prudence and moderation in the political and personal spheres mentioned earlier in connection with the *Federalist*'s closing citation of Hume. And these views of knowledge, history, and the virtues are being rejected by Jefferson's antagonists here.[108]

PRUDENCE AND SLAVERY

A number of Jefferson's writings announce the doctrine of natural rights and then tell us that particular deeds—say, the actions of the British or the institution of slavery—violate the doctrine. But rarely does Jefferson specify the kind of obligation to act or not to act that his theory entails or the boundary conditions (beyond natural rights) under which prudence would have to operate. Having examined the general features of Jefferson's position, I wish now to focus on the issue of slavery in order to show by steps how Jefferson's general position collapses. I begin by trying to spell out further the boundary conditions of Jefferson's moral theory. Then I look specifically at Jefferson's stance on slavery, first with respect to his ownership of slaves and then with respect to the institution of slavery.

Prudence and further Jeffersonian boundary conditions. It seems apparent that Jefferson accepts the "liberal" distinction between politics and morality. As is particularly evident in his discussions of freedom of religion, the theory of rights imposes restraints on the actions that individuals (whether singly or as incorporated into a government) can take against others. The politically relevant content of the "right to the free exercise of religion," for example, amounts to a prohibition against any interference with an individual's exercise, or lack of exercise, of religion. His theory of rights is, to use imprecise language, a theory of negative duties that isolates those aspects of a person's activities with which others are obliged not to interfere physically or directly. Morality is the province of positive moral duty (articulated by the virtues of the "true Christian-

---

[108] Davis, "The Emergence of Immediatism," writes that immediatism "was part of a larger reaction against a type of mind that tended to think of history in terms of linear time and logical categories, and that emphasized the importance of self-interest, expediency, moderation, and planning in accordance with economic and social laws. Immediatism shared with the romantic frame of mind a hostility to all dualisms of thought and feeling, an allegiance to both emotional sympathy and abstract principle, an assumption that mind can rise above self-interest, and a belief that ideas, when held with sufficient intensity, can be transformed into irresistible moral action" (p. 257).

ity"). The state is empowered to prevent people from physically or directly interfering with each other's rights. The state is not empowered to coerce morality (positive duties), for example, by forcing people to be benevolent; morality is a matter of choice. The distinction between one's external relations (physical or social) and one's person (or self), between the public and the private, is part of this distinction between duties.[109]

Slavery clearly violates the natural rights of the enslaved, as Jefferson tells us repeatedly.[110] Jefferson believes that when rights are not reciprocally recognized, might has replaced rights as the basis of justice. The oppressed then have a natural right to dissolve the political bonds that tie them to their masters, although, as Jefferson cautions in the Declaration of Independence, "Prudence indeed will dictate that governments long established should not be changed for light and transient causes."[111]

---

[109] See Jefferson's letter to P. S. Du Pont de Nemours of 24 April 1816 (pp. 1386–7). In Query XVII of the Notes Jefferson says, "The legitimate powers of government extend to such acts only as are injurious to others" (p. 285). Jefferson goes on to make it clear that an opinion about religious matters, no matter how odious to others, does not qualify as an injury to them. For it does not interfere with their right to formulate their own opinions.

[110] In the Summary View (1774) Jefferson says that the "infamous practice" of slavery deeply wounds "the rights of human nature" (p. 116). In his draft of the Declaration Jefferson wrote that the King "has waged cruel war against human nature itself, violating it's most sacred rights of life and liberty in the persons of a distant people who never offended him, captivating and carrying them into slavery in another hemisphere, or to incur miserable death in their transportation thither" (Autobiography, 22). In Query XVIII of the Notes we read: "The whole commerce between master and slave is a perpetual exercise of the most boisterous passions, the most unremitting despotism on the one part, and degrading submissions on the other.... The man must be a prodigy who can retain his manners and morals undepraved by such circumstances. And with what execration should the statesman be loaded, who permitting one half the citizens thus to trample on the rights of the other" (p. 288). In his sixth annual message to Congress Jefferson characterizes the slave trade as a "violation of human rights" (p. 528). In his letter to Edward Coles of 25 August 1814, Jefferson says that it is a "moral reproach" to the whites that the blacks have pleaded so long in vain (p. 1344). See the third of the "Answers and Observations for Démeunier's Article on the United States in the Encyclopédie Methodique, 1786," for further comments on the question.

[111] Cf. Query XVII of the Notes where we read of "religious slavery" (p. 285). With explicit reference to blacks, Jefferson writes in Query XIV of the Notes: "That disposition [in the slaves] to theft with which they have been branded, must be ascribed to their situation, and not to any depravity of the moral sense. The man, in whose favour no laws of property exist, probably feels himself less bound to respect those made in favour of others. When arguing for ourselves, we lay it down as a fundamental, that laws, to be just, must give a reciprocation of right: that, without this, they are mere arbitrary rules of conduct, founded in force, and not in conscience: and it is a problem which I give to the master to solve, whether the religious precepts against the violation of property were not framed for him as well as his slave? And whether the slave may not as justifiably take a little from one, who has taken all from him, as he may slay one who would slay him?" (p. 269).

We must conclude that, from the Jeffersonian standpoint, the slaves had a perfect right to revolt against their masters (to the best of my knowledge, Jefferson never implies anything different). It also follows that people have an obligation not to hold others in bondage, and that in principle the government has the authority to compel people to honor this obligation (what level of government—state or federal—ought to exert this authority is a separate matter). It does not necessarily follow that the government can coerce an individual to compel other individuals not to own slaves. However, it would be morally incumbent—insofar as the moral sense requires it in a way consistent with tranquillity—for an individual to try to abolish the institution of slavery.

At the beginning of this chapter I distinguished between two levels of the problem of Jefferson and slavery: the one concerning Jefferson's ownership of slaves, the second concerning his views on and actions about the institution of slavery. Given what I have said in the preceding paragraphs, Jefferson's stance toward the institution of slavery appears to be defensible only if it satisfies the following conditions: One must do nothing to extend or enlarge the institution (for then one is actively violating the rights of others), and one is morally obligated to do everything possible to help to abolish the institution. A wide spectrum of actions are, in principle, acceptable in satisfying the "do everything possible" demand; and the Jeffersonian actor will take a variety of goods as contributing to his or her tranquillity and as demanding their due. It is the task of prudence and moral sense to determine what is due others. Nevertheless, whereas Jefferson might not think that simply living in a nation in which slaveholding exists constitutes the doing of injustice on the part of nonslaveholding citizens, he would presumably hold the actor morally responsible for taking steps to help extirpate the institution.[112]

With respect to owning slaves, however, the situation differs, for a slave's master is violating the natural rights of the slaves. Here, too, Jefferson will retain a "do everything possible" demand, but presumably with greater insistence on the cessation of unjust action on the part of slaveholders. But Jefferson simply is not clear—and here the strains of his synthesis begin to show clearly—about just how much weight that insistence should have relative to the claims of other goods in a prudent life. In any event, he seems to make it clear that cessation of the injustice

---

[112] Jefferson's synthesis would require an account of this demand for responsibility in terms of the agent's summum bonum (tranquillity) and the moral sense. It will rapidly become evident that under the pressure of the case, however, his synthesis comes apart.

is not a good that outweighs all others; indeed, he seems to think its realization is desirable only if it is adequately coordinated with other ends, including the subsequent welfare of the aggrieved parties and the welfare of the nation as a whole. Jefferson seems to believe that there are conditions under which it is moral to violate someone else's natural rights. This is essentially how Jefferson describes his stance with respect to his own slaves. He grants (or it can be inferred from his views) that his slaves have a right to revolt against him; he grants that in principle he has an obligation to free them, for slavery is unjust; but he also believes that he has a moral obligation not to free them except under certain conditions. Until those conditions are satisfied, prudence requires various schemes to bring the hoped-for day closer. For example, at one point he argues that, in renting them out so as to generate income (and thus putting them at risk of being abused), he is acting in a way that is ultimately the most useful to himself and his slaves, and so acting as benevolently as possible.[113]

Of course, this position seems dangerously close to an easy rationalization for paternalism. Jefferson's position can be filled out a bit more in light of his "Opinion on the French Treaties."[114] Jefferson begins his argument by addressing himself to the "Moral law of our nature," which he claims is exactly the same between individuals in the state of nature as between societies. As individuals are not released from these "duties"

---

[113] See Jefferson's letter to N. Lewis, 29 July 1787 (in *Papers of Thomas Jefferson*, ed. Julian Boyd [Princeton, N.J.: Princeton University Press, 1950-], 21 vols.): "Nor would I willingly sell the slaves as long as there remains any prospect of paying my debts with their labour. In this I am governed solely by views to their happiness which will render it worth their while to use extraordinary cautions for some time to enable me to put them ultimately on an easier footing, which I will do the moment they have paid the debts due from the estate, two thirds of which have been contracted by purchasing them. I am therefore strengthened in the idea of renting out my whole estate" (11:640). And several lines further (p. 641): "I feel all the weight of the objection that we cannot guard the negroes perfectly against ill usage. But in a question between hiring and selling them (one of which is necessary) the hiring will be temporary only, and will end in their happiness; whereas if we sell them, they will be subject to equal ill usage, without a prospect of change. It is for their good therefore ultimately, and it appears to promise a relief to me within such a term as I would be willing to wait for." Consider the remark in the letter to Coles of 25 August 1814: "My opinion has ever been that, until more can be done for them, we should endeavor, with those whom fortune has thrown on our hands, to feed and clothe them well, protect them from all ill usage, require such reasonable labor only as is performed voluntarily by freemen, and be led by no repugnancies to abdicate them, and our duties to them" (p. 1346).

[114] I recognize that the "Opinion" was not written with the use to which I shall put it in mind. My purpose in calling on that document is to try to construct as solid a position as Jefferson's various writings permit before trying to show how that position fails.

when they form a society, neither are societies when they form treaties or alliances. Thus "compacts then between nation and nation are obligatory on them by the same moral law which obliges individuals to observe their compacts" (p. 423). Jefferson goes on to specify two conditions under which contracts (between societies or between individuals) can legitimately be broken by one party, namely, when the performance becomes impossible and when it becomes self-destructive (for in the latter case the law of self-preservation overrules the laws of obligation to others). The basis for all this is to be found, as always, in the moral sense that nature has implanted in us (p. 423). And the moral sense also informs us that moral obligations cannot be annulled simply because they have become useless or disagreeable. Danger can serve as a reason only if the danger is imminent and great (p. 424). The mere possibility of danger is insufficient to dissolve a party from its contract. "Obligation is not suspended, till the danger is become real, and the moment of it so imminent, that we can no longer avoid decision without forever losing the opportunity to do it" (pp. 424–5). At that point, performance of a moral obligation would contradict the law of self-preservation. As to how to determine precisely when either of these escape clauses should operate, Jefferson reminds us: "Questions of natural right are triable by their conformity with the moral sense & reason of man." Ultimately we cannot simply rely on the learned books of law; we know when to affirm their conclusions (or which to affirm when they disagree with one another) by appealing "to our own feelings and reason" (p. 428).

Prudence and slavery at home. Let us attempt to apply these principles to Jefferson's position on the slavery issue. Although the specific context of the "Opinion" concerns the question of the nonperformance of a contract—the breaking of a promise, in short—the doctrine of obligation there is explicitly said to have validity in the state of nature, that is, not to be simply a creature of convention. Because Jefferson believed that all humans possess by nature the same rights and because society is understood as a contract, a just political contract between individuals requires, on the political level, reciprocity or equality of treatment.[115] Conse-

---

[115] In the "Opinion" Jefferson calls upon Pufendorf, among others. In book 3 of *De Jure Naturae et Gentium* (1688), trans. C. H. Oldfather and W. A. Oldfather (Oxford: Clarendon Press, 1934), chap. 2 ("All Men are Accounted as Naturally Equal"), Pufendorf argues, in a way that must remind us of Jefferson, that superiority of intelligence or capability does not confer the right to rule the less fortunate, nor differences of

quently, a situation in which some members of a society have been enslaved can be understood as the nonperformance by their masters of the just contract that is implied by the fundamental principles of right. This nonperformance of a just contract—the enslaving of others—would be permissible only if obeying the contract (liberating the slaves and treating them as one's political equals) was either impossible or dangerous (in a sense that threatened one's self-preservation directly). With this in mind, let us now turn first to Jefferson's ownership of slaves and then to his stance relative to the institution of slavery.

Jefferson's ownership of slaves. Jefferson appeared to think that emancipation of his slaves was dangerous for both parties, as well as impossible. In his letter to Jefferson of 31 July 1814, Edward Coles both implores Jefferson to speak out forcefully against slavery and mentions that as a result of his own opposition to slavery he intends to leave the state and free his slaves.[116] Coles, in fact, did so; after many difficulties

property the right of resisting rule. Pufendorf then adds: "And this equality we can call an *equality of right,* which has its origin in the fact that an obligation to cultivate a social life is equally binding upon all men, since it is an integral part of human nature as such" (p. 333). Pufendorf goes to some lengths to show that "the old idea handed down from the Greeks, to the effect that certain men are slaves by nature, merits complete disapproval" (p. 340); of course he has Aristotle in particular in mind. Consider, too, Pufendorf's statement in vol. 2 of *De Officio Hominis et Civis Juxta Legem Naturalem,* trans. F. G. Moore (New York: Oxford University Press, 1927), chap. 3 ("On Natural Law"): "Thus then man is indeed an animal most bent upon self-preservation, helpless in himself, unable to save himself without the aid of his fellows.... Whence it follows that, in order to be safe, he must be sociable, that is, must be united with men like himself, and so conduct himself toward them that they may have no good cause to injure him, but rather may be ready to maintain and promote his interests. The laws then of this sociability, or those which teach how a man should conduct himself, to become a good member of human society, are called natural laws. So much settled, it is clear that the fundamental natural law is this: that every man must cherish and maintain sociability, so far as in him lies.... He who wishes an end, wishes also the means.... The remaining precepts are mere corollaries, so to speak, under this general law, and the natural light given to mankind declares that they are evident" (p. 19).

[116] For Coles's letter, as well as his reply of 26 September 1814 to Jefferson's reply of 25 August 1814, see *Sketch of Edward Coles,* by E. B. Washburne (Chicago: Jansen, McClurg, and Co., 1882), 21–31. In the 31 July 1814 letter to Jefferson, Coles says: "My object is to entreat and beseech you to exert your knowledge and influence in devising and getting into operation some plan for the gradual emancipation of slavery" (p. 22). Coles suggests that this is a "duty" that devolves on Jefferson in particular given Jefferson's prominent stand in favor of the rights of man. Even if Jefferson's words have no immediate effect, Coles argues, they will "leave human nature the invaluable Testament...how best to establish its rights" (p. 23), a testament sure to have a positive effect eventually. See also Benjamin Banneker's letter to Jefferson of 19 August 1791, in which Jefferson is again asked to speak out. Banneker contrasts the servitude of blacks with the desire of the whites to free themselves from British rule, and quotes the "self-

he not only freed his slaves in Illinois but also was instrumental in abolishing slavery from that state.[117] In his reply to Coles of 25 August 1814, Jefferson asks whether Coles is right in "abandoning this property [the slaves], and your country [Virginia] with it"; for "the laws do not permit us to turn them loose, if that were for their good: and to commute them for other property is to commit them to those whose usage of them we cannot control." In the meantime we should feed and clothe the slaves well, and "require such reasonable labor only as is performed voluntarily by freemen, and be led by no repugnancies to abdicate them and our duties to them." Jefferson urges Coles to stay in Virginia and to "become the missionary of this doctrine truly christian; insinuate & inculcate it softly but steadily, through the medium of writing and conversation" (p. 1346) until a critical mass of opinion in favor of emancipation is reached. Jefferson suggests, that is, that it is legally impossible to manumit one's slaves in Virginia—a claim that is not quite accurate—and that manumission would be detrimental to the slaves.[118] Because Coles was not advocating the sale of his slaves to other owners, Jefferson's point on that score is irrelevant. In Query XIV of the *Notes* Jefferson states the "emancipation is dangerous for blacks and whites" thesis in greater detail,

---

evident" phrase of the Declaration of Independence. Banneker reproaches Jefferson for still owning slaves though believing in the truths of the Declaration.

[117] For further details about Coles, see Miller, *Wolf by the Ears*, 205–8.

[118] The Virginia Act of 1806 (which repealed the Act of 1782) stipulated that manumitted slaves leave the state within one year, unless permitted to stay by the legislature. Many freed slaves were permitted to stay. Jefferson may be referring, however, to laws regulating manumission in cases in which their owners were in debt (the purpose of the laws being to prevent people from avoiding payment by shifting—to a relative who could be counted on returning the slaves, for example—their primary capital, slaves). See McColley, *Slavery*, 132: "The claims of creditors would, under Virginia law, have precluded or at least postponed such an emancipation, but even without these he had so many relatives committed to the plantation way of life that such an act [Jefferson's freeing all his slaves] would have amounted to a disinheritance"; and *A History of American Law*, by Lawrence M. Friedman, 2nd ed. (New York: Simon and Schuster, 1985): "The law [in Virginia] remained sensitive to the connections between slaves and the land. A Virginia Statute of 1794, for example, prohibited the sale of slaves to satisfy the master's debts, unless all other personal property had been exhausted. Legally, land could not be levied on until *all* the personal property had been sold to pay debts. Under this statute, then, the slaves were halfway between land and personality, in regard to creditors' rights" (p. 225). For some further discussion, see Mark Tushnet, *The American Law of Slavery 1810–1860: Considerations of Humanity and Interest* (Princeton: Princeton University Press, 1981), 188–228; Mary Locke, *Anti-Slavery in America, from the Introduction of African Slaves to the Prohibition of the Slave Trade, 1619–1808* (Boston: Ginn and Co., 1901), 74 ff., 122 ff.; Luther P. Jackson, "Manumission in Certain Virginia Cities," *Journal of Negro History* 15 (1930): 278–314; and A. Leon Higginbotham, Jr., *In the Matter of Color: Race and the American Legal Process* (New York: Oxford University Press, 1978), 47–50.

arguing that emancipation would be stymied by (1) the continued prejudices of the whites, (2) bitter recollections by the blacks of the injuries
they had sustained, and (3) "many other circumstances, [which] will
divide us into parties, and produce convulsions which will probably never
end but in the extermination of the one or the other race" (p. 264).
Emancipation will lead to racial war, and because the blacks are in the
minority, they will not benefit from emancipation. Ergo, it is not moral
to emancipate one's slaves.

In his famous letter to John Holmes of 22 April 1820, Jefferson says
that, with respect to slavery, "justice is in one scale, and self-preservation
in the other" (p. 1434). "Self-preservation" could be extended to refer
to the blacks, but it refers primarily here to the whites. Jefferson may
have had in mind the economic self-preservation of the whites as well as
their physical survival, which would be threatened by hordes of angry
former slaves.

As already noted, the "impossibility" reason for Jefferson's not emancipating his own slaves is not persuasive, at least not so long as moral
sense serves as the standard. With sufficient ingenuity and effort, he could
have found a way to bring this about, but he might have had to leave
Virginia, as Coles did. The "danger" rationale is not finally persuasive
either. Indeed, Jefferson emphasized in his letter to Coles that "the hour
of emancipation is advancing, in the march of time," either through the
voluntary efforts of whites or through a bloody revolution (encouraged
by foreign nations) comparable with that of Santo Domingo (p. 1345).
A similar thought animates Jefferson's letter to Holmes of 22 April 1820.
Thus not emancipating one's slaves seems as dangerous in the longer run,
on Jefferson's own grounds, as doing so in the short term. In any event,
according to the standards of the "Opinion," the danger must be immediate and direct to qualify as a reason for annulling a moral obligation.
Jefferson does not show that emancipation of his own slaves met that
criterion, and in fact it would not have done so, especially if Jefferson
had moved out of the state.

Of course, emancipating his slaves would have meant immense trouble
for Jefferson, as well as a drastic reduction in the level of his and his
family's material welfare. But disagreeableness and lack of utility relative
to one's own self-interest do not, according to Jefferson himself in the
"Opinion," qualify as legitimate reasons for annulling a moral obligation,
let alone one as serious as that in question. Indeed, in promoting the
revolution against Britain, Jefferson was prepared to sacrifice his own

property and the material welfare of his family (in fact, the British nearly captured Jefferson at Monticello, and while there took a number of his slaves and a good deal of his property). Nothing in the moral sense could warrant the continued enslavement by Jefferson of hundreds of blacks in the name of preventing economic hardship on the part of Jefferson and his family. Furthermore, there were alternatives to simply freeing slaves and throwing them out to fend for themselves, or to destroying one's farm in the name of emancipation. Jefferson formulated one such plan in France (it involved hiring the freed slaves as workers), but he abandoned it when he returned. Thomas Paine urged some similar alternatives.[119] An Epicurean, by contrast, could find good reason for not emancipating his slaves, particularly if prudence pointed out another boundary condition that would have to be met.

Jefferson's objections to emancipation of his own slaves, as well as to the unqualified emancipation of all slaves, are tied to a conviction mentioned in his letter to Coles, namely, that the blacks should be expatriated.[120] When in that letter to Holmes he remarks, to repeat, that "there is not a man on earth who would sacrifice more than I would to relieve us from this heavy reproach, in any *practicable* way" (p. 1434; Jefferson's emphasis), Jefferson explicitly stipulates that emancipation must be accompanied by the expatriation of the blacks. Practicality or utility must satisfy that condition as well, and not simply the general condition that the blacks not be endangered in an immediate way. The expatriation condition vastly complicated any scheme for emancipation and thus rendered emancipation far less likely. Because the expatriation condition is a sine qua non, for Jefferson, of emancipation of his own slaves or of any plan for general emancipation, let me say a few words

---

[119] See Jefferson's letter to E. Bancroft, 26 January 1788 (Boyd, *Papers of Thomas Jefferson*, 14: 492–4); and Thomas Paine, "African Slavery in America," in *Writings*, 1:4–9.

[120] Jefferson insisted from beginning to end that the emancipation of the slaves be accompanied by expatriation, that is, their removal either to Africa, the Caribbean, or some other place. This is one of his boundary criteria for prudential action here, which I discuss later. Jefferson's principle that all those born in a country are citizens of it applied only to whites ("A Bill Declaring who shall be deemed Citizens of this Commonwealth," p. 374), though the "natural right" of emigration belongs to "all men." On separating mothers from children, see his letter of 4 February 1824 to Jared Sparks: "I am aware that this subject involves some constitutional scruples. But a liberal construction, justified by the object, may go far, and an amendment of the constitution, the whole length necessary. The separation of infants from their mothers too, would produce some scruples of humanity. But this would be straining at a gnat, and swallowing a camel" (p. 1487). The expatriation requirement vastly complicated the task of solving the slavery problem; indeed, McColley concludes that it made general emancipation impossible (*Slavery*, 130).

about its presumed moral status before I consider the legitimacy of Jefferson's stance toward the institution of slavery.[121]

Why did Jefferson insist, from beginning to end, that the blacks be forcibly expatriated, that is, that they not form a permanent part of the American republic? In addition to the reason already mentioned—that Jefferson thought the hostility between blacks and whites so deep and so permanent as to destroy the bonds of trust and friendship required in a free republic—there is another, deeper, reason. I have already mentioned that Jefferson thought black persons ugly, and he very much feared the "degradation" of the whites as a result (by contrast, Jefferson encouraged the mixing of the whites and Indians, believing that the whites became more beautiful as a result).[122] Jefferson's pervasive fear of miscegenation goes far beyond physical beauty; for his "suspicion" that blacks are inferior to whites in body and mind would necessarily lead him to worry that mixing the two races would degrade the mental capacities of the whites, and indeed their very humanity.

My interpretation of Jefferson as an Epicurean helps explain Jefferson's fear of miscegenation. If there is no immaterial soul that belongs to all humans equally, "human nature" is material nature, and material nature can evolve through time.[123] The "moral sense" is the attribute that qual-

[121] For the details of Jefferson's expatriation plan, see Query XIV of the *Notes* (p. 264); the letter to Sparks of 4 February 1824 (pp. 1484–7); the letter to Coles, 25 August 1814 (p. 1345); letter to John Lynch of 21 January 1811 (p. 1241). In the letter to Monroe of 24 November 1801 (pp. 1096–9) Jefferson argues against resettling the blacks anywhere in North America lest a "blot or mixture" on the continent result. Presumably following this advice would entail forcible resettlement of freed blacks.

[122] Consider the remark in the letter to Chastellux of 7 June 1785: "I believe the Indian, then, to be, in body and mind, equal to the white man. I have supposed the black man, in his present state, might not be so; but it would be hazardous to affirm, that, equally cultivated for a few generations, he would not become so" (p. 801). For a sensitive discussion of Jefferson's views on the Indians, see Ralph Lerner's *The Thinking Revolutionary: Principle and Practice in the New Republic* (Ithaca: Cornell University Press, 1987), chap. 4.

[123] Similarly, Hume thought blacks almost certainly inferior to whites. See "Of National Characters," in *Essays Moral, Political, and Literary*, ed. Eugene F. Miller (Indianapolis: Liberty Press, 1985), 208, n.10: "I am apt to suspect the negroes to be naturally inferior to the whites. There scarcely ever was a civilized nation of that complexion, nor even any individual eminent either in action or speculation. No ingenious manufactures amongst them, no arts, no sciences.... Such a uniform and constant difference could not happen, in so many countries and ages, if nature had not made an original distinction between these breeds of men. Not to mention our colonies, there are NEGROE slaves dispersed all over EUROPE, of whom none ever discovered any symptoms of ingenuity. ... In JAMAICA, indeed, they talk of one negro as a man of parts and learning; but it is likely he is admired for slender accomplishments, like a parrot, who speaks a few words plainly." It is worth adding, however, that Hume disliked the institution of slavery, in part because of its evil effects on the character of the masters.

ifies an entity as human, but moral sense is as much a biological attribute as eyesight. Although Jefferson indicated—as already noted—that blacks possess moral sense, he also wondered whether evolution might have accorded blacks less virtue in mind and body than nature did to whites.[124] In the passage in the *Notes* just cited, Jefferson explicitly indicates that the results of an empirical study of blacks might "degrade a whole race of men from the rank in the scale of beings which their Creator may perhaps have given them." Jefferson goes on to indicate that nothing in nature contradicts the possibility that there are distinct races of men as there are of other animals, some being superior to others. Entertaining the hypothesis that blacks "are inferior to the whites in the endowments both of body and mind" may amount to entertaining the hypothesis that blacks are less human than whites, if "body and mind" include the moral sense. Consequently when Jefferson articulates his fear of a black person "staining the blood of his master" (*Notes*, Query XIV, p. 270), he is thinking of the possibility that mixing the races might actually make the whites less human, and that is not a possibility he was willing to risk. Jefferson might have seen his moral obligation as weakened by the "danger" miscegenation would present. Jefferson's views on politics and morals are thus heavily indebted to his views on nature—to his biology, in short. Equality, humanity, moral sense: these can only be "empirical" issues for Jefferson. If blacks turned out to be by nature "subhuman" (i.e., lacking moral sense), presumably they could be justly enslaved. Through the back door, as it were, Jefferson's Epicureanism and his "demystified" Christianity could join hands in "justifying" slavery. The science that liberates us from hierarchies could also reestablish hierarchies. This realization occurred to Jefferson, but he resisted abandoning his belief in the moral equality of blacks and whites.

The tensions within Jefferson's scheme of moral justification pointed to by his actions can be illustrated in another way. Let us assume that the distinction between long- and short-term time horizons can be mean-

---

[124] *Notes*, Query XIV, p. 270: "I advance it therefore as a suspicion only, that the blacks, whether originally a distinct race, or made distinct by time and circumstances, are inferior to the whites in the endowments both of body and mind. It is not against experience to suppose, that different species of the same genus, or varieties of the same species, may possess different qualifications. Will not a lover of natural history then, one who views the gradations in all the races of animals with the eye of philosophy, excuse an effort to keep those in the department of man as distinct as nature has formed them?" Jefferson's view that "the improvement of the blacks in body and mind, in the first instance of their mixture with the whites, has been observed by every one" (p. 267) suggests that he was inclined to the view that blacks are by nature inferior.

ingfully used here. Even if it were prudent to tolerate certain evils for the short term in the name of ultimately removing the evil, it could not be prudent to make the evil still worse in the name of extirpating it. Yet in at least one attested case—and some such case was inevitable—Jefferson did precisely this. Jefferson wrote in a letter that he had one of his slaves— Jame Hubbard—"severely flogged in the presence of his old companions" (in Jefferson's words) for having made repeated efforts to win his freedom.[125] Although the preservation of the institution of slavery requires that the slaves not revolt, one could not simultaneously condemn the institution on the basis that it violates the natural rights of the slaves and take actions that make the condition of the slaves still worse. One could hardly argue that Hubbard was improved by the flogging. It might be prudent in the nonmoral sense of the term to flog freedom-minded slaves, but it could not be "prudent" to do so in the sense of the term Jefferson wishes to espouse.

I have argued that Jefferson rationalized in justifying his prudent actions with respect to his ownership of slaves. By this I mean that he falsely claimed to be doing the best he could under the circumstances relative to the dictates of moral sense. His failure should not be interpreted as being merely a personal one but as pointing up a deep problem in his "synthesis." From a strictly Epicurean standpoint, Jefferson's actions might well have been perfectly "just" in the sense of most conducive to his tranquillity. The logic of Jefferson's stance here points to the Epicurean summum bonum as its justification, as well it might, given that in Jefferson's synthesis tranquillity remains methodologically primary; yet he takes his supplement to be crucial. The attempt to proffer the dictates of moral-sense theory *and* of happiness by way of justification puts intolerable strain on the synthesis and shows that the summum bonum cannot, for Jefferson, accommodate both Epicurean tranquillity and the enlarged circle of moral valuation entailed by moral sense.

---

[125] For the details of that episode, see William Cohen, "Thomas Jefferson and the Problem of Slavery," *Journal of American History* 56 (1969): 516; and Jefferson's letter to Reuben Perry (from which the words just quoted are taken) of 16 April 1812, in *Thomas Jefferson's Farm Book,* ed. Edwin M. Betts (Charlottesville: University of Virginia Press, 1987), 34–5. Jefferson claims that Hubbard "committed a theft" along the way. Compare the letter to William Gordon, 16 July 1788 (*Thomas Jefferson's Farm Book,* 505), where Jefferson says that Cornwallis "carried off also about 30 slaves: had this been to give them freedom he would have done right, but it was to consign them to inevitable death from the small pox and putrid fever then raging in his camp."

Let us now briefly examine Jefferson's stance relative to the institution of slavery.

Jefferson and the institution of slavery. In the letter to Coles of 25 August 1814, Jefferson recounts some of the efforts he had made prior to 1800 on behalf of the blacks. In particular he mentions his authorship of an act in the Virginia legislature for extending the protection of the laws to blacks. The effort was roundly rejected and vilified (p. 1344). Even the act of 1782 making manumission much easier—an act promoted by Jefferson—faced opposition.[126] These and other failed efforts rapidly convinced Jefferson that any public opposition to slavery was bound to be counterproductive,[127] hence his great efforts to keep the *Notes on the State of Virginia* from being published.[128] Jefferson feared not that the

---

[126] See Fredrika T. Schmidt and Barbara R. Wilhelm, "Early Pro-Slavery Petitions in Virginia," *William and Mary Quarterly* 30 (1973): 133–46; and Miller, *Wolf by the Ears*, 36.

[127] Miller notes that by 1777 Jefferson had suffered enough rebuffs to his efforts to commit him to a course of "prudent and pragmatic action" (*Wolf by the Ears*, 19). See also Winthrop D. Jordan, *White over Black* (New York: W. W. Norton, 1977), 435; Jefferson "had good reason to think that antislavery pronouncements might solidify the institution."

[128] Jefferson wrote the *Notes* in 1781 in answer to a number of queries put to him by François Marbois, secretary to the French legation. Desiring to get copies into the hands of several friends, Jefferson revised and enlarged the text and published it anonymously, in a private edition, in France in 1785 (see Jefferson's letter to Chastellux of 16 January 1784 [p. 786]). In the *Autobiography* Jefferson claims that the decision to publish the *Notes* in France was made simply because printing costs there were cheaper (p. 56). However, doing so also had the advantage of increasing the chances of keeping the *Notes* private. In his letter to Chastellux of 7 June 1785, Jefferson says that the *Notes* were not to be circulated, for "The strictures on slavery and on the constitution of Virginia, are not of that kind, and they are the parts which I do not wish to have made public, at least, till I know whether their publication would do most harm or good. It is possible, that in my own country, these strictures might produce an irritation, which would indispose the people towards the two great objects I have in view; that is, the emancipation of their slaves, and the settlement of their constitution on a firmer and more permanent basis." Jefferson contemplated the possibility of sending copies to "every young man at the College," for in the young lay his hope for change (pp. 799–800). In the letter to Madison of 1 September 1785, Jefferson remarks that "I am anxious to hear from you on the subject of my Notes on Virginia. I have been obliged to give so many of them here, that I fear their getting published" (p. 822). A copy did get in the hands of a French bookseller, and a poor French translation (with Jefferson's authorship stated) was scheduled for 1787. Jefferson could do little about it except try to improve the translation (see his letters to Madison of 8 February 1786 [p. 849]; to John Page of 4 May 1786 [pp. 852–3]; to George Wythe of 13 August 1786 [p. 858]). Jefferson then decided to print an accurate edition in English, with his authorship public, in 1787. Soon after, the book was published in America, and it quickly became the center of considerable controversy, concerning which see Jordan, *White over Black*,

"suspicions" expressed there about the inferiority of blacks would cause trouble but, rather, that the suggestions that blacks were equal to whites in the decisive sense, and so that slavery is immoral, would cause a backlash. In fact, Jefferson was bitterly attacked during the 1800 presidential election for his views on race.[129]

After 1777, Jefferson said very little in public against the institution of slavery, and made no efforts to improve the wretched lot of many "free blacks," even though on occasion he might have made a decisive difference.[130] As he put the matter in a letter to James Heaton, written in the last year of his life (20 May 1826):

A good cause is often injured more by ill-timed efforts of its friends than by the arguments of its enemies. Persuasion, perseverance, and patience are the best advocates on questions depending on the will of others. The revolution in public opinion which this cause requires, is not to be expected in a day, or perhaps in an age; but time, which outlives all things, will outlive this evil also. My sentiments have been forty years before the public. Had I repeated them forty times, they would only have become the more stale and threadbare. (p. 1516)[131]

---

441. Miller remarks (Wolf by the Ears, 57) that Jefferson's "suspicion" that blacks are inferior was much milder than that of his fellow Virginians "who regarded the inferiority of blacks as an indubitable fact, and who believed that slavery itself was a 'natural', Heaven-ordained institution."

[129] I refer to the tract by William L. Smith, "The Pretensions of Thomas Jefferson to the Presidency Examined" (Philadelphia, 1796). For discussion of the pamphlet, see McColley, Slavery, 126–7. Miller notes that when Jefferson's correspondence with Benjamin Banneker was published (without Jefferson's consent), Jefferson discovered that any intellectual relationship with a black person could cause him difficulties among whites (Wolf by the Ears, 78).

[130] Miller notes that if Jefferson had spoken out in 1806, a bill outlawing slavery in the District of Columbia might have passed (Wolf by the Ears, 132). Miller too suggests that with respect to the spread of slavery in the Louisiana territories, Jefferson did not do everything possible to limit slavery (p. 143), and indeed that after 1819 Jefferson became an ardent exponent of the establishment of slavery in the Louisiana Purchase territories (p. 209).

[131] Consider the sentences at the end of the "Answers to Démeunier's Queries," which Jefferson proposes should be included (without his name attached) in the Encyclopédie: Jefferson and Wythe were not present to offer the amendment concerning emancipation because "they saw that the moment of doing it with success was not yet arrived, and that an unsuccessful effort, as too often happens, would only rivet still closer the chains of bondage, and retard the moment of delivery to this oppressed description of men. What a stupendous, what an incomprehensible machine is man! who can endure toil, famine, stripes, imprisonment and death itself in vindication of his own liberty, and the next moment be deaf to all those motives whose power supported him thro' his trial, and inflict on his fellow men a bondage, one hour of which is fraught with more misery than ages of that which he rose in rebellion to oppose. But we must await with patience the workings of an overruling providence, and hope that that is preparing the deliverance of these, our suffering brethren" (p. 592).

Jefferson was convinced that if he pushed the issue publicly, he would only hasten the split between North and South, and between Federalists and Republicans, the result being the destruction of the Union and the perpetuation of slavery in the South. Jefferson adds that this letter, too, is to be kept private. Prudence requires silence about the prudential reasons for the silence.

Jefferson had a further constraint to his advocacy of means for general emancipation as well, and this second constraint was crucial to his position on the controversy leading up to the Missouri Compromise (1820). I refer to his view that no solution to the slavery issue could be permitted to destroy the Union, the continued existence of the Union being a precondition for the liberties of all the peoples existing within it. In that sense the moral duty to preserve the Constitution for the long run was higher than the moral duty to abolish slavery in the short run. Jefferson thought that the Constitution could be preserved only if the distinction between state and federal authority was retained. Hence slavery could be abolished only by a decision of the individual states, not by a decision of the federal government (even though the Constitution requires that each state have a "republican form of government"). Jefferson's problematic position on the Missouri controversy is simply an extension of that sequence of inferences drawn from the second constraining premise (the premise that the Union must be preserved above all).

Furthermore, there seems to be a scholarly consensus that had Jefferson taken a sustained and public abolitionist stand, his chances for election to public office would have been small or nonexistent.[132] It could be argued, then, that silence with respect to the institution was the price Jefferson paid for the privilege of serving his country. The opportunity for accomplishing great things—and, in Jefferson's eyes, for saving the Union by reversing Federalist policies—might have outweighed in Jefferson's mind the evil that his speaking out on slavery could perhaps

---

[132] See McColley, *Slavery*, pp. 115–6, 131; and Miller, *Wolf by the Ears*, 278: "It was also legibly written in the Book of Fate that had Jefferson made himself conspicuous as a fervent, militant, and uncompromising abolitionist on the model of William Lloyd Garrison, or had he even gone so far as to suggest that whites and blacks ought to enjoy equal rights as citizens of the United States, he would not have succeeded in doing the things in which he took the greatest pride and by which he wished to be remembered by posterity. Nor would he have had the slightest chance of becoming president of the United States." Of course, after his second election to the Presidency this rationale would have lost its force.

have averted. This would appear to be an example of "prudential" reasoning.[133]

Jefferson's position with respect to the institution of slavery, then, is conditioned by the expatriation requirement and by the requirement that the Union and its constitutional structures be preserved, and thus that the decision to emancipate be left to the states. His position is also conditioned by his perception that his own effectiveness in promoting a

---

[133] While discussing Jefferson's actions with respect to slavery, we should note that in the *Autobiography* Jefferson mentions the bill on the subject of slaves that was drawn up by the committee on revising Virginia's laws (p. 44). The bill did not contain a plan for a future and general emancipation, the intention being to introduce such a plan (in which "the freedom of all born after a certain day, and deportation at a proper age" was envisioned) in an amendment, but "it was found that the public mind would not yet bear the proposition, nor will it bear it even at this day" (p. 44). In his "Memorandum (Services to My Country)" Jefferson lists "the act prohibiting the importation of slaves" as one of his achievements (p. 702). See also his "Draft Constitution for Virginia" (June 1776): "No person hereafter coming into this country shall be held within the same in slavery under any pretext whatever" (p. 344). Jefferson's revised draft of 1783 (which he wrote when he thought that the 1776 Virginia Constitution was to be revised) included a plan for gradual emancipation. For another reference to that see part 3 of Jefferson's "Answers and Observations for Démeunier's Article," in which Jefferson says of his and Wythe's decision not to offer the amendment: "There were persons there who wanted neither the virtue to propose, nor talents to enforce the proposition had they seen that the disposition of the legislature was ripe for it." Wythe and Jefferson would feel "wounded, degraded, and discouraged" by the proposition that they were not present to act because they did not care about the issue (p. 592). Jefferson's draft of the Declaration contained a passage strongly condemning the slave trade and slavery, but the passage was dropped at the insistence of South Carolina and Georgia, with the implied approval of some of the northern states engaged in the slave trade (*Autobiography,* 18). Jefferson's "Report on Government for Western Territory" of 1784, which became the early draft of the Northwest Ordinance, provided that "after the year 1800 of the Christian aera, there shall be neither slavery nor involuntary servitude in any of the said states" (p. 377; the plan failed by one vote to pass Congress). Miller notes that almost all southerners, and all of Virginia's representatives, voted against the bill (*Wolf by the Ears,* 28–9). In his eighth annual message to Congress, Jefferson urged successfully that importation of slaves be outlawed by the earliest possible date permitted in the Constitution (1808), for these "violations of human rights which have been so long continued on the unoffending inhabitants of Africa, and which the morality, the reputation, and the best interest of our country, have long been eager to proscribe" (p. 528). However, Miller notes that because Jefferson stood by the doctrine of the freedom of the seas and did not let the British inspect ships showing the American flag, thousands of slaves were still brought to the United States after 1808 in violation of the ban and under the U.S. flag (*Wolf by the Ears,* 146). See *Wolf by the Ears,* 4–6, for Jefferson's early acts with respect to slavery (for example, in 1769 when elected to the Virginia House of Burgesses "one of his first [acts] was to attempt to make the manumission of slaves easier for owners"). Miller also tells us that Jefferson "had endorsed the Fugitive Slave Act of 1793 by which the federal government underwrote the system of involuntary servitude by committing itself to aiding in the return of fugitive slaves to their masters" (p. 229). Finally, Miller says (pp. 255–6) that Jefferson did nothing to educate his slaves and did not contribute to the Quaker effort to educate slaves, for Jefferson assumed that the blacks would be expatriated.

decision to emancipate depended on indirect strategies and by his perception, based on the general failure of his efforts before 1777 and on an assessment of the state of public opinion on the question of race, that prudence required an indirect, long-term approach rather than a direct, short-term approach to the problem of abolishing slavery.

The expatriation requirement cannot be defended on the "imminent danger" doctrine of the "Opinion on the French Treaties." At best, Jefferson only suspected that there was a possibility of danger to the whites if their "blood" were mixed with that of blacks, but that suspicion does not justify any of the draconian measures associated with Jefferson's plan for emancipation. Jefferson's suspicion that blacks and whites would find it difficult to live together was not without basis, as subsequent history shows; but it does not justify (on his own grounds in the "Opinion") expelling the native blacks any more than it does expelling the native whites. If blacks and whites are morally equal and being born in a certain place entails a right to citizenship (as Jefferson believed with respect to whites), then blacks possess that right as much as whites do.[134] However much Jefferson finds blacks lacking in beauty and unpleasant to see, that subjective feeling is not, on Jefferson's own grounds, a sufficient ground for violating moral obligation.

The "states' rights" condition is not justifiable either, and as a consequence Jefferson's position on the Missouri controversy is not justifiable. The basis for the argument that states and not the federal government possess the authority to determine who shall enjoy full civil rights can only be a purely technical one. That is, the state governments no more possess natural rights than the federal, county, or city governments do. The rationale for distributing powers among the different levels of authority is that doing so will create a mechanism that maximizes the chances that the natural rights of the individual will be protected.[135] The

---

[134] This principle would apply equally when whites are in the minority. It would mean that in South Africa, for example, native whites have, in principle, as much right to remain in the country as native blacks do, even though the forebears of one group may have inhabited the land long before the forebears of another group, or one group taken power by conquest from another group. None of this entails a right to any particular piece of property, of course.

[135] See Jefferson's letter to Joseph C. Cabell of 2 February 1816: "No, my friend, the way to have good and safe government, is not to trust it all to one, but to divide it among the many, distributing to every one exactly the functions he is competent to. Let the national government be entrusted with the defence of the nation, and its foreign and federal relations; the State governments with the civil rights, laws, police, and administration of what concerns the State generally.... It is by dividing and subdividing these republics from the great national one down through all its subordinations ... that all

distribution of powers thus is purely a "technical" matter; moral authority derives from the doctrine of natural rights, and only individuals
possess natural rights, not groups of individuals. Indeed, Jefferson did
not see the Missouri question as a moral one so much as a question of
power politics; the Federalists were using the slavery issue to increase
their own power.[136] Jefferson also thought that those who were genuinely
against slavery but in favor of the Missouri Compromise were acting
imprudently, that is, in a way that destroyed in the name of abstract
moral principle the means required to implement abstract principle.[137]

The principal problem with Jefferson's argument is that it seeks to
implement means to the end defined by abstract principle (the equality
of persons as defined by the natural-rights doctrine) that not only contradict that principle in the abstract but also have little chance from an
empirical standpoint of bringing about the end. Refusing to limit the
geographical spread of slavery could hardly have facilitated the abolition
of the institution, or even have made Jefferson's expatriation condition
any easier to carry out.[138] The means to the end have at this point

will be done for the best. What has destroyed liberty and the rights of man in every
government which has ever existed under the sun? The generalizing and concentrating
all cares and powers into one body" (p. 1380).

[136] In the letter to Holmes of 22 April 1820 (p. 1434) Jefferson denies that the extension
of slavery would create any new slaves. In the letter to Albert Gallatin of 26 December
1820, Jefferson repeats the point (pp. 1448–9), and adds that if there is any morality
at issue, it lies on his own side; by spreading the slaves over a larger surface "their
happiness would be increased, and the burthen of their future liberation lightened by
bringing a greater number of shoulders under it." Once Congress "goes out of the
Constitution to arrogate a right of regulating the conditions of the inhabitants of the
States" the floodgates are open and Congress will feel entitled to many usurpatory
actions (p. 1449). In *Wolf by the Ears* Miller says, with reference to Missouri's efforts
to prevent entry of free blacks into the state—despite the fact that "the United States
Constitution made free blacks citizens of the United States entitled to all the privileges
and immunities of white men"—that by Jefferson's silence on this issue, he "put himself
in the anomalous and morally untenable position of advocating the opening of the West
to black slaves and closing it to free blacks. Truly, for Jefferson, the Missouri controversy
proved to be a Pandora's box filled with ambiguities, contradictions, paradoxes, and
not a few sheer fantasies" (p. 248). Miller goes on to note that as the slavery issue was
dividing the Union, it was also uniting the South; as the one institution capable of doing
that, it prepared the way for the Civil War, as well as for the idea that the antislavery
movement in the North was a plot designed solely to destroy the South. Jefferson's
actions and words strengthened the planter aristocracy, Miller adds—the very aristocracy
that he had tried to destroy in the Revolutionary days.

[137] Consider, again, Jefferson's words to Holmes, 22 April 1820: "If they [the sons of the
revolutionary generation] would but dispassionately weigh the blessings they will throw
away, against an abstract principle more likely to be effected by union than by scission,
they would pause before they would perpetrate this act of suicide on themselves, and
of treason against the hopes of the world" (p. 1435).

[138] The most that can be said on behalf of Jefferson's "spread slavery further" view is

superseded the end itself. Conventional states' rights are here placed above the natural rights of individuals. Simply preserving the Constitution, even when the natural rights of many persons are being suppressed, supersedes the principles of the Declaration of Independence that the Constitution is presumably intended to implement. Prudence has become rationalization.

At this point, the rationale for upholding the administrative mechanisms set out in the Constitution has collapsed. The criteria of impossibility and imminent danger that, according to Jefferson in the "Opinion," permit the annulment of moral obligation, cannot apply here. The danger is a danger to the means of self-government, not to its ends—but the means possess moral legitimacy only if they can be shown to lead to the ends (at least over the long term), and Jefferson did not show this with respect to the Missouri question. Jefferson could argue that his position on the Missouri question, while committing him to the continued violation of the natural rights of blacks, preserved the constitutional structure that protects the freedom of whites. To argue in that way, however, is simply to indulge in a crude utilitarian calculus that dispenses with the individual rights of the numerical minority altogether. Alternatively, Jefferson could argue that preserving the Union was the necessary condition for preserving the mechanism that would one day permit blacks to enjoy freedom as well. But because he insisted from beginning to end on expatriation as a precondition for emancipation, the status of the blacks after their emancipation could hardly have been paramount in his mind. The various boundary conditions are not consistent with one another.

As already noted, there is no question that any movement for emancipation faced tremendous obstacles in the form of vested interests and racist opinion. And it is arguable that at some junctures indirect tactics may have been superior to a direct and sustained rhetorical attack by Jefferson on the institution. Therefore it is possible to reconcile, in principle, prudence and rights. But it seems that after his second term as president (and perhaps before) Jefferson employed few if any indirect tactics other than silence and inaction. He seemed to place a certain faith in the younger generation, which would presumably be molded by the

that in some states with a small proportion of slaves, such as Pennsylvania, abolition may indeed have been made easier by the fact that the vested interests in favor of the institution were relatively weak, as is argued by Adam Smith. See *Wealth of Nations*, 1:388.

egalitarian ideals of the Revolution and so would be free from the prejudices of their parents. Jefferson's assumptions about historical progress
resonate here. At other times, though, Jefferson was pessimistic about
the young.[139] In any event, Jefferson did not seem to give full weight to
the fact that the young needed to be inspired and led, and he above all
possessed the moral authority to lead.[140]

Jefferson's quandaries may be illustrated by the example of Gabriel's
attempted rebellion in Virginia in 1800. Gabriel was a freed black. Let
us suppose that Gabriel's rebellion had no chance of success (it would
not secure the long-term freedom of any of the slaves); that it would
almost certainly lead to the death of the leaders of the rebellion and the
reenslavement—this time under harsher circumstances, say, in the West
Indies—of all others involved; to the reenslavement of some free blacks
in the area, and generally to the imposition of further restrictions on free
blacks; and to the arousal of fear among the majority white population,
the result being a hardening of attitudes against blacks and so the diminution of the chances for general emancipation.[141] In a Jeffersonian
scheme, was Gabriel prudent in leading this rebellion? Are there any
conditions under which it is prudent to act "idealistically," without regard
to the probable consequences of one's actions? The answers to both
questions can be affirmative only if it is true that the conditions of enslavement or quasi-freedom (the latter characterized Virginia's "free"
blacks) were intrinsically worse than death and were agreed to be so by
all those about to risk death or increased suffering. In principle, Jefferson
would have to grant this much.

Are there any conditions under which it is prudent for one person to
violate the natural rights of another *and* for the other to respond in kind?
I raised this question earlier, when considering the possibility that Jefferson's decision to hold other people in slavery might be, in his terms,
morally prudent while the slave's decision to escape might be equally

---

[139] For the optimistic view, see Query XVIII of the *Notes* (p. 289); the letter to Richard
Price of 7 August 1785 (Boyd, ed., *Papers of Thomas Jefferson*, 8:356–7); and the letter
to Roger C. Weightman of 24 June 1826. For the pessimistic view, see the letter to
Holmes of 22 April 1820. The letter to Coles of 25 August 1814 contains both optimism
and pessimism.

[140] A point made by Davis, *Slavery in the Age of the Revolution*, 176.

[141] These consequences are not far from the historical truth. McColley notes that among
the other negative results of Gabriel's rebellion (negative for the blacks) "the conspiracy,
which had been a fruit of slavery itself, became the justification for further tightening
the hold of slavery on Virginia and choking off the small, but promising, progress of
gradual, voluntary emancipation" (*Slavery*, 111).

prudent. Suppose that one of Jefferson's slaves requested his freedom on the grounds that he was prepared to take whatever risks freedom entailed. Suppose that he had a usable skill with which to provide for himself once free, and so forth. Jefferson refused to grant him his freedom. The slave then forced Jefferson at the point of a knife to sign the emancipation papers. When Jefferson declared his intention of revoking the papers at the earliest possible moment, the slave killed him, cleverly concealed his deed, and succeeded in escaping to a life of freedom in the North.

Jefferson might have acted in full accord with his prudential morality, believing that it was genuinely better for the slave not to be free in the short run. Perhaps the slave did not have as good a knowledge as Jefferson did of the fate of "free" blacks in a hostile white society, and Jefferson did not want to set a precedent that would lead all his other slaves to demand their freedom—believing that an increase in the number of free blacks would only set back the cause of general emancipation and full equality.[142] Jefferson could retain his tranquillity in the belief that he was standing on principle in an effective way. The slave, in contrast, had a natural right to his freedom and wished to exercise his right in the belief that he would be more tranquil having done so. He would rather be dead than enslaved. I suggest that a case of this sort could be constructed so that both sides could be said to have acted according to Jeffersonian prudence.

But this seems to amount to a reductio ad absurdum of Jeffersonian prudence. I do not think that the conclusion to be drawn is that prudence should be rejected altogether as a category of moral reasoning. Rather, I have tried to suggest that Jefferson's account of his action and inaction relative to the institution of slavery is at times internally inconsistent and at times just unpersuasive—*if* one adopts the standpoint of the "Opinions" as the touchstone. That document is a moral-sense document,

---

[142] Douglass Adair points out that, possibly as early as 1774, Jefferson decided to offer Betty Hemings's boys their freedom once they reached a certain age, "though seemingly only two of them exercised" this option (*Fame and the Founding Fathers*, ed. T. Colbourn [New York: W. W. Norton, 1974], 185). Jefferson did not free Sally Hemings, one of Betty's daughters, and Adair conjectures that the reason was that the only way that someone of Sally's manners, style of behavior, and standards of taste—all of which "made her much too superior to associate with slaves in general"—could have survived in white society was to follow the "customary" path of "beautiful mulatto or quadroon girls." That is, either staffing a brothel in a southern city such as New Orleans or if "lucky," becoming the mistress of a wealthy young creole (p. 186). Adair notes that because Jefferson would have found such a possibility abhorrent, he decided not to free Sally. Was Jefferson's decision prudent? (It turns out, according to Adair, that Sally had a liaison anyhow, at Monticello—with Peter Carr.)

however; and when we remember Jefferson's Epicurean view to which
the moral-sense doctrine is a supplement, we see that his prevarications
are not so much a matter of personal failings as a symptom of the deep
incoherence of his theoretical structure. It is as though Jefferson felt
tugged in contrary directions by two of his principles: tranquillity and
rights.

PRUDENCE, RATIONALIZATION, AND JEFFERSON'S SYNTHESIS

My discussion in the preceding section indicates that Jefferson's appeals
to prudence with respect to both levels of the slavery problem—his ownership of slaves and the institution of slavery—ultimately amount to
rationalization on his part. In this section I wish to examine in slightly
greater detail the difference between prudence and rationalization and
to draw some conclusions. The issue of rationalization is complex philosophically, involving issues of self-deception, weakness of will, and the
like.[143] It is not my purpose here to work out the difference in the abstract
so much as to reflect on it in terms suggested by Jefferson's philosophy
as set out earlier.

To rationalize is to attempt to justify a blameworthy course or plan
of action in a way that in effect amounts to an excuse for continued
indulgence therein. Rationalization should be distinguished from a failure
of a prudent course of action to succeed. For sometimes even the best
efforts may fail. Rationalization should also be distinguished from making a mistake. I assume that a person who has made a mistake with
respect to the means to an end, and who truly wishes to reach that end,
would correct the choice of means as soon as the mistake is pointed out.
Someone who is rationalizing a course of action may not truly desire the
end being professed, or at least may sense (but fail to face up to) some
conflict between it and another end.

If wrongdoing cannot be avoided, rationalization has not occurred.
But, as Jefferson informs us, "unavoidable" must be narrowly defined.
If it is defined as "physically impossible to avoid" it reflects one sense in
which the world is imperfect (i.e., simply out of one's control) and does
not present the problem of rationalization, at least not immediately. But

---

[143] For a good sample of the philosophical discussion, see Phillip Bricker's "Prudence,"
Journal of Philosophy 77 (1980): 381–401; J. D. Mabbot, "Prudence," *Proceedings of
the Aristotelian Society*, Suppl. vol. 36 (1962): 51–64; and the reply in the same volume
by H. J. N. Horsburgh, 65–76.

when the issue is a good's desirability relative to another standard, reflecting the imperfection of the world in the sense that not all choiceworthy goods can be realized simultaneously, the possibility of rationalization arises. Jefferson would want to use the judgment of the enlightened Epicurean of sound moral sense as the standard. The "right" goods are those worthy of a self so conceived.

Rationalization may occur when the reasons offered for a course of action being prudent are not persuasive on impartial examination as measured by (1) the internal coherence of the individual's own scheme of constraints; or (2) the extent of the actual efforts made, given the particulars of the situation, to bring the real up to the level of the ideal over the long term; or (3) the soundness of the basic conception of the self that one would want to be. I have argued that on the slavery issue Jefferson has rationalized in the first two senses, and that his failure to act prudently reflects on the third.

The core difficulty is that Jefferson's synthesis of Epicurus and moral sense leaves him with *two* principles, tranquillity and the duty to treat others in a certain way. Unfortunately, when push comes to shove, as it does in the case of slavery, the two principles are incompatible. Consequently, the claim to have responded prudently to the challenge—that is, in such a way as to approximate the ideal (defined by tranquillity and natural rights, in this case) as much as the situation permits (the situation being defined by empirical factors as well as side constraints contextually generated, such as the "preservation of the Union" condition)—becomes rationalization. It is rationalization because it pretends that prudent action was succeeding in realizing *both* the summum bonum (the agent's tranquillity) and the dictates of moral sense, whereas in fact the latter was being sacrificed.

Correspondingly, I have tried to resist interpreting Jefferson's quandaries solely (1) as expressions of the view that there are some unsolvable quandaries in moral life, (2) as manifestations of a personal failure, or (3) as indications that Kant is right in rejecting the view that prudence is in no way a moral virtue because it inevitably leads to self-serving choices and rationalization. With respect to the last of these, it might be noted that it is difficult to deny that prudence plays and is widely felt to play some legitimate role not just in our own lives but also in political life. Considerations of happiness, utility, and consequences of choices do figure in our moral deliberations, particularly in political life.

The root problem, to repeat, concerns the relationship between Jefferson's Epicurean conception of happiness and its supplement, namely, the other-regarding moral-sense doctrine. To put it starkly: if it is prudent to do what Jefferson did in the Revolution—to risk fortune and sacred honor and all else—tranquillity cannot be the highest good.[144] Those actions render the agent vulnerable in ways that would surely sabotage tranquillity. Accommodation to the ruling power would have been more prudent. Or, again, if tranquillity is the highest good and Jefferson's stance with respect to his ownership of slaves and to the institution is prudent, prudence is purchased at the price of justice understood in Jefferson's moral-sense way. Self-interest rightly understood (along Epicurean lines) and duty rightly understood (along the moral-sense lines) do not, in the end, cohere. Jefferson seems not to have a coherent picture of the sort of person he would want to be that can survive the challenge of the slavery issue. That is, he seems unable to articulate a picture of an ideal self such that, in a most difficult situation, that self could be both happy and virtuous. To revert again to Coles, I do not see that Jefferson ultimately has a way of explaining how Coles, having exiled himself to a remote region and freed his slaves, could be both happy and just.

This incoherence in the synthesis creates fault lines that are visible elsewhere in Jefferson's thought. He seems unable to explain not just his stance on the slavery issue, but his own public service. If politics is drudgery, anxiety, and lack of tranquillity, why did he engage in it in the sustained way that he did?[145] I do not see that invoking prudence supplies a persuasive answer. Although Jefferson devoted enormous amounts of time and effort to public life, he would just as soon have us forget that effort and remember him instead for his accomplishments as

---

[144] It could be responded that, at the time of the Revolution, Jefferson did not think that tranquillity was the summum bonum. That is, one could attempt to explain away the inconsistencies by reference to presumed changes of view on Jefferson's part. I am relying on the interpretive principle set out in note 25 above. I am using the assumption of consistency over time to extract the latent tensions in Jefferson's words and deeds. As pointed out in footnote 25 and elsewhere in this chapter, Jefferson held certain key views with some constancy throughout his adult life.

[145] Compare Jefferson's letter to Martha J. Randolph of 11 February 1800: "Politics are such a torment that I would advise every one I love not to mix with them." In Sarah N. Randolph, *The Domestic Life of Thomas Jefferson, Compiled from Family Letters and Reminiscences* (Charlottesville: University Press of Virginia, 1985), 262. See also the letters to John Randolph of 25 August 1775, to George Washington of 28 May 1781, and to Alexander Donald of 7 February 1788 (all in Peterson, 749, 777, and 920).

a philosopher, writer, and conveyor of knowledge. I refer of course to his epitaph, which he so carefully scripted, trusting only himself to recognize what is worth memorializing. Serving as president of the United States and governor of an important state were too insignificant, in Jefferson's eyes, to be mentioned. Do not these striking omissions signal an inability to articulate how public service and individual happiness cohere? I suspect that the fault lines stretched through Jefferson's plans for public education[146] and more broadly through his ideas about the mythology that provides the political creed and, as it were, civic education of all citizens.[147]

I cannot embark here on a discussion of the etiology of the failure of Jefferson's synthesis or its significance for the coherence of the Enlightenment.[148] Although Jefferson's quandaries seem to anticipate—if they did not actually help to bring about—quandaries in contemporary American life, this subject too is beyond the boundaries of this discussion. In conclusion, I venture to prophesy—with an eye on Charles Taylor's recent and monumental attempt to show us a way to a new synthesis through an analysis of modernity's roots and history—that whatever new synthesis we propose must be bound by three imperatives. First, it must include a "legitimation" of liberal political structures that assumes the political equality and "rights" of all persons.[149] However much it is to be bent or straightened, that leg of Jefferson's triad will remain part of

[146] Jefferson's founding of the University of Virginia recognizes the great benefit of liberal education to individual happiness, and no doubt the importance of liberally educated persons to a republican nation. But would the "natural aristoi" educated along Jeffersonian lines find that contributing to the welfare of a liberal republic fits with the ends promoted by their liberal education?

[147] I refer to the problem signaled above: in Query XVII of the *Notes* Jefferson declares that "it does me no injury for my neighbour to say there are twenty gods, or no god" (p. 285). And yet when he turns to contemplate the slavery problem in the very next Query, he seems pressed to suggest a contradictory view, namely that it matters a great deal what his neighbors believe in matters of religion: "And can the liberties of a nation be thought secure when we have removed their only firm basis, a conviction in the minds of the people that these liberties are of the gift of God? That they are not to be violated but with his wrath?" (p. 289). In asking this question Jefferson seems to wonder whether the pronoun in the statement just quoted from Query XVII refers to him personally; if it did, however, the argument for freedom of religious belief would presumably need recasting.

[148] That Jefferson's position is an attempt at putting together a synthesis, indeed the synthesis of the elements in question, invites a MacIntyrean analysis, for Jefferson could be seen as trying (without much chance of success) to merge incompatible fragments of older traditions. (In *After Virtue* MacIntyre discusses Benjamin Franklin rather than Jefferson as critical to the development of the American Enlightenment.)

[149] As Charles Taylor asserts in *Sources of the Self: The Making of the Modern Identity* (Cambridge, Mass.: Harvard University Press, 1989), 395–6.

our body politic. Second, prudential moral deliberation in the political sphere seems equally inescapable (and that deliberation will be informed by everything from economics to history to psychology). The "second order" problem of implementing a theory of rights is not going to be solved by rejecting, on principle, prudential deliberation.[150] This second leg of his triad will remain in one shape or another. We are left, third, with the task of articulating a notion of the self, its virtues, and its happiness capable of avoiding Jefferson's quandaries. The issues will involve religion, materialism, and our view of history, as we have seen. Through their very deficiency, Jefferson's views may help us to define the problem to be solved. Even here, Jefferson may again exercise remarkable influence.

---

[150] Consider one of Taylor's concluding statements that follows a reflection on "the appalling destruction wrought in history in the name of the faith": "That is why adopting a stripped-down secular outlook, without any religious dimension or radical hope in history, is not a way of *avoiding* the dilemma [religion vs. secular humanism], although it may be a good way to live with it. It doesn't avoid it, because this too involves its 'mutilation.' It involves stifling the response in us to some of the deepest and most powerful spiritual aspirations that humans have conceived. This, too, is a heavy price to pay. This is not to say, though, that if we have to pay some price, this may not be the safest. Prudence constantly advises us to scale down our hopes and circumscribe our vision. But we deceive ourselves if we pretend that nothing is denied thereby of our humanity" (*Sources*, 520).

5

Practical philosophy and the Bill of Rights: perspectives on some contemporary issues

WILLIAM A. GALSTON

During the past generation, controversies over rights have generated a vast and diverse literature. Any effort, such as this one, that seeks to catalogue this outpouring is bound to become in some measure a third-order affair: a survey of surveys, a bibliography of bibliographies.[1] I cannot hope to break much new ground. My purpose, rather, is to undertake a high-altitude overflight, affording the reader a glimpse of the terrain below.

---

[1] For an admirable survey of postwar developments in academic philosophy, see Rex Martin and James W. Nickel, "Recent Work on the Concept of Rights," *American Philosophical Quarterly* 17 (July 1980): 165–80. The best recent survey from the standpoint of political theory is Jeremy Waldron's concluding essay in Waldron, ed., *Nonsense upon Stilts: Bentham, Burke and Marx on the Rights of Man* (London and New York: Methuen, 1987), chap. 6. This volume also includes a substantial bibliographical essay (pp. 222–30). Other important bibliographies of rights literature include Martin and Nickel, "Bibliography on the Nature and Foundations of Rights, 1947–1977," *Political Theory* 6 (1978): 395–413; Waldron, ed., *Theories of Rights* (Oxford: Oxford University Press, 1984), 202–5; Loren Lomasky, *Persons, Rights, and the Moral Community* (New York: Oxford University Press, 1987), 273–6; Jack Donnelly, *Universal Human Rights in Theory and Practice* (Ithaca: Cornell University Press, 1989), 271–91; and C. J. G. Sampford and D. J. Galligan, eds., *Law, Rights and the Welfare State* (London: Croom Helm, 1986), 200–7. In addition to the collections by Waldron and Sampford/Galligan just cited, key anthologies of essays on rights include D. D. Raphael, ed., *Political Theory and the Rights of Man* (London: Macmillan, 1967); David Lyons, ed., *Rights* (Belmont, Calif.: Wadsworth, 1979); A. I. Melden, ed., *Human Rights* (Belmont, Calif.: Wadsworth, 1970); Eugene Kamenka and Alice Erh-Soon Tay, eds., *Human Rights* (London: Edward Arnold, 1978); J. Roland Pennock and John W. Chapman, eds., *Human Rights: Nomos XXIII* (New York and London: New York University Press, 1981); R. G. Frey, ed., *Utility and Rights* (Minneapolis: University of Minnesota Press, 1984); Robert A. Goldwin and William A. Schambra, eds., *How Does the Constitution Secure Rights?* (Washington, D.C.: American Enterprise Institute, 1985); *The Monist* 52 (October 1968); *Social Philosophy and Policy* 1 (Spring 1984).

The first section offers a brief account of the historical traditions of public and philosophic discourse that have shaped the current discussion of rights. The second section looks more directly, and less briefly, at this discussion—specifically, at some of the epistemological, ontological, moral, and political objections raised against rights. The third section explores some implications of taking the Declaration of Independence seriously as a philosophic backdrop to the interpretation of the Bill of Rights. The fourth section inventories and investigates some recent philosophic supplements to, or substitutes for, the Declaration as a source of rights interpretation. The concluding section offers some brief reflections on ways in which the language of rights must be enriched if the liberal polity structured by rights is to be adequately defended.

Although the central purpose of this chapter is to survey current thinking about rights, a brief sketch of my own views may help orient the reader. I believe that rights must be viewed as historical achievements, as protections—devised and tested through time and practice—against many of the worst evils that can befall human beings, especially those they can inflict on one another. The task of practical philosophy is to reflect on that achievement: to search for underlying commonalities; to explore ambiguities of (and contradictions between) existing rights; and to inquire whether, given added experience and changed circumstances, the intuitions that initially guided the construction of particular rights might now warrant their extension or alteration.

In so reflecting, two unifying functions of rights emerge: protecting certain interests deemed to be central to our conception of minimally decent human lives, and securing adequate scope for the exercise of individual agency. What also emerges (and this is the note on which this chapter concludes) is the *incompleteness* of the language of rights. There is a gap between "I have a right to do *X*" and "*X* is the right thing to do" that can only be filled by a non–rights-based moral vocabulary. Equally important is the question of how we become agents capable of exercising rights responsibly; this is the point at which the discourse of rights gives way to issues of civic education and to the inquiry into the full range of influences on the formation of character in liberal societies.

HISTORICAL SOURCES OF RIGHTS

Contemporary discussions of rights are shaped by a complex historical inheritance. This section sketches the most important historical tributaries flowing into today's sea of rights.

The post-Reformation wars of religion serve as a useful point of departure. Three different responses to this turbulent period have helped constitute our understanding of rights. To begin with, doctrinal clashes had helped spark an outburst of cruelty that shocked Europe. Leading humanists, chief among them Montaigne, reacted (in Judith Shklar's formulation) by "putting cruelty first"—that is, by identifying cruelty as the prime vice, by focusing on the fear cruelty engendered as the core evil, and by attempting to shape new political understandings and institutions that would reduce the amount of cruelty and fear in the world. As Shklar puts it,

When one puts [cruelty] first one responds, as Montaigne did, to the acknowledgment that one fears nothing more than fear. The fear of fear does not require any further justification, because it is irreducible. It can be both the beginning and an end of political institutions such as rights. The first right is to be protected against the fear of cruelty. People have rights against this greatest of public vices.[2]

This focus on cruelty is echoed in the Eighth Amendment's prohibition of cruel and unusual punishment, and it makes a dramatic reappearance as one of the Atlantic Charter's "four freedoms"—freedom from fear—in response to the twentieth-century renewal of doctrinally driven brutality.

A second response to religious warfare was an enhanced focus on the value of human life and the formulation of rights of self-preservation. The locus classicus is of course Hobbes, but life is first among the Lockean triad as well, and it figures prominently in both the Declaration of Independence and the Fifth Amendment. In our time, H. L. A. Hart has restated this thesis as the "minimum content of natural law."[3]

A third response to the wars of religion was the development of doctrines of toleration, rights of religious conscience, and the conception of a sphere of privacy, free from government interference, of which religion was the first (and arguably remains the most important) occupant. Locke's various letters on toleration constitute the fullest (if by no means unique statement) of this thesis, the impact of which on the First Amend-

---

[2] Judith Shklar, *Ordinary Vices* (Cambridge, Mass.: Harvard University Press, 1984), 237.
[3] H. L. A. Hart, *The Concept of Law* (Oxford: Clarendon Press, 1961), chap. 9. Important discussions of Hobbesian arguments are found in Leo Strauss, *Natural Right and History* (Chicago: University of Chicago Press, 1953), chap. 5(A); Ian Shapiro, *The Evolution of Rights in Liberal Theory* (Cambridge: Cambridge University Press, 1986), chap. 2; Richard Tuck, *Natural Rights Theories: Their Origin and Development* (Cambridge: Cambridge University Press, 1979).

ment—indeed, on American constitutionalism generally—can hardly be overestimated.[4]

The impact of Protestantism on the development of rights theories extended far beyond these responses to religious conflict. In its more radical forms, Protestantism preached the fundamental equality of human beings and translated this principle into a consensual theory of legitimacy. Perhaps the classic formulation of this relationship appears in the 1647 Putney debates, when Colonel Rainboro, a leader of the radicals within the Parliamentary army, declared: "Really I think that the poorest he that is in England has a life to live as the richest he; and therefore truly, Sir, I think it's clear, that every man that is to live under a Government ought first by his own consent to put himself under that Government."[5] In our time Gregory Vlastos has defended a secularized version of this argument, in the form of a distinction between the intrinsic equality of human worth and the various inequalities of individual merit and accomplishment.[6]

The focus thus far has been on the consequences for rights of religious conflict. Parallel but equally consequential developments, of course, were occurring in the society and economy of early modern Europe: in particular, the breakdown of feudal and aristocratic systems under various pressures and their gradual replacement by conceptions of property as fungible individual holdings. The causal relationship of historical and doctrinal change in this area has been subject to endless debate, as have

---

[4] For a clear characterization of the American significance of Locke's religious thought, see Walter Berns, "Religion and the Founding Principle," in Robert H. Horwitz, ed., *The Moral Foundations of the American Republic* (Charlottesville: University Press of Virginia, 1977), 157–82. David A. J. Richards offers a survey with constitutional applications in *Toleration and the Constitution* (New York: Oxford University Press, 1986), chaps. 4 and 5. A valuable collection of diverse essays is found in Robert A. Goldwin and Art Kaufman, eds., *How Does the Constitution Protect Religious Freedom?* (Washington, D.C.: American Enterprise Institute, 1987). I have explored the roots and consequences of Locke's argument in "Liberalism and Public Morality," Alfonso J. Damico, ed., *Liberals on Liberalism* (Totowa, N.J.: Rowman & Littlefield, 1986), 129–47. Stephen Holmes has traced parallel developments in the thought of the sixteenth-century French thinker Jean Bodin, "Jean Bodin: The Paradox of Sovereignty and the Privatization of Religion," in J. Roland Pennock and John W. Chapman, eds., *Religion, Morality, and the Law: Nomos XXX* (New York: New York University Press, 1988), 5–45. The late George Kelly has done the same for Pierre Bayle in "Bayle's Commonwealth of Atheists Revisited," in ibid., 78–109.

[5] "Debates on the Putney Project," in Alphaeus Thomas Mason, *Free Government in the Making* (3d ed.; New York: Oxford University Press, 1965), 13.

[6] Gregory Vlastos, "Justice and Equality," in Waldron, ed., *Theories of Rights*, 41–76. See also Joel Feinberg, *Social Philosophy* (Englewood Cliffs, N.J.: Prentice-Hall, 1973), 88–94.

the roles of (inter alia) Hobbes and the Harringtonian civic republicans. Suffice it to say here that by no later than Locke's *Second Treatise,* an enormously powerful revision of medieval property theory had made its appearance, in which full-blown property rights were grounded in self-ownership and labor and were limited only modestly by the rightful claims of others and by the valid acts of consent-based representative governments. While the Declaration of Independence replaces the property leg of Locke's tripod with the more general pursuit of happiness, property rights binding on the national government reappear strongly in the Fifth Amendment, in language to be repeated and applied to the states in the Fourteenth.[7]

The encounter between systems of property rights and the dynamics of market economies, which roughly spanned the century between the 1830s and the 1930s, engendered important codicils to Locke's initial bequest. In Britain, liberal thought after John Stuart Mill developed ideas of what we would now call welfare rights and reconceptualized the relationship between individual holdings and the common good.[8] In the

[7] The literature on this topic is unfathomably vast. For the seventeenth-century context readers may begin with Strauss, *Natural Right and History,* chap. 5(B); Shapiro, *The Evolution of Rights in Liberal Theory,* chaps. 2 and 3; C. B. Macpherson, *The Political Theory of Possessive Individualism: Hobbes to Locke* (Oxford: Oxford University Press, 1962); James Tully, *A Discourse on Property: John Locke and his Adversaries* (Cambridge: Cambridge University Press, 1980); Richard Ashcraft, *Revolutionary Politics and Locke's Two Treatises of Government* (Princeton, N.J.: Princeton University Press, 1986); Richard B. Schlatter, *Private Property: The History of an Idea* (London, Eng.: Allen & Unwin, 1951). Important contemporary treatments include Alan Ryan, *Property* (Minneapolis: University of Minnesota Press, 1987), and *Property and Political Theory* (Oxford: Basil Blackwell, 1984); Lawrence Becker, *Property Rights: Philosophic Foundations* (London: Routledge and Kegan Paul, 1971); John W. Chapman, *Property* (New York: New York University Press, 1980); Jeremy Waldron, *The Right to Private Property* (Oxford: Clarendon Press, 1988). Two provocative and philosophically informed discussions within the constitutional context are Bruce A. Ackerman, *Private Property and the Constitution* (New Haven: Yale University Press, 1977), and Richard Epstein, *Takings* (Cambridge, Mass.: Harvard University Press, 1986).

[8] For useful historical surveys, see Stefan Collini, *Liberalism and Sociology: L. T. Hobhouse and Political Argument in England, 1880–1914* (Cambridge: Cambridge University Press, 1979); Michael Freeden, *The New Liberalism: An Ideology of Social Reform* (Oxford: Clarendon Press, 1978); and Gerald F. Gaus, *The Modern Liberal Theory of Man* (London & Canberra: Croom Helm, 1983), especially chap. 7. For philosophical arguments in favor of welfare rights, variously construed, see: Sampford and Galligan, eds., *Law, Rights and the Welfare State* (especially chapters by Raymond Plant and Wojciech Sadurski); Carl Wellman, *Welfare Rights* (Totowa, N.J.: Rowman and Littlefield, 1982); D. D. Raphael, "Human Rights, Old and New," in Raphael, ed., *Political Theory and the Rights of Man.* Martin P. Golding argues for an even stronger proposition; "If there are any rights at all, there are welfare rights [and] the notion of welfare rights has a theoretical primacy, conceptually and normatively, over option rights" ("The Primacy of Welfare Rights," *Social Philosophy and Policy* 1 [Spring 1984]: 135). For an effort to incorporate

United States, the Progressive movement in the first quarter of this century espoused a more collectivist and Hamiltonian doctrine of government economic policy, a move that laid the intellectual foundation for the New Deal.[9] As a broad generalization, it may be said that these developments had the effect of highlighting elements of the Lockean argument that had been largely suppressed during the late eighteenth and early nineteenth centuries: the requirements of at least limited "other-regardingness" and the residual economic power of popular governments. The ensuing tension between the moral logics of individual holdings and of the general welfare has continued to characterize American politics and jurisprudence to the present day.[10]

The sea of rights has been nourished by two other tributaries in the two centuries since the American Revolution. The one is Immanuel Kant's understanding of individual autonomy and dignity, which in our time has influenced conceptions of rights from Robert Nozick on the libertarian right to Jürgen Habermas on the participatory left. John Rawls, surely the most influential liberal theorist of our time, has moved decisively in the past decade toward a more Kantian understanding of moral personality. Kant's renewed appeal may be directly related to the interpretation (I would say misinterpretation) of pre-Kantian liberalism as rooted in self-interest and therefore as lacking in moral depth.[11]

The final source of the rights tradition is a conception of liberal individuality, shaped in response to the rise of liberal societies. One element of this tradition is the line running from Humboldt to Mill and

this concept into the U. S. Constitution, see Frank I. Michelman, "In Pursuit of Constitutional Welfare Rights: One View of Rawls' Theory of Justice," *University of Pennsylvania Law Review* 121 (1973), and "Constitutional Welfare Rights and *A Theory of Justice*," in Daniels, ed., *Reading Rawls*, 319–47. For an extension into the international arena, see Henry Shue, *Basic Rights: Subsistence, Affluence, and U.S. Foreign Policy* (Princeton, N.J.: Princeton University Press, 1980). Maurice Cranston offers a counterargument in "Human Rights, Real and Supposed," Raphael, ed., 43–53. Of course, Nozick's *Anarchy, State, and Utopia* may be read as a sustained critique of the proposition that rights and welfare can be conjoined. Waldron offers a useful summary discussion in *Nonsense upon Stilts*, 156–9.

[9] See especially Herbert Croly, *The Promise of American Life* (New York: Capricorn Books, 1964).

[10] Arguably, this tension can be resolved if both teachings are seen as rooted in a deeper Lockean conception of rational liberty or self-direction, and of government as having the right to provide all individuals with the internal and external requisites for the development and exercise of self-direction. See Rogers Smith, *Liberalism and American Constitutional Law* (Cambridge, Mass.: Harvard University Press, 1985).

[11] For more developed speculations along these lines, see my "Moral Personality and Liberal Theory: John Rawls's 'Dewey Lectures,' " *Political Theory* 10 (1982): 492–519.

Tocqueville, which focuses on the social conditions for the preservation of human distinctiveness against the weight of egalitarian "mass society." Another element is the more distinctively American heroic-Romantic tradition of Emerson, Thoreau, and Whitman, which (not without ambiguity) sees a rights-based democratic society as the arena within which various dramas of individuality may be enacted.[12] A third, developed most fully by Bernard Williams, sees personal character and integrity as in tension with both utilitarian consequentialism and Kantian abstraction. The point of our life, Williams argues, is to lead it as a distinct person with commitments to which we must hold fast, on pain of sacrificing what gives identity and meaning to life. From this standpoint, the purpose of moral theory and political institutions is to safeguard, as far as possible, the space within which these concrete individual life-projects can be adopted and carried out.[13]

In sum, I suggest that intellectual and institutional responses to three great historical events—religious conflict, the attenuation of feudal-aristocratic economies, and the rise of liberal societies—have engendered the categories within which most contemporary discussion of rights is carried out. But these events do not remain static and separate; on the contrary, what is most characteristic of the current discussion is the extent to which they intermingle in novel ways. For example, the much-disputed constitutional "right of privacy" would, if stabilized and solidified, lend to all manner of sexual relations the kind of protected sanctity once most characteristic of religious conscience. My point is only that a modest attention to history will help us understand why members of liberal societies today characteristically invoke certain concepts in response to the felt difficulties of our common life.

CONTEMPORARY CONTEXTS OF ARGUMENT

Rights stand at the epicenter of key debates in contemporary philosophy and politics. This section situates rights within the matrix of these debates. The main point is that in current circumstances, "taking rights seriously"

---

[12] For this, see especially George Kateb, "Democratic Individuality and the Claims of Politics," *Political Theory* 12 (August 1984): 331–60.

[13] See Bernard Williams, "Persons, Character and Morality," in *Moral Luck* (Cambridge: Cambridge University Press, 1981), 1–19, and "A Critique of Utilitarianism," in J. J. C. Smart and Bernard Williams, *Utilitarianism: For and Against* (Cambridge: Cambridge University Press, 1973).

entails a number of controversial, and in some cases unfashionable, commitments.

Epistemology. Let me begin on an epistemological note by distinguishing two ways of understanding the status of rights. In the first, which can be called the foundationalist view, rights rest on some general and enduring features of human beings: as moral agents, as created, as needy, or whatever. The basis on which any particular human beings are understood as "rights-bearers" makes it logically necessary to understand all human beings as rights-bearers. While it may be true that not all citizens or peoples or nations enjoy the full and free exercise of their rights, they nonetheless all possess them (equally). This element of universality is inherent in the very assertion of rights, or (to put it the other way around) to deny others their rights is to erode the ground on which one can claim one's own.

The other (antifoundationalist) view, espoused most prominently by Richard Rorty, is that the notion of rights as "resting on" something is a relic of the Greek/metaphysical, Christian/theological, Enlightenment/ rationalist picture of the self as an "ahistorical nature center, the locus of human dignity, surrounded by an adventitious and inessential periphery." From this standpoint, universalistic rights talk is "an attempt to enjoy the benefits of metaphysics without assuming the appropriate responsibilities." Instead, we must regard our rights as representing

something relatively local and ethnocentric—the tradition of a particular community, the consensus of a particular culture.... What counts as rational ... is relative to the group to which we think it necessary to justify ourselves—to the body of shared belief that determines the reference of the word "we."... The question of whether justifiability to the community with which we identify entails truth is simply irrelevant.[14]

Without entering into the details of this now-familiar controversy, let me pose what I take to be the central issue for present purposes: the relationship between the basis on which rights are asserted and the scope of their validity.[15] One view is that rights based on the consensus of a

---

[14] Richard Rorty, "The Priority of Democracy to Philosophy," in Merrill D. Peterson and Robert C. Vaughan, eds., *The Virginia Statute for Religious Freedom* (Cambridge: Cambridge University Press, 1988), 258–9.

[15] I am grateful to my colleagues at the University of Maryland's Institute for Philosophy and Public Policy, and especially to Robert Fullinwider and David Luban, for instructive discussion on this point.

particular community may still, without evident absurdity, be said to apply beyond the bounds of that community. The contrasting view, which I regard as more plausible, is that Rortean efforts to interpret universalistic norms as community values are likely to be incompatible with the community's own understanding of its transcommunity writ. At the very least, the communitarian interpretation is bound to conflict with the self-understanding of professedly universalistic cultures. As Jeremy Waldron observes,

A community like the United States cannot found itself upon something it takes to be a "self-evident truth" . . . and then go on to say glibly, "But that's just what we happen to think around here; different attitudes are distinctive of and valid for different societies." A person who says anything like that from within our society betrays our norms. . . . She does not keep faith with the *content* of our norm—namely, that it is *all people* (not simply all people who happen to live around here) who are said to have been created equal.[16]

This argument is very powerful within the American context, where a key locus of our rights discourse—the Declaration of Independence—announces that rights claims can (and must) be addressed, that is, to humankind as a whole. It is further reinforced by the United Nations' Universal Declaration of Human Rights, which addresses itself to "all members of the human family" and contends that disregard and contempt for rights have "outraged the conscience of mankind."[17] The point is not the (counterfactual) empirical claim that all nations have accepted and honored rights, but rather that rights are inherent possessions of every human being and binding on every government. This statement obviously does not prove that such universal claims are well founded, but it does suggest that it would be ill advised to dismiss them at the outset on abstract epistemological grounds.[18]

Ontology. The ontological critique of rights is somewhat more serious. It comes in two versions, individual and social. Michael Sandel has argued

[16] Jeremy Waldron, "Particular Values and Critical Morality," *California Law Review* 77 (May 1989): 576. See also Will Kymlicka, *Liberalism, Community, and Culture* (Oxford: Clarendon Press, 1989), 65–66; and William A. Galston, "Pluralism and Social Unity," *Ethics* 99 (July 1989): 725–6.

[17] Ian Brownlie, ed., *Basic Documents on Human Rights* (Oxford: Clarendon Press, 1981), 21.

[18] For a serious and intriguing effort to locate rights claims at the midpoint of the continuum of antifoundationalist particularity and rationalist universality, see Thomas L. Haskell, "The Curious Persistence of Rights Talk in the 'Age of Interpretation,' " *Journal of American History* (1988): 984–1012.

that our current understanding of rights rests on an untenable conception of the self as "unencumbered" by particular ties of birth and community membership. This conception suggests that the structure of the self is somehow anterior to, and detachable from, the choices that give the self its particular identity. But Sandel thinks this understanding is untrue to the facts: many loyalties and convictions are the product of unchosen ties—"constitutive attachments" that we could not repudiate without undermining our character and identity.[19]

Any sensible response to this argument must begin by accepting one of its essential premises. There *are* aims and allegiances that are not in the first instance chosen, that arise out of our history and circumstances, and that to a considerable extent constitute our individual identities.

Once this point is granted, defenders of rights must choose between two strategies. The first, espoused most directly by John Rawls, is to draw a sharp line between these constitutive relationships and the conception of the person required by the political conception of liberal justice—that is, to deny that liberal rights rest on any specific conception of the individual. Properly understood, liberalism is "political not metaphysical." The veil of ignorance through which our rights are specified has "no metaphysical implications concerning the nature of the self; it does not imply that the self is ontologically prior to the facts about persons that the parties are excluded from knowing." We enter the original position not by denying our constituted selfhood but by screening out, for justificatory purposes, knowledge of social position and other individual contingencies held to be morally arbitrary.[20]

Rawls's strategy contains a number of difficulties. To begin with, as Amy Gutmann has argued, it is one thing to say that rights do not presuppose a single metaphysical view of the individual, but quite another to say that they are compatible with all such views. There are some conceptions of the individual (viewed, e.g., as "radically situated") that rights as we understand them simply cannot accommodate.[21]

There is another objection: Rawls's own argument manifestly depends on a specific affirmative conception of the self. Persons must be seen as

---

[19] Michael Sandel, "The Procedural Republic and the Unencumbered Self," *Political Theory* 12 (1984): 90–1.

[20] John Rawls, "Justice as Fairness: Political not Metaphysical," *Philosophy and Public Affairs* 14 (1985): 237–9.

[21] Amy Gutmann, "Communitarian Critics of Liberalism," *Philosophy and Public Affairs* 14 (1985): 319. See also Rawls's own qualifications in "Political Not Metaphysical," 240n.

emotionally, intellectually, and ontologically capable of drawing an effective line between their public and nonpublic identities and of setting aside their particular commitments, at least to the extent needed to enter the original position and to reason in a manner consistent with its constraints.

This objection suggests an affirmative proposition. Liberal rights rest not on the unencumbered self (which Sandel rightly criticizes) but on the *divided* self. On the one side stands the individual's personal and social history, with all the aims and attachments it may imply. On the other side stands the possibility of critical reflection on—even revolt against—these very commitments. Crucial to the self as rights-bearer is the potential for such critical distance from one's inheritance and the possibility that the exercise of critical faculties may, in important respects, modify that inheritance. The liberal conception of the self requires the kind of reflective distance demonstrated by the ability to become aware of the contingency of one's own social position and of the latent contradictions of one's own society. Rawls must concede no less, the liberal theory of rights needs no more, and the communitarian critics of rights cannot in the last analysis deny the possibility of reflective distance, so understood.[22]

Charles Taylor has offered a critique of rights from the standpoint of what might be termed social ontology. Stripped to its essentials, his thesis is that the theoretical primacy of rights rests on a false ("atomistic") view of the relationship between the individual and the political community. In this view, the individual is seen as prior to the community, which in turn is understood as the product of individual choice. For Taylor, this thesis requires the denial both of the modern truth that respect for rights requires us to affirm the worth of certain human capacities and of the Aristotelian truth that people are social beings who can develop these capacities only in society. The conjunction of these truths yields an obligation to join and sustain a political community that is (at least) equiprimordial with the assertion of rights. It also yields a specific, nonneutral conception of the human good: to wit, the demand that we become beings capable of rightly exercising our rights by rising to self-consciousness

---

[22] The preceding six paragraphs are adapted from my "Pluralism and Social Unity," 720–2. Parallel arguments were developed at roughly the same time by Kymlicka in *Liberalism, Community, and Culture*, 55–6, and by Robert Post, "Tradition, the Self, and Substantive Due Process: A Comment on Michael Sandel," *California Law Review* 77 (May 1989): 557–8. Post very pertinently refers to George Herbert Mead's distinction between the socially constituted me-self and the critical I-self as support for such a position.

and overcoming fear, sloth, and ignorance—accomplishments that require not only society but society of a certain kind in which the needs of all members are taken seriously and in which the political instruments of common decision include (and are used by) everyone.[23]

If asserting rights really implied denying human sociability, their credibility would be shaky indeed, but there are reasons to doubt the necessity of this move. To begin with, as Stephen Holmes has argued, the early modern progenitors of rights doctrines never supposed that human beings were presocial in Taylor's sense:

Not even the liberals who consistently invoked the state of nature were so unrealistic as to deny the social nature of man. Locke, for one, never suggested that fully formed adults entered the world without any need for primary socialization. The social contract myth should be read politically, not descriptively. An emphasis on the voluntariness of social "bonds" was meant to discredit a specific set of involuntary relations characteristic of traditional European societies. To "atomize" human self-understanding was to attack "organic" chains of dependence and subordination as well as to undermine dangerous clan and sectarian groupings.[24]

At most, Taylor's social thesis shows that defenders of rights would be mistaken to claim that rights constitute the totality of politically relevant principles. But few (if any)[25] have ever advanced such claims. The point is, rights protect vital individual interests that political theory neglects at its peril. The difficulty of coordinating rights with other political values should not be underestimated, but this difficulty should not lead us to the extreme of devaluing rights or of systematically subordinating them to other considerations.[26]

In recent writings Taylor has added a layer of productive complexity to these issues. He distinguishes between ontological argument, which elucidates the general structure of relationships between individuals and the community, and advocacy, which takes a stand on specific issues such

---

[23] This paragraph summarizes the argument of Charles Taylor, "Atomism," in Alkis Kontos, ed., *Powers, Possessions, and Freedom: Essays in Honour of C.B. Macpherson* (Toronto: University of Toronto Press, 1979), 39–61.

[24] Stephen Holmes, "The Permanent Structure of Antiliberal Thought," in Nancy L. Rosenblum, ed., *Liberalism and the Moral Life* (Cambridge, Mass.: Harvard University Press, 1989), 238.

[25] Even Robert Nozick, widely considered to be the archetypical rights purist, acknowledges that rights might have to be violated to avoid "catastrophic moral horror." *Anarchy, State, and Utopia* (New York: Basic Books, 1974), 30n.

[26] This thesis is vigorously argued by Jeremy Waldron in Waldron, ed., *Nonsense upon Stilts: Bentham, Burke, and Marx on the Rights of Man* (London and New York: Methuen, 1987), 183–90.

as the status and content of rights. Ontological argument may be broadly divided into atomistic and holistic theses, while advocacy is arrayed along a continuum from individualism to collectivism. Taylor's point is that a holistic (e.g., Aristotelian) ontological commitment can be combined with a form of individualism at the level of advocacy. He invokes Humboldt as an example of this stance and goes on to argue, correctly in my view, that

> Humboldt was one of the important sources for Mill's doctrine of liberty. In the face of this, it is astonishing that anyone should read a defense of holism as entailing an advocacy of collectivism. But the rich tradition that Humboldt represents seems to have been forgotten by Mill's heirs in the English-speaking world.[27]

From this standpoint, a key task for contemporary rights theory is to bring together in one view a realistic understanding of the social formation of personality, with all the particular commitments and obligations this understanding may entail, and an appreciation of the continuing individuation of persons so formed. I may share much with others, and many of the goods I enjoy may be collective. Still, it is *I* who share and enjoy—an independent consciousness, a separate locus of pleasure and pain, a demarcated being with interests and convictions to be advanced or suppressed. My interpretation of my individual good, or the good of society, may be socially constituted, but it is nonetheless mine, and it may not be fully congruent with the good or conceptions of others. As we resist the hyperindividualism of thinkers who deny the existence of any social bonds with or natural duties to others, we must not fall into a hyperorganicism that forgets the ineradicable separateness of our individual existences.

Moral theory. Moral theory is a third significant arena of contemporary conflict over rights. The best-known difficulty here is the conflict, real or alleged, between individual rights and collective ends. From the classic Benthamite standpoint, of course, all talk of natural rights is "nonsense

---

[27] Charles Taylor, "Cross-Purposes: The Liberal-Communitarian Debate," in Rosenblum, ed., *Liberalism and the Moral Life*, 163. For another exploration of the differences between social ontology and social advocacy, see Bernard Yack, "Does Liberal Practice Live 'Down' to Liberal Theory?: Liberalism and Its Communitarian Critics," in Charles Reynolds and Ralph Norman, eds., *Community in America* (Berkeley: University of California Press, 1988).

upon stilts."[28] John Stuart Mill believed that personal liberty properly understood was compatible with general utility (again, properly understood)—a claim that has been exposed ever since to vast quantities of abuse and defense.[29] Today, many sophisticated utilitarians argue that their theory supports, and allows adequate scope for, rights as now understood, while others contend with equal fervor that a choice between them cannot be indefinitely avoided.[30] Ronald Dworkin and Robert Nozick, two theorists with very different substantive conceptions of rights, have converged on the claim that the purpose of individual rights as a general concept is to block certain appeals to collective goals.[31] John Rawls, of course, has criticized utilitarianism for not taking seriously the separateness of persons, and his own theory, as Dworkin suggests, accordingly (if tacitly) appeals to the very general right of each person to equal concern and respect.[32]

I cannot hope to advance, let alone resolve, the debate on a topic of such scope and complexity. Mutually independent and normatively weighty considerations often tug in opposing directions and, in the absence of a common denominator of value, must be balanced against each other through intuition and common sense in specific cases.[33]

---

[28] See especially Jeremy Bentham's *Anarchical Fallacies,* portions of which are reprinted in Waldron, *Nonsense upon Stilts,* 46–76.

[29] For a recent defense of Mill that manages to cite a substantial fraction of the writings on this subject, see John Gray, "John Stuart Mill on Liberty, Utility, and Rights," in J. Roland Pennock and John W. Chapman, eds., *Human Rights: Nomos XXIII* (New York and London: New York University Press, 1981), 80–116. Gray's note 11 is an especially valuable compilation of sources.

[30] An excellent collection of recent essays on this topic may be found in R. G. Frey, ed., *Utility and Rights* (Minneapolis: University of Minnesota Press, 1984). Other important contributions include Lawrence Haworth, "Utility and Rights," in Nicholas Rescher, ed., *Studies in Moral Philosophy* (Oxford: Basil Blackwell, 1968), 64–85; David Lyons, "Human Rights and the General Welfare," *Philosophy and Public Affairs* (Winter 1977): 113–28, and "Utility and Rights," in Jeremy Waldron, ed., *Theories of Rights* (Oxford: Oxford University Press, 1984), 110–36; T. M. Scanlon, "Rights, Goals, and Fairness," also in Waldron, *Theories of Rights,* 137–52; H. L. A. Hart, "Between Utility and Rights," in Alan Ryan, ed., *The Idea of Freedom: Essays in Honour of Isaiah Berlin* (Oxford: Oxford University Press, 1979), 77–98. Waldron's *Nonsense upon Stilts,* 228, offers a list of additional readings on this topic.

[31] Nozick, *Anarchy, State, and Utopia,* 28–35; Ronald Dworkin, *Taking Rights Seriously* (Cambridge, Mass.: Harvard University Press, 1978), chap. 7, and *A Matter of Principle* (Cambridge, Mass.: Harvard University Press, 1985), chap. 17.

[32] John Rawls, *A Theory of Justice* (Cambridge, Mass.: Harvard University Press, 1971); Ronald Dworkin, "The Original Position," in Norman Daniels, ed., *Reading Rawls* (New York: Basic Books, n.d.), 16–53. Rawls takes issue with Dworkin's interpretation in "Justice as Fairness: Political Not Metaphysical," 236–7n, but does not firmly reject it. Indeed, Rawls remarks, "Others may prefer his account."

[33] For discussions of such trade-offs, see Brian Barry, *Political Argument* (London: Rout-

Rights theorists are on strong ground when they appeal to sentiments of personal inviolability and to what G. A. Cohen has called self-ownership—the thought that "each person is the morally rightful owner of himself." As Cohen candidly acknowledges, many critics of rights

lose confidence in their unqualified denial of the thesis of self-ownership when they are asked to consider who has the right to decide what should happen to, for example, their own eyes. They do not immediately agree that, were eye transplants easy to achieve, it would then be acceptable for the state to conscript potential eye donors into a lottery whose losers must yield an eye to beneficiaries who would otherwise be not one-eyed but blind.[34]

Conversely, utilitarians are on strong ground when they insist that at some point numbers matter—that is, that the consequences (for others affected) of honoring an individual's right at some level of scope and severity, will come to appear intolerable. This position is only strengthened by the tendency of many theorists to trace the importance of rights to the importance of the interests they help defend: at some point it will come to seem unreasonable to protect A's interest in X at the expense of the equivalent interests of B, C, ... N.

Precisely this tension between the perspectives of the individual and the collectivity is reflected in the charter documents of the United States. The preamble to the Constitution depicts the purposes of the institutions it creates in decidedly collective terms: ensuring domestic tranquillity, providing for the common defense, and promoting the general welfare. Yet it also speaks of establishing justice and securing liberty, terms susceptible of a far more individualistic reading.

This tension is only heightened by the Bill of Rights. Many of its opponents held it to be unnecessary because (as Alexander Hamilton said) the Constitution is itself a bill of rights,[35] or even potentially harmful because (as James Madison feared) any incomplete enumeration of the people's rights might warrant the mistaken conclusion that the others

ledge & Kegan Paul), 1965, 3–8; James S. Fishkin, *Justice, Equal Opportunity, and the Family* (New Haven, Conn.: Yale University Press, 1983), 169–93; Charles E. Larmore, *Patterns of Moral Complexity* (Cambridge: Cambridge University Press, 1987), chap. 6.

[34] G. A. Cohen, "Self-Ownership, World Ownership, and Equality," in Frank S. Lucash, ed., *Justice and Equality Here and Now* (Ithaca: Cornell University Press, 1986), 109, 111.

[35] Clinton Rossiter, ed., *The Federalist* (New York: New American Library, 1961), no. 84, p. 515.

had been forfeited to the new government.[36] But to the best of my knowledge, none argued that a bill of rights would be inconsistent with the Constitution's principles and purposes. A tension between individual rights and collective purposes is thus built into the basic structure of American political institutions.

Indeed, the language in which some rights are expressed may be interpreted as bearing witness to this tension. Consider, for example, the Fourth Amendment, which protects individuals against "unreasonable" searches. The language of the amendment provides no standard of reasonableness, but one possible test is the balance between the extent of the contemplated violation of personal security and the weight of the public tranquillity, welfare, or defense interests at stake. That governments will constantly be tempted to justify intrusions by exaggerating or trumping up threats is true enough, but the task of weighing public against personal claims cannot be avoided. That task must, then, have an institutional locus, which Madison found in the judiciary:

If a [bill of rights is] incorporated into the constitution, independent tribunals of justice will consider themselves in a peculiar manner the guardians of those rights; they will be an impenetrable bulwark against assumption of power in the legislative and executive; they will be naturally led to resist every encroachment upon rights.[37]

A very different range of issues is raised by the charge that the emphasis on rights must give short shrift to, or inappropriately subordinate, the claims of duty. Leo Strauss has observed that "premodern natural law doctrines taught the duties of man; if they paid any attention at all to his rights, they conceived of them as essentially derivative from his duties. ... In the course of the seventeenth and eighteenth centuries a much greater emphasis was put on rights than had ever been done before."[38] Ronald Dworkin's influential trichotomy of goal-based, rights-based, and

---

[36] See Arthur E. Wilmarth, Jr., "The Original Purpose of the Bill of Rights: James Madison and the Founders' Search for a Workable Balance between Federal and State Power," *American Criminal Law Review* 26 (1989): 1290–1.

[37] Speech by Madison to the House of Representatives of 8 June 1789, quoted in Wilmarth, "The Original Purpose of the Bill of Rights," 1293.

[38] Leo Strauss, *Natural Right and History* (Chicago: University of Chicago Press, 1953), 182.

duty-based theories has lent plausibility to the suspicion that taking rights seriously may entail treating duties less than seriously.[39]

There is much to be said against this suspicion. First, without venturing into the endless technical discussions of the "correlativity of rights and duties," it is clear that many rights entail duties.[40] If I have a right to do X, then you have (at least) a duty not to prevent me from doing X. A system of permissions is simultaneously a system of exacting prohibitions.

Second, political philosophies emphasizing rights can coexist with moral philosophies that give pride of place to duty. It would be hard, for example, to accuse Kant of being unserious about duties, but in his political writings he tries to show how this focus might be combined with strict and extensive limits on the capacity of public authority to interfere with individuals.[41]

Third, some rights are simultaneously and equally duties. In the Declaration of Independence, for example, popular resistance to tyrannical oppression is characterized as both a right and a duty (discussed later).

Finally, rights are rarely intended as a complete and comprehensive moral vocabulary. John Rawls, for example, proposes a theory of justice that includes—indeed, gives pride of place to—philosophical justification for a wide range of traditional constitutional rights. At the same time, he speaks of the natural duty to uphold just institutions, and proposes the "capacity for a sense of justice" as the aspect of individual moral personality needed to sustain that duty.[42]

This point—the incompleteness of rights—may be defended from another perspective as well. As Jeremy Waldron observes, the proposition that I have a right to do X hardly exhausts what we may say about X,

---

[39] Ronald Dworkin, "The Original Position," 40. I cannot here assess Kymlicka's intriguing assertion that Dworkin has, in effect, subsequently repudiated this system of classification. See *Liberalism, Community, and Culture*, 75.

[40] For those inclined to take a deeper plunge into this topic, the place to begin is with Martin and Nickel, "Recent Work on the Concept of Rights," 165–7.

[41] I do not mean to suggest that this coexistence is altogether untroubled. For some reasons why not, see my "Defending Liberalism," *American Political Science Review* 76 (1982): 621–9, and *Kant and the Problem of History* (Chicago: University of Chicago Press, 1975), 195–202.

[42] For the philosophical underpinnings of constitutional rights, see his "The Basic Liberties and Their Priority," in Sterling M. McMurrin, ed., *The Tanner Lectures on Human Values: III* (Salt Lake City: University of Utah Press, 1982), 1–87. Natural duty is discussed in *A Theory of Justice*, sections 19 and 51. The capacity for a sense of justice is stressed in "Kantian Constructivism in Moral Theory: The Dewey Lectures 1980," *Journal of Philosophy* 77 (1980): 515–72.

morally speaking. There may be compelling moral reasons why I should not do X, and indeed my right to do it is in no sense a reason to. The right is addressed, in the first instance, to those other than myself and indicates the wrongness of interfering with me. To the extent that a right is a sufficient reason for action, it is such a reason for others, not for the rights-bearer.[43]

The moral incompleteness of rights extends far beyond duties. Joseph Raz has argued that rights-based theories cannot do justice to supererogation, the virtues, or morally significant reasons for action that transcend narrow duty, and that such theories have a hard time coming to grips with the social pursuit of intrinsically valuable goods that are collective rather than individual.[44] Raz's compelling argument is directed at the proposition that only rights are to be taken as fundamental and other moral categories are to be regarded as deriving from them. As he makes clear, however, his argument is not intended as a case against rights as such but as one in favor of a "pluralistic understanding of the foundation of morality" in which rights, duties, and intrinsic values are equally fundamental.[45]

Politics. World events of the late 1980s have fundamentally transformed the rights discussion. Classic Marxist animadversions against "bourgeois rights" have all but disappeared, as have the moral equivalence arguments ("you stress political rights, we ensure economic rights") characteristic of Leninist regimes in the post–World War II era. Throughout the former Eastern Bloc, traditional liberal rights are the focus of attention—in part because they were systematically repressed for so long, in part because they are crucial for the intellectuals who form the vanguard of the reform movements.

In one key respect, however, the debate has not changed. Rights are constitutive of liberalism as they are of no other political philosophy or

---

[43] Waldron, *Nonsense upon Stilts,* chap. 6. This is not to say, however, that there is a full-blown right to do wrong. Readers interested in this issue may consult Waldron, "A Right to Do Wrong," *Ethics* 92 (1981): 21–39, and the ensuing exchange between Waldron and myself, "On the Alleged Right to Do Wrong: A Response to Waldron" and "Galston on Rights," both appearing in *Ethics* 93 (January 1983): 320 ff.

[44] Joseph Raz, "Right-based Moralities," in Waldron, ed., *Theories of Rights,* 182–200.

[45] Ibid., 182. This immediately raises the question whether these basic moral categories form a harmonious system and if not, how the conflicts among them are to be adjudicated. Raz provides some sense of direction in *The Morality of Freedom* (Oxford: Clarendon Press, 1986), especially chaps. 11–15.

practice. Doubts about rights tend strongly to reflect broader reservations about liberalism itself.

These reservations have taken two forms. External reservations criticize liberalism and rights in the name of competing conceptions of politics and human life. Fascism, which upended the classic liberal preference for peace over war, was one such conception; today's Islamic fundamentalism is another. Internal reservations, by contrast, criticize liberal rights as inadequately realizing, or even thwarting, core principles that liberalism itself embraces (or at least does not wish to repudiate).

One such principle is democracy. In contemporary discussions, rights are seen as hostile to democracy in several respects. Democracy requires public, and public-spirited, action; rights sustain privacy and egoism. Democracy requires the ability of the people to carry out their decisions; rights thwart even overwhelming majorities. Democracy requires popular sovereignty; rights imply sources of moral authority beyond popular will and tend to empower unrepresentative and unresponsive institutions such as the judiciary.[46]

Supporters of liberal rights cheerfully plead guilty to portions of this indictment: rights do thwart majorities and do restrict popular sovereignty. These supporters go on to insist, with Jefferson and Lincoln, that democracy degenerates into the rule of force unless it is limited in this fashion or, to put the same point differently, that the moral force of democratic self-rule rests on a foundation of respect for individuals that limits the permissible scope of self-rule.

Liberals will be little troubled, at least in one important sense, by the "privacy" count of the indictment. An important purpose of rights is to establish a zone of noninterference protected from invasion, or redefinition, by even the most popularly based government. Liberals must therefore reject the democratic thesis of Benjamin Barber that the public has "the responsibility to legislate not only its own common destiny but

---

[46] See, for example, Benjamin R. Barber, *Strong Democracy: Participatory Politics for a New Age* (Berkeley: University of California Press, 1984), *The Conquest of Politics* (Princeton, N.J.: Princeton University Press, 1988), and "Liberal Democracy and the Costs of Consent," in Rosenblum, ed., *Liberalism and the Moral Life,* 54–68; Michael Walzer, "Philosophy and Democracy," *Political Theory* 9 (August 1981): 379–99, and "Liberalism and the Art of Separation," *Political Theory* 12 (August 1984): 315–30. Although this line of argument is most frequently associated with the participatory left, portions also make their appearance in the populist majoritarianism of the New Right, typically in response to what it views as "judicial activism." For an illuminating exposition and critique, see Stephen Macedo, *The New Right v. The Constitution* (Washington, D.C.: Cato Institute, 1987).

also the standards by which what is common and what is individual (what is public and what is private) are determined."[47]

Another sense of the privacy charge, however, is more fundamentally troubling. Liberals do not admit that the prime function of rights is to safeguard privacy. They point out that rights also protect opportunities for participation, including the rights to vote, to assemble, and to petition for redress. And clearly, freedom of speech and freedom of the press are "public-regarding" as well as (or, as some would argue, far more than) "private-regarding" rights.

Finally, the charge of egoism cannot be accepted, at least not as it stands. That the exercise of rights is consistent with a measure of self-interested behavior can hardly be denied, but rights do more than empower and protect individuals one by one. They form a system of conduct and constitute a regime. They ask each member of that regime to honor the rights of every other member and to respect all members as fellow rights-bearers. In a system of rights, then, permissible self-interest is constrained by prior moral commitments.[48]

There is, however, an important and cautionary practical point at the

---

[47] Barber, *The Conquest of Politics*, 7.

[48] For a more detailed discussion of the relationship between egoism and rights, see Waldron, *Nonsense upon Stilts*, 190–209. The philosophical version of this issue goes back at least to Hobbes. In *Morals by Agreement* (Oxford: Oxford University Press, 1986), David Gauthier tries to reinvigorate the Hobbesian argument that individuals moved by no more than rational self-interest would assent to moral constraints on their behavior, including the rights of others to certain kinds of noninterference. This thesis has been subjected to numerous searching criticisms, many of which are usefully collected in Ellen Frankel Paul et al., eds., *The New Social Contract: Essays on Gauthier* (Oxford: Basil Blackwell, 1988). In his post–*Theory of Justice* phase, John Rawls has denied with increasing fervor that rational self-interest, even when constrained by forms of ignorance and uncertainty, is enough to generate liberal principles. The distinction between the "Rational" (forming and pursuing a conception of the good) and the "Reasonable" (acting to honor fair terms of social cooperation) is intended to rule out the possibility that principles of justice can be selected "purely on the basis of a conception of rational choice as understood in economics or decision theory" ["The Basic Liberties and Their Priority, 21n]. Judith Shklar has also forcefully argued against the egoism thesis: "Since the eighteenth century, . . . critics of liberalism have pictured it as a doctrine that achieves its public goods, peace, prosperity, and security by encouraging private vice. Selfishness in all its possible forms is said to be its essence, purpose, and outcome. . . . Nothing could be more remote from the truth. The very refusal to use public coercion to impose creedal unanimity and uniform standards of behavior demands an enormous degree of self-control. Tolerance consistently applied is more difficult and morally more demanding than repression. . . . Far from being an amoral free-for-all, liberalism is, in fact, extremely difficult and constraining, far too much so for those who cannot endure contradiction, complexity, diversity, and the risks of freedom" (*Ordinary Vices* [Cambridge, Mass.: Harvard University Press, 1984], 4–5). Shklar's comments on Kantian liberal character, 232–236, are also pertinent in this connection.

heart of the democratic criticisms of rights. As the zone of individual rights expands, the space for popular determination of policy contracts. As Fred Siegel has summarized this argument:

Democratic politics ideally revolves around the compromises needed to secure widespread consent for government actions. Representative government, which encourages citizen participation, leaves the losers in a political contest with part of what they asked for or at least a feeling that their interests were considered. A judicialized politics, in contrast, bypasses public consent. Profoundly anti-democratic when it goes beyond vindicating the fundamental rights of citizenship, judicial politics alienates voters by placing public policy in the private hands of lawyers and litigants. And since rights are absolute, it polarizes by producing winner-take-all outcomes, in which the losers are likely to feel embittered. [Moreover,] the assertion of rights fences off the proponents of policies from the social costs those policies impose on the public at large.... What is lost, then, if rights are interpreted so expansively as to define policy, is a concern for the cumulative consequences of individually rendered rights-based decisions.[49]

Siegel's argument reminds (or should remind) proponents of rights that their hyperexpansion is questionable as a matter of theory and in practice may well lead to an erosion of support for the regime of basic rights and for their judicial protection. Clearly this debate cannot be fully joined until there is a specification of rights that marks off the arena of rights from the realm of policy. But any conception of rights that leads to interminable incursions into the public's democratic authority will end by undermining itself.[50]

The charge that rights are insufficiently democratic is frequently accompanied by the charge that they are insufficiently egalitarian. The latter charge assumes a number of related but distinct guises: that rights protect unacceptably unequal outcomes; that social and economic inequalities dilute the meaning of rights for the least-fortunate members of the community; and that as formal-legal powers they cannot be meaningful without collective efforts to provide everyone with the means to exercise them.

To some extent this is a debate not about the concept of rights but

---

[49] Fred Siegel, "Nothing in Moderation," *Atlantic* 265 (May 1990): 108–9.
[50] In the U.S. context, this issue is further complicated by the question of federalism. One indisputable outcome of the Civil War was the victory of a conception of national citizenship and of a mechanism for its protection. The question then becomes, What rights does national citizenship entail? The answer will draw the line between legitimate and illegitimate uses of state and local public power. National rights of voting, participation, and conscience are now regarded as settled and enforceable against local majorities. But issues such as abortion, pornography, and homosexuality remain embroiled in the struggle between proponents of uniform, judicially enforced national rights and proponents of local (hence variable) legislative authority.

about their substance. Much of it can be rephrased in the familiar di-
chotomy of liberty rights and welfare rights, and placed in the context
of the historic debate between classical liberalism and social democracy.[51]
If there are enforceable rights to a "social minimum" or to a fair share
of the social product as defined by generally accepted principles of justice,
then the charge of insufficient egalitarianism, which dines off the classic
Marxist distinction between "merely formal" political freedom and
"real" economic position, loses much of its force. (This is not to say that
the existence of such economic rights is obvious or incontestable.[52])

On the practical level, this argument may even be turned on its head.
Amartya Sen, whose concern for the well-being of the least advantaged
is both personal and passionate, has concluded on the basis of detailed
empirical-historical inquiry that extreme welfare deprivations such as
famines typically stem from the absence of classic liberal-democratic
political rights and can be prevented by the exercise of such rights:

> The diverse political freedoms that are available in a democratic state, including
> regular elections, free newspapers, and freedom of speech (without government
> prohibition or censorship), must be seen as the real force behind the elimination
> of famines.... The negative freedoms of newspapers and opposition parties to
> criticize, publish and agitate can be powerful in safeguarding the elementary
> positive freedoms of the vulnerable population.[53]

Another line of argument erodes the distinction between liberty and
welfare rights, and more broadly between negative rights of protection
against others and positive rights of claims against others, by observing
that the social enforcement of protective rights always involves a positive
claim on (or cost to) the community as a whole. If, for example, every
accused person has the right to a "speedy trial" and to "compulsory
process for obtaining witnesses in his favor," the community has an
obligation to furnish the wherewithal to make these rights effective and
real. And more generally, if individuals in society surrender a portion of
their right of self-protection in return for civil protection of their right
to life, then the community undertakes what may prove to be a very
costly obligation to guard all its members against violence.[54]

---

[51] See note 8 above.
[52] Ibid.
[53] Amartya Sen, "Individual Freedom as a Social Commitment," *New York Review of
Books* 37 (14 June 1990): 50.
[54] Norman Daniels has offered an even more far-reaching argument to the effect that the
equal political and social liberties affirmed in Rawls's first principle of justice will not
be truly choiceworthy unless their worth to all individuals is more or less equal, a

When all is said and done, however, proponents of rights must acknowledge the persistence of significant inequalities. Even if all (normal) human beings are equal in their possession of rights and in the means needed to exercise them,[55] a system of rights will allow a wide range of individual choice within which variations of preference, ambition, and talent are bound to manifest themselves in every sphere of endeavor. To give rights a central political position is to draw a line between required equality and permissible inequality. Partisans of a more comprehensive equality may object to the location of this line. If so, they must undertake to show that their own proposed boundary (which will require either the reduction or the redefinition of rights) is, on balance, more eligible.

Finally, the critique of rights may be examined from the standpoint of community. The core of the charge against rights here is that healthy political association requires a kind of sharing—not only agreement on common purposes, but also a network of affective ties. But whereas politics should connect us, rights divide us. They replace substantive purposes with formal procedures, and (worse) the warmth and intimacy of fellow-feeling with the chilly distance of opposing claims. This position does not necessarily mean that rights should be jettisoned altogether. It does at least require a fuller recognition of the extent to which a regime of rights is incomplete without, and depends on, a sense of mutual connection and shared fate among all members of the community.[56]

Proponents of rights need not resist the claim that an effective system

---

requirement that would require a substantial reduction in the range of economic and welfare inequalities permitted by Rawls's Difference Principle ("Equal Liberty and the Unequal Worth of Liberty," in Daniels, ed., *Reading Rawls,* 253–81). Another strategy would be to insulate the political process from such inequalities more effectively, which might well require reversing *Buckley* v. *Valeo,* which struck down legal restraints on the financing of political speech, and related decisions. See Rawls's discussion of this option in "The Basic Liberties and Their Priority," 74–9.

[55] And perhaps in other respects as well. This subject is discussed later.

[56] For a moderate and balanced statement of this position, see Charles Taylor, "Cross-Purposes," in Rosenblum, ed., *Liberalism and the Moral Life,* 159–82. A more radical critique of rights-based community is offered by feminists who argue that the essentially abstract and adversarial language of rights distorts, or makes impossible, discussion of crucial issues of compassion and degradation. Other feminists argue that the problem is not so much the language of rights as it is a political failure to define them appropriately and to extend their protections to all members of the community. See Susan Moller Okin's "Humanist Liberalism," in Rosenblum, ed., 21–53, and her "Feminism, the Individual, and Contract Theory," *Ethics* 100 (April 1990): 658–69. Two important recent collections bearing on this question are Deborah Rhode, ed., *Theoretical Perspectives on Difference* (New Haven, Conn.: Yale University Press, 1989), and the "Symposium on Feminism and Political Theory," *Ethics* 99 (January 1989): 219–406. See also the discussion in Waldron, *Nonsense upon Stilts,* 159–60.

of rights requires some sense of identification among individual bearers of rights. These proponents will observe that in the United States, a shared conception of individual rights goes some distance toward providing the common ground that makes such mutual identification possible—a phenomenon highlighted by U.S. naturalization procedures and by the typical sentiments of newly minted citizens. But while acknowledging the essential role of community in realizing the human good, defenders of rights will insist that a more basic role of political association lies in preventing disaster. As Jeremy Waldron has argued, we need rights most when affection fails. We need rights to reconsider damaged ties, to forge new ones, and to protect ourselves from the indifference or hostility of others.[57] Rights, then, are a kind of social safety net that secures our minimal expectations and wards off the worst case.

To summarize: Within the sphere of political discourse, three main lines of rights critique may be discerned. The first lies squarely within the liberal tradition. It accepts for the most part the liberal definition of rights and condemns the incompleteness or hypocrisy of liberal regimes that fail to extend these rights to all their members. This effort to generalize rights is frequently accompanied by an emphasis on the material conditions needed for the meaningful exercise of rights—for example, the public provision of qualified defense attorneys for accused indigents. The argument, though, is not that rights need to be reconceived, but that they need to be realized.

A second, more radical line of argument accepts the general concept of rights discourse but takes issue with standard conceptions of rights. One strand, discussed earlier, focuses on economic welfare rights rather than rights of social protection and political participation. A more far-reaching version, advanced by Roberto Unger, speaks of "destabilization rights" as empowering citizens to challenge all concentrations of capital and power.[58]

The third, most radical line of argument questions the entire category of rights as a way of describing and justifying political life. As we have seen, rights may be queried on the basis of (allegedly) competing sub-

---

[57] Jeremy Waldron, "When Justice Replaces Affection: The Need for Rights," *Harvard Journal of Law and Public Policy* 11 (Summer 1988): 625–47.

[58] See Roberto Unger, *False Necessity: Anti-Necessitarian Social Theory in the Service of Radical Democracy* (Cambridge: Cambridge University Press, 1987). For discussions of this thesis from various points of view, see Robin W. Lovin and Michael J. Perry, eds., *Critique and Construction: A Symposium on Roberto Unger's Politics* (Cambridge: Cambridge University Press, 1990). Lovin's "Introduction," 3–6, is a useful guide.

stantive values such as equality, democracy, community, affective ties, and gender specificity. They may also be subjected to an internal critique designed to demonstrate their futility. For example, Mark Tushnet has argued that rights are inherently unstable and vulnerable to changes in social setting, that they are indeterminate in principle, and that they represent empty, abstract reifications of meaningful human experiences.[59]

Clearly, defenders of rights must reject the most radical charges, although (as already discussed) they can cheerfully concede that rights form only a part of a comprehensive political morality and do not function well if applied apart from the other aspects of that morality. Conversely, defenders of rights must accept a substantial portion of the realization-of-rights thesis. But controversy is likely along two dimensions: whether X is truly necessary as a means to the exercise of rights, and whether on balance X promotes or undermines the regime of rights. (Debates over affirmative action revolve to some extent around these issues.)

The intermediate critique, centering on the content of rights, may well prove the most perplexing, especially when newly proposed rights come into practical conflict with older ones. For example, welfare rights can clash with established property rights, and the right of women and minorities not to be degraded may run afoul of the expansive definition of free speech characteristic of post–World War II constitutional jurisprudence. The extent to which one welcomes or resists these and other innovations will be strongly influenced by one's stance on broader issues such as the limits of liberal politics and the nature of a choiceworthy human life.

UNDERSTANDING THE BILL OF RIGHTS

History, philosophy, and the Declaration of Independence. How is the Bill of Rights to be understood today? Two kinds of answers can be given to this question. The first might be termed historical: From this perspective the concept of rights stems from concrete experiences of cruelty, oppression, and degradation imposed on victims typically (though not solely) by governments, and from the need for protection

---

[59] Mark Tushnet, "An Essay on Rights," *Texas Law Review* 62 (May 1984): 1363–1403. Tushnet also offers an external substantive critique to the effect that rights talk impedes advances by what he terms progressive social forces. His argument is in turn criticized by Michael J. Perry, "Taking Neither Rights-Talk nor the 'Critique of Rights' Too Seriously," *Texas Law Review* 62 (May 1984): 1405–16.

against these wrongs. The content of particular rights represents the accretion of social learning about the most important arenas of victimization and the most efficacious defenses against them. Different particular rights are related to one another functionally rather than conceptually: they cannot be derived from a single unifying principle but can be seen instead as performing linked but distinct tasks. Thus rights stand in the same relationship to one another as do tools in a carpenter's kit.

The other way of understanding the Bill of Rights may be termed philosophical. From this perspective, the rights we possess radiate from a common core: divine endowment, natural uniformities, central features of our humanity, or intuitively apprehended first principles. The specification of our rights arises through some conjunction of core principles and empirical circumstances, related to one another as major and minor premises, respectively.

Up to a point, of course, these two approaches are reconcilable. On the way "up" from the particular to the general, historical experience can provide both material and motivation for the dialectical inquiry into first principles. On the way "down," such experience may well prove indispensable for the specification of particular rights. Still, the contrast remains between understanding the Bill of Rights as being thoroughly inductive/particular and viewing it as containing an ineliminable element of philosophic generality.[60]

The dominant approach in America today is the philosophic. Indeed, commitment to this approach represents common ground among scholars who agree on nothing else. According to Walter Berns, for example, "Constitutional law and philosophy or political theory are not isolated from one another, and emphatically not in the United States."[61] Ronald Dworkin writes, "Constitutional law can make no genuine advance until it isolates the problem of rights against the state and makes that problem

---

[60] For parallel distinctions, see Judith Shklar, "The Liberalism of Fear," in Rosenblum, ed., *Liberalism and the Moral Life*, 26–8; Frithjof Bergmann, "Two Critiques of the Traditional Theory of Human Rights," in Pennock and Chapman, *Human Rights: Nomos XXX*, 57; Rawls, "The Basic Liberties and Their Priority," 6–7. Shklar and Bergmann espouse what I am calling the historical-inductive approach, while Rawls of course pursues the philosophical. I do not mean to suggest that these are necessarily opposed strategies of argument. It seems most plausible to see political theory as poised, sometimes uneasily, between philosophy and history, partaking of both but identified with neither. And indeed, history-preferring political theorists typically gesture toward more abstract philosophical argumentation, whereas philosophers draw on history as a source of intuitive judgments and quasi-"fixed points" for which their arguments must account.

[61] Walter Berns, "Equally Endowed with Rights," in Frank Lucash, ed., *Justice and Equality Here and Now* (Ithaca: Cornell University Press, 1986), 151.

part of its own agenda. That argues for a fusion of constitutional law and moral theory."[62]

The key difference emerges at the next step. Dworkin contends that the fusion he recommends "has yet to take place,"[63] whereas Berns maintains that it was present from the outset: our Constitution "is related to the Declaration of Independence as effect is related to cause, and the Declaration of Independence . . . is a political statement of a philosophical teaching concerning the nature of man, Providence, and nature itself."[64] If Berns is correct, the specific provisions embodied in the Bill of Rights would have to be read in light of the general theory of rights sketched in the Declaration.

Berns's thesis is of course not novel. In its essentials, it is Abraham Lincoln's understanding: the Declaration of Independence is the statement of principle that the Constitution works out and applies; the declaration is the "apple of gold," the Constitution, "the picture of silver"; the picture was "made for the apple."[65] Even Garry Wills, who trenchantly criticizes the Berns-Lincoln understanding, is at pains to repudiate the oft-refuted but never quite slain Progressive thesis that the Constitution somehow represents a departure from the declaration.[66]

At first glance, anyway, the Berns-Lincoln thesis holds out the possibility of a secure and compelling philosophic foundation for our constitutional rights. By contrast, Dworkin's approach, which would require reflection de novo on foundational issues, threatens to plunge us into the abstruse and interminable debates of contemporary moral philosophy. But early impressions may not be the whole story. In the subsection that follows I want to complicate matters somewhat by rereading the Declaration of Independence. My suggestion is that, taken as foundational, this document bequeaths a range of perplexities and ambiguities to which contemporary students of rights are compelled to respond.

Rereading the Declaration of Independence. Consider, to begin with, the account of the source and basis of rights in the Declaration of In-

---

[62] Ronald Dworkin, *Taking Rights Seriously* (Cambridge, Mass.: Harvard University Press, 1977), 149.
[63] Ibid.
[64] Berns, "Equally Endowed with Rights," 151.
[65] Quoted in Harry V. Jaffa, "Abraham Lincoln," in Morton J. Frisch and Richard G. Stevens, eds., *American Political Thought: The Philosophic Dimension of American Statesmanship* (New York: Charles Scribner's Sons, 1971), 139.
[66] Garry Wills, *Inventing America: Jefferson's Declaration of Independence* (Garden City N.Y.: Doubleday, 1978), xix and chap. 27.

dependence, namely, endowment by the "Creator." To be sure, this phrase must be read in light of the preceding reference to the "Laws of Nature and of Nature's God." No special revelation is required to apprehend the Creator's endowing activity; to learn our rights, we need read not the Bible but (only) the book of nature. Still, to state the obvious, this deist confidence in rational religion is not so widely shared as it was two centuries ago (and it was controversial then). Nor is it clear that the contemporary understanding of nature will lead toward the moral and political conclusions linked to the Enlightenment's Newtonian-mechanical conception. Indeed, the relationship between nature and morality has become notoriously problematic.

In his well-known letter to Henry Lee, Jefferson stated that the Declaration of Independence "was intended to be an expression of the American mind," the authority of which rested on "the harmonizing sentiments of the day."[67] But the American mind is not now what is was then, and such harmony as then existed has given way to discord. What is (for many of us) the *non–self-evidence* of the Declaration's point of departure thus compels us to pose the foundational question again: In virtue of what can we be said to have rights?

But let me, for the moment, set the foundation to one side and focus on the structure. Rights are not first, but second, in the enumeration of creation; equality comes first. What, then, is the relationship between our equality and our rights? One piece of the answer is evident: As human beings we are *equally* endowed with rights. My right to life does not differ, qualitatively or quantitatively, from yours.

Does equality of rights exhaust the meaning of the Declaration's equality? No less authoritative an interpreter than Abraham Lincoln thought it did:

The authors of that notable instrument... did not intend to declare all men are equal *in all respects*. They did not mean to say that all were equal in color, size, intellect, moral developments, or social capacity. They defined with tolerable distinctness, in what respects they did consider all men are created equal—equal in "certain inalienable rights, among which are life, liberty, and the pursuit of happiness."[68]

But there exists another possible line of interpretation that would give equality some force independent of rights. It is rooted in Locke's critique

---

[67] Letter to Henry Lee, 8 May 1825, in Morton J. Frisch and Richard G. Stevens, eds., *The Political Thought of American Statesmen* (Itasca, Ill.: F. E. Peacock, 1973), 12.

[68] Quoted in Jaffa, "Abraham Lincoln," 136.

of Filmer and restated ringingly in virtually the last words Jefferson ever wrote: "The general spread of the light of science has already laid open to every view the palpable truth, that the mass of mankind has not been born with saddles on their backs, nor a favored few booted and spurred, ready to ride them legitimately, by the grace of God."[69] Human beings are equal in the negative but strong sense that neither God nor nature provides adequate warrant for the rule of some over others. Because all arguments for subordination have been discredited, each person must be considered the ruler of himself or herself, and equal to every other person in this critical respect. It is this primordial self-rule that explains why government derives its just powers from the consent of the governed: there is no other warranted source of public authority.

It also explains why there are limits on what majorities acting through government may do. Because the rightful power of the majority rests on a moral ground "independent of force," the majority, "oppressing an individual, is guilty of a crime, abuses its strength, and by acting on the law of the strongest breaks up the foundations of society."[70]

Finally, the idea of primordial self-rule allows us to ask whether our rights do not rest on, without exhausting, this underlying equality—for example, whether liberty is a right precisely because we owe no one either natural or divine fealty. This point may of course be turned around: if equality and rights are distinguishable endowments, then rights may add something to, may not be exhausted by, bare equality. Utilitarianism, which in its classical form affirms equality while denying natural rights, bears witness to this possibility. Such rights express not just the equality but also the separateness and importance of each person as someone entitled not only to be counted with, but also to advance claims against, all the rest.

The notion of endowment helps clarify the nature of rights. It tells us, for example, that the rights under discussion in the Declaration of Independence are not human constructions and are not subject to the spatiotemporal variations characteristic of such constructions. The notion suggests, further, that these rights are to be known through rational apprehension, a suggestion further bolstered by the determinateness of the endowment: *certain* inalienable rights—that is, rights that are denumerable and specifiable rather than open-ended.

[69] Letter to Roger C. Weightman, 24 June 1826, in Frisch and Stevens, eds., *The Political Thought of American Statesmen*, 13.
[70] Jefferson, letter to P. S. Du Pont de Nemours 24 April 1816, in ibid., 31.

The Declaration goes on to provide a famous (and in at least one respect unexpected) list of such rights. Worthy of more than the usual notice, however, is the explicit incompleteness of its enumeration: "*among these* are Life, Liberty, and the pursuit of Happiness." What are the others? How do we discover them? The document itself gives us no guidance—a difficulty mirrored in the Bill of Rights, where the enumeration in the first eight amendments is explicitly declared incomplete in the ninth.[71] Both the Declaration of Independence and the Bill of Rights, then, invite us—indeed, require us—to engage in a process of inquiry to complete the roster of our basic rights. This is one of the key points at which American constitutionalism is compelled to confront moral and political philosophy.

Whereas the possession of rights is an inalienable endowment, the ability to exercise them depends on circumstances that must be contrived or "instituted." The securing of rights becomes the chief purpose of government, and thus the standard by which all forms of government are to be judged. Rights are not only moral facts but moral ends.

This simple observation resolves one perplexity only to create another. It is frequently alleged that a rights-based regime is inherently defective in that it lacks shared purpose and a guiding conception of the common good. In one respect, anyway, this charge is flatly mistaken: rights *are* shared ends, and the Declaration suggests that they constitute (or conduce to) the common good. The claim, not fully explicit but clear in the logic of the text, is this: The two greatest human aspirations are safety and happiness. Our safety is best promoted by a government that secures the rights to life and liberty, while our happiness is best promoted by a regime that allows us to pursue happiness rather than seeking to provide it for us (for example, by establishing a general public definition of happiness and furnishing the means for its attainment).

Although the movement from rights as facts to rights as ends resolves the problem of the common good on one level, it reinstitutes it on another. Government secures rights by creating a general system of rights, but there is no guarantee that in practice the rights of every individual will be compatible with those of all the rest. Robert Nozick has distinguished

---

[71] For a number of compelling arguments to the effect that the Ninth Amendment means what it says, see Randy E. Barnett, ed., "Symposium on Interpreting the Ninth Amendment," *Chicago-Kent Law Review* 64 (1988): 37–268. For a wider debate, see Barnett, ed., *The Rights Retained by the People: The History and Meaning of the Ninth Amendment* (Fairfax, Va.: George Mason University Press, 1989).

two ways of understanding public rights. In the first, rights are understood as absolute and inviolable side constraints, and no individual may be deprived of rights in order to satisfy other claims and considerations. In the second, rights are understood as goals to be achieved, and public policy is therefore understood as a "utilitarianism of rights" in which the point is to maximize the exercise of rights over the community as a whole.[72] From this perspective, some rights might have to be modified or even abrogated to create the most extensive possible security of our rights taken as a total system.

This original ambiguity has roiled our politics and jurisprudence ever since. One historical example is President Lincoln's controversial selective suspension of habeas corpus during the Civil War. A contemporary example is the Supreme Court's acceptance of police barricades on highways at which all motorists are stopped and administered sobriety tests. On one plausible reading of the Fourth Amendment, this procedure fails to satisfy the requirement of "probable cause," and the security of persons against "unreasonable searches" is therefore breached. But because drunk driving is among the most significant modern threats to the right to life announced in the Declaration of Independence, the Court was willing to accept as the best defense of rights, all things considered, a procedure it might well have struck down as violating a basic right in other contexts.

Thus far I have spoken of individual rights. But these are not the only rights defended in the Declaration. The document's opening sentence proclaims the necessity of dissolving the political bands connecting one *people* with another. A bit later, the right of altering or abolishing forms of government is assigned to the people as a whole. For current purposes, the key point is that a "people" is not necessarily coextensive with the full citizenry of an existing political community; communities may include several peoples, linked politically. A people, then, is an internally unified collectivity standing between individuals and the political community.

This transition from individuals to subnational peoples is critical because (to state the obvious) the Declaration is not simply invoking a Lockean right of revolution. The object is not to alter or abolish Britain's form of government but to separate from it. There must, then, be some basis on which a subnational community can invoke a right of separation. One need not go all the way down Garry Wills's road to agree that

---

[72] Robert Nozick, *Anarchy, State, and Utopia* (New York: Basic Books, 1974), 28–9.

peoples are in part constituted by bonds of birth, affection, and memory.[73] That is why the colonists appealed to their "British brethren" on grounds of history and consanguinity as well as justice. The "necessity" of the separation of peoples announced at the beginning of the Declaration is explained at the end as the attenuation of affective ties between them. The collapse of Canada's Meech Lake accords, which would have granted Quebec special cultural rights within the Canadian federation, and the recrudescence of subnational ethnic loyalties in Central Europe may well provide new arenas in our time for such acts of political self-assertion and for tests of their validity.

The Declaration of Independence is justly regarded as the locus classicus of American rights talk. Yet the declaration itself makes clear that rights do not exhaust, or fill, the politically relevant portion of the moral universe. For example, resistance to despotism is said to be not only a right but a "duty." The reason, not spelled out, would seem to be this: if certain rights are inalienable, linked indissolubly to our humanity, then as human agents we are forbidden to surrender the capacity to exercise them. We do not have the right to forfeit our rights; we have the duty to fight for them.

Resistance to the invasion of rights is more than coolly deontological. At one point the Declaration talks of the "manly firmness" with which colonial legislatures had opposed the king's usurpations. The suggestion is that standing up for one's rights is an element, or sign, of self-respect, and that failing to do so is evidence of weakness of character.[74]

One is required to respect others as well as oneself, by assuming a measure of intelligent goodwill among them and by acknowledging one's moral responsibility toward them. There is a "candid world" to which it makes sense to submit the facts—whose opinions, indeed, *require* a "decent respect."

As the last sentence of the Declaration emphasizes, securing a gov-

---

[73] Wills, *Inventing America,* chaps. 21–3. For a sophisticated discussion of this issue, see Nathan Tarcov, "American Constitutionalism and Individual Rights," in Robert Goldwin and William Schambra, eds., *How Does the Constitution Secure Rights?* (Washington, D.C.: American Enterprise Institute, 1985), 105–8.

[74] For reflections on the relationship between modern rights and the classical account of "spiritedness," see Nathan Tarcov, "The Spirit of Liberty and Early American Foreign Policy," in Catherine H. Zuckert, ed., *Understanding the Political Spirit: Philosophical Investigations from Socrates to Nietzsche* (New Haven, Conn.: Yale University Press, 1988); and Joseph Cropsey, "The United States as Regime and the Sources of the American Way of Life," in *Political Philosophy and the Issues of Politics* (Chicago: University of Chicago Press, 1977).

ernment that secures rights is likely to be neither costless nor bloodless. The struggle for life jeopardizes life; the struggle against confiscation risks fortunes. Rights require sacrifice, secured by a "mutual pledge," buttressed by "sacred Honor," and protected by "divine Providence."

In the Declaration's account, rights make sense and function only within a multidimensional moral universe. To ignore their embeddedness (and onesidedness) is to risk forgetting what gives them their limit and point. One might suggest that something like this has happened in much of contemporary rights discourse.

CONTEMPORARY THEORIES OF RIGHTS

What do rights do? Many contemporary thinkers have focused on the functions that rights perform in our moral and political life. This functional analysis frequently, and not unjustly, constitutes the point of departure for broader arguments about the foundation and content of rights.

Among these thinkers the most common theme is that of *protection*. The details differ, of course. As we have seen, Judith Shklar emphasizes the fear that individuals feel in the face of potentially cruel concentrations of power. Rights, then, represent the standpoint of the potential victims and, when adequately institutionalized, serve to protect these individuals against the various horrors that powerful cruel forces can inflict upon them.[75]

Jeremy Waldron has made a similar, if more general, point: a human right is "a moral position in relation to a particularly important type of individual interest" and helps secure that interest against dangerous invasion by others, especially (but not only) the state. In Waldron's view, rights emerge as crucial, and are most likely to come into play, when bonds of affection and identification become frayed. Rights are "fallbacks"—guarantees that individuals will continue to enjoy opportunities to make their own way even when the content of their choices renders them highly unpopular, even outcasts, in the eyes of their community.[76]

Ronald Dworkin has translated this concern for individual protection

---

[75] Shklar, *Ordinary Vices,* chap. 6; "The Liberalism of Fear," in Rosenblum, ed., *Liberalism and the Moral Life,* chap. 1; "Injustice, Injury, and Inequality: An Introduction," in Lucash, *Justice and Equality Here and Now,* 13–33; "Giving Injustice Its Due," *Yale Law Journal* 98 (April 1989): 1135–51.
[76] Waldron, *Nonsense upon Stilts,* 179; "When Justice Replaces Affection," 625–47.

into the language of moral philosophy. The idea of individual rights, he argues, is

parasitic on the dominant idea of utilitarianism, which is the idea of a collective goal of the community as a whole. Individual rights are political trumps held by individuals. Individuals have rights when, for some reason, a collective goal is not a sufficient justification for denying them what they wish, as individuals, to have or to do, or not a sufficient justification for imposing some loss or injury upon them.

Dworkin goes on to argue, as do other theorists, that when we say someone has a right to do something, we imply that it would be wrong (for the government as well as other individuals) to interfere with that person's doing it, or at least that some special grounds would be needed to justify interference in this arena. Rights protect individuals from the moral as well as physical force of collectivities.[77]

The broad thesis that rights function as protections does not by itself specify what it is that rights protect. Further specifications may usefully be divided into two general categories. *Interest* theories suggest that rights protect goods and activities that (tend to) benefit individuals. Such theories usually go on to argue that the goods and activities so protected are "high order," essential for individual well-being. (Without some ranking of goods and activities, it becomes difficult to explain why some enjoy the special protection characteristic of rights while others are left to the vagaries of individual effort or public policy.)

Will theories, by contrast, assert that the prime function of rights is to protect individual "authority, discretion, or control" in certain areas of life. In this view, it is the individual's own decision-making capacity that is protected against external intervention, even when others believe that this capacity is being exercised in a manner that contradicts the interests of the rights-bearing agent. Will theories can readily (and typically do) serve as fulcrums for arguments against paternalism.

Of course, will and interest theories need not be viewed as antithetical. It might be argued that specific rights would not have been embraced unless they were somehow linked to interests with which most individuals can identify, and that this general linkage is compatible with specific choices—exercises of right—that work against the interests of the agents.[78]

---

[77] Dworkin, *Taking Rights Seriously,* pp. xi, 188.
[78] For a clear discussion of will and interest theories, see James Nickel, *Making Sense of*

Joel Feinberg offers a functional analysis of rights that is compatible with but goes beyond individual protection. Rights, he argues, are intrinsically connected to the activity of claiming—that is, of protesting against being wronged and of demanding one's due. Claiming, in turn, is essential to the full expression of our humanity:

> Having rights enables us to "stand up like men," to look others in the eye, and to feel in some fundamental way the equal of anyone. To think of oneself as the holder of rights is not to be unduly but properly proud, to have that minimal self-respect that is necessary to be worthy of the love and esteem of others.[79]

Conversely, as Thomas Hill goes on to argue, to undervalue one's rights is to manifest the vice of "servility." Within this context, rights may be seen as serving the quasi-Aristotelian moral function of enabling us to hit the mean between servility and the opposing vice of arrogance (overvaluing one's own claims vis-à-vis others).[80]

Philosophic foundations of rights. To ascribe certain functions to rights is not necessarily to say that individuals have rights. For this reason, contemporary philosophy typically combines pragmatic analysis of rights with exploration of their ground.

One possibility is to regard rights as bedrock—that is, as grounds of moral and political argument for which no further argument is needed. For example, having divided all political theories into the triad of rights based, goal based, and duty based, Ronald Dworkin begins his exposition of liberalism as resting on each individual's right to "equality of concern and respect" with the statement, "I presume we all accept the following postulates of political morality."[81] Now it is possible to offer a kind of support for a fundamental postulate—namely, the plausibility of the understanding of particulars that flows from it—and Dworkin characteristically avails himself of this strategy. Of course at some point in every argument explanation ceases, to be succeeded by "Here I stand." Still, one may wonder whether Dworkin has pushed the argument back far

---

Human Rights, 19–23. Nickel links these categories to the Kantian and utilitarian traditions, respectively, not implausibly; but there are also non-Kantian will theories and nonutilitarian interest theories. See, for example, Joseph Raz's discussion of the links between rights and interests in *The Morality of Freedom,* chap. 7.

[79] Joel Feinberg, "The Nature and Value of Rights," in David Lyons, ed., *Rights,* 84, 87.
[80] Thomas E. Hill, Jr., "Servility and Self-Respect," in ibid., 111–24.
[81] Dworkin, *Taking Rights Seriously,* 272.

enough to render the particulars compelling to those who stumble at the threshold of the first principle.[82]

As indicated in the previous section, Dworkin defines rights in opposition to utilitarian considerations. Several recent thinkers have dissented from this formulation of the issue, arguing historically (in the case of John Stuart Mill) or conceptually that utilitarian theory, suitably complicated in structure or maximand (or both), is compatible with a robust understanding of individual rights.[83] Antiutilitarians characteristically reply that utilitarian rights theories are too clever by half, reaching the "correct" conclusions via convoluted paths that other accounts can straighten out. As Rolf Sartorius has argued, "The basic problem for any form of utilitarian theory no matter how cleverly constructed is that when it does yield the required principles of moral right it will do so for the wrong reasons."[84]

In the course of his argument for utilitarian property rights, Alan Ryan confronts this issue directly. Utilitarians can give good utilitarian reasons for opposing, say, compulsory transplant surgery, he observes, but many skeptics think these reasons miss the point. One possibly better reason is directly moral: such surgery treats people as resources, as mere means to an end. Ryan comments, "I do not think that utilitarianism can do very much to accommodate the idea that this is intolerable. . . . There may be some rights—the right not to be sacrificed, say—for which utilitarianism cannot offer a very compelling rationale."[85]

What might a more compelling rationale look like? If it is not to be

---

[82] In fairness, I should note that Dworkin may more recently have shifted toward the view that rights are one possible specification of a higher-order "plateau" in political argument, namely, the commitment to equality in highly abstract form. See his "Comment on Narveson: In Defense of Equality," *Social Philosophy and Policy* 1 (Autumn 1983): 24–40.

[83] For Mill in general, see John Gray, "John Stuart Mill on Liberty, Utility, and Rights," and David Lyons, "Human Rights and the General Welfare," in Lyons, ed., *Rights*. (Lyons seems to have shifted ground significantly in "Utility and Rights," Waldron, ed., *Theories of Rights*, 110–136.) For a theory of property rights inspired to a considerable extent by Mill and to a lesser extent by Bentham, see Alan Ryan, "Utility and Ownership," in Frey, *Utility and Rights*, 175–95. L. W. Sumner offers a propaedeutic to a utility-based rights theory in his "Rights Denaturalized," Frey, ed., 20–41. Two of the most sophisticated attempts to move this ball forward are James Griffin, "Toward a Substantive Theory of Rights," in Frey, ed., *Utility and Rights*, 137–60, and T. M. Scanlon, "Rights, Goals, and Fairness," in Waldron, ed., *Theories of Rights*, 137–52.

[84] Rolf Sartorius, "Persons and Property," in Frey, ed., *Utility and Rights*, 196–214.

[85] Ryan, "Utility and Ownership," 192–3. The logic of this argument yields a mixed theory of rights in which some stand on utilitarian, and others on nonutilitarian, foundations. The challenge is to weld the foundational arguments together in a consistent fashion.

found through a process of aggregation, it might be located in certain general features of individuals. Many contemporary philosophers have explored this possibility. Following a recent essay by Hugo Adam Bedau, I shall divide their proposed answers triadically: rights may be seen as rooted in nonmoral facts about individuals, in moral facts, or in an intermediate category of quasi-moral facts.[86]

Robert Nozick has argued that the requisite moral conclusion about individuals—their inviolability—follows from a key nonmoral fact about individuals—their existential separation:

> There is no *social entity* with a good that undergoes some sacrifice for its own good. There are only individual people, different individual people, with their own individual lives. Using one of these people for the benefit of others, uses him and benefits the others. Nothing more.... The moral side-constraints upon what we may do, I claim, reflect the fact of our separate existences. They reflect the fact that no moral balancing act can take place among us; there is no moral outweighing of one of our lives by others so as to lead to a greater overall *social* good. There is no justified sacrifice of some of us for others.[87]

Put formally, Nozick's argument appears to be the following:

(P1)   Every justification for penalizing some individuals to benefit others rests on the existence of some "social entity" of which benefit and harm can be predicated.

(P2)   No such social entity exists.

(Ergo)   There is no valid justification for penalizing some individuals to benefit others.

Nozick is justified in asserting P2. On the level of inner feeling he is obviously correct. Aristotle made this point in his critique of the *Republic:* if you understand what happiness is, you see immediately that it makes no sense to predicate it of a community unless all or most of the individuals that constitute that community are happy. Even if the communitarians are correct, even if character and consciousness are decisively shaped by membership in society, it is still the individual—a demarcated locus of sensation, desire, purpose, and reason with a separate life to lead—who is being shaped.

But P1 seems arbitrary. Consider the oft-discussed case of the innocent person whose life is deliberately sacrificed to save ninety-nine other innocents. Thinkers who are willing to justify this act do not need to claim

---

[86] Hugo Adam Bedau, "Why Do We Have the Rights We Do?" *Social Philosophy and Policy* 1 (Spring 1984): 56–72.

[87] Nozick, *Anarchy, State, and Utopia,* 32–3.

that the one hundred persons form some mystical social entity that feels pleasure and pain. The decision is between two states of affairs, each involving the same disjoint individuals. To conclude that it is better that the ninety-nine live is not necessarily to engage in illusory reification. To say that the death of the one-hundredth person does not sufficiently respect the fact of a separate existence begs the question, because the issue is precisely to determine what rights separate existence generates. Thus when Nozick says that side constraints "reflect" our separate existence, the vague relationship between moral conclusion and factual premise obscures the wide range of possible relationships between them.[88]

Another well-known effort to derive rights from nonmoral facts is offered by Alan Gewirth, who argues that the bare conception of purposive intentional agency is enough to yield the desired conclusion. The argument proceeds in two broad steps (here I vastly oversimplify a very subtle case): First, every agent engaged in purposive activity must ascribe to one's self basic rights to freedom and well-being. Second, no agent can consistently claim rights for one's self without acknowledging the symmetrical claim of all other agents.

Gewirth's thesis has been subjected to a number of penetrating criticisms, which I shall not recapitulate here. Many of these have converged on one central point: Gewirth's point of departure—rational prudential agency—is too parsimonious to get him where he wants to go. As Martin Golding has put it, "The prudent amoralist [Gewirth's rational agent] neither asserts nor denies any rights-claims, nor does he ever have to assert or deny them. He cannot assert or deny them, because the terminology of rights is not part of his vocabulary."[89] Many of the argu-

---

[88] The preceding two paragraphs are adapted from my *Justice and the Human Good* (Chicago: University of Chicago Press, 1980), 130–1. For a parallel argument that the fact of separateness is not nearly strong or specific enough to yield Nozick's conclusion, see H. L. A. Hart, "Between Utility and Rights," in Ryan, ed., *The Idea of Freedom*, 82–6. For even more wide-ranging reflections on the vicissitudes of separateness, see Raz, *The Morality of Freedom*, chap. 11. As Raz notices, Nozick gestures toward the Kantian principle that individuals are ends and not means alone. Nozick does not really use it as a free-standing argument, however, but traces it back to separateness. This distinction reflects a fundamental choice, discussed later, between grounding rights in moral or nonmoral facts about individuals: Kantian "endness" is a moral fact, while Nozick's separateness is a nonmoral fact.

[89] Martin P. Golding, "From Prudence to Rights: A Critique," in Pennock and Chapman, eds., *Human Rights: Nomos XXIII*, 175. For other versions, see the essays by Richard B. Friedman and Arval Morris, in ibid.; Bedau, "Why Do We Have the Rights We Do?" 65–6 and note 21; and my own *Justice and the Human Good*, 49–51. Gewirth's unrepentant reply is found in *Human Rights: Essays on Justification and Applications* (Chicago: University of Chicago Press, 1982), 67–78.

ments against Gewirth's particular claims apply with equal force to the general strategy of deriving morally forceful rights from deliberately demoralized facts about human beings. Carried to extremes, the quest for theoretical parsimony, elegance, and indubitability ends by depriving itself of resources essential to its success.[90]

I turn now to the second strategy, that of grounding rights on moral facts about individuals. One example of this is H. L. A. Hart's well-known argument that if there are any general social rights (e.g., the right to worship as one pleases), it follows that there is at least one natural right—the equal right to be free.[91] Bedau parses this, sensibly enough, as a modern version of the Hobbesian thesis that to have a social right pursuant to a contract "presupposes having a prior general moral right to make the contract in the first place. This right to contract with another cannot, of course, itself be generated by some prior contract on pain of infinite regress. It must be a right, therefore, that everyone has *de novo*."[92] A difficulty (and not the only one) with this argument is that it comes perilously close to presupposing what was to be proved. Anyone who doubts that we have a particular social right (or any at all) will obviously be unimpressed by the regression to its necessary precondition.

John Rawls has proposed a different moral basis for rights. Liberal politics, he suggests, rests on a distinctive conception of "moral personality"

characterized by two moral powers and by two corresponding highest-order interests in realizing and exercising these powers. The first power is the capacity for an effective sense of justice, that is, the capacity to understand, to apply and to act from (not merely in accordance with) the principles of justice. The second moral power is the capacity to form, to revise, and rationally to pursue a conception of the good.[93]

---

[90] For a less parsimonious argument of similar form, see Nickel, *Making Sense of Human Rights*, 84–90. Nickel's argument is somewhat more successful because it rests on a conception of "fundamental interests" to be protected through a system of rights. This conception verges on, if it does not reach, the category of quasi-moral facts, discussed later. A similar characterization applies to Loren Lomasky's argument in *Persons, Rights, and the Moral Community*. Lomasky in effect combines Gewirth's emphasis on agency with Nozick's focus on separateness (via Bernard Williams's notion of integrity) into a conception of individuals as distinct and irreplaceable "project pursuers." Rights safeguard the conditions of project pursuit.

[91] H. L. A. Hart, "Are There Any Natural Rights?" in Lyons, ed., *Rights*, 14–25.

[92] Bedau, "Why Do We Have the Rights We Do?" 64.

[93] Rawls, "Kantian Constructivism in Moral Theory," 525.

The realization and exercise of the moral powers require, as necessary conditions, certain "primary goods," among which are the "basic liberties (freedom of thought and liberty, and so on)."[94] From this perspective, our rights define and defend the circumstances in which worthwhile human lives (as worth is broadly conceived within the liberal tradition) may be lived. These rights would thus be chosen by agents in circumstances that represent both the determination to advance rational self-interest and to honor fair terms of social cooperation.[95]

This argument connects attractively with elements of post-Lockean liberalism as various as the views of Humboldt and T. H. Green. The argument may also be seen as moving in the right direction—from the more controversial (rights in need of justification) to the less controversial (liberal conception of moral agency). Two kinds of objections may nonetheless be raised. Many loyal citizens of liberal regimes may find it difficult to subscribe to the Rawlsian definition of moral personality, and even those who do may wonder whether the rights Rawls purports to derive from it are fully conducive to developing and exercising the moral powers in question. Many wonder, for example, whether these powers can be adequately developed in a society in which the right of self-expression is regarded as near-absolute. Recent debates about the National Endowment for the Arts and rap music groups reflect these liberal worries, not just illiberal moralism (as defenders of free speech often suppose).[96]

The third, and to me most promising, strategy for justifying rights connects them to quasi-moral facts: widely shared empirical features of human individuals (their nature, reason, needs, and purposes) that are invested with moral significance. As Bedau puts it, "Built into their very description and analysis will be certain norms, or the adequate basis for certain norms, that will serve to dictate or direct certain kinds of conduct by anyone who understands the original concept and who applies it to himself and his world." Bedau goes on to argue:

The best explanation for the human rights we have must take its cue from the role these rights play in our lives, not only in our actual lives but in any possible human life, any life we could recognize as a life you or I might have lived.... Our common human predicament and roughly similar environmental circum-

---

[94] Rawls, "The Basic Liberties and Their Priority," 22.
[95] Ibid., 20.
[96] For some reflections on these and related questions, see my "Moral Personality and Liberal Theory: John Rawls's 'Dewey Lectures,'" *Political Theory* 10 (November 1982): 492–519, and "Pluralism and Social Unity."

stances and biological structure guarantee that our needs and capacities are far more homogeneous than heterogeneous. . . . I take it as an anthropological fact, resting in turn on biological facts, that members of the human species share a certain equipotentiality for socialization and self-determination, that can be best expressed in terms of common human capacities.[97]

This sort of modest naturalism, though still a minority view, is gaining momentum in contemporary philosophy and serves as a retort to fashionable forms of relativism and antifoundationalism. H. J. McCloskey contends that "the basic, fundamental human rights are self-evidently so [and] to become aware that persons possess such rights, we need simply reflect on the nature of human persons and on the concept of a moral right."[98] Steven Collins has sought to define "a set of basic predicaments which define what it is to be human [and which] neither vary cross-culturally nor develop historically."[99] In the course of a discussion of Aristotle's ethics, Martha Nussbaum has catalogued certain "spheres of experience" to which human beings generally must respond with concepts and actions.[100] Susan Moller Okin has argued for a list of generally shared human needs and capabilities as the best way of understanding not only why we have rights but also what rights we have.[101] In her view, the key needs are basic sustenance, physical security, and respectful treatment; the key capabilities are making choices, learning, and establishing relationships with other humans. Martin Golding has situated human rights in certain basic features of human beings and of the circumstances in which they are placed. These are, in his analysis, the capability to engage in voluntary activity; the existence of human desires and interests; the capability to engage in conscious purposive activity; the ability to com-

---

[97] Bedau, "Why Do We Have the Rights We Do?" 67, 71. (I have altered the order of some of the sentences to bring out the point of the argument.)

[98] H. J. McCloskey, "Respect for Human Moral Rights," in Frey, *Utility and Rights*, 126.

[99] Steven Collins, "Categories, Concepts or Predicaments?" in Michael Carrithers, Steven Collins, and Steven Lukes, eds., *The Category of the Person: Anthropology, Philosophy, History* (Cambridge: Cambridge University Press, 1985), 73. See, more generally, pp. 71–6.

[100] Martha C. Nussbaum, "Non-Relative Virtues: An Aristotelian Approach," in Peter A. French, Theodore E. Uehling, Jr., and Howard K. Wettstein, eds., *Midwest Studies in Philosophy, Vol. XIII: Ethical Theory: Character and Virtue* (Notre Dame, Ind.: University of Notre Dame Press, 1988), 32–53. Other recent works inspired by Aristotle include Stephen Salkever, *Finding the Mean* (Princeton, N.J.: Princeton University Press, 1990), and Ian Shapiro, *Political Criticism* (Berkeley: University of California Press, 1990).

[101] Susan Moller Okin, "Liberty and Welfare: Some Issues in Human Rights Theory," in Pennock and Chapman, eds., *Human Rights*, 230–56.

municate demands and to respond to them; the possibility of clash between demands; and the fact of human community.[102]

These efforts may be understood as part of a broad and expanding
tendency to see rights as defending essential human interests. Writing
from widely varying standpoints, theorists such as Golding, Richard
Flathman, T. M. Scanlon, John Kleinig, Stanley Benn, Jeremy Waldron,
and Joseph Raz have converged on the thesis that rights find not only
their justification but also their content and point in the defense of basic
interests.[103] There are differences among them, to be sure. Raz, Golding,
and Benn have gone further than others in the direction of an objective
or perfectionist account of essential interests. Golding, for example, insists that the "personal good" a right defends must also be a "genuine
good" and that persons can be mistaken about the content of their genuine good.[104] Raz sees rights as "nested in" key aspects of individual
well-being and contends as follows:

Since our well-being depends in part on having appropriate goals, it cannot be
merely a matter of satisfying some or all of the desires we have. It consists, it is
true, in success in the aspects of our lives we care about. But we care not merely
about having our wants satisfied, but about having *reasonable* wants. We value
our lives, judge them to be successful, in proportion to their being occupied with
worthwhile pursuits.[105]

I do not mean to suggest that distinguishing between genuine and
merely apparent good, reasonable and unreasonable wants, worthwhile
and worthless pursuits, essential and inessential interests is either un-
problematic or risk free. Liberals have typically been leery of such distinctions, with reason. Still, if rights are to be viewed in conjunction with
human goods and interests, some differentiation among goods and in-

---

[102] Martin Golding, "Towards a Theory of Human Rights," *The Monist* 52 (October 1968):
521–49. In form (and to a lesser but still considerable degree, in content) Golding's
account resembles H. L. A. Hart's discussion of the "minimum content of natural law"
in *The Concept of Law* (Oxford, Eng.: Clarendon Press, 1961), chap. 9. That discussion
seems to me more promising as a basis for rights than does Hart's "Are There Any
Natural Rights?" discussed earlier.

[103] Martin Golding, "The Primacy of Welfare Rights," *Social Philosophy and Policy* 1
(Spring 1984): 135; Richard E. Flathman, *Toward a Liberalism* (Ithaca: Cornell University Press, 1989); T. M. Scanlon, "Rights, Goals, and Fairness"; John Kleinig, "Human Rights, Legal Rights, and Social Change," in Kamenka and Tay, eds., *Human
Rights*, 44–5; Stanley I. Benn, "Human Rights—For Whom and for What?," in ibid.,
59–73; Waldron, *Nonsense upon Stilts*, 179; Joseph Raz, "Liberating Duties," *Law and
Philosophy* 8 (1989): 3–21.

[104] Golding, "The Primacy of Welfare Rights," 135.

[105] Raz, "Liberating Duties," 12, 14 (emphasis added).

terests is crucial. The alternative is the relativization of rights, or their hyperexpansion to cover the entire sphere of human endeavor. In neither case could rights perform what most thinkers agree is their core function: the morally compelling defense of a vital but limited zone in which the essential conditions not of human perfection but of human decency are secured and enjoyed.

For example, Richard Flathman, who systematically links rights to human interests and who emphasizes the freedom to pursue interests in their full diversity, nonetheless recognizes the need for principles of selection among interests:

Interests and desires, objectives and purposes, are rankable and are in fact ranked by the individuals whose interests they are and by the members of their societies. ... Judgments can be made as to which of them should be served when conflicts develop among them; as to which of the choices or policies, all of which would accord with the principle of prima facie good, would accomplish the *most* good. ... Hence it would also be a feature of a theory of rights grounded in this principle that it would be possible to make judgments as to which interests, desires, and so on should be protected by rights and which should not.[106]

Rights, says Flathman, not only establish a sphere of special protection within which individuals can act but also provide a "distinctive type of warrant for particularly valuable actions within that sphere."[107] Defenders of rights who wish to link them to fundamental human interests must then attend systematically to the basis on which highest-order interests are to be identified.[108] Thus theories of rights represent continuations of, not alternatives to, the conceptions of human nature at the heart of the Western philosophic tradition.[109]

---

[106] Richard E. Flathman, *The Practice of Rights* (Cambridge, Eng.: Cambridge University Press, 1976), 179.

[107] Ibid., 182.

[108] As Lawrence Haworth puts it, "When it is said that a person has a right to do something, this is to be understood as the proposal that he be protected in his efforts to do it, and that others be discouraged in some way from interfering. ... The proposal is reasonable to the extent that it can be supported by good reasons. ... The required reasons would be criteria of importance for actions." "Utility and Rights," in Richard E. Flathman, *Concepts in Social and Political Philosophy* (New York: Macmillan, 1973), 469. For an influential effort to provide criteria of importance, see T. M. Scanlon, "Preference and Urgency," *Journal of Philosophy* 72 (1975): 655–70.

[109] There is one stream of contemporary thought that is obviously and self-consciously a continuation of traditional argumentation, namely, Catholic natural-rights theories. The best-known representative of this school is John Finnis, *Natural Law and Natural Rights* (Oxford, Eng.: Clarendon Press, 1980). See also Germain Grisez, especially *The Way of Lord Jesus*, Vol. 1: *Christian Moral Principles* (Chicago: Franciscan Herald Press, 1983); and R. Hittinger, *A Critique of the New Natural Law Theory* (Notre Dame:

The content of rights. I turn now from the foundation of rights to their content. Here the discussion may usefully be divided into general (philosophic) rights and particular rights, such as those found in the Bill of Rights.

I will not tarry long at the first category. For present purposes, it must suffice to observe that several influential but mutually incompatible proposals have surfaced in the past generation. As we have seen, H. L. A. Hart argued that there is an *ur*-right: the equal right of all to be free. Ronald Dworkin responded by rejecting any general right to liberty and proposed instead a fundamental right possessed by all individuals to equal concern and respect from which particular rights, including specific kinds of liberties, may be inferred.[110] Joel Feinberg has suggested that a triad of fundamental rights exists: the right to fair treatment, the right not to be treated cruelly or inhumanely, and the right not to be subjected to degradation and exploitation (even when such treatment is both painless and acceptable to the victim).[111] Taking as his point of departure the clash of human interests, the great variety of human conceptions of the good, and the *libido dominandi* (lust for domination) that inclines some to impose their interests and conceptions on others, Stuart Hampshire argues that society most requires a form of procedural justice that substitutes rule-guided discussion and negotiation for conquest and terror. From this standpoint, the core human right is that of participating (or at least being fairly represented) in the procedures by which deep conflicts are adjudicated.[112]

Under the rubric of particular rights, the area of agreement among contemporary thinkers is more substantial:

1. A right to life is generally acknowledged although, according to the Fifth Amendment, life may be forfeit (as may liberty and property) under certain conditions. Contemporary controversy over the right to life revolves around its scope and reach. Prochoice and prolife advocates disagree whether fetuses are "persons" within the meaning of the right.

University of Notre Dame Press, 1987). For these references (and much else), I am indebted to Knud Haakonssen, "Natural Law," in Lawrence C. Becker, ed., *Garland Encyclopedia of Ethics* (New York: Garland Press, 1991).

[110] Dworkin, *Taking Rights Seriously,* chap. 12.

[111] Joel Feinberg, *Social Philosophy* (Englewood Cliffs, N.J.: Prentice-Hall, 1973), 96–7.

[112] Stuart Hampshire, *Innocence and Experience* (Cambridge, Mass.: Harvard University Press, 1989), 72–8, 107–9. Although the form of adjudication enjoys universal validity, Hampshire suggests, its content will be strongly influenced by the "practices, the moral principles, and the precedents that prevail in a particular culture or community" (p. 61).

Those who favor the death penalty point to the language of the Bill of Rights, while those who oppose it argue that the right to life cannot be squared with the state's taking of life.

2. Also subject to general agreement is a range of rights of personal protection: against slavery and personal servitude; against cruel and unusual punishment and torture; against arbitrary searches, arrest, imprisonment, and seizure or confiscation; and against invasions of religious, intellectual, and expressive freedom. (There is, to be sure, debate at the margin of some of these protections. For example, what does the right of free exercise of religion require in certain complex cases, and how is it related to valid secular goals the state may wish to promote? Does the freedom of expression in all instances protect pornographic, racist, or abusive communications?)

3. These rights of personal protection are bolstered by the right of all persons to the equal protection of the laws and by the various rights that define and help ensure fair trials. (It is worth recalling that fully half the amendments in the Bill of Rights deal with the rights of accused persons.)

4. Even if there is no general right to (or presumption in favor of) liberty, rights secure a wide range of particular liberties: among them, the freedoms to travel, to marry or not marry, to choose and follow a profession, to associate with others, and to own and freely dispose of personal property. Taken together, these rights not only secure areas of liberty but also provide concrete opportunities for the pursuit of happiness invoked in the Declaration of Independence. Many rights relating to particular liberties, of course, engender problems of application. Is the right to travel infringed by foreign-policy limitations on access to terrorist nations? Is the right to marry infringed by a particular state's definition of marriageable partners?

5. Finally, rights of participation help to secure and protect all other rights and to ensure that government remains rooted in the consent of the people, as the principles of liberal legitimacy require. These rights include fair access to citizenship for all residents within a political jurisdiction; equal treatment of all citizens; free political speech and assembly and the ability to bring grievances before public authority for redress; the receipt of all information needed to carry out the activities of citizenship; and a fair opportunity to gain offices of public trust and responsibility.[113]

---

[113] These five headings summarize what I believe most Americans would intuitively take

Throughout this enumeration, I have indicated that even well-established rights give rise to controversies over their application. Other rights are more controversial still; their very existence is in dispute.

1. Above and beyond particular liberties and immunities, is there a "right of privacy" that protects individuals against public interference in, say, matters of sexual orientation, practice, and expression? Within U.S. constitutional adjudication, this question has arisen in areas such as contraception and homosexuality and has frequently revolved around interpretations of the Ninth Amendment. But the issue is much broader and older than the public conflicts of the past quarter-century. It found classic expression in John Stuart Mill's famous "harm principle" and in the much-discussed distinction between public- and private-regarding action. It resurfaced in the debate between H. L. A. Hart and Lord Devlin over legal restrictions on homosexuality, which reverberated across the Atlantic. And it continues to roil the waters of American politics today. Partisans of privacy rights appeal to equal respect for the dignity of each person and to mistrust of government intrusion; opponents insist not only that local majorities have rights to defend their own moral conceptions but also that liberal society cannot safely be as latitudinarian in matters of sexual conduct as the partisans believe.[114]

2. A second contested right is that of property. As I suggested earlier,

---

to be the incontrovertible heart of the matter. They are also congruent with, and systematize, Benjamin Constant's famous description of the "liberty of the moderns": "It is the right to be subjected only to the laws, and to be neither arrested, detained, put to death or maltreated in any way by the arbitrary will of one or more individuals. It is the right of everyone to express their opinion, choose a profession and practice it, to dispose of their property, and even to abuse it; to come and go without permission, and without having to account for their motives or undertakings. It is everyone's right to associate with other individuals, either to discuss their interests, or to profess the religion which they and their associates prefer, or even to occupy their days or hours in a way which is most compatible with their inclinations or whims. Finally it is everyone's right to exercise some influence on the administration of the government, either by electing all or particular officials, or through representations, petitions, demands to which the authorities are more or less compelled to pay heed." Biancamaria Fontana, *Political Writings* (Cambridge: Cambridge University Press, 1988), 310–1. For the most nuanced discussion of Constant's contribution to liberal rights, see Stephen Holmes, *Benjamin Constant and the Making of Modern Liberalism* (New Haven, Conn.: Yale University Press, 1984), especially chaps. 1 and 2.

[114] On all this, see Richard A. Wasserstrom, ed., *Morality and the Law* (Belmont, Calif.: Wadsworth, 1971); Ronald Dworkin, *A Matter of Principle* (Cambridge, Mass.: Harvard University Press, 1985), chap. 17, and *Taking Rights Seriously*, chap. 10; *California Law Review* 77 (May 1989): 479–594; Stephen Macedo, *Liberal Virtues: Citizenship, Virtue, and Community in Liberal Constitutionalism* (Oxford: Clarendon Press, 1990), 193–7.

the modern form of this contest is rooted in the European conflict between classical liberalism and social democracy, and in the parallel American conflict between laissez-faire and Progressive nationalism. Today some philosophers affirm a far-reaching right of property, while others either deny such a right or place it on the shifting sands of social utility.[115] Questions of "personal" property (housing, transportation, clothing, and the like) are uncontroversial. The issue is debated along two other dimensions. Some affirm, while others deny, that there is a right to private ownership of the means of production (a dispute detachable from the question of whether socialized production is prudent and efficient).[116] And some advance, while others resist, the proposition that the typical activities of the modern regulatory state amount to public "taking" of private property without just compensation, and thus to practical nullification of a core moral entitlement.[117]

3. A third area of contestation is that of "welfare rights"—guaranteed entitlements to basic levels of material provision and opportunity. As I suggested earlier,[118] this category of proposed rights emerged in the European struggle to address some of the unwanted consequences of market economies. It was crystallized in Articles 23 through 26 of the post–World War II Universal Declaration of Human Rights, which enumerated guarantees of employment, material decency, adequate leisure, and education. It surfaced in the United States in the 1960s and 1970s in the effort to read John Rawls's "Difference Principle," requiring distributional arrangements to maximize the well-being of the least-advantaged groups, into the Fourteenth Amendment.

Amid what has become a rather murky debate, three points seem evident. First, unlike other kinds of interests protected by rights, the ability of governments to secure individual material welfare depends to a considerable degree on each country's overall level of material well-being and on its specific circumstances.

Second, whatever their standing may be in liberal theory (and views

---

[115] Nozick, *Anarchy, State, and Utopia*, 150–82; Lomasky, *Persons, Rights, and the Moral Community*, chap. 6; Nickel, *Making Sense of Human Rights*, 100, 151–6; Rolf Sartorius, "Persons and Property," in Frey, ed., *Utility and Rights*, 196–214; Alan Ryan, "Utility and Ownership," in ibid., 175–95.
[116] Nickel, *Making Sense of Human Rights*, 152–6.
[117] See Richard Epstein, *Takings: Private Property and the Power of Eminent Domain* (Cambridge, Mass.: Harvard University Press, 1985).
[118] See footnote 8.

differ sharply), minimum welfare guarantees cannot easily be located in (or crammed into) the Bill of Rights, or indeed any other provisions of the U.S. Constitution as it now stands.

Third, although welfare is not a free-standing and independent claim within the U.S. constitutional framework, specific welfare provisions may enjoy a kind of derivative status as the means needed to carry into practice the rights that are guaranteed explicitly or by clear implication. The right to public provision of legal counsel for indigent defendants is one clear case. More broadly, it might well be argued that citizenship guarantees are devalued unless all persons are given the opportunity to equip themselves to exercise the privileges and responsibilities of citizenship. From this perspective, access to education verges on an implied derivative right for all.

A final observation: Liberal conceptions of citizenship stress the duty of independence—the obligation of all (unimpaired) adults to provide for themselves and their families. In modern market economies, the individual's ability to fulfill this duty is in part a function of circumstances outside each person's control (as became painfully evident during the Great Depression). From this standpoint, entitlements to collective material provision might well be regarded as latent and contingent—that is, as activated if and when economic circumstances make it impossible for individuals to achieve full independence through their own efforts.

The bearers of rights. The central, least-problematic case for the analysis of rights is the normally developed adult human being. Matters become more complex when we move to what Kent Greenawalt has called "borderlines of status": children, people with disabilities, fetuses, animals, and even vegetation and inanimate nature. Each of these cases has given rise to complex and emotionally charged debates. No one doubts that children and people with disabilities have important rights; the chief difficulty is to define the rights of normal adults, if any, that members of these categories lack and conversely the rights, if any, that are peculiar to them. The question of fetal rights is, of course, entangled with the intractable abortion debate. Proponents of animal rights have tended to argue that because animals can feel pleasure and pain, they possess much the same right to have their subjective sensations taken into account as do human beings. (Not surprisingly, utilitarians have an easier time with animal rights that Kantians do.) Rights questions involving plants and inanimate objects have come to the fore with the rise of environmental concerns, although in these cases most theorists believe that moral categories other than rights are more useful and revealing.[119]

A final issue—heatedly debated in the United States in the controversy over affirmative action and increasingly salient for Canada and Europe as well—is whether groups as well as individuals may reasonably be regarded as rights-bearers. (As we have seen, a remote antecedent of this debate is the distinction, evident in the Declaration of Independence, between the rights of individuals and of "peoples.") Although a strong case can be made that the treatment of individuals is the appropriate benchmark of justice, many dissenters have argued that liberalism cannot proceed in complete disregard of the fact of subnational group identity and the history of intergroup injustice. On the practical level, the United States has adopted a somewhat obfuscatory muddle-through policy that has left many people on both sides unsatisfied. The debate over the Civil Rights Act of 1990 has once again raised the linkage between group rights and quotas, an issue that is sure to roil American politics for years to come.[120]

CONCLUSION

Throughout this chapter I have stressed the connection between rights and liberalism. Historically, to the present day, doubts about rights have been embedded in broader reservations about the liberal enterprise. Over time, of course, the scope and focus of these critiques have changed. Liberalism today is engaged neither in a grand contest with patriarchal monarchy and feudal aristocracy like that of the seventeenth and eighteenth centuries nor in a desperate struggle with fascism and communism like that which dominated so much of the twentieth century. Most con-

[119] The literature on these topics is now vast, and I cannot even begin to cover it. Useful points of departure are Loren Lomasky, *Persons, Rights, and the Moral Community*, chaps. 7 and 8; Kent Greenawalt, *Religious Convictions and Political Choice* (New York: Oxford University Press, 1988), chaps. 6 and 7; Joel Feinberg, *Rights, Justice, and the Bounds of Liberty* (Princeton, N.J.: Princeton University Press, 1980), 159–206; Flathman, *Toward a Liberalism*, chap. 6; Kurt Baier, "When Does the Right to Life Begin?" in Pennock and Chapman, eds., *Human Rights*, 201–29.

[120] Once again, the literature in this area is vast and burgeoning. For a start, see Marshall Cohen, Thomas Nagel, and Thomas Scanlon, eds., *Equality and Preferential Treatment* (Princeton, N.J.: Princeton University Press, 1977), especially Owen Fiss's "Groups and the Equal Protection Clause"; Ellen Frankel Paul et al., *Equal Opportunity*; Nathan Glazer, "Individual Rights Against Group Rights," in Kamenka and Tay, eds., *Human Rights*, 87–103; Kymlicka, *Liberalism, Community, and Culture*, chaps. 7–10; and Robert K. Fullinwider, *The Reverse Discrimination Controversy: A Moral and Legal Analysis* (Totowa, N.J.: Rowman & Allanheld, 1980), chap. 5.

temporary critics are inclined to argue not that liberal rights are misguided or covertly repressive but that they are one-sided and incomplete—that societies wholly preoccupied with claiming and exercising rights cannot provide scope for a fully rounded and worthy human existence.

Much must be conceded to these critics. The premise "I have a right to do X" does not remotely warrant the conclusion that "X is the right thing to do." Liberal theorists have not worked nearly hard enough to flesh out the conception of "rightness" that forms an indispensable complement to rights, and contemporary liberal education has done little to fill this gap. Nor have liberals paid enough attention to the role of responsibilities, duties, and virtues in the constitution of personal and social life. They have acknowledged grudgingly, or not at all, the essential contributions to liberalism of associations (such as religion and the family) that are not themselves structured by the concept and practice of rights. Finally, contemporary liberals have not focused adequately on the kinds of goals and goods that liberal societies characteristically pursue and on the resulting balance that must be struck between goal-based and rights-based considerations. These and similar considerations lie at the heart of liberalism's future agenda.

Let me translate these concerns into the language of rights. Broadly speaking, there are three kinds of obstacles to the achievement of individual purposes and the attainment of a choiceworthy life. First, other individuals may intervene to prevent us from pursuing our good; rights are the best protection against such threats the human race has yet devised. Second, we may be thwarted by a scarcity of external goods— things available for use or other individuals ready to cooperate. Here rights can be of considerable assistance, but other things are needed as well—principles of distributive justice, sentiments of social solidarity, and institutions that artfully link individual and collective goods. Finally, we may be thwarted by deficiencies of mind or character. Here rights have relatively little to say, because the underlying issue is how we become agents capable (among other excellences) of exercising rights prudently and responsibly. This is the point at which the discourse of rights gives way to the classic questions of *paideia* (moral education), and at which we must concern ourselves with the full range of influences on the formation of character in liberal societies.

For centuries liberals have argued that coercion deprives acts of moral meaning. Unless individuals can freely originate, and hence identify with, their deeds, their compliance with external norms is worth little. Rights protect individuals' ability to choose their acts and to embrace those acts as their own.

The liberal emphasis on internally produced action is not misplaced, but it is incomplete. Fully worthy acts have both an internal dimension (self-origination) and an external dimension (correctness or appropriateness). Liberal practical philosophy has long excelled at the defense of individual choice; it must now learn how to provide standards for the appropriate exercise of rights. Without such criteria, a system of rights cannot coherently distinguish between liberty and license. In the long run, prospects for societies without the inner resources to defend such a distinction cannot be considered to be bright.

6

The development of modern American legal theory and the judicial interpretation of the Bill of Rights

WILLIAM W. FISHER III

The legal interpretation of the Bill of Rights is largely controlled by the United States Supreme Court. Members of Congress occasionally vote against bills and presidents sometimes veto acts in the belief that they violate provisions of the Bill of Rights, thereby preventing the Supreme Court from passing on those issues.[1] And the sheer number of cases that arise each year in which statutes or administrative edicts are challenged on constitutional grounds prevents the Supreme Court from reconsidering all the rulings made by state and lower federal courts.[2] But on most

I am grateful for the comments of Victor Brudney, Gerald Frug, Benjamin Kaplan, Frank Michelman, Martha Minow, Lloyd Weinreb, and the participants in the three workshops at the Woodrow Wilson Center. Stephen Choi, John Hockley, Eliseo Neuman, and Christopher Younger helped revise the manuscript for publication.

[1] Some state constitutions contain provisions that authorize their legislatures or executives to request from their supreme courts "advisory opinions" regarding the constitutionality of proposed legislation. See, for example, Massachusetts Constitution Chap. III, Art. II. The federal Constitution, however, does not contain such a provision and, since 1793, the United States Supreme Court has consistently refused to issue advisory opinions. Paul Bator, Daniel Meltzer, Paul Mishkin, and David Shapiro, *The Federal Courts and the Federal System*, 3d ed. (Westbury, N.Y.: Foundation Press, 1988), 65–6.

[2] The Supreme Court currently receives approximately 4,800 petitions for certiorari per year. Of those cases, it hears (and issues full, written opinions in) approximately 170 and disposes summarily of an additional 80. See "The Supreme Court, 1988 Term—Leading Cases," *Harvard Law Review* 103 (November 1989): 398; Bator et al., *The Federal Courts and the Federal System*, 59–60. The Court thus refuses to consider on the merits approximately 95 percent of the cases presented to it. A significant number of the petitions it denies involve constitutional rulings by lower courts with which a majority of the justices would disagree if they had the time to address them.

matters of importance, the Supreme Court sooner or later has the last word.

At least three circumstances, it is commonly and accurately believed, influence the Supreme Court's construction of the Bill of Rights. First, the language of the provisions themselves sets loose limits on the range of plausible interpretations. Second, the prejudices and convictions of the justices powerfully affect how the Bill of Rights is construed. Third, the Court is influenced to some degree by actual or apparent shifts in public opinion. This chapter seeks, among other things, to demonstrate the importance of a fourth source of guidance: understandings diffused in legal scholarship and in the legal community at large concerning the nature and proper derivation of rights in general.

The argument is divided into three sections. The first contends that the agenda of twentieth-century American legal theory has been substantially determined by two groups of scholars: the "Legal Realists" and their intellectual heirs, the members of the Conference on Critical Legal Studies. The Realists developed—and the Critical Legal Studies scholars then amplified—several challenges to conventional understandings of the nature and functions of legal doctrine. Most seriously, they called into question three related ideals cherished by most Americans: the notion that, in the United States, the people select the rules by which they are governed; the conviction that the institution of judicial review reinforces rather than undermines representative democracy; and the faith that ours is a government of laws, not of men.

The second section argues that most aspects of the five major schools of American legal theory that have arisen since World War II are best understood as efforts to meet the challenges first presented by Legal Realism. The defensive strategies adopted by the five schools have varied. Some have responded to the Realists' contention that legal doctrine is insufficient to constrain judicial decision making by urging the courts to interpret or modify doctrine in the light of a particular moral or economic theory. Others have sought refuge in theories of the legal process, contending that, if the courts would confine their attention to certain sorts of issues and resolve them in a certain spirit, their decisions would be predictable and justifiable. Still others have contended that, although much of contemporary law is illegitimate, legal doctrine in general and legal rights in particular could be refashioned into effective engines of social justice. None of these strategies has been wholly successful. The result is that contemporary American legal scholarship consists of an unstable melange of arguments drawn from disparate, contending theoretical traditions.

The third section explores connections between these various academic perspectives and the Supreme Court's handling of three representative aspects of the Bill of Rights: the clause in the First Amendment protecting "freedom of speech," the clause in the Fifth Amendment regulating "takings" of private property, and the principle (which the Supreme Court purports to have derived from several of the first ten amendments) that certain sexual and familial freedoms should be shielded from government interference. The thesis of the section is that the arguments the justices have employed in reaching and justifying their decisions in those areas have been influenced to a substantial (and hitherto unrecognized) extent by the five theories that for the past half century have dominated legal scholarship. That influence has not been wholly beneficial. Partly because of the defensive and conflicted character of the legal theories themselves and partly because of the selective and haphazard manner in which the justices have invoked them, difficult issues have been confused or obscured by this procedure as often as they have been clarified.

LEGAL REALISM AND ITS REPERCUSSIONS

The story begins in the 1920s with the formation of a loose alliance of law teachers who came to be known as Legal Realists. The exact composition of the group is a matter of some dispute. There was substantial disagreement among its members, and most were at least ambivalent about being affiliated with an academic movement. But, in retrospect, we can identify approximately forty scholars, most of them teachers at Columbia, Yale, Harvard, and Johns Hopkins universities, who developed and popularized a novel approach to law, adjudication, and legal education.[3]

---

[3] Until recently most legal historians accepted with few modifications the list of Legal Realists compiled by Karl Llewellyn in the course of his famous effort to define the movement. See Llewellyn, "Some Realism about Realism—Responding to Dean Pound," *Harvard Law Review* 44 (June 1931): 1226–7, n.18. The discovery that Llewellyn himself had previously compiled several much longer lists has encouraged historians of the movement to define it more expansively. See N. E. H. Hull, "Some Realism about the Llewellyn–Pound Exchange over Realism: The Newly Uncovered Private Correspondence, 1927–1931," *Wisconsin Law Review* 6 (1987): 921.

The Realists' critique. The most important component of that approach was what Karl Llewellyn, the foremost of the Realists, described as a "method of attack"—a multifaceted effort to discredit "formalism," the style of legal reasoning that dominated the academy and, to a lesser extent, the judiciary around the turn of the century. Formalism, as the Realists described it (tendentiously but not altogether unfairly), revolved around the following propositions: A judge should derive the answer to a difficult case by canvassing the decisions reached previously by other courts in similar cases ("similarity" being defined extremely generously), inducing from those precedents a few abstract and general principles, and then applying those principles to the facts of the problem before him. Neither the judge's views regarding the social policy implications of alternative resolutions of the controversy nor his sense of the "equities" of the case has any legitimate place in his decision making. Conscientious adoption of this method by the judiciary would generate unique correct answers to every dispute and, eventually, would purify legal doctrine as a whole of anomalies and inconsistencies.[4]

In the Realists' view this theory of adjudication was fundamentally misconceived. In its pure form it was impracticable; judges could not honestly resolve cases this way. Most judges, especially trial judges, recognized its unworkability. To the extent that some judges had been swayed by this ideal, they had been led astray—for example, into declaring unconstitutional (as violative of "freedom of contract") Progressive Era legislation designed to protect workers from exploitation.

The foundation of the Realists' critique was a positivist theory of the nature of law. They denounced the various "metaphysical" definitions of law that circulated in the formalist literature, offering in their place the empirical definition developed by Oliver Wendell Holmes: "The prophecies of what the courts will do in fact, and nothing more pretentious, are what I mean by law."[5] More specifically, the Realists argued

---

[4] For less summary accounts of formalist legal theory, also known as "classical legal thought," see Thomas Grey, "Langdell's Orthodoxy," *University of Pittsburgh Law Review* 45 (Fall 1983): 1; and Duncan Kennedy, "Toward an Historical Understanding of Legal Consciousness: The Case of Classical Legal Thought in America, 1850–1940," *Research in Law and Sociology* 3 (1980): 3.

[5] Oliver Wendell Holmes, Jr., "The Path of the Law," *Harvard Law Review* 10 (March 1897): 457. For Realist writings defending this definition, see, for example, Jerome Frank, "What Courts Do in Fact," *Illinois Law Review* 26 (February 1932): 645; Karl Llewellyn, *The Bramble Bush: On Our Law and Its Study* (New York: Columbia School of Law, 1930), 3; Herman Oliphant, "Stare Decisis—Continued," *American Bar Association Journal* 14 (March 1928): 159.

that an accurate statement of the law governing a given case consists of an assessment of the probability that a judge or jury would grant relief to the plaintiff. "[A] right ... exists to the extent that a likelihood exists that A can induce a court to squeeze, out of B, A's damages."[6]

In making such prophecies, the Realists claimed, legal doctrine—"traditional legal rules and concepts"[7]—had limited value. A few Realists sometimes argued that doctrine played no role whatsoever in courts' decision making and thus was useless in predicting outcomes.[8] Most took a more moderate position, arguing that judges sometimes to some degree paid attention to the "paper rules," but that they were also influenced powerfully by other considerations.[9]

The Realists explained on two grounds the limited role of doctrine in determining how cases were decided. First, invoking recent developments in philosophy, they argued that deductive logic and analogical reasoning were more flexible and open-ended analytical tools than the formalist scholars assumed; it was therefore naive to believe it possible either to derive particular legal rules from general concepts and particular outcomes from the application of rules to facts or to derive the answer to one case from a prior decision in a related case.[10] Second, the Realists insisted that extant legal doctrine was internally inconsistent. "Legal Principles—and rules as well—are in the habit of hunting in pairs"; to any given dispute, at least two are likely to be equally relevant, and to

[6] Karl Llewellyn, "A Realistic Jurisprudence: The Next Step," *Columbia Law Review* 30 (April 1930): 448.
[7] Llewellyn, "Some Realism about Realism," 1237.
[8] See, for example, Frank, "What Courts Do in Fact," 654–6.
[9] See, for example, Felix Cohen, *Ethical Systems and Legal Ideals: An Essay on the Foundations of Legal Criticism* (New York: Harcourt, Brace, 1933), 240–9; Jerome Frank, Review of *The Bramble Bush* by Karl Llewellyn, *Yale Law Journal* 40 (May 1931): 1123–4; Llewellyn, "A Realistic Jurisprudence," 444.
[10] On the indeterminacy of deductive logic, see, for example, Felix Cohen, "Modern Ethics and the Law," *Brooklyn Law Review* 4 (October 1934): 43; Walter Wheeler Cook, "Scientific Method and the Law," *American Bar Association Journal* 13 (June 1927): 305–6; John Dewey, "Logical Method and the Law," *Cornell Law Quarterly* 10 (December 1924): 17; and Edward Purcell, *The Crisis of Democratic Theory: Scientific Naturalism and the Problem of Value* (Lexington: University Press of Kentucky, 1973), 89. For an important antecedent of this argument, see *Lochner* v. *New York*, 198 *United States Reports* 45, 76 (1905) (Justice Holmes dissenting) ("General propositions do not decide concrete cases"). On the indeterminacy of analogical reasoning, see Cohen, *Ethical Systems*, 244–5; Llewellyn, *The Bramble Bush*, 67–71; Wilfred Rumble, *American Legal Realism: Skepticism, Reform, and the Judicial Process* (Ithaca, N.Y.: Cornell University Press, 1968), 55–63.

point in opposite directions.[11] Precedents, they contended, are arranged in similar patterns.[12] Thus, even if equipped with effective logical implements, judges could not derive determinate answers from the "traditional rules."[13]

In response to the question, If doctrine does not determine outcomes, what does, the Realists answered: hunches. "The vital motivating impulse for decision is an intuitive sense of what is right or wrong in the particular case."[14] The principal determinant of an intuition of this sort, they argued, is "the personality of the judge,"[15] which, in turn, is composed of some traits and attitudes common to the social class from which the judge was drawn and some more idiosyncratic "biases."[16] Prejudices of these sorts, the Realists argued, affect the judge's response to a given dispute in two ways: they influence his assessment of the credibility of the parties and witnesses and thus mold his perception of the "facts" of the case, and they shape his sense of how the law ought to respond to those facts.[17]

Why then do judges pretend, when they write opinions explaining their decisions, that they are merely applying settled law? Drawing on recent developments in psychology and sociology, the Realists answered that judicial opinions serve the functions of rationalization and legiti-

---

[11] Walter Wheeler Cook, Review of *The Paradoxes of Legal Science* by Benjamin Cardozo, *Yale Law Journal* 38 (1929): 406.

[12] See Llewellyn, *The Bramble Bush*, 68.

[13] See Laura Kalman, *Legal Realism at Yale, 1927–1960* (Chapel Hill: University of North Carolina Press, 1986), 22.

[14] Joseph Hutcheson, "The Judgment Intuitive: The Function of the 'Hunch' in Judicial Decision," *Cornell Law Quarterly* 14 (April 1929): 274.

[15] Frank, "What Courts Do in Fact," 655.

[16] Although some Realists—most notably, Jerome Frank—argued that life experiences peculiar to each judge molded his biases, most members of the movement emphasized the more systemic and social determinants of judges' "prejudices." Differences of opinion on this point reflected and contributed to disagreement among Realists regarding the degree to which decision making by different judges was or could be consistent. For a spectrum of views on these issues, see Felix Cohen, "Transcendental Nonsense and the Functional Approach," *Columbia Law Review* 35 (June 1935): 843–5; Jerome Frank, *Law and the Modern Mind* (1930; Gloucester, Mass.: Peter Smith, 1970), 114; Charles G. Haines, "General Observations on the Effects of Personal, Political and Economic Influences in the Decisions of Judges," *Illinois Law Review* 17 (May 1922): 96; Harold D. Lasswell, "Self-Analysis and Judicial Thinking," *International Journal of Ethics* 40 (April 1930): 354; Llewellyn, "Some Realism about Realism," 1242–3; Max Radin, "The Theory of Judicial Decisions: Or How Judges Think," *American Bar Association Journal* 11 (June 1925), 359; Hessel Yntema, "The Hornbook Method and the Conflict of Laws," *Yale Law Journal* 37 (February 1928): 480. For secondary accounts, see Kalman, *Legal Realism at Yale*, 6; Purcell, *Democratic Theory*, 88–9.

[17] Frank, *Law and the Modern Mind*, 114.

mation. By making each decision "seem plausible, legally decent, legally right, . . . indeed, legally inevitable,"[18] opinions "dull . . . lay understanding and criticism of what the courts do in fact" and conceal from the judges themselves the true bases of their rulings.[19]

The Realists' program. Those, then, are the principal features of the Realists' assault on what they regarded as orthodox legal theory. The Realists' proposals for reshaping American law—and, specifically, their suggestions regarding how judges should decide cases—were less systematic and insightful. Indeed, the weakness of their affirmative program contributed significantly to the deterioration of the movement in the early 1940s. Among their desultory reflections on "ought-questions," however, were a few crucial insights and recommendations that were to figure prominently in legal scholarship after World War II.[20]

The Realists' detractors accused them of being nominalists—of believing that universals and abstractions are nothing more than convenient devices for the communication of ideas and that the only respect in which the various referents of a general term are truly alike is that they happen to be called by the same name.[21] As applied to some members of the movement, the charge is accurate.[22] The majority, however, took a more moderate position: They believed that it was possible to identify or develop generalizations—specifically, legal concepts and rules—that cap-

[18] Llewellyn, "Some Realism About Realism," 1238–9.

[19] Cohen, "Transcendental Nonsense," 812, 815–6. For other versions of this argument, see Frank, *Law and the Modern Mind,* 159; Max Lerner, "Constitution and Court as Symbols," *Yale Law Journal* 46 (June 1937): 1317; Karl Llewellyn, *Cases and Materials on the Law of Sales* (Chicago: Callahan and Company, 1930), xi; Leon A. Tulin, "The Role of Penalties in Criminal Law," *Yale Law Journal* 37 (June 1928): 1052. On occasion, Realists supplemented this account of the function of judicial opinions with acknowledgment that the obligation to develop "plausible" rationales for their pronouncements limited to some degree the range of options open to a judge in a given case. But this conception of the disciplining function of opinions was a distinctly subordinate theme in their writings.

[20] The phrase in quotation marks is derived from Llewellyn's most famous article, in which he provides a refreshingly honest assessment of the limited contributions of the Realists to "a program in the normative aspect." "Some Realism about Realism," 1254.

[21] For versions of the accusation, see Lon Fuller, "American Legal Realism," *University of Pennsylvania Law Review* 82 (March 1934): 443–7; Roscoe Pound, "The Call for a Realist Jurisprudence," *Harvard Law Review* 44 (March 1931): 707–8; Morris Cohen, "Justice Holmes and the Nature of Law," *Columbia Law Review* 31 (March 1931): 361. (Morris Cohen was an important forerunner of Legal Realism; his articles in the 1920s cut paths trod by many members of the movement. In the 1930s, however, Cohen criticized ever more sharply the writings of his erstwhile followers.)

[22] See Cook, "Scientific Method and the Law," 305; Herman Oliphant, "Facts, Opinions, and Value-Judgments," *Texas Law Review* 10 (February 1932): 134.

tured or corresponded to natural categories of human behavior and ways of controlling it. But they insisted that, to be meaningful and useful, such generalizations must be empirically based (derived from universally verifiable data) and narrow (incorporating only a small collection of manifestly similar situations or propositions).[23]

The philosophic stance just described undergirded three related proposals for transforming the substance and practice of law, which may be described collectively as "particularism." First, the Realists argued that scholars and judges should jettison most of the accepted "black letter" rules and develop "working rules" that would more accurately describe "the actual behavior of courts."[24] Such empirically grounded rules would undoubtedly be much more specific than the propositions that currently dominated treatises and judicial opinions, because in practice most judges adjusted their decisions to accommodate the peculiarities of the controversies they confronted.[25] The principal virtue of detailed "real rules" of this sort is that they would enable lawyers to advise their clients more intelligently.[26]

Second, the Realists argued that most extant legal concepts had to be disaggregated if they were to be of any use in describing the behavior of courts or facilitating legal reform. Concepts like "title," "property right," and "due process" were hopelessly general.[27] Relying heavily on the work of Wesley Hohfeld, the Realists insisted that all legal relationships, properly understood, consisted of combinations of elemental entitlements that came in eight (and only eight) varieties—rights, privileges, powers, immunities, duties, no-rights, liabilities, and disabilities.[28] The existence of

---

[23] See, for example, Frank, Review of *The Bramble Bush*, 1124, n.12. For discussion of the respects in which these convictions were derived from contemporaneous movements in philosophy and the natural and social sciences, see Purcell, *Democratic Theory*, 21–3.

[24] Cohen, "Transcendental Nonsense," 839. See also Cook, "Scientific Method and the Law," 308–9; Llewellyn, "Realistic Jurisprudence," 443, 448, 453.

[25] Llewellyn, "Some Realism about Realism," 1240–1; Wesley Sturges and Samuel O. Clark, "Legal Theory and Real Property Mortgages," *Yale Law Journal* 37 (April 1928): 713–4.

[26] Cohen, "Transcendental Nonsense," 839–40.

[27] Indeed, because they tended to forestall thought, such concepts, the Realists contended, were worse than useless. See Llewellyn, "Realistic Jurisprudence," 453; Oliphant, "Stare Decisis—Continued," 159; Tulin, "The Role of Penalties," 1063.

[28] Wesley Newcomb Hohfeld, "Some Fundamental Legal Conceptions as Applied in Judicial Reasoning," *Yale Law Journal* 23 (November 1913): 16; idem, "Fundamental Legal Conceptions as Applied in Judicial Reasoning," *Yale Law Journal* 26 (June 1917): 710. For secondary accounts, see Duncan Kennedy and Frank Michelman, "Are Property and Contract Efficient?" *Hofstra Law Review* 8 (Spring 1980): 748–58; Joseph Singer, "The

any one of these entitlements necessarily implied the existence of one other (its "correlative") and the nonexistence of a third (its "opposite"). Beyond that, however, there existed no inexorable or natural pattern of these relationships; it in no sense "followed" from the fact that X enjoyed a particular legal privilege that X should also enjoy corresponding legal rights or powers. So, for example, the answer to the question whether picketing a place of business violates any right of the owner of the business could be derived neither from the abstract concept of "ownership" nor from the fact that the owner had the legal privilege of hiring whom he or she pleased, but rather could be obtained only through a conscious "policy" decision.[29] Disaggregation of a legal concept thus permitted and necessitated assessment of the social desirability of each of the myriad entitlements it had hitherto encompassed and concealed.[30] "Any part [of the law] needs constantly to be examined for its purpose, and for its effect, and to be judged in the light of both and their relation to each other."[31]

Third, the Realists argued that such policy decisions must be "partic-

---

Legal Rights Debate in Analytical Jurisprudence from Bentham to Hohfeld," *Wisconsin Law Review* (1982): 986–9.

[29] Walter Wheeler Cook, "Privileges of Labor Unions in the Struggle for Life," *Yale Law Journal* 27 (April 1918): 785–96.

[30] Articles adopting Hohfeld's argument and putting it to the purposes described in the text include Charles E. Clark, "Relations, Legal and Otherwise," *Illinois Law Quarterly* 5 (December 1922): 26; Cook, "Privileges of Unions"; Arthur L. Corbin, "Jural Relations and their Classification," *Yale Law Journal* 30 (January 1921): 226; Frederick Green, "The Relativity of Legal Relations," *Illinois Law Quarterly* 5 (June 1923): 187; Underhill Moore, "Rational Basis of Legal Institutions," *Columbia Law Review* 23 (November 1923): 609; and Max Radin, "A Restatement of Hohfeld," *Harvard Law Review* 51 (May 1938): 1141.

[31] Llewellyn, "Some Realism about Realism," 1236. For a similar argument, see Morris Cohen, "Property and Sovereignty," *Cornell Law Quarterly* 13 (December 1927): 21. It was this assertion that *each piece* of the legal order must be assessed from an instrumental standpoint that most distinguishes the Realists' program from the formalist style the Realists attacked. Like virtually every other American legal theorist, the architects of formalism were instrumentalists in the most basic sense: they believed that the legal system existed in order to advance certain secular ends, that it should be judged on the basis of its effectiveness in securing those goals, and that judges had a responsibility to increase that effectiveness. But the formalists tended to confine their instrumentalist inquiries to highly general and abstract questions—for example, whether a regime of private property and freedom of contract or a regime in which "all things are held in common" was more socially desirable. See *Coppage v. Kansas*, 236 U.S. 1, 17 (1915); and Grey, "Langdell's Orthodoxy," 14–5. The principal innovation first of Holmes (see *The Common Law* [Boston: Little, Brown, 1881], 69), then of so-called Sociological Jurisprudence (see G. Edward White, *Patterns of American Legal Thought* [Charlottesville, Va.: Michie, 1978], 100–115; and Purcell, *Democratic Theory*, 76–7), and finally of Legal Realism was not to resurrect instrumentalism but to lower dramatically the level of generality at which it was applied.

ular" in an additional sense: they must refer to specific sets of socioeconomic circumstances. It makes no sense to develop a rule governing all contracts or even all mortgages. The contexts in which contracts and mortgages are entered into and enforced vary dramatically; a set of entitlements appropriate in one might be entirely inappropriate in another.[32]

Different groups of Realists extended this last argument in two different directions. The first set argued that social reality is so variegated that even narrow rules are unhelpful; each dispute should be decided on its own facts. The responsible adjudicator, they claimed, should employ a variety of procedural devices to develop a rich understanding of the "social setting" and idiosyncratic circumstances of each "individual case" that came before him and then, keeping in view and attempting to neutralize "his own prejudices, biases, antipathies, and the like," determine the best resolution of the controversy.[33] The second group believed that social reality, though complex, could be managed sensibly with narrow rules. On the basis of a thorough study of a particular industry or social practice, including examination of how its participants responded to different legal regimes, they claimed, a judge could and should, in the course of a particular decision, announce a specific legal norm, which would then guide and aid courts confronted in the future with similar problems.[34]

---

[32] See Thurman W. Arnold, Review of *The Law of Trusts and Trustees* by George Gleason Bogert, *Columbia Law Review* 36 (April 1936), 687; Earnst G. Lorenzen and Raymond J. Heilman, "The Restatement of the Conflict of Laws," *University of Pennsylvania Law Review* 83 (March 1935): 561; Oliphant, "Stare Decisis—Continued," 159–60; Edwin W. Patterson, "The Restatement of the Law of Contracts," *Columbia Law Review* 33 (March 1933): 425; Sturges and Clark, "Legal Theory and Real Property Mortgages," 701.

[33] Frank, *Modern Mind,* 157–8, nn. 26–7. See also Hutcheson, "Judgment Intuitive," 274; Oliphant, "Return to Stare Decisis," 159–62. In some of his early writings Roscoe Pound seemed to take this extreme position, arguing that judges should strive for "reasonable and just solutions of individual cases." "The Scope and Purpose of Sociological Jurisprudence," *Harvard Law Review* 25 (April 1912): 515. He gradually retreated from this stance (see White, *Patterns of Legal Thought,* 114–15) until by the 1930s he was denouncing the Realists for their fascination with "the unique single case" (see "Call for Realist Jurisprudence," 707).

[34] The principal exponents of this view were Felix Cohen and Karl Llewellyn. See Cohen, *Ethical Systems,* 238 (criticizing his fellow Realists for "an unrealistic view of single cases as divorced from the uniformities which lend them significance"); Karl Llewellyn, *The Common Law Tradition in Deciding Appeals* (Boston: Little, Brown, 1960), 121–6; idem, "On Warranty of Quality and Society," *Columbia Law Review* 37 (March 1937): 369; idem, "On the Good, the True, the Beautiful, in Law," *University of Chicago Law Review* 9 (February 1942): 249–50, 260 (suggesting that case-by-case adjudication leads only to a "welter" and that "wise" rules, in which "the situation [is] rightly grasped,

The second major component of the Realists' affirmative program is captured by the phrase *purposive adjudication*. For guidance in decision making, many Realists argued, courts should depend primarily on consciously articulated social policies. Those Realists who saw any value in rules thought they ought to function, not as powerful constraints on adjudication, but as tentative expressions of how particular sets of policies impinged on particular social problems. Those Realists who saw rules as altogether unhelpful believed that the deliberate pursuit of social policies through the resolution of individual controversies was the only stabilizing force in adjudication.[35]

Direct reference to their purposes was both the key to *wise* construction of legal rules and the only way in which rules could be applied to facts with any degree of consistency and determinacy. Even the best rules were incapable of " 'decid[ing] concrete cases' by any deductive process, because their edges are unclear, because, also, two or more of them can commonly overlap a situation in conflicting ways."[36] The most that the best rules could do was "focus" and guide the analysis of "problems of policy" in concrete cases and "suggest *lines* of wise *direction* of solution, for consideration."[37] In sum, to think that a judge could decide a case by reading the rule and ignoring its "reason" was senseless.

Because awareness of the purposes of legal rules was so important to their interpretation, the Realists argued, "only the rule which shows its reason on its face has ground to claim maximum chance of *continuing* effectiveness."[38] That insight, in turn, had important implications for the design of both statutory and common-law norms. Legislators who wished to provide citizens and judges meaningful guidance should make their objectives clear when drafting and adopting statutes.[39] Judges who wished the norms they announced to be of any use in the future likewise should make explicit the policies on which they rested. In Llewellyn's charac-

---

the criterion rightly seen, [and] the effect neatly devised to purpose," should be formulated to deal with recurring social problems).

[35] See, for example, Karl Llewellyn, *Jurisprudence: Realism in Theory and Practice* (Chicago: University of Chicago Press, 1962), 217.

[36] Llewellyn, "The Good, the True, the Beautiful," 260.

[37] Ibid. (emphasis in original).

[38] Ibid., 250 (emphasis in original).

[39] Llewellyn's largely unsuccessful effort to adhere to this proposition when drafting the Uniform Commercial Code is described in Zipporah Batshaw Wiseman, "The Limits of Vision: Karl Llewellyn and the Merchant Rules," *Harvard Law Review* 100 (January 1987): 465.

teristically eccentric prose, the "rightest and most beautiful type of legal rule, is the singing rule with purpose and with reason clear."[40] Only rules of that sort were capable of providing guidance to other judges, to lawyers, and to "the interested layman,... the law-consumer,... the law-supporter,... the man whose law our law is."[41]

But even "singing" common-law rules, the Realists contended, were ephemeral in one crucial respect. The articulation of the objectives of a rule made it *possible* for courts in subsequent cases to follow it (more or less). But if those courts disagreed with the policies, they could and should modify the rule.[42] It was this last attitude—that judges engaged in common-law adjudication have the right and duty constantly to reconsider and revise the policies announced by their predecessors and the rules in which those policies were expressed—that doomed the project, first sketched by Oliver Wendell Holmes, Jr., of rebuilding legal doctrine from the ground up. Holmes had substantially anticipated the Realists in his contention that responsible decision making requires the conscious application of policies to the facts of individual cases.[43] Holmes, however, had believed that the accretion of answers to such particular questions would gradually give rise to a detailed, consistent, and relatively stable body of doctrine that would inform private parties what they could and could not do and enable them to adjust their conduct accordingly.[44] The

---

[40] "The Good, the True, the Beautiful," 250.

[41] Ibid., 260.

[42] Ibid., 264. Llewellyn, *Common Law Tradition*, 426. Llewellyn's vision of the appropriate role of judges in reconceiving the "purposes" of *statutes* was more ambiguous than this picture of common-law adjudication. See Wiseman, "Limits of Vision," 499–501 (describing his awkward position concerning the "mandatory" character of his proposed statements of the purposes of the Uniform Commercial Code); Llewellyn, "The Good, the True, the Beautiful," 251 (referring to a judge's obligation to remain within the "limits" of his office).

[43] See, for example, Oliver Wendell Holmes, Jr., "Privilege, Malice, and Intent" (1894), reprinted in *Collected Legal Papers* (New York: Peter Smith, 1952), 120 ("Whether, and how far, a privilege shall be allowed is a question of policy.... When the question of policy is faced it will be seen to be one which cannot be answered by generalities, but must be determined by the particular character of the case").

[44] The most famous expression of this belief is Holmes's argument that, after the question whether a particular sort of behavior constituted "negligence" had been submitted to several different juries, the courts should extract from the juries' answers a rule of law, which thereafter would govern all such cases. The net result would be that "the featureless generality, that the defendant was bound to use such care as a prudent man would do under the circumstances" would gradually give way to a matrix of more specific, "fixed" rules prescribing what a person might and might not do in certain situations. *The Common Law*, 110–24.

Realists' conviction that even highly specific common-law rules should be continually reexamined compelled them to renounce Holmes's ambition.[45]

If the content of each of the myriad particular rules that constitute legal doctrine ought to be determined by a conscious policy decision, and if the interpretation and application of any rule require reference to its purposes, lawmakers (legislators and judges) must have a clear and coherent vision of which policies are important and which are not. Unfortunately, it is on this crucial point that the Realists' writings are least satisfactory. Few members of the movement devoted significant attention to the content of the principles or policies that lawmakers should strive to implement,[46] and the reflections of those who did take up such topics suffered from two general defects: eclecticism and excessive dependence on customary practices and standards.

Virtually every time a Realist discussed the concerns that ought to guide reformulation of the legal rules governing a particular subfield or problem, he stressed the variety of conflicting policies that bore on the issue. Felix Cohen, atypical of the Realists on some questions, was representative on this one. In his most influential article, "Transcendental Nonsense and the Functional Approach," Cohen described as follows the way adjudication ought to proceed:

The realistic judge ... will frankly assess the conflicting human values that are opposed in every controversy, appraise the social importance of the precedents to which each claim appeals, open the courtroom to all evidence that will bring light to this delicate practical task of social adjustment, and consign to Von Jhering's heaven of legal concepts all attorneys whose only skill is that of the conceptual acrobat.[47]

The judge's task will be complex and "delicate," Cohen believed, for two reasons. First, legal decisions touch countless aspects of social life, and every one of those contacts can and must be assessed from an ethical standpoint. "All human goods, all parts of the good life, may be affected

---

[45] On rare occasions Realists spoke wistfully of the possibility of "raising the [legal] walls within which men must live and work by just laying one [decisional] brick upon another, letting a keener awareness of the needs of life and labor which they are to house guide our hands." Oliphant, "Stare Decisis—Continued," 160. But most often their sense of the instability of each such brick led them to despair of completing the building.

[46] Indeed, the Realists' writings on ethics are so thin that some of their critics suspected them of deliberately disguising a political agenda. See Fuller, "American Legal Realism," 448.

[47] Cohen, "Transcendental Nonsense," 842.

by the legal order and are therefore relevant to our standards of legal criticism."[48] Second, our "standards of legal criticism" must themselves be inclusive. "Modern ethics has made it clear that no realm of values can be set apart from the fulsomeness of life. Justice, like beauty, or health, can be defined only in terms of the full set of human values, the things that men approve or enjoy for their own sake."[49] Given this outlook, it is not surprising that Cohen concluded that "most errors of juristic criticism arise from illicit simplification of the questions we ought to face."[50]

One aspect of the Realists' outlook that may have contributed to the approach just described is their ambivalence concerning the origins and status of moral propositions. A few members of the movement forthrightly adopted the stance of ethical relativism, insisting that "human experience discloses no ultimates" and that "ultimates are phantoms drifting on a stream of daydreams."[51] Most, however, equivocated on this issue. For example, Llewellyn, in the article in which he confronted most directly the problem of value, acknowledges that he is incapable of supporting his vision of the Good through the exercise of "Reason" and that "every man of conscience must hold his own perceptions of Justice to be the basic ones."[52] Yet he suggests that his vision is grounded in "faith," and that "faith is a good foundation."[53] Similarly, Felix Cohen admits that, as far as his own "vision ... extends," two "theories of ethics ... appear equally valid as explanations of the world of value": relativistic naturalism, which holds that "intrinsic goodness is relative, definable,

---

[48] Cohen, *Ethical Systems*, 272.
[49] Cohen, "Modern Ethics," 50. Consistent with this position, Cohen spent a substantial portion of his magnum opus denouncing as hollow, misleading, or incomplete "standard[s] of valuation ... which restrict themselves to such limited aspects of legal results as the maintenance of peace, freedom, justice, 'social' interests, or 'natural rights.' " *Ethical Systems* 55, 69–111.
[50] Ibid., at 287. For similar assertions of the multiplicity of values a conscientious judge must take into account, see Cohen, "Property and Sovereignty," 15–21; Llewellyn, "The Good, the True, the Beautiful," 250–64.
[51] Moore, "Rational Basis of Legal Institutions," 612. For similar views, see Joseph W. Bingham, "The Nature of Legal Rights and Duties," *Michigan Law Review* 12 (November 1912): 2–3; Walter Nelles, Review of *Ethical Systems and Legal Ideals* by Felix Cohen, *Columbia Law Review* 33 (April 1933): 767. Some critics and historians of Realism have suggested that most if not all members of the movement were ethical relativists. See, for example, Morris Cohen, "Justice Holmes and the Nature of Law," 357; Purcell, *Democratic Theory*, 91–2. As the text following this note suggests, that characterization of the Realists is misleading.
[52] "The Good, the True, the Beautiful," 255–6.
[53] Ibid., 255, 257.

and identical with a relation to an approving individual"; and "the theory that intrinsic goodness is absolute, indefinable, and equivalent in application to positive pleasantness."[54] But although he concedes that "between these incompatible alternatives, we have discovered no rational basis of choice," he "[flies] forth on the pinions of faith" and does his best to persuade the reader of the merits of the second theory.[55]

The ambivalence acknowledged by Cohen and Llewellyn colors most Realist writings; the authors seem torn between a conviction that values are not susceptible of proof and a residual belief (perhaps traceable to the ideology of Progressivism[56]) that there do exist objective standards of justice and the "public good," which the law could and should strive to advance.[57] In view of their tenuous hold on the notion that justice means more than personal taste, it is not surprising that few Realists had the confidence to exclude from the world of values any conceivable social good.

Most Realists sensed that, by arguing that a wide variety of policies will bear on any given problem, they were putting judges—and themselves, as critics of particular doctrines—in an uncomfortable position. How is a judge or scholar to weigh or choose between competing purposes? One member of the movement, Felix Cohen, confronted and tried to resolve this problem. After insisting on the breadth of the set of values that shapers of the law should take into account, Cohen set out to integrate those values into a coherent standard. The proper "starting point," he argued, is "the nonverbal agreement of men as to the content of the good life, whether determined broadly for a civilization or narrowly for a particular class or community." That vision should then be subjected to "continued refinement" through "critical analysis of possible ethical

---

[54] Cohen, *Ethical Systems*, 227.

[55] See also ibid., 229: "And if it is alleged that the values he seeks to attain are ephemeral and evanescent, rationally devoid of objective significance, he will reply that it is human happiness he loves, and that if this love can have no ulterior justification it can need none, that if the kingdom of heaven within us be a dream it is, like life itself, a dream from which we can never wake."

[56] See White, *Patterns of American Legal Thought*, 109.

[57] Because these attitudes set the tone rather than provided the substance of most Realists' writings, it is difficult to identify clear-cut manifestations of them. For signs of this complex outlook, see, Oliphant, "Facts, Opinions, and Value-Judgments," 136–7 (arguing that legal scholars should confine themselves, for the time being, to empirical research but that devotion to that enterprise does not imply that a researcher is "deficient in moral sense"); Purcell, *Democratic Theory*, 42–3 (describing the struggle of John Dewey [an important contributor to Legal Realism] to develop "a convincing naturalistic method of value criticism and justification").

systems." Specifically, reflection upon "the nature of goodness" pointed toward "the hedonistic hypothesis" (by which he meant a version of utilitarianism) as the most plausible and attractive general ethical criterion. That insight, in turn, provided the makings of a standard for criticism and decision making: "The political task of hedonism is plain,—in thought, the translation of the books of the law into the universal language of human joys and sufferings,—in practice, the struggle for the attainment of the ideals thus discovered."[58]

Felix Cohen, alas, was unique. The remaining Realists attempted in one of two ways not to solve but to evade the dilemma created by their ethical pluralism. The first tactic was simply to delay the project of considering "oughts."[59] A significant number of Realists purported to concentrate their energies on "identify[ing] . . . the social consequences of particular legal measures and devices," disclaiming any ambition to "evaluate" those impacts.[60] They justified thus limiting their analyses on the ground that tracing the impacts of alternative legal regimes was an important and difficult job, demanding considerable time and attention. "When that task is well under way, there will be other seasons and other specialists more appropriate for doing the tasks of evaluation."[61]

The second tactic also involved a self-conscious turn from reflection upon ideals to examination of social reality, but for the purpose not of postponing the task of evaluation but rather of deriving substantive values from customary practices and beliefs. There were many variants of this move; what they shared was the assumption that it was possible to

[58] Cohen, *Ethical Systems*, 145, 187–8, 220, 229.
[59] See Llewellyn, "Some Realism about Realism," 1236 (identifying, as one of the Realists' "common points of departure," "the *temporary* divorce of Is and Ought for purposes of study") (emphasis in original).
[60] Oliphant, "Facts, Opinions, and Value-Judgments," 137. See also Cook, "Scientific Method and the Law," 308–9; Yntema, "The Rational Basis of Legal Science," 943; Kalman, *Legal Realism at Yale*, 20–1 and n. 85 (describing the authors of the three articles just cited, along with Underhill Moore, as "the scientific wing of the realists"). Projects undertaken in this spirit included empirical studies of various systems of criminal penalties and more abstract explorations of economics and psychology with a view to illuminating the relationship between legal regimes and the behavior of institutions and people. See Karl Llewellyn, "The Effect of Legal Institutions upon Economics," *American Economic Review* 15 (December 1925): 682; Edwin Patterson, *Jurisprudence: Men and Ideas of Law* (Brooklyn, N.Y.: Foundation Press, 1940), 548–52; John Schlegel, "American Legal Realism and Empirical Social Science: From the Yale Experience," *Buffalo Law Review* 28 (Winter 1979): 459; idem, "American Legal Realism and Empirical Social Science: The Singular Case of Underhill Moore," *Buffalo Law Review* 29 (Spring 1980): 195.
[61] Oliphant, "Facts, Opinions, and Value-Judgments," 137.

determine what the law ought to be by studying how people in fact behaved and what they in fact valued.[62]

The most common defense of the foregoing assumption rested on a traditional Marxist conception of the nature and function of law: Although "changes in material culture...precede and control changes in ...non-material culture," including "legal institutions," the latter all too often "lag behind" the former.[63] If legal analysts wish to shorten that lag, they must first acquire a thorough understanding of the evolving ways in which different institutions and industries operated. And the ambition of bringing the law more into conformity with underlying material conditions provided Realists who took this route a normative criterion for legal criticism and decision making.[64]

This functionalist argument seems to have been supplemented in the minds of a few Realists by a conviction that the customary mores of a particular community should guide the resolution of controversies among members of the community. Llewellyn, in particular, believed that "indwelling" in "every fact-pattern of common life"—inherent in the circumstances themselves and the ways in which people perceive and respond to them—was an "immanent law," which a lawmaker could and should strive to "uncover and implement."[65] No other Realist was

[62] The argument that positive law derives from custom has very deep roots in Anglo-American law. For a few of the tendrils, see E. Donald Elliott, "The Evolutionary Tradition in Jurisprudence," *Columbia Law Review* 85 (January 1985): 38. The Realists were probably most influenced by Holmes's early writings, in which he emphasized the customary roots of the common law. In his later writings Holmes retreated from this stance, for reasons the Realists, partly because of their particularism, unfortunately failed to consider. See Morton Horwitz, "The Place of Justice Holmes in American Legal Thought," unpublished manuscript, at 30–3, 38–40, 46–69.

[63] Moore, "Rational Basis of Legal Institutions," 614.

[64] For defenses and applications of this method, see, for example, Llewellyn, "Some Realism about Realism," 1236 (arguing that Realists shared a "conception of society in flux, and in flux typically faster than the law, so that the probability is always given that any portion of the law needs reexamination to determine how far it fits the society it purports to serve"); William Douglas, "A Functional Approach to the Law of Business Associations," *Illinois Law Review* 23 (March 1929): 675; Moore, "Rational Basis of Legal Institutions." For a criticism of it, see Fuller, "American Legal Realism," 448–53.

[65] Llewellyn, *Common Law Tradition,* 122. See also Note, "Legal Theory and Legal Education," *Yale Law Journal* 79 (May 1970): 1170. As Richard Danzig has argued, the clearest manifestation of this view of the proper origins of law is Article II of the Uniform Commercial Code, which was drafted in substantial part by Llewellyn. Danzig, "A Comment on the Jurisprudence of the Uniform Commercial Code," *Stanford Law Review* 27 (February 1975): 621. Many of the crucial provisions of the article do not purport to establish a rule of decision, but instead direct judges to decide controversies among merchants on the basis of commercial practice and customary standards of fair dealing. The code does not mandate slavish deference to business practice; not all provisions are based upon custom and those that are frequently advert not to average levels of conduct

so explicit as Llewellyn on this score, but many seem to have shared his orientation.

To summarize, three attitudes both stimulated and hampered the Realists' efforts to rebuild American legal doctrine: (1) particularism, encompassing the related propositions that only narrow, empirically grounded "working rules" were helpful in predicting courts' decisions; that both analytical precision and wise policy-making required the disaggregation of extant legal concepts; and that detailed knowledge of particular socioeconomic contexts was a precondition to sensible lawmaking; (2) purposive adjudication—the conviction that legal rules could be intelligently applied only by keeping constantly in view the shifting mix of social policies they served—and (3) ethical pluralism—the belief, partly rooted in ambivalence regarding the existence of objective standards of justice and the public good, that myriad, often conflicting social values were implicated by every legal issue—conjoined with hope that deference to customary values and practices would provide a way of reconciling competing concerns.

The implications of Realism. During the period between the two world wars, Legal Realism enjoyed a substantial following in American law schools. A large proportion of the younger law teachers found the new ideas compelling or at least intriguing, and many of the best students at the schools in which the Realists flourished found their ideas captivating. By the end of the 1930s, however, a scholarly reaction had begun. Published attacks on Legal Realism became more common and venomous, and opposition intensified to the appointment of Realist professors at leading law schools.[66]

Some of the increasingly hostile reaction was provoked by the ways in which many Realists carried themselves; most were younger faculty, and their flamboyance and irreverence infuriated their older colleagues.[67] Some of the reaction was related to developments in international politics; in the opinion of many older legal scholars, the Realists' thoroughgoing positivism and flirtation with ethical relativism were helping to erode Americans' faith that the law could and should be measured against any

---

but to the behavior of "commercially *decent* dealers." But "commercial standards" provide the principal criteria of decision making.

[66] See White, *Patterns of Legal Thought,* 140–1; and Kalman, *Legal Realism at Yale,* 120–44.

[67] Morton Horwitz, *The Crisis of Legal Orthodoxy, 1870–1960* (forthcoming, Oxford University Press), chap. 6.

rational moral standard, thereby weakening the nation's intellectual defenses against the fascism overrunning Europe.[68] And some of the response derived from domestic politics; the support most Realists had lent the New Deal—in particular, their denunciation of the decisions of the Supreme Court invalidating early New Deal statutes—aroused the wrath of those who regarded FDR's policies as protototalitarian.[69]

In the face of these attacks many Realists retreated. Several publicly disavowed positions they had taken (or might have been thought to have taken) in the early 1930s. Some went so far as to repudiate legal positivism, the foundation of the Realist critique, embracing a revived natural-law theory. Others in one way or another retired from the scholarly battlefield.[70]

By the end of World War II, Legal Realism as a coherent movement in legal scholarship was dead. But several of the arguments the Realists had developed or popularized survived the cessation of hostilities and have continued to nag legal scholars to the present day. In particular, three implications of the Realist critique have constituted standing challenges to central principles of American legal culture.

First and most obviously, the conception of adjudication that dominates most Realist writings is inconsistent with a truly democratic system of government. The heart of democratic theory is the proposition that laws should rest, mediately or immediately, on the consent of the governed.[71] If, as the Realists argued, judges deciding individual controversies often derive little if any guidance either from statutes (enacted by elected representatives of the people) or from common-law rules (implicitly democratically ratified through the legislature's inaction)—if, in other words, judges (most of whom are neither elected nor accountable to the people) routinely "make law"—then that proposition is regularly violated.

---

[68] Imprudent or deliberately inflammatory arguments by a few Realists fueled these fires. For example, in 1934 Frederick Beutel argued that a legal analyst need not concern himself with the ends to which his science is put; an efficient legal system could be devoted to any number of purposes, including "race power, national aggrandizement, or spiritual or intellectual advancement." "Some Implications of Experimental Jurisprudence," *Harvard Law Review* 48 (December 1934), 178–9. It is not surprising that members of the legal establishment, like Lon Fuller and the increasingly conservative Dean Roscoe Pound of Harvard Law School, found such statements dangerous. Purcell, *Crisis of Democratic Theory*, 159–71.

[69] Ibid., 171–2.

[70] Ibid., 172–6.

[71] See, for example, John Locke, *The Second Treatise of Government* in *Two Treatises of Government*, 2d ed. (Cambridge: Cambridge University Press, 1967), 373–8.

Second, for similar reasons the legitimacy of the institution of judicial review—the power of the judiciary to invalidate legislation it deems inconsistent with the Constitution—is called into question by the Realist attack. Since the late eighteenth century an important project of American political and legal theorists has been the effort to demonstrate that the practice of judicial review, although unmentioned in the federal or state constitutions, is nevertheless consistent with those documents and in particular does not represent the usurpation of lawmaking authority by the judiciary.[72] Common to most (albeit not all) of the theories they developed for that purpose was the notion that judges, when exercising their power, are in some way bound by the language of the constitutions themselves, which, in turn, derive their authority from the will of the people. The Realists' image of judges as guided primarily not by the provisions of the documents they purport to be construing but by a combination of idiosyncratic hunches and class biases seriously undermines most of those theories.

Third, the Realists' critique casts doubt on the attainability of the venerable Anglo-American political ideal of "the rule of law." Originating in the writings of Aristotle, Locke, Montesquieu, and Dicey,[73] that ideal is founded on an image of how government power could and should be constrained: the state may legitimately impose its will upon persons only through the promulgation (by lawmakers who do not know the identities of those affected) and enforcement (by judges who are free from bias and immune to pressure) of general, clear, well-publicized rules that are capable of being obeyed.[74] Important (though much debated) subsidiary

---

[72] See, for example, Alexander Hamilton, *The Federalist* No. 78 (1788) (Cambridge, Mass.: Harvard University Press, 1961), 489–96; William Nelson, "Changing Conceptions of Judicial Review: The Evolution of Constitutional Theory in the States, 1790–1860," *University of Pennsylvania Law Review* 120 (June 1972): 1166.

[73] See Judith Shklar, "Political Theory and the Rule of Law," in Allan Hutchinson and Patrick Monahan, eds., *The Rule of Law: Ideal or Ideology* (Toronto: Carswell, 1987) (describing the different versions of the Rule of Law that derive from Aristotle and Montesquieu and criticizing contemporary incarnations of the ideal); David Epstein, *The Political Theory of the Federalist* (Chicago: University of Chicago Press, 1984) (discussing the Lockean version of the ideal).

[74] There exists no single canonical statement of the ideal, but a good sense of its contours may be obtained by collating the following discussions: Lon Fuller, *The Morality of Law* (New Haven: Yale University Press, 1964), chap. 2; Friedrich Hayek, *The Political Ideal of the Rule of Law* (Cairo: N.B.E. Press, 1955), lecture III; Duncan Kennedy, "Legal Formality," *Journal of Legal Studies* 2 (June 1973), 31–2, 38–9; John Rawls, *A Theory of Justice* (Cambridge, Mass.: Harvard University Press, 1971), 235–42; Joseph Raz, *The Authority of Law: Essays on Law and Morality* (Oxford: Clarendon Press, 1979), chap. 11.

propositions include: similar cases must be treated similarly;[75] no person is above the law;[76] legal rules (especially criminal rules) should not be retroactive;[77] and any person adversely affected by or accused of violating a law has a right to a day in court to have his or her claims heard.[78] Adherence to these principles, it is said, not only makes democracy feasible but fosters productive activity and promotes individual liberty (by enabling private parties to plan their activities with knowledge of how other persons and the state will respond to their behavior)[79] and reduces arbitrariness and inequality in the imposition of collective force on individuals.[80]

The Realists' critique and affirmative program threaten several crucial components of the foregoing vision. Their particularized image of adjudication implies that the state does and should impose its will on citizens, not through the promulgation of general rules knowable in advance but through specific edicts. Because those edicts often cannot be anticipated, the exercise of government power is commonly at least partially retroactive. And because different judges confronting similar controversies will, in the Realists' view, frequently disagree, like cases are not treated alike.

[75] See, for example, Friedrich Hayek, *The Constitution of Liberty* (Chicago: University of Chicago Press, 1960), 153–4; Rawls, *Theory of Justice*, 237–8. Compare Fuller, *Morality of Law*, 41–4 (excluding equality of treatment from his definition of the "inner morality of the law"); Raz, *Authority of Law*, 226–27 (arguing that this principle is tautological or unattainable).

[76] See *United States* v. *Nixon*, 418 *United States Reports* 683, 715 (1974).

[77] This proposition is usually thought to be a derivative of the principal statement insofar as laws that apply to actions committed prior to their enactment cannot be "obeyed." See Fuller, *Morality of Law*, 51–62; Rawls, *Theory of Justice*, 238. For a dissenting view, see Raz, *Authority of Law*, 214 (arguing that a retroactive statute does not conflict with the rule of law if its enactment can be foreseen).

[78] See Rawls, *Theory of Justice*, 238–9; Raz, *Authority of Law*, 217. This proposition is described as subsidiary because, in the opinion of most proponents of the rule of law, such procedural protections are instrumental to the achievement of the substantive ideal of general rules fairly and equally applied and have no independent, noninstrumental value.

[79] See, for example, Friedrich Hayek, *Law, Legislation and Liberty: A New Statement of the Liberal Principles of Political Economy* (Chicago: University of Chicago Press, 1978), 2: 133–52; Rawls, *Theory of Justice*, 235–6; Max Weber, *Economy and Society: An Outline of Interpretive Sociology* (New York: Bedminster Press, 1968), Chap. 7, sec. 8. Compare Robert Gordon, "Critical Legal Histories," *Stanford Law Review* 36 (January 1984): 78–80 (summarizing and agreeing with the Realists' criticism of this asserted benefit of the rule of law).

[80] See, for example, Montesquieu, *De l'Esprit des Lois* (Geneva: Barrillot et fils, 1748), book VI, chaps. 1–6; Rawls, *Theory of Justice*, 240.

The amplification of Realism. The three challenges just reviewed have remained at or near the surface of the consciousness of most American legal theorists—and particularly theorists of constitutional law—since World War II. In part, the continuing power of these arguments derives simply from the forcefulness of the Realists' critique. But it also derives in part from the successful efforts of subsequent generations of legal scholars to sustain and advance the arguments initiated by the Realists.

Two groups of modern scholars have been especially influential in this regard. The first is the large and still-growing Law and Society movement. Established in 1964, the Law and Society Association has sought to foster work that crosses the disciplinary boundary between law and sociology.[81] In two related respects, the founders of the organization invoked and promised to apply Legal Realist principles. First, they shared the Realists' disdain for "paper rules" and their fascination with "the law in action"— the ways in which government power is actually brought to bear on individuals.[82] Second, like many Realists they believed that empirical research, uncorrupted by preconceptions, can reveal how law does in fact operate.[83]

The scholarship that has been generated by the movement over its twenty-five–year history is variegated, and much of it has little bearing on the overall development of American legal thought, but one important strand of writing associated with the Law and Society Association has been instrumental in reinforcing the original Realist challenges. Investigation of the law in action, a number of scholars associated with the movement concluded, revealed a persistent bias in the application of statutes, regulations, and common-law rules. In the words of one early article, "The law is not a neutral instrument, but rather . . . is oriented in favor of those groups or classes in society having the power to bend the legal order to their advantage."[84] Many articles and books that emerged from the movement developed the same theme.[85] The principal signifi-

[81] Robert B. Yegge, "The Law and Society Association to Date," *Law and Society Review* 1 (November 1966): 3–4.
[82] G. Edward White, "From Realism to Critical Legal Studies: A Truncated Intellectual History," *Southwestern Law Journal* 40 (June 1986): 830–1.
[83] For a less naive understanding of the nature and power of empirical research, see David Trubeck, "Where the Action Is," *Stanford Law Review* 36 (January 1984): 575.
[84] Jerome Carlin, Jon Howard, and Sheldon Messinger, "Civil Justice and the Poor: Issues for Sociological Research," *Law and Society Review* 1 (November 1966): 12.
[85] See, for example, Stewart Macaulay, *Law and the Balance of Power: Automobile Manufacturers and Their Dealers* (New York: Russell Sage Foundation, 1966); Mark Gal-

cance of this assertion for our purposes is that it threatened to corrode further the ideal of the rule of law. If legal rules are regularly designed and interpreted to enhance the interests "of those in positions of wealth and authority,"[86] the primary promise of that ideal—that all persons stand equally before the law—is a sham. Donald Black put the point crisply: The "central finding [of legal sociology] that the handling of cases is socially relative—that discrimination is ubiquitous—devastates any claim that the rule of law prevails, that like cases are treated in like fashion."[87]

Even more important than the impact of the Law and Society movement have been the amplification and modification of the Realist message by the Conference on Critical Legal Studies (CLS). Since its organization in 1977, the CLS "movement," as it appropriately has come to be called,[88] has attracted or fomented the most politically and methodologically radical work in American legal scholarship.[89] Again, it is important to emphasize that the movement is diverse and not susceptible of easy summary. But three of the many theses developed under its auspices are important to the development of modern legal scholarship.

First, scholars associated with the movement have argued that American legal culture—and American political culture more generally—is riven by fundamentally contradictory aspirations or commitments. As already suggested, sensitivity to the tensions and inconsistencies in legal doctrine was a defining characteristic of the Legal Realists; one of their favorite games was to demonstrate that for many seemingly authoritative legal rules there existed equally valid counter-rules. Scholars affiliated with the CLS movement make similar assertions on a grander scale. Conflicts between individual rules are merely manifestations, they claim, of deeper and more general contradictions running throughout entire doctrinal fields.[90]

anter, "Why the 'Haves' Come Out Ahead: Speculations on the Limits of Legal Change," *Law and Society Review* 9 (1974): 95; Lawrence Friedman, "Legal Culture and Social Development," *Law and Society Review* 4 (August 1969): 29.

[86] Carlin et al., "Civil Justice," 12.

[87] Donald Black, *Sociological Justice* (New York: Oxford University Press, 1989), 96–7.

[88] See, for example, Roberto Unger, *The Critical Legal Studies Movement* (Cambridge, Mass.: Harvard University Press, 1986).

[89] For accounts of the origins and history of the organization, see John Henry Schlegel, "Notes Toward an Intimate, Opinionated, and Affectionate History of the Conference on Critical Legal Studies," *Stanford Law Review* 36 (January 1984): 391; Mark Kelman, *A Guide to Critical Legal Studies* (Cambridge, Mass.: Harvard University Press, 1987), 1.

[90] See Schlegel, "Notes Toward a History of CLS," 407.

As Mark Kelman, one of the more prominent members of the movement has observed, "three central contradictions in liberal thought" have
been identified by the CLS scholars:

(1) the contradiction between a commitment to mechanically applicable rules as
the appropriate form for resolving disputes (thought to be associated in complex
ways with the political tradition of self-reliance and individualism) and a commitment to situation-sensitive, ad hoc standards (thought to correspond to a
commitment to sharing and altruism); (2) the contradiction between a commitment to the traditional liberal notion that values or desires are arbitrary, subjective, individual, and individuating while facts or reason are objective and
universal *and* a commitment to the ideal that we can "know" social and ethical
truths objectively (through objective knowledge of true human nature) or to the
hope that one can transcend the usual distinction between subjective and objective
in seeking moral truth; and (3) the contradiction between a commitment to an
intentionalistic discourse, in which human action is seen as the product of a self-
determining individual will, and determinist discourse, in which the activity of
nominal subjects merits neither respect nor condemnation because it is simply
deemed the expected outcome of existing structures.[91]

Some CLS scholars contend that underlying these three tensions is an
even deeper trauma, an experience common to all participants in contemporary Western culture. As Duncan Kennedy, the originator of this
argument, put it:

Most participants in American legal culture believe that the goal of individual
freedom is at the same time dependent on and incompatible with the communal
coercive action that is necessary to achieve it. Others (family, friends, bureaucrats,
cultural figures, the state) are necessary if we are to become persons at all—they
provide us the stuff of our selves and protect us in crucial ways against destruction.
...But at the same time that it forms and protects us, the universe of others
(family, friendship, bureaucracy, culture, the state) threatens us with annihilation
and urges upon us forms of fusion that are quite plainly bad rather than good.
...Through our existence as members of collectives, we impose on others and
have imposed on us hierarchical structures of power, welfare, and access to
enlightenment that are illegitimate, whether based on birth into a particular social
class or on the accident of genetic endowment. The kicker is that the abolition
of these illegitimate structures, the fashioning of an unalienated collective existence, appears to imply such a massive increase of collective control over our
lives that it would defeat its purpose.[92]

---

[91] Kelman, *A Guide to Critical Legal Studies*, 3. Kelman explicates these contradictions
and documents their importance to American legal culture in chaps. 1–3 of the book.
[92] Duncan Kennedy, "The Structure of Blackstone's Commentaries," *Buffalo Law Review*
28 (Spring 1979): 211–12.

Although Kennedy himself has since renounced reliance on this particular version of the "fundamental contradiction," others in the movement continue to see it as one of the principal sources of the many fault lines in American legal thought.[93]

The second and most notorious of the claims associated with Critical Legal Studies is what has come to be called (somewhat misleadingly) the "indeterminacy thesis." This is not an assertion that legal decision making is unpredictable in practice—that "you can never tell what a judge will do." Most CLS scholars freely admit that experienced lawyers can predict with confidence how courts will or would resolve (at least in the near future) most of the myriad disputes in which Americans become involved.[94] But the CLS scholars contend that this predictability derives not from the coherence of the legal order or the grip exerted on judges by the legal norms they are interpreting and applying but from two related aspects of the culture in which lawyers work. First, a combination of "shared understandings of proper institutional roles and the extent to which the status quo should be maintained or altered, . . . 'common sense' understandings of what rules mean, . . . conventions (the identification of rules and exceptions), and politics (the differentiation between liberal and conservative judges)" often provides answers that the relevant rules by themselves would be incapable of supplying.[95] Second, "mainstream legal thought" accords one of the terms in each pair of contradictory impulses a privileged or dominant status. Specifically, legal norms associated with the ideals of individualism, formal realizability, the subjectivity of values, and free will are treated as paradigmatic and presumptively applicable, whereas legal norms associated with the ideals of altruism, sensitivity to context, the objectivity of ethical truths, and determinism are usually treated—despite their ubiquity—as exceptional and in need of special justification.[96] Together, these two circumstances operate to stabilize and render reasonably predictable legal decision making.

---

[93] See Peter Gabel and Duncan Kennedy, "Roll over Beethoven," *Stanford Law Review* 36 (January 1984): 15–7.

[94] For an effort by a judge to estimate the proportion of cases whose resolution can be predicted with confidence, see Harry T. Edwards, "The Role of a Judge in Modern Society: Some Reflections on Current Practice in Federal Appellate Adjudication," *Cleveland State Law Review* 32 (1983): 389–92.

[95] Joseph William Singer, "The Player and the Cards: Nihilism and Legal Theory," *Yale Law Journal* 94 (November 1984), 22.

[96] Kelman, *A Guide to Critical Legal Studies*, 4; Gerald Frug, "The Ideology of Bureaucracy in American Law," *Harvard Law Review* 97 (April 1984): 1276.

But—and here is the real import of the indeterminacy thesis—the conventions that channel adjudication are sufficiently tenuous that the subordinate term of each of the dyads is always available to overturn or confound the dominant term and to prompt lawmakers to alter dramatically their responses to particular sorts of cases. There is no coherent, integrated justificatory system underlying and shaping the legal order as a whole.[97] As a result it is almost always possible for an irreverent scholar or lawyer, using arguments drawn from and common within "mainstream legal discourse," to argue that a given case should be resolved in any of a variety of different ways.[98]

The last of these contentions represents a substantial extension of the Realists' critique. The Realists, of course, made much of the indeterminacy of legal doctrine but thought that the problem was remediable. They believed that general adoption of the technique of purposive adjudication—pursuant to which the objectives served by legal norms would be routinely articulated and used to guide the interpretation and application of those norms—could render the activity of adjudication far more predictable and sensible. The Critical Legal Studies scholars argue that the system of principles and policies to which lawmakers would be likely to appeal when defining those objectives is itself incoherent, and therefore that adoption of the Realists' remedy would be ineffectual.

The third thesis associated with the CLS movement also substantially extends an element of the Realist critique. A minor theme in the Realist canon was a demonstration of the power of legal discourse—specifically, the classical language commonly used by turn-of-the-century judges in their opinions—to legitimate the outcomes of cases and the legal order as a whole. The CLS scholars, reflecting their indebtedness to Antonio Gramsci, the Frankfurt School, and the general tradition of Critical Marxism, devote far greater attention to the ideological functions of law.[99]

---

[97] See Kelman, *A Guide to Critical Legal Studies,* 13.

[98] For variants of the argument, see Mark Kelman, "Interpretive Construction in Substantive Criminal Law," *Stanford Law Review* 33 (April 1981): 591; Mark Tushnet, "Legal Scholarship: Its Causes and Cure," *Yale Law Journal* 90 (April 1981): 1205; Alan D. Freeman, "Truth and Mystification in Legal Scholarship," *Yale Law Journal* 90 (April 1981): 1229; Peter Gabel, "Intention and Structure in Contractual Conditions," *Minnesota Law Review* 61 (1977): 601.

[99] See Alvin Gouldner, *The Two Marxisms: Contradictions and Anomalies in the Development of Theory* (New York: Oxford University Press, 1980); Schlegel, "Notes Toward a History of CLS," 398; Kelman, *A Guide to Critical Legal Studies,* 302, n. 17. This sensitivity to the ideological significance of doctrine is one of the principal features differentiating Critical Legal Studies scholars from the Law and Society scholars from whom they drew much of their inspiration. See White, "From Realism to CLS," 833.

Over the course of American history, they argue, conventional legal language has operated in many ways to retard skeptical and imaginative thinking about law. It has helped to obscure the contradictory impulses in the legal order as a whole. (Indeed, some CLS scholars argue that the history of American legal thought is best described as a succession of unstable efforts to "mediate" or hide the fundamental divisions in liberal legalism.)[100] Conventional legal discourse, they claim, has also reduced popular appreciation of the indeterminacy of legal norms. Finally, it has stunted utopian thought, making it harder for participants in legal culture to imagine truly radical departures from the status quo.[101] One of the central objectives of critical legal scholarship must be to free Americans from these mental fetters.

The theses developed and popularized by the Critical Legal Studies movement are threatening for many reasons. Perhaps most obviously they reinforce all the challenges to orthodox legal thought originally generated by Legal Realism—the implicit attack on democratic theory, the delegitimation of the institution of judicial review, and the erosion of the ideal of the rule of law. In addition, scholars associated with the movement have derived from their overall program an attack more focused and explicit than that offered by the Realists on the theory and practice of legal rights.

The "critique of rights," as it has come to be called, has three main themes—each an outgrowth of some aspect of the CLS agenda. First, CLS scholars argue that legal rights—at least the sort of rights that figure in contemporary American legal discourse—are indeterminate. Their inability to provide answers to real cases derives partly from the ways in which rights are conventionally construed and applied by the courts. Too often judges attempt to resolve difficult controversies by "balancing" the individual rights at stake against the relevant "social interests" or by assessing the relative weight of two or more inconsistent rights; not surprisingly, such a procedure frequently fails to produce determinate solutions.[102] More fundamentally, abstract rights (e.g., the right to equal

---

[100] See Duncan Kennedy, "The Rise and Fall of Classical Legal Thought," unpublished manuscript, 1975; Elizabeth Mensch, "The History of Mainstream Legal Thought," in David Kairys, ed., *The Politics of Law* (New York: Pantheon Books, 1982), 18–39.

[101] See Alan Freeman, "Anti-discrimination Law: A Critical Review," in Kairys, ed., *The Politics of Law*, 96–116; Kelman, *A Guide to Critical Legal Studies*, 6 and chaps. 8–9.

[102] See Mark Tushnet, "An Essay on Rights," *Texas Law Review* 62 (May 1984): 1371–5.

concern and respect) are indeterminate when applied to real problems (e.g., the scope of parents' and children's entitlements against one another) because the implications of those rights depend on matters of social context (e.g., whether children need their biological parents to develop into autonomous persons) about which Americans are in radical disagreement.[103]

Second, CLS scholars contend that use of the language of rights to describe our social world or to argue about how it should be changed stunts our imaginations.[104] "Rights discourse," they claim, fails to capture the depth and texture of our experiences and thus restricts our capacity for genuine communication.[105] More seriously, the language of rights, by allowing us to pretend that judicially enforced rules both guarantee us some measure of autonomy and secure for us meaningful opportunities for community, obscures the fundamental and ineradicable contradiction between our yearning for freedom and our desire for solidarity. The result is to reassure us, falsely, "that we have been delivered from existential tragedy" and thereby to inhibit our efforts to imagine and establish a better world.[106]

The most developed version of the latter argument has been advanced by Peter Gabel, one of the early members of the movement. Gabel contends that all participants in contemporary Western culture experience both a "desire to be recognized by others in an empowering, life-giving way" and an expectation that others will withhold that recognition. Partly to reduce the pain associated with anticipated rejection, we play roles, denying to each other our genuine desires through the assumption of false selves. The activity of role playing is, however, unstable—constantly threatened by individuals' need for more authentic, less mediated social contact. The activity of describing our relationships in terms of rights—in particular, the attribution of control over our roles to the state—serves to stabilize the general social practice of role playing and the associated condition of alienation. Gabel summarizes his argument as follows:

"Rights consciousness"... is intended to secure the denial of desire in the face of contingency and the fear of loss by representing our false selves as legally

---

[103] Ibid., 1375–82. See also idem, "Critical Legal Studies and Constitutional Law: An Essay in Deconstruction," *Stanford Law Review* 36 (January 1984): 623.
[104] See Peter Gabel, "Reification in Legal Reasoning," *Research in Law and Sociology* 3 (1980): 25; Robert Gordon, "New Developments in Legal Theory," in Kairys, ed., *The Politics of Law*, 281.
[105] See Tushnet, "Essay on Rights," 1382–4.
[106] Kelman, *A Guide to Critical Legal Studies*, 62–3, 289–90.

compelled. We guard ourselves against the risk of taking existential action against our alienation by repeatedly telling ourselves that our alienation is inevitable, while at the same time denying that this alienation exists. And by acting toward each other as if we believe all this and that it must be believed, we coerce each other into remaining passive observers of our own suspended experience, hiding together inside the anonymity of artificial self-presentations that perpetually keep us locked in a state of mutual distance.[107]

Third, CLS scholars contend that the discourse of rights is less useful in securing progressive social change—in serving "the party of humanity," in Mark Tushnet's words—than liberal politicians and theorists generally suppose. To some extent this argument reduces simply to a critique of the ways in which the Bill of Rights happens to have been interpreted recently by the United States Supreme Court. So, for example, CLS scholars point out that current constitutional doctrine heavily favors so-called negative liberties (entitlements to be free of government interference) over positive liberties (entitlements to government protection or aid) and thus reinforces the pernicious "public/private distinction," one implication of which is that government is generally not thought to be responsible for providing persons the resources they need to exercise their liberties effectively.[108] To similar effect they argue that current free-speech doctrine, by according protection to commercial speech and obscenity and by limiting government regulation of private contributions to political campaigns, may on balance be more regressive than progressive. More generally, CLS scholars argue that disingenuous use of the language of rights—that is, "strategic" invocation of the language by those who believe it to be indeterminate—is likely to backfire either when true believers come to recognize and resent the disingenuousness or when social conservatives commandeer the indeterminacy argument themselves.[109] Finally, over the course of American history the political establishment has so often successfully employed strategic concessions of limited sets of rights to co-opt genuinely radical social movements that rights themselves should generally be regarded as untrustworthy.[110]

Rights are indeterminate, rights limit our imaginations, rights inhibit political and social change. Combined with the more general criticisms CLS scholars make of American law, these assertions provide powerful

---

[107] Peter Gabel, "The Phenomenology of Rights-Consciousness and the Pact of the Withdrawn Selves," *Texas Law Review* 62 (May 1984): 1563, 1581.
[108] See Tushnet, "Essay on Rights," 1392.
[109] Ibid., 1384–94.
[110] Gabel, "Phenomenology of Rights," 1591–7.

challenges to theorists who see merit in contemporary legal and constitutional practice.

THE STRATA OF POSTWAR LEGAL THEORY

To recapitulate, Legal Realism posed three threats to American legal and constitutional theory. First, the Realists' depiction of judges as relatively unconstrained by statutes or precedent clashed with the principle, central to democratic theory, that the citizenry should write the rules by which it is governed. Second, the Realists' contention that courts have substantial discretion when construing constitutional provisions endangered the conventional justifications of the institution of judicial review. Third, the Realists' celebration of particularized, context-specific adjudication implied that the ideal of the rule of law was both unattainable and undesirable. After World War II, American lawyers' awareness of these threats was sustained by a series of studies of "the law in action" associated with the Law and Society movement, and by a set of even more radical critiques of contemporary legal culture catalyzed by the Conference on Critical Legal Studies.

Since the 1950s the stakes of these debates have been sharply increased by the reemergence of the United States Supreme Court as a leader of social and political reform. In 1936, responding to popular outcry and increased pressure from President Roosevelt (as well as to the criticisms of its decision making advanced by the Realists), the Court ceased demanding that statutes and administrative edicts regulating social and economic affairs conform to the justices' conceptions of "freedom of contract" and federalism.[111] For the next two decades the Court remained aloof from most major political and social controversies. Beginning in 1954, however, it abandoned its passive stance and, in field after field, began to wield the power of judicial review aggressively. It declared unconstitutional racially segregated public schools and approved judicially mandated busing of students to overcome the effects of decades of officially sponsored discrimination. In an effort to give life to the principle of one person, one vote, the Court insisted on the reapportionment of federal and state electoral districts. It buttressed the rights of criminal defendants—for example, by forbidding the introduction into evidence of material secured in violation of a reinvigorated Fourth Amendment,

[111] See Alpheus Mason, *The Supreme Court from Taft to Burger* (Baton Rouge: Louisiana State University Press, 1958), 74–128.

by requiring that all defendants be given the effective assistance of counsel, and by demanding that suspects once placed in custody be given prophylactic warnings concerning the likelihood that their admissions would be used against them. And, in ways detailed in the next section of this chapter, the Court substantially enlarged the meaning of freedom of speech and created an entirely new category of constitutional rights pertaining to sexual and familial autonomy.[112] In short, during the past half-century judicial review has become an extremely important and controversial institution—and that situation, in turn, has made the amplified Realist challenges all the more salient.

This section describes the efforts of successive generations of legal theorists to meet those challenges. Many scholars have tried their hands at this task, and the fruits of their efforts are extensive and diverse. The bulk of the work, however, consists of variations on one of five themes. Adopting the (sometimes misleading) labels assumed by their originators, these approaches are Legal Process Theory, Law and Economics, Kantian Liberalism, Theories of the Good, and Perspectives of "Outsiders."

As the ensuing discussion will show, the five schools differ on many issues. They all share, however, the aspiration to refute the more sweeping of the arguments advanced by Legal Realism and Critical Legal Studies. They do not—because they cannot—repudiate all aspects of the Realist vision; several features of Realism are now permanently embedded in American legal culture. But they all attempt to deny or deflect the most politically and methodologically radical of the contentions of the Realists and their successors; they all seek to demonstrate, in one way or another, that if the courts behave responsibly, adjudication can be reasonably constrained, judicial review can be legitimate, the rule of law can be a reality, and justice can be secured.

Not surprisingly none of the five schools of scholarship has attained those objectives, but each has succeeded in the more limited sense of providing American judges and lawyers a vocabulary—a way of practicing and talking about law that seems to avoid both the manifest naïveté of Classicism and the supposedly cynical or nihilist implications of Realism and Critical Legal Studies. Contemporary American legal discourse, as a result, consists of a mélange of arguments drawn from each of the postwar perspectives. In oral arguments in appellate cases, in discussions

---

[112] See, for example, Robert McCloskey, *The Modern Supreme Court* (Cambridge, Mass.: Harvard University Press, 1972); and Laurence Tribe, *American Constitutional Law* (Mineola, N.Y.: Foundation Press, 1988), 785–1153, 1436–1672.

in law school classrooms, in op-ed essays in major newspapers, one frequently finds assertions drawn from all five approaches. To the uninitiated, the net effect is often disorienting.

Before the five approaches are analyzed, a few disclaimers must be made. In keeping with the overall focus of this volume—namely, a focus on the history of the Bill of Rights—this chapter is concerned principally with constitutional theory. Consequently, movements in legal scholarship that have as yet borne little on the question of how the Constitution should be construed are neglected in the following pages. Next, the organization of this section is not meant to suggest either that the divisions among the five schools are always crisp and unbridgeable or that all the members of each school agree on major issues. A number of important scholars have at various times sought to straddle two or more divides, and disagreements within each group have sometimes been fratricidal. Finally, the aim here is to identify major movements that have made relatively durable contributions to American legal thought. Thus, small clusters of scholars whose ideas passed relatively quickly from the scene are ignored.[113]

Legal Process Theory. The first and, until recently, most influential body of writing focuses on the process of judicial decision making. The central contention of scholars in this tradition is that, if conducted in conformity with certain guidelines and confined to certain sorts of disputes, adjudication should be reasonably disciplined, constrained, and determinate. So long as judges behave appropriately, private parties will be able to predict how the state will respond to their actions. In other words, citizens will be able to ascertain what their legal rights are and can be confident that those rights will be respected.

Since the early nineteenth century, American legal scholars had toyed with ideas of this sort,[114] but it was not until the 1950s that they were

---

[113] A good example of such a cluster is the "Law, Science, and Policy Movement" initiated by Harold Lasswell and Myres McDougal at Yale Law School in the early 1940s. Repudiating the ethical relativism attributed to Legal Realism (in favor of a recommitment to "clearly defined democratic values") while proclaiming their adherence to an "empirical" and "scientific" approach to the study of law, Lasswell and McDougal for a time were able to attract a number of followers. See White, "From Realism to Critical Legal Studies," 825–7. As the shallowness of their arguments became more apparent, however, the movement lost momentum and ultimately "failed to establish itself as a conversational presence in ongoing professional exchange." Bruce Ackerman, *Reconstructing American Law* (Cambridge, Mass.: Harvard University Press, 1984), 41.

[114] See, for example, Francis Lieber, *Legal and Political Hermeneutics* (Boston: Little, Brown, 1839).

elaborated into a full-blown legal theory. During that decade, many influential law professors subscribed to, and imparted to their students, a distinctive vision of how courts ought to conduct their business. Not all of them would have described the vision the same way, but the following composite picture would have found favor with most.

To begin with, responsible judges approach their job in a dispassionate spirit. Aware of the danger that their feelings and prejudices will affect their deliberations, they should seek to purge themselves of such influences before they address difficult cases. Reason, not emotion, must be their guiding light. Felix Frankfurter, in what must have seemed to his colleagues an irritatingly condescending letter written to them on the occasion of his retirement from the Supreme Court, aptly described this orientation:

> My years on the Court have only deepened my conviction that its existence and functioning according to its best historic traditions are indispensable for the well-being of the nation. The nature of the issues which are involved in the legal controversies that are inevitable under our constitutional system does not warrant the nation to expect identity of views among the members of the Court regarding such issues, nor even agreement on the routes of thought by which decisions are reached. The nation is merely warranted in expecting harmony of aims among those who have been called to the Court. This means pertinacious pursuit of the processes of Reason in the disposition of the controversies that come before the Court. This presupposes intellectual disinterestedness in the analysis of the factors involved in the issues that call for decision. This in turn requires rigorous self-scrutiny to discover, with a view to curbing, every influence that may deflect from such disinterestedness.[115]

Only by sustaining this stance of "disinterestedness" and humility, Frankfurter suggested in another context, would judges be able to make fine, unbiased discriminations among closely balanced arguments and thereby resolve disputes according to law and not according to their personal views.[116]

But disinterestedness alone was not sufficient, the Legal Process theorists conceded. It was also crucial that judges when making determi-

---

[115] Felix Frankfurter, Letter to "My Dear Brethren," 28 September 1962, reprinted in 371 *United States Reports* x (1962).

[116] Felix Frankfurter, "Some Reflections on the Reading of Statutes," *Columbia Law Review* 47 (May 1947): 535, 544. For similar statements by other Legal Process theorists, see Henry Hart, "The Supreme Court, 1958 Term—Foreword: The Time Chart of the Justices," *Harvard Law Review* 73 (November 1959): 84; Erwin Griswold, "The Supreme Court, 1959 Term—Foreword: Of Time and Attitudes—Professor Hart and Judge Arnold," *Harvard Law Review* 74 (November 1960): 85.

nations attend to the right sort of considerations. At this point, the Legal Process theorists took their cue from the Legal Realists themselves. It was hopeless, most acknowledged, to try to derive the solution to a difficult case from the language of the precedent, statutory provision, or constitutional clause being construed; responsible adjudication demanded that the underlying purpose of the norm at issue be identified and used to guide the outcome. In the most influential article to develop this point, Lon Fuller contended that it is never "possible to interpret a word in a statute without knowing the aim of the statute." When the meaning of statutory language seems to be obvious, that is only because the objective of the norm is obvious. When the relevant purposes are not plain, judges must be "sufficiently capable of putting [themselves] in the position of those who drafted the rule to know what they thought 'ought to be.' It is in the light of this 'ought' that we must decide what the rule 'is.' "[117]

But what if—as in many constitutional cases—the principles and purposes underlying the norms judges are called on to construe are not ascertainable? Such cases are troubling because they compel judges to become, at least to some extent, lawmakers. But the problematic character of such "judicial legislation" can be reduced, Legal Process theorists argued, if the judges at least avoid the pitfall of *ad hoc* decision making. Here they departed sharply from the Legal Realists, most of whom had argued that highly contextual decision making was both necessary and desirable. By contrast, Legal Process scholars urged judges to stand back from the particularities of individual controversies and render "principled decisions." In the most famous passage in this theoretical tradition, Herbert Wechsler explained: "A principled decision . . . is one that rests on reasons . . . that in their generality and their neutrality transcend any immediate result that is involved."[118]

Two further aspects of the judicial process could assist judges in achieving such unbiased, principled decision making. First, they could and should consult with their colleagues before coming to any conclusions. Such collegial deliberations would facilitate "the maturing of collective thought," making apparent which of each judge's impulses were idio-

---

[117] Lon Fuller, "Positivism and Fidelity to Law: A Reply to Professor Hart," *Harvard Law Review* 71 (February 1958): 664, 666.
[118] Herbert Wechsler, "Toward Neutral Principles of Constitutional Law," *Harvard Law Review* 73 (November 1959): 19.

syncratic and which were principled.[119] Second, judges should strive to identify and advance principles that were not only "general" and "neutral," but also comported with the shared commitments and aspirations of the American public.[120]

Deciding cases on the right bases was not enough, however. It was also crucial that judges fully explain the rationales of their rulings. One of the principal inspirations of Legal Process Theory was irritation at the sparsely or clumsily reasoned Supreme Court decisions of the late 1940s and early 1950s. When judges fail to articulate the reasons for their rulings, the Legal Process theorists insisted, they not only provide citizens inadequate guidance as to their legal rights but also prevent the public from critically examining their rulings. The result is a failure to "make law, in the sense in which the term 'law' must have in a democratic society."[121]

The last component of Legal Process Theory as it was originally developed in the 1950s was an analysis of the sorts of disputes that were suitable for resolution through adjudication. The techniques just reviewed would make possible reasonably constrained, determinate resolution of many controversies, the Legal Process theorists argued, but not all. Some kinds of problems were best left to other branches of government. For example, Professors Henry Hart and Albert Sacks argued (in an unpublished but extremely influential manuscript) that decisions whose resolution depended ultimately either on the expression of "preferences" or upon political compromise should be addressed either by legislatures or the public at large "by a count of noses at the ballot box." By contrast, types of decision (like the appointment of judges or the making of tariff policy) in which consistency and predictability are less important than context-specific exercises of informed discretion are best left to the executive. Only problems "which are soluable by methods of reason" should be entrusted to the courts.[122]

---

[119] See Hart, "Time Chart of the Justices," 100; and Griswold, "Of Time and Attitudes," 85.

[120] See G. Edward White, "The Evolution of Reasoned Elaboration: Jurisprudential Criticism and Social Change," *Virginia Law Review* 59 (February 1973), 286–91.

[121] Alexander Bickel and Harry Wellington, "Legislative Purpose and the Judicial Process: The Lincoln Mills Case," *Harvard Law Review* 71 (November 1957): 5. See also White, "Evolution of Reasoned Elaboration," 286–7.

[122] Henry Hart and Albert Sacks, *The Legal Process: Basic Problems in the Making and Application of Law*, tentative ed. (Cambridge, Mass., 1958). For another effort in the same vein (originally written in 1957 but not published [posthumously] until 1978), see

To summarize, the Legal Process theorists argued that judges could avoid most of the pitfalls identified by the Legal Realists and their heirs if they confined their attention to certain sorts of disputes; approached those disputes in a dispassionate spirit; attended closely to the purposes underlying the norms they were construing; founded their decisions on general, neutral principles; and explained the bases of their rulings to the public. Since 1960 the influence of this set of ideas in legal scholarship and teaching has gradually diminished, but has by no means dissipated altogether. In law review articles and casual conversations in classrooms and among law teachers, assertions traceable to the movement crop up constantly.[123] And periodically a major legal or constitutional theorist will rework these themes into a novel structure.

One such reconfiguration bears special mention because, as will be seen, it has had an unusually strong influence on the judicial interpretation of the Bill of Rights. In the late 1970s and early 1980s a small but prominent group of scholars ventured what they described as a "representation-reinforcing" theory of constitutional adjudication.[124] In the most influential of the works in this vein, John Ely argued that the judiciary, when called on to interpret and apply constitutional provisions, should concentrate its energies on perfecting representative democracy. The genius of the American system of government, Ely contended, is that it allows for the translation of the popular will into the laws by which we are all governed—with one crucial limitation: namely, that no social group may be systematically prevented from securing a fair share of the benefits or protections provided by government. This ideal, he argued, is the central underlying purpose of the federal Constitution; the framers were "overwhelmingly concerned with participational goals." And in most circumstances the electoral apparatus and separation of powers prescribed by the Constitution are sufficient to achieve this ideal with little or no guidance from the judiciary. Unfortunately, all systems of

---

Lon Fuller, "The Forms and Limits of Adjudication," *Harvard Law Review* 92 (December 1978): 353.

[123] See, for example, Paul Bator, "Legal Methodology and the Academy," *Harvard Journal of Law and Public Policy* 8 (1985): 338.

[124] John Ely, *Democracy and Distrust: A Theory of Judicial Review* (Cambridge, Mass.: Harvard University Press, 1980); Jesse Choper, *Judicial Review and the National Political Process: A Functional Reconsideration of the Role of the Supreme Court* (Chicago: University of Chicago Press, 1980). For critical analyses of this body of writing, see Richard Parker, "The Past of Constitutional Theory—and Its Future," *Ohio State Law Review* 42 (1981): 223; Laurence Tribe, "The Puzzling Persistence of Process-Based Constitutional Theories," *Yale Law Journal* 89 (1980): 1063.

representative democracy are susceptible to certain diseases. Elected officials, in hopes of muting criticism and keeping their jobs, are sometimes tempted to suppress dissent and debate, thereby retarding the maturation and expression of the sovereign will. For similar reasons legislatures often delegate excessive authority to administrative agencies and other bodies, hoping thereby to limit their responsibility for those agencies' actions. Population growth, inevitably uneven, eventually leads to serious departures from the principle of one person, one vote, and the party in power is generally reluctant to correct the imbalance. Perhaps most seriously, divisions between social (especially racial) groups sometimes result in permanent exclusion of "discrete and insular minorities" from the political process.

The job of the judiciary, Ely argued, is to detect and cure these ills. It should "clear the channels of political change" by preventing the government, unless it has a very good reason, from interfering with free speech. It should force legislatures to give clear and specific instructions to any agencies they establish. It should compel reapportionment of imbalanced districting systems. Last but not least, it should scrutinize all statutes that make it easier for a majority coalition to isolate, oppress, or ignore a discrete minority. If undertaken for one of these purposes, the exercise of judicial review is justified both by its conformity with the underlying ideals of the Constitution and by the judiciary's special competence in detecting and curing problems of this sort. If undertaken for other purposes, Ely contended, the exercise of judicial review is illegitimate.[125]

Law and Economics. In the mid-1960s, articles invoking the methodologies of economics began to appear with increasing frequency in legal periodicals. Some of these essays sought merely to clarify the impacts of alternative legal doctrines in hopes of aiding policymakers obliged to choose between them.[126] The more ambitious and influential papers, however, advanced and applied a normative theory. Legal rules, they asserted, should be designed and interpreted to maximize net social wel-

---

[125] Ely, *Democracy and Distrust,* chaps. 4–6.

[126] Most of the criticisms of economic analysis of law presented in the next few pages are inapplicable to scholarship in this vein. The use of the tools of economics to illuminate the choices available to lawmakers has much to recommend it. However, because analysis of this sort does not address the central concern of modern legal theory—namely, what criteria should guide lawmakers once they are aware of their options—it will not be considered further in this essay.

fare—defined as the total output of all goods and services, measured by the prices consumers are willing and able to pay for them.[127] In effect, the authors of the latter group of articles took seriously the Realists' contention that all responsible adjudication is self-consciously purposive, but sought to avoid the indeterminacy associated with the Realists' program by repudiating the Realists' purposive eclecticism. A single ideal—the criterion of allocative efficiency—should be judges' exclusive guide both in formulating and then in construing doctrines.[128] Adjudication practiced in this spirit, they contended, would be both predictable and socially beneficial.

The article that, in retrospect, is generally seen as the inspiration for this scholarly movement is "The Problem of Social Cost," published in 1960 by Ronald Coase.[129] Coase observed that if no "transaction costs" prevented two persons from entering into a contract determining their respective entitlements, it would not matter from the standpoint of allocative efficiency what rule the legal system selected to govern their affairs, because they would agree on and abide by the socially optimal rule.[130] The effect (though, it seems, not the intention) of Coase's essay was to provoke an ever-growing cadre of legal scholars to try to identify the legal rules that would advance allocative efficiency in situations in which transaction costs did prevent the achievement of optimal solutions through free bargaining. Some doctrinal fields—such as contracts, torts, property, and antitrust law—seemed to invite economic scrutiny.[131] But

---

[127] For a few of the statements and defenses of this proposition, see Guido Calabresi and Douglas A. Melamed, "Property Rules, Liability Rules, and Inalienability: One View of the Cathedral," *Harvard Law Review* 85 (April 1972): 1094; A. Mitchell Polinsky, *An Introduction to Law and Economics* (Boston: Little, Brown, 1983), 7; Richard Posner, "The Ethical and Political Basis of the Efficiency Norm in Common Law Adjudication," *Hofstra Law Review* 8 (Spring 1980): 487; idem, "Utilitarianism, Economics, and Legal Theory," *Journal of Legal Studies* 8 (January 1979): 103.

[128] See, for example, Polinsky, *Introduction to Law and Economics*, 105–17.

[129] *Journal of Law and Economics* 3 (October 1960): 1. For discussion of the historical significance of Coase's article, see Duncan Kennedy, "Cost-Benefit Analysis of Entitlements Problems: A Critique," *Stanford Law Review* 33 (February 1981): 395–8.

[130] In most contexts, the choice of a non-optimal rule will have *distributional* consequences, because the party favored by the rule will have to surrender something of value to induce the other party to agree to the optimal rule. Most lawyer-economists contend, however, that such "transfer payments" have no bearing on net social welfare. See, for example, Richard Posner, *Economic Analysis of Law,* 3d ed. (Boston: Little, Brown, 1986), 436.

[131] Partial lists of the essays addressing these fields follow. Contracts: John H. Barton, "The Economic Basis of Damages for Breach of Contract," *Journal of Legal Studies* 1 (June 1972): 277; Charles J. Goetz and Robert E. Scott, "Liquidated Damages, Penalties and the Just Compensation Principle: Some Notes on an Enforcement Model and a Theory of Efficient Breach," *Columbia Law Review* 77 (May 1977): 544;

the lawyer-economists soon brought their tools to bear on such seemingly unlikely fields as criminal law, family law, environmental law, landlord-tenant law, civil procedure, and (last but not least) constitutional law.[132]

From the outset, the dominant style of economic analysis has been plagued with serious methodological difficulties. For example, the developers of the method have never been able to resolve satisfactorily the so-called offer-asking problem: When measuring the "wealth" fostered by a particular legal rule, should the value of the goods or states of affairs it affects (such as habitable apartments or protection against sexual assault) be priced on the basis of the amount of money consumers would be willing and able to pay to obtain them or the amount of money consumers would demand in return for surrendering them?[133] At least

George Priest, "Breach and Remedy for the Tender of Nonconforming Goods under the Uniform Commercial Code: An Economic Approach," *Harvard Law Review* 91 (March 1978): 960. Torts: Guido Calabresi, "Some Thoughts on Risk Distribution and the Law of Torts," *Yale Law Journal* 70 (March 1961): 499; idem, *The Cost of Accidents: A Legal and Economic Analysis* (New Haven: Yale University Press, 1970); William Landes and Richard Posner, *The Economic Structure of Tort Law* (Cambridge, Mass.: Harvard University Press, 1987); Steven Shavell, *Economic Analysis of Accident Law* (Cambridge, Mass.: Harvard University Press, 1987). Property: A. Mitchell Polinsky, "Resolving Nuisance Disputes: The Simple Economics of Injunctive and Damages Remedies," *Stanford Law Review* 32 (July 1980): 1075. Antitrust: Kenneth E. Elzinga and William Breit, *The Antitrust Penalties: A Study in Law and Economics* (New Haven: Yale University Press, 1976); Louis Kaplow, "The Patent-Antitrust Intersection: A Reappraisal," *Harvard Law Review* 97 (June 1984): 1813.

[132] Partial lists of the essays addressing these fields follow. Criminal law: Issac Ehrlich and Joel Gibbons, "On the Measurement of the Deterrent Effect of Capital Punishment and the Theory of Deterrence," *Journal of Legal Studies* 6 (January 1977): 35; Gary S. Becker, "Crime and Punishment: An Economic Approach," *Journal of Political Economy* 76 (1968): 169. Family law: Elizabeth M. Landes, "Economics of Alimony," *Journal of Legal Studies* 7 (January 1978): 35; Elizabeth M. Landes and Richard Posner, "The Economics of the Baby Shortage," *Journal of Legal Studies* 7 (June 1978): 323. Environmental law: Richard Stewart and James Krier, *Environmental Law and Policy: Readings, Materials, and Notes*, 2d ed. (Indianapolis: Bobbs-Merrill, 1978). Landlord-tenant law: Richard S. Markovits, "The Distributive Impact, Allocative Efficiency, and Overall Desirability of Ideal Housing Codes: Some Theoretical Clarifications," *Harvard Law Review* 89 (June 1976), 1815. Civil procedure: Richard Posner, "An Economic Approach to Legal Procedure and Judicial Administration," *Journal of Legal Studies* 2 (June 1973): 399; Steven Shavell, "Suit, Settlement, and Trial: A Theoretical Analysis Under Alternative Methods for the Allocation of Legal Costs," *Journal of Legal Studies* 11 (January 1982): 55. Constitutional law: See the next section of this chapter.

[133] Among the reasons these figures often diverge are the following: (1) consumers who enjoy an entitlement and are asked to sell it are wealthier than consumers who do not enjoy the entitlement and are asked to purchase it, and the value people place on entitlements commonly varies with their total wealth; (2) people commonly (albeit "irrationally") refuse to ignore "sunk costs" (irretrievable investments) when deciding whether to spend more to obtain a commodity or entitlement; and (3) people typically place higher values on goods "in the hand" with which they are familiar than goods

as serious is the problem of "general indeterminacy." When an analyst must apply the method to two or more legal problems, it often makes a difference where she starts. If, for example, she begins by determining the optimal rule governing industrial pollution and then, taking as given the entitlements produced by that analysis and the associated effects on landowners' wealth, she determines the optimal rules governing land-owners' liability to injured trespassing children, the combination of rules she produces may be different from the combination she would have generated if she proceeded in the opposite order. The more numerous the rules to be considered sequentially, the more serious the problem. The lawyer-economists have yet to propose a plausible way of addressing the difficulty.[134]

But the most serious of the methodological difficulties concerns not technical problems of these sorts but the weakness of the justification for using wealth maximization as the legal system's principal objective.[135] Had they contented themselves with advocating "Pareto-superior" doctrinal reforms,[136] the lawyer-economists would have had a relatively easy justificatory job; the notion that it is good to make some people better off without making anyone worse off (by their own lights) is relatively noncontroversial. Only a few of the scholars in this camp, however, content themselves with the criterion of Pareto superiority; most urge lawmakers to adopt reforms that would make some persons worse off,

---

"in the bush," regardless of the probability that they will obtain the latter. See Mark Kelman, "Consumption Theory, Production Theory, and Ideology in the Coase Theorem," *Southern California Law Review* 52 (1979): 669. The most serious of the analytical difficulties caused by the divergence of "offer" and "asking" prices is that it will sometimes be efficient to leave an entitlement in the hands of whichever of two claimants is first assigned it; under such circumstances, it will be impossible, using the wealth-maximization criterion, to decide which party should get the entitlement. See T. De Scitovszky, "A Note on Welfare Propositions in Economics," *Review of Economic Studies* 9 (November 1941): 77; C. Edwin Baker, "The Ideology of the Economic Analysis of Law," *Philosophy and Public Affairs* 5 (Fall 1975): 3; Kennedy, "Cost-Benefit Analysis," 401–22.

[134] For discussion of the problem and its implications, see Lucian Bebchuk, "The Pursuit of a Bigger Pie: Can Everyone Expect a Bigger Slice?" *Hofstra Law Review* 8 (Spring 1980): 671; Kennedy, "Cost-Benefit Analysis," 422ff.

[135] See Coleman, "Economics and the Law: A Critical Review of the Foundations of the Economic Approach to Law," *Ethics* 94 (July 1984): 649; Anthony Kronman, "Wealth Maximization as a Normative Principle," *Journal of Legal Studies* 9 (1980): 227; and Ronald Dworkin, "Is Wealth a Value?" *Journal of Legal Studies* 9 (1980): 323.

[136] As Bruce Ackerman explains, "under this principle of evaluation, Outcome A is said to be Pareto-superior to Outcome B *if and only if* at least one person believes himself better off under A and *nobody* believes himself worse off." *Economic Foundations of Property Law* (Boston: Little, Brown, 1975), xi (emphasis in original).

but would confer upon others benefits that, in toto, exceed those losses.[137] Defending the latter, more ambitious, criterion is no easy job, and few of the lawyer-economists make a serious effort to do so. The majority of them either acknowledge the difficulty and move on,[138] assert baldly that the wealth-maximization criterion is functionally equivalent to the "Pareto superiority" test,[139] or simply ignore the difficulty altogether.

The only serious effort to provide an undergirding for the wealth maximization test has been made by Richard Posner, the most prolific and prominent member of the movement. The heart of Posner's argument is the assertion that because all (or almost all) persons are sometimes benefited and sometimes burdened by most legal rules, it is in the long-term best interest of everyone to select the rules that will maximize net social welfare. For example, almost every adult in the United States sometimes drives an automobile and sometimes walks across streets. Ex ante (in other words, before it is known who will be the drivers and who will be the pedestrians when pedestrians are run over), every person thus has an interest in the selection of a legal rule governing automobile accidents that will minimize the total of the costs of accidents (hospital and repair bills, etc.) and the costs of taking precautions to avoid accidents (the price of better brakes and traffic signals, the losses attributable to forgone strolls downtown, etc.).[140] Among the weaknesses of this argument, the most obvious is that many persons do not stand an equal chance of being benefited and being burdened by a given legal rule. Some people drive more than they walk, some walk more than they drive. Unless the persons disproportionately benefited by the choices of optimal over extant legal rules compensate persons burdened by such choices (a corrective device few lawyer-economists advocate), the persons burdened have no reason to agree to the adoption of the wealth-maximization criterion.[141] The difficulty is plain enough that few of the legal scholars working this terrain subscribe to Posner's theory.

What explains, then, the substantial and apparently still growing pop-

---

[137] In the typical analysis, the benefits to the gainers are measured by their monetary values to the gainers, while the injuries to the losers are measured by their monetary values to the losers. Because adoption of such a reform would put the gainers in a position from which they *could,* if they wished, compensate the losers for their losses and still be better off than before, this criterion is sometimes referred to as "*potential* Pareto superiority."

[138] See, for example, Robert Cooter and Thomas Ulen, *Law and Economics* (Glenview, Ill.: Scott, Foresman, 1988), 51.

[139] See Polinsky, *Introduction to Law and Economics,* 7, n.4.

[140] See Posner, "The Ethical and Political Basis of the Efficiency Norm," 487.

[141] See Bebchuk, "Pursuit of a Bigger Pie," 673–7.

ularity among legal scholars of this approach? The most plausible answer, as Arthur Leff has suggested, is that the wealth-maximization criterion, whatever its problems, offers some relief from the complexity and doubts thrust on the legal profession—and on legal scholars in particular—by Legal Realism. The wealth-maximization criterion, shaky as it is, appears to provide a neutral, apolitical, scientific standard of judgment—a standard that legal scholars can use in differentiating good rules from bad, and that judges can use in making the innumerable hard choices they now realize they must make. Especially for lawyers increasingly dissatisfied with the platitudes of Legal Process Theory, economic analysis has provided a way "to go on talking."[142]

Kantian liberalism. The third and fourth movements in legal theory have both been stimulated by developments in academic philosophy. In the late 1960s, utilitarianism came under increasing attack by a group of political philosophers who looked for guidance principally to the work of Kant. Quickly the new crew came to dominate the field. In 1977 H. L. A. Hart summarized the shift in orientation as follows:

I do not think that anyone familiar with what has been published in the last ten years, in England and the United States, on the philosophy of government can doubt that this subject, which is the meeting point of moral, political and legal philosophy, is undergoing a major change. We are currently witnessing, I think, the progress of a transition from a once widely accepted old faith that some form of utilitarianism, if only we could discover the right form, *must* capture the essence of political morality. The new faith is that the truth must lie not with a doctrine that takes the maximisation of aggregate or average general welfare for its goal, but with a doctrine of basic human rights, protecting specific basic liberties and interests of individuals, if only we could find some sufficiently firm foundation for such rights to meet some long familiar objections. Whereas not so long ago great energy and much ingenuity of many philosophers were devoted to making some form of utilitarianism work, latterly such energies and ingenuity have been devoted to the articulation of theories of basic rights.[143]

Many legal scholars—especially those ill suited by taste or aptitude for economic analysis—found the resurgence of the Kantian perspective

---

[142] Arthur A. Leff, "Economic Analysis of Law: Some Realism about Nominalism," *Virginia Law Review* 60 (March 1974): 459.

[143] H. L. A. Hart, "Between Utility and Rights," *Columbia Law Review* 79 (June 1979): 828, reprinted in Alan Ryan, ed., *The Idea of Freedom: Essays in Honour of Isaiah Berlin* (Oxford: Oxford University Press, 1979), 77 (emphasis in original). See also Michael Sandel, *Liberalism and Its Critics* (Cambridge: Cambridge University Press, 1984), 1–5.

liberating. It offered them a powerful analytic, a set of firm, seemingly well grounded principles that enabled them to criticize and reform legal doctrines while permitting (indeed, requiring) them to avoid discussing the hopelessly controversial question of how persons ought to live. Articles urging courts engaged in common-law or constitutional adjudication to pay attention to the ruminations of the new Kantian philosophers began to appear in ever greater numbers in law reviews.

The developers of this new style of legal scholarship differed on many issues but shared a set of related convictions: The right is prior to the good. It is appropriate, indeed imperative, for the state to establish and guarantee a framework of fundamental rights and liberties, but it is inappropriate for the state to affirm particular ends, particular ways of living. The job of government in general and courts in particular is to devise rules that accord persons the respect they are due as autonomous moral agents without making judgments concerning their aspirations or life-styles.[144] Two examples of this new style of legal writing should convey its flavor and suggest the diversity of views it can encompass.

In 1969 Frank Michelman argued in a prominent article in the *Harvard Law Review* that the Supreme Court, when construing the Fourteenth Amendment in cases implicating de facto discrimination against the poor, should attend to and incorporate John Rawls's theory of distributive justice. The nub of Rawls's argument was the proposition that inequality in the distribution of "primary goods" is legitimate if and only if, by increasing incentives for productive effort, it leaves the least-advantaged group in the society no worse off than under conditions of perfect equality in the distribution of those goods.[145] Rawls's argument, Michelman contended, should be used by the courts to develop a theory of "just wants," which could then be used to test the constitutionality of legislation ad-

---

[144] See, for example, Bruce Ackerman, *Social Justice in the Liberal State* (New Haven, Conn.: Yale University Press, 1980), 11, 57–8, 327–78; Ronald Dworkin, *Taking Rights Seriously* (Cambridge, Mass.: Harvard University Press, 1977), vii; Charles Fried, *Right and Wrong* (Cambridge, Mass.: Harvard University Press, 1978), 13–17, 146–7; David Richards, *A Theory of Reasons for Action* (Oxford, Eng.: Clarendon Press, 1971), 87; and idem, "Human Rights and Moral Ideals: An Essay on the Moral Theory of Liberalism," *Social Theory and Practice* 5 (1980): 461, 465–8.

[145] At the time Michelman wrote his essay, Rawls had not yet published *A Theory of Justice*, in which he develops his theory, but had outlined his argument in several articles. For explication (and criticism) of Rawls's theory, see Benjamin R. Barber, "Justifying Justice: Problems of Psychology, Politics, and Measurement in Rawls," in Norman Daniels, ed., *Reading Rawls: Critical Studies on Rawls' A Theory of Justice* (Stanford, Calif.: Stanford University Press, 1989), 301–3; Thomas Scanlon, "Rawls' Theory of Justice," *University of Pennsylvania Law Review* 121 (May 1973): 1057–61.

versely affecting the poor. If they adopted such a method, the courts might well conclude, for example, that access to public office "should never be blocked by economic vicissitude" and that "each child must be guaranteed the means of developing his competence, self-knowledge, and tastes for living."[146]

In 1981, Charles Fried set out to apply the insights of Rawls, Ronald Dworkin, and Robert Nozick to a classic common-law issue: the nature and scope of contractual duties. Repudiating the view that "legal obligation can be imposed only by the community, and in so imposing it the community must be pursuing its goals and imposing its standards," Fried contended that an implication of the notion that "individuals have rights" is that "contractual obligations [are] essentially self-imposed." Freely made promises give rise to moral obligations that the state should enforce, because the maintenance of a convention that promises are kept is essential to enable persons to pursue their own ends effectively, and abuse of that convention (making and then reneging on a promise) represents an improper "use" of another person. By contrast, the imposition of obligations on persons who have not freely made promises illegitimately curtails their freedom—unless, of course, they have behaved in ways that appropriately expose them to liability in tort. On these premises Fried ventured novel suggestions concerning a variety of venerable problems in contract law—such as what constitutes the proper measure of damages and what should be done when one of the contracting parties has been operating under a mistake of fact. The overarching message was that, when administering this body of law, courts should disregard the realm of "the good, which is the domain of aspiration," and concern themselves exclusively with the realm of "the right, which sets the terms and limits according to which we strive"—leaving to us the choices of how to operate within those limits.[147]

Theories of the good. In the 1980s, the tides of American political philosophy began to turn once again. A fresh group of scholars found the Kantians' conception of the self (as a subject prior to its ends and

---

[146] Frank Michelman, "The Supreme Court, 1968 Term—Foreword: On Protecting the Poor Through the Fourteenth Amendment," *Harvard Law Review* 83 (November 1969): 15–6. For a critique of Michelman's effort, see Mark Tushnet, "Truth, Justice, and the American Way: An Interpretation of Public Law Scholarship in the Seventies," *Texas Law Review* 57 (November 1979): 1316–19.

[147] Charles Fried, *Contract as Promise: A Theory of Contractual Obligation* (Cambridge, Mass.: Harvard University Press, 1981). The quotations appear on pp. 2, 16, and 8.

independent of its culture) unrealistic and their vision of a just society unpalatable. Michael Sandel, one of the leaders of the young Turks, summarizes their principal contentions as follows:

Recalling the arguments of Hegel against Kant, the communitarian critics of modern liberalism question the claim for the priority of the right over the good, and the picture of the freely-choosing individual it embodies. Following Aristotle, they argue that we cannot justify political arrangements without reference to common purposes and ends, and that we cannot conceive our personhood without reference to our role as citizens, and as participants in a common life.[148]

By the latter half of the decade, legal scholars had begun to pick up the new themes. Repudiating the strictures of Dworkin and Fried, a growing group of younger law teachers began speculating freely about the sort of societies that would most conduce to "human flourishing" and urging courts and legislatures to adopt reforms that would accelerate achievement of those societies.

The utopian visions of this new generation have come in various shapes and sizes. Examples include Margaret Jane Radin's Hegelian theory of "personhood" and the forms of property ownership that would make possible its widespread realization;[149] Kathleen Sullivan's vision of "normative pluralism";[150] Joseph Singer's "social vision" in which cruelty is prevented, misery alleviated, "illegitimate hierarchies" democratized, and alienation overcome;[151] and my own version of egalitarian socialism.[152]

One theory, however, has attracted a disproportionate number of followers and thus deserves special attention. Since the mid-1960s, a number of prominent historians of the American Revolution have been arguing that the liberal political tradition, traceable to the writings of Hobbes and Locke, was not, as had long been assumed, the lens through which the colonists viewed the events of that period. Rather, the reigning ideology (or, as some of the revisionist historians preferred to say, the vocabulary in which political discourse was conducted) was a variant of classical republicanism. Originating in the writings of Aristotle and Ma-

---

[148] Sandel, *Liberalism and Its Critics*, 5.
[149] See Margaret Jane Radin, "Property and Personhood," *Stanford Law Review* 34 (May 1982): 957; idem, "Market-Inalienability," *Harvard Law Review* 100 (1987): 1849; idem, "Residential Rent Control," *Philosophy and Public Affairs* 15 (Fall 1986): 350.
[150] See Kathleen Sullivan, "Rainbow Republicanism," *Yale Law Journal* 97 (July 1988): 1713.
[151] See Singer, "The Player and the Cards," 66–70.
[152] See William W. Fisher, "Reconstructing the Fair Use Doctrine," *Harvard Law Review* 101 (June 1988): 1744–94.

chiavelli, modified by Harrington and the Commonwealthmen, republicanism, they argued, centered on the following notions: a good life is a virtuous life; virtue consists partly in a willingness to subordinate one's private ends to the common weal; man is a political being whose self-realization comes only through active participation in public life; material and psychic "independence" is a prerequisite to responsible citizenship; and a system of government embodying those ideals is perennially threatened by such diverse dangers as the spread of luxury, exercise of patronage, maintenance of standing armies, and (perhaps) serious inequality of wealth.[153]

To a group of young law teachers casting about for an alternative to liberalism as a template for doctrinal criticism and reform, this newly excavated set of ideas was attractive for several reasons: It comported with their hostility to the excessive individualism of the Kantian school. It had an authentic American heritage and, so it seemed, had been influential in shaping the federal Constitution. Finally, it relieved them of the formidable task of developing a theory of the good on their own.

The result was a spate of articles, beginning in the mid-1980s, arguing that one or another field of law should be modified or altogether reconstructed in light of the lessons of republicanism. Among the recommen-

---

[153] See, for example, Bernard Bailyn, *The Ideological Origins of the American Revolution* (Cambridge, Mass.: Harvard University Press, 1967); Gordon Wood, *The Creation of the American Republic, 1776–1787* (Chapel Hill: University of North Carolina Press, 1969); Pauline Maier, *From Resistance to Revolution: Colonial Radicals and the Development of American Opposition to Britain 1765–1776* (New York: Knopf, 1972); and J. G. A. Pocock, *The Machiavellian Moment: Florentine Political Thought and the Atlantic Republican Tradition* (Princeton: Princeton University Press, 1975). This brief summary flattens important differences among the various historians who contributed to the so-called republican revival concerning the nature and power of the political discourse they recovered. For more detailed accounts of their arguments, see Robert E. Shalhope, "Republicanism and Early American Historiography," *William & Mary Quarterly*, 3d Ser., 39 (April 1982): 334; and William W. Fisher, "Ideology, Religion, and the Constitutional Protection of Private Property: 1760–1860," *Emory Law Journal* 39 (Winter 1990): 67–75.

Recently the view that classical republicanism was both the principal spring for the Revolution and a powerful force in American political thought in the ensuing years has been challenged by a number of historians. See, for example, Morton White, *The Philosophy of the American Revolution* (New York: Oxford University Press, 1978); Gary Nash, *The Urban Crucible: Social Change, Political Consciousness, and the Origins of the American Revolution* (Cambridge, Mass.: Harvard University Press, 1979); Joyce Appleby, *Capitalism and a New Social Order: The Republican Vision of the 1790s* (New York: New York University Press, 1984); and John Diggins, *The Lost Soul of American Politics: Virtue, Self-Interest, and the Foundations of Liberalism* (New York: Basic Books, 1984). Legal scholars have yet to take much notice of this historiographic shift.

dations that emerged from these analyses were these: cities and other arenas for the exercise of citizenship should be accorded more autonomy and power; greater protection should be accorded a more expansively understood zone of religious practice; pornography and other forms of expression corrosive of civic virtue should be more closely regulated; statutes prohibiting homosexual sodomy should be deemed unconstitutional on the ground that they threaten the spheres of privacy essential to the cultivation of republican virtues and impermissibly "denigrate" one important group of citizens; businesses should be discouraged from moving their bases of operation, thereby disrupting local communities; and courts should be more skeptical of statutes that derive from logrolling or pluralistic bargaining than they are of statutes that issue from an empathetic process of rational deliberation in which all the participants seek to identify and advance the common good.[154]

In working out these arguments the law teachers confronted various aspects of classical republicanism that, in the modern world, seemed neither attractive nor practicable. In its original form, republicanism was perfectly compatible with—indeed, may have depended on—a system of slavery. The ideology as a whole had a disturbingly martial and pugnacious cast; in the original persuasion, women were certainly not seen as candidates for republican citizenship. A system of *representative* democracy did not mesh well with the republican vision. Most generally, republicanism seemed to presume or demand a culturally homogeneous population; it thus seemed ill-suited to a large, diverse population like that of the modern United States. As a result, much of the recent effort of scholars working this vein has been devoted to demonstrating that republicanism can be purged of its noxious elements without losing its

---

[154] See, for example, Cass Sunstein, "Interest Groups in American Public Law," *Stanford Law Review* 38 (November 1985): 29; Frank Michelman, "The Supreme Court, 1985 Term—Foreword: Traces of Self-Government," *Harvard Law Review* 100 (November 1986): 4; Suzanna Sherry, "Civic Virtue and the Feminine Voice in Constitutional Adjudication," *University of Virginia Law Review* 72 (April 1986): 543; Frank Michelman, "Law's Republic," *Yale Law Journal* 97 (July 1988): 1493; Cass Sunstein, "Beyond the Republican Revival," *Yale Law Journal* 97 (July 1988): 1539; and Mark Tushnet, *Red, White, and Blue: A Critical Analysis of Constitutional Law* (Cambridge, Mass.: Harvard University Press, 1988). Proposing reforms of particular doctrinal regimes was not the only use to which legal scholars put republicanism. Some scholars contented themselves with employing republicanism as a device for illuminating the defects of liberalism as an "ideal type," or suggesting the range of argumentative possibilities rather than providing a template for doctrinal change. See Richard Fallon, "What Is Republicanism, and Is It Worth Reviving?" *Harvard Law Review* 102 (May 1989), 1703–20. But the utopian use of republicanism has been the most common and influential.

value as a criterion of legal criticism and guide for change. Whether they will be successful in that venture is uncertain.[155]

It should be apparent that although the proposals of the economists, Kantian scholars, and theorists of the good differ radically, the strategy of the three groups is similar in one important respect. The members of all three follow the Realists in their insistence upon the impossibility of deriving answers to difficult cases from the materials of positive law. But unlike the Realists, who encouraged judges to take into account a limitless array of moral and political concerns, the members of these three modern groups seek to supply judges with a more clearly defined criterion—a principle or vision that, conscientiously applied, would lend coherence and predictability to the judges' rulings.

Perspectives of "Outsiders."[156] The newest of the five varieties of twentieth-century legal theory derives from the work of a small but growing cluster of scholars who belong to groups long excluded from the legal academy. During the past decade, women and members of racial and ethnic minorities for the first time have begun to be hired as faculty in significant numbers by major law schools. The legal theories in general circulation have seemed unsatisfactory to many of these newcomers. Drawing on their heritages and personal histories, they have begun to develop novel perspectives on the meaning and function of law. The newcomers by no means agree on all important issues. Feminist scholars argue about such crucial questions as the extent to which men and women, as a result of either their biology or social positions, think (and ought to think) differently.[157] Black scholars disagree on such important matters as the extent to which law schools should be engaged in affir-

---

[155] For skeptical assessments, see Sullivan, "Rainbow Republicanism"; and Fallon, "What Is Republicanism," 1733–5.

[156] The term "outsiders" is employed here in the same sense and for the same purposes it is used by Mari Matsuda: " 'Outsiders' is used throughout the remainder of this article to encompass various outgroups, including women, people of color, poor people, gays and lesbians, indigenous Americans, and other oppressed people who have suffered historical underrepresentation and silencing in the law schools. 'Outsiders' is an awkward term, used here experimentally to avoid the use of 'minority.' The outsiders collectively are a numerical majority in this country. The inclusive term is not intended to deny the need for separate consideration of the circumstances of each group. It is a semantic convenience used here to discuss the need for epistemological inclusion of the views of many dominated groups." "Affirmative Action and Legal Knowledge: Planting Seeds in Plowed-up Ground," *Harvard Women's Law Journal* 11 (Spring 1988): 1n.2.

[157] Compare, for example, Ann Scales, "The Emergence of Feminist Jurisprudence: An Essay," *Yale Law Journal* 95 (June 1986): 1373; with Joan Williams, "Deconstructing Gender," *Michigan Law Review* 87 (February 1989): 797.

mative action in faculty hiring.[158] Nevertheless, some important methodological and substantive commitments can be found in the work of most of the new teachers, and members of the group have a sense of participating in a common enterprise.

The starting point for most of the essays in this vein is an original conception of the process by which the values advanced by the law should be developed: instead of trying to imagine the sort of social and political system that would be selected by persons deliberating behind a "veil of ignorance" or seeking to derive a theory of human flourishing from introspection concerning their own needs and aspirations, lawmakers should engage in conversations with members of groups traditionally deprived of a political role or voice. Mari Matsuda explains the advantages of this method:

> When notions of right and wrong, justice and injustice, are examined not from an abstract position but from the position of groups who have suffered through history, moral relativism recedes and identifiable normative priorities emerge. This article, then, suggests a new epistemological source for critical scholars: the actual experience, history, culture, and intellectual tradition of people of color in America.[159]

Similarly, Martha Minow argues that a judge or other lawmaker who makes a concerted effort to assume the perspective of persons and groups he would otherwise consider alien will find his horizons vastly enlarged.[160] The notion is not merely that, by viewing the world through the eyes of the others, lawmakers will understand it better, but that they will gain access to the wisdom of those who have had to confront and struggle against oppression and exploitation. "*Praxis*, deliberate action consciously reflected upon, is the most trustworthy source of sure knowledge." Persons "on the bottom" have disproportionate amounts of such knowledge, and the law should take account of their insights.[161]

---

[158] Compare, for example, Richard Delgado, "Commentary: The Imperial Scholar: Reflections on a Review of Civil Rights Literature," *University of Pennsylvania Law Review* 132 (March 1984): 561, with Randall Kennedy, "Racial Critiques of Legal Academia," *Harvard Law Review* 102 (June 1989): 1745.

[159] Mari Matsuda, "Looking to the Bottom: Critical Legal Studies and Reparations," *Harvard Civil Rights—Civil Liberties Law Review* 22 (Spring 1987): 325. See also idem, "Affirmative Action and Legal Theory," 8.

[160] Martha Minow, "The Supreme Court, 1986 Term—Foreword: Justice Engendered," *Harvard Law Review* 101 (November 1987): 72. See also Patricia Williams, "Alchemical Notes: Reconstructing Ideals from Deconstructed Rights," *Harvard Civil Rights—Civil Liberties Law Review* 22 (Spring 1987): 410–29.

[161] Muhammad Kenyatta, "Critical Footnotes to Parker's 'Constitutional Theory,'" *Harvard Blackletter Journal* 2 (Spring 1985): 51.

In the minds of some of the new theorists, this conception of how lawmakers should set their agendas is reinforced by an "antifoundationalist" epistemology, derived in part from the Critical Legal Studies movement. It is hopeless, so the argument goes, to try to generate values from reflection on human nature, the nature of women, the meaning of freedom and equality, or any other abstract ideal. Our identities—as persons, as Americans, as blacks, as men or women—are socially constructed; we have no "essential," immutable attributes or rights from which a utopian program can be derived. Thus the only plausible way to develop answers to hard problems (great or small) is to explore and debate the meanings of the shared commitments of the communities to which we belong and in which we must continue to make ourselves. Through the exchange of anecdotes, narratives, and data that draw on and illuminate our common experiences—not through the derivation of theorems from universally agreed-on postulates—we must select our goals. In short, discussions within our groups and across the boundaries of our groups provide our only hope for identifying a set of common ends.[162]

What sort of goals—what sort of legal system—would general adoption of this method produce? Not all the advocates of the approach venture answers to that question, and the responses of those who do so are not uniform. A few principles, however, enjoy substantial support.

Central to the visions of most of the new scholars is what Ruth Colker refers to as the "anti-subordination perspective." Above all, the law must be organized and wielded so as to combat and offset the exploitation and domination of some groups by others. So, for example, we should dispense with the rule that a plaintiff alleging a violation of the equal-protection clause must prove that the defendant *intended* to discriminate on some invidious basis; it should be sufficient to show that the defendant's "policy or action had a disparate impact on members of plaintiff's race or sex."[163] In a similar vein, Frances Olsen argues that, when adjudicating or considering a sex-discrimination case, we should be wary of abstract debates such as whether "gender-blind" or "gender-

---

[162] See Joan Williams, "Feminism and Post-Structuralism," *Michigan Law Review* 88 (May 1990): 1776 (reviewing *The Female Body and the Law* by Zillah Eisenstein); Minow, "Justice Engendered." Not all feminists share this orientation. Robin West, for example, calls for the construction of "feminist jurisprudence," which she defines as "a jurisprudence built upon feminist insights into women's true nature." "Jurisprudence and Gender," *University of Chicago Law Review* 55 (Winter 1988): 4.

[163] Ruth Colker, "Anti-subordination Above All: Sex, Race and Equal Protection," *New York University Law Review* 61 (December 1986): 1007, 1014.

conscious" policies are superior; the sole issue should be which outcome, in the particular set of circumstances presented in the case, would improve women's position.[164]

To date, feminist scholars have been disappointingly vague concerning how this anti-subordination principle might be implemented. A few proposals may be found in the feminist literature. For example, Joan Williams has sketched an ambitious plan for reorganizing work roles in American society—enabling all persons to escape the current situation in which they are confronted with only two choices: "the traditional male life pattern or women's traditional economic vulnerability."[165] And, as detailed later, Catharine MacKinnon, among others, has proposed the suppression of a particular kind of pornography that contributes to the subordination of women. The essays of most feminist legal scholars, however, terminate in discouragingly general calls for the reorganization of legal reasoning and decision making so as to incorporate more fully the values of compassion, connectedness, and intimacy.[166]

The proposals of minority scholars have been more concrete, albeit also more conventional. Central to the essays of most minority law teachers—especially those associated with what has come to be called Critical Race Theory—is the notion that we must preserve and strengthen legal rights. It is this orientation that differentiates most minority law teachers from the adherents of Critical Legal Studies. The three criticisms of rights popularized by CLS scholars—that they are indeterminate; that they stunt the imaginations of the persons they supposedly benefit; and that, on balance, they inhibit social and political progress—leave most minority scholars unpersuaded. The extant system of legal rights, they concede, is unstable and often manipulated to advance the interests of the wealthy

---

[164] Frances Olsen, "From False Paternalism to False Equality: Judicial Assaults on Feminist Community, Illinois 1869–1895," *Michigan Law Review* 84 (June 1986): 1522. Muhammad Kenyatta proposes a similar circumvention of the rancorous debate over affirmative action: "The doctrines of color-blindness and of race-conscious affirmative action are reconciled at a higher doctrinal level wherein we are concerned to overcome patterns of racial dominance and subordination because those patterns are inimical to democratic values that we hold dear." Kenyatta, "Critical Footnotes to Parker's Theory," 51.

[165] Williams, "Deconstructing Gender," 801, 822–43.

[166] See, for example, West, "Jurisprudence and Gender"; Kathy Ferguson, *The Feminist Case Against Bureaucracy* (Philadelphia: Temple University Press, 1984); and Carrie Menkel-Meadow, "Portia in a Different Voice: Speculations on a Women's Lawyering Process," *Berkeley Women's Law Journal* 1 (Fall 1985): 39.

and powerful.[167] But the solution, they argue, is to strengthen and modify those entitlements, not to dispense with them entirely.

Such a reformed regime would have three advantages. First, although the establishment and enforcement of legal rights is surely not sufficient to eliminate racism and sexism, it is helpful in combating those evils. As Richard Delgado writes: "Rights do, at times, give pause to those who would otherwise oppress us; without the law's sanction, these individuals would be more likely to express racist sentiments on the job. It is condescending and misguided to assume that the enervating effect of rights talk is experienced by the victims and not the perpetrators of racial mistreatment."[168] Second, the impact of rights discourse on social psychology is likely, on balance, to be beneficial to minorities. The organization of human relationships in terms of entitlements may perpetuate alienation—may reinforce the distance between persons—but it at least accords everyone a modicum of respect. To members of minority groups, the language of rights is liberating and empowering, not enervating—a source of solidarity, not paralysis.[169] Third, rights discourse has less hegemonic power than CLS scholars pretend. Few "outsiders" are deluded by the language into believing that the current distribution of wealth and power is legitimate; the vast majority are able to sustain a "dual consciousness"—recognizing and capitalizing on the revolutionary potential of legal rights while remaining skeptical of the overall social and political order in which rights are currently embedded.[170]

So, given a free hand, what sorts of rights would the minority scholars institute? More expansive and well-enforced civil rights, of course—rights to be free of invidious discrimination in private relations as well as public

---

[167] See, for example, Matsuda, "Looking to the Bottom," 323, 327; and Williams, "Alchemical Notes," 409.

[168] Richard Delgado, "The Ethereal Scholar: Does Critical Legal Studies Have What Minorities Want?" *Harvard Civil Rights—Civil Liberties Law Review* 22 (Spring 1987): 305. See also Williams, "Alchemical Notes," 410. For a parallel argument by a feminist scholar, see Elizabeth M. Schneider, "The Dialectic of Rights and Politics: Perspectives from the Women's Movement," *New York University Law Review* 61 (October 1986): 589.

[169] See Williams, "Alchemical Notes," 408, 416, 431; Harlon Dalton, "The Clouded Prism," *Harvard Civil Rights—Civil Liberties Law Review* 22 (Spring 1987): 440; Matsuda, "Looking to the Bottom," 340–1; and Delgado, "The Ethereal Scholar," 305.

[170] See Delgado, "The Ethereal Scholar," 311; Matsuda, "Looking to the Bottom," 333–4, 338, 341; and Williams, "Alchemical Notes," 430. For an unusual acknowledgment by a minority scholar of the legitimating power of rights, see Frances Lee Ansley, "Stirring the Ashes: Race, Class and the Future of Civil Rights Scholarship," *Cornell Law Review* 74 (September 1989): 996.

affairs. But so-called economic rights are at least as important to them. Rights to education, jobs, housing, and a minimal standard of living figure prominently in their proposals.[171] Finally, at least one scholar has proposed a reconfiguration of the traditional rights of privacy and property:

> [Our objective should be] not to discard rights, but to see through or past them so that they reflect a larger definition of privacy, and of property: so that privacy is turned from exclusion based on *self*-regard, into regard for another's fragile, mysterious autonomy; and so that property regains its ancient connotation of being a reflection of that part of the self which by virtue of its very externalization is universal. The task is to expand private property rights into a conception of civil rights, into the right to expect civility from others.[172]

Of the five groups of contemporary theorists, the Outsiders accept the most of the amplified Realist challenge. In their skepticism concerning the power of legal doctrine to constrain judicial decision making, their belief that the values advanced by the law should be subject to continual debate and frequent modification, and their conviction that the extant legal and political order is fundamentally unjust, they are indebted to the Legal Realists and their successors, the participants in the Conference on Critical Legal Studies. But, as should by now be evident, in three crucial respects the Outsiders refuse to follow Realism and CLS. First, they are less attracted than the Realists or their heirs by ethical pluralism; stable "normative priorities," they believe, can and should be identified and implemented. Second, most of the Outsiders are not persuaded by the critique of rights; judicially enforced civil rights, in particular, they regard as beneficial, not misleading or pernicious. Third, they are unconvinced that legal discourse is an effective vehicle of cultural hegemony; they are thus less wary than CLS scholars of using traditional legal arguments and tactics in their campaign for social justice. In short, most of the Outsiders retain a faith in the rule of law. Whether that faith will survive the political struggles of the 1990s is uncertain.

---

[171] See, for example, Kenyatta, "Critical Footnotes to Parker's Theory," 52; and Matsuda, "Looking to the Bottom," 357.

[172] Williams, "Alchemical Notes," 432 (emphasis in original). Notably absent from the proposals of the minority scholars are suggestions that we reshape American culture along the lines suggested by classical republican theory. The localism, informality, and potential for exclusivity associated with the republican tradition strike them as not only undesirable but noxious, an invitation for the cultivation and expression of racism. See, for example, Williams, "Alchemical Notes," 424; Delgado, "The Ethereal Scholar," 315, 321; and Kenyatta, "Critical Footnotes," 52.

INTERPRETATIONS OF THE BILL OF RIGHTS

This section examines the ways in which legal scholars and the United States Supreme Court during the modern period have tried to make sense of selected provisions of the Bill of Rights. The analysis of the positions that scholars have taken is intended to extend the argument of the last section. The central thesis is that the principal proposals made by law teachers concerning the proper construction of those constitutional provisions represent applications or elaborations of the five general perspectives that have dominated legal theory in general since World War II. The analysis of the judges' interpretations of those provisions is intended to show, among other things, that the cacophonous debates of the scholars have had echoes in legal doctrine. The Supreme Court has incorporated in its opinions many fragments of the scholars' recommendations. The result, not surprisingly, has been a hodgepodge. The Court has been influenced, of course, by many pressures other than the importunities of law professors. But the combination of the diversity of the professors' proposals and the Court's tendency to pick up bits and pieces from each has contributed to the jumbled, intellectually unsatisfying character of current doctrine.

Freedom of speech. The second clause of the First Amendment provides: "Congress shall make no law ... abridging the freedom of speech, or of the press." Until the early twentieth century the Supreme Court made little of this provision. In the 1920s, goaded by some famous dissents by Justice Holmes,[173] the Court began to use the provision increasingly often to strike down both federal and state statutes. Since 1940 the coverage of the First Amendment has been extended well beyond the obviously relevant category of political speech to include such expressive activities as defamation of public figures,[174] commercial advertising,[175] some forms of pornography, and the burning of the American flag.[176] Most legal

---

[173] See, for example, *Abrams* v. *United States*, 250 *United States Reports* 616, 630 (1919); *Gitlow* v. *New York*, 268 *United States Reports* 652, 673 (1925).
[174] See *New York Times* v. *Sullivan*, 376 *United States Reports* 254 (1964). In *Gertz* v. *Welch*, 418 *United States Reports* 323 (1974), some of the restrictions on defamation suits brought by public officials were also imposed on defamation suits brought by private individuals against media defendants.
[175] See *Virginia State Board of Pharmacy* v. *Virginia Citizens Consumer Council*, 425 *United States Reports* 748 (1976).
[176] See *Texas* v. *Johnson*, 491 *United States Reports* 397 (1989).

scholars have applauded the increasingly expansive judicial interpretation of the First Amendment. The grounds on which they have expressed approval have varied considerably, however, and much turns on precisely why freedom of speech, broadly understood, deserves protection.

In the enormous body of legal literature on the subject, five arguments stand out. The first, closely connected to Legal Process Theory, emphasizes the importance of freedom of expression to the functioning of a representative democracy. The scholar who did most to develop and popularize this perspective was Alexander Meiklejohn. In an influential collection of books and essays published between 1945 and 1965, Meiklejohn argued that if a democratic system is to work well, its citizens must have access to the information they need to form intelligent opinions on issues of public importance and freedom to debate the significance of that information. Laws that inhibit the free flow of information or opinions pertaining to political questions should therefore be subject to scrutiny by the courts.[177] Scholars who have followed in Meiklejohn's wake have disagreed concerning how broadly "speech pertaining to political questions" should be defined,[178] but have adhered to his central assertion that political speech deserves special protection.

An important extension of Meiklejohn's position that makes clearer its connection to the Legal Process tradition can be found in the work of John Ely. In his conception of the purpose of the First Amendment, Ely is avowedly unoriginal: its "central function," he insists, is that of "assuring an open political dialogue and process." On the question of why it should be the job of the *courts* to shield those processes, however, Ely has something to add. Drawing both on his general theory of the afflictions to which representative democracies are subject and on the larger body of literature pertaining to institutional competence, Ely argues that two reasons support entrusting this crucial job to the judiciary. First, "ins have a way of wanting to make sure the outs stay out"; "elected officials" cannot be trusted to "police inhibitions on expression and other

[177] See, for example, Alexander Meiklejohn, *Free Speech and Its Relation to Self-Government* (New York: Harper & Row, 1948); and *Political Freedom: The Constitutional Powers of the People* (New York: Oxford University Press, 1965).

[178] Compare, for example, Robert Bork, "Neutral Principles and Some First Amendment Problems," *Indiana Law Journal* 47 (Fall 1971): 1 (arguing that only political speech narrowly defined should be shielded from regulation); with Lillian BeVier, "The First Amendment and Political Speech: An Inquiry into the Substance and Limits of Principle," *Stanford Law Review* 30 (January 1978): 299 (arguing that preservation of room for free debate on political issues requires shielding some forms of nonpolitical speech).

political activity" because they are often the sources of those inhibitions. Second, because of their special backgrounds and modes of deliberation, "unelected judges are likely to be somewhat more objective than elected officials about the dangers posed by an alien view."[179] Building on this composite rationale, Ely proposes a two-part test for evaluating First Amendment challenges:

> Where the evil the state is seeking to avert is one that is independent of the message being regulated, where it arises from something other than a fear of how people will react to what the speaker is saying, ... a "specific-threat" approach [i.e., a context-specific evaluation of the danger posed to legitimate governmental purposes of the defendant's mode of communicating] is the only one that can be coherent. [By contrast,] where state officials seek to silence a message because they think it's dangerous, ... we [should] insist that the message fall within some clearly and narrowly bounded category of expression we have designated in advance as unentitled to protection.[180]

If it follows these guidelines, Ely argued, the Supreme Court will ensure that the room for the debate and dissent essential to the operation of an "open and effective democratic process" will be preserved "through our future periods of actual or perceived crisis"—without either endangering national security or exceeding the Court's legitimate authority within the constitutional system.[181]

The second of the five scholarly approaches to the First Amendment has had a smaller following but may now be gaining adherents. In 1973, taking his cue from a famous decision by Judge Learned Hand,[182] Richard Posner argued that the law pertaining to freedom of expression was just as suitable for reformation on the basis of economic analysis as any other legal doctrine. His ensuing discussion of the First Amendment was grounded in a curious form of relativism: there exists no test of the "truth" of an idea, he insisted, other than its acceptance by most people after they have been exposed to it and its alternatives. Ordinarily, there-

---

[179] Ely, *Democracy and Distrust*, 106, 112. Ely is careful not to make too much of the second of these two arguments, pointing out that "judges by and large are drawn from the same political and social ranks as elected officials, and are subject to many of the same anxieties." His preferred reason plainly is the first.

[180] Ibid., 111–12.

[181] Ibid., 105, 116.

[182] In *United States* v. *Dennis*, 183 F.2d 201 (2d Cir. 1950), *aff'd*, 341 *United States Reports* 494 (1951), Hand ruled that judges confronted with a government's claim that a particular example of speech should be suppressed, should "ask whether the gravity of the 'evil,' discounted by its improbability, justifies such invasion of free speech as is necessary to avoid the danger."

fore, ideas should be permitted to compete freely for acceptance.[183] Two circumstances, however, provide justifications for restricting freedom of expression: First, if suppression of a particular form of speech would eliminate undesirable externalities (or achieve positive economic effects) greater in magnitude than the resultant "cost of the reduction in the stock of ideas," the First Amendment should be construed to permit it. Second, regulation of speech may be economically efficient and therefore should be permitted by the courts when designed to overcome "market failures" that prevent free competition in ideas from exposing important facts.

As is his wont Posner applied these proposed standards for the most part in a Panglossian fashion. Most of the Supreme Court's recent free-speech rulings comport, he contended, with the efficiency criterion.[184] Posner's approach was not altogether toothless, however. For example, he denounced the Supreme Court's decision in the *Red Lion* case (upholding an FCC rule that broadcasters must afford opportunities for rebuttal to persons opposed to the broadcasters' views)[185] as "economic nonsense." The physical limitation of the electromagnetic spectrum does not, as the Court had asserted, necessarily lead to monopolization of television markets. In any event, Posner argued, it is far from clear that monopolization of a television market would result in diminution in the diversity of ideas made available to viewers.[186] The number of law teachers who, like Posner, contend that allocative efficiency should be the exclusive or dominant criterion in interpreting the First Amendment re-

---

[183] *Economic Analysis of Law*, 627. This notion is derived in part from Justice Holmes's dissenting opinion in *Abrams*, in which he proclaimed that "the best test of truth is the power of the thought to get itself accepted in the competition of the market." 250 *United States Reports* at 630.

[184] For example, he argued that the Supreme Court's decision to permit the states to award damages to victims of defamation who are not public figures makes economic sense because defamatory statements "inflict costs that are both concentrated . . . and at least crudely measurable; the falsity of the defamation may be readily demonstrable, implying that a legal determination of the truth may be a pretty good substitute for market determination; and (a related point) competition may not be an effective remedy—how do I compete with *Time* magazine if it libels me?" By contrast, the Court's insistence that public figures, to recover, must prove that the defendant had "actual knowledge of (or reckless indifference to) the falsity of the defamation is defensible on the not implausible assumption that the publication of criticisms of public figures has benefits not fully captured by the publisher"—namely, the advantage to the public of being given information about their political and cultural leaders. Ibid., 631.

[185] *Red Lion Broadcasting Co. v. Federal Communications Commission*, 395 *United States Reports* 367 (1969).

[186] *Economic Analysis of Law*, 634.

mains small,[187] but the number who include economic arguments in their lectures and articles is large and growing.

First Amendment scholars who consider themselves Kantian liberals denounce both the Legal Process and the economic approaches as insufficiently sensitive to and protective of persons' fundamental individual rights to speak and listen. Not surprisingly, they consider the economic approach, grounded in utilitarianism, especially misguided and pernicious. Bruce Ackerman, for example, fears the "illiberal uses" that might be made of the economists' theory of market failure. "[A] clear-thinking utilitarian," he warns, "might conclude that government regulation of speech would sometimes maximize the production of happiness-inducing ideas."[188] Legal Process Theory is treated with somewhat greater respect by the Kantians, partly because the two schools share an interest in the conditions essential to effective operation of a representative democracy. But the teleological orientation of Legal Process Theory nevertheless repels the Kantian scholars. This reaction is illustrated by Dworkin's treatment of Justice Brennan's concurring opinion in the *Richmond Newspapers* case, which held that representatives of the press must be given access under certain circumstances to criminal trials.[189] Distancing himself from Chief Justice Burger's theory of the case (which emphasized the customary practice of affording the press access), Brennan, invoking Madison's famous passage on freedom of speech,[190] argued that special

[187] See Ronald Coase, "The Market for Goods and the Market for Ideas," *American Economic Review, Papers and Proceedings* 64 (May 1974): 384; idem, "Advertising and Free Speech," *Journal of Legal Studies* 6 (January 1977): 1; Fred S. McChesney, "Commercial Speech in the Professions: The Supreme Court's Question and Questionable Answers," *University of Pennsylvania Law Review* 134 (December 1985): 45. Posner himself substantially expanded his initial argument in "Free Speech in an Economic Perspective," *Suffolk University Law Review* 20 (Spring 1986): 1.

[188] Ackerman, *Social Justice*, 265–6. Similarly, Ronald Dworkin believes that theorists or judges committed to maximizing net social welfare will find it difficult to object even to "extraordinary and indefensible" decisions like the Supreme Court's ruling in *Snepp* v. *United States*, 444 *United States Reports* 507 (1980)—in which a former employee of the CIA was forced to turn over to the agency all the profits he made from a book that, in defiance of his original employment contract, he had refused to submit to the agency for approval. But more important than the weakness of the utilitarian approach in advancing the cause of liberalism, Dworkin contends, is its failure to accord adequate attention to the central concern of the federal Constitution: defining "the conditions under which citizens shall be deemed to form a community of equals." Dworkin, "Is the Press Losing the First Amendment?" reprinted in *A Matter of Principle* (Cambridge, Mass.: Harvard University Press, 1985), 381–2, 392–3, 396.

[189] *Richmond Newspapers* v. *Virginia*, 498 *United States Reports* 555 (1980).

[190] "A popular government, without popular information or the means of acquiring it, is

protection for the press was necessary "to preserve the very structure of democracy." Dworkin, though conceding that this perspective is "both more important and more complex" than Burger's, ultimately rejects it on the ground that it invites a balancing process in which the public's interest in information is weighed against "competing interests" and thus in the end is not fundamentally different from Mill's utilitarian approach.[191]

How then do they think the First Amendment should be construed? Different scholars within the Kantian camp (indeed, the same scholars at different times) have responded differently, but their analyses have the same structure. The first step is isolating an individual right—usually a right extracted in some way from the overall structure of the Constitution. The next, usually harder step is showing how respect for that right (or respect for that right among other rights) mandates substantial (albeit perhaps not absolute) respect for freedom of speech in a particular setting.

Dworkin's handling of the problem of pornography is typical. Dismissing various "goal-based strategies" for defining the limits of permissible government regulation of pornographic material, Dworkin insists that a philosophically sound approach to the issue must commence with a recognition of persons' "right to moral independence." Implicitly drawing on his overall conception of liberalism,[192] Dworkin defines that right as follows: "People have the right not to suffer disadvantage in the distribution of social goods and opportunities, including disadvantage in the liberties permitted to them by the criminal law, just on the ground that their officials or fellow-citizens think that their opinions about the right way for them to lead their own lives are ignoble and wrong."[193] Respect for this right requires shielding pornography from government regulation to the extent that such regulation is motivated by either of two impulses: (1) the belief that "the attitudes about sex displayed or nurtured in pornography are demeaning or bestial or otherwise unsuitable to human beings of the best sort" or (2) the desire to relieve citizens of the disgust they experience—disgust grounded in the belief that pornog-

---

but a prologue to a farce or a tragedy; or perhaps both. . . . A people who mean to be their own governors, must arm themselves with the power knowledge makes."

[191] "Is the Press Losing?" 390–2.

[192] Dworkin, "Liberalism," reprinted in *A Matter of Principle*, 191 (arguing that a liberal government must "treat its citizens as equals," which requires, in turn, that it "must be neutral on what might be called the question of the good life").

[193] Dworkin, "Do We Have a Right to Pornography?" reprinted in *A Matter of Principle*, 353.

raphy is demeaning—when members of their community "read dirty books or look at dirty pictures." The right is not violated, however, by regulations of pornography motivated either by the public's desire "not to encounter genital displays on the way to the grocer" or by the public's interest in reducing crime (assuming that a link between pornography and crime could be established). Unfortunately, Dworkin concedes, legitimate and illegitimate motives are often inextricably combined in the inception of antipornography statutes. Under such circumstances, a permissible, plausible stance for a society committed to respect for the right of moral independence would be a compromise: modest regulation of pornography would be deemed acceptable (for example, restriction of the time, place, and manner in which it is displayed and sold), but regulations that caused the producers and consumers of pornography to "suffer *serious* damage through legal restraint" would not.[194] Other legal scholars in the Kantian tradition organize their arguments differently but place similar emphasis on fundamental individual rights when trying to provide answers to concrete problems.[195]

Of the five groups of modern legal theorists, the scholars who aspire to develop theories of the good have, as yet, contributed least to the debate over the proper meaning of the First Amendment. Recently, however, a few promising arguments have appeared in the literature, and others will probably be made public shortly. A narrowly focused but rich example is a student essay published in 1988 by Dan Kahan, then president of the *Harvard Law Review*. Kahan argues that the long-standing debate over the constitutionality of group libel laws should be resolved (in favor of such laws) through greater attention to the insights of communitarian political theory. Group libel laws are statutes or local ordinances that proscribe speech or expressive action designed to promote

---

[194] Ibid., 354–7. Dworkin's own analysis of the *Snepp* case is similar in structure and outcome. See "Is the Press Losing?" 395–7.

[195] Bruce Ackerman's style is more colloquial and his argument depends more on a hypothetical ideal deliberative process, but otherwise his view of freedom of speech is similar to Dworkin's. See *Social Justice in the Liberal State*, 177–8. For other examples of Kantian perspectives on the First Amendment, see Rawls, *A Theory of Justice*, 225–6 (arguing that the "first principle of justice" demands that "all citizens should have the means to be informed about political issues, . . . should be in a position to assess how proposals affect their well-being and which policies advance their conception of the public good, . . . [and] should have a fair chance to add alternative proposals to the agenda for political discussion"); and Thomas Scanlon, "A Theory of Free Expression," *Philosophy and Public Affairs* 1 (Winter 1972): 204 (justifying freedom of speech as mandated by government's obligation to respect individuals' autonomy).

hatred of particular racial, ethnic, or religious groups.[196] Since 1952, when the Supreme Court upheld the constitutionality of one such statute, group libel laws have come under increasing attack by liberal legal scholars, and some lower courts have refused to enforce them. Kahan contends that the law is drifting in the wrong direction.

> The communitarian case for restricting group defamatory expression . . . begins with the insight, ignored by contemporary liberalism and by the liberal justification of free speech, that group membership is a precondition of individual autonomy. In this view, the capacity to engage in reflective, deliberative choices about how to live is made possible only by virtue of the common meanings implicit in the constitutive communities to which the individual belongs. Tolerating vilification of such groups, then, fails to respect the personhood of the vilified citizens; and in failing to respect equally the personhood of all members of the political community, toleration erodes the conception of the good that animates American political life. Preserving the conditions of freedom therefore requires permitting localities to restrain group-defamatory expression as a form of speech incompatible with the principle of equal membership.[197]

A parallel effort to bring the outlook of classical republicanism to bear on the First Amendment can be found in Mark Tushnet's recent book on constitutional law. Tushnet's argument is tentative—apparently because, although Tushnet is a hot critic of liberalism, he is only a lukewarm advocate of republicanism as an alternative. Nevertheless, several important insights can be gleaned from his analysis. For example, he points out that most of the arguments that have been or might be deployed in support of limitations on private contributions to political campaigns draw in some way on the republican tradition. Unfortunately, most of those arguments ultimately rest, Tushnet contends, on an unappealing conception of "instrumental rationality" as the proper form of deliberation on both public and private matters. But one of the arguments elicits his qualified approval. Limitations on campaign contributions, it has been claimed, force candidates' supporters to participate actively in the political process, through "direct discussion, canvassing, and the like," instead of merely writing checks. The net effect is partially to "break the connection between the economic market, where wealth is accumulated and the private interest prevails, and the political process, in which wealth

---

[196] An example of the kind of activity targeted by such statutes is the 1978 march and demonstration by a self-proclaimed group of Nazis in the largely Jewish village of Skokie, Illinois.

[197] Note, "A Communitarian Defense of Group Libel Law," *Harvard Law Review* 101 (January 1988): 700–1.

should not be spent and the public interest should prevail." That effect advances republican values in two respects: it "stresses the importance of equality in wealth as the basis for independence in political judgment"; and it "emphasizes the intrinsic value of political activity [and] encourages people to divert attention from the market and private interest to politics and the public interest." Tushnet goes on to insist that it is doubtful that such legislation—or any legislation, for that matter—will suffice to re-create a republican society in the United States. But, he suggests, something is better than nothing.[198]

The new group of scholars who style themselves Outsiders has yet to develop a general theory of the First Amendment. One important aspect of the interpretation of the provision, however, has attracted their critical attention. Since the early 1980s, a group of feminist scholars led by Catharine MacKinnon have been insisting that state and local governments should be much more aggressive in penalizing the production and dissemination of pornography and that the Constitution should not be construed to prevent such regulation.

The argument—and MacKinnon's version of it, in particular—is grounded in a sweeping critique of sexual relations in the contemporary United States. MacKinnon contends that men dominate women in countless major and minor ways. Rape, battery, and sexual harassment are only the most visible of the means by which they achieve and exercise such dominance. Indeed, much of what most men think of as normal, healthy heterosexual relations manifest and perpetuate the violent subordination of women.

The male centrally features hierarchy of control. Aggression against those with less power is experienced as sexual pleasure, an entitlement of masculinity. For the female, subordination is sexualized, in the way that dominance is for the male, as pleasure as well as gender identity, as femininity. Dominance, principally by men, and submission, principally by women, will be the ruling code through which sexual pleasure is experienced. Sexism will be a political inequality that is sexually enjoyed, if unequally so.[199]

---

[198] Tushnet, *Red, White, and Blue*, 280–8. His defense of the constitutionality of restrictions on commercial speech ends on a similar note: "Most of the time regulation of commercial speech is unlikely to serve republican values, but sometimes it will. Perhaps the best we can hope for is a constitutional doctrine that inquires directly whether the regulations serve those values." Ibid., 292.

[199] Catharine MacKinnon, *Feminism Unmodified* (Cambridge, Mass.: Harvard University Press, 1987), 6–7. See also pp. 85–93.

The pornography industry, MacKinnon argues, reinforces this pattern of violence and oppression in four ways. First, it degrades and injures the women who act in the films and pose for the pictures. Some are physically coerced into participating; others are forced by the absence of employment alternatives; still others are induced by the men on whom they are financially or emotionally dependent. All emerge from the experience worse off.[200] Second, pornography encourages the men who consume it to behave more violently toward women and to acquiesce in the violent abuse of women by other men (e.g., by acquitting defendants accused of "date rape").[201] Third, pornography is itself a form of violence against women.

> Pornography not only teaches the reality of male dominance. It is one way its reality is imposed as well as experienced. It is a way of seeing and using women. Male power makes authoritative a way of seeing and treating women, so that when a man looks at a pornographic picture—pornographic meaning that the woman is defined as to be acted upon, a sexual object, a sexual thing—the *viewing* is an *act,* an act of male supremacy.[202]

Finally, pornography silences women. By ratifying and normalizing the power of men to dominate women, it reduces the capacity of women to challenge the hierarchy of gender.[203]

In sum, MacKinnon contends, some way ought to be devised to halt the production and dissemination of pornography. The principal objection to such an initiative has been that it would violate the First Amendment and the tradition of respect for freedom of speech the amendment embodies. MacKinnon has two responses to the objection. First, the myriad injuries sustained by women as a result of consumption of pornography by men are at least as serious as the sorts of harms the Supreme Court has long accepted as sufficient justifications for suppressing other forms of speech.[204] If the annoyance suffered by suburbanites forced to listen to political sound trucks driving past their homes is enough to

---

[200] See Catharine MacKinnon, "Pornography, Civil Rights, and Speech," *Harvard Civil Rights—Civil Liberties Law Review* 20 (Winter 1985): 32–8. See also Sandra Grove, "Constitutionality of Minnesota's Sodomy Law," *Law and Inequality* 2 (August 1984): 521.

[201] MacKinnon, "Pornography, Civil Rights, and Speech," 43–54. See also Margaret Baldwin, "The Sexuality of Inequality: The Minneapolis Pornography Ordinance," *Law and Inequality* 2 (August 1984): 639–40.

[202] MacKinnon, *Feminism Unmodified,* 130. See also Andrea Dworkin, *Pornography: Men Possessing Women* (1981).

[203] MacKinnon, *Feminism Unmodified,* 129.

[204] MacKinnon, "Pornography, Civil Rights, and Speech," 21.

warrant permitting the state to ban the trucks, surely the assaults and degradation suffered by women at the hands of men whose conceptions of sexuality have been shaped or reinforced by pornography is sufficient to sustain a law removing such material from circulation. Second and more fundamentally, MacKinnon argues that the First Amendment should be construed not merely to protect from government interference the voices of persons already willing and able to speak, but also to give voices to persons who currently are silent. Partly as a result of the widespread dissemination of pornography, "women's minds and bodies" are now "enslav[ed]"; to free them, to enable them to become "speakers" instead of simply "speech," the state may and should reach into what has traditionally been considered the private sphere and disrupt the hierarchy of gender. In short, suppressing pornography, far from exceeding the state's legitimate power under the Constitution, is the least it can do.[205]

Constitutional theory comes to the attention of Supreme Court justices in several ways. The lawyers for clients whose cases are accepted for review commonly canvass the relevant secondary literature and, in their briefs and oral arguments, press on the Court their favorite academic perspectives. Each justice has several law clerks to assist him or her in preparing for the arguments and in writing opinions. Recent graduates of the more prestigious American law schools, the clerks come to their jobs chock full of their former professors' theories and eager to test them against real problems. Last but not least, several of the justices read broadly in legal scholarship and are likely to draw on arguments they find congenial. Through one or more of these routes several aspects of the five major academic approaches to freedom of speech have found their way into Supreme Court decisions. No one theory has come to dominate the case law, but at least three of the five have had a significant impact.

The most influential of the approaches has been Legal Process Theory. Two related features of the work of Meiklejohn, Ely, and their ilk have found favor with the justices. First, in several opinions, the Court has insisted on the "structural function" of the First Amendment—its role in preserving conditions essential to the smooth operation of representative democracy. In the *Consolidated Edison* case, for example, Justice Powell relied partly on Meiklejohn's theory in striking down an order

---

[205] MacKinnon, *Feminism Unmodified*, 129–30, 206–13.

by the New York Public Service Commission forbidding public utility companies from including in their billing envelopes inserts discussing controversial questions of public policy. If we wish to foster "a more capable citizenry and more perfect polity," Powell contended, we must be skeptical of all government restraints on public discussion.[206] Justice Brennan, concurring in the *Richmond Newspapers* case, discussed earlier, was equally adamant: "The First Amendment embodies more than a commitment to free expression and communicative interchange for their own sakes; it has a *structural* role to play in securing and fostering our republican system of government."[207]

The second feature of Legal Process Theory to which the Court has been sympathetic is the privileged place it accords speech addressed to what would conventionally be considered political questions. Since 1960 a majority of the Court has been especially solicitous of expression falling into that category. For example, in ruling that an advertisement expressing opposition to a proposed income-tax amendment to the Massachusetts Constitution did not lose its entitlement to First Amendment protection merely because it emanated from a private corporation, Justice Powell, writing for the Court, emphasized the fact that the matter in dispute impinged directly on "governmental affairs." On issues of that sort, the state "has a special incentive to repress opposition and often wields a more effective power of suppression." Accordingly, the judiciary should be especially vigilant in protecting such speech.[208]

The impact on the case law of the second and third of the scholarly

---

[206] *Consolidated Edison Co.* v. *Public Service Commission of New York,* 447 *United States Reports* 530, 534 (1980).

[207] 448 *United States Reports* 555, 587 (1980) (citing *inter alia* Meiklejohn and Ely). See also *Columbia Broadcasting System* v. *Democratic National Committee,* 412 *United States Reports* 94 (1973) ("The interest of the public is our foremost concern. With broadcasting, where the available means of communication are limited in both space and time, the admonition of Professor Alexander Meiklejohn that 'what is essential is not that everyone shall speak, but that everything worth saying shall be said' is peculiarly appropriate."); *Houchins* v. *KQED, Inc.* 438 *United States Reports* 1, 30 (1978) (Justice Stevens, dissenting); *Herbert* v. *Lando,* 441 *United States Reports* 153, 184 (1979) (Justice Brennan, dissenting); *Board of Education* v. *Pico,* 457 *United States Reports* 853, 867 (1982) (relying partly on the views of Madison and Meiklejohn to limit the discretion of a local school board to remove from the library books it finds politically offensive).

[208] *First National Bank of Boston* v. *Bellotti,* 435 *United States Reports* 765, 776–7 (1978) (quoting Thomas Emerson and citing Meiklejohn). See also *Saxbe* v. *Washington Post Co.,* 417 U.S. 843, 862–863 (1974) (Justice Powell, dissenting); *Virginia State Board of Pharmacy* v. *Virginia Citizens Consumer Council,* 425 *United States Reports* 748, 765 (1976); *Time, Inc.* v. *Firestone,* 424 *United States Reports* 448, 471 (1976) (Justice Brennan, dissenting); *Carey* v. *Brown,* 447 *United States Reports* 455, 467 (1980).

approaches has been more diffuse and difficult to trace, but nevertheless significant. Richard Posner's work on the First Amendment has never been cited by the Supreme Court. The overall utilitarian perspective, however, has affected the Court's deliberations—most noticeably by contributing to the Court's ever increasing reliance since World War II on "balancing tests" when confronted with difficult problems.[209] This has been especially true in the context of "time, place, and manner" regulations. When a challenged statute is designed not to discourage a particular message but to limit the way in which the message is expressed, the Court in recent years has typically tried to assess the constitutionality of the statute by determining whether the degree to which it advances other public policies is sufficient to offset its adverse impact on freedom of expression. The underlying principle, the Court seems to assume, is that the First Amendment should be construed in the way that maximizes net social utility. So, for example, in *Konigsberg* v. *State Bar of California,* Justice Harlan, writing for the Court, held broadly:

General regulatory statutes, not intended to control the content of speech but incidentally limiting its unfettered exercise, have not been regarded as the type of law the First or Fourteenth Amendment forbade . . . when they have been found justified by subordinating valid governmental interests, a prerequisite to constitutionality which has necessarily involved a weighing of the governmental interest involved.[210]

But it is not only when considering "time, place, and manner" rules that the Court employs such balancing tests. Even when confronted with statutes that restrain speech in traditional ways—by penalizing the communication of particular messages or silencing some speakers altogether—the Court sometimes tries to weigh the adverse impact on freedom of expression against the value of the ends advanced by the statutes. For example, in *F.C.C.* v. *League of Women Voters,* the Court struck down a statute prohibiting editorials by public broadcast stations, but not until it had assessed the strength of the government's asserted interest in ensuring that the public received a balanced presentation of

[209] See, for example, T. Alexander Aleinikoff, "Constitutional Law in the Age of Balancing," *Yale Law Journal* 96 (April 1987): 966–8.

[210] 366 *United States Reports* 36, 50–1 (1961). For examples of reliance upon such balancing tests when reviewing statutes restricting the "time, place, and manner" of speech, see *Metromedia* v. *City of San Diego,* 453 *United States Reports* 490 (1981) (Justice Brennan, dissenting); *City of Renton* v. *Playtime Theaters,* 475 *United States Reports* 41 (1986); *San Francisco Arts & Athletics* v. *United States Olympic Committee,* 483 *United States Reports* 522 (1987).

views on matters of public concern. Justice Brennan summarized the
Court's mode of analysis as follows:

[Broadcast restrictions] have been upheld only when we were satisfied that the
restriction is narrowly tailored to further a substantial governmental interest,
such as ensuring adequate and balanced coverage of public issues. . . . Making
that judgment requires a critical examination of the interests of the public and
broadcasters in light of the particular circumstances of each case.[211]

By contrast, the anti-consequentialist orientation of the Kantian school
of scholarship has contributed to an equally prominent line of decisions
eschewing balancing tests and insisting that First Amendment rights must
be respected regardless of the social costs. Justice Black was the most
consistent champion of this approach. For example, in the famous *Communist Party* case, he denounced the majority's reasoning as follows: "I
see no way to escape the fateful consequences of a return to the era [of
the Alien and Sedition Acts] in which all government critics had to face
the probability of being sent to jail except for this Court to abandon
what I consider to be the dangerous constitutional doctrine of 'balancing'
to which the Court is presently adhering."[212]

Black has not been alone in taking this stance. For example, in *Miami
Herald Publishing Co.* v. *Tornillo,* the Court considered a Florida statute
requiring newspapers to afford a "right of reply" to political candidates
whom the papers criticize. Chief Justice Burger sympathetically reviewed
the various "public policy" arguments advanced in favor of the statute:
high barriers to entry into the newspaper business and the development
of national news services have resulted in monopolization of most markets by one or two papers (each typically a member of a large chain),
threatening the diversity of views to which the public is exposed; compelling the major papers to afford space to politicians they attack is thus
consistent with the ideal that underlies the First Amendment—namely,
"a profound national commitment to the principle that debate on public
issues should be uninhibited, robust, and wide-open." Appealing as these
arguments may be, Burger held, they must fall before "the express provisions of the First Amendment and the judicial gloss on that Amendment
developed over the years." The fact is that the statute requires editors

---

[211] 468 *United States Reports* 364, 380–1 (1984).
[212] *Communist Party* v. *Subversive Activities Control Board, 367 United States Reports* 1,
64 (1961). Though fiercely committed to this position, Black was not altogether consistent. See Harry Kalven, Jr., "Upon Rereading Mr. Justice Black on the First Amendment," *U.C.L.A. Law Review* 14 (August 1967): 441–4.

and publishers to print something they wish not to print. It therefore violates the rule that private newspapers are entitled to say or not say what they please.[213] Rights are rights; the "structural function" of the First Amendment be damned.

To date, the communitarian perspective on freedom of speech has had little impact on the Supreme Court's rulings, but there are signs in a few opinions of its growing popularity. In the *Jaycees* case, for example, the Court relied to some extent on an appreciation of the "stigmatizing injury" to women—the threat to their sense of participation in the community—posed by private all-male clubs in upholding against a First Amendment challenge a state statute requiring such clubs to admit women.[214] Similar themes play a part in the dissenting opinions of Justices Rehnquist and Stevens in the recent flag-desecration cases. The burning of the national flag, both justices contend, threatens the culturally integrating power of the symbol and citizens' sense of themselves as members of a cohesive national community.[215] As republicanism and other variants of communitarian theory gain in prominence in legal scholarship, we can expect to see more and clearer invocations of such outlooks by the Court.

The only one of the five academic perspectives that thus far seems to have had no impact whatsoever on the Supreme Court's deliberations is feminist theory. The Court did have one opportunity to confront directly the arguments of Catharine MacKinnon and her adherents. In *American Booksellers Association* v. *Hudnut,* an Indianapolis city ordinance that adopted many of MacKinnon's proposals for more stringent suppression of pornography was challenged as violative of the First Amendment. In a forthright opinion by Judge Easterbrook, the federal Court of Appeals for the Seventh Circuit agreed with the challenge and declared the statute unconstitutional.[216] Easterbrook's reasoning (condensed by Frank Michelman) proceeded as follows:

A good society is a free society. A free society is open to ideological challenge by cultural "outsiders." Political speech is a serviceable and (by comparison with alternatives) benign instrumentality of ideological challenge. Governments tend to act on behalf of the ideological powers that be. Hence, governmental restric-

---

[213] 418 *United States Reports* 241, 247–58 (1974).

[214] *Roberts* v. *United States Jaycees, 468 United States Reports* 609, 625 (1984). For a communitarian reading of the decision, see Note, "Group Libel Laws," 699.

[215] *Texas* v. *Johnson, 491 United States Reports* 397, 421–39 (1989). For a communitarian reading of the case, see "The Supreme Court—Leading Cases," *Harvard Law Review* 103 (November 1989): 253–9

[216] 771 *Federal Reports, Second Series* 323 (7th Circuit 1985).

tions on political speech are in general a social evil. Such restrictions are especially constitutionally indefensible when they select utterances for suppression on the basis of message content or viewpoint, because such selectivity can have no other justifying purpose than the illicit one of "thought control." Pornography is political expression in that it promulgates a certain view of women's natures and thus of women's appropriate relations and treatment in society; the Indianapolis ordinance is precisely designed to suppress that particular view by censoring pornography; therefore the Indianapolis ordinance is an instance of both the general social evil (governmental restrictions on political expression) and its particularly obnoxious manifestation (viewpoint-discriminatory suppression) identified by the instrumented argument.[217]

The decision was appealed, thus presenting the Supreme Court a perfect opportunity to assess the merits of MacKinnon's constitutional theory. Three justices (one short of the number necessary) voted to note probable jurisdiction and set the case for oral argument; the remainder voted to affirm summarily the ruling of the Seventh Circuit.[218] Until such time as the Court decides to reconsider that judgment, the feminist theory will remain beyond the pale of constitutional doctrine.

To summarize, for the past thirty years, the Supreme Court's interpretation of the First Amendment's guarantee of freedom of speech has been influenced by at least three of the five lines of academic commentary on the subject. The net result, it is generally conceded, has been an eclectic mix of theories and "tests."[219] Some subsets of the field are more confused than others. For example, the cases attempting to define obscenity are a notorious muddle, while the cases prescribing when public and private figures may be permitted to bring actions for defamation are clearer. But the field as a whole has yet to be stabilized by any overarching vision. Some observers are content with such a state of affairs;[220] most think we can do better.

---

[217] Frank Michelman, "Conceptions of Democracy in American Constitutional Argument: The Case of Pornography Regulation," *Tennessee Law Review* 56 (Winter 1989): 302–3.

[218] 475 *United States Reports* 1001 (1986). Chief Justice Burger and Justices Rehnquist and O'Connor would have set the case for argument. The silent affirmance infuriated MacKinnon: "The Supreme Court just told us that it is a constitutional right to traffic in our flesh, so long as it is done through pictures and words, and a legislature may not give us access to court to contest it. The Indianapolis case is the *Dred Scott* of the women's movement." *Feminism Unmodified*, 213.

[219] See, for example, Laurence Tribe, *American Constitutional Law*, 2d ed. (Mineola, N.Y.: Foundation Press, 1988), 785–94.

[220] See, for example, Steven Shiffrin, "The First Amendment and Economic Regulation: Away from a General Theory of the First Amendment," *Northwestern University Law Review* 78 (December 1983): 1212.

Takings of property. A crucial constitutional question since the founding of the nation has been the extent to which the state and federal legislatures are permitted to impair private property rights. From the beginning the courts have recognized that governments must be accorded some latitude in setting and modifying the entitlements associated with the ownership of land and other commodities. The courts have refused, however, to acquiesce in all legislative interferences with private property rights.[221]

Until the end of the nineteenth century, the combination of the fact that most regulations of private property emanated from the state governments, not the federal government, and the Supreme Court's ruling that the Bill of Rights was inapplicable to the states[222] had the effect of minimizing the relevance to these disputes of the Fifth Amendment's ban on uncompensated "takings" of private property. In the few cases in which the Supreme Court undertook to review challenges to allegedly confiscatory legislation, it based its rulings either on broad principles of natural law[223] or on the contracts clause of Article I, Section 10.[224] In 1897 the Supreme Court held for the first time that the due-process clause of the Fourteenth Amendment "incorporated" against the states the takings clause of the Fifth Amendment.[225] Since that date the stream of cases invoking the clause to challenge legislative or judicial impairments of property rights has steadily increased.

Before World War II, legal scholars paid relatively little attention to the so-called takings doctrine. Since the 1950s, however, the body of academic writing dealing with the issue has mushroomed. The ambition of the large majority of the authors has been to define a principled line that would enable the courts to differentiate permissible "regulation" of private property from impermissible (if uncompensated) expropriation thereof. The bulk of the literature falls into four categories, which correspond closely to the first four of the five schools of postwar legal theory.[226]

---

[221] For a review of the early history of the courts' treatment of such issues, see Fisher, "Ideology, Religion, and the Constitutional Protection of Private Property," 95–121.

[222] See *Barron* v. *Baltimore,* 32 *United States Reports* 243 (1833).

[223] See, for example, *Fletcher* v. *Peck,* 10 *United States Reports* 87, 135, 143 (1810).

[224] The clause forbids states to "pass any ... law impairing the Obligation of Contracts." Early Supreme Court decisions invoking the clause include *Dartmouth College* v. *Woodward,* 17 *United States Reports* 518 (1819).

[225] *Chicago, Burlington and Quincy Railroad* v. *Chicago,* 166 *United States Reports* 226 (1897).

[226] As yet, no scholar seeking to develop the perspectives of outsiders has taken up the question of the proper interpretation of the takings clause. However, the relevance of

The first approach is exemplified by the work of Joseph Sax. In an influential article published in 1964 Sax criticized the tests that the Supreme Court had been using to evaluate takings cases, arguing instead for the following approach:

> The rule proposed here is that when economic loss is incurred as a result of government enhancement of its resource position in its enterprise capacity, then compensation is constitutionally required; it is that result which is to be characterized as a taking. But losses, however severe, incurred as a consequence of government acting merely in its arbitral capacity are to be viewed as a noncompensable exercise of the police power.[227]

By activity in an "enterprise capacity," Sax meant activity in which the government participates in the market as a competitor and which is designed to "enhance...the economic value of some governmental agency." So, for example, when a government constructs and operates an airport, it should be compelled to compensate the owners of the nearby houses who are forced either to endure increased noise and light or to sell their houses at a loss.[228] By activity in an "arbitral capacity," Sax meant efforts to "mediat[e] conflicts between competing private economic claims," from which the government itself reaps no benefit. So, for example, local zoning regulations forcing industries to shut down to avoid annoying nearby homeowners do not run afoul of the Constitution.[229]

Why should the courts adopt this interpretation of the Fifth Amendment rather than some other? Sax offered two main answers, and both reflect his indebtedness to the then-powerful Legal Process Theory. First, "enterprise activities," unlike "arbitral activities," create a serious risk that the democratic process will be corrupted. Government officials, when making what amount to procurement decisions, will often be tempted to "reward...the faithful or punish...the opposition." Discrimination of this sort—unrelated to the advancement of the public good—is plainly

---

that provision to the power of government to redistribute wealth (one of the larger ambitions of many of the scholars in this group) is likely to attract their attention soon.

[227] "Takings and the Police Power," *Yale Law Journal* 74 (November 1964): 63. In a subsequent article, Sax modified this distinction somewhat but retained the central features of his theory. See "Private Property and Public Rights," *Yale Law Journal* 81 (December 1971): 149.

[228] Similarly, if the reason why the federal government in 1942 ordered the closure of privately owned gold mines was to induce experienced miners to go into more essential war work, from which the government itself was the principal beneficiary, it should have been required to indemnify the owners of the mines. See *United States* v. *Central Eureka Mining Company*, 357 *United States Reports* 155 (1958).

[229] Sax, "Takings and the Police Power," 62–72.

not something government should be about, and the courts should do what they can to eliminate the temptations to engage in it. By contrast, in the mediation of disputes between private parties, government officials have many fewer opportunities for such illicit action; a prophylactic rule requiring that adversely affected persons be compensated is thus unnecessary.[230] This first argument, it should be plain, is a close cousin of the idea of "representation reinforcement" that figures so prominently in the work of such theorists as John Ely and Jesse Choper.

Sax's second rationale for his proposed test represents an outgrowth of the related idea of "institutional competence." Government officials, he argued, are reasonably well qualified to decide contests between two private claimants. In such contexts, officials can be expected to show "restraint and detached reflection" and to take care before disrupting "established interests." By contrast, when making decisions from which the government stands to gain, officials act as judges in their own cases. Under such circumstances there is a serious risk that they will manifest excessive zeal. In short, decisions of the former sort legislative and executive officials are well equipped to make on their own. Only if restrained by the judicially imposed obligation to compensate adversely affected parties, however, can they be trusted with decisions of the latter sort.

The second of the four approaches to the takings doctrine is grounded in utilitarianism and, in its more recent avatars, in the distinctive methodology of law and economics. The approach can be traced to a famous 1967 article in which Frank Michelman argued (among other things) that a judge called on to determine whether the Fifth Amendment had been violated in a particular case might plausibly select as her criterion of judgment the maximization of net social welfare.[231] If that were her ambition, Michelman contended, the judge should begin by estimating and comparing the following economic impacts: (1) the net efficiency gains secured by the government action in question (in other words, "the excess of benefits produced by [the]measure over losses inflicted by it");[232] (2) the cost of measuring the injuries sustained by adversely affected

---

[230] Ibid., 64–5.
[231] Frank Michelman, "Property, Utility, and Fairness: Comments on the Ethical Foundations of 'Just Compensation' Law," *Harvard Law Review* 80 (April 1967): 1165. Bruce Ackerman's discussion of the utilitarian approach largely tracks Michelman's analysis. See *Private Property and the Constitution* (New Haven, Conn.: Yale University Press, 1977), chap. 3.
[232] Though Michelman was not entirely clear on this point, if his formula is to make sense,

parties and of providing them monetary compensation;[233] and (3) the "demoralization costs" incurred by not indemnifying them. Michelman's definition of the third of these terms was original and critical; to ascertain the "demoralization costs" entailed by not paying compensation, the judge should measure

the total of... the dollar value necessary to offset disutilities which accrue to losers and their sympathizers specifically from the realization that no compensation is offered, and... the present capitalized dollar value of lost future production (reflecting either impaired incentives or social unrest) caused by demoralization of uncompensated losers, their sympathizers, and other observers disturbed by the thought that they themselves may be subjected to similar treatment on some other occasion.

Once the judge has calculated these impacts, Michelman contended, her job is straightforward. If (1) is the smallest figure, she should contrive some way to enjoin the action—for example, by declaring it to be violative of the constitutional requirement that private property be taken only for a "public use." If (2) is the smallest figure, she should not enjoin the action but should require that the parties hurt by it be compensated. If (3) is the smallest figure, she should allow the government to proceed without indemnifying the victims.[234]

Applying this composite test, Michelman suggested that some of the guidelines employed by the Supreme Court, though seemingly simplistic or senseless, turn out to have plausible utilitarian justifications. For example, the rule that "physical invasion" by government of private property is always deemed a taking, though apparently a clumsy device for separating mild from severe encroachments on private rights, turns out to have important redeeming features: it identifies a set of cases in which settlement costs (the costs of both ascertaining liability and measuring the resultant damages) are likely to be modest and in which, because of the "psychological shock, the emotional protest, the symbolic threat to all property and security" commonly associated with bald invasions,

"net efficiency gains" must means gains exclusive of the "demoralization costs" discussed later.

[233] Not included in these so-called settlement costs are the compensation awards themselves, which, from an economist's standpoint, constitute transfer payments irrelevant to the calculation of net social utility.

[234] Michelman, "Property, Utility, and Fairness," 1214–15.

"demoralization costs" are likely to be high—precisely the circumstance in which compensation is most appropriate.[235]

In a number of recent articles, other scholars have proposed various modifications of Michelman's original theory.[236] Some have met with general approval within the circle of lawyer-economists; others are controversial. Debate over how exactly the Fifth Amendment should be construed so as to advance the ideal of allocative efficiency is likely to continue for the foreseeable future, but there is little doubt that the economic perspective on the field will remain influential.

As was true in the context of freedom of speech, the Kantian tradition in legal scholarship has generated not a single, integrated analysis of the takings doctrine but a family of analyses similar in orientation and structure. The first of the set was also developed by Frank Michelman. After deploying his seminal utilitarian theory Michelman went on to inquire how the takings doctrine might be reconstructed on the basis of John Rawls's theory of distributive justice. The premises of Rawls's theory, Michelman observed, are the notions that the "good" should be understood in terms of "individually experienced satisfactions" and that the claims of different individuals to satisfaction cannot be ranked. From

---

[235] Ibid., 1227–9. Similarly, the courts' sensitivity in takings cases to the percentage of the total value of the plaintiff's holdings destroyed by the government action in question (rather than to the absolute amount of the economic injury) makes some sense on the following plausible assumptions: "(1) that one thinks of himself not just as owning a total amount of wealth or income, but also as owning several discrete things whose destinies he controls; (2) that deprivation of one of these mentally circumscribed things is an event attended by pain of a specially acute or demoralizing kind, as compared with what one experiences in response to the different kind of event consisting of a general decline in one's net worth; and (3) that events of the specially painful kind can usually be identified by compensation tribunals with relative ease." Ibid., 1234.

[236] For example, a number of writers have argued that Michelman was wrong in suggesting that the judge, when measuring "demoralization costs," should include the diminution in investment and "productive activity" caused by not making the victims whole; indeed, assuring owners that they will be indemnified if and when the public needs their property causes them to *over*invest in capital improvements—a phenomenon economists refer to as "moral hazard." Inducement of efficient kinds and levels of activity requires that economic actors "bear all real costs and benefits of their decisions" including the risk of future changes in pertinent legal rules. See Lawrence Blume, Daniel Rubinfeld, and Perry Shapiro, "The Taking of Land: When Should Compensation Be Paid?" *Quarterly Journal of Economics* 99 (1984): 71; Lawrence Blume and Daniel Rubinfeld, "Compensation for Regulatory Takings: An Economic Analysis," *California Law Review* 72 (July 1984): 569; Louis Kaplow, "An Economic Analysis of Legal Transitions," *Harvard Law Review* 99 (January 1986): 509; and William Fischel and Perry Shapiro, "Takings, Insurance and Michelman: Comments on Economic Interpretations of 'Just Compensation' Law," *Journal of Legal Studies* 17 (June 1988): 269. For a more detailed review of this body of literature, see William Fisher, "The Significance of Public Perceptions of the Takings Doctrine," *Columbia Law Review* 88 (December 1988): 1776–81.

these propositions Rawls had derived (as of 1967) two general principles of justice: (1) the presumption that social arrangements should give no preference to anyone, but should assure each member of the society the maximum liberty consistent with preservation of equal liberty for all others; and (2) the legitimacy of a departure from such a state of affairs if and only if everyone has a chance to attain the better positions in the resultant unequal society and the departure in question is likely to benefit everyone in the society, including its most disadvantaged member.[237]

What would those principles entail if scrupulously applied to the problem of government regulation of private property? Michelman contended that they would yield the following doctrine: compensation is always constitutionally required unless denying it in a particular type of case would work out best for everyone over the long haul.[238] The application of this criterion, Michelman observed, yields (somewhat surprisingly) a set of guidelines remarkably similar to the guidelines suggested by the utilitarian approach. In only two situations would the two theories diverge: (1) when a decision not to compensate victims of governmental action is not widely publicized (in which case "demoralization costs" will be low but the decision might still be unfair); and (2) when people do not behave like the reasonable, patient, farseeing folk who inhabit the Kantian model (in which case "demoralization costs" might be quite high even though a decision not to compensate would be fair).[239]

In his book on the takings doctrine Bruce Ackerman offered a different construction of the Kantian theory. Ackerman used as his foundation not Rawls's theory of distributive justice but a more general Principle of Exploitation—derived, he argued, from Kant's categorical imperative: "the idea that policymakers are not to conceive of their fellow citizens as merely means to the larger end of maximizing social utility, but are instead to treat them as ends in themselves." The natural implication of this proposition, Ackerman contended, is a doctrine sharply different from either extant constitutional law or Michelman's proposal:

The restrained Kantian's approach to compensation will be in some respects more, and in some respects less, demanding than that of his Utilitarian counter-

---

[237] Michelman, "Property, Utility, and Fairness," 1218–29.

[238] Somewhat more precisely: "A decision not to compensate is not unfair as long as the disappointed claimant ought to be able to appreciate how such decisions might fit into a consistent practice which holds forth a lesser long-run risk to people like himself than would any consistent practice which is naturally suggested by the opposite decision." Ibid., 1223.

[239] Ibid., 1223–4.

part. When there is reason to believe that $P < B - C$ [where P is the costs of processing compensation claims, B is the social benefit of the project, and C is other project costs], the Kantian will *always* insist upon compensation while the Utilitarian will only sometimes do so; in contrast, when $P > B - C$, the Kantian will *never* insist upon compensation, while the Utilitarian sometimes will.[240]

Ackerman went on to outline other variations on the Kantian approach. For example, he argued that skepticism regarding legislators' willingness to respect citizens' rights adequately will naturally draw a Kantian judge toward a stance of judicial activism rather than judicial restraint, and an activist stance in turn will alter somewhat the judge's perspective on the just-compensation question. But the requirement that a judge mandate the achievement of Pareto superiority whenever feasible remained the centerpiece of his analysis.[241]

Members of the fourth group of scholars contend that, when construing the Fifth Amendment, judges, instead of striving to remain neutral as to alternative theories of the good, should identify and advance a particular conception of "human flourishing." A closely textured analysis of this sort has been elaborated over the past decade by Margaret Jane Radin. Drawing on the personality theory of property—in particular, Hegel's insight that "the entity we know as a person cannot come to exist without both differentiating itself from the physical environment and yet maintaining relationships with portions of that environment"— Radin contends that objects of ownership vary (along "a continuum") in their importance to individuals' selfhood. At one extreme are things "indispensable to someone's being"; at the other extreme are things "wholly interchangeable with money." She insists that judges when shaping common-law and constitutional doctrines should be sensitive to this fundamental phenomenon.[242] Specifically, when applying the takings clause, judges should abide by two guidelines: First, government expropriation of discrete objects should be more likely to give rise to compensation than regulations that generate comparable adverse financial impacts but leave the regulated objects in their owners' possession and control. The reason: "In order to lead a normal life, there must be some continuity relating to 'things.' One's expectations crystallize around certain 'things,' the loss of which causes more disruption and disorientation than does a simple decrease in aggregate wealth." Second, judges should

---

[240] Ackerman, *Private Property and the Constitution*, 72, 76.
[241] Ibid., 77–80, 222, n.11.
[242] Radin, "Property and Personhood," *Stanford Law Review* 34 (May 1982): 977, 987.

be more willing to declare unconstitutional uncompensated (or even compensated) expropriations of objects central to their owners' personhood (like family homes, backyards, heirlooms, and kidneys) than expropriations of objects deemed fungible by their owners (like real estate held for investment purposes).[243] Radin's proposal is by far the most developed analysis of the takings doctrine from the standpoint of an overt theory of the good, but other proposals are beginning to appear,[244] and we can expect to see more in the near future.[245]

The four approaches just reviewed represent the principal scholarly options in analyses of the takings problem. Sometimes an author will attempt a more or less explicit combination of two or even three perspectives.[246] But few stray outside these channels. As was true of the First Amendment, each of the four scholarly approaches has had an impact on the Supreme Court's decisions and opinions, but none has been adopted in toto by the Court. Partly as a result, current doctrine governing takings of private property is even more chaotic and unpredictable than current doctrine governing freedom of speech.

Joseph Sax's theory has attracted the Supreme Court's attention on a number of occasions. For example, in the 1987 *Keystone Coal* case, Justice Stevens, writing for the Court, invoked Sax's expansive notion of

---

[243] Ibid., 1004, 1005–8. For a student note advocating adoption of Radin's proposal, see "The Supreme Court, 1983 Term—Leading Cases," *Harvard Law Review* 98 (November 1984): 235–6.

[244] For example, in a recent article C. Edwin Baker relies in part on an appreciation of the "personhood function of property" and the sorts of freedom ownership makes possible in defending against attack by "new conservatives" the Supreme Court's treatment of property rights as less deserving of vigorous defense than civil rights. "Property and Its Relation to Constitutionally Protected Liberty," *University of Pennsylvania Law Review* 134 (April 1986): 741.

[245] Although the "republican revisionists" have not yet applied their theory to this problem, the possibilities for advancing their agenda of more equal distribution of wealth and greater autonomy and power for local communities through judicious interpretation of the Fifth Amendment will soon become apparent to them. For a preliminary effort in this vein, see Michelman, "Property as a Constitutional Right," *Washington and Lee Law Review* 38 (Fall 1981): 1097.

[246] By far the most ingenious and influential such combination is Richard Epstein's recent book, *Takings* (Cambridge, Mass.: Harvard University Press, 1985). Epstein's fiercely libertarian argument is grounded for the most part in a strong theory of individual rights—specifically in a novel reading of chapter 5 of Locke's *Second Treatise*. But recently Epstein has acknowledged (to the dismay of his Kantian supporters) that his proposal can also be defended on the ground that it both advances the greatest good of the greatest number and contributes to the republican effort to curb self-interested factions. See Epstein, "A Last Word on Eminent Domain," *University of Miami Law Review* 41 (November 1986): 256–8; idem, "Beyond the Rule of Law: Civic Virtue and Constitutional Structure," *George Washington University Law Review* 56 (November 1987): 169–71.

the sorts of land-use regulations to which an owner ought not feel immune in support of the proposition that bans on "uses of property that are tantamount to public nuisances" should ordinarily not be deemed takings.[247] Two other justices have relied on Sax's argument in dissenting opinions objecting to what they regarded as overly generous interpretations of the Fifth Amendment.[248] But more important by far than these relatively casual invocations of Sax's argument was the Court's reliance on his theory in *Penn Central Transportation Co. v. New York City.* Justice Brennan's majority opinion in that case has long been regarded as seminal, partly because Brennan overtly sought therein to outline "the factors that have shaped the jurisprudence of the Fifth Amendment." In the course of his survey, Brennan twice looked for guidance to Sax. In the second and more substantial of those references he summarized and adopted Sax's characterization and treatment of "enterprise activities": "Finally, government actions that may be characterized as acquisitions of resources to permit or facilitate uniquely public functions" have been held, and should continue to be held, to constitute takings. Brennan then ruled that the conduct challenged in the case—the declaration by New York City that Grand Central Station is a historical landmark and thus cannot be altered by its owner—did not violate Sax's test.[249]

The impact on the case law of the utilitarian line of scholarly criticism has been even more striking. The most general and important effect has been the partial corrosion during the past twenty years of the so-called noxious-use exception to the ban on uncompensated takings. In the early twentieth century the Supreme Court consistently and confidently ruled that when a state forbids the continuation of a use of land or other property that would be harmful to the public or to neighbors, it is not obliged to indemnify the owner. For example, in *Miller v. Schoene,* the Court upheld on this basis a Virginia statute that required the owner of

---

[247] *Keystone Bituminous Coal Assn. v. DeBenedictis,* 480 *United States Reports* 470, 491 and n.20 (1987).

[248] In *Loretto v. Teleprompter Manhattan CATV Corp.,* Justice Blackmun expressly relied on Sax's denunciation of the distinction between physical invasions of property and noninvasive regulations of property to criticize the majority's perpetuation of that distinction. 458 *United States Reports* 419, 442 (1982). A few years later, in *Nollan v. California Coastal Commission,* Justice Brennan quoted extensively from one of Sax's articles in an effort to discredit the majority's insistence that the conditions imposed by a state agency on the grant of a building permit must advance the same "legitimate state interest" that would have been advanced by denial of the permit outright. 483 *United States Reports* 825, 863–64 (1987).

[249] 438 *United States Reports* 104, 128, 135 (1978).

ornamental cedar trees to cut them down because they produced cedar rust that endangered apple trees in the vicinity.[250] As legal scholars became increasingly familiar with the economic analysis of doctrinal problems—and, in particular, with Ronald Coase's assertion that, in all cases of conflicting land uses, it is senseless to characterize one such use as the cause of harm to the other—they pointed out that the Court's handling of cases like *Miller* was at best naive.[251] In the face of this chorus of criticism, the Court retreated. Its renunciation of the "noxious use" test was most complete and overt in Brennan's 1978 opinion in *Penn Central:*

> We observe that the [land] uses in issue in *Hadacheck, Miller,* and *Goldblatt* were perfectly lawful in themselves. They involved no "blameworthiness, . . . moral wrongdoing or conscious act of dangerous risk-taking which induce[d society] to shift the cost to a particular individual." These cases are better understood as resting not on any supposed "noxious" quality of the prohibited uses but rather on the ground that the restrictions were reasonably related to the implementation of a policy—not unlike historic preservation—expected to produce a widespread public benefit and applicable to all similarly situated property.[252]

For better or worse, however, the Court since *Penn Central* has drifted back toward its original view. The justices' invocations of the distinction between "noxious" and "innocent" uses have been more tentative and awkward than in the period before 1960, but nevertheless have been increasing.[253]

The Court's opinion in *Loretto* v. *Teleprompter Manhattan CATV Corp.* furnishes a more straightforward illustration of the power of the utilitarian perspective. At issue in the case was a New York statute empowering a cable television company to install fixtures on the sides and roofs of privately owned buildings. In holding that such a "permanent physical occupation" of private property, no matter how trivial, always constitutes a taking, Justice Marshall relied twice on Michelman's 1967 article—first, for Michelman's analysis of the historical development of the physical-occupation rule; and second for his defense of the rule as

---

[250] 276 *United States Reports* 272 (1927). Similarly, in *Goldblatt* v. *Town of Hempstead,* the Court deemed not to be a "taking" a city ordinance banning excavations below the level of the water table, despite the fact that the ordinance effectively forced the petitioner to close down his sand and gravel business. 369 *United States Reports* 590 (1962).
[251] See, for example, Michelman, "Property, Utility, and Fairness," 1198–9.
[252] 438 *United States Reports* 104, 133–4, n.30 (1977).
[253] See, for example, *Keystone Bituminous Coal Assn.* v. *DeBenedictis,* 480 *United States Reports* at 491; *Nollan* v. *California Coastal Comm.,* 483 *United States Reports* at 825.

an effective way to identify situations involving both low settlement costs and high demoralization costs.[254]

Finally, a disturbing illustration of the way that pieces of academic theories can have unexpected impact on Supreme Court decision making can be gleaned from the fate of another aspect of Michelman's analysis. Toward the close of his article Michelman provided a brief, avowedly utilitarian defense of the venerable and much-maligned "diminution in value" test for determining whether a statute had effected a taking. The true justification of the test, he argued, is that, like the physical-invasion test, it mandates compensation in situations in which property owners will experience severe psychological injury. Recognition of its true purpose, Michelman went on to argue, requires that we reconceive the test slightly:

> More sympathetically perceived, however, the test poses not [a] loose question of degree; it does not ask "how much," but rather . . . it asks "whether or not": whether or not the measure in question can easily be seen to have practically deprived the claimant of some distinctly perceived, sharply crystallized, investment-backed expectation.[255]

In his *Penn Central* opinion, Justice Brennan several times invoked the language with which Michelman closed his discussion—without recapitulating, however, the argument on which it was based.[256] Cut loose from its moorings, Michelman's proposed test has since been put to some surprising uses. For example, in *Kaiser-Aetna v. United States,* the owner of a resort and marina in Hawaii argued that, by granting it permission to convert a shallow, landlocked lagoon into a bay accessible to pleasure boats, the Army Corps of Engineers had forfeited the right subsequently to declare the bay a navigable waterway open to the public—unless, of course, it compensated the marina owner. Emphasizing the amount of money the petitioner had invested in the project, Justice Rehnquist and a majority of the Court agreed. A well-established factor in assessing takings challenges, Rehnquist held, is the extent to which the challenged government action "interfere[s] with reasonable investment backed expectations." In the case at bar, the interference plainly had been substantial.[257] Whatever one thinks of the merits of the ruling, it is considerably removed from Michelman's original point—namely, that

---

[254] 458 *United States Reports* at 427, n.5, 436.
[255] "Property, Utility, and Fairness," 1233.
[256] See 438 *United States Reports* at 124, 127–8.
[257] 444 *United States Reports* 164, 175–6 (1979).

total or nearly total devaluation of a distinct property interest (something that plainly did not occur in *Kaiser-Aetna*) should be deemed a taking because of its likely psychic impact on the owner of the property.[258] The third and fourth schools of takings scholarship thus far have had less impact on the case law, but their power may well be increasing. The standard-bearer of the Kantian approach is likely to be Justice Scalia, who seems well on his way to becoming the intellectual leader of the (growing) conservative wing of the Court. Scalia's distinctive view of the Fifth Amendment is well illustrated by his dissenting opinion in *Pennell* v. *City of San Jose,* decided in 1988. At issue in the case was a rent-control ordinance that authorized hearing officers, when determining the rents that the owners of particular apartments would be permitted to charge, to take into account the "hardship" that the tenants of those apartments would suffer as a result of a rent increase. A majority of the Court held that the landlords' constitutional challenge to the statute was premature, insofar as there was no evidence that the provision in question had yet been invoked to limit rent increases. Justice Scalia, in an opinion joined by Justice O'Connor, argued that the challenge was not premature and then went on to argue that the ordinance did indeed constitute an unconstitutional taking of the landlords' property. He began his analysis by firmly grounding the Fifth Amendment in notions of fairness: "We have repeatedly observed that the purpose of this provision is to bar Government from forcing some people alone to bear burdens which, in all fairness and justice, should be borne by the public as a whole."[259] Traditional land-use regulation passes muster under this test, Scalia argued, because the targets of the regulation are themselves the "cause" of some injury to their neighbors; insofar as they are to blame, it is fair for the state to impose on them the financial burden of correcting the problem in question. Even traditional price regulation and rent control, he suggested gingerly, may be justifiable on this basis, because, by reaping exorbitant profits or rents, the persons targeted by such regulations "can

---

[258] For other instances in which the Supreme Court has relied on the utilitarian approach in general and Michelman's formulation of it in particular, see *Kirby Forest Industries* v. *United States,* 467 *United States Reports* 1, 14 (1984) (invoking Michelman's theory of the relevance of settlement costs); *Andrus* v. *Allard,* 444 *United States Reports* 51, 66 (1979).

[259] 108 *Supreme Court Reports* 849, 861–2 (1988). See also ibid., 864 (arguing that the "essence" of the takings clause "is simply the unfairness of making one citizen pay, in some fashion other than taxes, to remedy a social problem that is none of his creation").

be viewed as responsible for the economic hardship" of the consumers of goods and housing—hardship the state may legitimately seek to alleviate. But in no way can the particular landlords who happen to have poor tenants living in their apartments be deemed responsible for the poverty of the latter. To force those landlords to subsidize their tenants thus compels them to pay for a social problem for which they are not to blame. If the state wishes to improve the lot of poor tenants, it should collect the necessary funds from "the public at large," not from innocent landlords.[260] Most of the major themes of the Kantian perspective—that fairness and justice, not maximization of net social utility, should guide constitutional adjudication and that blameless persons should not be treated as the means to the advancement of general social policies—are clearly evident in these passages. As Scalia gains more confidence and votes, his view of the Fifth Amendment can be expected to increase in influence.

Theories of the good have, to date, received even less attention from the Supreme Court. In only one case do they appear to have had an impact. At issue in *Hodel* v. *Irving* was a 1983 federal statute providing that, in order to ameliorate the increasing fractionalization of the ownership of Indian lands, henceforth small shares (i.e., shares that represent less than 2 percent of the acreage of a particular tract and earn their owners less than $100 per year) may not be devised by will and, in the absence of a will, may not descend through intestate succession but instead, upon the deaths of their owners, shall escheat to the Indian tribe. Despite the fact that the owners of such shares enjoyed full control and use of them during their lifetimes and could convey their interests to others before their deaths, the Supreme Court struck down the statute as an uncompensated taking. One of the few indications of the considerations that impelled the Court to rule this way was its observation that "in one form or another, the right to pass on property—to one's family in particular—has been part of the Anglo-American legal system since feudal times."[261] A generous reading of that passage suggests that the Court may be becoming more sensitive to the culturally conditioned "personhood" functions of property—the ways in which the power to control and dispose of objects may, in American society, assist individ-

---

[260] Ibid., 862–3.
[261] 481 *United States Reports* 704, 716 (1987).

uals in defining themselves and their constitutive familial relationships. Interference with those functions, even if the resultant economic burdens are trivial, should be deemed offensive.

To summarize, the Supreme Court has partially assimilated arguments derived from four of the five traditions of postwar legal theory. Insofar as their arguments have had any impact, the scholars should perhaps be gratified, but the overall shape of the contemporary takings doctrine should give them pause. All observers, including the justices themselves, agree that the rules governing permissible and impermissible regulations of private property are a "muddle."[262] No overarching theory integrates the field. Instead, the Supreme Court in recent years has instructed lower courts to analyze takings challenges on an ad hoc basis, taking into account a loosely formulated and admittedly incomplete set of factors. The result, not surprisingly, has been a "crazy-quilt pattern" of decisions that leaves litigants uncertain as to their rights and unable confidently to arrange their affairs.[263] That the Supreme Court has drawn selectively from several incommensurable scholarly traditions is surely not the only source of the problem, but has contributed to it.

Rights of sexual and familial autonomy. In 1965 the Supreme Court confronted for the second time a challenge to a Connecticut statute forbidding the sale or use of contraceptives.[264] Justice Douglas, writing for the Court, held that, although no provision of the Constitution expressly accorded individuals a right to be free from legislation of this sort, such a right could be derived from the "penumbras" of the First, Third, Fourth, Fifth, and Ninth Amendments. Together those provisions created a "zone of privacy" that a legislature may not invade—a zone that includes the freedom of married couples, within "the sacred precincts of marital bedrooms," to practice birth control.[265]

---

[262] See, for example, Carol Rose, "*Mahon* Reconstructed: Why the Takings Doctrine Is Still a Muddle," *Southern California Law Review* 57 (May 1984): 561.

[263] Dunham, "*Griggs* v. *Allegheny County* in Perspective: 30 Years of Supreme Court Expropriation Law," *Supreme Court Review*, (1962): 63.

[264] Over the dissents of Justices Douglas, Harlan, and Stewart, the Court dismissed the first such challenge on technical grounds. See *Poe* v. *Ullman*, 367 *United States Reports* 497 (1961).

[265] *Griswold* v. *Connecticut*, 381 *United States Reports* 479, 484–6 (1965). In concurring opinions, other members of the Court offered slightly different rationales for the ruling. Justice Goldberg, joined by Justice Brennan and Chief Justice Warren, emphasized the Ninth Amendment, which, in their view, established that the rights protected by the Constitution are not exhausted by the express protections in the first eight amendments. Ibid., 487. Justices Harlan and White looked for guidance primarily to the due-process

Over the course of the next twenty years the Supreme Court constructed on this foundation an elaborate doctrinal edifice. The right to use contraceptives was extended to unmarried persons and then to adolescents.[266] A host of related activities and choices were held to be protected from "unwarranted" government interference—for example, the decision to marry,[267] cohabitation with members of one's extended family,[268] and parents' control over the education and upbringing of their children.[269] Last but not least, the Court sharply curtailed the power of the state to interfere with a woman's freedom to decide whether to carry a fetus to term or to obtain an abortion.[270]

In the past five years, however, the structure has begun to teeter. As the composition of the Court has changed, it has backed away from the more liberal interpretations of the so-called right of privacy. In 1986, for instance, a majority of the Court refused to recognize a constitutional right to engage in consensual homosexual sodomy.[271] Three years later, in the course of upholding a Missouri statute that imposed significant restrictions on women's access to abortion, four justices made clear their opposition to the right of abortion itself.[272] It now seems unlikely that the Court will expand the set of privacy rights it shields from legislative abrogation. How many of the rights that gained protection during the 1970s and 1980s will survive the 1990s is highly uncertain.

A substantial proportion of the constitutional scholarship published since 1965 has focused on the cases in which the Court developed and elaborated the right of privacy. The grounds on which the scholars have celebrated or criticized the Court's rulings have varied, but most of the arguments have drawn on one of the five schools of postwar legal theory.

A significant body of commentary, most of it published during the 1970s, sought to measure the Court's rulings against the standards of

---

clause of the Fourteenth Amendment. Ibid., 499–500, 502. Justices Stewart and Black dissented, contending that the statute, though "uncommonly silly," did not violate any constitutional provision. Ibid., 507–31.

[266] *Eisenstadt v. Baird*, 405 *United States Reports* 438 (1972); and *Carey v. Population Services International*, 431 *United States Reports* 678 (1977).

[267] *Zablocki v. Redhail*, 434 *United States Reports* 374 (1978).

[268] *Moore v. City of East Cleveland*, 431 *United States Reports* 494 (1977) (plurality opinion).

[269] *Stanley v. Illinois*, 405 *United States Reports* 645 (1972); *Wisconsin v. Yoder*, 406 *United States Reports* 205 (1972).

[270] *Roe v. Wade*, 410 *United States Reports* 113 (1973); and *Planned Parenthood of Central Missouri v. Danforth*, 428 *United States Reports* 52 (1976).

[271] *Bowers v. Hardwick*, 478 *United States Reports* 186 (1986).

[272] *Webster v. Reproductive Health Services*, 109 *Supreme Court Reporter* 3040 (1989).

Legal Process Theory. A few of the scholars who took this route concluded that at least some of the decisions were defensible. For example, Harry Wellington, then dean of Yale Law School, began his analysis of the cases by reiterating the major requirements of responsible adjudication: judges should decide difficult constitutional cases on the basis of "principles, general in form and universal in application," that cohere with the "conventional morality" shared by most Americans. Striking down legislation inconsistent with such principles is a legitimate exercise of the power of judicial review—even when the principles cannot fairly be derived from the text of the Constitution itself—because some agency should be responsible for keeping government as a whole within bounds, and the judiciary, unlike the legislature, has the detachment and long perspective necessary to discern the society's general commitments and defend them against the "prejudices and passions of the moment." Applying these strictures to the Court's recent decisions, Wellington concluded that the right of a married couple to use contraceptives and the right of a woman whose pregnancy results from rape to obtain an abortion should indeed be protected from legislative tampering, but that it was at best doubtful whether the right of unmarried couples to use contraceptives or the right of women whose pregnancies were voluntary to secure abortions could be fairly derived from "conventional morality."[273] In a set of early articles Michael Perry employed a similar approach to commend all of the Court's rulings to date and to urge it to go even further.[274]

Most scholars inspired by Legal Process Theory, however, were far more skeptical of the tack the Court was taking. The reaction of Archibald Cox to the original abortion ruling was typical:

My criticism of *Roe* v. *Wade* is that the Court failed to establish the legitimacy of the decision by not articulating a precept of sufficient abstractness to lift the ruling above the level of a political judgment based upon the evidence currently available from the medical, physical, and social sciences. Nor can I articulate

[273] "Common Law Rules and Constitutional Double Standards: Some Notes on Adjudication," *Yale Law Journal* 83 (December 1973): 243–9, 292–311.

[274] Michael Perry, "Abortion, The Public Morals, and the Police Power: The Ethical Function of Substantive Due Process," *U.C.L.A. Law Review* 23 (August 1976): 713–33; idem, "Substantive Due Process Revisited: Reflections on (and Beyond) Recent Cases," *Northwestern University Law Review* 71 (September 1977): 417, 447–8. Since the late 1970s, Perry has modified his constitutional theory considerably. See Michael Perry, *The Constitution, the Courts, and Human Rights: An Inquiry into the Legitimacy of Constitutional Policymaking by the Judiciary* (New Haven, Conn.: Yale University Press, 1982); idem, *Morality, Politics, and Law* (New York: Oxford University Press, 1988).

such a principle—unless it be that a State cannot interfere with individual decisions relating to sex, procreation, and family with only a moral or philosophical State justification: a principle which I cannot accept or believe will be accepted by the American people. The failure to confront the issue in principled terms leaves the opinion to read like a set of hospital rules and regulations, whose validity is good enough this week but will be destroyed with new statistics upon the medical risks of childbirth and abortion or new advances in providing for the separate existence of a foetus. . . . Constitutional rights ought not to be created under the Due Process Clause unless they can be stated in principles sufficiently absolute to give them roots throughout the community and continuity over significant periods of time, and to lift them above the level of the pragmatic political judgments of a particular time and place.[275]

When interpreting the Constitution, Cox insisted, the proper province of the judiciary was the "declaration of virtually absolute and enduring principle[s]," not the making of context-specific, "judgemental balance[s] of shifting evidence or values."[276] Tested by that standard, the decision plainly went too far.

John Ely's criticism of *Roe* was more innovative—and, indeed, seems to have been one of the catalysts for his later reconfiguration of the elements of Legal Process Theory. General principles grounded in conventional morality, Ely contended, have less to recommend themselves than his colleagues had suggested. "A neutral and durable principle may be a thing of beauty and a joy forever. But if it lacks any connection with any value the Constitution marks as special, it is not a constitutional principle and the Court has no business imposing it." Ely hastened to add that he was no literal interpretivist; the Court, he freely conceded, should not limit itself to the enforcement of rights clearly delineated in the Constitution itself.[277] But—and here one sees the outlines of what would later become his full-blown constitutional theory—there were only a limited set of circumstances in which the construction of unenumerated rights would be appropriate: First, the Court could legitimately derive rights "from the system of government, and the citizen's role therein, contemplated by the Constitution." Second, "the Court is entitled, indeed . . . obligated, to seek out the sorts of evils the framers meant to combat and to move against their twentieth century counterparts." Third and

---

[275] Archibald Cox, *The Role of the Supreme Court in American Government* (New York: Oxford University Press, 1976), 113–4.

[276] Ibid., 114.

[277] For an example of a critique of *Roe* that, in contrast to Ely's position, does derive from a strictly interpretivist constitutional theory, see Robert Bork, *The Tempting of America* (New York: Free Press, 1990), 111–16.

finally, the Court might accord special protection to interests "that are unlikely to receive adequate consideration in the political process, specifically, the interests of 'discrete and insular minorities' unable to form effective political alliances." None of these responsibilities, however, could support the creation of a right to an abortion. In short, Ely concluded, once one appreciated the limited roles the judiciary ought to play in American society, one would recognize that the abortion decision was not "bad constitutional law" but "*not* constitutional law."[278]

In contrast to the deep body of scholarship drawing on Legal Process Theory, the germane writing emanating from the Law-and-Economics movement is extremely thin. Indeed, the constitutional right of privacy seems to be one of the few doctrinal areas that has almost completely escaped the economists' scrutiny. One article, however, bears at least obliquely on the abortion controversy and warrants brief mention here because of its notoriety. In 1978 Elizabeth Landes and Richard Posner suggested that the "shortage" of babies available and "suitable" for adoption in the United States could be alleviated if we replaced the expensive and slow bureaucratic system by which orphaned or unwanted babies are currently allocated to couples with a market regime. Awarding babies to the highest bidders would not only provide an efficient mechanism for getting them into the hands of people who wished to care for them, but would also provide an incentive for pregnant women who otherwise would obtain abortions to carry their babies to term and to abstain from unhealthy activities during pregnancy. Under such a system, Landes and Posner claimed, everyone would be better off. Couples desperate to adopt children would get them faster. Babies needing support and love would get them faster. Society would save the costs of administering the adoption agencies and of suppressing the black market in children. Last but not least, the rate of abortion could be expected to decline.[279] Maximizing allocative efficiency, the authors implied, might entail neither forbidding abortion nor legalizing it, but adjusting the system of incentives for childbearing to reduce the willingness or necessity of women to abort their fetuses. The Landes and Posner article, as one might expect, produced a small storm in legal scholarship. A few com-

---

[278] Ely, "The Wages of Crying Wolf: A Comment on *Roe* v. *Wade*," *Yale Law Journal* 82 (April 1973): 927, 929, 933, 935–6, 947, 949 (emphasis in original).
[279] Landes and Posner, "The Economics of the Baby Shortage," *Journal of Legal Studies* 7 (June 1978): 343. See also Posner, *Economic Analysis of Law*, 141–3.

mentators treated the argument with respect.[280] Most held it up as an example of the moral bankruptcy of the economic approach to law.[281] In recent years Richard Posner seems to have retreated from the position, but it remains one of the most visible essays in the Law-and-Economics literature.

The next two schools of postwar legal thought—Kantian Liberalism and Theories of the Good—are, by comparison, well represented in the literature pertaining to the constitutional right of privacy. A good example of the former is the work of David Richards. In a series of articles published in the late 1970s and early 1980s, Richards sought to extract from the writings of Locke, Rousseau, and, above all, Kant a general theory of human rights and then to bring that theory to bear on the issues of sexual and familial freedom. His argument proceeded from two fundamental principles: First, "every person has a capacity for autonomy"—the ability to shape his life and to select and pursue his own goals. Second, "every person has the right to equal concern and respect in his pursuit of autonomy." Acknowledgment of these propositions, Richards contended, requires the state to adhere to "a morally neutral theory of the good for individual persons." One implication of that obligation is that the state may not legitimately interfere with a citizen's activities on "paternalistic grounds" unless the citizen is behaving sufficiently "irrationally"—that is, in a manner that is likely to impair severely and permanently his ability to pursue his own "system of ends as determined by his appetites, desires, capacities, aspirations, and the like."[282]

This theory of human rights, Richards argued, "formed the moral basis of the American innovation of judicial review" and thus constituted an "unwritten Constitution" implicitly adopted by "the Founders." The responsibility of the judiciary, when construing the Constitution in the twentieth century, is to "elaborate" the theory to take account of "contemporary circumstances."[283] Some of the Supreme Court's recent decisions, Richards contended, were consistent with that responsibility. For example, because the right to use contraceptives is "associated with the

---

[280] See, for example, J. Robert S. Prichard, "A Market for Babies," *University of Toronto Law Journal* 34 (Summer 1984): 341.

[281] See, for example, Kelman, "Consumption Theory, Production Theory, and Ideology," 688, n.51.

[282] David A. J. Richards, "The Individual, the Family, and the Constitution: A Jurisprudential Perspective," *New York University Law Review* 55 (April 1980): 8, 10, 18–19.

[283] David A. J. Richards, "The Theory of Adjudication and the Task of the Great Judge," *Cardozo Law Review* 1 (Spring 1979): 171.

protection and enhancement of personal autonomy in making strategic life decisions," the Court's original ruling in *Griswold* and its subsequent extension of the doctrine to "sexually active adolescents" were justifiable.[284] For similar reasons, it was proper for the Court to recognize and protect individuals' right to use pornography in the privacy of their own homes and to live together with members of their biological families. If the justices better appreciated the theory of human rights, Richards insisted, they would go further. For example, they would extend the zone of protected activities to include "consensual adult homosexuality and the right of unrelated people to live together"—both of which can be forbidden only on the basis of illegitimately paternalistic conceptions of individuals' welfare.[285]

The question of the constitutional status of abortion put Richards's theory to a more difficult test. He began his analysis of the issue by brushing aside, as grounded in unacceptable forms of paternalism, two arguments usually advanced in support of criminalization of abortion— that it unduly endangers the woman's life and that there is "a necessary moral link between sex and procreation." He then confronted a more serious claim—namely, that "abortion involves an additional moral feature, the alleged moral personality of the fetus, who has, correspondingly, a 'right to life.' " Given his commitment to protecting and cultivating the ability of all human beings to become self-directing moral agents, Richards might have been expected to find this claim an insurmountable objection to the legalization of the practice. He circumvented it, however, on the ground that "there is something very problematic, indeed philosophically incoherent, in attributing appetites, emotions, or conscious responsiveness to a fetus in the early stages of pregnancy." A fetus, he insisted, has only a "potentiality" for autonomy, not the "capacity" for autonomy—and thus lacks the rights enjoyed by persons after birth.[286]

Not all scholars who work in the Kantian tradition think that the abortion question can be resolved so easily. For most, the apparent clash between the right of a fetus to life and the right of a woman to control over her own body seems more troubling. When individual rights and social interests compete, Kantian scholars typically contend, the former

---

[284] Richards, "The Individual, the Family," 55.
[285] Ibid., 36–7. See also Richards, "Sexual Autonomy and the Constitutional Right to Privacy: A Case Study in Human Rights and the Unwritten Constitution," *Hastings Law Journal* 30 (March 1979), 957.
[286] Richards, "The Individual, the Family," 34 n.160.

must prevail. But when two rights collide (and both pertain to matters of such importance), how is one to decide which should take precedence?

In two recent articles[287] and in his 1990 Holmes lecture at Harvard Law School, Ronald Dworkin outlined a strategy subtler and more ingenious than that of Richards for evading the issue. As long as the question of the constitutional status of abortion is framed in terms of the competing rights of fetuses and women, Dworkin argued, it will continue to elicit unhelpful and divergent answers. To advance in our understanding of the problem, we must somehow shift the debate away from the analytical "space" occupied by the competing rights of individual persons. Such a displacement might be effected, he suggested, by attending more closely to the interest of government in "the sanctity of human life." Invoking some passing remarks by Justices Rehnquist and Scalia in the recent *Cruzan* case[288] and appealing to our common intuition that it is somehow wasteful and wrong to halt an ongoing life of any kind, Dworkin suggested that we incorporate into our analysis an appreciation of the government's stake in preserving life—a stake not derivative of the rights or interests of any particular person. What would recognizing such a state interest entail? Dworkin answered that it might lead to either of two policies: First, the state might compel all citizens to abide by the views of the majority concerning when life begins and what sorts of protections it deserves. Second, the state might seek to cultivate in all citizens an appreciation of the sanctity of life and a willingness to abide by their own sincerely held views regarding when it begins. Of these two options, Dworkin insisted, the latter treats persons with greater respect and is more likely to generate a citizenry genuinely committed to the protection of life.[289]

The fourth group of scholars find unconvincing the Kantians' manipulation of the concepts of autonomy, neutrality, and respect. The proper way to decide cases implicating sexual or familial freedom, they argue, is to develop a substantive vision of "human flourishing" and a theory of the sorts of social and political institutions that would conduce to its

---

[287] Ronald Dworkin, "The Great Abortion Case," *New York Review of Books* (29 June 1989): 49–53; idem, "The Future of Abortion," ibid. (28 September 1989): 47–51.

[288] *Cruzan v. Director, Missouri Department of Health,* 110 *Supreme Court Reporter* 2841, 2852–3, 2859 (1990) (alluding to the state's "interest in the protection and preservation of human life," which "has always accorded the state the power to prevent, by force if necessary, suicide").

[289] Ronald Dworkin, "The Sanctity of Life," Oliver Wendell Holmes, Jr., Memorial Lecture, Harvard Law School, 24 September 1990.

widespread achievement—and then to use the courts to nudge American society in the direction of that ideal. In an influential early article in this vein Kenneth Karst argued that attributes crucial to persons' self-realization—"caring, commitment, intimacy, self-identification"—are best developed in the context of "intimate associations"—"close and familiar personal relationship[s]" comparable to marriages or families. Recognition of the importance of the values such associations cultivate should prompt courts to shield them from government interference. So, for example, unless the state could show that a particular homosexual relationship resulted in demonstrable damage to others—for example, that "a male homosexual teacher, by virtue of his homosexual status alone, created special risk of seduction of children assigned to his classes"—it should not be permitted to penalize or otherwise interfere with such a relationship.[290] In a collaborative article J. Harvie Wilkinson and G. Edward White deployed a similar, though somewhat less sweeping, theory of the prerequisites of "individuality" and then used the theory to defend most of the Court's privacy decisions.[291]

Michael Sandel, one of the originators of the modern communitarian perspective, has been unusually explicit regarding the deficiencies of the Kantian approach and the importance of developing an alternative mode of analysis. It is senseless, he argued in a recent article, to try to determine the constitutionality of statutes that regulate sexual activities or procreation by asking whether they are "neutral among competing visions of the good life." Instead one must confront forthrightly "the morality (or immorality)" of the activities the state seeks to regulate. Pursuing this line, Sandel criticized both the majority and the dissenting justices in the *Hardwick* case for failing to recognize that homosexual relationships advance the same "important human goods" advanced by conventional marriages. Sandel claimed that framing the issue in terms of the moral worth of the conduct in question not only would have been philosophically more coherent but also would have been more likely to cultivate in the American public a genuine "appreciation of the lives homosexuals live" than abstract analyses of autonomy.[292]

---

[290] Karst, "The Freedom of Intimate Association," *Yale Law Journal* 89 (March 1980): 624, 629, 663, 685.

[291] Wilkinson and White, "Constitutional Protection for Personal Lifestyles," *Cornell Law Review* 62 (March 1977): 563, 611–7.

[292] Michael Sandel, "Moral Argument and Liberal Toleration: Abortion and Homosexuality," *California Law Review* 77 (May 1989): 521–2, 535, 537.

The developers of the fifth and final scholarly perspective have advanced even more thoroughgoing criticisms of the ways in which the Supreme Court has addressed problems of sexual freedom. A group of feminist theorists led by Catharine MacKinnon, Sylvia Law, and Frances Olsen have argued that analysis of such problems in terms of the definition and protection of zones of privacy reinforces the misguided notion that, in the "private" sphere, persons should be free to interact without government interference. Far from liberating all persons to shape their own lives as they please, such an approach, particularly when applied to sexual relations, merely enhances the power of men to dominate women:

> It is probably not coincidence that the very things feminism regards as central to the subjection of women—the very place, the body; the very relations, heterosexual; the very activities, intercourse and reproduction; and the very feelings, intimate—form the core of what is covered by privacy doctrine. From this perspective, the legal concept of privacy can and has shielded the place of battery, marital rape, and women's exploited labor; has preserved the central institutions whereby women are deprived of identity, autonomy, control and self-definition; and has protected the primary activity through which male supremacy is expressed and enforced.[293]

The pernicious effects of the mode of analysis the Court adopted in *Roe v. Wade* were made evident, the feminists argue, by its subsequent rulings in *Harris v. McRae* and *Webster v. Reproductive Health Services* that the Constitution does not prevent Congress from denying public funding for abortions or a state from banning the use of public facilities and employees for abortions.[294] If the Constitution merely guarantees persons immunity from government interference with their choices and actions, those decisions make sense; their practical effect, however, is to impair severely the ability of poor women to obtain abortions and thereby to perpetuate their vulnerability and subordinate status.[295]

Improving this state of affairs, the feminist theorists contend, would require doctrinal and social reform of many sorts, but at a minimum we ought to alter the way we think about the constitutional status of abortion. Specifically, two changes in perspective are imperative: First, we

---

[293] MacKinnon, *Feminism Unmodified*, 101. See also Frances Olsen, "Unraveling Compromise," *Harvard Law Review* 103 (November 1989): 111–13.

[294] 448 *United States Reports* 297 (1980); 109 *Supreme Court Reporter* 3040 (1989).

[295] MacKinnon, *Feminism Unmodified*, 93, 97; and Olsen, "Unraveling Compromise," 113–17. See also Laurence Tribe, "The Abortion Funding Conundrum: Inalienable Rights, Affirmative Duties, and the Dilemma of Dependence," *Harvard Law Review* 99 (November 1985): 338 (making a similar argument).

should cease discussing access to abortion as a derivative of the right to privacy and instead recognize it as crucial to the establishment of equality between men and women. Enabling (not merely permitting) women to control their own sexuality and reproduction is imperative if we wish to "value women's lives equally with men's" and put "an end to the subordinate status of women."[296] Second, we must reexamine our attitudes about the nature and strength of the state's interest in protecting fetal life. The assumption made all too often even by supporters of women's access to abortion is that, from the moment of conception, a fetus is in some sense a human being with rights and interests independent of its mother. Such a view fails to recognize both "the active role that mothers play in procreation"—in other words, the importance of their actions not only before but *after* conception to the creation of children—and the degree to which the determination of when life begins is "culturally created": "The possibility of valuing fetal life from an early stage exists because of the systematic undervaluation of women's lives. If women were taken seriously, early fetal life would not be valued by society at large unless and until the woman carrying the fetus valued it."[297] Rethinking the problem along these lines would make evident the need to preserve the constitutional right to an abortion and to ensure that all women could avail themselves of that right—and might even move us a few steps toward the achievement of genuine equality of the sexes.

Those then are the five modes of analysis that have dominated scholarly discussion of the privacy cases. Two of the perspectives appear not to have attracted the Supreme Court's attention. Neither Posner's and Landes's proposal for instituting a market in adoptive babies nor the feminist theorists' suggestions for radically reforming the constitutional right to abortion have noticeably affected the deliberations of any justice. The other three approaches, however, have figured prominently in the Court's analyses.

Not surprisingly, the division in the ranks of scholars influenced by Legal Process Theory has reinforced a division among the Supreme Court justices about the proper approach to cases implicating sexual or familial freedom. The scholars who have argued for the legitimacy of reliance on

---

[296] Olsen, "Unraveling Compromise," 119. See also Sylvia A. Law, "Rethinking Sex and the Constitution," *University of Pennsylvania Law Review* 132 (1984): 1014–17. This argument builds on the proposals for doctrinal reform originally made by Donald Regan. See "Rewriting *Roe v. Wade*," *Michigan Law Review* 77 (August 1979): 1569.

[297] Olsen, "Unraveling Compromise," 121, 128.

general principles grounded in our nation's traditions and common values have found a sympathetic audience in those justices eager to expand the zones of constitutional protection. For example, in *Moore* v. *City of East Cleveland,* Justice Powell, writing for a plurality of the Court, emphasized the high value that Americans have traditionally placed on extended families as a justification for striking down a zoning ordinance that, as applied, prevented a woman from living with her son and two grand-children.[298] Likewise, in *Wisconsin* v. *Yoder,* Chief Justice Burger argued that an important consideration in determining whether Amish parents should be accorded a constitutional right to withdraw their children from the public schools was Americans' nearly universal agreement on the general principle that the upbringing of children was the responsibility of their parents: "The history and culture of Western civilization reflect a strong tradition of parental concern for the nurture and upbringing of their children. This primary role of the parents in the upbringing of their children is now established beyond debate as an enduring American tradition."[299] Similar arguments can be found in many other Supreme Court opinions shielding sexual or familial activities from government interference.[300] To some extent, at least, the popularity of this mode of analysis can be traced to the support it has received from a prominent group of scholars.

As indicated earlier, however, a second group of scholars has drawn on Legal Process Theory to criticize some or all of the privacy decisions, and in recent years the members of the Court who are hostile to expansive, judicially created rights of sexual and familial autonomy have looked increasingly for support and guidance to the writings of the latter group. For example, since she was named to the Court, Justice O'Connor has expressed growing dissatisfaction, if not with the outcome of the original abortion decision, at least with the mode of analysis on which the ruling was based. Particularly misguided, in her view, is the holding in *Roe* that the strength of a state's interests in the protection of maternal health and the preservation of fetal life—and consequently the state's constitutional authority to regulate or ban abortions—is different in each of the three

---

[298] 431 *United States Reports* at 503–5.
[299] 406 *United States Reports* at 232.
[300] See, for example, *Griswold* v. *Connecticut*, 381 *United States Reports* at 495–6 (Justice Goldberg concurring); *Ginsberg* v. *New York*, 390 *United States Reports* 629, 639 (1968); *Zablocki* v. *Redhail*, 434 *United States Reports* at 383–6 (emphasizing the respect Americans have long accorded the freedom to marry); *Bellotti* v. *Baird*, 443 *United States Reports* 622, 638 (1979).

trimesters of a pregnancy. In what may eventually prove a highly influential dissenting opinion in the *City of Akron* case, Justice O'Connor
made explicit the extent to which her objection was derived from Legal
Process Theory: "It is clear that the trimester approach violates the fundamental aspiration of judicial decisionmaking through the application
of neutral principles 'sufficiently absolute to give them roots throughout
the community and continuity over significant periods of time.' "[301]

Justice White has drawn on the same body of writing in pressing for
even more dramatic doctrinal change. One of the two dissenters in *Roe*,
White has been campaigning against the decision ever since. In his dissenting opinion in *Thornburgh* v. *American College of Obstetricians and
Gynecologists*, he listed the three main reasons he thinks *Roe* should be
overruled:[302] First, although the Supreme Court, when construing the
Constitution, need not limit itself to "the 'plain meaning' of the Constitution's text or to the subjective intention of the Framers," it ought not to
rely on the justices' "own, extra constitutional, value preferences," but instead should strive to identify and protect against legislative encroachment
the "values and principles that are implicit (and explicit) in the structure of
rights and institutions the people have themselves created."[303] Second,
even if it were legitimate for the Court to incorporate into the Constitution
values its members consider "implicit in the concept of ordered liberty" or
"rooted in this nation's history and tradition," the right of a woman to obtain an abortion plainly would not satisfy either of those tests.[304] Third, the
interest of a state in protecting "potential human life" is substantial
throughout a pregnancy; only on the basis of an "arbitrary," unprincipled
judgment can that interest be deemed not "compelling" prior to the mo-

---

[301] *City of Akron* v. *Akron Center for Reproductive Health*, 462 *United States Reports*
416, 458 (1983) (quoting Cox, *The Role of the Supreme Court*, 114). In place of the
Roe doctrine, O'Connor proposed a more general and ostensibly "neutral" rule under
which a regulation would be unconstitutional if and only if it "unduly burden[s]" the
right to seek an abortion. Ibid., 453. For other cases in which Justice O'Connor had
developed this position, see *Thornburgh* v. *American College of Obstetricians and Gynecologists*, 476 *United States Reports* 747, 828–9 (1986); *Planned Parenthood Ass'n* v.
Ashcroft, 462 *United States Reports* 476, 505 (1983); and *Webster* v. *Reproductive
Health Services*, 109 *Supreme Court Reporter* at 3060–4.

[302] 476 *United States Reports* at 786–97. For the original statement of White's views, see
Doe v. *Bolton*, 410 *United States Reports* 179, 221–3 (1973).

[303] 476 *United States Reports* at 789, 794, 796, n.5 (quoting *Palko* v. *Connecticut*, 302
United States Reports 319, 325–6 [1937]).

[304] Ibid., 790–1 (quoting *Griswold* v. *Connecticut*, 381 *United States Reports* at 501). In
Bowers v. *Hardwick*, Justice White, writing for the Court, makes much the same ar-
gument concerning a putative "fundamental right to engage in homosexual sodomy."
See 478 *United States Reports* at 190–6.

ment the fetus becomes "viable."[305] Each of these arguments, as White acknowledged in his citations, parallels an argument made previously by John Ely, either in his article criticizing *Roe* or in his book on constitutional theory.[306]

The influence of the Kantian scholars on the Court's rulings can be traced in two ways. First, on occasion, individual justices have drawn explicitly upon legal scholarship in the Kantian tradition when defining or defending rights of privacy. For example, in his concurring opinion in *Thornburgh*, Justice Stevens chastised Justice White for failing to recognize that a woman must have control over her own body if she is to be free to define and pursue her ends in life:

If Justice White were correct in regarding the postconception decision of the question whether to bear a child as a relatively unimportant, second-class sort of interest, I might agree with his view that the individual should be required to conform her decision to the will of the majority. But if that decision commands the respect that is traditionally associated with the "sensitive areas of liberty" protected by the Constitution, ... no individual should be compelled to surrender the freedom to make that decision for herself simply because her "value preferences" are not shared by the majority.[307]

In an accompanying footnote Stevens quoted extensively from two essays by Charles Fried developing the notion that respect for individuals' autonomy requires that they be left free to develop their own "life plan[s]."[308] In subsequent opinions Justice Blackmun has relied on the same passages in giving shape to his own privacy theory.[309]

The second impact of the Kantian tradition is harder to document but at least as important. In the eight years between the original decision in *Griswold* and the explosive ruling in *Roe*, the focus of the Court's concern gradually shifted from the protection of privacy in the traditional sense of "freedom from surveillance or disclosure of intimate affairs" to the

---

[305] 476 *United States Reports* at 794–5.
[306] Justice White's citations to Ely appear in 476 *United States Reports* at 795, 796, n.5.
[307] 476 *United States Reports* at 777.
[308] Ibid., 777, n.5: "What a person is, what he wants, the determination of his life plan, of his concept of the good, are the most intimate expressions of self-determination, and by asserting a person's responsibility for the results of this self-determination we give substance to the concept of liberty." Charles Fried, *Right and Wrong* (Cambridge, Mass.: Harvard University Press, 1978), 146–7. See also Fried, Correspondence, *Philosophy and Public Affairs* 6 (Spring 1977): 288–9 (the concept of privacy embodies the "moral fact that a person belongs to himself and not others nor to society as a whole").
[309] *Bowers* v. *Hardwick*, 478 *United States Reports* at 203–6 (Justice Blackmun dissenting); *Webster* v. *Reproductive Health Services*, 109 *Supreme Court Reporter* at 3072–3 (Justice Blackmun dissenting).

protection of autonomy, that is, the right to make certain sorts of choices free from private or government interference.[310] In his opinion for the Court in *Carey* v. *Population Services International*, Justice Brennan explained the change in orientation as follows:

> *Griswold* did state that by "forbidding the *use* of contraceptives rather than regulating their manufacture or sale," the Connecticut statute...had "a maximum destructive impact" on privacy rights. This intrusion into "the sacred precincts of marital bedrooms" made the statute particularly "repulsive." But subsequent decisions have made clear that the constitutional protection of individual autonomy in matters of childbearing is not dependent on that element. *Eisenstadt v. Baird*, holding that the protection is not limited to married couples, characterized the protected right as the "*decision* whether to bear or beget a child." Similarly, *Roe v. Wade* held that the Constitution protects "a woman's *decision* whether or not to terminate her pregnancy." These decisions put *Griswold* in proper perspective. *Griswold* may no longer be read as holding only that a State may not prohibit a married couple's use of contraceptives. Read in light of its progeny, the teaching of *Griswold* is that the Constitution protects individual decisions in matters of childbearing from unjustified intrusion by the State.[311]

Undoubtedly, this shift in the Court's rhetoric and concerns was prompted by many considerations, including the difficulty of justifying the Court's more innovative decisions in the areas of abortion and non-marital sex on the basis of popular attitudes concerning privacy in the traditional sense.[312] But at least partial credit must go to the popularity in legal scholarship during the 1970s and '80s of "voluntarist" theories—theories stressing the obligation of the state to leave citizens free to shape their lives as they choose.

As was suggested earlier, however, not all political or legal theories that counsel according persons freedom of choice regarding sexual or familial matters rest on the notions that the state must respect individuals' autonomy and remain neutral as to alternative life-styles. Some of the arguments that take this tack are founded on the radically different notions that certain ways of living are better than others, that social and political institutions should be organized so as to encourage people to live good lives, and that the judiciary should contribute to the project of reorganizing society in conformity with that vision by striking down

---

[310] See Sandel, "Moral Argument," 525–31.
[311] 431 *United States Reports* 678, 687 (1977) (citations omitted).
[312] See Robert Post, "Tradition, the Self, and Substantive Due Process: A Comment on Michael Sandel," *California Law Review* 77 (May 1989): 556–7.

statutes that interfere with its achievement. So far the latter perspective has had less impact than the Kantian view on the Supreme Court's deliberations, but during the past decade signs of its influence have become more common. An especially clear invocation of the utopian perspective is the following passage from the opinion of the Court in *Roberts* v. *United States Jaycees,* in which Justice Brennan sought to explicate the "freedom of intimate association" protected by the Court's recent decisions:

The Court has long recognized that, because the Bill of Rights is designed to secure individual liberty, it must afford the formation and preservation of certain kinds of highly personal relationships a substantial measure of sanctuary from unjustified interference by the State. Without precisely identifying every consideration that may underlie this type of constitutional protection, we have noted that certain kinds of personal bonds have played a critical role in the culture and traditions of the Nation by cultivating and transmitting shared ideals and beliefs; they thereby foster diversity and act as critical buffers between the individual and the power of the State. Moreover, the constitutional shelter afforded such relationships reflects the realization that individuals draw much of their emotional enrichment from close ties with others. Protecting these relationships from unwarranted state interference therefore safeguards the ability independently to define one's identity that is central to any concept of liberty.[313]

The idea that gives shape and power to Brennan's argument is that the formation of "deep attachments and commitments to the necessarily few other individuals with whom one shares not only a special community of thoughts, experiences, and beliefs but also distinctively personal aspects of one's life"[314] is not merely one of the options an autonomous individual might consider when deciding how to arrange his or her affairs, but a good thing—something the Court, in its interpretation of the Constitution, should strive to encourage.[315]

A similar perspective is evident in Justice Blackmun's dissenting opinion in *Hardwick,* the case in which a majority of the Court refused to extend constitutional protection to private consensual homosexual con-

---

[313] 468 *United States Reports* at 618–19 (citations omitted).
[314] Ibid., 620.
[315] Prior intimations of such a theory—on which the Court in *Roberts* relied in part—can be found in *Smith* v. *Organization of Foster Families,* 431 *United States Reports* 816, 844–5 (1977) (stressing the importance of the "emotional attachments" arising out of the "familial relationship" "even in the absence of blood relationships"); *Stanley* v. *Illinois,* 405 *United States Reports* at 651–2 (same); and *Moore* v. *City of East Cleveland,* 431 *United States Reports* at 503–6, 508 (emphasizing the strength of the emotional ties between members of an extended family).

duct. Michael Sandel, in his essay on the case, chastises Blackmun for adhering to a sterile "voluntarist" theory.[316] It is true that some passages in the opinion do draw upon the Kantian approach; for example, Blackmun quotes and relies on Charles Fried's depiction of the self-owning and self-directing individual.[317] However, as Robert Post observes, other portions of the opinion forthrightly identify and seek to advance a particular vision of a rewarding and virtuous life.[318] The reason we should protect freedom of choice in matters of sexuality, Blackmun insists, is not because it "contribute[s], in some direct and material way, to the general welfare," but because it fosters "sexual intimacy," which in turn is a "sensitive, key relationship of human existence, central to family life, community welfare, and the development of human personality." Citing the work of Kenneth Karst, he contends that the "richness" of "intensely personal bonds" depends in part on the ability of the participants "to '*choose*' the form and nature" of those bonds.[319] In short, Blackmun argues, the case should have been decided differently not because freedom of choice is desirable in and of itself but because, in the context of sexual relations, it contributes to "the happiness of individuals" and "a harmony in living."[320]

The eclecticism of Justice Blackmun's dissent poses anew the question with which this section began. Should we be pleased or dismayed to find in Supreme Court opinions shards of the various seemingly incommensurable normative theories developed by law teachers? A generous view of Blackmun's analysis is that, by demonstrating in a particular context the interdependence of the values of liberty and self-creation emphasized by the Kantian teachers and the values of intimacy, community, and "human flourishing" emphasized by teachers in the fourth camp, it achieves greater insight and power than any single school of legal scholarship.[321] A fairer judgment, in my view, is that, by eliding fundamental

---

[316] Sandel, "Moral Argument," 530–1.

[317] 478 *United States Reports* at 204. For the passages in question, see note 308 above.

[318] Post, "Tradition and the Self," 554–5.

[319] 478 *United States Reports* at 204–5 (citing both Karst and *Paris Adult Theatre I v. Slaton*, 413 *United States Reports* 49, 63 [1973]). For another invocation of Karst's work in a related context, see *Rowland v. Mad River Local School District*, 470 *United States Reports* 1009, 1015 n.9 (1985) (Justices Brennan and Marshall dissenting from the denial of certiorari).

[320] 478 *United States Reports* at 204–5.

[321] For an analysis of the jurisprudence of Justice Brennan that adopts such a line, see Frank Michelman, "A Tribute to Justice William J. Brennan, Jr.," *Harvard Law Review* 104 (November 1990): 22.

issues (e.g., whether the state should be neutral as to alternative theories of the good or should seek to advance a particular vision) and by tolerating or enhancing ambiguity in the meanings of crucial concepts (e.g., autonomy), Blackmun's dissent and opinions like it impede more than they advance our understanding of the issues at stake. Especially in view of the importance of "constitutional discourse" in helping to "constitute the terms of political discourse in American public life,"[322] the net effect is regrettable.

[322] Sandel, "Moral Argument," 538.

7

The British, the Americans, and rights

ALAN RYAN

Both the style and the content of this chapter differ somewhat from those of the other chapters in this volume. Although I hope the discussion never descends to the level of mere propaganda, at least some of what follows may well sound a little like the editorial pages of our better newspapers. For the similarities and differences in British and American views of the law and politics of a bill of rights or the Bill of Rights are not of academic interest alone, and it is impossible to write of them without displaying one's political allegiances along with one's intellectual commitments.

The question whether Britain ought to adopt a written constitution or a bill of rights with statutory force has lately been hotly debated. Comparisons with the theory and practice of American politics have been deployed as weapons on both sides of the contest between the defenders of the unwritten constitution and would-be reformers. That argument has always divided mildly social-democratic academics, journalists, and unattached intellectuals, on the one hand, from conservative politicians (of all political parties), on the other. What is novel is not so much that appeals to American experience are the common coin of this argument as that British writers now draw so heavily on American resources in political theory, political science, and jurisprudence and that American writers feel so much at home in British controversies. It was the American Ronald Dworkin who provided British professors of law with the text for their attack on former Prime Minister Margaret Thatcher: "Liberty in Britain is sick."[1] Conversely, the violent political controversies sur-

---

[1] K. D. Ewing and C. A. Gearty, *Freedom Under Thatcher* (Oxford: Clarendon Press, 1989), 16, quoting Ronald Dworkin, "Devaluing Liberty," *Index on Censorship* (London: Index on Censorship, 1988), 8.

rounding some recent nominations to the U.S. Supreme Court have more than ever convinced British opponents of a written constitution that the innovation would "politicize" a judiciary hitherto above the political clamor.

This chapter straddles the Atlantic in comparing and contrasting British and American attitudes to bills of rights, to judicial review, and to the interplay of party politics and judicial politics. Its focus is British, but its implications are equally American. Its focus is unavoidable. My background and political attachments are British; indeed, my views on the role of a bill of rights in contemporary politics are those of an Englishman of a particular age and political complexion. Of course, my views have American analogues. An American of my age and political allegiances who looks back to the 1950s probably shares my ambivalence about a Supreme Court that sparked the modern civil rights movement with its famous decision in *Brown* v. *Topeka Board of Education* at the same time as it refused to interfere with the activities of the House Un-American Activities Committee. All the same, we must remember how different the perspective is from different sides of the Atlantic. Americans older than I take for granted the Supreme Court's role in American politics, with all that it entails; Britons older than I take it for granted that grafting a statutory bill of rights and American judicial habits onto the British political system would be impossible or pointless.

Age makes a lot of difference to British views. Younger writers of a centrist persuasion are more likely than I to believe that by one route or another it is possible to give basic rights more solid statutory protection. This is not only, or even primarily, because they are impressed by American practice and the U.S. Bill of Rights. They look to European institutions rather than American ones. Britain is a signatory to the European Convention on Human Rights, but the convention is not part of British law, and its provisions cannot be invoked in a British court. The simplest way to give statutory protection to human rights, thus in a sense creating a British bill of rights, is for a British government to make the European Convention part of ordinary British law. Nonetheless, American free-speech and criminal-justice decisions are also much cited in defense of the view that a bill of rights and new judicial habits would do much for the liberty of the British.[2] Optimists seek to combine European legislation

---

[2] Ewing and Gearty, *Freedom Under Thatcher*, e.g., 35–7 (*Miranda* v. *Arizona*) and 197–8 (*New York Times Co.* v. *U.S.*).

on human rights and an American-style judiciary ready and able to defy
the wishes of both the executive and legislative branches of government.
Pessimists fear that British judges would emasculate any bill of rights,
no matter what its origins might be, because British judges are too tender
toward the powers that be, and not tender enough toward the poor,
the inarticulate, or the dissident.

The fact that Britain has no written constitution nor any constitutional
provision corresponding to the U.S. Bill of Rights is cause and effect of
many other large differences in history and political culture that cumu-
latively mean that politicians and judges in the two countries work in
strikingly different environments. What concerns us here is judicial control over the executive.[3] Differences between American and British practice in that area, however, can hardly be understood without
understanding how far British habits are part of a more general lack of
concern for the strict separation of powers.[4] That unconcern in turn is
yet another aspect of the British willingness to concentrate power in the
hands of government, and that readiness to concentrate power in the
executive in turn has implications for the nature of British political parties
and for the whole political culture. It is a cliché that it is hard to set
limits on comparative analysis of this kind; when comparing some of the
most important features of a centralized, power-concentrating, strongly
two-party political system with the same features of a federal, power-
dispersing, weakly two-party political system, it is a cliché with some
force.

Some issues can quickly be disposed of. In the absence of the Second
Amendment no one in the United States would think that people possessed an inalienable right to own an assortment of handguns, shotguns,
and rifles. The British certainly think no such thing. British laws on the
ownership, registration, safekeeping, and lawful use of firearms are tough,
universally supported, and almost universally obeyed. In Britain, as any-

---

[3] See Dennis J. Galligan, *Discretionary Powers* (Oxford: Clarendon Press, 1990), 219ff.,
and more generally, Stanley de Smith and Rodney Brazier, *Constitutional and Administrative Law*, 6th ed. (Harmondsworth, England: Penguin Books, 1990), 546ff.

[4] The innumerable differences between British and American political institutions that stem
from the fact that the British executive sits in Parliament are too large a subject to tackle
here. American readers will still find the discussion of cabinet government in Walter
Bagehot, *The English Constitution*, worth reading. Conversely, Britons must beware of
exaggerating the United States's enthusiasm for an independent judicary. Thirty-nine states
submit their judges to popular election, and only a handful share with the federal government and Britain the belief that judges should hold office *"dum se bene gesserint,"*
and not at the mercy of legislature or people.

where, the occasional madman runs amok. If one does so with a gun, however, it is not because the gun was handy. When Michael Ryan killed more than a dozen policemen, neighbors, family, and finally himself in Hungerford in 1987, he did so with weapons that had been previously registered, kept under lock and key, and formerly used only at a gun club.[5] Historians of ideas have written interestingly in recent years about the eighteenth-century obsession with "the militia question," and have reminded us how frightened eighteenth-century defenders of freedom were of the liberticide possibilities of a standing army under the control of a probably absolute monarch.[6] But the subject is essentially of anti-quarian interest. The National Rifle Association does not propose the abolition of the United States's standing army when it defends the citizens' right to bear arms. Nobody in Britain believes that British civil liberties would be enhanced by the abolition of British firearms legislation, and this is the last mention of the Second Amendment in this chapter.

Many important contrasts between the United States and Britain are a subclass of contrasts between the United States and most Western liberal democracies. In the past forty years other countries have achieved by legislative action alone much the same results that have been achieved in the United States by the idiosyncratic American mix of legislation and Supreme Court initiative. British, indeed any European, politicians expect the cabinet to propose and Parliament to legislate; Americans have looked to the decisions of the nine wise men in Washington. The contrast is not absolute. Many of the crucial decisions of the Supreme Court have been provoked by the federal government's determination to bring recalcitrant state governments up to the standards of the rest of the country in the matter of voting rights for minorities, access to education, and work for both sexes and all races. Conversely, British judges have acted where Parliament has not, extending the protection of the law against rape to married women, for instance, and, as we shall see, the British Parliament has been forced to act on the prodding of the European Court of Human Rights. Still, the contrast remains broadly valid.

A skeptic about the part played in recent American history by the ten amendments that make up the Bill of Rights narrowly construed might observe that the creative use of the equal-protection and due process clauses of the Fourteenth Amendment has been even more significant

---

[5] *The Times* (London), 20 August 1987.
[6] John Robertson, *The Scottish Enlightenment and the Militia Issue* (Edinburgh: J. Donald, 1985).

than that of the first ten amendments. Thus school desegregation was launched by the famous decision in *Brown* v. *Topeka Board of Education* on the basis of the Fourteenth Amendment; so were redistricting and new-voter registration rules for the elimination of racial bias. In making transatlantic comparisons, however, it seems artificial to separate out the Court's use of different parts of the Constitution, when it is their combined impact that has been so impressive, and the fact of their absence that strikes critics of the British political and legal system. The point of the Fourteenth Amendment is to ensure among other things that the individual states live up to the requirements of the Bill of Rights; without it, there would be fewer rights to be "equally protected."

In any case, the point at issue here is the larger contrast between British and American political culture and behavior. It is inconceivable that sweeping changes in civil rights could *originate* in the British courts, or that British judges could keep up the reforming momentum that characterized the Supreme Court in the field of civil rights. In Britain, similar results could only be achieved by legislation. Legislation there certainly has been. Successive race relations acts since 1968 have made it an offense to discriminate in employment, and have opened clubs and organizations of a sufficient size or with a "public" purpose to would-be members of all races and both sexes.[7] The outcome is like that in the United States, allowance being made for the American history of slavery, Jim Crow legislation, and the obstacles that a federal constitution puts in the way of a uniform settlement.[8] The same is true of other issues, such as nonracial discrimination in employment, the right of religious minorities such as Sikhs to wear headgear other than uniform caps when driving buses or collecting tickets on the railways, and so endlessly on. Given that Britain and the United States are ethnically and culturally diverse societies facing many similar problems it is not surprising that British law and American law are often very similar. Still, the fact that the law is established by such different processes has important political consequences. One is that American conservatives complain of the activism of the Supreme Court, while the British left complains that the

---

[7] The applicable legislation is the *Race Relations Act*, 1965, 1968, 1976; legislation for sex equality has been slower arriving, the Equal Pay Act of 1970 and the Sex Discrimination Act of 1975 being the operative laws here.
[8] De Smith and Brazier, *Constitutional and Administrative Law*, 431–6, discuss the interpretative difficulties of these acts.

courts narrow the effect of legislation once Parliament has been moved to act.

THREE CIVIL LIBERTIES ISSUES

Even though racial issues are perhaps the most striking examples of the Supreme Court's taking the initiative in reform, this chapter concentrates on civil liberties of the kind dealt with by the Supreme Court on the basis of First, Fourth, and Fifth Amendment rights. Whatever the failings of British race relations, governments have not been reluctant to legislate against overt discrimination. The issues that remain contentious are issues of freedom of speech, freedom of assembly, guarantees against police misconduct, and only to a lesser extent social issues. I therefore contrast British and American attitudes toward three issues. On the first, the advantage has been all in Britain's favor—actually, all in the United Kingdom's favor;[9] on the second, the advantage is unequivocally in the United States's favor; and on the third it is difficult to know what to think. The first issue is abortion; if the British experience has not been easy, it has been much easier than that of the United States.[10] The second issue is the regulation of the police and the protection of the rights of the accused; Britain has discovered that it is harder to legislate an equivalent of what was achieved by *Miranda* than anyone had previously imagined.[11] The third is the balancing of free speech with considerations of public order and national security. It is an open question whether the occasional absurdities of U.S. practice—such as the appearance in court of the American Civil Liberties Union to defend the right of members of the Ku Klux Klan to process through black neighborhoods in hoods and robes—are a fair price to pay for lively political debate or whether these things go better in Britain, where the police have far more power to control who says what and where in the name of public order.[12]

---

[9] The British Parliament does not always legislate for the whole of the United Kingdom; homosexual law reform, for instance, was initially confined in its application to mainland Britain and was not the law of "the United Kingdom of Great Britain and Northern Ireland." Much legislation for Scotland has to be cast differently, too, in virtue of the differences between the Scottish and English legal systems. Legislation for Scotland passes through the Scottish Grand Committee of the House of Commons, though this is a matter of courtesy.

[10] Mary Ann Glendon, *Abortion and Divorce in Western Law* (Cambridge, Mass.: Harvard University Press, 1987).

[11] Ewing and Gearty, *Freedom Under Thatcher*, 34–7.

[12] Ibid., 84–7.

Some free expression cases are easy to make up one's mind on; the recent behavior of the British government and judges in the area of the censorship of the press and other media for the sake of "national security" contrasts instructively with American attitudes since the *Pentagon Papers* case.[13] The ridicule that the British government so abundantly incurred by its actions in the *Spycatcher* case would not have been risked by the U.S. government during the past twenty years.[14] In the *Spycatcher* case, Peter Wright, a retired employee of MI-5, the British secret service, set out to supplement his pension by publishing a fairly racy memoir of his career; among other things it contained the allegation that MI-5 had engaged in a dirty-tricks campaign to bring down the Labour government in the mid-1960s. Wright was not a left-winger exposing the wickedness of his former employers, but a right-winger concerned that MI-5 had been ineffective in stopping the left from infiltrating everywhere in British politics, administration, and defense.[15] The British government tried to stop publication, both in Australia where Wright had by that time gone to live, and in Britain. It also tried to prevent newspapers from publishing extracts from the book, and at one point set out to stop them from printing anything about the allegations made in the trial in Australia. Until late in the process British courts granted the government injunctions against newspapers that tried to publish extracts from the book, and even broke new ground in finding that an injunction against one newspaper was an injunction against all. The courts' behavior was not absolutely indefensible; they were granting interim injunctions before a full trial and could properly say that they were not judging the merits of the government's eventual case at trial, where, after all, the government lost. But the government's behavior was certainly indefensible. Nor did most of the judges cover themselves in glory in their attitudes toward freedom of the press. For the most part, they seemed to regard newspapers as at best a necessary evil, and Lord Ackner, one of the Law Lords who heard the case on appeal, went so far as to dismiss the First Amendment's protection of press freedom as a misfortune for American governments that had thereby been deprived of all control over the press.[16]

[13] *New York Times Co. v. U.S.* (403 US, 413) (1971). But see Simon Lee, *Judging Judges* (London: Faber and Faber, 1988), chap. 15, 110–19, and his *"Spycatcher," The Times* (London), 14 August 1987, for a defense of the judiciary.
[14] Lee, *Judging Judges*, and Geoffrey Robertson, *Freedom, the Individual and the Law*, 6th ed. (Harmondsworth, Eng.: Penguin Books, 1989), 263–5, 289–90.
[15] Peter Wright, *Spycatcher* (New York: Viking, 1987).
[16] Ewing and Gearty, *Freedom Under Thatcher*, 197–8.

In this chapter, I have not tried to draw up a comprehensive list of issues addressed by the Bill of Rights in order to contrast the ways these issues are dealt with in British and American practice. Still less have I tried to trace all these differences to their roots in British and American political culture, jurisprudence, and political philosophy. The sheer quantity of material would make such a project the work of a lifetime.[17] A less obvious reason for not embarking on any such project ought to be mentioned in passing, however. In many areas comparison is pointless because the British have for years taken no interest in the specific freedoms established in the U.S. Bill of Rights. Take the formerly vexed issue of religious liberty. The First Amendment prohibits the creation of an established church. Britain, by contrast, has not just one but *two* established churches, because the Church of England is established in England and the Presbyterian Church in Scotland. There are public arguments aplenty about the place of religious knowledge in the school curriculum; there have lately been intense arguments about the extent to which non-Christian religions should be protected by the (largely unenforced) laws against blasphemy and seditious libel that protect the Christianity of the Church of England.[18] The mere existence of an established church causes little or no comment.[19]

Whether this silence reflects a lack of interest in religious liberty is a moot point. The British, like Europeans generally, are less likely to profess any religious belief and much less likely to attend any place of worship than are the inhabitants of the United States.[20] This lack of religious commitment is not in itself evidence of a lack of concern for freedom of religious choice but a manifestation of a certain skepticism about the value of legislating for a rigorous separation of church and state. The British believe that liberal religious attitudes are more readily promoted by establishing a church that nobody takes much notice of than by constitutionally prohibiting the mingling of church and state. The latter incites fanatical secularists to agitate for the right of Jews and atheists

---

[17] Geoffrey Robertson, *Freedom, the Individual and the Law* is the classic source; this is the successor to the late Harry Street's book of the same title, and a work that, over twenty-five years, has become a sort of legal conscience to the British.

[18] This is a smoldering issue lately inflamed by the Rushdie affair. For a dramatic account see W. J. Weatherby, *Salman Rushdie: Sentenced to Death* (New York: Carroll and Graf, 1990).

[19] I must qualify this statement by observing that the 1990 conference of the Social and Liberal Democrats did indeed call for the disestablishment of the church. *The Observer* (London), 23 September 1990.

[20] *Gallup Report* (Princeton, N.J., 1990), no. 288, 15–17.

not to pay for the Christmas decorations of Christians, an agitation that may square with the letter of the law but is also unmannerly social behavior.[21]

Legislation for separation excites others to try to expel from the classroom even those elements of religious instruction that would allow children to locate themselves in the cultural tradition in which they happen to have been born and would render Western art, architecture, music, and poetry rather more intelligible than they generally are. These efforts predictably incite fundamentalists to try to bring bigotry back into the classroom, and so relentlessly on. Such conflicts seem to most Britons a high price to pay for the absence of an established church. No doubt many Americans think the British equally wrong-headed. Whatever the truth on this particular matter, the point remains that there is no simple way of mapping British concerns even onto the literal wording of the Bill of Rights, let alone onto what the Bill of Rights has become under judicial reinterpretation.

The theme that runs through this chapter is that British and American attitudes to individual rights differ in innumerable ways that Britons and Americans rarely notice until they are brought up against the contrast.[22] It may or may not be significant that Americans are citizens of the United States, whereas Britons are subjects of Her Majesty the Queen. It seems at all events to be true that the British are more trusting of government, more willing to see governments act, and less quick to insist on their rights. Many years ago, *The Civic Culture* dressed up the common-sense thought that the British expect governments to govern, whereas Americans expect them to respect the rights of the citizenry, by awarding British respondents to its questions on "democratic competence" strikingly high marks for "subject competence" and less strikingly lower marks for "citizen competence." Unsurprisingly, American respondents did better on "citizen competence" and less well on "subject competence."[23] The burden of my argument is that Britain has not had a "culture of rights" in the sense in which the United States has had, but that over the past twenty years Britain has been acquiring elements of such a culture, provoked by

[21] As in the notorious case of repeated court battles over the display of a Christmas crèche and a Hanukkah menorah in public places in Pittsburgh.

[22] Americans are horrified to discover that there is no right of assembly or free speech in British law. The British are startled by the American view that whenever anything goes wrong somebody's rights must have been violated.

[23] Gabriel Almond and Sidney Verba, *The Civic Culture* (Boston: Little, Brown, 1965), 173.

political events, as well as by developments in international law and the legal framework of the European Community, and by some more or less autonomous developments in political theory and jurisprudence.

THE UNMETAPHYSICAL BRITISH

It is these thoughts about the contrast between British and American politics and jurisprudence that the body of this chapter will develop. Generalizations about the "spirit" of a nation's politics are always unwise. Still, it is hard to resist the thought that British politics has had a distinctive character shaped by the common sense of British jurisprudence and political philosophy and shaping, in turn, the practice of British politicians and judges. This character has been passionate in its attachment to legal or customary rights and friendlier to individual eccentricity and nonconformity than American social and legal theory and political culture have been. Yet alongside this practical attachment to individual liberty, there has been widespread skepticism of any attempt to found politics on a constitution embodying natural rights, whether these are understood as the dictates of reason, the laws of God, or rules inscribed in human hearts.[24] The philosophical apparatus and the targets of the skeptics have varied, but the hostility has been constant.

This skepticism has been common currency across the political spectrum, employed both to curb the enthusiasms of the radical and to undermine the resistance of the conservative. Burke remains the patron of conservative skeptics. He famously complained that he had never encountered "man" and could make no sense of the rights of man; Frenchmen, Americans, and Englishmen enjoyed and ought to enjoy many rights guaranteed to them by their own political and legal systems, but that was another matter. If the rights of Britons were sacred, it was because there were good reasons for treating the settled rights enjoyed in all political societies as sacred, not because they were also "Rights of Man."[25] Radical skeptics have been as common as conservatives. Bentham and Mill held religious and political views very different from Burke's, but were equally unwilling to found their political theory on

---

[24] See Louis Hartz, *The Liberal Tradition in America* (New York: Harcourt Brace, 1955), 9–17, for repeated reminders of the way American liberalism has been hostile to the "diversity" that English liberalism and conservatism both fostered.

[25] Edmund Burke, *Reflections on the Revolution in France* (Garden City, N.Y.: Doubleday, 1961), 71ff.

natural rights. Whereas Burke thought that radicals would undermine the customary rights, especially the property rights, of those whose rights were already well entrenched, Bentham and Mill thought that the well entrenched would mistake their local and accidental entitlements for the dictates of eternal reason and natural law.[26] To distinguish sharply between nature and custom was the first step toward treating the legal system as something to be shaped and reshaped for rational purposes.

We must not exaggerate the extent to which this skepticism united radicals and conservatives. Conservative hostility to theories of natural rights has differed from the hostility of radicals like Bentham in one very crucial respect. The common law has been revered by conservatives and treated with suspicion by radicals. Doubts about natural law and natural rights thus look very different from different sides of the political debate. Radicals dislike the way conservatives pass off the common law as a branch of the law of nature, whereas conservatives dislike the way radicals contrast the local, traditional, judge-developed common law with the universal, eternal natural law that is inscribed in every bosom, not only in the bosoms of the judges. When both deplore appeals to natural rights, therefore, they are not always deploring the same thing.

A further complicating factor in offering any quick account of the differences between British and American attitudes toward bills of rights in general and the U.S. Bill of Rights in particular is the way in which those attitudes have changed over time. The emphasis in the academic literature on the differences between British and U.S. jurisprudence is quite novel, as is the current emphasis on the U.S. Bill of Rights and its political role. Whatever the rhetoric surrounding the achievement of independence and the creation of the U.S. Constitution, the British and the Americans seem for a long time to have taken much the same view of the genesis and status of bills of rights. Commentators thought that such bills encapsulated liberties and privileges that were antecedently secured by the common law but had come under attack and expected such bills particularly to stress liberties recently under threat from overweening monarchs. They did not think that they had any more special standing than that. The way the Supreme Court treated civil liberties cases until the 1950s did little to suggest that it held a different view.

In the eyes of British commentators, British and American law stood

---

[26] J. S. Mill, *Utilitarianism, Liberty, and Representative Government* (London: Dent, 1912), 69.

together as traditionalist, common-law systems quite different in character from rationalist continental legal systems. The continental legal systems were not founded on the thought that citizens already had rights embodied in the common law, but on the thought that citizens had those rights that an authoritative legal code gave them. A. V. Dicey spent many years popularizing this view. He did not merely identify British and American theory and practice; he could hardly contain his sense that continental Europe was at best digging its way out of a tyrannical darkness into which Britain and America had never fallen. In Dicey's view, the British had always possessed a great many rights, and the Americans had inherited them. The British and the Americans took it for granted that authority had legal limits, that there were things that kings, courtiers, and even parliaments could not do; Europeans with a long history of absolute monarchy had to resort to fragile rationalist devices to effect the same results. It is a recent development, sparked by the more adventurous jurisprudence of the Supreme Court after *Brown,* that assimilates American and European practice, leaving Britain in lonely isolation.[27]

The recent academic view of the U.S. Constitution in general and the Bill of Rights in particular has stressed the defense of *individual* rights to the exclusion of everything else, as if the U.S. Bill of Rights embodies something like the moral theory of Immanuel Kant and as if its political purpose is to ensure that governments treat individuals as "ends in themselves." The common law has always been inhospitable to this kind of individualism, however, and this has meant that there is some tension between what present-day commentators tell us the Bill of Rights means and any plausible historical account of its genesis and its place in the legal system of its own time.[28] Nor is there much scope to resolve this tension by analysis of the document itself. If the French Declaration of the Rights of Man and of the Citizen is indeed a rationalist document animated by moral individualism in the way the English Declaration of Rights of 1689 was not and the U.S. Bill of Rights may not have been, appeal to the text alone cannot demonstrate this. As a historical matter it thus remains an open question whether the U.S. Bill of Rights embodied the modern theory of individual rights or not. As a philosophical matter it is an equally open question how far an adequate theory of judicial interpretation allows judges, lawyers, and the citizenry to ignore historical

---

[27] See A. V. Dicey, *The Law of the Constitution,* 9th ed. (London: Macmillan, 1939), 200n.
[28] Dworkin's various accounts are canonical; *Taking Rights Seriously,* 2d ed. (London: Duckworth, 1978) offers innumerable illustrations.

origins in deciding the contemporary meaning of the law.[29] These questions are a reflection in history and philosophy of the political argument between believers in "original intent" and those who think judges may interpret the text creatively and in the light of present needs.

The French Declaration of the Rights of Man and of the Citizen plainly did embody from the beginning a modern, individualistic, conception of natural rights, as well as a more sweeping view of the state's authority than anything the American Founders would have tolerated. Unsurprisingly, post–World War II declarations of human rights, such as the European Convention on Human Rights, have steered clear of metaphysical questions. They have aspired to become part of the fundamental positive law of the signatory states. The new terminology of human rights implies that these rights possess that status without commitment to their ultimate metaphysical, philosophical, or theological standing.[30]

How sharp is the distinction between the common-law vision of a bill of rights and the natural law? In one respect, not very sharp. The common law employs the idea of "natural justice," in the sense of rules of justice that require no particular legal framework for their justification and are implicit in almost all procedures for doing justice. Blackstone's account of the way divine law and natural law underpin common law depends on the existence of these rules of natural justice for its plausibility, and both judges and sovereigns have in their time appealed to a view of that connection very like Blackstone's. In other respects, the difference is marked. The common law's root principle is tradition rather than nature; when it appeals to nature it is to natural law rather than individual natural rights. The common law is based less on rights than on rules, forms of action, and procedures for arriving at right decisions, and their naturalness has less to do with reason than with reasonableness.

Constitutional interpretation in Britain has always operated differently from the interpretation of the continental codes over the past two centuries within which declarations of rights have recently found their natural and usual place. British constitutional writers find themselves discussing cases such as *Bushell's Case* (1670), which established the right of juries to return whatever verdict their consciences dictated and

---

[29] Ronald Dworkin, *Law's Empire* (Cambridge, Mass.: Harvard University Press, 1987), 68ff.

[30] Paul Sieghart, *The Lawful Rights of Mankind* (Oxford: Oxford University Press, 1985), ix–xi; and James W. Nickel, *Making Sense of Human Rights* (Berkeley: University of California Press, 1987).

is thus fundamental to the right of trial by jury, or *Entick* v. *Carrington* (1768), which established the immunity to unwarrantable search and seizure later enshrined in the Fourth Amendment.[31] They do not discuss large principles and admissible exceptions to them.

To a writer like Dicey, this jurisprudential tradition was an aspect of the good fortune of the British. Without a written constitution, the British had more rights than others, and they were more secure in their possession of them. It was the spirit, custom, and temper of the country, with its long history of devotion to its particular customary rights, Dicey believed, that ensured that the rule of law prevailed:

> We may say that the constitution is pervaded by the rule of law on the ground that the general principles of the constitution (as for example the right to personal liberty, or the right of public meeting) are with us the result of judicial decisions determining the rights of private persons in particular cases brought before the courts; whereas under many foreign constitutions, the security (such as it is) given to individuals results, or appears to result, from the general principles of the constitution.

Dicey agreed that foreigners "have often been in nowise to blame" for starting with abstract principles and deriving rights from them, but he was quite clear that the British had done better with their inductive, common-law, judge-made tradition.[32]

Dicey's discussion confirms that when appeals to the common law were the vehicle of resistance to arbitrary royal power in England, these episodes of resistance did not reflect the individualistic, rationalistic, and liberal distrust of authority that was embodied in appeals to the "rights of man." There is thus a double contrast: first, a contrast between the attitudes embodied in the English Declaration of Rights of 1689 and the attitudes embodied in the U.S. Bill of Rights; and, second, a contrast between the outlook these two documents share and the outlook of the French declarations. Dicey was right that the English Declaration of Rights of 1689 and the U.S. Bill of Rights were similar insofar as they took their shape from the activities of government that they wished to stop, and they were different insofar as the American Declaration of Independence had relied on Enlightenment doctrines of individual natural rights that were later to be reflected in the Constitution as well. Because these philosophical doctrines dropped out of sight when judges began to

---

[31] Even before the Incitement to Disaffection Act of 1934, it was widely agreed that *Entick* v. *Carrington* had been substantially qualified by statutory exceptions. See note 69 below.
[32] Dicey, *Law of the Constitution*, 197–8.

apply the law to the cases before them, it seemed to Dicey that Britain and the United States remained on one side of the larger divide, while continental legal systems remained on the other.[33]

THE SOCIAL CONTRACT AND ITS PROBLEMS

There is still one important and long-standing difference between the British and the American political and legal cultures. A highly individualistic and contractarian conception of legitimacy underpins much American thinking but has not in the same way taken root in Britain. American political theorists and jurists have since the foundation thought naturally and easily of government authority as something granted by the citizenry on terms that included the protection of preexisting rights, and thus as something to be withdrawn if the government violated those rights. I do not mean that American legal philosophers and political theorists have naively subscribed to the Lockean theory of the social contract. They have for all that subscribed to an essentially contractual conception of authority; within that conception, the role of a bill of rights in setting out the terms of the contract between rulers and ruled is obvious.[34]

British legal and political theory has not been wholly anticontractual. British monarchs take a coronation oath, and for many hundreds of years holders of public office, the incumbents of clerical livings, and the Fellows of Oxford and Cambridge colleges, all had to take various oaths before they were admitted to office. The ancient and uncontractual conception of the English realm as an organic unity of king, lords, and commons thus coexisted with a habit of asking for loyalty oaths and with a highly developed legal system within which the law of contract occupied a prominent place. Yet, British writers have done what they could to draw the individualistic and potentially anarchic teeth of contractualism.

Thus Burke agreed that society was founded on a contract, and promptly argued that it was for such exalted purposes that no individual could decide that it had been broken.[35] Hobbes created a sovereign by

---

[33] Ibid., 200n.

[34] Louis Hartz's *American Liberal Tradition* treats as inescapable and as deeply embedded in the American culture and psyche what Herbert Croly's *Promise of American Life* (Evanston, Ill.: Northwestern University Press, 1989) deplored as a simple-minded Jeffersonian liberalism. Both exaggerate: Croly and Hartz were not at all intimidated by the extreme individualism of their fellow countrymen. Still, they exaggerate what is genuinely there; they do not fabricate an image out of nothing.

[35] Burke, *Reflections,* 110–11.

contract and ensured that the sovereign was never in a position to be accused of breach of contract; once entered into, it was a contract that bound the subjects and not the sovereign.[36] Hume, Bentham, Mill, and the English Idealists simply denied that contractual notions played any useful part in explaining political authority.[37]

The contrast with American conceptions of government legitimacy then comes through very clearly. In 1908, Herbert Croly lamented the difficulty of persuading Americans to see that government existed to further a common good, not to protect the idea of "equality for all, privilege for none."[38] Americans today, eighty years later, point out with more or less enthusiasm that American governments are authorized to pursue the common good only within a framework of indefeasible rights.[39] The relative failure of this individualism and contractualism to dominate in Britain has, in contrast, allowed a broadbrush conception of authority as founded on the pursuit of the common good to prevail. Such a conception leaves wide open the question of how far the pursuit of the collective good should be constrained by the rights of individuals.

In fact it has not been difficult to defuse the tension between a concern for rights and a concern for the common good. The establishment of proper legal protection is generally an important element in the common good. Radical utilitarians applaud positive legal rights as conventional devices that give individuals security for themselves and render the behavior of others predictable and unthreatening. Radicals demand deliberate legislation that achieves these ends more effectively and for more people; conservatives claim that the process of unplanned evolution by which the common law adapts to the life of the citizenry, assisted only at the margin by statutory invention, will do more than a bill of rights for the liberty and happiness of the subject. All parties take it for granted that the task of government is to use its power for the public good— even if conservatives think this task requires the government *not* to alter present arrangements. Nobody believes that this pursuit should be constrained by rights originating in some other conception of the proper tasks of government.

No brisk sketch of such contrasts can carry very much conviction. All I want to say is that British *anti*contractualism and British antipathy to

[36] Thomas Hobbes, *Leviathan* (London: Dent & Co., 1961), 90–2.
[37] Mill, *Utilitarianism, Liberty, and Representative Government*, 71.
[38] Croly, *Promise of American Life*, 57–63.
[39] Dworkin, *Taking Rights Seriously*.

the idea that the preexisting rights of man set limits to government authority have been the conventional wisdom. Conservatives who loathe Bentham's utilitarianism settle for Burke's; socialists who loathe Burke's defense of property and prescription look beyond the rights of labor to the consensual pursuit of a socialist common good. American students of British politics find it hard not to flinch at this failure to take rights seriously; many British writers have boasted of it. Others have taken rights seriously but would have been appalled at what recent writers have thought this required. Dicey thought he took rights perfectly seriously, but he would never have accepted Ronald Dworkin's view that we can take rights seriously only in something like the modern welfare state.

Although one must not exaggerate the differences in outcomes between the British and American political orders, it is worth recalling what a difference in political tactics the differences in ideology and structure impose. I learned my political allegiances and my political theory during the 1950s; I have always thought that the only ultimate security for political rights is a liberal political culture. I have never trusted the judiciary to protect the political rights of the ordinary citizen, but have assumed that if one wanted the liberalization of existing legislation about access to government information, the censorship of plays, films, and books, the legality of homosexuality, police powers of arrest and detention, the powers of the security services, and other civil liberties issues, one had to persuade the major political parties to bring forward appropriate legislation.[40] Letter writing and agitating in the media, or even in the streets, might be required to achieve the desired end, but these were matters for political action and decision, not for bodies detached from politics and *au delà de la mêlée*. The legal donkey work by the National Association for the Advancement of Colored People after the war and before *Brown* has no analogue in Britain. Conversely, no Briton would suffer the frustration of an American reformer competing with endless other interest and pressure groups and never quite knowing how much influence any given legislator might have on any given result.

---

[40] We were wrong. Under Roy Jenkins's benign gaze as home secretary, it was private members who secured the liberalization of the laws on abortion and homosexuality and abolished the jurisdiction of the lord chamberlain over what went on on stage. Both major parties were terrified of alienating their activists—on the one side, Tory ladies in flowery hats who called for hanging and flogging to be reintroduced, and on the other side, Catholic voters whose economic interests made them natural Labour voters and whose cultural allegiances inclined them elsewhere. The situation had many affinities with contemporary U.S. politics.

British reformers thus look to elect the "right" party and rely on its ability to push a reforming program through Parliament. What this reliance on prime ministerial, cabinet, and party authority leaves out is what a bill of rights puts in. There is a danger that even the "right" kind of government will act illiberally—or at least with too little respect for individual rights.[41] There is a risk that *all* governments may succumb to similar pathologies, such as an undue credulity about what their security services tell them about supposed dissidents, or an inability to see that the investigative press whose efforts they lauded in opposition has not become malign when it keeps up the same investigative efforts once they are in power. Like many people whose political views have always been those of the center-left, I have come to think that even though a bill of rights cannot enforce itself, and will surely be sabotaged by judges with an undue tenderness for the executive, Britain now needs such a charter.

Some writers suppose that the statutory protection of civil rights is essential for political reasons; they suppose that the British electorate will in future elect a government of the left only if it pledges itself to such a charter. Others think Britain ought to display its attachment to human rights by following the rest of Europe in incorporating the European Convention into British law.[42] I think, rather, that it is because the British political system weights the scales in favor of the executive, and provides few counterweights in Parliament, that even an imperfect, judiciary-dependent method of redressing that balance in favor of the ordinary citizen would be valuable. Still, I have only qualified hopes for, let us say, the effect of incorporating the European Convention on Human Rights into British domestic law, and the skepticism I have come to abandon may come over more eloquently than the views I have come to hold. That is an artifact of my age and political experience; unabashed centrists twenty years younger would be more optimistic about the prospects for securing a British bill of rights and about the good it would do, whereas diehard members of the Labour party twenty years older will treat all this as academic nonsense.

---

[41] It was a Labour home secretary who deported the American journalists Agee and Hosenball, a Labour attorney general who allowed surreptitious jury vetting by the police and prosecution, and a Labour government that employed the Official Secrets Act against the *Daily Telegraph* journalist Jonathan Aitken. See Geoffrey Robertson, *Freedom, the Individual and the Law*, 326–7 (Agee and Hosenball), 300–1 (jury vetting), 134 (Aitken).

[42] In fact, Australia and Canada also offer examples of what is needed, as well as grounds for anxiety. Ewing and Gearty, *Freedom Under Thatcher*, 260–9.

In the next section of this chapter, I argue briskly that the standard vision of British liberty has always more or less ignored the Declaration of Rights of 1689—although it was the model for the U.S. Bill of Rights—and on that foundation launch into my main theme, that Britain has always been attached to parliamentary supremacy and a strong executive, and has until recently flourished under that mixture. I then go on to express my doubts about how adequate that political recipe is today.

"BRITISH LIBERTY" AND THE NONHISTORY OF THE DECLARATION OF RIGHTS

It is an old British habit to invent industrial techniques that are then exploited more successfully by foreign competitors. One might add the Declaration of Rights of 1689 to the list of inventions made in Britain and then forgotten. At all events, the century from 1689 to 1789 was not one in which the British spent much time debating the literal terms of the Declaration of Rights or its underlying conceptual implications. Victorian Whig writers like Macaulay held the Glorious Revolution of 1688 to be glorious just because it was the last revolution the British needed to make. In the eighteenth century, Blackstone praised its success in balancing the powers of Commons, lords, and monarch and in securing the independence of the judiciary.[43] Both Blackstone and Macaulay thought the revolution had created a constitution capable of producing from within its own resources all further changes needed for its own perfection. In this, they provided a model for subsequent American self-congratulation. The liberties of the British that the Glorious Revolution had secured were recognized to be limited. It secured, on Blackstone's reading, a balance of power that meant that no part of the political system could arrogate absolute power. What the unwritten constitution could not do was set out a list of the fundamental rights of the subject.

More surprisingly, neither did the Declaration of Rights when it was finally passed by Parliament and signed into law by William III in 1689. Although it certainly listed a number of rights the Crown was forbidden to abrogate, the list was very selective, and its purpose of restricting the freedom of the sovereign was much more evident than any notion of liberating the "individual." In form, the declaration opened in the manner of the U.S. Declaration of Independence by listing the misdeeds of "the

---

[43] Quoted in ibid., 4.

late King James the Second," who "by the Assistance of diverse evill Councellors Judges and Ministers imployed by him did endeavour to subvert and extirpate the Protestant Religion and the Laws and Liberties of this Kingdome."[44] It continued with a list of rights that simply parallels the illegalities of James II. Of that list, the right to petition the king and the prohibition on excessive bail, excessive fines, and "cruell and unusuall Punishments" are the closest relatives of the U.S. Bill of Rights. The prohibition on "raising or keeping a Standing Army within the Kingdome in time of Peace unless it be with the Consent of Parlyament" and the declaration that "the Subjects which are Protestants may have Arms for their Defense suitable to their Conditions and as allowed by Law" reflect the complaint that James II had created a standing army and disbanded Protestant militias so that when the time came to return Britain to the Roman Catholic fold, there should be no resistance.[45]

If the U.S. Constitution, including the Bill of Rights, is primarily concerned with ensuring that the federal government should have enough but not too much power, the English Declaration of Rights was above all a statement of the terms of the settlement with William and Mary that put an end to the constitutional interregnum. In that sense, and perhaps only in that sense, it was functionally similar to its American successor. In much else, it was not. There is here no thought of avoiding a national religious establishment, for instance. The declaration was particularly concerned to secure that Britain remained a Protestant country; a large part of the text concerns the form of the coronation oath and the new monarch's declaration against the doctrine of transubstantiation.[46]

The other major concern of the Declaration of Rights was the balance of power between king and Parliament, and here, too, it was unlike its American successor in looking less to achieve a balance than to settle the issue in favor of Parliament. As for the rights of the individual citizen, the declaration ensured that future monarchs could not discriminate against Protestants in favor of Catholics. It did not settle the question of the toleration of dissenters, who found their social position, political rights, and religious freedoms intermittently worsened once the new regime was established. Catholics were decisively excluded from political life, and Jews remained excluded.

---

[44] Charles Grant Robertson, *Select Statutes, Cases and Documents,* 2d ed. (London: Methuen, 1913).
[45] Ibid., 133.
[46] Ibid., 135ff.

Readers looking for the antecedents of the U.S. Bill of Rights are often surprised by the declaration's provision that future monarchs have *no* right to exempt Catholics from penal legislation. Dicey ingeniously suggested that in establishing the rule of law—in Dicey's sense of the subordination of everyone to the law—it was appropriate to curtail the royal power of exempting anyone from its rigors.[47] This is fair comment, but it is a reminder that the rule of law can be consistent with a high degree of illiberalism.

American writers sometimes observe with surprise that it is only in the twentieth century that the U.S. Bill of Rights has really come into its own. In that respect the first century-and-a-half of the history of the United States was not unlike the history of Hanoverian Britain. Political writers of the eighteenth century wrote at length about the success—or lack of it—of the revolutionary settlement in bringing liberty to the British. Generally, they did so without treating the Declaration of Rights as especially important. Dissenters came closest because they naturally concentrated on the final settlement's failure to enshrine religious liberty in the law.[48] Other critics of the new political and social settlement complained that it was insufficiently free, but not because they thought it violated the natural rights of dissenters and their like. "Country party" Whigs, for instance, whose "country" label suggests their hostility to what went on in London and under the influence of the court, saw Britain heading for corruption and absolute monarchy. They certainly thought British liberty was in danger. They deplored the creation of a standing army, even though Britain was so rarely at peace that its creation never flouted the letter of the Declaration of Rights. Otherwise, they concentrated on the corrupting effects of the national debt, the inflationary dangers of the newly chartered Bank of England, and the court's resulting ability to subvert the independence of Parliament by bribery and jobbery. None of these was mentioned in the Declaration of Rights, and the threat to freedom that they posed was more subtle than anything the declaration envisaged.

These "corrupt" activities were arguably much less of a threat to freedom than James II's tampering with the courts had been. Indeed, David Hume produced a sophisticated account of the revolution's success that incorporated a positive defense of the new corruption. He argued

---

[47] Dicey, *Law of the Constitution,* 193n.
[48] The Toleration Act of 1694 gave some relief to Trinitarian Dissenters, but this was never extended to Unitarians and was eroded by successive acts against occasional conformity.

that Britain now enjoyed a kind of liberty that had been unknown in the ancient or medieval world, but was wholly appropriate to the modern world. It rested on the cheerful adaptability to a modern market economy that he baptized "the brisk march of the spirits."[49] Hume never thought that this new freedom had much to do with entrenching a fixed list of rights and immunities. The prosperous, unideological society that had grown up under the Hanoverian settlement would preserve the liberty on which prosperity depended and would avoid "the friar, the stake and the gibbet" of Catholic Europe. Moderate liberty was protected by a balance of social forces that prevented the Crown from dominating the representatives of the common people and prevented the common people from establishing the kind of tumultuous democracy that had ruined ancient Athens. It was a balancing act whose future was not entirely predictable, and for all his liberalism, Hume held that if things went wrong and the balance was lost, better the moderate, absolute monarchy of France than a passionate democracy and Cromwell's Commonwealth.[50]

In this scenario, Whig values find a home, although Whig myths do not. What the enemies of James II had achieved in 1688–89 was valuable, even though their belief that James II had broken any kind of contract with his subjects was absurd. The stability, predictability, security of property, and avoidance of cruelty that Whig constitutionalism valued were, indeed, valuable. But they were not valuable because they were part of the original contract or because they were dictates of natural law or of God or reason; their value was essentially utilitarian. Reasonable people wish to live in a society in which these values are sustained and where they can live in peace. What such persons are unlikely to feel is that any one of these values is so sacred that it demands a fanatical adherence. "Liberty or death" is not a Humean thought.[51]

Hume's sophisticated account of the success of the regime that the Glorious Revolution had put in place hardly needed to refer to its character as a revolution, and even less to the role of the Declaration of Rights. It was the moderation and law-abidingness of Hanoverian Britain that were impressive, not the fiction that the English had recovered their natural rights by ejecting the tyrannical James II. In the late nineteenth

---

[49] David Hume, *Essays, Moral, Political, and Literary* (Oxford: Oxford University Press, 1963), 485–6.
[50] Ibid., 496–7, and 53.
[51] Ibid., 29ff.

century Dicey made the same case.[52] He was a more sober stylist than Hume and less eager to mock the historiography of the Whigs. Still, Dicey's history is not Lockean and his language not that of the social contract. The British enjoyed the blessings of liberty, but not because their natural rights were respected. They were free because they might do whatever it was not unlawful to do; thanks to the good sense and liberalism of the British political temper, the range of what was not unlawful was wider in Britain than in almost any other country. Britain was governed by the "rule of law," but what the rule of law meant was that nobody could be punished *without* having broken a definite law, and that nobody was above the law.[53]

The rule of law left parliamentary supremacy intact. Parliament could pass laws on absolutely anything it might choose, and no court was competent to declare its acts invalid. It is in the acceptance of that fact that the great breach between British and American practice lies. In calm conditions, most people were happy to believe that Parliament was too sensible to pass liberticide laws, that judges would find some way of drawing their sting if Parliament did pass them, and that juries would dig in their heels if judges did not. In calm conditions these complacent beliefs were not put to the test.

In less calm conditions, the British experienced the desire for a new beginning that animated the American revolutionaries. Nor is it surprising in the light of their shared traditions that British radicals appealed for the restoration of their natural rights and their embodiment in the law of the land. Even then, Britain and America remained far apart in their hopes for the subsequent protection of their freedom. Until very recently, nobody on the British left would have thought of the judiciary as the guardians of civil liberties. In troubled times, the British judiciary usually sided with the conservative instincts of the government of the day rather than with a popular desire for change.[54] If judges were not to be a threat to the liberties of the ordinary Briton, they would have to be constrained by positive legislation that allowed very little room for judicial interpretation. That brings us back to a running theme of this chapter, the way

---

[52] Dicey, *Law of the Constitution*, 183ff.

[53] Ibid., 189, quoting Montesquieu's dictum, "La liberté est le droit de faire tout ce que les lois permettent."

[54] A representative instance is the Treason Trial of 1794. See any account of the life and times of William Godwin, who did much to discredit Chief Justice Eyre's attempt to extend the law of treason to every attempt to demand parliamentary reform, for example, Don Locke, *A Fantasy of Reason* (London: Routledge, 1982), 77–85.

in which radical energies in Britain focused not on arguments about rights, but on the need to put new governments in power and for them to produce new legislation.

LEGAL POSITIVISM AND RIGHTS

Bentham was eager to give constitutions to almost anyone who asked for one. He was a defender of codification, and wanted to give every citizen a digest of his rights and duties. Yet Bentham's argument for codification is not an argument for a bill of rights, *as interpreted by the judiciary,* and Bentham deplored the American taste for rights.[55] A constitution that evaded the question of where sovereignty lay invited endless squabbling and would give excessive power to the lawyers who moderated such squabbles. The American break with Britain was good for everyone, because the British Empire was a waste of money, and the Americans would govern themselves better than they would be governed from Westminster. It did not follow that the American *theory* of government was to be admired. A superstitious belief in the "government of laws not of men" would end in the government of lawyers, not men. That American politics was harmed by its obsession with rights is not only a British view; Herbert Croly and many American commentators have had doubts about their role in American political life. Still, it is impressive that so standard a criticism of American political ideology and practice should come so early in the history of the Republic and from a radical. The only sound theoretical basis of government in Bentham's view was a clear understanding that rights were the gift of the sovereign and that an acceptable sovereign would make a gift of utility-promoting rights. The way this fostered freedom was simply that the best way to bestow this gift was often by doing nothing, or at least by doing nothing more than preventing the ill-intentioned from interfering with the freedom of their fellow citizens.

J. S. Mill never broke with this analysis. *Utilitarianism* and *On Liberty* discuss rights at length, but Mill emphasized that these were not natural rights.[56] Mill was ready to talk about moral rights, understood as interests of such importance that society ought to secure them to us by peculiarly

[55] H. L. A. Hart, "Bentham and the United States of America," in *1776: The Revolution in Social Thought,* ed. Ronald H. Coase (Chicago: University of Chicago Press, 1979), 555–6, 561–2.

[56] Mill, *Utilitarianism, Liberty, and Representative Government,* 71.

stringent rules.[57] This allowed him to do what Bentham neither did, nor could do, nor wished to do, and that was to base his political philosophy on a genuine moral individualism, as opposed to the computational individualism implied in utilitarianism. But Mill remained a legal positivist; he put no more faith in lawyers than Bentham had done and never suggested that liberty would be best protected by a bill of rights and an energetic judiciary. Yet, Mill knew many American liberals and shared their political and social anxieties. He was interested in the effect of legal and political institutions in just the way the American Founders had been, and he shared the fear of popular despotism that led them to set up a constitution with an elaborate separation of powers and to entrench a bill of rights. His hopes for and fears of democracy in Britain were strongly influenced by what he thought he knew of the United States. Like Jefferson and Tocqueville, Mill feared the tyranny of the majority and had no difficulty understanding the concept of elective despotism. His *Considerations on Representative Government* show how fertile he was in devising institutional checks on the power of the numerical majority. Proportional representation and a parliament with no power to *make,* as distinct from the power to *approve or disapprove,* law was one element. The expertise of bureaucrats, the protection of disinterested intelligence, the erection of obstacles to any majority that threatened to form itself into a compact mass—these were Mill's remedies. To the modern American eye, a bill of rights and judicial review are conspicuous by their absence.[58]

One result of the very different American and British attitudes to written constitutions, judicial review, and reforming interpretations of a bill of rights is a difference in the academic jurisprudence of constitutional interpretation. There are institutional reasons for some of these differences. Mill addressed an audience of liberal intellectuals, practitioners of the higher journalism, politicians, and public servants; the professorial elite of Harvard Law School address their former students now serving on the bench or clerking for those who serve on the bench. Mill thus addressed a political elite while his American successors address a judicial elite. But when all institutional differences are taken into account, there remains the difference between the American taste for discovering new rights in old places and the British skepticism about that process.

---

[57] Ibid., 132.
[58] Ibid., 256ff.

It would be pointlessly repetitive to offer a condensed history of the way legal positivism developed in English jurisprudence after the utilitarian radicals. One qualification ought perhaps to be added to what I have said. I have suggested that enthusiasts for bills of rights are often moved by a belief in natural rights and that legal positivists are skeptical about their value. I must add that there can be no question of any logical connection here. It is easy to imagine the connection running quite differently. A believer in natural rights might insist that we should allow the judiciary to discover our rights by the light of experience and reason, and insist that they need no document to guide them. A positivist might follow Tom Paine in declaring that he did not know what his rights were until he had seen them in print, and that he wanted to see the most important ones written down with particular clarity.

Still the fact remains that since 1945 legal positivists have had to defend themselves against the charge of "not taking rights seriously" enough.[59] The charge can be generalized into a national accusation: British jurisprudence is attached to a positivist conception of law that reflects the British tradition of parliamentary supremacy, judicial reticence, and a noncontractarian, unindividualist conception of law. This tradition cannot say anything convincing about our rights, and does not know how to draw on the law in the interest of members of society who have escaped the notice of legislators. Whether this is an argument for a jurisprudence built upon natural law is another matter. It is certainly a call for an expansive jurisprudence and a criticism of its opposite.

Reconciling positivism and natural law. It is for other essayists in this volume to say anything informed about issues in American jurisprudence strictly considered. Here I shall say a little about the way a positivist may respond to the complaint that positivism gives too narrow an account of the law and fails to understand the role in American constitutional practice of the principles essential to the preservation of equal liberty.[60] Insofar as this is nothing more than the complaint that the positivist does not believe that natural law lies behind constitutional law and natural right behind the Bill of Rights, the positivist would think there was no case to answer. The essence of legal positivism is the claim that law is

---

[59] Notably, of course, by Ronald Dworkin in the book of that title.

[60] It is a striking characteristic of Professor Dworkin's work, however, that he believes there is some *via tertia* between positivism and natural law, and that his theory of interpretation walks it.

generated by human lawgivers and human institutions. Insofar as it is
the complaint that positivism cannot account for the way in which moral
principles enter into the law and determine what judges will count as
law, and courts will enforce as law, positivists are likely to be conciliatory—that is, they are prepared to agree that in the interpretation of the
letter of the law judges employ principles of "reasonableness" that overlap with the precepts of natural law, and that when judges decide what
rights the parties to cases have they will have an eye to the point of the
law. That point will often include the aim of securing many of the rights
that theorists have labeled "natural" rights.[61]

The natural hazards of human existence—such as our vulnerability to
violence, our dislike of uncertainty, and our need to see to our physical
survival—explain our need for rules to prevent force and fraud and to
establish property and regulate its acquisition and transfer. The same
need will surely generate laws about marriage and the family, and the
dangers of ideological conflict may very well generate laws about the
public practice of religion. Unlike traditional theories of natural law,
however, this account of what is "natural" in the law does not favor
monogamy over polygamy, monandry over polyandry, and does not favor
freedom of religion over an ecclesiastical establishment. It is an account
that generates a much wider range of "reasonable" law than traditional
natural law did. How sharp the contrast is with modern natural-law
theories is a more open question. Lon Fuller, for example, claimed to be
arguing from a natural-law perspective when he wrote that beyond a
certain level of arbitrariness and uselessness, law is not law at all. Fuller's
conception of natural law, however, concentrated on procedural rationality and irrationality, rather than substantive wickedness. The positivist
can certainly accept that sufficiently arbitrary judicial rulings would not
be law so much as ravings from the bench, and he can agree that short
of that they may provoke such disobedience and dissension that they
violate the purpose of having a legal system in the first place.[62] What the
positivist will resist is the suggestion that bad laws are not laws at all;
but what many writers in the field of human and civil rights want to
defend is just that suggestion.

Legal positivists do not lack resources for explaining the point of rights
in general. Of course, it is part of the positivist case that morally important

---

[61] H. L. A. Hart, *The Concept of Law* (Oxford: Clarendon Press, 1961), 195ff.; compare
Lon Fuller, *The Morality of Law* (New Haven: Yale University Press, 1964).
[62] Fuller, *Morality of Law*, 98–116.

rights do not become part of the law simply by virtue of being morally important. Positivism is a natural ally of "strict construction" in the sense that positivists draw a sharp line between the rights it would be good to see secured by the law and the rights that actually are secured by the law, and this is what makes positivism suspect to theorists who take a large view of what can be extracted from the U.S. Constitution. All the same, positivists can give, and have given, persuasive accounts of why *rights* have a special status in moral thinking, and why many moral rights should also enjoy legal protection. Although, as we shall see, J. S. Mill in the nineteenth century and Joseph Raz recently have found a special role for rights in a utilitarian framework, there are equally persuasive nonutilitarian explanations for the status of rights.

A libertarian argument for the special status of rights starts from such phenomena as promises. When we make a promise we bind ourselves to behave in a particular way in the future, and so limit our freedom by actions of our own that aim to do precisely that. This limitation implies that in advance of making the promise, we must have been free to dispose of our future in this way and must have possessed the power to bind ourselves by our own words.[63] To say this, however, is just to say that we have a natural right to liberty. The limits of that right are set by reflecting on the fact that everyone has the same right; it follows that we all possess a natural right to as much liberty as is consistent with a like liberty for all. This "natural" right is a fundamental moral right rather than a legal right. It is, however, not surprising that the French Declaration of the Rights of Man places it at the center of the rights that the French Revolution proposed to enshrine in the French Constitution.

This is only one way of arguing for a right to liberty, grounded independently of utilitarian considerations. It is, however, a famous one, and has distinguished origins in the writings of Thomas Hobbes and Immanuel Kant. The bearing of this argument on the attractions of a bill of rights is indirect but simple. A bill of rights sets the terms on which any person or institution is entitled to exercise authority; each can act only within the limits the bill sets down. Why might we enshrine these terms in a bill? Because authority is not self-justifying. The difficulty of justifying all forms of authority lies in the fact that authority curtails our liberty. If we have a moral right to liberty, authority is legitimate only

---

[63] H. L. A. Hart, "Are There Any Natural Rights?" in *Political Philosophy*, ed. Anthony Quinton (Oxford: Oxford University Press, 1968), 53–66.

if it protects that liberty, or curtails it only to the extent demanded by important purposes to which we freely assent. From John Locke to John Rawls, this has been the view of authority espoused by American liberals. A bill of rights enshrines this understanding. It marks the peculiar importance of liberty and reflects in the law our intuitive belief that we have a *right* to act freely except for very good reasons.[64]

It is evident, therefore, that even though legal positivists accept neither the contractarian view of the origins of government, nor the view that valid law must embody natural law, nor the view that government authority is limited by the subjects' natural rights, positivists can agree that rights are a central element in morality, that the law should protect these moral rights, and that government's authority is diminished to the extent that it fails to do so. The attractions of a bill of rights, understood as positive legislation to achieve this end, are obvious. What accounts for the traditional British skepticism on this front is not, therefore, legal positivism alone, but the conjunction of legal positivism and the British belief in parliamentary supremacy. The orthodox view was summed up in Dicey's account of the rule of law. The primary sense in which the rule of law operated in Britain was that nobody was subject to anything other than the law and that nobody was above the law.[65] What of the secondary sense; could it be expected that the laws would respect our liberty? The answer was reassuring, although it rested on less-reassuring premises. The sense in which the English subject had *a right* to freedom of assembly, freedom of speech, freedom of publication and self-expression was only that he could lawfully do what the law did not prohibit. Liberty was what was left after the law had spoken.

Although his freedom was in this sense residual, a long series of battles with the executive had left the British subject freer than anyone in the world. Parliament would not stand for executive encroachment on individual liberty; if some mistake was made and encroachment occurred, Parliament or the judiciary would soon put a stop to it. Though the full-fledged theory of the separation of powers was not part of the operating theory of the British constitution, the independence of the judiciary from the executive was. The courts would not cooperate with executive misbehavior, and Parliament could curb an overenthusiastic executive. The difference from American sentiments on the subject could not be more

---

[64] Ibid., 60ff.
[65] Dicey, *Law of the Constitution*, 183.

marked. Moreover, the British view emphasizes the importance of executive authority should it be needed. A time of emergency is not the moment to have to assemble executive authority, and a prudent polity will leave much power latent in executive hands. So long as public and government opinion are friendly to freedom, executive authority will not be abused. This said, it became possible to celebrate the blessings of parliamentary sovereignty in a liberal society. It is the attractions of this view of the British political and legal system that make reformers skeptical of the virtues of a bill of rights for Britain.

PARLIAMENTARY SUPREMACY AND ITS FRIENDS

There are three main arguments for parliamentary supremacy, two of them positive, and one an argument *ad terrorem* drawn from the politics of the United States. The distinction between a positive enthusiasm for the British model and a dislike of most of the alternatives to it is not absolute. Most of the enthusiasts for the British parliamentary system of the past one hundred years have been as vigorous in their condemnation of other political systems as in the defense of the British system. The positive arguments begin with the benign role of the modern political party in a properly functioning British polity. In a disciplined two-party system, parliamentary sovereignty is really party sovereignty. For all the unattractive features of party competition—party bosses, professional politicians, the tendency of entrenched parties to shut out new groups and new ideas—party government has many virtues. But these virtues can only appear where responsibility for what happens can be laid firmly at the feet of a governing party. This demands something very like the British system of cabinet government and parliamentary supremacy. Given those conditions, party government will achieve many goods.

A party that knows that if it succeeds at the polls it will genuinely have to govern has an incentive to think sensibly about its policies and consider whether they will work, whether they will arouse excessive resistance, and how they will appear to the electorate when the time comes to appeal to them again. Party responsibility leads to a respect for the rules of the game and the civil liberties of the citizens, too. Politicians must reckon with the time they will spend out of power. They would make a great mistake if they tampered with the political rights of their opponents, because the results would certainly rebound upon them.

Again, there are pressures for moderation, even for (one might say) moderation-in-moderation. A party in power has to think how much of its platform it really wishes to see enacted, which forces it to consider where it ought to compromise and where it ought not. The secret of good government, however, is to compromise at the right moment. This is recognized in a properly functioning two-party system. The electorate needs a clear choice of party and needs not to be unduly confused by compromises made before the election takes place. The manifestos of British political parties have satisfied this requirement by being explicit about the parties' intentions. Once a party is in power and its program is passed into law, however, its policies need at least the grudging assent of their opponents, if not their approval, and so a measure of conciliation is required. When the system works properly and the major parties alternate in office, reforms put in place by a government of one party usually come to commend themselves to the electorate and are not thrown out by an incoming government of the other party. A premature compromise between the parties would probably have prevented the reforms from being introduced in the first place, but a sensitive appreciation of the limits of the system and the need to appeal to an electorate whose center of gravity lies in the center of the political spectrum results in reforms being implemented in a way that makes them widely acceptable.

This picture is, of course, a pollyannaish caricature, but it hardly exaggerates the arguments of writers on Parliament in the 1950s. From such a perspective, the American two-party system seems extraordinarily irresponsible, and American political parties quite hopeless at setting out a clear policy line for which they can be held responsible by the electorate. The fact that American political parties operate in a federal system that disperses power in a way the British system does not obviously accounts for a great deal of this difference, and even forty years ago British writers never quite suggested that the American party system had been created in a spirit of pure mischief. Still, the argument always leads to the same conclusions, whether the tone is one of unmitigated self-congratulation or merely one of gratitude for the greater simplicity of the British political scene. A two-party system of the British kind ideally sets clear policy choices before the electorate, gives political parties a clear route to implement those choices, and allows the electorate thereafter to hold its leaders accountable for what they did when they held power.

The role of political parties in a system where they seize all of the reins of power provides a second argument for the nonseparation of powers. The point of a two-party system is to offer the electorate alternative routes to reform and improvement. If the electorate's choice is to make a difference, the winners must have power to act. They cannot be held up by outside bodies, by judicial interference, or even by the electorate's attempts to change its mind. The British dislike referenda and recall and have little taste for judicial review. Governments exist to govern; reforming governments exist to reform. Power can be used creatively and for good purposes, and no good comes of dispersing it so thoroughly that governments are hamstrung. This is an argument that has periodically appealed to Americans of many persuasions.

The American Political Science Association has for decades had a working group devising legal and constitutional schemes for a more responsible party system in the United States. The Progressive movement of the early twentieth century more was attracted by individual leadership than by the collective leadership provided by political parties; nonetheless, Progressives thought that the executive and legislative branches should put their minds together to legislate for some useful end, and that once they had done so that should end the matter until the electorate spoke again.

In British discussion this argument relies heavily on negative examples. In the 1950s the negative example was supplied by France and Italy, where government crisis was the order of the day and the complacent British could claim that both nations changed their prime ministers more often than their underwear. There was a great deal of self-delusion in all this. It emerged in due course that the apparent instability of French and Italian politics had actually masked the way that both countries had pursued more consistent policies than the supposedly stable British had done, while the continuity of British government turned out to have been an illusion. The French and the Italians constantly shuffled their governments, but a small team of very able finance ministers pursued policies that remained remarkably stable from year to year. British governments were more stable than their European counterparts, but only at the price of repeated alterations of economic policy and repeated changes of finance ministers. Meanwhile, both France and Italy were largely run by skilled civil servants whose conception of national renewal and economic revival lent the management of their society a coherence that British party competition had not. The incorruptibility and liberalism of British governments were still impressive, but there was no reason to think that *all* the virtues were located in one regime.

In addition to these European examples, the United States was often drawn on. Although the United States seemed to have flourished in spite of its terrible institutional arrangements, it was hard to deny that they were terrible. The absence of party discipline meant that no issue that involved deep social divisions, most notably race relations, could be resolved in Congress. It seemed to British observers faintly shameful to rely on the Supreme Court to achieve the desegregation of schools and the extension of the vote to the black population of the southern states. The ability of special-interest groups to block legislation they did not like seemed equally shocking. That the American Medical Association could discredit as "socialist medicine" even the most modest advance toward a national health service that European countries had for years taken for granted was further evidence of the silliness of a system in which the government did not have enough centralized power actually to govern.

The more sophisticated gloss on the defects of dispersing power is that it has unjust distributive results. The pluralistic and slow-moving nature of American politics meant that legislation would pass easily on issues about which there was an overwhelming consensus and might not pass at all on any other issue. It is easy to waste money on military procurement, harder to spend it usefully in the cities and on decent education. Over the past twenty years British observers have admired the American concern for individual rights, while still taking a dim view of the system's apparent inability to act promptly and efficiently on economic policy and much else. In the 1950s it was harder to regard lethargic and much compromised policy making as the price of a libertarian polity, for the United States seemed a lot less liberal than Britain. British observers found the cold-war United States hardly more liberal than the Soviet Union: hysterical patriotism, unfounded fears about the Soviet Union's ambitions for world conquest, a foreign policy that expressed itself in Latin American invasions and support for bloodthirsty dictators all looked very nasty.

The skeptical view that paper guarantees do no good precisely when they are needed the most was much reinforced by the spectacle U.S. politics presented in the 1950s. Neither the federal system, nor the separation of executive and legislature, nor a hundred and sixty years of constitutional government stopped Congress from violating the Fifth Amendment rights of witnesses or stopped employers from violating the First Amendment rights of their employees. Nor did the Bill of Rights and the Supreme Court help the victims of congressional investigations.

The Court kept silent until the anti-Communist hysteria was over. This reluctance to protect possible dissidents was not new. Knowledgeable critics of the history of civil liberties in the United States looked back to the Supreme Court's decision that the Espionage and Sedition Acts of World War I were constitutional, although the acts were so wide in their scope and so draconian in their penalties that they punished any public opposition to the war and made mere bad-mouthing the government an offense. As Eugene Debs rightly said before being sentenced to ten years' imprisonment under the Sedition Act, "Either there is a First Amendment and the Sedition Act is unconstitutional, or the Sedition Act is constitutional and there is no First Amendment."[66] The Supreme Court had done nothing to save the Chicago anarchists judicially murdered in 1887, and it did very little to save the victims of the postwar "Red Scare" either.[67] Of course, to concentrate only on these failures would be silly. My intention is to suggest the *worst* that British spectators could say against American political practice, and this is a deliberately highly colored picture—the Supreme Court was already warming up for active redistricting and in a few years would restrict the right of politicians and public figures to sue for libel in a way that was only possible on the basis of First Amendment rights of free expression. Still, it is easy to see how anyone predisposed to favor the British system of government would in the 1950s be skeptical of the libertarian advantages to be expected from the existence of the Bill of Rights and a Supreme Court to enforce it.

The failures of British liberties. The other side of all this has been a large measure of self-deception and a certain blindness to the realities of the British parliamentary system. The self-deception comes in many shapes and sizes, but an obvious example is British readiness to overlook legislation such as the Official Secrets Act of 1911. The act was the product of a pre–World War I panic about espionage and showed from the beginning the stigmata of the haste with which it was drafted and introduced. The bill introducing it was passed through all its stages inside a day; among its many defects was the fact that the wide terms in which it defined official secrets made an official secret out of any information that was gained by working in the civil service. It was an offense to reveal

---

[66] "Speech to the Jury," in *Debs*, ed. Ronald Radosh (Englewood Cliffs, N.J.: Prentice-Hall, 1971), 78.

[67] On the former, see Paul Avrich, *The Haymarket Tragedy* (Princeton: Princeton University Press, 1984).

even such innocuous details as the price of a cup of coffee in a Treasury canteen.[68]

The cheerful assumption was that the political establishment would never want to use the provisions of the act other than to prevent the leaking of information that would genuinely damage the security or the economic welfare of the country. This was wishful thinking. The act offered considerable scope to any ministry that wanted to employ it to save ministerial embarrassment in Parliament or in front of the press. This opening was often exploited. Ministers could hardly threaten newspapers with the act every time they feared a loss of face, but the fear of prosecution was a powerful deterrent to civil servants who might be tempted to wash their department's dirty linen in public, and made investigative journalism more hazardous than it might otherwise have been.

The Official Secrets Act is not the only cause of the British government's obsession with secrecy. The British system of ministerial accountability protects from public scrutiny senior civil servants who would in the United States have to answer to congressional committees for their views. Senior civil servants have accepted that complete discretion on their side is the price of their ministers' absolute responsibility. The underdevelopment of the parliamentary committee system compared with the committee system of the U.S. Congress has been both the cause and the consequence of the doctrine that ministers alone speak for their departments and that what goes on within their departments is not to be discussed outside them. The adversarial character of the British parliamentary system locks into place here, too. The result is that, until recently, there has been little pressure for anything resembling the American Freedom of Information Act, and little room for a judiciary that inclined toward fresh-air government to act. One consequence is that to American eyes the British political system seems to combine a high degree of informal leakiness with a high degree of formalized secrecy.

Secrecy has often been protected without recourse even to a badly drawn statute. The so-called D-notice system by which newspapers are encouraged to accept a system of semivoluntary self-censorship relies entirely on the willingness of newspaper owners and editors to cooperate with the government of the day in deciding what news is safe to print. The government of the day possesses a D-notice committee of security officials and civil servants, the membership of which is not publicized,

---

[68] Robertson, *Freedom, the Individual, and the Law*, 132.

which meets to consider what information ought to be suppressed, and then transmits its decisions to the press and the broadcasting media. Its advantage from the point of view of both government and media is that it is informal and flexible, and it raises none of the difficulties that would arise were the government to have only the recourse of applying for injunctions against specific publications over specific items or prosecuting them after the event. The system is in principle the prior censorship American courts have declared unconstitutional. In practice, the difference between British and American outcomes is not as great as that bald contrast suggests. There are innumerable secret and semisecret committees in Washington, and innumerable plans and projected actions that the federal government places under embargo. More of this is covered by specific legislation than in Britain, and the realm of executive discretion is narrower, but the difference in what gets published may not be great.

The D-notice system is an informal one, but it is hard to believe that the presence of the Official Secrets Act in the background is anything but a powerful incentive for British editors and newspaper proprietors to cooperate with the government. The government offers the press Hobson's choice—and editors and owners rightly suspect if they are hauled into court they will find the judges more inclined to side with the government than the papers. Once again we must not exaggerate. The deference to executive authority that allows the D-notice system to operate would have made for a cautious press even in its absence. It is an expensive business to defend oneself even against a government seeking a civil injunction rather than a conviction in the criminal courts. Conversely, if the judiciary was more inclined to stand up to the government, more journalists and their employers would be willing to risk prosecution.

It is sometimes thought to be silly to stress security legislation; all societies behave more or less illiberally when they believe their national security is threatened. Britons who look to American legislation like the Freedom of Information Act and to the willingness of American courts to uphold the right of ordinary citizens to see previously classified information as a model for what they would want to see in Britain forget that the legislation was imposed on an executive that the country had come to distrust thoroughly, and has mostly been employed to allow people to correct damaging misinformation about themselves. It is a safe bet that if the legislation had been in force during the 1950s, government departments would have energetically resisted any attempt at trawling through their files, and would have been supported by the courts.

The bill of indictment against British self-congratulation does not rely exclusively on the wickedness of the Official Secrets Acts, whether in the 1911 or 1989 version. An equally ill-drawn piece of legislation was the Public Order Act of 1936. It had been preceded by the Incitement to Disaffection Act, 1934, which allowed police to search premises on suspicion that their occupants possessed literature that might diminish the armed services' enthusiasm for their task. This act had the somewhat melancholy distinction of bringing back into British law the "general warrant," which had been discredited during the Wilkesite uproar of the 1760s and which the Fourth Amendment of the Bill of Rights attempted to keep out of the United States.[69] The Public Order Act and a number of associated acts that dealt with the wearing of uniforms for intimidatory effect were intended to stop street fighting between fascist and Communist mobs in the East End of London—a wholly laudable aim. What they used as a means to this end was another matter entirely. Every police officer with whom I have discussed the question maintains that the bill gave the police such wide and undefined powers that any police officer who can keep a straight face while telling a court that he apprehended a breach of the peace can prevent any individual or group he chooses from meeting, demonstrating, chanting slogans, or otherwise doing most of the things the First Amendment protects in the United States. Once again, self-deception does not consist in lawyers' being unaware that the police have such a wide discretion, but in the readiness with which they have allowed themselves to be convinced that this discretion would never be abused.

The British have usually believed that the adversarial structure of British politics achieves all that American constitutional checks achieve. So long as the country as a whole is liberal in sentiment, the constant parliamentary scrutiny that British governments face is a powerful deterrent to any encroachment on popular liberty. The American system of government does not expose the executive to such constant scrutiny, and it therefore demands the constitutional checks that are so abundantly provided. Conversely, a liberal executive can curb an illiberal public opinion. No Parliament can pass legislation the government of the day

---

[69] It is an exaggeration to suggest that the "General Warrant Cases" had simply settled the issue until then; the Obscene Publications Act of 1857 gave wide powers of search to police looking for obscene publications, and the Official Secrets Act of 1911 gave to superintendents of police the power to issue warrants without going to court. See E. C. S. Wade's appendix to Dicey, *Law of the Constitution*, 580–1, 584–5.

opposes. The government has control over the timetable; it can obstruct and delay any attempt to pass law over its resistance. Unimaginably and in extremis, it could secure the dissolution of Parliament. No British government faces what American presidents so often face, namely, legislation passed over its veto. Illiberal law is likely to be passed if and only if the executive wants it. The theory of adversarial restraint outlined earlier explains how determined opposition, widely supported in the country at large, will persuade a government not to want it. The problem is that the mechanism has lately seemed not to work.

In ordinary times the British executive is unchallengeable. The legislative process does not consist of a beleaguered orator trying to collect the last few votes needed to see a bill through Parliament. For part of the eighteenth century, and much of the nineteenth, that was an apt image; for the twentieth century it is not. To the casual British observer the American scene is astonishingly reminiscent of the most disorderly periods of the mid-nineteenth century, and the spectacle of congressional leaders pleading, cajoling, bribing, and threatening their supposed followers is always good for a certain high-toned mockery in the better British press. But after a dozen years of tightly disciplined Conservative government, many commentators yearn for a little American disorder in the British parliamentary scene, even though party politicians and civil servants alike maintain in all sincerity that the British political system could not stand it. At all events, since the end of World War I the British system of legislation has been strikingly orderly. Once the cabinet has decided on a piece of legislation, that, to all intents and purposes, is that. The amending process does not expose legislation to alteration by the opposition; it largely allows the government of the day to fine-tune its legislation.

Once again, the cliff-hanging process so familiar in Congress is absent; there are no last-minute conferences among back-benchers, no crucial amendments suddenly brought onto the stage. According to Michael Zander's calculations, "94 percent of all amendments moved successfully in Committee and 96 percent of those moved successfully on Report were moved by the Minister, and almost all those moved successfully by back-benchers or the Opposition concerned very small points." Most of the legislation that goes through Congress with so much drama, and almost all the legislation that goes through Parliament with so little drama, raises no issues of a constitutional or civil libertarian kind. Still, the crucial point remains. In Britain, as opposed to the United States, the one direction from which a threat can come is the executive. Were there to be such a threat—critics would amend that phrase to "when such threats occur"—there is little prospect that British liberties will be rescued by a revolt from the floor of the House of Commons, and little prospect that the government will suffer second thoughts.[70]

Nor have the other mechanisms of control over the executive proved effective. Perhaps the most famous, and at the same time the least effective, method of control over the executive is the doctrine of ministerial responsibility. According to this doctrine, a government minister is answerable to Parliament for the conduct of every last member of the department for which the minister is responsible. Again, according to this doctrine, any serious misconduct in the department should be followed by the minister's resignation, even if it was not humanly possible to oversee the conduct complained of. The idea behind such strict liability is that prudence dictates extremely careful behavior. The legal fiction is that the minister does whatever the department actually does in the minister's name; the moral theory is that this system enables Parliament and the citizenry to pin blame where it belongs. The home secretary is liable not only for misbehavior on the part of the Metropolitan Police, who are directly responsible to the Home Office, but even for the misbehavior of other police forces, who are supposed to be kept up to the mark by the inspector of Constabulary, backed by Home Office review. The reality is that only one minister since World War II has been forced to resign because of the misconduct of his department, and that was a junior minister, Minister of Agriculture Thomas Dugdale, whose civil servants had mishandled the return to its owners of a country estate requisitioned for military purposes during the war. There is much doubt whether even that case was a bona fide example of the Commons' forcing a resignation, the latest account of the affair suggesting that Dugdale was pushed out by the government itself in response to a conspiracy among Tory backbenchers.

Given the feebleness of institutional constraints and the potential ferocity of the law, the last, characteristically British, explanation for the apparently liberal character of British political life is sociological. The American political system brings together in Washington people from all parts of an entire continent. They have many disagreements of culture, interest, style, and ideology. Although they are agreed on broad political

[70] Michael Zander, *A Matter of Justice* (Oxford: Oxford University Press, 1989), 262–3.

principle, they may still have widely divergent views about the proper behavior of politicians and about the wisdom of legislation on contentious moral, religious, and other issues widely thought of as "private." It is enough to observe that Nelson Rockefeller and Ronald Reagan belonged to the same political party. The Founders of the American Republic devised a constitution to deal with just such diversity. A well-ordered republic could organize these divergent passions to hold one another in check, but there was no doubt that an elaborate constitutional structure was required to make such a system work. It is here that we find the much-discussed connection between the federal structure of the system and its attachment to individual rights. The Founders had to allow opinion to control opinion and state to control state in the hope that individuals would find room to live their own lives in the space so created. It may help to explain why the Bill of Rights ends with two essentially negative clauses, the Ninth Amendment reminding readers that a bill cannot enumerate all the rights that citizens possess, and the Tenth assigning all legitimate authority not explicitly given to the central government to other—state—governments.

The British notion of checks is social, not legal. It rests on the thought that legal restraints fail when they are most needed, while internal, cultural restraints operate in the privacy of a politician's soul. The British political elite is permeable but homogeneous. Outsiders can join, but they join by being socialized into the mores of the elite. Labour cabinets as much as Tory cabinets are full of people who went to school together or attended the same universities (or colleges within those universities); the senior civil servants with whom they deal will have come from much the same background and will have much the same view of the world as their political masters. They may belong to the same London clubs, and they will certainly read the same newspapers, listen to the same radio programs, and have rather similar friends. What prevents politicians from abusing their trust is not the law but the same pressures that stop academics from stealing each other's work and inhibit bank tellers from robbing their customers.

Whether this vision is entirely persuasive is a hard question. Within limits it is not implausible, though it was probably truer of a brief period earlier in this century when politics was ceasing to be dominated by aristocrats who had little in common with most of their civil servants but had not yet become wide open to lower-middle-class political careerists. This vision is not a reassuring one, for it suggests that if the upper-middle-class sense of decency fails, civil liberties might be in danger. In any event, it is not clear that these safeguards are particularly effective. Just as skeptical observers might point to the loss of civil liberties in the United States as soon as the United States entered World War I, or the internment of harmless West Coast Japanese after Pearl Harbor, so they might point to the British government's harsh treatment of conscientious objectors in World War I and the deportation of German refugees in World War II as evidence that cultural restraints work smoothly when under no stress, but that they work no better than legal measures once tempers are lost.

The unwritten constitution. Once we appeal to the qualities of the political culture to explain the liberalism of Britain, we are well into the familiar terrain of the virtues of the unwritten constitution. One of its virtues is negative. British political writers have always been scornful of continental codes that begin by announcing that the subject is to enjoy the widest possible liberty, and then take away the force of what is said by adding, "save where it is necessary to restrict that liberty for the sake of the public utility." Many critics of the European Convention on Human Rights complain that it essentially does just this. It was Dicey's great argument against most continental constitutions, and it was Margaret Thatcher's against contemporary cries for a written bill of rights.[71] The point is simple. The value of paper guarantees depends entirely on how they are construed. Dicey distrusted European judges. Americans who have read Felix Frankfurter's wartime account of why the children of Jehovah's Witnesses must be made to salute the American flag may feel that the U.S. Supreme Court sometimes does no better. The European Convention allows governments to abridge our rights for the sake of the nation's integrity, and no doubt the rights of Americans must be similarly abridged when the nation is at war. But it is hard to see the point of forcing upon people who conscientiously deplore them rituals whose only purpose is to express an unfeigned allegiance to the Great Republic. It is harder still to see the point of forcing children to pay lip service to their country while they cause real pain to their parents.[72]

There is a plausible positive defense of the unwritten constitution. Written constitutions encourage legalistic quibbling; they tempt govern-

---

[71] Dicey, *Law of the Constitution*, 197ff.
[72] *West Virginia Board of Education* v. *Barnett* (319 U.S. 646–70).

ments into elaborate maneuvers to skirt constitutional traps; they heighten tensions by turning every policy decision into a potentially litigious issue.[73] The American experience with abortion rights is an obvious example. Entire social and economic programs also demonstrate the point. Franklin Roosevelt found the Supreme Court a constant obstacle to the recovery program of his first term in office. The best anyone has ever said about the slow and clumsy system of government that results is that it is a luxury that a prosperous but deeply divided country can well afford.[74] People at the time did not share that relaxed view; in the middle of the worst depression in the country's history, they were far from feeling that they could afford a leisurely approach to reconstruction. The British argument is that unwritten constitutions allow governments to act, knowing that if the sense of the community is with them they will be able to act successfully and with dispatch, and that if the sense of the community is against them they will get nowhere.[75]

One example of a measure that failed because it was in this broad sense at odds with the unwritten constitution is the industrial relations legislation of Edward Heath's Conservative government of 1970–74. There are many possible explanations of the failure of Heath's Industrial Relations Act of 1971. The simplest and most brutal is that the trade unions had the power to prevent it from working and used their power. Another is that the public that later sided with Margaret Thatcher over her industrial relations policies was in 1971 unconvinced that the new regulations were in a broad sense constitutional. They breached no particular law or principle, but they seemed to violate the social compact within which industrial relations had been carried on since 1945, and they did so in the absence of overriding necessity.

In essence the British had achieved in 1945 the kind of tripartite compact among a reforming government, organized labor, and organized capital that Herbert Croly had urged upon the United States in his *Promise of American Life*. It was taken for granted that labor unions protected

---

[73] Fred Siegel, "Nothing in Moderation," *Atlantic* (May 1990): 108ff.

[74] Robert A. Dahl, *A Preface to Democratic Theory* (Chicago: University of Chicago Press, 1953), 149–51.

[75] I do not mean that no American believes this; many do. A marked distaste for legalism was characteristic of writers such as Dewey, Holmes, Croly, the young Lippmann, and their friends. It made Dewey, for one, a rather casual defender of civil liberties in wartime, for all his role in founding the American Civil Liberties Union. Morton White, *American Social Thought: The Revolt Against Formalism* (New York: Oxford University Press, 1976); Christopher Lasch, *The New Radicalism* (New York: W. W. Norton, 1965), chap. 6.

their members' interests first and foremost, that industrialists were primarily concerned with the profits of their individual firms, and that responsibility for coordination had to rest on the government. Yet it was also assumed that all parties were amenable to appeals for self-restraint for the sake of the general good. Unfortunately Edward Heath came to power in 1970 on the slogan "stand on your own two feet." In intention this slogan merely meant that inefficient British industries should stop looking to the government for subsidies. In practice it was felt to be a unilateral breach of the tripartite compact as well as an incitement to unrestrained selfishness.

Following that up with legislation that made much strike action illegal was thought by trade unionists to amount to a declaration of war: Heath had told the unions to stand on their own two feet and had then tried to tie their feet together. Thirteen years later, Margaret Thatcher succeeded where Edward Heath had failed because she benefited from a period of five or so years in which union leaders had seemed to think that they were entitled to operate an alternative government to that which the electorate had installed. This union view was an equally glaring breach of the old understanding and it deprived the union movement of the broad support of the electorate.[76]

There are other reasons for praising unwritten constitutions, many of them accepted by Americans impatient with the slow pace of reform in the United States. Whether they have wanted the promotion of interstate travel, the creation of a modern banking system, or the development of a national health service, reformers have wanted a stronger executive. All those who hold that reform requires strong executive authority and want to see governments act with speed and decisiveness must be tempted by the argument from the unwritten constitution, no matter which side of the Atlantic they encounter it. The one obstacle to its easy acceptance by liberal reformers is the fear that if strong executives clean up the streets and produce a physically healthy population, they may behave like Bismarck, let us say, in other entirely illiberal ways. It is here that a faith in public opinion has to substitute for legal checks. If the public has a strong feeling for its liberties and is ready to turn on politicians who unduly restrict its freedom, it needs fewer additional guarantees.

A delicate line must be trodden here. If people are to know what to

[76] James Prior, *A Balance of Power* (London: Hamish Hamilton, 1986), chaps. 4, 9.

expect, the constitution cannot be so unwritten that nobody can predict what will happen if the government tries to legislate in hitherto untrodden areas. To put it differently, an unwritten constitution must be backed up by a more predictable social framework. Even then, injustices may readily occur. The eighteenth- and nineteenth-century British treatment of capital cases displays the dangers in the field of penal legislation. There were innumerable petty offenses for which the penalty was, in principle, death. Every so often someone would in fact be executed for something generally felt to be too trivial to deserve the penalty. Most juries and prosecutors sorted things out in such a way that cases did not come to trial or noncapital charges were substituted, or juries refused to convict in flat disregard of the facts. The result was less inhumane than it threatened to be. Yet it remained an unsatisfactory system of justice. In contentious times, say, during the 1790s, it gave judges a fine chance to terrify political dissidents. In less contentious times, the system was too arbitrary and unpredictable to be tolerated. The question is how far the analogy extends and how far liberties taken for granted in their unwritten form need to be restated in a new, written form.

The views just sketched form part of a traditional, rather conservative vision of the British political order. Elements of it have been attacked more or less continuously by politicians and intellectuals from the Liberal and Labour parties. One area in which the argument has been particularly intense is relevant to comparisons between British and American experience. This area is the question of how wise it is to rely on the judiciary as defenders of the liberty of the ordinary citizen. The British and American experiences have been interestingly the reverse of one another. In the United States, questions about judicial interpretation of the Constitution and judicial extension of the protections and privileges guaranteed in the Bill of Rights have stemmed from what conservatives have denounced as "judicial activism." In Britain, it is rare for conservatives to criticize the actions of the judiciary, but it has become common for the left and particularly the "soft" or center-left to argue in favor of a bill of rights precisely because of judicial inactivism. The scene is utterly confused and defies simple explanation or description. In its early years the Labour party was interested in constitutional matters and argued for revisions of the electoral system, alterations in the system of criminal justice, and much else. Some of its aspirations forced the party to take an interest in such issues. Given the way that the appeals procedure in Britain terminates in the House of Lords, a party that contemplates abolishing the House of Lords, as the Labour party does, has to think what changes that entails in the structure of the judiciary and in legal procedure.

The early history of the Labour party left it alienated from the judiciary. The party found that even after it had won immunities for trade union activity from a grudging Parliament, those immunities were then interpreted in the narrowest possible way by the courts. Labour critics often blamed the recruitment process that guaranteed that judges would be drawn from a narrow social background and argued that any constitutional arrangements that left such people in power would be hostile to the cause of labor. But the Labour party's interest in such issues began and ended with abolishing the House of Lords and with changing the legal standing of trade unions in ways that could not be subverted by the judiciary. The Labour party held that all the party needed was a majority in the House of Commons and a clear reforming program to carry out. Given the party's perception of the judiciary, it was bound to be hostile to judicial review and to a written constitution that would allow judges to invalidate Labour legislation.[77] Sidney Webb, in fact, wrote a constitution for a socialist commonwealth of Great Britain but did not imagine that one of his tasks was to devise ways in which judges might keep socialist governments in check.

Judicial review. The subject of judicial review is a complicated and difficult one. In the British context applications for judicial review arise when a plaintiff believes that central or local government has acted *ultra vires.* In theory, occasions for complaint ought to be rare. Parliament possesses a "select committee on statutory instruments" that scrutinizes delegated legislation that might raise constitutional or other political questions to ensure that it is within the letter as well as in the spirit of the enabling legislation. Most regulations issued by government departments under delegated authority are, in fact, of mind-numbing dullness for anyone not immediately affected by them. Judges have in the past been reluctant to review such regulations at all. The doctrine of parliamentary supremacy means that judges cannot challenge the validity of an act of Parliament and they have often treated regulations made under delegated authority as if they were acts of Parliament and shared that

---

[77] Peter Archer, "The Constitution," in *Fabian Essays on Socialism,* ed. Ben Pimlott (London: Heinemann, 1984), 117–31.

immunity to review. The judiciary long held that they could act to invalidate an administrative decision only if it was so unreasonable that no sane person could have made it, or if it was malicious. It is hard to prove either of those things in a court of law.

Recently judges have been reacting to the increasing quantity of legislation and regulation by extending the range of what they will review. They have asserted a right to judge the merits of a minister's thinking as well as its consistency with his or her powers narrowly construed. Unreasonable regulations have been struck down on the grounds of their unreasonableness. Judges, however, have remained extremely reluctant to become embroiled whenever regulations embody some decided government view about the security of the state or the "public interest." In these areas, judges continue to display the traditional reluctance to go behind the minister's decision. Because these are the most "political" cases and the ones that cause the most heated arguments, it is not surprising that radicals remain contemptuous of judicial review.

The gap left in the British defense of freedom by the failure of judicial review to provide more remedies is no small matter. Most of the regulations that affect a citizen's existence are perfectly innocuous. They are churned out by civil servants, not so much as glanced at by their political masters, and raise no question of any interest to anyone other than the fishermen, pharmaceutical companies, building restorers, or other groups to whom they are addressed. More worrisome are blanket decisions with a strong "bill of rights" flavor taken by ministers in an unargued exercise of delegated authority. Most Americans find it alarming that so much power over the broadcasting media is placed in the political hands of a British home secretary, who can, in effect, declare persons and subjects undiscussable on television or on the radio with little legal redress.

It was the fiat of the home secretary, Douglas Hurd, that forbade television and radio companies to present live interviews with the spokesmen for the Irish Republican Army. Of course, a row ensued in the House of Commons and the press protested, but there appeared to be no way of bringing Hurd's right to issue such an instruction before a court. If there had been, the home secretary could have disarmed the court by appealing to national security. As with delegated legislation, so with the powers of ministers, British courts have held that where Parliament delegates responsibility, Parliament intends the minister to have sweeping powers. In any event, the domination of Parliament by the executive means that if any court were tempted to intervene it could be stopped by a statutory statement that the decision is immune from legal review. In the United States such a declaration would be unconstitutional; in Britain it is unchallengeable.

Although British courts have been very self-denying, governments have gone out of their way to make it hard for them to be anything else. The most extreme example is the Immigration Act of 1971, which explicitly rules out the possibility of taking a home secretary to court who "certifies that he personally directed that the applicant be excluded because exclusion would be conducive to the public good, or if entry was refused in obedience to such a direction."[78] This power appears to have been used only once, as soon as it was acquired. Two American journalists, Mark Hosenball and Philip Agee, were deported because of their known opposition to the Vietnam War. Hosenball appealed to the European Commission on Human Rights, but enthusiasts for the European Convention on Human Rights have always been dismayed by the fact that the commission decided that the home secretary had not violated Hosenball's human rights. The commission was no more willing than British courts have been to challenge the government's understanding of national security, although it has on other occasions objected to various features of the act and to the way in which it is implemented.[79]

The act is a good example of how it is possible in Britain to bar an appeal against any but the lowest level of administrative decision making. There is an appeals procedure for aliens denied entry to Britain or deported from the country; when that procedure is exhausted, aggrieved aliens may appeal for judicial review. But the grounds for appeal are so narrow—one would have to show malice or spectacular unreasonableness on the part of the Home Office—that there is little point in seeking it.

The procedures laid down by the act give complainants almost no information about the grounds for an unfavorable decision. People appealing against a refusal of admission or against a deportation order are largely forced to guess at the case against them, which obviously makes an appeal more difficult to mount. That this refusal of information is a violation of "natural justice" does not seem to be denied; the government relies on its right to employ procedures that violate natural justice when national security requires such measures. Hearing their complaint against deportation, the appeals court held that Hosenball and Agee had no right

---

[78] De Smith and Brazier, *Constitutional and Administrative Law*, 450.
[79] Ibid., 451n.

to demand treatment in accordance with natural justice. Shocking though this appears, it is in fact a case in which U.S. practice is no more fastidious than British. The Supreme Court has ruled that the treatment aliens applying for admission receive is not to be judged by the constitutional standards applicable to American citizens. A broad-brush appeal to the "national interest" is all the immigration authorities need to justify their treatment of aliens; the authorities are not obliged to follow natural justice as they would be if they were dealing with citizens. It remains surprising that home secretaries should have armored themselves against criticism quite so completely. Given the willingness of British judges to side with the government and to accept the government's conception of the general interest as determinative, it looks very much like overkill.

It bears repeating that only in the field of civil liberties is the judicial record so depressing. In other areas the past twenty years have seen increasing boldness on the part of British judges. Although they remain unwilling to criticize Parliament's decisions or attack ministers' ideas of good policy, they have looked for ways to help individuals, businesses, and local authorities stand up to the central government. When ministers or their civil servants make decisions that rely on disputed facts, courts will listen to a claim that the facts are other than was claimed. In 1977 Tameside Local Education Authority resisted a ministerial order to introduce nonselective secondary education on the grounds that the minister had no grasp of the impact on the authority's area; the minister appealed to the courts to enforce his order. The court held that he had not shown that the authority was unreasonable in its refusal and declined to enforce the order. It is the courts' behavior in contested issues of civil liberties that leads critics to complain of the inactivism of British courts compared with American courts.

It is a recent development that finds radicals complaining of this inactivism. Radicals had never previously looked for much help from the judiciary. As I have said, political radicals have always looked to Parliament to legislate in the desired direction, just as conservatives have looked to Parliament to hold off the changes they feared. The radicals' skepticism has social sources. These have as much to do with culture, lifestyle, sexual preference, and artistic license as with *political* free speech. The radicals' complaint was that judges are almost always socially reactionary, and thus bound to be unreliable on matters of literary freedom, censorship, and anything to do with public morality. The exhibit relied on almost to death is the 1961 prosecution of Penguin Books under the Obscene

Publications Act—the so-called Trial of Lady Chatterley. This trial was notable for a wonderful moment when prosecuting counsel asked the jury to consider the book's effect "on their maidservants," a gaffe that may have cost the prosecution its case, and one that certainly did much to convince the young people who were about to launch London's "swinging sixties" that their elders were astonishingly out of touch. But before the trial of Lady Chatterley, the House of Lords had done quite enough to outrage even the mildly liberal on matters of sex. A Soho shopkeeper named Shaw had published a *Ladies Directory,* that is, a prostitutes' address book.[80] The publication was not in the ordinary sense obscene. To stop its circulation and send Shaw to jail, the House of Lords reinvented a common-law offense that had been unheard of since its invention by the conservative eighteenth-century judge, Lord Mansfield. This new crime was "conspiracy to corrupt public morals." The announcement of its existence amounted to a statement by the Law Lords that they possessed a reserve power to declare otherwise noncriminal behavior a threat to the moral fabric of the nation and to impose on it whatever penalities seemed appropriate. Happily, the judgment seems to have been a momentary aberration, though one that other judges were happy enough to defend.

It is easy to see how this judgment affects writers and artists who have no First Amendment to hide behind. Where American writers can venture into court to challenge local obscenity statutes in the name of their First Amendment freedoms, British writers and intellectuals armed with nothing but the common sense of the British public have wanted to keep well away from judges—even though juries have shown an engaging tendency to ignore the more hysterical summings-up to which they have been subjected. It has, for example, become almost impossible to get a conviction for obscenity out of a jury for anything other than child pornography. The result is not entirely satisfactory. Knowing they will not secure convictions if the case goes to jury trial, the police seek instead destruction orders from local magistrates. Magistrates generally have a less-relaxed attitude to pornography than juries. Pornographers no doubt prefer the destruction of their stock in trade to a jail term but the process essentially amounts to the sublegal harassment of anyone who oversteps the boundaries of local toleration. It is a characteristically messy British result and,

[80] H. L. A. Hart, *Law, Liberty and Morality* (London: Oxford University Press, 1963), 6–12.

like much else in Britain, is more or less acceptable according to the personalities involved. A puritanical chief constable whose moral standards are at odds with his community's will be at least irritating and at worst oppressive; a sensible chief constable in tune with his locality may shield local sensibilities from offensive displays without excessive interference.

In the last ten years anxiety has focused less on the fields of obscenity, blasphemy, and the like than on government-inspired restrictions of liberty—the extension of police powers in the Police and Criminal Evidence Act of 1984 and its successors, the erosion of the right to silence in provisions made for Northern Ireland that the government would wish to extend to mainland Britain, and the government's attempt to throw a veil of censorship over absolutely every aspect of the operations of the security services. It has also focused on the distinctive political aspects of First Amendment issues—the right of assembly and political expression—and their erosion by the police with the encouragement of magistrates' courts. To this there has been no American analogue.

The experiences of Britain and the United States during the 1980s are mirror images of each other. What caused violent political rows in Britain caused none in the United States, and the single most contentious issue in U.S. politics had been settled in Britain a decade before. When Ronald Reagan's government tried to roll back trade union powers, for instance, it did so through the courts, one case at a time, with the solicitor general filing brief after brief to try, mostly unsuccessfully, to reduce bargaining rights or employment privileges secured under older federal law. The air traffic controllers' strike certainly aroused strong feelings, but nothing on the scale of the British miners' strike of 1984–85, and with nothing of the latter's political impact. Again, although everyday American crime kills far more people than do the Northern Ireland troubles (drug-related deaths in Washington, D.C., alone are far higher than violent deaths in the whole of Ulster) the United States has not suffered the effects of a simmering civil war during this century.

The two great political controversies that centered on the Supreme Court were reverse discrimination and abortion. The former rarely surfaces as an issue in Britain; in the absence of any constitutional right to equal treatment and due process, aggrieved job applicants who believe they have been turned down in favor of less-qualified minority applicants have to sue under explicit employment statutes, and these usually allow the employer more discretion than U.S. employers are allowed. Abortion, as we shall see, is the sort of issue Britain handles more successfully than the United States—doubtless because it is easier to do so in a smaller, more homogeneous, and less religiously passionate society, but partly because British political arrangements make it easier to strike a deal that takes the subject off the boil. So whereas the United States has become excited about a large cultural and moral issue that the courts, Congress, and state legislatures cannot resolve, Britain has turned to the judiciary out of a sudden perception that the politics of the 1980s have damaged British civil liberties in quite new ways.

This is a wholly new state of affairs. Radicals who formerly hoped to keep away from judges and never trusted them as an engine of social or cultural enlightenment were in the past no happier about their political enlightenment. Despite occasional counterexamples, such as Lord Scarman's report on the 1981 outbreak of rioting and vandalism in the black inner London suburb of Brixton, which came down heavily against aggressive policing, radicals expected the judiciary to side with the powers that be. If the solicitor general comes into court and swears that publication of extracts from *Spycatcher* will damage the interests of the country, radicals expect judges to hand out injunctions against all and sundry; nor are radicals surprised when judges invent new restrictions on press freedom, such as the thought that an injunction against one newspaper is an injunction against all newspapers.[81] Of course, this is what radicals have always believed. Because they share the judiciary's tenderness toward established authority, conservatives do not usually feel threatened in the way the left does, although the Conservative press is quite capable of eloquent outrage when a Labour solicitor general silences a *Telegraph* journalist. In the *Spycatcher* case, even the most Thatcherite newspapers reacted ferociously to judicial intervention.[82]

BRINGING INTERNATIONAL DECLARATIONS BACK HOME

Discussions of a bill of rights for Britain have lately contrasted the British lack of a written constitution with the state of affairs among European countries where the European Convention has been naturalized into local law. British radicals and conservatives are articulate in their complaints about Britain's deficiencies and the deficiencies of proposed reforms. The decent center is even more articulate than they, since it is the decent

[81] Robertson, *Freedom, the Individual and the Law*, 150–9; Lee, *Judging Judges*, 112–13.
[82] Lee, *Judging Judges*, 112.

center that hopes that naturalizing the European Convention and a *somewhat* more liberal and adventurous judiciary will work a small miracle for British civil rights. As we shall see, it is easy enough to discover what the articulate left and right think of the prospects of a British bill of rights, with or without a small revolution in judicial behavior. On the wider stage, however, it is simply impossible to say anything about the attitude of the British public to the postwar spate of charters and declarations of human rights, and impossible to know what the public thinks of proposals for incorporating them into British law, because 95 percent of the British public is almost certainly completely ignorant of their existence.

Educated opinion is predictable. Those who glory in the unwritten constitution and would hate to see further codification are contemptuous of international declarations in all shapes and forms. Some of those who are eager to embrace the European Convention are rationalists who think it is a good idea to spell out the background rules that legitimate government and constrain its activities. Others think that Britain was once a model for other nations and is now an illiberal slum and desperately hope that British law can be brought up to the level of the rest of Europe.[83]

Britain has signed most of the appropriate postwar charters. The UN Declaration of Human Rights of 1948 plays no role in British law or politics, because it makes no provision for violations of the rights it sets out to be taken to any court. The UN Declaration has been discussed in texts in political theory and jurisprudence, mostly by commentators pointing out the difference between negative universal rights (the familiar life, liberty, and the pursuit of happiness—the implementation of which only requires nonintervention by government or others with power) and positive rights (such as the right to holidays with pay and medical treatment according to need, which require positive action by the appropriate authority if they are to be enjoyed by the right-holder). The implication is that because the possibility of meeting these social and economic demands depends on the level of economic performance achieved in any given society, it is wrong to treat such positive rights as universal rights on a level with the negative rights.[84]

The document that has made a good deal of difference both in practice and especially in discussion of the need for a British bill of rights is the

---

[83] Ewing and Gearty, *Freedom Under Thatcher*, 264–75.
[84] Maurice Cranston, *What Are Human Rights?* (London: Bodley Head, 1973), 65ff.

European Convention on Human Rights, dating back to 1951.[85] Indeed, it could with only slight exaggeration be said that "the United Kingdom has, since 1953 in fact, been subject to a modern bill of rights with its own machinery for interpretation, and during that time United Kingdom law and practice has on occasion been modified so as to conform to it."[86] The convention is backed up by a commission (which scrutinizes cases to see whether they are well founded or whether they can be dealt with by conciliation) and a court (which takes cases that the commission certifies as well founded, and which can and does tell the governments of the twenty-seven signatory states that their law is at odds with the convention) behind it, and a procedure for aggrieved parties to employ in bringing their cases before the court. It is regularly used by disgruntled citizens of the European Community (EC) countries, and unfavorable decisions are extremely embarrassing to governments found guilty of violating their citizens' rights. Although the court has immense prestige, as befits a court sitting in judgment on independent sovereign states, its proceedings are fairly informal. The court takes no risks with its reputation, however; the elaborate screening process ensures that trivial cases never reach it, and it never hears cases where it has no standing.[87]

The British government was one of the first to ratify the convention, but has remained unwilling to enact the convention into British law.[88] The other EC countries have ratified it and incorporated it into their domestic law. In the case of Britain, plaintiffs disgruntled at their treatment by the British legal system may, after exhausting all domestic resources, take their case to the European Court. The British government acknowledges the standing of the court by appearing before it, and indeed by legislating the procedures to be used in "going to Strasbourg"; but the court's judgment supplies a remedy only for the individual plaintiff, and does not establish new British law. Only the government can supply a general remedy by new legislation; thus far the British government has always done so, although often with ill grace. The effect of incorporation would be to make statutes subordinate to the convention and directly challengeable in a British court for their incompatibility with it.

The British principle of the supremacy of Parliament and British prickliness on the subject of legal sovereignty have always made it difficult to

---

[85] It came into force for the signatory states in 1953.
[86] De Smith and Brazier, *Constitutional and Administrative Law*, 426.
[87] Ibid., 426–31.
[88] Ibid., 430–1.

envisage subordinating British statutes to judicial review. Judges used to say that they did not know how they would proceed if matters changed in this regard. The British accession to the Treaty of Rome in 1971, however, has caused some weakening of that attitude, for the treaty subordinates British commercial law to the law of the European Community. Here the old rule that a later statute always trumps an earlier act is decisively done away with, and the assumption that Parliament must have intended to override any treaty with which its acts are inconsistent is explicitly repudiated. That is a small dent in sovereignty compared with the provisions of the European Convention, for these cover political, intellectual, and social freedoms that come closer to the heart of any government's control over its citizens.

The European Convention is the only example of a declaration of human rights that has made much impact on British thinking, either politically or intellectually. Statements of the "rights of peoples," such as the African Charter of 1981, the Algiers Declaration of 1976, or the International Convention on the Suppression of Apartheid of 1974, are known to specially interested persons and to lawyers, but to almost nobody else. It is hard to generalize, but British opinion is, if anything, hostile to declarations of right that go much beyond the recognition of individual immunities against governmental and other forms of brutality. Such purported rights as the rights of peoples to form a nation are not subjects of wide public interest, and most legal commentators treat assertions of such rights with great caution.

The burden of this chapter is that reliance on a bill of rights—based on an individualistic, quasi–natural rights conception of the law—is alien to the British political tradition but is becoming less alien. Indeed, it would seem that the "American" view of rights is acquiring intellectual respectability and political plausibility by the day. To put it differently, if Britain and the United States a century ago shared a common, common-law understanding of their adherence to the rule of law and the principles embodied in their bills of rights, they have since diverged, and Britain is now importing an American understanding of what it means to show a concern for social and political rights. Such a claim obviously must be qualified, but not qualified to death.

Until recently, when governments have been attacked for the wickedness of their activities or for their failure to secure the liberty of the citizenry, concern has centered on the activities in question, not on the violation of rights. Homosexual law reform sprang from a humanitarian feeling that the law against homosexual activities even in private and even between consenting adults served no purpose, was unenforceable except by means that were more repugnant than anything they were likely to prevent, and injured those whose sexual natures were thwarted in a peculiarly painful way.[89] None of these claims rested on the assertion of a *right* to sexual self-expression. Again, the censorship of stage productions by the Lord Chamberlain (a measure dating back to George II's troubles with the London theater) discredited itself when audiences no longer saw why God could not appear on stage and why actresses could not say four-letter words when everyone in the audience could and did. Pointless interference was just that—pointless.[90] The reforming view was more nearly utilitarian than rights based. It also produced very different results from the corresponding movement in the United States. The American emphasis on freedom of choice implies that where choice is protected as a right, nobody may interfere, and no other considerations than the freedom of the bearers of the right can be considered. American homosexuals campaigned more aggressively and energetically and demanded much greater public toleration of public expressions of their sexual preferences than British homosexual law reformers did. Advocates of easier access to abortion based their case on a right to choose that seemed to forbid governments to invoke any considerations beyond the freedom of choice of pregnant women.

SUCCESSES AND FAILURES

Advocates of these two very different ways of approaching civil liberties agree on the effects they will have. Utilitarians are willing to balance a variety of social goods against one another without giving absolute priority to any. So greater freedom for homosexuals can properly be balanced by some regard for the sensitivities of people who strongly disapprove of deviant sexual preferences. Rights theorists are absolutists. If homosexuals have a right to sexual self-expression, those who dislike homosexuality must simply control their distaste. In general, utilitarians will readily set considerations of decorum and the soothing of affronted feelings against the demands of liberty, while rights theorists will not.

The non—rights-based view of matters has had some striking successes to its credit, for instance, the British treatment of abortion. This is not

---

[89] Hart, *Law, Liberty and Morality*, 69–71.
[90] It was abolished by a private members bill in 1967.

to say that the British policy on abortion has wholly kept the peace and resulted in the humane and rational treatment of unwanted pregnancies throughout the British Isles. Right-to-life groups periodically succeed in getting a member of Parliament to put forward a bill to repeal the existing act in whole or in part—in practice, only in part, because there is no hope of anything more, and more serious challenges have failed—but apart from occasional episodes of this sort, the subject does not dominate politics.[91] It is widely acknowledged that, as with many other matters on which ultimate commitments differ dramatically, the best one can hope for is a practical solution that alienates as few of the population as possible. Nobody is happy with the increase in the number of abortions that have been performed over the past few years, any more than anyone welcomes the increase in the divorce rate since the easing of divorce. The public sentiment is that less misery is caused by the present regulations than by any alternative that can be put into place. The basis of this relative success is that few Britons wish to turn the issue into an argument between an unborn fetus's absolute immunity against injury and death and the mother's absolute control over her body. By the same token it can be argued that British practice violates the rights of both the mother and the fetus; the law criminalizes abortion, which violates the mother's rights, and it allows innumerable exceptions to that criminalization, which violates the fetus's rights.

The benefit of *not* arguing about rights in this case is clear. It would not be popular to assert that a mother had the right to do whatever she liked with her own body, including the contents of her womb; nor would it be popular to assert that the state was entitled to decide in detail just what she could do with her own body. The European Convention is inevitably at its feeblest on issues of this sort, for all it can do is assert in general terms the importance of respecting the individual's physical and moral integrity before going on to allow the state to regulate the individual's control of her body for reasons that include "public morality." Unsurprisingly, the European Commission has declined to agree that the absence of a right to abortion was a defect in the law of member states and a breach of the European Convention. The looser notion— that abortion was inevitable, unpleasant, but in many cases less unpleasant than the alternatives—carried the day in Britain in 1967 and has done ever since. Physicians and nurses who have conscientious objections

---

[91] Glendon, *Abortion and Divorce*, 42–6.

to performing abortions or assisting in them are not compelled to do so. The thought is that there is so much room for misery and real conscientious pain of one sort and another that regulations have to be framed to do as little damage as possible. No British commentator can make any sense at all of *Roe v. Wade,* where dubious premises have had to be worked very hard to produce a commonsensical outcome.[92]

Certainly British opinion would have been entirely hostile to the Connecticut legislation on birth control that provoked the original legal challenge that led to *Griswold* and the announcement that there was a constitutional right to privacy implicit in the Fourth Amendment immunity to unreasonable search and seizure. British opinion has always emphasized the value of privacy and the importance of not permitting the state to intrude into intimate areas of life. Lord Devlin, for instance, whose essay *The Enforcement of Morals* is a *locus classicus* of the judicial view that there are *no* areas that are simply and in principle outside the reach of the law, argued all along that the law's concern for "public morals" had to be tempered by a concern for privacy and family life.[93] What British commentators find hard to believe is that the U.S. Bill of Rights really contains a right to abortion, or that the way to deal with abortion is to treat it as a question of conflicting rights rather than a delicate issue of public policy. What American commentators find equally hard to accept is the British view that it makes perfectly good sense to declare abortion prima facie illegal, and then to spell out a wide range of exceptions that permit abortion in much the same situations that *Roe v. Wade* allowed.[94]

This case, and homosexual law reform, are only two in which the old British attitude to civil liberties still finds both popular support and substantial intellectual support.[95] It is more nearly true that over the past two decades the old confidence in the power of liberal common sense has diminished. Many issues have undermined that confidence, not least the long-drawn-out horrors of Northern Ireland. In the course of that conflict, the British government has been found guilty by the European Court of Human Rights of using cruel and degrading treatment barely short of torture to obtain evidence from suspected terrorists, has abol-

---

[92] Ibid., 51–2.
[93] Patrick Devlin, *The Enforcement of Morals* (Oxford: Clarendon Press, 1963).
[94] Laurence Tribe, *A Clash of Absolutes* (New York: W. W. Norton, 1990).
[95] It was a decision by the European Commission on Human Rights that forced the British government to extend the liberalizing legislation to Northern Ireland.

ished the right of accused persons to remain silent without suffering any adverse inferences as to their guilt or innocence, has diminished the habeas corpus rights of persons taken in for questioning in order to give the police a longer period of uninterrupted questioning to try to get a confession, has abolished trial by jury in cases involving terrorism, and has materially restricted the freedom of movement of the Irish in mainland Britain.[96] What has caused an almost continuous uproar since 1979 has been the conjunction of this erosion of civil liberties with the determined executive style of Margaret Thatcher's three administrations.

Elective despotism rediscovered. It is usually the liberals and the left who find themselves arguing for the statutory entrenchment of civil liberties. Since 1979, some of the pressure for a statutory defense of the public's right to know what the government is doing has come from liberal young civil servants who have gone out of their way to publicize what they have thought of as the assorted wickednesses of the Thatcher government. But the first recent demand for a bill of rights and for devices for tying the hands of *any* government came from a different and very unlikely direction. Lord Hailsham put back into British circulation the notion that Thomas Jefferson first introduced to the Americans, that of "elective dictatorship."[97]

As a Conservative politician who had never been particularly scrupulous in his charges against the Labour party, Lord Hailsham carried little weight. It is true that the ability of the British executive to carry its policies through Parliament with little obstruction amounts in many ways to elective dictatorship, as this chapter has already observed. Ordinarily, it is held to be a consequence of the British two-party system that what Britain operates is alternating party dictatorships, which happily are operated by liberal-minded persons, aware of both the prudential and principled arguments for exercising their dictatorial powers with moderation. Lord Hailsham's pained announcement of his discovery was therefore treated as a case of party politics as usual. It is a touching feature of British politics that Conservative critics of a Labour government always protest that it has no mandate for its actions and is in violation of the constitution, no matter what it sets out to do.

Still, Hailsham was quite right to notice that a two-party system, in

[96] Ewing and Gearty, *Freedom Under Thatcher*, 217–21.
[97] Lord Hailsham, *The Dilemma of Democracy: Diagnosis and Prescription* (London: Collins, 1978).

which politics goes on in the same adversarial fashion as the law, raises the question of how one can tell when the fight has ceased to be within the rules. Politics is not like a boxing match, in which the opponents try to knock each other senseless within the Marquis of Queensberry's rules and do not use their fists to persuade the referee to adjust the rules as well. The aim of political parties is not only to operate within current understandings but to change the fundamental rules and understandings on which their society rests. Given what was said earlier about the inability of Parliament to hold up a government's legislative program, it is natural to turn elsewhere for some constraint on what a government may try to push through Parliament. It is equally natural to resist such a move for all the reasons we have already spelled out.

Hailsham was hostile to the Labour party's desire to secure what it described as an "irreversible and massive transfer of wealth and power" to the working people of Britain. Had he known how unseriously this rhetoric was taken by those who uttered it, he might have been less anxious. What he wanted to enshrine into law was not so much the civil rights dear to the left but the right to acquire, hold, and not part with individual private property. The U.S. Constitution would certainly have done more to achieve that than any Labour government would find tolerable. As one authority observes, if the "American constitutional Bill of Rights had been transported to Britain along with Marshall Aid in the late 1940s...its terms would also have made it more difficult for Parliament to nationalize industries and implement town and country planning policies."[98] Civil liberties in the usual sense were not wholly absent from Hailsham's concerns, however. At the time he was writing, the print unions were aggressively looking for an editorial role in the papers they worked for. In this they were, rather extraordinarily, encouraged by Michael Foot, the employment minister of the day and a one-time journalist as well as a historian of dissenting journalism. Many people thought that the trade unions had quite enough power over their lives without gaining the power to censor the press as well. But others thought that Hailsham's conception of a free press was too narrow: it embraced the freedom of the proprietors and their editors but had no thought of opening access to the previously silent.

Hailsham's anxieties were taken care of, as far as he was concerned, by the return of a Conservative government. The more pressing source

[98] De Smith and Brazier, *Constitutional and Administrative Law*, 424.

of anxiety about civil liberties, and one whose impact has become more alarming, has been Northern Ireland. There are three rather distinct areas of disquiet. The first is the way the police, the government, and the army have behaved in the province itself. Detention without trial was originally tried as a way of pulling IRA sympathizers out of the population, but it turned out to alienate the Catholic population more effectively than any amount of IRA organizing. The army's methods of interrogating suspects were taken to the European Court of Human Rights as verging on torture. They were declared not to be torture, but they were condemned as inhumane and intolerable. There are periodic accusations that the police have been shooting IRA suspects on sight rather than scrupulously trying to catch them uninjured for a proper trial, and inquiries into the accusations have not carried conviction. A matter that goes to the heart of Northern Ireland's status as something close to a territory under military occupation is the way the British government has taken the province under direct rule for the past fifteen years. Even if essential, it is a violation of the ordinary rights of local self-government.

The second is the ancillary legislation created to make the task of the security forces easier and to give the population in Ulster and on the mainland more protection. The most important item is the Prevention of Terrorism Act, which gives the police such far-reaching powers of detention and interrogation that it has to be renewed every year. Once again, the law is not in itself intolerable in the light of the threat really posed to civilian life and limb by IRA bombers and assassins. But the extension of police powers and the lowering of the standards required for arrest and detention are intrinsically alarming, and anyone who is at all anxious about what the police may do under cover of preventing terrorism will be alarmed by the sweepingness of the measure. If Britain is a long way from following Latin American countries in which the suppression of terrorism has been made the excuse for a reign of terror by the military and police, the existence of such regimes is enough to give any nation cold feet.[99]

The third is the way in which the situation in Northern Ireland reinforces the political habits of a government already inclined to panic in the face of "law and order" issues. In Ulster there really is a low-key civil war going on. In the rest of the United Kingdom there is nothing of the sort. But when the National Union of Mineworkers (NUM)

---

[99] Ewing and Gearty, *Freedom Under Thatcher*, 230ff.

launched its disastrous and ill-advised strike in 1984, it touched a raw nerve. Arthur Scargill had been the hero of the NUM in 1974 when his so-called flying pickets were able to congregate in such numbers outside coalmines and power stations that the police were forced to tell the management to close down in the face of intimidation. He expected to close down the industry and the power stations again and foolishly advertised the fact. His offer to conduct the coal strike as if it were a civil war frightened and angered the public, and in a way militarized the conflict from the very beginning. No doubt Margaret Thatcher's government would have fought the strike with all the weapons it could plausibly use, and would have made sure that Scargill could not humiliate it in the way he had humiliated Edward Heath's government a decade earlier. But the government's support for the various chief constables whose "interforce task forces" prevented striking miners from organizing, traveling, and congregating in force was more enthusiastic than it would have been before the Northern Irish conflict. The government reacted with outrage to any suggestion that police measures violated the miners' freedom of speech, travel, and assembly, and was equally deaf to any suggestion that the police were guilty of provoking much of the violence that marked the strike. Margaret Thatcher's description of the mineworkers as "the enemy within" suggests the frame of mind in which her government approached the strike.

It is difficult to write dispassionately about Margaret Thatcher's years in office. The bossiness of which so many commentators complain looks less dreadful when contrasted with the feebleness of James Callaghan's government, and her outspoken and confrontational style seems less threatening compared with the emollient half-truths by which Harold Wilson kept the peace in the Labour party. All the same, it is hard to deny that under her government the powers of the authorities steadily increased and the ability of the citizen to call them to account or otherwise resist them diminished.

How far this authoritarian movement was a consequence of her intention to demolish British socialism is another question. It has undoubtedly become harder to pursue what used to be the ordinary activities of trade unions in Britain; aside from the alteration in the terms of conflict stemming from successive industrial relations acts, picketing has become more circumscribed than it used to be, and the police have become much more aggressive in policing industrial disputes—as the National Graphical Association learned to its cost when it tried to enforce a closed shop against Eddie Shah, the owner of a free local newspaper published at Warrington in Lancashire and later against Rupert Murdoch's papers when Murdoch moved out of Fleet Street and set up new printing works in Wapping. Besides being tougher on pickets on site, the police have become adept at stopping buses and cars bringing demonstrators and pickets to reinforce a local strike. Their warrant for so doing has been the old and new versions of the Public Order Acts, which permit the police to suspend ordinary freedom of assembly and movement to prevent a breach of the peace.[100] It is beyond the scope of this chapter to compare British and American practices in this field. British industry has always been more heavily unionized than American industry (although union membership has dropped dramatically in both countries). Mass picketing was thus more common in Britain than in the United States, although and perhaps for that reason British strikes were never as violent, and the effect of recent legislation has not been to deprive British workers of rights they would have retained in the United States so much as to make the two countries more similar.

Most complaints against Thatcher had little to do with the strictly economic front. The two areas of greatest concern were freedom of speech in connection with national security and with issues of criminal justice. The *Spycatcher* trial was perhaps the occasion that caused the loudest denunciations of the government's unconcern for the freedom of the press. The prosecution of the junior civil servant Clive Ponting for leaking defense ministry documents about the sinking of the Argentine cruiser, the *Admiral Belgrano,* was another, if less dramatic, example.[101] Turning from the First to the Fourth Amendment, the government was attacked for its failure to control police and security-service wiretapping and other forms of interception of communications. In Dicey's sense, the government has usually proceeded according to "the rule of law" inasmuch as it has consistently taken to itself by parliamentary means the legal authority to allow the police and the security services to eavesdrop on people they define (more or less according to their own preconceptions) as subversive. In a sense that owes less to Dicey, a government that legislates away the fundamental political freedoms of the people is an unlawful government. A bill of rights is intended to give such governments a hard

---

[100] Ibid., 103ff.
[101] Clive Ponting, *The Right to Know: The Inside Story of the Belgrano Affair* (London: Sphere, 1985).

time by allowing the government's conception of the general interest to be challenged in the courts.

The public demand for a moderating influence of this kind was mostly articulated by a new political grouping. After 1974 British politics were more angry and uncivil than they had been during most of the 1950s and '60s. The Labour party began to slide to the left, and the Conservative party by an odd reaction began to move sharply to the right. Some Labour voters deserted outright to the Conservatives, many more abstained, and the result was that the Conservatives enjoyed overwhelming parliamentary majorities with 40 percent of the actual vote and barely 30 percent of the electorate. This circumstance left large numbers of voters alienated from both traditional parties. Politics abhors a vacuum, and into the center stepped the Alliance, that is, the allied Liberal and Social Democratic parties.

The Alliance was briefly more popular than either of the major parties, but in a way that did not translate into votes. Voters liked its policies and its conciliatory style, but thought it had no chance of forming a government and were therefore not going to "waste" their votes on it. The Alliance's attention naturally turned to proportional representation and from that, in turn, to the superior political and civil liberties performance of the rest of Europe. At the end of the 1980s there arrived Charter 88, a movement inspired by the tricentennial of the Glorious Revolution and the Declaration of Rights and organized by an unlikely combination of former Marxists, Alliance and Labour party activists, and free-floating intellectuals, all under the benign patronage of Lord Scarman. The otherwise somewhat confusing conjunction of items on the shopping list of Charter 88 and the Alliance owes much to the feeling that the British have neither lived up to the professions of 1688 nor to the recent achievements of their fellow-Europeans. Americans would feel entirely at home with these demands for a bill of rights and with the emphasis on a restatement of the rights of citizenship, but it is hard to imagine an American audience agreeing, without prompting, that one of the rights of the citizen was to vote by proportional representation.

The Alliance was the natural home of all who felt that Thatcher's counterrevolution was an irrational and unduly abrasive way of improving industrial relations and encouraging initiative, and who did not fancy the class-war scenario that the wilder elements in the Labour party offered in its place. So it was not surprising that the Alliance advocated a bill of rights and the incorporation of the European Convention into

British law. As it became increasingly clear through the 1980s that Thatcher's taste for law and order would lead to a criminal justice bill giving the police more sweeping powers of detention than they had ever had in British history, and that the government also intended to restrict the accused's right to keep silent, to take draconian powers to censor the media for the sake of security in Ireland, and to preserve government secrets that the whole non-British world already knew, the soft center became increasingly attracted to the idea of setting up a judicial barrier to government excesses of this kind.

Why the center placed so much faith in the judiciary is mysterious in view of the behavior of the judiciary during this period. It took a revolt by the jury to acquit Clive Ponting; only two British judges stood up to the government in the *Spycatcher* affair, and during the mining strike of 1984–85, magistrates allowed the police a free hand in controlling strikers without any hint from senior judges that the police were abusing the latitude given them by the Public Order Act of 1936. The Public Order Act of 1986 tidied up the provisions of the 1936 act, without suggesting that it gave any cause for anxiety. Certainly, there was no judicial pressure for improvement. Nor had the judiciary taken a liberal view of the rights of those detained by the police in their interpretation of the Police and Criminal Evidence Act of 1984.[102] Perhaps the best explanation is that when Lord Scarman was given the task of inquiring into the Brixton riots of 1981 mentioned earlier, he concluded that a large part of the trouble lay in the heavy-handed actions of the police, and that the British citizenry were inadequately safeguarded against excessive force, let alone against illegalities and cover-ups of other kinds.

An aspect of this lack of protection that bears on the question whether the British need a bill of rights is that in British law the police are not penalized for committing illegalities on the way to court. Evidence obtained improperly is admissible in court, so that the most obvious incentive to good behavior has been thrown away. Moreover, there are many local and national laws that would never survive appeal in the United States; nineteenth-century laws against vagrancy can be used to pick up anyone the police do not like the look of, and it is not unduly difficult for the police to find something to charge the vagrant with if they do so. The use of the so-called sus law, which allows the police to detain anyone "on suspicion" that they have committed, or might be

---

[102] Ewing and Gearty, *Freedom Under Thatcher*, 29ff.

about to commit, a crime was the major black grievance against the police and the main cause of the Brixton riots. The argument between those who think that a British bill of rights would do some good and those who think it would not tends to hang on their view of the chances of finding many more Lord Scarmans among the judiciary.

The judiciary's previous record is not conclusive evidence. The British have behaved somewhat like their colleagues in South Africa, where the judiciary has been scrupulous in keeping the government to the rule of law in Dicey's sense, but legislation has been utterly illiberal. Like the South African judiciary, British judges have been sticklers for law and precedent; they will not let the police act without having the law on their side, but police action with a plausible legal color is not closely scrutinized. Judicial ideology has been that the citizenry should have every liberty the law allows, and that if the law allows very few, the citizenry will have very few and had better apply to Parliament for redress. New laws requiring the judiciary to balance freedom of speech, freedom of the press, freedom of assembly, immunity to unreasonable search and seizure, and the rest against the requirements of law and order would certainly be implemented scrupulously, although it is an open question whether they would be implemented with generosity. Skeptics doubt whether British judges would show much generosity, and many skeptics doubt whether the Supreme Court of the United States will provide an encouraging model for them in the present decade.

The impact of a bill of rights depends as heavily on how judges decide to interpret it in Europe as it does in Britain, and as heavily in the United States as on the other side of the Atlantic. All the objections to giving judges a free hand that were noted earlier remain as strong as ever. Judges are more likely to give the benefit of the doubt to people in authority than to troublemakers of dubious political views and dubious racial origin. The American jurisprudential doctrine of "legal realism"—the idea that what the law *is* is simply what the judges will *decide*—is an exaggeration, but it exaggerates something undeniable.[103] According to an American adage, the Supreme Court "follows the election returns," and judicial liberalism and judicial conservatism occur pretty much as they occur in the country at large. No doubt the process occurs with something of a time lag, but hardly anyone denies that it occurs. If that

[103] Hart, *Concept of Law*, 132–44.

is so, a certain skepticism seems in order for any British attempt to import American law and practice.

Nonskeptical reactions to a bill of rights. That nonskepticism also has some appeal has been demonstrated by the success of Charter 88. When Charter 88 was formed, Margaret Thatcher was quick to deride it as yet another attempt to undermine her authority, and one that voters would ignore as they had ignored all previous challenges to her authority. The Labour party was equally quick to deride it as a plot to hold up the activities of a reforming Labour administration. It soon emerged that the Labour party had miscalculated public opinion. Although the British public is no more interested in the niceties of constitutional reform than any other democratic electorate, there is widespread anxiety that the Labour party has not entirely purged itself of assorted authoritarian leftists—sympathizers with the IRA, members of the Militant organization, and other Trotskyite groupings. The prospect of some entrenched safeguards against the influence of these groups on a future Labour government is attractive to many voters.

The deputy leader of the Labour party, Roy Hattersley, for years has held out against all such proposals, largely for the old reason that there would never be a one-party Labour administration again under any system of proportional representation. Lately he has been forced to concede that a Labour government will have to do *something* to guarantee civil liberties. He has suggested that the next Labour government will enact a people's charter enshrining the rights of assembly, speech, and publication that have been particularly at risk, and giving individuals clearer protection against arbitrary arrest and detention by the police. Charter 88's generalized anxiety about executive authority is not shared by the Labour leadership. Indeed, one would not expect such anxiety to commend itself to the leaders of any party, British or American.

The picture I have tried to present is complex. At its heart is the fact that the British have long taken it for granted that politics is a party battle in which success is a matter of winning a general election and keeping a parliamentary majority intact until major legislative goals are met. Until recently, it was assumed that a social consensus on the rules of the political game constrained all parties and guaranteed that politicians would respect the traditional British freedoms. The familiar rights that Parliament had defended against James II and the American Founders had enshrined in the Bill of Rights were thought to be safer in Britain than anywhere in the world, just because they were guaranteed by a consensus and not by "a piece of paper." Against the background of those settled expectations partisan politics could flourish. It was expected that Conservatives would legislate to give a free rein to propertied interests, would be antipathetic to principled defenses of freedom of speech and assembly, would place law and order above a fastidious concern to avoid unwarrantable search and seizure, and would expect the judiciary to accept the government's view of the national interest in cases involving security and defense. It was equally expected that the Labour party would legislate to offset the existing advantages of property and enhance the freedom of working class organization; might (but might not) engage in the principled expansion of sexual, artistic, and intellectual liberties; and would expect the judiciary to scrutinize everything it did with a mildly hostile eye, except in matters of national security, where it would expect to get the benefit of the same doubt that all other governments receive. Liberal voters hoped that what they could not achieve by electing a Liberal government they could bring about by persuading one of the major parties that its popularity depended on enacting part of the Liberal agenda. The parallels with, and differences from, politics in the United States are evident.

The partisan quality of British politics interests political theorists because it raises the question of what underlying pattern of moral argument supports the competing programs. This chapter has argued that the British have assumed that the task of government is to promote the general interest and have thought of individual rights as constituents of the general interest more than as constraints upon it. Each party argues that it can pursue the general interest more effectively than its competitors (the Labour party's class character is less than skin-deep), but naturally understands the general interest rather differently from its opponents. The cultural attachments and high-principled commitments to rights reflected in American politics enter by being taken into the computation of the general interest. This difference explains the unwillingness of British political theorists to make the theory of government a theory of rights. Until recently, many British writers have been impatient with arguments based on rights altogether—or, at any rate, with arguments that make rights "a thing independent of utility."[104] There has been some change of heart. The events of the past twenty years have unsettled assumptions about

---

[104] Mill, *Utilitarianism, Liberty, and Representative Government*, 132–5.

the lack of a need for a bill of rights and have undermined old beliefs about the effectiveness of British public opinion in restraining government illiberalism and authoritarianism. Conversely, belief in the importance of rights has grown stronger, and political theorists have become readier to discuss rights in a nonutilitarian framework, even in something close to a framework of natural rights.[105]

This change of heart manifests itself in the reception into British intellectual life of the political ideas of John Rawls and Ronald Dworkin.[106] American ideas have flourished in a foreign marketplace because they speak to contemporary British political and intellectual needs. Though Ronald Dworkin has lived in England for twenty years, John Rawls has not, and Rawls has had an equally important influence on recent political ideas. It is important to distinguish between Dworkin's pure jurisprudence and his underlying moral theory. British readers have largely rejected Dworkin's claims about the judicial process but have found the moral theory very attractive. Most British readers find Dworkin's theory of constitutional interpretation alien. Critics complain that they cannot tell whether Dworkin subscribes to some version of the theory of natural law—according to which what "really" underlies the U.S. Constitution is the law of nature—or whether he is only an elaborately disguised legal positivist, according to whom one's (legal) rights are determined by local law, the elaborate disguise being a matter of the interpretation of the law.[107] Similarly, in the case of John Rawls, British readers have thought some elements of his ideas much more important to an American audience than any other, but have found Rawls's theory of justice and rights not in the least limited by its national origins.

Students of British law sometimes dismiss Dworkin's views on judicial interpretation as inapplicable to Britain, though they are ready to admit that they may be apt in an American context. Sometimes they argue that no theory of law that tries to set out a *general* theory of adjudication and interpretation can afford to be so at odds with the practice of British judges.[108] British judges are surely judges, and what they engage in is adjudication. What critics find morally attractive but unacceptable as

---

[105] This is enigmatically put, but Chapter 5 of this volume illuminates my point more elegantly than any discussion I might insert here.
[106] Will Kymlicka, *Contemporary Political Philosophy* (Oxford: Clarendon Press, 1990).
[107] Neil MacCormick, *Legal Right and Social Democracy* (Oxford: Clarendon Press, 1982), chap. 7.
[108] Lee, *Judging Judges*, 20–32.

jurisprudence is Dworkin's insistence that determinations of right are wholly different from consequentialist decisions about future judicial policy, and Dworkin's subsequent claim that the judge's task is to *find* a right answer embedded in the law, not to work out what a good rule for the future would be. British judges consistently employ consequentialist arguments and do not flinch from what this implies. The House of Lords has issued a "practice statement" declaring its readiness not to be bound by its previous decisions, and nobody doubts that judges do, must, and ought to *make* law as well as discover it.[109]

What remains attractive about Dworkin's thinking is the depth of his commitment to individual liberty—even if it is called liberal equality— and his reiterated insistence that without such a commitment, law and rights are not taken seriously. This commitment is, in a British context, rhetorically powerful as well as intellectually persuasive, for Dworkin's writing displays a wide-eyed incomprehension of the way that British law does *not* recognize the fundamental rights that the U.S. Bill of Rights does. It is the depth of Dworkin's conviction that British civil liberties are treated in an arbitrary and unpredictable fashion by both governments and judges just because they do not employ an adequate theory of rights that makes his rather rare, sidelong observations about British politics so effective.[110]

In the background of Dworkin's observations lies the monumental work of John Rawls. It is doubtful whether anyone anywhere can properly be called a disciple of Rawls—a circumstance that doubtless comes as a relief to Rawls himself. For all the regard in which Rawls's work is held in Britain, it is also doubtful whether even now British political theorists share their American colleagues' conviction that a political theory must be a theory of rights in its foundations rather than in passing. Nonetheless, the thought has struck home that liberals and radicals need a theory of rights that will set limits—on the one hand, to the extent to which individuals can refuse to cooperate in social reform and stand pat on their proprietary rights and, on the other hand, to the extent to which individuals can be conscripted for good social purposes. The individualism that sustains the defense of the liberties and immunities protected by the U.S. Bill of Rights and spelled out in traditional theories of natural right has become deeply attractive to a British audience.

---

[109] Ibid., 3–17.
[110] For example, his "Why Britain Needs a Bill of Rights," *The Observer* (London), 30 September 1990, and *A Bill of Rights for Britain?* (London: Chato & Windus, 1990).

There is another explanation of the support that Rawls and Dworkin have found in Britain. Theories of politics based on rights have frequently been attacked for being essentially conservative. They provide people with defenses against attack or the active ill-will of others, but they supply no remedy against bad luck or natural misfortune. Individuals may have all their rights respected and still fare very badly. It is this problem that is remedied in the theories of Rawls and Dworkin. Rawls's theory of justice provides the least-advantaged people with a *right* to fare as well as they possibly can. Conservative critics, both in Britain and America, dislike the doctrine for exactly this reason, and still want to distinguish sharply between a concern for *rights,* which sustains the rule of law, and *benevolence,* which sustains a welfare state. The rhetorical advantage of appealing to rights is obvious, and so long as the moral high ground on which they are established is tolerably secure, demanding one's welfare *rights* is clearly more morally impressive than asking one's betters to be benevolent.

As to how welfare rights can be integrated into a theory of rights there is much debate, and nobody supposes that the last word has been said on either side of the Atlantic. Indeed, there are plenty of diverse resources to draw on. The considerations of security and predictability that Mill emphasized are one obvious basis, as is the thought that liberty is of no use to anyone who lacks the resources to take advantage of that liberty. Anatole France's famous quip that "the law in its impartial majesty forbids rich and poor alike to sleep under the bridges of Paris" is a much-used weapon in such discussions. Again, the concept of urgency or need can be invoked to draw a line between what would truly be charity given by the better-off and what is a matter of justice. It is an injustice to remain indifferent to the claims of need, which is as much as to say that the needy have a right to assistance from the well-off.

The intellectual interest of rights theories is a matter of the philosophical quality of arguments for a wider or narrower account of our rights. The political interest lies in the fact that a "culture of rights" is a seamless garment. The habit of arguing in terms of rights and their protection is not likely to be confined to one area of political debate, and it is not likely to be confined to one set of institutions. The British think of the United States as a litigious society, while Americans think of the British as too ready to accept what they are told about their entitlements. To the degree that British utilitarianism is permeated by or replaced by something nearer the U.S. belief in rights, this difference will lessen. One can readily imagine British lawyers taking on some of the characteristics of U.S. "public interest" lawyers and pressing the courts to act more aggressively over entitlements to health care, unemployment benefits, educational access, and much else.

Another traditional doubt about the political value of constantly appealing to rights was the fear that rights talk was excessively individualistic. The question of how the rights of individuals relate to the rights, if any, of groups, cultures, nations, and peoples remains a vexed issue.[111] Although Dworkin's best-known accounts of the nature of rights stress their *individualistic* quality—they are "trumps" held by individuals—his account of the content of rights supports more group rights than appears at first sight. Dworkin claims that our fundamental right is the right to equal concern and respect, and this means that anyone who is discriminated against on the ground of race or creed or sex in a matter that is properly regulated by the law can demand redress. The law cannot undertake to secure parity of esteem in private matters, let alone parity of liking. The law can secure, and on Dworkin's reading of the U.S. Constitution the law is committed to securing, equality of treatment by public bodies and equality of access to economic and other advantages regulated by law. The procedures used to achieve this equality of concern and respect may even *look* like reverse discrimination and a rectificatory inequality of treatment, as when colleges and universities admit minority students with lower test scores than white students. Dworkin's gloss on such procedures is that they do not confer unequal rights on minorities because their effect is to secure equality of concern and respect in the face of unequal antecedent treatment. It is unclear whether Dworkin supposes that a similar right to equal concern and respect is part of British law; at times he certainly suggests that any modern legal system rests on the same basic rights. It is this suggestion that disregarded minorities have a right to redress, and that this right may even exist in British law, that helps Dworkin's theory to find acceptance in Britain, where it was long felt that the American concern for the political and legal rights listed in the Bill of Rights went along with a splendid unconcern for the survival, let alone the welfare, of outgroups.

British readers have been skeptical about the way the theory has been applied to some cases of reverse discrimination, notably the *Bakke* case.[112]

---

[111] James Crawford, *The Rights of Peoples* (Oxford: Clarendon Press, 1986).
[112] Lee, *Judging Judges*, 20–5, is a slapdash but representative account of why Dworkin's views strike British readers as alien and unpersuasive.

The thought that groups can have rights by virtue of possessing a way of life that needs protecting or by virtue of protecting their role in the life of the whole society is one that has begun to spread, most recently because of the work of Joseph Raz.[113] Here the apparent conflict between the loose utilitarianism of British public life and the rigidity of rights theories has been subdued. Raz's account of rights is an "interest" theory of rights, in which rights are explained in the way they were explained in Mill's *Utilitarianism,* in terms of the protection of vital interests.[114] A twist to the argument, however, is that one of these vital interests is an interest in a fair share of the cultural and other resources of one's society. The thought that underlies much of Raz's work is that everyone enters the world with a right to a fair share of its resources and opportunities and is therefore owed a fair contribution from other people. Thus the question of what duties a right to work imposes and on whom it falls does not produce the answer that someone must find jobs for all the unemployed; rather, *all* of us must contribute on equitable terms to whatever rational scheme for overcoming unemployment can be devised.

In this way, the welfare rights that are set out in the UN Declaration and in the European Convention get a grounding beyond their mere enactment into positive law. The legal right rests on a moral right not on a maximizing utilitarian calculation or on other non–rights-based considerations. Viewed thus, the connection of rights and freedom ceases to be a matter of beginning with a few obvious immunities—life, liberty, and the pursuit of happiness—and branching out to an expanded conception of freedom.[115] The broader conception based on the right to a fair share of the advantages of our culture and its resources dominates from the outset. This account of freedom resembles more traditional theories in picking out some political rights as peculiarly important and in yielding less clear results for welfare rights and even less clear results for claimed rights to public assistance for religion. Thus the special status of First, Fourth, and Fifth Amendment rights springs from the kinds of vulnerability and weakness that they are particularly intended to shield, and the kind of political relationship between rulers and ruled that they are particularly designed to promote. Rights to welfare, which some writers have dismissed as not being rights at all, are less determinate,

---

[113] Joseph Raz, *The Morality of Freedom* (Oxford: Clarendon Press, 1986).
[114] Ibid., 180–3.
[115] Though this is how I have generally proceeded myself; see, for example, "Socialism and Freedom," in *Fabian Essays on Socialism,* 101–16.

because it is less clear what a fair share of society's resources comes to and because it is often unclear how best to achieve the welfare goals we have in mind. Common sense emerges unshaken. The common assumption that the right not to starve is a genuine, rock-bottom welfare right is easy to sustain, because there are many effective ways to prevent people starving in societies such as Britain or the United States. The right to public funds for religious education is much more disputable, because it is unclear that this claim amounts to a legitimate call on the purses of the irreligious, and unclear that children would suffer grievous harm from a secular education. There might, of course, be other reasons for such public funding quite unrelated to the rights of children.

CONCLUSION

Let me risk my reputation by offering some concluding predictions. The first is that, in Britain, the argument over the incorporation of the European Convention will continue until it is incorporated. The last parliamentary attempt to do this was defeated only because the government imposed a three-line whip (the strictest party discipline) against a private member's bill, but there will come a time when the government either will not dare to impose a three-line whip or will be unable to keep its troops in line.[116] The second prediction is that the effects of the European Convention's incorporation will be disappointing. The convention does exactly what Dicey (and Margaret Thatcher)[117] maintained that all such statements of rights must do: It states a right in general terms and then allows government to abridge that right on so many grounds of security, public order, national need, and even public morality that everything turns on the courts' perception of the government's good faith, the courts' reasonableness in applying those exceptions, and the courts' commitment to the initial rights. Unless British judges become much less inclined to support the government of the day than they have been, there is no reason to think that governments that choose to behave as Thatcher's government behaved will be much impeded. The remarks of Lord Templeman, who explicitly raised the question of the consistency of the British government's stand in the *Spycatcher* case with the requirements of the European Convention, ought to disillusion anyone who expects great

---

[116] De Smith and Brazier, *Constitutional and Administrative Law*, 430–1.
[117] See Thatcher's letter of 26 May 1989 in reply to Lady Ewart-Biggs's letter commending Charter 88's program and distributed to members of Charter 88.

things from incorporation. (Templeman had no doubt that the considerations of national security mentioned by the convention gave the government the right to stop the press from publishing excerpts from the
book.)[118] The third prediction is that the incorporation of the European
Convention will be worth having simply because it will force the courts
to balance statutorily declared rights against government claims. At present, the unwritten constitution allows such considerations to enter only
insofar as judges balance one aspect of the public interest (for example,
the public interest in a free press) against another (for example, the public
interest in national security or in the prevention of terrorist outrages).

The fourth prediction is that such incorporation will lead to some
interesting and innovative legislation and interpretation as Parliament
and the judiciary come to terms with the convention's impact on parliamentary supremacy. Incorporation will have an impact on judicial review
of administrative action, as well as on the willingness of judges to review
subordinated legislation. If incorporation will not make an enormous
difference in the large and contentious cases, such as the *Spycatcher* case
or the trial of Clive Ponting, it will make a small revolution in less exciting
cases. Of course, to what extent all this comes to pass depends on the
future of British relations with the rest of Europe and on the character
of the British judiciary over the next decade or so. Both of these matters
are outside the scope of a single historical and philosophical chapter.

[118] Lee, *Judging Judges,* 114 (quoting Lord Templeman).

Appendix:
The Constitution and the Bill of Rights

Constitution of the United States of America

PREAMBLE

We the people of the United States, in order to form a more perfect union, establish justice, insure domestic tranquillity, provide for the common defense, promote the general welfare, and secure the blessings of liberty to ourselves and our posterity, do ordain and establish this CONSTITUTION for the United States of America.

ARTICLE I

Section I. All legislative powers herein granted shall be vested in a Congress of the United States, which shall consist of a Senate and a House of Representatives.

Section II. The House of Representatives shall be composed of members chosen every second year by the people of the several States, and the electors in each State shall have the qualifications requisite for electors of the most numerous branch of the State Legislature.

No person shall be a Representative who shall not have attained to the age of twenty-five years, and been seven years a citizen of the United States, and who shall not, when elected, be an inhabitant of that State in which he shall be chosen.

Representatives and direct taxes shall be apportioned among the several States which may be included within this Union, according to their respective numbers, *which shall be determined by adding to the whole number of free persons, including those bound to service for a term of years and excluding Indians not taxed, three-fifths of all other persons.* The actual enumeration shall be made within three years after the first meeting of the Congress of the United States, and within every subsequent

NOTE: Passages that are no longer in effect are printed in italic type.

440

term of ten years, in such manner as they shall by law direct. The number of Representatives shall not exceed one for every thirty thousand, but each State shall have at least one Representative; *and until such enumeration shall be made, the State of New Hampshire shall be entitled to choose three, Massachusetts eight, Rhode Island and Providence Plantations one, Connecticut five, New York six, New Jersey four, Pennsylvania eight, Delaware one, Maryland six, Virginia ten, North Carolina five, South Carolina five, and Georgia three.*

When vacancies happen in the representation from any State, the Executive authority thereof shall issue writs of election to fill such vacancies.

The House of Representatives shall choose their Speaker and other officers; and shall have the sole power of impeachment.

Section III. The Senate of the United States shall be composed of two Senators from each State, *chosen by the legislature thereof,* for six years; and each Senator shall have one vote.

Immediately after they shall be assembled in consequence of the first election, they shall be divided as equally as may be into three classes. The seats of the Senators of the first class shall be vacated at the expiration of the second year, of the second class at the expiration of the fourth year, and of the third class at the expiration of the sixth year, so that one-third may be chosen every second year; *and if vacancies happen by resignation or otherwise, during the recess of the legislature of any State, the Executive thereof may make temporary appointments until the next meeting of the legislature, which shall then fill such vacancies.*

No person shall be a Senator who shall not have attained to the age of thirty years, and been nine years a citizen of the United States, and who shall not, when elected, be an inhabitant of that State for which he shall be chosen.

The Vice-President of the United States shall be President of the Senate, but shall have no vote, unless they be equally divided.

The Senate shall choose their other officers, and also a President *pro tempore,* in the absence of the Vice-President, or when he shall exercise the office of President of the United States.

The Senate shall have the sole power to try all impeachments. When sitting for that purpose, they shall be on oath or affirmation. When the President of the United States is tried, the Chief Justice shall preside: and no person shall be convicted without the concurrence of two-thirds of the members present.

Judgment in cases of impeachment shall not extend further than to removal from office, and disqualification to hold and enjoy any office of honor, trust or profit under the United States: but the party convicted shall nevertheless be liable and subject to indictment, trial, judgment and punishment, according to law.

Section IV. The times, places and manner of holding elections for Senators and Representatives shall be prescribed in each State by the legislature thereof; but the Congress may at any time by law make or alter such regulations, except as to the places of choosing Senators.

The Congress shall assemble at least once in every year, and such meeting *shall be on the first Monday in December, unless they shall by law appoint a different day.*

Section V. Each house shall be the judge of the elections, returns and qualifications of its own members, and a majority of each shall constitute a quorum to do business; but a smaller number may adjourn from day to day, and may be authorized to compel the attendance of absent members, in such manner, and under such penalties, as each house may provide.

Each house may determine the rules of its proceedings, punish its members for disorderly behavior, and with the concurrence of two-thirds, expel a member.

Each house shall keep a journal of its proceedings, and from time to time publish the same, excepting such parts as may in their judgment require secrecy; and the yeas and nays of the members of either house on any question shall, at the desire of one-fifth of those present, be entered on the journal.

Neither house, during the session of Congress, shall, without the consent of the other, adjourn for more than three days, nor to any other place than that in which the two houses shall be sitting.

Section VI. The Senators and Representatives shall receive a compensation for their services, to be ascertained by law and paid out of the treasury of the United States. They shall in all cases except treason, felony and breach of the peace, be privileged from arrest during their attendance at the session of their respective houses, and in going to and returning from the same; and for any speech or debate in either house, they shall not be questioned in any other place.

No Senator or Representative shall, during the time for which he was elected, be appointed to any civil office under the authority of the United States, which shall have been created, or the emoluments whereof shall have been increased, during such time; and no person holding any office under the United States shall be a member of either house during his continuance in office.

Section VII. All bills for raising revenue shall originate in the House of Representatives; but the Senate may propose or concur with amendments as on other bills.

Every bill which shall have passed the House of Representatives and the Senate, shall, before it become a law, be presented to the President of the United States; if he approve he shall sign it, but if not he shall return it with objections to that house in which it originated, who shall enter the objections at large on their journal, and proceed to reconsider it. If after such reconsideration two-thirds of that house shall agree to pass the bill, it shall be sent, together with the objections, to the other house, by which it shall likewise be reconsidered, and, if approved by two-thirds of that house, it shall become a law. But in all such cases the votes of both houses shall be determined by yeas and nays, and the names of the persons voting for and against the bill shall be entered on the journal of each house respectively. If any bill shall not be returned by the President within ten days (Sundays excepted) after it shall have been presented to him, the same shall be a law, in like manner as if he had signed it, unless the Congress by their adjournment prevent its return, in which case it shall not be a law.

Every order, resolution, or vote to which the concurrence of the Senate and House of Representatives may be necessary (except on a question of adjournment) shall be presented to the President of the United States; and before the same shall take effect, shall be approved by him, or being disapproved by him, shall be repassed by two-thirds of the Senate and House of Representatives, according to the rules and limitations prescribed in the case of a bill.

Section VIII. The Congress shall have power

To lay and collect taxes, duties, imposts, and excises, to pay the debts and provide for the common defense and general welfare of the United

States; but all duties, imposts and excises shall be uniform throughout the United States;

To borrow money on the credit of the United States;

To regulate commerce with foreign nations, and among the several States, and with the Indian tribes;

To establish an uniform rule of naturalization, and uniform laws on the subject of bankruptcies throughout the United States;

To coin money, regulate the value thereof, and of foreign coin, and fix the standard of weights and measures;

To provide for the punishment of counterfeiting the securities and current coin of the United States;

To establish post offices and post roads;

To promote the progress of science and useful arts by securing for limited times to authors and inventors the exclusive right to their respective writings and discoveries;

To constitute tribunals inferior to the Supreme Court;

To define and punish piracies and felonies committed on the high seas and offenses against the law of nations;

To declare war, grant letters of marque and reprisal, and make rules concerning captures on land and water;

To raise and support armies, but no appropriation of money to that use shall be for a longer term than two years;

To provide and maintain a navy;

To make rules for the government and regulation of the land and naval forces;

To provide for calling forth the militia to execute the laws of the Union, suppress insurrections, and repel invasions;

To provide for organizing, arming, and disciplining the militia, and for governing such part of them as may be employed in the service of the United States, reserving to the States respectively the appointment of the officers, and the authority of training the militia according to the discipline prescribed by Congress;

To exercise exclusive legislation in all cases whatsoever, over such district (not exceeding ten miles square) as may, by cession of particular States, and the acceptance of Congress, become the seat of government of the United States, and to exercise like authority over all places purchased by the consent of the legislature of the State, in which the same shall be, for the erection of forts, magazines, arsenals, dock-yards, and other needful buildings;—and

To make all laws which shall be necessary and proper for carrying into execution the foregoing powers, and all other powers vested by this Constitution in the government of the United States, or in any department or officer thereof.

Section IX. The migration or importation of such persons as any of the States now existing shall think proper to admit shall not be prohibited by the Congress prior to the year 1808; but a tax or duty may be imposed on such importation, not exceeding $10 for each person.

The privilege of the writ of habeas corpus shall not be suspended, unless when in cases of rebellion or invasion the public safety may require it.

No bill of attainder or ex post facto law shall be passed.

No capitation, or other direct, tax shall be laid, unless in proportion to the census or enumeration herein before directed to be taken.

No tax or duty shall be laid on articles exported from any State.

No preference shall be given by any regulation of commerce or revenue to the ports of one State over those of another; nor shall vessels bound to, or from, one State, be obliged to enter, clear, or pay duties in another.

No money shall be drawn from the treasury, but in consequence of appropriations made by law; and a regular statement and account of the receipts and expenditures of all public money shall be published from time to time.

No title of nobility shall be granted by the United States: and no person holding any office of profit or trust under them, shall, without the consent of the Congress, accept of any present, emolument, office, or title, of any kind whatever, from any king, prince, or foreign state.

Section X. No state shall enter into any treaty, alliance, or confederation; grant letters of marque and reprisal; coin money; emit bills of credit; make anything but gold and silver coin a tender in payment of debts; pass any bill of attainder, ex post facto law, or law impairing the obligation of contracts, or grant any title of nobility.

No State shall, without the consent of Congress, lay any imposts or duties on imports or exports, except what may be absolutely necessary for executing its inspection laws: and the net produce of all duties and imposts, laid by any State on imports or exports, shall be for the use of the treasury of the United States; and all such laws shall be subject to the revision and control of the Congress.

No State shall, without the consent of Congress, lay any duty of tonnage, keep troops or ships of war in time of peace, enter into any agreement or compact with another State, or with a foreign power, or engage in war, unless actually invaded, or in such imminent danger as will not admit of delay.

ARTICLE II

Section I. The executive power shall be vested in a President of the United States of America. He shall hold his office during the term of four years, and, together with the Vice-President, chosen for the same term, be elected as follows:

Each State shall appoint, in such manner as the legislature thereof may direct, a number of electors, equal to the whole number of Senators and Representatives to which the State may be entitled in the Congress; but no Senator or Representative, or person holding an office of trust or profit under the United States, shall be appointed an elector.

The electors shall meet in their respective States, and vote by ballot for two persons, of whom one at least shall not be an inhabitant of the same State with themselves. And they shall make a list of all the persons voted for, and of the number of votes for each; which list they shall sign and certify, and transmit sealed to the seat of government of the United States, directed to the President of the Senate. The President of the Senate shall, in the presence of the Senate and House of Representatives, open all the certificates, and the votes shall then be counted. The person having the greatest number of votes shall be the President, if such number be a majority of the whole number of electors appointed; and if there be more than one who have such majority, and have an equal number of votes, then the House of Representatives shall immediately choose by ballot one of them for President; and if no person have a majority, then from the five highest on the list said house shall in like manner choose the President. But in choosing the President the votes shall be taken by States, the representation from each State having one vote; a quorum for this purpose shall consist of a member or members from two-thirds of the States, and a majority of all the States shall be necessary to a choice. In every case, after the choice of the President, the person having the greatest number of votes of the electors shall be the Vice-President. But if there should remain two or more who have equal votes, the Senate shall choose from them by ballot the Vice-President.

The Congress may determine the time of choosing the electors and the day on which they shall give their votes; which day shall be the same throughout the United States.

No person except a natural-born citizen, *or a citizen of the United States at the time of the adoption of this Constitution,* shall be eligible to the office of President; neither shall any person be eligible to that office who shall not have attained to the age of thirty-five years, and been fourteen years a resident within the United States.

In case of the removal of the President from office or of his death, resignation, or inability to discharge the powers and duties of the said office, the same shall devolve on the Vice-President, and the Congress may by law provide for the case of removal, death, resignation, or inability, both of the President and Vice-President, declaring what officer shall then act as President, and such officer shall act accordingly, until the disability be removed, or a President shall be elected.

The President shall, at stated times, receive for his services a compensation, which shall neither be increased nor diminished during the period for which he shall have been elected, and he shall not receive within that period any other emolument from the United States, or any of them.

Before he enter on the execution of his office, he shall take the following oath or affirmation:—"I do solemnly swear (or affirm) that I will faithfully execute the office of the President of the United States, and will to the best of my ability preserve, protect and defend the Constitution of the United States."

Section II. The President shall be commander in chief of the army and navy of the United States, and of the militia of the several States, when called into the actual service of the United States; he may require the opinion, in writing, of the principal officer in each of the executive departments, upon any subject relating to the duties of their respective offices, and he shall have power to grant reprieves and pardons for offenses against the United States, except in cases of impeachment.

He shall have power, by and with the advice and consent of the Senate, to make treaties, provided two-thirds of the Senators present concur; and he shall nominate, and by and with the advice and consent of the Senate, shall appoint ambassadors, other public ministers and consuls, judges of the Supreme Court, and all other officers of the United States, whose appointments are not herein otherwise provided for, and which shall be established by law: but Congress may by law vest the appointment of such inferior officers, as they think proper, in the President alone, in the courts of law, or in the heads of departments.

The President shall have power to fill up all vacancies that may happen during the recess of the Senate, by granting commissions which shall expire at the end of their next session.

Section III. He shall from time to time give to the Congress information of the state of the Union, and recommend to their consideration such measures as he shall judge necessary and expedient; he may, on extraordinary occasions, convene both houses, or either of them, and in case of disagreement between them, with respect to the time of adjournment, he may adjourn them to such time as he shall think proper; he shall receive ambassadors and other public ministers; he shall take care that the laws be faithfully executed, and shall commission all the officers of the United States.

Section IV. The President, Vice-President and all civil officers of the United States shall be removed from office on impeachment for, and on conviction of, treason, bribery, or other high crimes and misdemeanors.

ARTICLE III

Section I. The judicial power of the United States shall be vested in one Supreme Court, and in such inferior courts as the Congress may from time to time ordain and establish. The judges, both of the Supreme and inferior courts, shall hold their offices during good behavior, and shall, at stated times, receive for their services a compensation which shall not be diminished during their continuance in office.

Section II. The judicial power shall extend to all cases, in law and equity, arising under this Constitution, the laws of the United States, and treaties made, or which shall be made, under their authority;—to all cases affecting ambassadors, other public ministers and consuls;—to all cases of admiralty and maritime jurisdiction;—to controversies to which the United States shall be a party;—to controversies between two or more States;—*between a State and citizens of another State*;—between citizens of different States;—between citizens of the same State claiming lands under grants of different States, and between a State, or the citizens thereof, and foreign states, citizens or subjects.

In all cases affecting ambassadors, other public ministers and consuls, and those in which a State shall be party, the Supreme Court shall have original jurisdiction. In all the other cases before mentioned, the Supreme Court shall have appellate jurisdiction, both as to law and fact, with such exceptions, and under such regulations, as the Congress shall make.

The trial of all crimes, except in cases of impeachment, shall be by jury; and such trial shall be held in the State where the said crimes shall have been committed; but when not committed within any State, the trial shall be at such place or places as the Congress may by law have directed.

Section III. Treason against the United States shall consist only in levying war against them, or in adhering to their enemies, giving them aid and comfort. No person shall be convicted of treason unless on the testimony of two witnesses to the same overt act, or on confession in open court.

The Congress shall have power to declare the punishment of treason, but no attainder of treason shall work corruption of blood, or forfeiture except during the life of the person attainted.

ARTICLE IV

Section I. Full faith and credit shall be given in each State to the public acts, records, and judicial proceedings of every other State. And the Congress may by general laws prescribe the manner in which such acts, records, and proceedings shall be proved, and the effect thereof.

Section II. The citizens of each State shall be entitled to all privileges and immunities of citizens in the several States.

A person charged in any State with treason, felony, or other crime, who shall flee from justice, and be found in another State, shall on demand of the executive authority of the State from which he fled, be delivered up, to be removed to the State having jurisdiction of the crime.

No person held to service or labor in one State, under the laws thereof, escaping into another, shall, in consequence of any law or regulation therein, be discharged from such service or labor, but shall be delivered up on claim of the party to whom such service or labor may be due.

Section III. New States may be admitted by the Congress into this Union; but no new State shall be formed or erected within the jurisdiction of any other State; nor any State be formed by the junction of two or more

States, or parts of States, without the consent of the legislatures of the States concerned as well as of the Congress.

The Congress shall have power to dispose of and make all needful rules and regulations respecting the territory or other property belonging to the United States; and nothing in this Constitution shall be so construed as to prejudice any claims of the United States, or of any particular State.

Section IV. The United States shall guarantee to every State in this Union a republican form of government, and shall protect each of them against invasion; and on application of the legislature, or of the executive (when the legislature cannot be convened), against domestic violence.

ARTICLE V

The Congress, whenever two-thirds of both houses shall deem it necessary, shall propose amendments to this Constitution, or, on the application of the legislatures of two-thirds of the several States, shall call a convention for proposing amendments, which, in either case, shall be valid to all intents and purposes, as part of this Constitution, when ratified by the legislatures of three-fourths of the several States, or by conventions in three-fourths thereof, as the one or the other mode of ratification may be proposed by the Congress; provided *that no amendments which may be made prior to the year one thousand eight hundred and eight shall in any manner affect the first and fourth clauses in the ninth section of the first article;* and that no State, without its consent, shall be deprived of its equal suffrage in the Senate.

ARTICLE VI

All debts contracted and engagements entered into, before the adoption of this Constitution, shall be as valid against the United States under this Constitution, as under the Confederation.

This Constitution, and the laws of the United States which shall be made in pursuance thereof; and all treaties made, or which shall be made, under the authority of the United States, shall be the supreme law of the land; and the judges in every State shall be bound thereby, anything in the Constitution or laws of any State to the contrary notwithstanding.

The Senators and Representatives before mentioned, and the members of the several State legislatures, and all executive and judicial officers, both of the United States and of the several States, shall be bound by oath or affirmation to support this Constitution; but no religious test shall ever be required as a qualification to any office or public trust under the United States.

ARTICLE VII

The ratification of the conventions of nine States shall be sufficient for the establishment of this Constitution between the States so ratifying the same.

Done in Convention by the unanimous consent of the States present, the seventeenth day of September in the year of our Lord one thousand seven hundred and eighty-seven and of the Independence of the United States of America the twelfth. In witness whereof we have hereunto subscribed our names.

[Signed by]
G° WASHINGTON
Presidt and Deputy from Virginia
[and thirty-eight others]

Amendments to the Constitution

ARTICLE I*

Congress shall make no law respecting an establishment of religion, or prohibiting the free exercise thereof; or abridging the freedom of speech, or of the press; or the right of the people peaceably to assemble, and to petition the government for a redress of grievances.

ARTICLE II

A well-regulated militia being necessary to the security of a free State, the right of the people to keep and bear arms shall not be infringed.

---

*The first ten Amendments (Bill of Rights) were adopted in 1791.

ARTICLE III

No soldier shall, in time of peace, be quartered in any house without the consent of the owner, nor in time of war, but in a manner to be prescribed by law.

ARTICLE IV

The right of the people to be secure in their persons, houses, papers, and effects, against unreasonable searches and seizures, shall not be violated, and no warrants shall issue but upon probable cause, supported by oath or affirmation, and particularly describing the place to be searched, and the persons or things to be seized.

ARTICLE V

No person shall be held to answer for a capital, or otherwise infamous crime, unless on a presentment or indictment of a grand jury, except in cases arising in the land or naval forces, or in the militia, when in actual service in time of war or public danger; nor shall any person be subject for the same offense to be twice put in jeopardy of life or limb; nor shall be compelled in any criminal case to be a witness against himself, nor be deprived of life, liberty, or property, without due process of law; nor shall private property be taken for public use without just compensation.

ARTICLE VI

In all criminal prosecutions, the accused shall enjoy the right to a speedy and public trial, by an impartial jury of the State and district wherein the crime shall have been committed, which district shall have been previously ascertained by law, and to be informed of the nature and cause of the accusation; to be confronted with the witnesses against him; to have compulsory process for obtaining witnesses in his favor, and to have the assistance of counsel for his defense.

ARTICLE VII

In suits at common law, where the value in controversy shall exceed twenty dollars, the right of trial by jury shall be preserved, and no fact tried by a jury shall be otherwise reexamined in any court of the United States, than according to the rules of the common law.

ARTICLE VIII

Excessive bail shall not be required, nor excessive fines imposed, nor cruel and unusual punishments inflicted.

ARTICLE IX

The enumeration in the Constitution, of certain rights, shall not be construed to deny or disparage others retained by the people.

ARTICLE X

The powers not delegated to the United States by the Constitution, nor prohibited by it to the States, are reserved to the States respectively, or to the people.

ARTICLE XI [adopted 1798]

The judicial power of the United States shall not be construed to extend to any suit in law or equity, commenced or prosecuted against one of the United States by citizens of another State, or by citizens or subjects of any foreign state.

ARTICLE XII [adopted 1804]

The electors shall meet in their respective States, and vote by ballot for President and Vice-President, one of whom, at least, shall not be an inhabitant of the same State with themselves; they shall name in their ballots the person voted for as President, and in distinct ballots the person voted for as Vice-President, and they shall make distinct lists of all persons voted for as President, and of all persons voted for as Vice-President, and of the number of votes for each, which lists they shall sign and certify, and transmit sealed to the seat of government of the United States, directed to the President of the Senate;—the President of the Senate shall, in the presence of the Senate and House of Representatives, open all the certificates and the votes shall then be counted;—the person having the greatest number of votes for President shall be the President, if such number be a majority of the whole number of electors appointed; and if no person have such majority, then from the persons having the highest numbers not exceeding three on the list of those voted for as President, the House of Representatives shall choose immediately, by ballot, the President. But in choosing the President, the votes shall be taken by States, the representation from each State having one vote; a quorum for this purpose shall consist of a member or member from two-thirds of the States, and a majority of all the States shall be necessary to a choice. And if the House of Representatives shall not choose a President whenever the right of choice shall devolve upon them, before *the fourth day of March* next following, then the Vice-President shall act as President, as in the case of the death or other constitutional disability of the President.

The person having the greatest number of votes as Vice-President shall be the Vice-President, if such number be a majority of the whole number of electors appointed; and if no person have a majority, then from the two highest numbers on the list the Senate shall choose the Vice-President; a quorum for the purpose shall consist of two-thirds of the whole number of Senators, and a majority of the whole number shall be necessary to a choice. But no person constitutionally ineligible to the office of President shall be eligible to that of Vice-President of the United States.

ARTICLE XIII [adopted 1865]

1. Neither slavery nor involuntary servitude, except as a punishment for crime whereof the party shall have been duly convicted, shall exist within the United States, or any place subject to their jurisdiction.

2. Congress shall have power to enforce this article by appropriate legislation.

ARTICLE XIV [adopted 1868]

1. All persons born or naturalized in the United States, and subject to the jurisdiction thereof, are citizens of the United States and of the State wherein they reside. No State shall make or enforce any law which shall abridge the privileges or immunities of citizens of the United States; nor shall any State deprive any person of life, liberty, or property, without due process of law; nor deny to any person within its jurisdiction the equal protection of the laws.

2. Representatives shall be apportioned among the several States according to their respective numbers, counting the whole number of persons in each State, excluding Indians not taxed. But when the right to vote at any election for the choice of Electors for President and Vice-President of the United States, Representatives in Congress, the executive and judicial officers of a State, or the members of the legislature thereof, is denied to any of the male inhabitants of such State, being twenty-one years of age and citizens of the United States, or in any way abridged, except for participation in rebellion, or other crime, the basis of representation therein shall be reduced in the proportion which the number of such male citizens shall bear to the whole number of male citizens twenty-one years of age in such State.

3. No person shall be a Senator or Representative in Congress, or Elector of President and Vice-President, or hold any office, civil or military, under the United States, or under any State, who, having previously taken an oath, as a member of Congress, or as an officer of the United States, or as a member of any State legislature, or as an executive or judicial officer of any State, to support the Constitution of the United States, shall have engaged in insurrection or rebellion against the same, or given aid or comfort to the enemies thereof. But Congress may, by a vote of two-thirds of each house, remove such disability.

4. The validity of the public debt of the United States, authorized by law, including debts incurred for payment of pensions and bounties for services in suppressing insurrection or rebellion, shall not be questioned. But neither the United States nor any State shall assume or pay any debt or obligation incurred in aid of insurrection or rebellion against the United States, or any claim for the loss or emancipation of any slave; but all such debts, obligations, and claims shall be held illegal and void.

5. The Congress shall have power to enforce, by appropriate legislation, the provisions of this article.

ARTICLE XV [adopted 1870]

1. The right of citizens of the United States to vote shall not be denied or abridged by the United States or by any State on account of race, color, or previous condition of servitude.

2. The Congress shall have power to enforce this article by appropriate legislation.

ARTICLE XVI [adopted 1913]

The Congress shall have power to lay and collect taxes on incomes, from whatever source derived, without apportionment among the several States, and without regard to any census or enumeration.

ARTICLE XVII [adopted 1913]

1. The Senate of the United States shall be composed of two Senators from each State, elected by the people thereof, for six years; and each Senator shall have one vote. The electors in each State shall have the qualifications requisite for electors of [voters for] the most numerous branch of the State legislatures.

2. When vacancies happen in the representation of any State in the Senate, the executive authority of such State shall issue writs of election to fill such vacancies: Provided, that the Legislature of any State may empower the executive thereof to make temporary appointments until the people fill the vacancies by election as the Legislature may direct.

3. This amendment shall not be so construed as to affect the election or term of any Senator chosen before it becomes valid as part of the Constitution.

ARTICLE XVIII [adopted 1919; repealed 1933]

1. *After one year from the ratification of this article the manufacture, sale, or transportation of intoxicating liquors within, the importation thereof into, or the exportation thereof from the United States and all territory subject to the jurisdiction thereof, for beverage purposes, is hereby prohibited.*

2. *The Congress and the several States shall have concurrent power to enforce this article by appropriate legislation.*

3. *This article shall be inoperative unless it shall have been ratified as an amendment to the Constitution by the legislatures of the several States, as provided by the Constitution, within seven years from the date of the submission thereof to the States by the Congress.*

ARTICLE XIX [adopted 1920]

1. The right of citizens of the United States to vote shall not be denied or abridged by the United States or by any State on account of sex.

2. The Congress shall have power to enforce this article by appropriate legislation.

ARTICLE XX [adopted 1933]

1. The terms of the President and Vice-President shall end at noon on the 20th day of January, and the terms of Senators and Representatives at noon on the 3d day of January, of the years in which such terms would have ended if this article had not been ratified; and the terms of their successors shall then begin.

2. The Congress shall assemble at least once in every year, and such meeting shall begin at noon on the 3d day of January, unless they shall by law appoint a different day.

3. If, at the time fixed for the beginning of the term of the President, the President-elect shall have died, the Vice-President-elect shall become President. If a President shall not have been chosen before the time fixed for the beginning of his term, or if the President-elect shall have failed to qualify, then the Vice-President-elect shall act as President until a President shall have qualified; and the Congress may by law provide for the case wherein neither a President-elect nor a Vice-President-elect shall have qualified, declaring who shall then act as President, or the manner in which one who is to act shall be selected, and such persons shall act accordingly until a President or Vice-President shall have qualified.

4. The Congress may by law provide for the case of the death of any of the persons from whom the House of Representatives may choose a President whenever the right of choice shall have devolved upon them, and for the case of the death of any of the persons from whom the Senate may choose a Vice-President whenever the right of choice shall have devolved upon them.

5. Sections 1 and 2 shall take effect on the 15th day of October following the ratification of this article.

6. This article shall be inoperative unless it shall have been ratified as an amendment to the Constitution by the Legislatures of three-fourths of the several States within seven years from the date of its submission.

ARTICLE XXI [adopted 1933]

1. The eighteenth article of amendment to the Constitution of the United States is hereby repealed.

2. The transportation or importation into any State, Territory, or Possession of the United States for delivery or use therein of intoxicating liquors, in violation of the laws thereof, is hereby prohibited.

3. This article shall be inoperative unless it shall have been ratified as an amendment to the Constitution by conventions in the several States, as provided in the Constitution, within seven years from the date of submission thereof to the States by the Congress.

ARTICLE XXII [adopted 1951]

1. No person shall be elected to the office of President more than twice, and no person who has held the office of President, or acted as President, for more than two years of a term to which some other person was elected President shall be elected to the office of President more than once. But this article shall not apply to any person holding the office of President when this article was proposed by the Congress, and shall not prevent any person who may be holding the office of President, or acting as President, during the term within which this article becomes operative from holding the office of President or acting as President during the remainder of such term.

2. This article shall be inoperative unless it shall have been ratified as an amendment to the Constitution by the legislatures of three-fourths of the several States within seven years from the date of its submission to the States by the Congress.

ARTICLE XXIII [adopted 1961]

1. The District constituting the seat of Government of the United States shall appoint in such manner as the Congress may direct:

A number of electors of President and Vice-President equal to the whole number of Senators and Representatives in Congress to which the District would be entitled if it were a State, but in no event more than the least populous State; they shall be in addition to those appointed by the States, but they shall be considered for the purposes of the election of President and Vice-President, to be electors appointed by a State; and they shall meet in the District and perform such duties as provided by the twelfth article of amendment.

2. The Congress shall have the power to enforce this article by appropriate legislation.

1. The right of citizens of the United States to vote in any primary or other election for President or Vice-President, for electors for President or Vice-President, or for Senator or Representative in Congress, shall not be denied or abridged by the United States or any State by reason of failure to pay any poll tax or other tax.

2. The Congress shall have the power to enforce this article by appropriate legislation.

1. In case of the removal of the President from office or of his death or resignation, the Vice-President shall become President.

2. Whenever there is a vacancy in the office of the Vice-President, the President shall nominate a Vice-President who shall take office upon confirmation by a majority vote of both Houses of Congress.

3. Whenever the President transmits to the President pro tempore of the Senate and the Speaker of the House of Representatives his written declaration that he is unable to discharge the powers and duties of his office, and until he transmits to them a written declaration to the contrary, such powers and duties shall be discharged by the Vice-President as Acting President.

4. Whenever the Vice-President and a majority of either the principal officers of the executive departments or of such other body as Congress may by law provide, transmit to the President pro tempore of the Senate and the Speaker of the House of Representatives their written declaration that the President is unable to discharge the powers and duties of his office, the Vice-President shall immediately assume the powers and duties of the office as Acting President.

Thereafter, when the President transmits to the President pro tempore of the Senate and the Speaker of the House of Representatives his written declaration that no inability exists, he shall resume the powers and duties of his office unless the Vice-President and a majority of either the principal officers of the executive department[s] or of such other body as Congress may by law provide, transmit within four days to the President pro tempore of the Senate and the Speaker of the House of Representatives their written declaration that the President is unable to discharge the powers and duties of his office. Thereupon Congress shall decide the issue, assembling within forty-eight hours for that purpose if not in session. If the Congress, within twenty-one days after receipt of the latter written declaration, or, if Congress is not in session, within twenty-one days after Congress is required to assemble, determines by two-thirds vote of both Houses that the President is unable to discharge the powers and duties of his office, the Vice-President shall continue to discharge the same as Acting President; otherwise, the President shall resume the powers and duties of his office.

ARTICLE XXVI [adopted 1971]

1. The right of citizens of the United States, who are eighteen years of age or older, to vote shall not be denied or abridged by the United States or by any State on account of age.

2. The Congress shall have power to enforce this article by appropriate legislation.

About the authors

WILLIAM W. FISHER III is professor of law, Harvard University, and director of the Harvard Program on Legal History. He is the author of "Reconstructing Fair Use Doctrine," *Harvard Law Review* 101 (June 1988): 1744–94, and "Ideology, Religion, and the Constitutional Protection of Private Property: 1760–1860," *Emory Law Journal* 39 (Winter 1990): 65–134.

WILLIAM A. GALSTON is professor, School of Public Affairs, and senior research scholar, Institute for Philosophy and Public Policy, University of Maryland. His publications include *Kant and the Problem of History* (1975), *Justice and the Human Good* (1980), and *Liberal Purposes* (1991).

CHARLES L. GRISWOLD, JR., is chairman and professor of philosophy, Boston University. He is the author of *Self-Knowledge in Plato's Phaedrus* (1988) and editor of *Platonic Writings, Platonic Readings* (1988). He was a fellow at the Woodrow Wilson Center in 1989, at work on a book on the moral thought of Adam Smith.

KNUD HAAKONSSEN is senior research fellow, History of Ideas Program, Research School of Social Sciences, the Australian National University. A Wilson Center fellow in 1988, he is the author of *The Science of a Legislator: The Natural Jurisprudence of David Hume and Adam Smith* (1981) and editor of Thomas Reid's *Practical Ethics; Being Lectures and Papers on Natural Religion, Self Government, Natural Jurisprudence and the Law of Nations* (1989).

JAMES H. HUTSON is chief, Manuscripts Division, Library of Congress. He is the author of *John Adams and the Diplomacy of the American Revolution* (1980) and *To Make All Laws: Congress of the United States, 1789–1989* (1989).

MICHAEL J. LACEY is director, Division of United States Studies, Woodrow Wilson Center, and the editor of *Religion and Twentieth-Century American Intellectual Life* (1989) and *The Truman Presidency* (1989).

JACK N. RAKOVE is professor of history, Stanford University. He is the author of *The Beginnings of National Politics: An Interpretive History of the Continental Congress* (1982) and *James Madison and the Creation of the American Republic* (1990). He is also the editor of *Interpreting the Constitution: The Debate over Original Intent* (1990).

ALAN RYAN was a reader in politics at Oxford University before he moved to the United States in 1988. He is now professor of politics, Princeton University. His books include *The Philosophy of John Stuart Mill* (rev. ed., 1987), *Property and Political Theory* (1984), and *Russell: A Political Life* (1988).

Index